EQUITY TODAY

This book presents a clear, carefully analysed picture of the operation of equity today, across the common law world. Rather than revisit the abstract debate as to whether or not equity has 'fused' with the common law, it focuses on specific equitable principles and doctrines. Expert contributors step back and take a wider view of those doctrines, examining how they can best be understood today and how they might develop in the future. This will prove invaluable to practitioners and courts (at first instance as well as appellate level), allowing them to navigate the constantly growing mass of case law. Drawing on expertise from across the worlds of academia, practice and the bench, this seminal collection provides the most illuminating picture available of how equity operates.

Note on the cover image:

In *Principles of Equity* (1902), Ashburner, referring to common law and equity, wrote that 'the two streams of jurisdiction, though they run in the same channel, run side by side and do not mingle their waters.' But in *United Scientific Holdings Ltd v Burnley BC* [1978] AC 904, 925, Lord Diplock said that: 'As at the confluence of the Rhône and Saône, it may be possible for a short distance to discern the source from which each part of the combined stream came, but there comes a point at which this ceases to be possible. If Professor Ashburner's fluvial metaphor is to be retained at all, the waters of the confluent streams of law and equity have surely mingled now.' The cover image is of the confluence of those two rivers in Lyon and includes the futuristic building housing the Musée des Confluences. The extent to which the metaphorical waters of common law and of equity can be distinguished today is a matter of real controversy and is one of the key issues addressed in this volume.

Equity Today

150 Years after the Judicature Reforms

Edited by
Ben McFarlane
and
Steven Elliott KC

•HART•
OXFORD • LONDON • NEW YORK • NEW DELHI • SYDNEY

HART PUBLISHING

Bloomsbury Publishing Plc

Kemp House, Chawley Park, Cumnor Hill, Oxford, OX2 9PH, UK

1385 Broadway, New York, NY 10018, USA

29 Earlsfort Terrace, Dublin 2, Ireland

First published in Great Britain 2023

A catalogue record for this book is available from the British Library.

A catalogue record for this book is available from the Library of Congress.

ISBN: HB: 978-1-50996-007-1
ePDF: 978-1-50996-009-5
ePub: 978-1-50996-008-8

Typeset by Compuscript Ltd, Shannon

Preface

LONG LUNCHES ARE the source of many imaginative ideas, very few of which are put into practice. One such meal helped to mark the 150th anniversary, in 2018, of the original publication of Edmund Snell's *The Principles of Equity*. It gathered together many of the contributors to the current edition of *Snell's Equity*. Buoyed by the food and company, and keen to make further use of the word 'sesquicentennial', we came up with the idea of a conference and book to be published in 2023, to coincide with the 150th anniversary of the reforms set in train by the Supreme Court of Judicature Act 1873.

At the time, 2023 was sufficiently far away for us all to agree that this was an excellent idea, and that a conference could bring together students, academics, practitioners and judges, not only to mark and marvel at, but also to ponder and puzzle over, the continued vitality of equity. Our aim was not to give a primarily historical account of the fate of equity in that century and a half, but rather to look at how equity operates today, and how it may develop in the future. Of course, examining the historical context in which particular equitable doctrines developed is a crucial part of understanding the contemporary law, and such analysis takes its place in this book along with conceptual, functional, doctrinal and comparative analyses of equity today.

A crucial factor in realising our post-prandial plan was the financial support of the University of Oxford, made available to Ben McFarlane on becoming Professor of English Law in 2019. That post is associated with St John's College, Oxford and we benefitted greatly from its excellent facilities and incredibly helpful Conference and Events team, led by Susanna Power. Our initial enthusiasm would certainly have been curbed had we known that travel would still be very difficult in spring 2022, but we were able to adapt to a hybrid format with the invaluable assistance of THAT Event Company, and we benefitted too from liaising closely with Natalie Mrockova, Aruna Nair and Luke Rostill, who organised the Modern Studies in Property Law conference 2022, which took place immediately before our own. We were also fortunate to have the assistance of three very able graduate students, Asang Wankhede, Luke Broadway and Alex Chan. In producing the book, we benefitted from the superlative research assistance of Eleni Katsampouka, and we are very grateful to Sinéad Moloney and Sasha Jawed at Hart Publishing.

We are also very grateful to all the chairs and speakers at the conference. We remain particularly grateful to those speakers, from Canada, the United States, Singapore and Australia, who were able to join us only remotely, and thus had the fuss of producing a paper without the corresponding fun of being at the conference. In addition to the papers which now appear as chapters of this volume, Hanoch Dagan and Irit Samet presented their work on 'The Beneficiary's Ownership Rights in the Trust Res in a

Liberal Property Regime', which will appear shortly in the *Modern Law Review*, and John Mee spoke on 'The Meanings of Unconscionability in Proprietary Estoppel', a paper which could not be finalised without access to the Supreme Court's decision in *Guest v Guest* [2022] UKSC 27, which unfortunately was handed down too late for discussion in any of the chapters of this book. Along with the Privy Council's examination of trustees' powers of indemnity in *Equity Trust (Jersey) Ltd v Halabi* [2022] UKPC 36, which also appeared in October 2022, *Guest v Guest* shows both the continued importance of equitable principles, and that the lively controversies over their application are not confined to academics. These two features of equity today are sufficient in themselves to justify this book.

In organising its chapters, we have adopted the basic scheme of *Snell's Equity*, and so have Parts on Equity and Equities; Maxims and Doctrines; Equitable Protection; Equitable Remedies; Trusts; Administration of Assets; and Securities. It would be impossible to have a taxonomy of which all readers (or, indeed, authors; or, possibly, editors) would approve, but following *Snell's Equity* is at least a nod to the conception of the book. One of the aims of the conference was to bring comparative analysis to bear, and so we are fortunate to have a further, final Part on International Perspectives.

The curtain-raiser for the conference was Ben McFarlane's inaugural lecture, which also begins the book. Like many of the following chapters, it grapples with a key question, exposed with surgical precision in an inaugural lecture given by Professor (now Lord) Burrows: when, if ever, is it justifiable to say that 'We Do This at Common Law, but that in Equity'? McFarlane uses the operation of the trust as the basis from which to draw broader lessons about equity, and Jessica Hudson's chapter similarly has the trust as a focus, presenting it as an excellent example of equity's distinctive, and continuing, role as a gloss on authority, rather than as a limit to legal power. The following chapters, by Chee Ho Tham and Aruna Nair, look at specific contexts, respectively assignment of choses of action and registration of land, where the distinction between common law and equity continues to be critical in practice, and each considers the conceptual justifications for treating equitable assignment, and equitable interests in land, differently from their common law counterparts.

The next Part contains only one chapter, but William Swadling's sceptical analysis of the utility of maxims surveys equity as a whole and demonstrates the need to think clearly and critically about the application of equity today. As in *Snell's Equity*, the Part entitled 'Equitable Protection' considers a distinctive and commercially important part of equity: the law of fiduciaries. Lord Briggs considers claims not only against fiduciaries, but also against accessories, and finds good reasons for maintaining, in general, the traditional strictness of equity's rules. Matthew Conaglen considers the fiduciary duties of agents, as part of a broader survey on the impact of the Judicature reforms on accounting rules, and shows how modern day courts may fall into error if failing to understand the historical context of nineteenth-century decisions.

The consideration of equitable accounting provides a neat segue into the next Part, which contains five explorations of equitable remedies. Justice Edelman argues that, even over 150 years later, a possibility raised by Lord Cairns' Act, and then the Judicature reforms, has yet to be fully realised: money awards for wrongdoing in equity should be recognised as damages. Looking to the different remedy of rescission, and taking a judicial statement that only a Supreme Court decision can reconcile the authorities as a challenge rather than a warning, Steven Elliott also looks for simplicity and coherence, proposing a unified model that draws on each of common law and equity. In looking at negotiating damages, John McGhee also crosses the jurisdictional divide, putting forward an analysis based on the nature of the claimant's interest which aims to answer the difficult question of when such damages will be available. In contrast, each of Janet O'Sullivan and Paul Davies focusses on what might be seen as specifically (or, at least, originally) equitable remedies: respectively specific performance and injunctions. In doing so, each author encourages courts to be bolder in exercising their remedial powers, thereby showing how the unification of court procedure has allowed courts more scope to apply the powerful specific remedies of equity.

Given their centrality to equity, it is no surprise that trusts are discussed in a number of the chapters already mentioned, nor that they also have their own distinct Part. This features David Fox's analysis of how we came to the now trite conclusion that a beneficiary's interest is protected in the trustee's insolvency. The path was much more complex than a simple stipulation that the beneficiary's right was thus protected because it was 'property' and Fox warns us of the risks of trying to impose categories which we now think of as fundamental on the reasoning of eighteenth- and nineteenth-century courts. Trusts, of course, involve the administration of assets, but they are not the only form which such administration can take and, as Simon Douglas shows in his analysis of devastavit, the law applying to a personal representative charged with a deceased estate has roots in common law as well as in equity. Security rights are of course another area where common law and equity currently mix, but one of the key questions for law reformers is whether equity is needed in a codified security regime. Magda Raczynska examines this question in her chapter, exploring the 'tempestuous' relationship between commercial law and equity, which also features prominently in the final Part of the book.

That concluding Part offers the International Perspectives which were a key part of the conference discussions. Alexandra Popovici and Lionel Smith draw on civil law, but their analysis of the concept of equity and how it differs from, but informs, equity (ie the specific body of rules examined in the other chapters of the book: given a capital E in their chapter) is a general one and clearly applicable to common law systems too. The following chapter, by Henry Smith, focusses on the law in the United States and amply demonstrates the benefits noted in the preceding chapter of equity as a body of rules, by showing, in the context of property law, what is lost when judges overlook the possibility of drawing on specifically equitable solutions. Simone Degeling's examination of how various equitable doctrines, particularly equitable estoppel, deal with lost opportunities of the claimant is concerned chiefly, but not exclusively, with Australian law. It certainly has broader lessons, including for English law, and is an excellent example of Justice Edelman's point that advances can be made by asking how common law and equity answer functionally identical questions.

The final two chapters are linked as each undertakes an impressive comparative survey of equity today, noting how jurisdictions with a common heritage have parted ways when dealing with that tricky relationship between equity and commercial law. Justice Newbury takes a view 'from 30,000 feet' of how each of Canada, Australia and England has dealt with dishonest or misleading statements made by one contracting party to the other, relating to the parties' rights under the contract, or to its performance. Whilst finalised well before the Supreme Court delivered its judgments, Justice Newbury's defence of the notion of unconscionability in understanding the operation of equitable estoppel is certainly in tune with the approach of the majority in *Guest v Guest*. In her consideration of equity's proper role in commerce, Man Yip looks closely at developments in Hong Kong and Singapore, observing how the unique cultures, experiences and judicial attitudes in particular jurisdictions can influence the operation of equity today.

When putting together the conference programme, we were careful to avoid any suggestion of a party line: the chapters in this book reflect and contribute to the ongoing debate as to the proper role of equity in modern legal systems. Certainly, as shown by even this brief summary, none of the chapters proceeds on the basis that equitable rules and principles can be different *simply* because of their jurisdictional basis. Rather, there is much to be gained from looking across the divide between common law and equity. At the same time, the specific historical contexts in which such doctrines developed, the particular functions they play today, or the characteristic form of the legal relations they involve, may all contribute to providing a current justification for those doctrines differing from their supposed common law equivalents. As a result, it remains necessary for practitioners and judges, as well as students and academics, to pay attention to the distinctive features of equity, and the type of careful academic analysis undertaken in this book can have important practical effects.

Ben McFarlane
Steven Elliott KC
October 2022

Contents

PART IV
EQUITABLE REMEDIES

PART V
TRUSTS

PART VI
ADMINISTRATION OF ASSETS

PART VII
SECURITIES

PART VIII
INTERNATIONAL PERSPECTIVES

List of Contributors

Lord Briggs of Westbourne is a Justice of the United Kingdom Supreme Court.

Matthew Conaglen is Professor of Equity and Trusts at the University of Sydney Law School.

Paul S Davies is Professor of Commercial Law at University College London and a barrister at Essex Court Chambers.

Simone Degeling is Professor of Law at the University of New South Wales.

Simon Douglas is an Associate Professor of Law at the University of Oxford and a Fellow of Jesus College.

The Honourable Justice Edelman is a Justice of the High Court of Australia.

Steven Elliott KC is a barrister at One Essex Court.

David Fox is Professor of Common Law at the University of Edinburgh.

Jessica Hudson is an Associate Professor of Law at the University of New South Wales.

Ben McFarlane is Professor of English Law at the University of Oxford and a Fellow of St John's College.

John McGhee KC is a barrister at Wilberforce Chambers.

Aruna Nair is an Associate Professor of Law at the University of Oxford and a Fellow of Hertford College.

The Honourable Madam Justice Newbury is a Justice of the Court of Appeal of British Columbia.

Janet O'Sullivan is Associate Professor, Faculty of Law, University of Cambridge and a Fellow and Vice-Master of Selwyn College.

Alexandra Popovici is Professeure agrégée at the Faculté de droit, Université de Sherbrooke.

Magda Raczynska is an Associate Professor of Law at University College London.

Henry E Smith is Fessenden Professor of Law at Harvard Law School.

Lionel Smith is Downing Professor of the Laws of England at the University of Cambridge and a Fellow of Gonville and Caius College.

William Swadling is Professor of Law at the University of Oxford and a Fellow of Brasenose College.

Chee Ho Tham is Professor of Law at the Yong Pung How School of Law, Singapore Management University.

Man Yip is Professor of Law at the Yong Pung How School of Law, Singapore Management University.

Table of Cases

Australia

British Virgin Islands

Canada

Cayman Islands

European Court of Justice

France

Hong Kong

India

Ireland

Jersey

New Zealand

Singapore

United Kingdom (Including Appeals from other Jurisdictions to the Privy Council)

United States

Table of Legislation

Statutes

Australia

British Virgin Islands

Canada

France

India

British Virgin Islands

EU Legislation

Part I

Equity and Equities

1

The Persistence of Equity: Lessons from the Trust

BEN McFARLANE

I. AN OVERVIEW AND TWO VIEWS

A. Overview

THIS CHAPTER AIMS to use the example of the trust to address the question that motivates this book: 150 years after the Judicature Act 1873, is there any reason (other than simple curiosity as to the historical origin of a particular rule or principle) to continue to distinguish between common law and equity?[1] As well as examining the trust, and equity more generally, it considers a still broader question: does the role of equity today reveal anything of wider significance about the nature of English law, and therefore of the common law as applied in jurisdictions around the world? Certainly, the continued presence, and prominence, of a body of rules and principles referred to as 'equity' is one of the more striking features of English law.

The chapter compares two approaches to these questions. The first will be referred to as the 'pragmatic view'; the second as the 'formal view'. It is not suggested that these views are the only two which might be taken, nor that there is only one view which could be called 'pragmatic', and only one which could be called 'formal'. The particular pragmatic view examined here, however, is a popular one, and a key aim of this chapter is to reveal some of its deficiencies, and show the possibilities opened up by adopting a particular type of formal view. One such advantage of this specific formal view, it will be argued in section II, is that it can answer a long-standing puzzle as to the nature and operation of the trust. As will

[1] This chapter is closely based on my inaugural lecture as Professor of English Law at the University of Oxford, delivered on 31 March 2022, but has fewer jokes. A video of the lecture itself is available at the YouTube site of the Oxford Faculty of Law: www.youtube.com/watch?v=TNUQ96ik2tQ. I am particularly grateful to Lord Burrows for chairing the lecture and for Professor Chen-Wishart, Dean of the Faculty of Law, for introducing it. I am also grateful to David Foster for his comments on a draft of this chapter and his permission to cite from (what was at the time) forthcoming work, and to Ernesto Vargas Weil and Giorgia Bucaria for assistance with some civil law perspectives.

be explored in section III, this shows in turn that, at least in some contexts, we should continue to distinguish between common law and equity as, in doing so, we are distinguishing between two fundamentally different forms of right. On this view, the contribution of equity goes beyond the undeniable practical benefits it has delivered in English law, and extends to the recognition of new legal concepts, which may be of use even beyond common law borders.

B. The Pragmatic View

A pragmatic view focusses essentially on outcomes, on ends rather than means.[2] The particular pragmatic view examined here does not attempt to give a principled defence of the historic distinction between common law and equity. Rather, it acknowledges the (undeniable) practical benefits that products of equity, such as the trust, have conferred on those bound by, or choosing to use, English law. On this view, continued use of the distinction between common law and equity is justifiable as long as those terms mark *some* practical difference in the operation of particular rules – so, for example, an equitable property right is usefully distinguished from a legal property right given its different effect on third parties. Such a view may draw support from the relatively haphazard origins and early development of equity, which was conceived not as a coherent system but was rather based on a series of initially ad hoc interventions aimed at avoiding practical outcomes which, for varying reasons, seemed unjust. It can further be linked to a broader view of English law as a whole as characteristically unconcerned with conceptual tidiness, given that fundamental parts of it have been established and refined by judges as a by-product of the very practical work of settling disputes.[3] The rules, therefore, were not worked

[2] J Goldberg, 'Pragmatism and Private Law' (2012) 125 *Harvard Law Review* 1640 uses the label 'brass-tacks pragmatism' to refer to three such analyses of private law: OW Holmes, 'The Path of the Law' (1897) 10 *Harvard Law Review* 457; K Llewellyn, 'Some Realism About Realism – Responding to Dean Pound' (1931) 44 *Harvard Law Review* 1222; and D Kennedy, 'Form and Substance in Private Law Adjudication' (1976) 89 *Harvard Law Review* 1685. Goldberg (ibid 1641–42) notes that such views aim to be 'hardheaded in the particular sense of pushing past the surface to get to what is "really" at stake' and are as a result sceptical about traditional private law distinctions (such as that between common law and equity). Goldberg argues instead for approaches which are based on 'inclusive pragmatism', which 'makes room for conceptual legal analysis without equating the study of law with logic or botany'. Certainly, the formal view proposed here is not unconcerned with practical consequences, and so may fall within the scope of 'The New Private Law' which Goldberg identifies as 'inclusively pragmatic'. For more on the consequences of the New Private Law for equity, see B McFarlane, 'Equity' in A Gold et al (eds), *The Oxford Handbook of the New Private Law* (Oxford, OUP, 2021). Note that, in his own inaugural lecture as Professor of English Law, published as 'From Principles to Pragmatism: Changes in the Function of the Judicial Process and the Law' (1980) 65 *Iowa Law Review* 1249 (and also as *From Principles to Pragmatism* (Oxford, Clarendon Press, 1978)) Patrick Atiyah at 1251 adopted a linked, but slightly different definition of 'pragmatism' and associated it with judicial decisions 'designed to achieve justice in the particular circumstances of the case, irrespective of the possible impact of the decision in the future.' Atiyah then linked equity and its conferral of judicial discretion to this sense of pragmatism. This chapter takes, in effect, the opposite approach, arguing that the true effect of many equitable doctrines can be understood only if we consider their formal role in the legal system.

[3] See, eg, R Pound, 'What is the Common Law?' (1937) 4 *University of Chicago Law Review* 176, 186–87: 'Behind the characteristic doctrines and ideas of the common-law lawyer there is a significant frame

out in theory and then formalised in codes and written constitutions devised by legislators or – even worse – academics.[4] As a result, we should not expect notions worked out pragmatically over the years, such as the effect of an equitable property right on a third party, to be capable of neat classification. On this view, in considering the persistence of equity, the lesson to be taken from the trust is simply that, despite the conceptual shakiness of its foundations, equity has allowed English law to respond in a flexible and pragmatic way to the needs of commercial and social life, unencumbered by the doctrinal scruples that would hold back less pragmatic jurisdictions.

A very useful exposition of the pragmatic view was given by Maitland, in writing for a primarily German audience at the start of the twentieth century.[5] It should be immediately noted that Maitland was not endorsing that view; the attention paid in other parts of his work to the correct conceptual understanding of the nature of the trust shows that, rather, Maitland himself adopted a view both of the trust and of equity more broadly which was closely concerned with the form of the court's intervention and thus of the parties' rights.[6] Rather, Maitland eloquently exposes how such a pragmatic view was commonplace amongst English lawyers. In considering how such a lawyer would react if asked by a German counterpart whether to classify the trust within the law of property, or the law of obligations, Maitland stated: '[t]o this elementary question I know of no reply which would be given at once and as a matter of course by every English lawyer.'[7] Nonetheless, Maitland showed, the possibility of setting up a trust conferred practical benefits in a wide variety of contexts: for example, it allowed groups as varied as the Catholic Church, the Jockey Club, and Lincoln's Inn to hold property without needing to take the formal step of incorporation. Maitland emphasised a cheerful absence of intellectual rigour on the part of the English lawyers, thus hinting that these significant practical benefits were related to, and could even depend on, this willingness not to worry about conceptual matters

of mind. It is a frame of mind which habitually looks at things in the concrete, not in the abstract; which puts its faith in experience rather than in abstractions.' See too, from a civilian perspective, K Zweigert and H Kotz, *An Introduction to Comparative Law*, T Weir tr, 3rd edn (Oxford, OUP, 1998) 265: 'With their practical empiricism and habit of going step by step from case to case the English would have regarded it as dangerous and unnatural to prescribe the outcome of comparable cases in advance by making general regulations to cover the whole area of life: "we'll cross that bridge when we come to it".'

[4] See, eg, J Getzler, 'Legal History as Doctrinal History' in M Dubber and C Tomlins (eds), *The Oxford Handbook of Legal History* (Oxford, OUP, 2018) 171, 185: 'The common law until well into the eighteenth century may be described as a type of tacit or craft knowledge, learnt by doing, and resistant to formal or rational doctrinal statement.'

[5] As noted in Getzler's very helpful examination of this 'late, great, sprawling and challenging essay' (J Getzler, 'Frederic William Maitland – Trust and Corporation' (2016) 35 *University of Queensland Law Journal* 171, 171), the essay in question was originally published in German as 'Trust und Korporation' (1905) 32 *Grunhut's Zeitschrift fur das Privat- und Offentliche Recht der Gegenwart*. It first appeared in English, as 'Trust and Corporation' posthumously in H Fisher (ed), *The Collected Papers of Frederic William Maitland, vols I-III* (Cambridge, CUP, 1911) vol III 321–404. It appears too as ch IV in HD Hazeltine, G Lapsley, PH Winfield (eds), *Maitland: Selected Essays* (Cambridge, CUP, 1936). Pinpoint citations in this chapter will be taken from D Runciman and M Ryan (eds), *Maitland: State, Trust and Corporation* (Cambridge, CUP, 2012) 75–130.

[6] Note however that Maitland's formal view was not the same as the formal view advocated in this chapter: see section II below.

[7] Runciman and Ryan (n 5) 76.

(such as the exact nature of the rights of individual members of an unincorporated association).[8] 'Shameful though it may be to say this,' Maitland confessed, speaking of English lawyers, 'we fear the petrifying action of juristic theory.'[9] So, Maitland explained to his German audience:

> [F]or the ordinary thought of Englishmen 'equitable ownership' is just ownership pure and simple, though it is subject to a peculiar, technical and not very intelligible rule in favour of *bona fide* purchasers … let the Herr Professor say what he likes, so many persons are bound to respect the rights [of the beneficiary] that practically they are almost as valuable as if they were *dominium* (ownership).[10]

On the pragmatic view, then, in considering the persistence of equity, the lesson to be taken from the trust is simply that equity persists because it has allowed English law to respond in a flexible way to the needs of commercial and social life; there is little to be gained from considering the precise nature of a beneficiary's rights under the trust and how they might differ from the rights of a party with unencumbered title to property. Such a pragmatic view can be applied to equity more broadly: whilst attention to 'juristic theory' would prevent any country having two separate sets of courts within a single jurisdiction, English law has in practice benefitted from the flexibility which allows parties further means by which to structure their transactions, and gives courts additional ways of responding to situations not covered by the parties' own arrangements.

Indeed, the organisation of the English court system before the Judicature reforms, whilst '[f]rom any managerial point of view … ludicrous',[11] was crucial to the existence of equity, and evidence of, at the least, a willingness to proceed without conceptual order. From a purely conceptual perspective, there would seem to be no obvious reason for having a separate court of Chancery, operating not as an appeal court to overturn common law judgments or otherwise issue instructions to common law judges, but rather to make orders against individuals.[12] Starting from scratch, no-one would design a system of dual, and sometimes duelling, jurisdictions. And yet, the legacy of that structure, the 'productive paradox of two rival court systems',[13] includes some real practical benefits. Certainly, the importance of the trust, and of other equitable creations, has only increased since Maitland's time. For example, Worthington has stated that trusts and equitable charges are 'often assumed to be equity's greatest legacy to the law. Their enormous commercial significance goes

[8] See too N McCormick, *Legal Reasoning and Legal Theory* (Oxford, Clarendon Press, 1978) 4: 'By and large English lawyers and writers have tended to think of it as almost a virtue to be illogical, and have ascribed that virtue freely to their law: "being logical" is an eccentric continental practice, in which common-sensical Englishmen indulge at their peril.'

[9] Runciman and Ryan (n 5) 106.

[10] ibid 94. Maitland adds in a footnote there: 'Some writers even in theoretical discussion have allowed themselves to speak of the [beneficiary] as "the real owner", and of the trustee's ownership as "nominal" and "fictitious". See Salmond, *Jurisprudence*, 278.'

[11] J Hackney, *Understanding Equity and Trusts* (London, Fontana Press, 1987) 15.

[12] F Maitland, *Equity; also, The Forms of Action at Common Law: Two Courses of Lectures*, edn by A Chaytor and W Whittaker (Cambridge, CUP, 1909) 9 – see too Swadling's chapter in this volume.

[13] B McFarlane and R Stevens, 'The Nature of Equitable Property' (2010) 4 *Journal of Equity* 1, 9.

without saying.'[14] The utility of a particular type of trust, the *Quistclose* trust,[15] was recently seen by Lady Arden as depending on, and demonstrating

> … the flexibility of equity. That flexibility makes an important and beneficial contribution to the legal system … because it enables equity to respond to the need for different sorts of transactions, and also because in that way it contributes to the development of society and to the growth of its economy.[16]

Moving beyond equity, the pragmatic view could be seen as resting on a wider characteristic of English law, or perhaps even Englishness more generally. For example, in a speech given by Queen Elizabeth II, on the occasion of her Golden Jubilee, to both Houses of Parliament,[17] the late Queen reflected on what qualities might be seen as distinctively British. One of the points she emphasised was that 'we are a moderate, pragmatic people, more comfortable with practice than theory.'[18]

It is dangerous of course to generalise, particularly given the quite different nature of Scots law; on the pragmatic view, nonetheless, the practical benefits of some important parts of *English* law, including both equity and the trust, could be seen as resulting from a relative lack of concern as to underlying coherence. Indeed, in their introduction to a collection of Maitland's work which contains his essay cited above, Runciman and Ryan expand on Maitland's observation that '[w]e Englishmen never clean our slates'[19] and write that the English 'were rarely afforded the vantage point from which to judge whether the law by which they lived made sense as a set of ideas, not least because they were too busily and successfully living by it.'[20]

C. The Formal View

It is no surprise, given that it is based on an inaugural professorial lecture, that the purpose of this chapter is to put forward a different view: it will be referred to here as the *formal* view, as it depends on a close analysis of *how* precisely equity intervenes, and therefore of the particular form of the rights that arise as a result. It is not suggested that only one type of formal view is possible; a different formal view could ask the same question as to the conceptual nature of the parties' rights, but reach a

[14] S Worthington, 'The Disappearing Divide Between Property and Obligation: The Impact of Aligning Legal Analysis and Commercial Expectation' (2007) 42 *Texas International Law Journal* 917, 921.

[15] Named for *Barclays Bank Ltd v Quistclose Investments Ltd* [1970] AC 567 (HL).

[16] *Prickly Bay Waterside Ltd v British American Insurance Co Ltd* [2022] UKPC 8, [2022] 1 WLR 2087 [32].

[17] A reply to the addresses of both Houses of Parliament. The text is available at news.bbc.co.uk/1/hi/uk_politics/1959753.stm.

[18] ibid. See too T Weir, 'The Common Law System' in R David (ed), *International Encyclopedia of Comparative Law* (Leiden, Brill, 1974, No 82) vol II, ch 2, 77: 'The Englishman is naturally pragmatic, more concerned with result than method, function than shape, effectiveness than style; he has little talent for producing intellectual order and little interest in the finer points of taxonomy.'

[19] Runciman and Ryan (n 5) 67. See too Maitland's more general observation in 'Trust and Corporation' (ibid, 89) that '[m]en often act first and think afterwards.'

[20] Runciman and Ryan (n 5) xiii.

different answer. It is suggested, however, that the specific formal view adopted here provides a useful understanding both of the nature of the trust, and of the persistence of equity more generally.

Whilst accepting the practical benefits that the trust, and equity, have conferred, the formal view aims to show that each has a sound conceptual underpinning and that, if it is to continue to deliver such benefits by developing to meet new practical challenges, this underpinning must be understood. To focus solely on the pragmatic benefits of the trust would be to miss a very valuable contribution it has made to our list of legal concepts: the idea of a right that has as its subject matter another person's right. It is the particular *form* of such a right that makes it hard to classify as within either the law of property or the law of obligations. The difficulty of classification does *not* arise because an interest in conceptual order is alien to equity, or to English law, but rather because equity, by recognising rights with a particular form, requires us to re-think certain distinctions and, in particular, to recognise that classificatory schemes derived from other systems (such as the divide between *in personam* and *in rem* rights) may not capture the formal complexity of English law.[21] The formal view thus aims to show that an exclusive focus on the practical benefits conferred by the trust, and by equity, in fact undervalues the contribution of those ideas, by missing the formal concepts they have added.

The formal view is not an attempt to ignore, or to re-write, the past. Indeed, the concept on which this chapter focusses, the idea of a right relating to another's right, can be clearly linked to the role of equity as a secondary or supplementary system and thus to the historical arrangement of the English courts. Nor does it deny the practical way in which that concept has developed, as a result of an accretion of judicial decisions. It does however depend on the key point that such conceptual ideas can be valid even where they have not been definitively posited by any legislature or court. This argument is consistent with the broader nature of English law, as a common law system, as it is often the case that principles have to be extracted, by careful analysis, from a mass of decisions. This point was made very clearly in the inaugural lecture of Wade,[22] when he argued that a coherent set of principles of English administrative law, although they had never been explicitly set out by the judges, could be extracted from the case law:

> The law is always working on inarticulate major premises – and so inarticulate are they that our highest judicial authorities may hold opposite opinions about them. Every student and practitioner of the law must have reflected upon this tantalising, fascinating mystery.[23]

As Wade put it, this means that the underlying justifications which can give English law coherence 'slowly crystallise beneath the surface'[24] of judgments: practitioners, judges, and academics can all play a role in bringing those principles to light.

[21] See section II.C. This observation is consistent with the analysis of Fox's chapter in this volume.
[22] The first holder of the statutory Professorship of English Law established in 1961.
[23] HWR Wade, 'Law, Opinion, and Administration' (1962) 78 *LQR* 188, 196.
[24] ibid 197.

II. THE TRUST

A. The Puzzle

It is helpful to start with another inaugural lecture, delivered by Burrows in 2001.[25] It made the fundamental point that, in seeking to explain a difference between two rules or principles, it is never enough simply to state that one came from common law, and the other from equity. Referring to the jurisdictional origin of the rule or principle cannot by itself justify a divergence, as there is no reason why common law and equity should continue to give competing answers to the same question. As Burrows notes, the practical imperative of treating like cases alike can be met only if we have a defensible means of identifying like cases, and it is not defensible to assume that two cases are different *simply* because one concerns an equitable right and the other a legal right.

Like all the best points, this is both very simple and has profound consequences, a number of which are dealt with in other contributions to this book.[26] Burrows identified and examined three categories in private law, focussing on the third where, in his view, common law and equity are in conflict, and reform is necessary to bring consistency and coherence to the law. The lecture is thus a fine example of the practical benefits of adopting a conceptual analysis: the convenience and pragmatic attraction of English law is impaired if there are competing legal and equitable rules, and uncertainty as to which should be applied.

For present purposes, however, it is Burrows' first category that is the most important. This category comprises cases where common law and equity *do* work coherently together and, moreover, it makes sense to use the labels of common law and equity to refer to the different rules. Understanding this category is therefore crucial to understanding the persistence of equity 150 years after the Judicature reforms. Burrows describes the prime example of a case in this first category as follows:

> I particularly have in mind here that greatest invention of equity, the trust. It is very hard – albeit not impossible as is shown by the approach in some other jurisdictions – to describe the trust without at some stage relying on, and referring to, the split between legal and equitable title.[27]

The argument in this chapter is that the trust is, indeed, an excellent example of the coherent co-existence of common law and equity; but that this coherence can only be seen if we reject the language of 'the split between legal and equitable title'. Of course, it is commonplace to refer to a trustee as having legal title, to a beneficiary as having equitable title, and to distinguish between legal property rights on the one hand and equitable property rights on the other.[28] The problem, however, is that, as Burrows

[25] A Burrows, 'We Do This at Common Law but That in Equity' (2002) 22 *OJLS* 1. The author is now of course Lord Burrows JSC.

[26] See, eg, Edelman's and Elliott's chapters in this volume.

[27] Burrows (n 25) 5.

[28] See, eg, Foxton J in *Serious Fraud Office v Litigation Capital Ltd* [2021] EWHC 1272 (Comm) [292], noting that the '"equitable property" approach to trusts, although subject to significant academic challenge, remains a substantial presence in the decided cases.'

made very clear, *simply* adding the adjective 'equitable' cannot in itself explain why a different outcome obtains. If, for example, we say that A has title to some property at law, but that B has title in equity, then common law and equity seem to be giving different answers to one of the most fundamental questions addressed by a legal system: who is the owner? An essay by F Scott Fitzgerald contains the line that 'the test of a first-rate intelligence is the ability to hold two opposed ideas in the mind at the same time, and still retain the ability to function',[29] but the title of that essay is telling and, in any case, it cannot be the mark of a good legal system to say that one party owns at common law, and another in equity. This point was memorably made by Maitland, with a touch of the hyperbole permitted in lectures: 'Think what this would mean were it really true. There are two courts of co-ordinate jurisdiction – one says that A is the owner, the other says that B is the owner. That means civil war and utter anarchy.'[30]

As soon, then, as we aim for the conceptual rigour which Burrows rightly identified as necessary to meet the basic aim of coherence in the law, the trust raises a puzzle: on its conventional understanding as depending on a split between legal and equitable ownership, it seems to be an egregious example of common law and equity giving different answers to the same, fundamental question. Rather than being an example of Burrows' first category, where common law and equity co-exist coherently, the trust, as often presented, seems to be a clear case of conflict.

A chief aim of this chapter, however, is to show that Burrows was correct in seeing the trust as a paradigm for the role of equity in the modern law. The key point, revealed by adopting the formal view, is that, in asking if a party (B) has a right under a trust, equity does not repeat the common law question, and ask if B has title to any property; rather, equity asks a fundamentally *different* question. The difference in the questions asked by common law and equity allows for different, but still coherent, answers to be given. And it is not just that there is *a* difference in the questions: the *nature* of the difference will tell us something of wider importance as to the general nature of equity, and its role in the modern legal system. We will consider these points further in section III, but it is first necessary to see how the pragmatic view might deal with the puzzle raised by the trust.

B. Limits of the Pragmatic View

One response to the puzzle of the trust, which might be given by a supporter of the pragmatic view, is simply to point to its success in practice: to stop worrying and learn to love the trust. Maitland's invocation of the 'ordinary thought of Englishmen' provides an example. Even if B (the beneficiary) is, in effect, an owner, B's vulnerability to the bona fide purchaser defence means that the distinction between legal and equitable property rights can work: the protection available to the holder of

[29] F Scott Fitzgerald, 'The Crack Up', first published in the Feb–April 1936 issues of *Esquire* magazine.
[30] Maitland (n 12) 17.

the equitable flavour of property right is weaker than that available to the holder of the legal equivalent. So, English law extends the options of the parties[31] (and of the courts)[32] by offering two types of property right and, in the case of the trust, two types of title. These are not, in practice, confused as the rules as to their acquisition, as well as the rules as to their content and enforceability, are different. There is also some logic to the system: whilst equitable property rights are generally easier to acquire than their legal counterparts, and more flexible as to their content, their enforceability against third parties is more limited.

The first point to make is that, on this pragmatic view, whilst it is coherent to distinguish between legal property rights on the one hand, and equitable property rights on the other, this does not demonstrate that the trust must fall into Burrows' first category: it does not provide a reason why we should continue to use the labels of 'legal' and 'equitable'. On this pragmatic view, the use of 'equitable' to refer to the weaker variety of property right tells us only about the historical jurisdictional origin of such rights, rather than identifying anything about the nature of the rights themselves. It would therefore seem perfectly acceptable, and perhaps more transparent, to drop the labels of common law and equity, and instead refer to two different types of property right, each with its own rules as to content, acquisition, and enforcement against third parties.

The second, linked point is that whilst this pragmatic analysis is, like Maitland's 'ordinary thought of Englishmen', avowedly conceptually unambitious, it is also limited even in its own, pragmatic terms: it breaks down rather quickly when specific practical questions arise. It tells us that there must be *a* difference between the effect of legal property rights on the one hand, and equitable property rights on the other, but tells us nothing about the extent of, or reasons for, this variation. For example, consider a case where A holds title to a painting on trust for B. Acting without authority under the trust, A then transfers title to the painting, as a gift, to C. C later makes a gift of that same painting to D. When receiving the painting, and throughout the time C held it, C did not know, and had no reason to believe, that the painting had been held by A on trust. In such a case, is it possible for B to make a claim against C? What if C received some benefit from the painting, such as a loan fee, but had spent that money on C's everyday expenses before becoming aware that the painting had been transferred by A in breach of trust? In such a case, of course, C is not a bona fide purchaser for value and so, adopting Maitland's 'ordinary thought', it might be argued that C should therefore be liable to B in the same way as C would be liable to an owner when innocently receiving and dealing with a stolen painting: in conversion in the first example, and/or in an action for money had and received in the second. That is not, however, the current position in English law: it seems instead that, in each

[31] As noted by, eg, Lady Arden in the quotation from *Prickly Bay* (n 16) (see section I.B above). See too H Dagan and I Samet, 'Express Trust: The Dark Horse of the Liberal Property Regime' in S Degeling, J Hudson and I Samet (eds), *Philosophical Foundations of the Law of Express Trusts* (Oxford, OUP, 2023).

[32] Through the possibility of recognising a non-express trust.

case, B has no claim against C,[33] as B's equitable 'title' under a trust of the painting is treated differently from a case of simple ownership.[34]

Similarly, should there also be a difference in how an equitable property right, as opposed to a legal property right, affects a third party (X) who carelessly damages that property? In a case where A holds title to a physical thing on trust for B, does the difference between A's right and that of B require that X is liable only to A, and so does not have to pay damages in relation to consequential loss suffered only by B? The answer given by the Court of Appeal in the (much-criticised)[35] decision of *Shell UK Ltd v Total UK Ltd*[36] was No: the nature of the trust was such that B was in practice entitled to the economic benefit of the property, and so was regarded as the 'the "real" owner'. The Court thus held it would be 'legalistic'[37] to deny B the protection against a careless third party that would be available where B is simply an owner of property. The analysis of the Court in *Shell* is a fine example of the pragmatic view[38] and its tendency to focus on ends rather means: if, in practice, it is B who enjoys the economic benefit of particular property, why should B be denied the protection usually given to an owner? It is also an almost direct application of Maitland's 'ordinary thought of Englishmen': where there is no bona fide purchaser involved, the beneficiary should be given the same protection as an outright owner of property.[39]

Contrast *Shell*, however, with the decision in *Akers v Samba*,[40] where the Supreme Court concluded that section 127 of the Insolvency Act 1986 (which operates to render void[41] a disposition of a company's property occurring after that company's winding-up has commenced) applies quite differently according to whether that transaction consists in the company's losing an equitable property right, rather than a legal property right. It was held that, if A, acting without authority under the trust, transfers to C shares held on trust for B, this is not a 'disposition' of B's property. Such a disposition would of course occur where the directors of a company transfer to a third party shares that the company held outright. The essential reasoning in *Akers* is thus in

[33] See, eg, *Independent Trustee Services Ltd v GP Noble Trustees Ltd* [2012] EWCA Civ 195, [2013] Ch 91 [76]; *Agip (Africa) Ltd v Jackson* [1990] Ch 265 (Ch) 290–91. See too *Farah Constructions Pty Ltd v Say-Dee Pty Ltd* [2007] HCA 22, (2007) 230 CLR 89.

[34] See, eg, L Smith, 'Property, Unjust Enrichment and the Structure of Trusts' (2000) 116 *LQR* 412.

[35] See, eg, P Turner, 'Consequential Economic Loss and the Trust Beneficiary' (2010) 69 *CLJ* 445; J Edelman, 'Two Fundamental Questions for the Law of Trusts' (2013) 129 *LQR* 66; B Häcker, '"Substance over Form": Has the Pendulum Swung Too Far?'; W Swadling, 'In Defence of Formalism'; and B McFarlane, 'Form and Substance in Equity', all in A Robertson and J Goudkamp (eds), *Form and Substance in the Law of Obligations* (Oxford, Hart, 2019).

[36] [2010] EWCA Civ 180, [2011] QB 86.

[37] ibid [132] (Waller LJ).

[38] See too the analysis of Millett LJ in *Trustee of the Property of FC Jones v Jones* [1997] Ch 159 (CA): sums credited to the bank account of A (Mrs Jones) were the traceable proceeds of a disposition of partnership assets which was void as made after an initial act of bankruptcy. Millett LJ (at 170) stated that the bank account 'in reality belonged to the trustee [in the bankruptcy of the partnership]' so that the trustee in bankruptcy (B) was 'entitled to the money in [Mrs Jones's] account'. For the difficulties with this analysis, see McFarlane and Stevens (n 13) 21–22.

[39] For a similarly pragmatic view, see Mummery LJ in *R v Tower Hamlets LBC, ex parte von Goetz* [1999] QB 1019 (CA) 1023, citing with approval the analysis of Carnwath J at first instance that an equitable lease is 'for all practical purposes, an interest as good as a legal interest'.

[40] [2017] UKSC 6, [2017] AC 424 [83].

[41] Subject to the exercise by the court of a power to allow the disposition nonetheless to take effect.

direct conflict with that in *Shell*: in *Akers*, a disposition of the trust property was not seen as a disposition of B's property, whereas in *Shell* damage to the trust property was seen as damage to property of which B was the 'real' owner.

The immediate point here is not as to whether the reasoning in either *Shell* or *Akers* is correct;[42] it is rather as to the difficulties that courts face when deciding on the impact of B's right on a third party. A pragmatic analysis, identifying *some* difference between such a right and a legal property right, neither explains why that difference exists, nor tells us the nature and extent of the divergence. Indeed, it is telling that, in *Akers*, the conceptual point which determined the outcome in the Supreme Court – that the unauthorised transfer by the trustee was not a 'disposition' of the company's property – went unconsidered not only at first instance[43] and by a very strong Court of Appeal[44] but also during the Supreme Court hearing itself, and was a matter first raised only after that hearing, when the Justices invited written submissions from counsel on the point.[45] *Akers* also demonstrates that the practical difficulties caused by the absence of a clear conceptual understanding of the trust extend to legislators, such as the drafters of section 127 of the 1986 Act, as it can make it difficult to know in advance how terms, such as 'a disposition of a company's property', will be applied by the courts in relation to equitable property rights.[46]

C. The Proposal

In order to understand the trust, and to answer important *practical* questions as to its operation, such as those canvassed in section II.B, it is necessary to move beyond a pragmatic view and engage instead with the form of the parties' rights. The proposal of this chapter, adopting a particular type of formal view, is that, where A holds on trust for B, B should not be seen as having 'equitable title', but rather as having a right that relates to the right that A holds on trust.[47]

[42] This will be discussed in section III.A.

[43] *Akers v Samba* [2014] EWHC 540, (2014) 16 ITELR 808.

[44] *Akers v Samba* [2014] EWCA Civ 1516, [2015] Ch 451.

[45] This set of events is consistent with the point made by J Penner, 'An Untheory of the Law of Trusts, or Some Notes Towards Understanding the Structure of Trusts Law Doctrine' (2010) 63 *Current Legal Problems* 653, 662 where he argues that, in relation to trusts, 'demonstrable errors' are made 'all the way up to highest courts'. See too *Criterion Properties v Stratford UK Properties LLC* [2004] UKHL 28, [2004] 1 WLR 1846, where it was only in the House of Lords that the 'faulty elision of two different issues' relating to the authority of a company's directors (see Lord Nicholls at [2]), which had occurred in the courts below, was pointed out.

[46] In his 2017 Chancery Bar Association Lecture, Lord Justice Briggs (as he then was) states that it would have come as a surprise to an insolvency lawyer to discover that the protection of section 127 has the 'flaw' that it does not apply where the company loses an equitable interest under a trust: see Lord Justice Briggs, '*Akers v Samba*: Equity's Darling Reigns Supreme' (2017) [59], available at www.chba.org.uk/for-members/library/annual-lectures/equitys-darling-reigns-supreme/view.

[47] This is a view I have developed in previous work, such as B McFarlane, *The Structure of Property Law* (Oxford, Hart, 2009); McFarlane and Stevens (n 13); B McFarlane and R Stevens, 'What's Special About Equity? Rights About Rights' in D Klimchuk, I Samet and H Smith (eds), *Philosophical Foundations of the Law of Equity* (Oxford, OUP, 2020).

The need to adopt a formal view was clearly appreciated by Maitland, who grappled with the paradox inherent in the conventional view that the trust involves the split between legal and equitable title. Maitland's solution was to regard the notion of equitable title as, in some important respects, misleading: whilst B's rights under a trust have come to have many of the same practical effects as the rights of an owner,[48] the core technique of equity in protecting those rights against third parties was to recognise situations where a third party could come under a new duty to B. It would be a mistake, therefore, to see that protection of B against third parties as depending on B's having title, or a property right; rather, the initial obligation of T to B could give rise to a new obligation of a third party to B, and so B's protection was in fact the result of a series of personal rights of B.[49] In Milsom's pithy phrase, 'equity has proved that from the materials of obligation you can counterfeit the phenomena of property'.[50]

The analysis in this chapter gives two cheers to Maitland.[51] One cheer for his recognition of the need to investigate the formal nature of B's rights under a trust, and thus to go beyond the pragmatic view which he identified as common amongst English lawyers. The second cheer is for his insight that it simply cannot be possible for equity, as a secondary or supplementary system, to contradict the common law position and claim that it is B who is the true owner of the trust property. Whilst B's rights may have some of the same effects as ownership, or of a legal property right, this need not depend (either as a matter of the development of the law, or of current analysis) on seeing B's right as a right *in rem*. In his chapter in this volume, for example, Fox shows how B's protection in A's insolvency – often said to depend on, and prove, the proprietary status of B's rights – was developed by the courts independently of any such classification of B's rights.[52] This is not of merely historical interest, as it also shows that there is no necessary conceptual link between protection in insolvency and the holding of a right *in rem*. As Mitchell has pointed out,[53] for example, a legatee of an unadministered estate has no right in any specific property of the deceased, but this does not mean that general creditors of the personal representative have any access to the deceased estate to meet the debts of the personal representative.

The third cheer is withheld, however, as the claim that B has only a purely personal right is very difficult to defend.[54] This can be seen most simply by considering the different treatment of the following three cases.

Example 1: A has a freehold of land and enters a contract with B to allow B a limited use of that land for two years. One year later, A sells A's freehold to C, who is aware of A's contract with B, but makes no promise to respect that contract.

[48] Maitland (n 12) 117.

[49] ibid 120.

[50] SF Milsom, *Historical Foundations of the Common Law*, 2nd edn (London, Butterworths, 1961) 6.

[51] See too B McFarlane, 'The Essential Nature of Trusts and Other Equitable Interests: Two and a Half Cheers for Hohfeld' in S Balganesh, T Sichelman and H Smith (eds), *The Legacy of Wesley Hohfeld: Edited Major Works, Select Personal Papers, and Original Commentaries* (Cambridge, CUP, 2022).

[52] See Fox's chapter in this volume.

[53] C Mitchell, '*Commissioner of Stamp Duties v Livingston* (1965)' in B Sloan (ed), *Landmark Cases in Succession Law* (Oxford, Hart, 2019).

[54] As shown in the responses to Maitland's analysis: see, eg, A Scott, 'The Nature of the Rights of the "Cestui Que Trust"' (1917) 17 *Columbia Law Review* 269.

Example 2: A has a freehold of land and holds that title on trust for B. X, who is aware of the trust, enters the land and takes possession of it without permission from A or B.

Example 3: A again has a freehold of land and holds that title on trust for B. A then sells A's freehold to C, who is aware that this is a breach of the trust.

In each case, the third party interferes with the performance of A's duty to B, and has acted with knowledge of that prior duty. In the first two cases, however, equity gives B no claim against the third party.[55] What then is different about the third case, where a claim can be made?

The significance of the third case, and the answer to the puzzle about the nature of the trust, can be seen by asking what it is A, the trustee, actually holds on trust for B. The standard term to use is the 'trust property' and it is tempting therefore to think that A (with legal title) and B (with equitable title) are making competing claims to the same asset. So, in a case such as *Shell*, it is natural to identify the trust property as the land (including of course the pipelines on it) damaged as a result of the fire caused by the defendant's lack of care. This is consistent with the Court of Appeal's view that, in *Shell*, B was the 'real' owner of those pipelines. However, the analysis in *Shell* is confused even on its own terms. The consequential loss suffered by B in that case was identified by the Court as purely economic loss, and thus prima facie covered by the 'exclusionary rule' preventing recovery in the tort of negligence; yet, of course, if the pipelines really were the property of B, then any loss suffered by B as a result of the damage to them would not be purely economic loss.

It is important, therefore, to look more closely at the form of the trust. Its subject matter, in a case such as *Shell*, is not the land itself, but is rather A's estate in the land. In a significant recent consideration of the historical development of the trust, Foster notes how the notion of 'privity of estate' played a pivotal role both in allowing B's right to affect third parties, and to determine which third parties were so bound. As Foster puts it:[56]

> The core idea was that the trust attached to the estate vested in the trustee and would bind the trustee's successors in title ... Privity of estate came to an end, however, when one entered the land by virtue of an estate arising by operation of law, which was not derived from an act of the trustee ... Where the trustee was disseised of the trust lands, for example, the disseisor took the lands free of the beneficiary's rights (even where they had prior notice of the trust's existence).[57]

[55] For Example 1, see, eg, *Keppell v Bailey* (1834) 2 My & K 517, 547; 39 ER 1042, 1053; *Lloyd v Dugdale* [2001] EWCA Civ 1754, [2002] 2 P & CR 13. For application of the same analysis where the A–B contract relates to the use of property other than land, see, eg, *Port Line Ltd v Ben Line Steamers Ltd* [1958] 2 QB 146 (QB); Z Chaffee, 'Equitable Servitudes on Chattels' (1928) 41 *Harvard Law Review* 945. For Example 2, see, eg, the authorities set out in n 57 below.

[56] D Foster, 'Historical Conceptions of the Express Trust, *c* 1600–1900' in S Degeling, J Hudson and I Samet (eds), *Philosophical Foundations of the Law of Express Trusts* (Oxford, OUP, 2023).

[57] *Lord Compton's Case* (1587) 3 Leo 196; *Chudleigh's Case* (1594) 1 Co Rep 120a, 122a; *Sir Moyle Finch's Case* (1600) 4 Co Inst 85; G Gilbert, *The Law of Uses and Trusts* (London, E and R Nutt and R Gosling, 1734) 168–69; T Lewin, *A Practical Treatise on the Law of Trusts and Trustees* (London, A Maxwell, 1837) 13, 124; G Spence, *The Equitable Jurisdiction of the Court of Chancery* (London, V and R Stevens and GS Norton, 1849) vol II, 196 (footnote taken from Foster's text).

The historical role of the trustee's estate can also be shown in an example used by Maitland: the effect, prior to statutory intervention, on B of the loss of A's estate by escheat.[58] A's estate simply ceased to exist, and the superior lord (in some cases the Crown) took advantage by re-asserting its own prior rights and thus without making any use of A's estate. As a result, that superior lord could not be bound by the trust.[59]

Foster also notes the importance of the analysis by Lewin, the author of what is still a leading work on trusts, in modifying the technical notion of 'privity of estate' to focus instead on whether the third party had 'derived their claim from the trustee'.[60] This idea, which can be separated from the technical notion of privity of estate, is helpful in understanding the difference between Examples 2 and 3 above. In Example 3, where A, the trustee, makes an unauthorised transfer to C of a freehold held on trust for B, then C's rights clearly derive from the estate that A held on trust for B, and so it is possible (subject to defences such as the bona fide purchaser defence) for B to bring a claim against C. In contrast, in Example 2, where X trespasses on, or carelessly damages, the land, then whilst A may have a claim against X, there is no such direct claim for B, as X does not 'derive their claim from the trustee'.[61]

Foster notes that Lewin's analysis fell out of favour partly because of its apparent reliance on the concept of an estate.[62] This made it awkward to apply the analysis to cases where the subject matter of the trust was not an estate in land but, instead, chattels or a chose in action, such as a bank account. Instead, amongst writers on trusts 'there emerged a tendency to discuss the trust simply in terms of "equitable ownership" and to refer to the beneficiary as the "true owner" of the trust property'.[63] With the increased popularity of Austin's emphasis on the distinction between rights *in rem* and rights *in personam*, there then arose the classic debates of the late nineteenth and early twentieth century as to which of those categories best fits with B's rights under the trust: as we have seen, Maitland's analysis supported the *in personam* view. One reason for the long-running nature of this debate is that, as Fox notes,[64] it is doubtful that *either* of those Austinian concepts is helpful when seeking to understand how, and why, B's rights were allowed by the courts to affect third parties. A second reason is that, as can be seen in the outcomes of Examples 2 and 3, the cases seem to provide fuel both for a view of B's rights as purely personal, and for a view of them as proprietary.

[58] Maitland (n 12) 120.

[59] HF Stone, 'The Nature of the Rights of the Cestui Que Trust' (1917) 17 *Columbia Law Review* 467, 480–81 draws a distinction between escheat and forfeiture of an estate to the Crown, on the basis that the Crown can be bound by a pre-existing trust in the case of A's being subject to forfeiture, as it then acquires the very estate held on trust. Foster (n 56), however, notes that the position in relation to forfeiture was not as clear as Stone suggests.

[60] Foster (n 56), section II.B, discussing T Lewin, *A Practical Treatise on the Law of Trusts and Trustees* (London, A Maxwell, 1837) 18–19. Lewin states for example (ibid at 18) that: 'A trust is *annexed in privity to the estate*, that is, must stand or fall with the interest of the person by whom the trust is created.'

[61] Where X takes possession of the land, X may acquire a new estate in the land as a result; but that estate is of course different from the estate held on trust and does not derive from A.

[62] Foster (n 56) section III.A, referring, eg, to the criticism of Lewin's analysis in A Underhill, *A Concise Manual of the Law Relating to Private Trusts and Trustees* (London, Butterworths, 1878) 1 where it is stated that Lewin's approach 'would seem applicable to real estate only'.

[63] Foster (n 56) section III.A.

[64] See Fox's chapter in this volume.

The argument of this chapter is that, in hindsight, a mistake was made in regarding Lewin's analysis as dependent on the notion of an estate, and thus as applicable only to cases involving land. The value of the analysis can be seen by reconsidering the 'trust property'. When we consider land, it is necessary to distinguish between the thing itself and the rights held in it. This is clear because, whilst Maitland's Englishman might ordinarily think of himself as an owner of land, his lawyer (or even his estate agent) will quickly tell him that he has, in fact, either a freehold or leasehold estate. So, where the subject matter of a trust appears to be land, it is in fact A's estate, the freehold or leasehold, which is held on trust for B. The crucial point, which extends beyond land, and beyond estates, is that we *always* have to distinguish between the thing and the rights held in it.[65] So, where O thinks of himself as selling his car to P, we know that O is in fact transferring his title to the car to P. Similarly, if a chattel is the subject matter of a trust, then it is A's *right* to the chattel that is held on trust for B.[66]

The irony is that the type of analysis preferred by Lewin in fact becomes even *more* useful when we move away from land to cases where a chose in action, such as a bank account, is held on trust. In such cases, it makes little sense to think of 'ownership' or 'rights *in rem*'. After all, if A has a bank account, this does not give A ownership of, or title to, any specific property: it simply means that A has a personal right against A's bank. If A then declares a trust of that right in favour of B, it would seem to breach any number of rules, from *nemo dat* to the first law of thermodynamics, if A, a holder of a *right in personam*, could thus confer on B a right *in rem*.

It is, however, possible to align the trust of a bank account with the case of chattels and land, if we again focus on the *right* held by A. On the conceptual view of the trust preferred in this chapter, the subject matter of a trust is always a specific right (or rights) held by A, and the third parties against whom B may be able to make a trust-based claim are those who acquire either that right, or a right that depends on it. The term 'trust property' is one which can reasonably be used, but only as long as we remember that the subject matter of the trust is always a right, rather than any independently existing thing. Terms such as 'trust property' or 'trust assets' are simply shorthand for the rights held on trust.[67]

D. Some Advantages of the Proposal

The first advantage of the conceptual view proposed here, which identifies the subject matter of a trust as the rights held on trust, is that it can justify Burrows' view that the trust provides an example of the coherent interaction of common law and equity.

[65] See, eg, W Swadling, 'Property' in A Burrows (ed), *English Private Law*, 3rd edn (Oxford, OUP, 2013) para [4.02].

[66] This is apparent in cases where it is claimed that a trust arises following a theft: the right which the thief can hold on trust is the precarious title acquired by the thief through taking possession. For discussion, see, eg, R Chambers, 'Trust and Theft' in E Bant and M Harding (eds), *Exploring Private Law* (Cambridge, CUP, 2010).

[67] As was expressly noted by Kiefel CJ, Keane and Edelman JJ in *Carter Holt Harvey Woodproducts Australia Pty Ltd v Commonwealth of Australia* [2019] HCA 20, (2019) 268 CLR 524 [24]. See too Briggs J, as he then was, in *Re Lehman Bros International (Europe) Ltd* [2010] EWHC 2914 (Ch) [241], noting that B can have a beneficial interest even where A holds a purely personal right, such as a bank account.

In a case, for example, where A holds a freehold of land on trust for B, B is not making a claim to the land which competes with the claim of A. B is not denying that A holds the freehold estate; rather, A's holding of that right is essential to B's claim. In finding that B has a right under a trust, then, equity does not contradict the common law's position that A has the freehold. This is why, for example, X continues to owe a duty to A, rather than to B, not to trespass on the land and why A still has the power to make a valid transfer of the freehold to C: as long as A's transfer to C complies with the general rules regulating such transfers, it will pass title to C whether or not that transfer is authorised under the trust.[68] There is then a separate question of whether C, having acquired that right from A, is also now under a duty to B in relation to it. This model also explains why, in *Akers v Samba*, the unauthorised transfer of the shares from A to C was not a disposition of B's property, even if its effect was that B no longer had a right under a trust of the shares.[69] A simply exercised A's power, as holder of the shares, to transfer A's rights to C; certainly, there was no transfer of *B*'s right to C. It is, therefore, a mistake to think of cases in which C takes trust property free from B's claim as exceptions to the *nemo dat* principle.[70] In such cases, A is *not* giving B's right to C. Rather, A simply transfers A's right to C and the separate question of whether B can assert B's right under the trust against C is answered in C's favour.

The second advantage of the proposal is that, in contrast to Maitland's analysis, it can help to explain equity's different treatment of Example 1 and Example 3, as given in section II.C. The difference lies in the content of the duty owed by A to B. In Example 3, in the case of the trust, the duty relates to the entirety of the right (the freehold) held by A on trust for B; in Example 1, the case of the contractual licence, in contrast, A's duty is simply one to give, and not revoke, A's permission for B to make a limited use of A's land. Regarding a trust as requiring A's duty to relate to the entirety of a specific right or rights held by A not only helps to explain which third parties may be subject to a claim by B, but also helps to explain when A's duty to B gives B only a personal right against A, rather than a beneficial interest. Indeed, it can be argued that the distinctive characteristic of all 'equitable property rights', whether arising under a trust or not, is that A's duty relates to a specific right or power of A.[71]

[68] See Hudson's chapter in this volume, section II.B.i.

[69] Note the model also explains why, if money is mistakenly paid to a trustee (who is not acting as an agent) and the money had not yet been paid out to any beneficiary, a restitutionary claim can be brought against the trustee, as confirmed in *Skandinaviska Enskilda Banken AB (Publ) v Conway* [2019] UKPC 36, [2020] AC 1111. Contrary to Lord Reed's suggestion at [89], this is not because the 'common law ignores the equitable interest of the beneficiaries': it is rather because the transfer reversed by the restitutionary claim was between the payor and the trustee, not the payor and any beneficiary. For further consequences of this model for our understanding of the position of a trustee, see B McFarlane, 'Trusts, Property, and Rights' in S Degeling, J Hudson and I Samet (eds), *Philosophical Foundations of the Law of Express Trusts* (Oxford, OUP, 2023).

[70] For such a *nemo dat* analysis, see, eg, P Birks, 'Notice and Onus in *O'Brien*' (1998) 12 *Trust Law International* 2 (discussing the Court of Appeal's decision in *Barclays Bank plc v Boulter* [1998] 1 WLR 1 (CA), later overturned by the House of Lords: [1999] 1 WLR 1919 (HL)). The flaws in this analysis are discussed by B McFarlane and A Televantos, 'As Complex as ABC? Bona Fide Purchasers of Equitable Interests' in P Davies and T Chen-Han (eds), *Intermediaries in Commercial Law* (Oxford, Hart, 2022).

[71] See further McFarlane, *The Structure of Property Law* (n 47) and McFarlane and Stevens, 'The Nature of Equitable Property' (n 13).

As noted by Justice Edelman, writing extra-judicially,[72] the proposal is consistent with some earlier accounts of the trust, which see it as 'an obligation annexed to the ownership of the property'.[73] The contrast is between a trust and the situation where, for example, A owes a debt to B: in the latter case, A's duty is simply to pay a sum of money to B, and that duty is not linked to any specific right held by A. It is this linking of the duty to the right which provides a conceptual account consistent both with B's having a right which is different from a standard personal right and with equity's not contradicting the position that it is A who holds the right forming the subject matter of the trust.[74] It is unfortunate that a misplaced desire to fit B's rights within Austinian categories has obscured equity's remarkable development of a special type of right, arising only where A holds a specific right, and is under a duty to B in relation to that very right.

This leads to a third advantage of the proposal: it reveals the dangers, noted by both Foster[75] and Fox,[76] of applying the '*in personam*' or '*in rem*' labels to B's rights under a trust. This can be seen by considering Lord Sumption's use of the latter term in *Akers v Samba*.[77] For the formal view adopted in this chapter, there are two key points about that decision. One was discussed above: A's unauthorised transfer of the shares to C was not a disposition of B's property. The second is the preliminary point that the Court was able to apply a law other than the *lex situs* of the shares to determine B's rights. As Lord Mance stated, 'in the eyes of English law, a trust may be created, exist and be enforceable in respect of assets located in a jurisdiction, the law of which does not recognise trusts in any form'.[78] Lord Mance drew on a long and consistent line of authorities in reaching that conclusion, and a significant part of the reasoning in those cases is that, in relation to each of jurisdiction and choice of law, the question of whether B has a right under a trust of, for example, land or shares is *not* governed by the same rules as the different question of whether a party has the right to the land itself, or to the shares themselves.[79] In claiming such a right under a trust, B is not claiming the asset held on trust, but is rather claiming that the holder of the asset is under a particular duty to B. This provides one reason why, in *Webb v Webb*, each of an English[80] and a European[81] court held that, in claiming that A held title to French land on trust for him, B's claim did not have as its object a right *in rem* in immovable property, and so the French courts did not have exclusive jurisdiction under what is now article 24(1) of the Recast Brussels Regulation.

[72] Edelman (n 35) 72–73.

[73] Using the language of the Indian Trusts Act 1882, s 3.

[74] W Swadling, 'Unjust Enrichment, Value, and Trusts' (2021) 137 *LQR* 56, 70–71 argues that A's being under a duty to B not to use A's right for A's benefit does not in itself make A a trustee. As Swadling notes, it is indeed important that there are other cases, as where A is the executor of a deceased's estate, where such a duty arises. Even if there is no trust in such a case, parties who benefit from the performance of the duty, such as a legatee, receive practically valuable protection against third parties, and in A's insolvency, not available to the holder of a purely personal right: see, eg, *Commissioner of Stamp Duties v Livingston* [1965] AC 694 (PC).

[75] Foster (n 56).

[76] See Fox's chapter in this volume.

[77] (n 40) [82].

[78] ibid [34].

[79] See further S Agnew and B McFarlane, 'The Nature of Trusts and the Conflict of Laws' (2021) 137 *LQR* 405.

[80] *Webb v Webb* [1991] 1 WLR 1410 (Ch).

[81] Case C-294/92 *Webb v Webb* [1994] ECR I–1717.

It is therefore puzzling that, in *Akers v Samba*, Lord Sumption, whilst accepting that a claim depending on B's equitable interest under a trust was not governed by the *lex situs*, at the same time stated that such an interest has

> the essential hallmark of any right in rem, namely that it is good against third parties into whose hands the property or its traceable proceeds may have come, subject to the rules of equity for the protection of bona fide purchasers for value without notice ...[82]

In the confidence with which it is made, as well as its content, this statement calls to mind Maitland's Englishman who, in his ordinary thinking, regards B as the owner of the asset held on trust, subject only to the technical rule of bona fide purchase. There are two particularly telling points, drawn from Lord Sumption's own analysis, which make the use of the '*in rem*' language particularly inapt. First, the specific focus is not on all third parties interacting with the trust property, but rather on recipients of that property (or its traceable proceeds): this is consistent with the distinction drawn above between Example 2 and Example 3, and the two particular types of third party represented by X on the one hand and C on the other. In contrast, a right *in rem* is more usually understood to be prima facie binding on *all* third parties interacting with the asset.[83] Second, even in those cases where C acquires the trust property then, as Lord Sumption noted later in his judgment, 'the question becomes whether the conscience of the transferee is affected'.[84] This observation is consistent with the analysis above, as the extent of C's knowledge may be decisive in determining if C has come under a duty to B; but it again shows how B's initial right operates differently from a standard right *in rem*, where strict prima facie liability is imposed on third parties, without any examination of their conscience.[85]

III. LESSONS FOR EQUITY

A. Lessons from the Trust

The particular formal view proposed here is that the trust does not involve common law and equity disagreeing about ownership of the asset held on trust; but nor is it a case of a simple personal duty being owed by the trustee to the beneficiary. Rather, the trust involves the recognition of a different type of right, transcending the *in personam*/*in rem* divide, arising where A's duty to B relates specifically to a right

[82] *Akers* (n 40) [82], citing Lord Browne-Wilkinson in *Westdeutsche Landesbank Girozentrale v Islington LBC* [1996] AC 669 (HL) 705.

[83] The qualification 'prima facie' is important: contrary to the analysis of, for example, C Langdell, 'A Brief Survey of the Equitable Jurisdiction' (1887) 1 *Harvard Law Review* 55, 60, a right can be *in rem* in this sense even if it is subject to a defence such as the bona fide purchaser defence. It is not, therefore, the possibility of such a defence that prevents B's interest coming within this definition of a right *in rem*: it is rather the fact that the interest is not even prima facie binding on third parties (such as X in Example 2) who do not acquire any right from A.

[84] *Akers* (n 40) [89].

[85] As noted in section III.C of Henry Smith's chapter in this volume, the legal system as a whole loses a potentially valuable tool if all rights are seen as either proprietary or personal, thus overlooking the possibility of a different means, in equity, for a claim to be made against a third party.

held by A. The analysis then is not purely negative, aiming to avoid a confrontation between common law and equity. Rather, it aims to show that the immensely valuable practical contribution equity has made by its development of the trust is based not just on pragmatism, but on a conceptual coup, the development of a new type of right. Indeed, the continued adaptability of the trust depends in some cases on this conceptual point. For example, the potential practical benefits of the 'data trust' would be lost[86] if English law adopted the mistaken view that, since data is not property, it cannot be held on trust.[87] Rather, as long as such trusts involve specific *rights* relating to data being held subject to a duty, data trusts are possible[88] and can provide a modern-day example of the pragmatic benefits of equity.[89]

This model thus explains why the trust is an example of the coherent interaction of common law and equity: put simply, in recognising that B has a right under a trust, equity is not giving a different answer to the fundamental question of who has title. Rather, where, for example, A holds a freehold on trust for B, the fact that A has the rights and powers associated with the freehold is not an obstacle to B; the benefits accruing to B under the trust *depend* on A's having those rights and powers. Equity does not deny A those rights and powers but instead imposes a duty on A to exercise them for the benefit of B, rather than for A's own benefit. This is the sense in which the trust operates by a 'process of cumulation, and not division'.[90] It is also consistent with Maitland's analysis of equity as a secondary or supplementary system: a court of equity did not intervene by way of appeal or judicial review, overturning a common law decision or directing common law judges to act in a particular way. Its orders were rather addressed to the parties themselves.[91] This is consistent with a view which sees the recognition of the trust not as denying A's entitlements, but rather acknowledging them, and directing A to act in a particular way in relation to them.[92]

[86] For such benefits, see, eg, S Delacroix and N Lawrence, 'Bottom-up Data Trusts: Disturbing the "One Size Fits All" Approach to Data Governance' (2019) 9 *International Data Privacy Law* 236.

[87] That view was adopted by Reed, BPE Solicitors and Pinsent Masons, 'Data Trusts: Legal and Governance Considerations' (2019) in a report for the Open Data Institute, 12, available at theodi.org/wp-content/uploads/2019/04/General-legal-report-on-data-trust.pdf.

[88] See Delacroix and Lawrence (n 86) and J Lau, J Penner and B Wong, 'The Basics of Private and Public Data Trusts' (2020) *Singapore Journal of Legal Studies* 90.

[89] Note that linking the trust to cases where A holds a specific right does also provide a limit to the flexibility of equity. This is an under-explored aspect of the courts' consideration, in cases such as *AA v Persons Unknown* [2019] EWHC 3556 (Comm), [2020] 4 WLR 35 and *Ruscoe and Moore v Cryptopia Ltd* [2020] NZHC 728, 22 ITELR 925 of trusts relating to cryptocurrency as the courts should be clearer as to what rights, if any, are held by a holder of cryptocurrency. There is a tendency in such cases to link the availability of a trust to a characterisation of cryptocurrency as property, which is misguided, given that it is clear that a purely personal right can be held on trust: see further K Low, 'Trusts of Cryptocurrency' (2021) 34 *Trust Law International* 191; McFarlane, 'Trusts, Property, and Rights' (n 69).

[90] See N Jones, 'Trusts in England after the Statute of Uses: A View from the 16th Century' in R Helmholz and R Zimmerman (eds), *Itinera Fiduciae: Trust and Treuhand in Historical Perspective* (Berlin, Duncker & Humblot, 1998) 190. See too Brennan J in *DKLR Holding Co (No 2) Ltd v Commissioner of Stamp Duties* (1982) 149 CLR 431 (HCA) 474: 'An equitable interest is not carved out of a legal estate but impressed upon it.'

[91] Maitland (n 12) 9. See too Swadling's chapter in this volume, section V.C.

[92] See, eg, *Re Transphere Pty Ltd* (1986) 5 NSWLR 309 (NSWSC) 311 (McLelland J): 'Where a legal owner holds property on trust for another, he has at law all the rights of an absolute owner but the beneficiary has the right to compel him to hold and use those rights which the law gives him in accordance with the obligations which equity has imposed on him by virtue of the existence of the trust.'

Such a view may also be helpful in addressing civilian objections which are based on the fear, misguided but stoked by the language of the split between legal and equitable title, that the trust involves fragmenting ownership between trustee and beneficiary.[93]

On a pragmatic view, it can be said that equity mitigates, or corrects, the common law: certainly, the practical outcomes to which common law rules would lead are modified by the existence of equitable intervention so that, as the Court of Appeal noted in *Shell*, for example, it is the beneficiary of a trust who in practice enjoys the economic value of the trust property.[94] However, this misses a fundamental formal point about the role of equity: it is not the common law rule or principle that is modified, but only its practical outcome in particular circumstances. Importantly, the rule itself is left intact. To take the case of *Shell*, and to challenge again the pragmatic analysis of the Court of Appeal, it simply cannot be the case that B is the 'real' owner of the land, as title to the land is acquired through registration. That statutory rule is not modified by recognising a trust: it is *not* the case that the statutory rule (that title to the estate in the land depends on registration) is unjust because of its generality and correction, in the Aristotelian sense of equity,[95] is required. Rather, the rule is upheld: it is A, the registered party, who has title (and the consequent rights and powers in relation to third parties); but A is under a duty to B to exercise those rights and powers in a particular way.[96] The trust thus provides a fine example of equity's supplementary or secondary role, with its intervention depending on, rather than denying, pre-existing common law entitlements.[97]

Such an analysis also provides a response to a standard, but potentially fatal, objection to the persistence of equity. If equity is seen as correcting the common law, the objection is that such correction should simply occur directly: by way of changing the common law rules themselves. On a pragmatic view, there is really no good answer to that objection.[98] Consider, for example, developments in the English law of penalties. By 1873, limits imposed on a party's ability to enforce an agreed damages

[93] See P Matthews, 'The Compatibility of the Trust with the Civil Law Notion of Property' in L Smith (ed), *The Worlds of the Trust* (Cambridge, CUP, 2013).

[94] *Shell* (n 36) [132].

[95] Based on Aristotle's discussion of *epiekeia*. For consideration of this sense of equity, see Popovici and Smith's chapter in this volume, section III.A.

[96] As noted in section II.A of Nair's chapter in this volume, the registration system sharply distinguishes in such a case between A, who has a registrable estate (and so access to the protections which come with registration) and B, who does not. As Nair notes, the 2002 Act distinguishes between legal and equitable rights in establishing this divide and that distinction cannot be justified in purely pragmatic terms (such as the value of the rights concerned).

[97] For the argument that a distinctive characteristic of equity is its control of the acquisition or enforcement of rights, see McFarlane and Stevens, 'What's Special About Equity? Rights About Rights' (n 47).

[98] The type of pragmatic view favoured by certain legal realists, for example, was often associated with scepticism as to the value of the distinction between law and equity: see, eg, Z Chafee, *Foreword to Selected Essays on Equity*, edn by ED Re (New York, Oceana, 1955) 4. The argument was not that equitable methods of proceeding were unwelcome, but rather that they should not be limited to traditionally equitable areas: see, eg, R Pound, 'The End of Law as Developed in Legal Rules and Doctrines' (1913) 27 *Harvard Law Review* 195, 226–27 and, later, D Laycock, 'The Triumph of Equity' (1993) 56 *Law and Contemporary Problems* 53.

clause had long been seen as equitable,[99] but the Supreme Court in *Cavendish Square Holding BV v Makdessi* re-interpreted the rule against penal clauses as a creature of common law.[100] From a pragmatic perspective, this might be praised as a clear-sighted simplification, directly adjusting the parties' powers to make enforceable agreements. To understand the *practical* significance of the change, however, a formal approach is necessary. Where the rule against penalties is seen as an equitable one, this means that the parties' powers to create valid rights and duties under an agreed damages clause are not denied, but rather than a party can be prevented from asserting the rights arising under such a clause in particular circumstances. The existence of the right is not denied; rather, its enforcement is regulated. This means, for example, that conditions can be imposed on the enforcement of the right, or the term can be enforced up to a limit set by the court.[101] In contrast, on the common law analysis, the right and correlative duty simply do not exist,[102] as the parties lack the power to create such legal relations. This is not to say that the law as a whole is necessarily in a worse state if the rule is regarded as a common law one that denies the parties the power to create such a right; it is rather to say that, as in relation to trusts, the divide between common law and equity reflects an important formal difference, and the practical consequences of moving from one analysis to another may be missed if those formal differences are not borne in mind. As Henry Smith has shown in his analysis of the law in the United States,[103] the 'flattening' involved in overlooking the differences between common law and equity can cause important practical problems.

B. Looking Beyond the Trust

One of the most forceful expositions of a pragmatic view of the relationship between common law and equity can be seen in Atiyah's analysis[104] of the Court of Appeal's decision in *Crabb v Arun District Council*.[105] As shown by the title of his case note, Atiyah's view was that, in allowing Crabb to succeed in his claim that the council was

[99] See, eg, *Wyllie v Wilkes* (1780) 2 Doug KB 519, 523; 99 ER 331, 333; *Sloman v Walter* (1784) 1 Bro CC 418, 28 ER 1213. For full discussion of the history, see P Turner, '*Lex Sequitur Equitatem*: Fusion and the Penalty Doctrine' in J Goldberg, H Smith and P Turner (eds), *Equity and Law: Fusion and Fission* (Cambridge, CUP, 2019) and N Tiverios, *Contractual Penalties in Australia and the United Kingdom: History, Theory and Practice* (Sydney, Federation Press, 2019).

[100] *Cavendish Square Holding BV v Makdessi* [2015] UKSC 67, [2016] AC 1172. Compare the different approach taken in Australia: whilst in *AMEV-UDC Finance Ltd v Austin* (1986) 162 CLR 170 (HCA), the distinct equitable doctrine was said to have 'withered on the vine', its vitality was asserted in *Andrews v Australia and New Zealand Banking Group Ltd* [2012] HCA 30, (2012) 247 CLR 205. See further N Tiverios and B McFarlane, 'Controlling Private Punishment in Three Dimensions: Penalties and Forfeiture in England and Australia' in E Bant et al (eds), *Punishment and Private Law* (Oxford, Hart, 2021).

[101] See, eg, the analysis of Nicholls LJ in *Jobson v Johnson* [1989] 1 WLR 1026 (CA) 1038–41.

[102] Or, at least, the right cannot be enforced: the analysis in eg, *Makdessi* (n 100) does not make entirely clear if the penal term is void or simply unenforceable.

[103] See Smith's chapter in this volume. See too H Smith, 'Equity as Meta-Law' (2021) 130 *Yale Law Journal* 1050 especially 1096–97, 1136–38.

[104] P Atiyah, 'When Is an Enforceable Agreement Not a Contract? Answer: When It Is an Equity' (1976) 92 *LQR* 174.

[105] [1976] Ch 179 (CA).

bound to grant him a right of way over its land, the Court had, in effect, modified the classic requirement of consideration, but had been too timid to challenge that rule directly, and so had used proprietary estoppel as a convenient equitable cover to reach the desired practical outcome. A more principled court, in Atiyah's view, would have foregone the equitable fig leaf and taken on the outmoded requirement of consideration directly.[106] The central difficulty with this analysis, as shown by Millett's spirited rebuttal,[107] is that it focusses too much on ends rather than means, assuming that, because the case resulted in the enforcement of an agreement, it must be seen as part of contract law. Taking a formal view is again necessary to understand the nature of the equitable intervention, and its interaction with common law.

On such a view, there are significant differences between finding a contract and permitting a proprietary estoppel claim: the latter is not the equitable equivalent of the former, just as a beneficial interest under a trust is not the equitable equivalent of ownership. Where a contract is found, A is under an immediate duty to B to honour A's side of the bargain and any judicial remedies will aim to give effect to that duty, whether or not B has suffered any loss from its breach.[108] If there is no contract, equity does not undermine that position by proceeding nonetheless to impose such a duty. In contrast, as Hoffmann LJ pointed out in an influential analysis,[109] equitable estoppel, where it operates as a cause of action, does not hold that the promise imposed an immediate duty on A, but rather 'looks backwards' and considers whether, given A's promise and B's reliance on it, it would *now* be unacceptable for A to be wholly free to withdraw from that promise. This explains, for example, why the contractual requirement of intention to come under a legally binding duty does not apply to proprietary estoppel: the equitable doctrine, after all, imposes no such duty.[110] Contrary to Atiyah's analysis, proprietary estoppel does not allow a contractual claim to proceed in the absence of consideration; rather, it recognises a quite different type of claim. This can be seen, as in the case of the trust, by focussing on the form of the parties' legal relations. It seems again that equity makes a useful addition to the forms available at common law: whereas the contractual requirements determine when A is under an enforceable duty to B to perform A's side of

[106] Atiyah (n 104) 179–80.

[107] P Millett, 'Crabb v Arun District Council – A Riposte' (1976) 92 *LQR* 342. As counsel for Crabb in the case, Millett understandably wished to rebut the notion that the case could simply have been pleaded as a contractual claim. As Millett noted (at 346) 'the apparent similarity of the results achieved [in a contractual claim and a proprietary estoppel claim]' is 'deceptive' as the claims 'are different, require different facts to be proved, and have different consequences'.

[108] See, eg, *Williams Bros v Ed T Agius Ltd* [1914] AC 510 (HL).

[109] *Walton v Walton* (CA, 14 April 1994): the case is unreported but Hoffmann LJ's analysis has been relied on in, eg, *Thorner v Major* [2009] UKHL 18, [2009] 1 WLR 776 [52]–[57] (Lord Walker), [101] (Lord Neuberger) and *Cowper-Smith v Morgan* [2017] SCC 61, [2017] 2 SCR 754 [26] and [28] (McLachlin CJ). See further B McFarlane, 'The Importance of Looking Back' in P Davies and J Pila (eds), *The Jurisprudence of Lord Hoffmann* (Oxford, Hart, 2015).

[110] As noted by Wilson LJ in *Sutcliffe v Lloyd* [2007] EWCA Civ 153, [2007] 2 EGLR 13 [38]: it is 'misconceived in law' to require A to have suggested to B that A's promise was legally binding as '[e]quity intervenes to make the promise unable to be revoked (and able to be enforced) not at the time when it is made but only at a significantly later stage, namely in the events both that the promisee should have acted to his detriment in reliance upon it and that the promisor should have unconscionably sought to withdraw from it. Equity does not require the promisor, in making the promise, to mis-state the law in this regard'.

an agreement, proprietary estoppel instead recognises when a court may give effect to a liability of A to ensure that A does not, without justification, leave B to suffer a detriment as a result of B's reasonable reliance on A's seriously intended promise to B. Indeed, it is in some ways fitting – albeit in other ways confusing – that the very word 'equity' is used to refer to the right B acquires where a proprietary estoppel arises, and thus to distinguish it from the claim-right B acquires where B has the benefit of an enforceable contract.[111]

IV. CONCLUSION

Less than 50 years after the Judicature reforms, Maitland stated that it would have been 'a belated, a reactionary measure' to include equity as a separate subject in an undergraduate law degree.[112] Over 100 years after those reforms, calls were made for the end of practitioner works on equity.[113] Yet, as we hit the 150th anniversary, there has been significant academic interest in recognising the benefits that equity can bring to a modern system of private law. Some have emphasised the substantive contribution of equity, for example in allowing the positive law to accord more closely with morality;[114] others have focussed on the functional advantages of a secondary system.[115] This chapter has argued instead for a formal analysis, which focusses on the specific nature of the legal relations involved where equity intervenes. Such an analysis is not inconsistent with either the substantive or functional views and, indeed, can provide support for them. The key point remains that identified by Burrows: to justify distinct equitable rules and principles, different from their common law 'equivalents', we need to identify the distinct questions which those rules and principles are answering and show how they differ from the questions posed at common law.

In the case of the trust, this chapter has argued, equity gives precisely the same answer as common law to the question of ownership of, or title to, property; it then goes on and, consistently with its role as a secondary or supplementary system, asks the further question of whether that party is under a particular type of duty in relation to that ownership or title. As Burrows claimed, common law and equity do co-exist coherently in such a case, but precisely because there is *not* a split between legal and equitable title. Rather, there is a difference between the question of title and the question of whether the holder of the title is under a particular type of duty. On this view,

[111] See, eg, *Crabb v Arun* (n 105) 192 (Scarman LJ): '[Mr Crabb] has the benefit of no enforceable contract … If the plaintiff has any right, it is an equity arising out of the conduct and relationship of the parties.' For an interpretation of such an 'equity' as showing that A is under a liability, rather than a duty to B, see, eg, B McFarlane, 'Equitable Estoppel as a Cause of Action: Neither One Thing nor One Other' in S Degeling, J Edelman and J Goudkamp (eds), *Contract in Commercial Law* (Sydney, LawBook Co, 2016).

[112] Maitland (n 12) 21.

[113] J Hackney, 'Snell's Equity (13th edn) (Review)' (2001) 117 *LQR* 150, 154 notes that the basic message of the organisation of P Birks, *English Private Law* (Oxford, OUP, 2000) – with its absence of a chapter on equity – is '"thank you, but no more *Snells*"'.

[114] See, eg, I Samet, *Equity: Conscience Goes to Market* (Oxford, OUP, 2018).

[115] See, eg, Smith, 'Equity as Meta-Law' (n 103).

then, the persistence of equity depends on the formal differences between the legal relations recognised by particular common law rules and principles on the one hand, and equitable rules and principles on the other. If English law is to continue to enjoy the practical benefits arising from equity, by giving clear answers to difficult questions as to the nature and operation of equitable concepts such as the trust, it is vital that those formal differences are kept in mind. The trust, and equity more broadly, thus provide examples of a still more general point: if English law is to continue to be successful in practice, we need not only pragmatists, but also Professors.

2

Equity's Gloss on Authority

JESSICA HUDSON*

I. INTRODUCTION

LAW SHOULD PREVENT, or at least respond to, the abuse(s) of power. There are a range of legal rules that implement this commitment, and upon which legal institutions and relationships depend for their function. Companies, agencies, express trusts, deceased estates, and other private and public power-holding arrangements can only fulfill their various mandates if there are legal rules that create *and control* legal powers. This chapter considers what contribution, if any, is made by the sub-set of power-controlling rules that can be traced to the body of rules administered by Courts of Equity prior to the Judicature Acts.[1]

Historically, the jurisdictional divides and constraints prior to the Judicature reforms meant that only courts of equity had the necessary rules of pleading, procedure and evidence to interrogate the consciences of the 'suitors'[2] before it,[3] and to adjudicate upon matters and develop rules that concerned the power-holder's subjective or internal reasons for action. The existence and content of the terms of an orally declared trust, for example, could only have been ascertained in equity. Further, some equitable controls, such as fraud on a power, are concerned with the power-holder's actual or subjective state of mind and thus could only have been developed and adjudicated upon in equity.[4] In addition to all this, some unauthorised exercises of power could only be addressed by equitable remedies, such as orders reversing the consequences of execution, for delivery up of documents, re-conveyance of title, and/or for consequential money orders.

* I am grateful to the organisers and participants of the International Fiduciary Law Workshop hosted by Melbourne Law School, December 2021, where an earlier version of this chapter was presented. I am grateful to Elise Bant, Rachel Leow, Ben McFarlane, Paul Miller, Charles Mitchell and Lionel Smith for discussing some of the ideas in this chapter with me, and to Alexander Stefas for his fantastic research assistance. All errors are mine.

[1] Judicature Act 1873.

[2] *Kakavas v Crown Melbourne Ltd* [2013] HCA 25, (2013) 250 CLR 392 [16].

[3] See generally M McNair, 'Equity and Conscience' (2007) 27 *OJLS* 659.

[4] J Hudson, 'One Thicket in Fraud on a Power' (2019) 39 *OJLS* 57.

History might explain why controls on power with particular normative content originated as equitable rules.[5] However, 150 years after the Judicature reforms, it is no longer possible to justify equity's distinct control of power according to the separate administration of law and equity, the inadequacies of the common law, or the distinctiveness of equity's normative content. The political and constitutional constraints on the development of the common law that once required equity's mitigation or correction are no longer applicable today. Further, the common law has evolved in a manner such that equity's normative content is no longer distinct. There is a plethora of statutory rules that model the same or very similar content to equitable rules, such as statutory rules requiring power to be exercised for a proper purpose, in good faith and free from conflict,[6] or common law rules concerning the exercise of contractual discretionary powers.[7] All this was predicted by Frederic Maitland, stating that 'lawyers will cease to inquire whether a given rule be a rule of equity or a rule of common law: suffice that it is a well-established rule administered by the High Court of Justice'.[8]

Despite Maitland's prediction, the equitableness of a rule still matters, determining, for example, how a rule operates, the applicability of discretionary factors and the remedies available.[9] How do we explain and justify equity's continued unique existence without pointing to the historically separate administration of law and equity or relying on an outdated and pejorative view of the common law?

This chapter develops a novel account of how equity's modality as a discretionary gloss on authority supports a symbiosis between power-generating rules (whether sourced in common law, statute or equity) and equity's power-controlling rules. Key to that account is the distinction, to be developed in more detail below, between a *legal power* understood as a person's ability to affect a change to the legal status of another, and *authority* understood as the lawfulness of that action. While often confused, these are different legal concepts that are defined by distinct sets of legal rules, albeit with some points of overlap that can make the core distinction hard to perceive and will be explained further below. Power-generating rules define the existence and scope of a legal power by prescribing what a power-holder must do to effect the change she wants. Power-controlling rules condition a power-holder's authority according to certain standards or criteria, such as a power-holder's adherence with the terms of the relevant mandate.

Some of equity's power-controlling rules, such as the excessive execution rule and the rule against fraud on a power, have sometimes been understood as power-generating rules that define the existence and scope of legal power, the non-satisfaction of which means that a power-holder's actions are ineffective to produce

[5] L Smith, 'Equity is not a Single Thing' in D Klimchuk, I Samet and H Smith (eds), *The Philosophical Foundations of the Law of Equity* (Oxford, OUP, 2020).

[6] See, eg, the statutory duties imposed upon directors and other corporate officers under various companies legislation, eg, the Companies Act 2006.

[7] See, eg, *Braganza v BP Shipping Ltd* [2015] UKSC 17, [2015] 4 All ER 639.

[8] FW Maitland, *Equity – A Course of Lectures*, 2nd edn (Cambridge, CUP, 1936) 1.

[9] See, eg, *Cavendish Square Holding BV v Makdessi* [2015] UKSC 67, [2016] AC 1172 [32]; *Andrews v Australia and New Zealand Banking Group* [2012] HCA 30, (2012) 247 CLR 205 [10]–[11], [61]–[63].

the legal consequence she intended, ie invalid, void or null. This chapter advocates a different understanding of these two equitable rules: they are not a gloss on power as they do not define or limit the scope of a legal power in the sense of prescribing what a power-holder must do to effect the change she wants. Equally, they do not disable the exercise of power or negate the consequences of execution. They are better understood as power-controlling rules, that, like other equitable rules with a secondary or meta-law function, determine the circumstances in which it is lawful for a legal entitlement to be exercised. It is in this sense that the excessive execution rule and rule against fraud on a power operate as a gloss on authority: they condition the lawfulness of execution on the power-holder's objective and subjective adherence with the terms according to which a power is held. They also determine when there is an equity for proprietary or personal relief against the power-holder and/or a third party, to reverse the consequence(s) of execution. Equity's gloss is discretionary as any relief is subject to certain equitable defences and discretionary factors.

The main argument is that law's ends are served by equity's modality as a discretionary gloss on authority because it allows the overall legal system to maintain otherwise inconsistent commitments to the rule of law arising from a legal system's generation of legal powers. Equity's modality preserves the stability, certainty and predictability of the legal rules that generate legal power, all while providing a response to the abusive exercise of power and preserving law's guidance function, when that is dependent upon power being exercised in accordance with some applicable set of terms. Equity's enduring role is to support the common law to fulfill its ends by preserving the guidance function of its power-generating rules, all while implementing the overall legal system's commitment to preventing, and if not responding to, the abuse of power.

The analysis proceeds as follows. Section II explains how a legal system's choice to recognise legal powers necessitates inconsistent commitments to the rule of law. Section III explains why outsourcing to equity one of these commitments allows the overall legal system to pursue both.

II. LEGAL POWERS AND THE RULE OF LAW

A. Equity's Authority Derived from the Rule of Law

This chapter draws on work which derives equity's authority from the rule of law.[10] This approach employs a relatively thin conception of the rule of law according to which law's ends, whatever they are, are best served by rules that count for people as normative reasons for action, rather than just signposting the potential for coercive

[10] A sample includes D Klimchuk, 'Equity and the Rule of Law' in L Austin and D Klimchuk (eds), *Private Law and the Rule of Law* (Oxford, OUP, 2014); M Harding, 'Equity and Institutions' in D Klimchuk, I Samet and H Smith (eds), *The Philosophical Foundations of the Law of Equity* (Oxford, OUP, 2020) ch 16; M Harding, 'Equity and the Rule of Law' (2016) 132 *LQR* 278; B McFarlane, 'Form and Substance in Equity' in A Robertson and J Goudkamp (eds), *Form and Substance in the Law of Obligations* (Oxford, Hart, 2019) ch 9; H Smith, 'Equity as Meta-Law' (2021) 130 *Yale Law Journal* 1050.

state action.[11] This ideal gives shape to various characteristics or requirements for the form or mode of legal rules, such as that law must be accessible, a reliable guide for individual action, and contribute to the conditions under which people have a disposition to be guided by and engage with it.

Accepting that the law's ends, whatever they are, depend upon its normative force, scholars have argued that equity furthers those ends by enhancing the conditions in which people may engage with law, in particular, by regulating how people use the legal entitlements afforded to them by the *ex ante* body of law. The assumption is that people may be less likely to respect and be guided by law if the legal entitlements it generates can be used unscrupulously in unfair or exploitative ways. Some secondary body of rules is needed to prevent people from abusing or exploiting the legal entitlements in a manner that undermines law's ends. To this end there are a range of equitable rules, such as equitable estoppels, and relief against forfeiture,[12] that operate as a form of 'meta-law',[13] 'adjective',[14] or 'gloss',[15] to prevent the unconscientious exercise of legal entitlements. It is this modality that preserves another rule of law commitment to ensuring the accessibility and stability of the legal rules defining the *ex ante* legal entitlement. This is because equitable rules do not change the underlying legal entitlement or legal rules that generate it, and so 'allow the rest of law to be simpler and more general than it otherwise could be.'[16]

Previous scholarship has not examined equity's control of legal power directly. This should not be surprising because the modality of some of equity's power-controlling rules have been (mis)understood as defining the existence and scope of power, and this prevents them being understood as secondary or meta-law. This chapter shows, however, that equity's power-controlling rules do not define the existence and scope of power, and rather operate as a discretionary gloss on authority. As with some other equitable rules, the enduring contribution made by equity's control of legal power is its modality as a discretionary gloss on authority that allows for the overall legal system to maintain inconsistent commitments to the rule of law that arise from a legal system's choice to generate legal powers. To explain this idea further, it is first necessary to explain why legal powers demand inconsistent commitments to the rule of law.

i. *Legal Powers*

A legal power is being used in this chapter to describe a person's ability or capacity to effect an intended change to her and/or another's legal status via her actions

[11] See, eg, J Raz, *The Authority of Law* (Oxford, Clarendon Press, 1979) ch 1; J Raz, *The Authority of Law: Essays on Law and Morality*, 2nd edn (Oxford, OUP, 2009) ch 11, 210; J Finnis, *Natural Law and Natural Rights*, 2nd edn (Oxford, OUP, 2011) ch 10; J Gardner, *Law as a Leap of Faith: Essays on Law in General* (Oxford, OUP, 2012) ch 8, 205–11.

[12] See further B McFarlane, 'Equity and the Justification of Private Rights' in S Degeling, M Crawford and N Tiverios (eds), *Justifying Private Rights* (Oxford, Hart, 2020) 221, 239–40; J Hudson, B McFarlane and C Mitchell, *Hayton, McFarlane and Mitchell: On Equity and Trusts*, 15th edn (London, Sweet & Maxwell, 2022) chs 1–3.

[13] Smith, 'Equity as Meta-Law' (n 10) 1054.

[14] Harding, 'Equity and the Rule of Law' (n 10).

[15] Maitland (n 8) 20.

[16] Smith, 'Equity as Meta-Law' (n 10) 1071.

in manifesting her intention to effect that change.[17] Examples include a power to contract with another; an agent's power to act on behalf of a principal; a titleholder's power to transfer, or otherwise deal with her title to specific property, including settle that title on express trust; a beneficiary's power to disclaim her interest, and in the case of a trust by transfer, the trustee's power to accept her role as such; and powers to vary the terms of an express trust or contract. This sense of a legal power is narrower than the Hohfeldian sense of A's ability to effect a legal change to her own and/or B's legal status via *any* of A's volitional actions[18] irrespective of whether that change is triggered by A's manifestation of her intention to effect that change.

A power is *legal* when it is generated by legal rules (statute, common law or equity) that define the scope of power by prescribing the actions a power-holder must take to effect the intended change. For example, a titleholder's power(s) to deal with her title is defined by the rules providing for the actions that a titleholder must take to effect some intended change, such as to transfer her title to land,[19] create a security interest in personal property,[20] assign a legal or equitable chose in action.[21] Legal rules also define the legal consequences of the power-holder's actions, such as the rules of property law and tort law that provide for the legal entitlements that constitute the title to land or other specific property acquired by the transferee. Power-generating rules are not mandatory or prescriptive in the sense that they prohibit action or require action to be taken.[22] They are, however, prescriptive in that they must be complied with for the power-holder to effect the intended change. If an owner of land, for example, wants to transfer her title to land, she must comply with the relevant transfer rules, or else her actions will be ineffective to produce the effect she intended: the transfer of title.

Across these and other contexts, power-generating rules afford a power-holder freedom in the form of a temporal horizon for action.[23] These rules allow a power-holder to make decisions and pursue action by manifesting her intention to effect a specific change to hers and/or another's legal status. Legal powers are generated in the pursuit of a range of law's ends. The legal rules that confer powers on titleholders, such as to transfer that title, for example, instantiate the law's commitment to giving titleholders control and determination of who will have ownership and control of the property.[24] Another example are contractual powers, which give legal effect to the parties' intentions

[17] See further N MacCormick and J Raz, 'Voluntary Obligations and Normative Powers' (1972) 46 *Proceedings of the Aristotelian Society*, Supplementary Volumes 59, 80; J Raz, *Practical Reason and Norms* (Oxford, OUP, 1990) 102–04; C Essert, 'Legal Powers in Private Law' (2015) 21 *Legal Theory* 136.

[18] W Hohfeld, 'Fundamental Legal Conceptions as Applied in Judicial Reasoning' (1913) 23 *Yale Law Journal* 16, 44–46.

[19] See, eg, Land Registration Act 2002, pt 3.

[20] See, eg, Companies Act 2006, pt 25.

[21] Law of Property Act 1925, s 136; *William Brandt's Sons & Co v Dunlop Rubber Co Ltd* [1905] AC 454 (HL) 462; *Corin v Patton* (1990) 169 CLR 540 (HCA) 556–59.

[22] As to this distinction, see further HLA Hart, *The Concept of Law* (Oxford, OUP, 1961) 27–29, 33–35.

[23] MacCormick and Raz, 'Voluntary Obligations and Normative Powers' (n 17) 81; L Austin, 'The Power of the Rule of Law' in L Austin and D Klimchuk (eds), *Private Law and the Rule of Law* (Oxford, OUP, 2014) 276–81.

[24] See further J Harris, *Property and Justice* (Oxford, OUP, 2002); L Katz, 'Exclusion and Exclusivity in Property Law' (2008) 58 *U Toronto Law Journal* 275; H Dagan, *A Liberal Theory of Property* (Cambridge, CUP, 2021) 60–64.

to defer specification for how one or more parties are obliged to act to some future choice of one party. As has been explained by Lord Sales, they are a 'mechanism … [to] allow for adjustment of a long-term relationship to accommodate changing circumstances over time …'.[25] Similarly, powers to vary the terms of an express trust, such as a power of appointment,[26] may give legal effect to the parties'[27] intentions to defer definition of specific terms to one or another party's choice in the future.

Legal powers also play a vital constitutive function for a range of relationships and institutions that, in one way or another, rely upon legal power. The existence and operation of express trusts, agency relationships, companies, deceased estates and mortgages, for example, all depend upon a person(s) having the ability to effect a change to the legal status of another by manifesting their intention to effect that change. Indeed, companies and other entities with artificial legal personality depend upon the law's recognition of legal powers that allow for the legal entity to act through its individual organs to whom its powers are allocated.[28]

There are other forms of power generated by social or physical phenomena, some of which equity controls, including powers arising from a party's ascendency or influence.[29] Much can be said about equity's control of factual or informal powers although they are beyond the scope of this chapter, which just asks how equity defines and controls the abuse of legal power.

ii. Legal Powers Distinguished from Other So-Called 'Powers'

Before moving on to explain how a legal system's choice to generate legal powers gives rise to inconsistent rule of law commitments, it is important to distinguish a legal power from other juridical phenomena sometimes also referred to as 'power'.

The label of 'power' sometimes refers to a power-holder's 'authority' in the sense of the range for the lawful exercise of power.[30] Indeed, the labels of authority and power are used interchangeably in cases and commentaries.[31] While this is confusing, the core juridical distinction[32] holds true as between a *legal power* understood

[25] P Sales, 'Use of Powers for Proper Purposes in Private Law' (2020) 136 *LQR* 384.

[26] See, eg, *Duke of Portland v Topham* (1864) 11 HL Cas 32; *Cloutte v Storey* [1911] 1 Ch 18 (CA).

[27] In addition to settlor's power to settle her property on trust, the trustee in a trust by transfer, and beneficiary each have their own role in determining the existence of the trust and its terms *as between them*, see further, J Hudson and C Mitchell, 'Justificanda' in S Degeling, J Hudson and I Samet (eds), *The Philosophical Foundations of the Law of Express Trusts* (Oxford, OUP, 2023).

[28] R Leow, 'Understanding Agency as a Proxy Power' (2019) 78 *CLJ* 99; R Leow, *Corporate Attribution in Private Law* (Oxford, Hart, 2022).

[29] See, eg, *Royal Bank of Scotland v Etridge (No 2)* [2001] UKHL 44, [2002] 2 AC 773; *Thorne v Kennedy* [2017] HCA 49, (2017) 263 CLR 85.

[30] See, eg, *Mills v Mills* (1938) 60 CLR 150 (HCA) 158–86; *Great Investments Ltd v Warner* [2016] FCAFC 85, (2016) 243 FCR 516; *Wellington Capital Ltd v Australian Securities and Investments Commission* [2013] FCAFC 52, 94 ACSR 293; R Nolan, 'Powers – General Principles' in J McGhee (ed), *Snell's Equity*, 34th edn (London, Sweet & Maxwell, 2020) para [10-001].

[31] 'Authority' refers to a legal power in *Richard Brady Franks Ltd v Price* (1937) 58 CLR 112 (HCA) 142; *Grimaldi v Chameleon Mining NL (No 2)* [2012] FCAFC 6, (2012) 200 FCR 296 [254]; *Wong v Burt* [2005] NZCA 174, [2005] 1 NZLR 91 [27].

[32] As to the distinction between power and authority, see generally W Seavey, 'The Rationale of Agency' (1920) 29 *Yale Law Journal* 859, 861; A Corbin, 'The Authority of an Agent: Definition' (1925) 34 *Yale Law Journal* 788, 794; F Reynolds, P Watts, and W Bowstead, *Bowstead and Reynolds on Agency*, 21st edn (London, Sweet & Maxwell, 2019) para [1-013].

as a power-holder's freedom to effect legal consequences via her actions in manifesting her intention to do so and as generated by the relevant power-generating rules; and *authority* understood as the lawfulness of the power-holder's actions assessed according to some other set of power-controlling rules that restrict a power-holder in the consequences she can lawfully pursue via execution.

A titleholder, for example, has a legal power to transfer her title to another, the existence and scope of which is defined by the relevant power-generating rules pertaining to the transfer or assignment of the subject property. These rules prescribe the conditions the power-holder must satisfy if she is to effect the legal consequence she manifests an intention to achieve, ie the transfer of her title to another. Whether or not the titleholder's actions are effective to produce the intended change is different to whether her actions are lawful, ie within her authority. If the titleholder is a trustee, for example, then there is an additional set of power-controlling rules that circumscribe her authority to exercise her legal power as titleholder. As shown by the cases concerning a trustee's unauthorised transfer of trust property to a third party, these other legal rules do not negate or deny the legal consequence(s) of the trustee's exercise of power, they rather make action that would otherwise have been lawful and authorised, unlawful and unauthorised.

The elision of power and authority can, in part, be explained by the use of the label of 'power' to refer to an authority or permission in trust instruments, company constitutions, other formal mandates and applicable legislation. An express trustee's actions and ensuing effects, for example, are said to be 'authorised' or 'unauthorised by the *power[s]*'[33] to sell, mortgage or invest trust property as contained in the terms of trust or applicable legislation. A director's or other agent's actions are likewise said to be 'authorised' (or not) by 'the powers' as provided for in a company constitution or applicable legislation. In these instances, the label of 'power' in the relevant terms is not being used to refer to a power-holder's freedom to effect legal consequences via her actions in manifesting her intention to do so. As Browne-Wilkinson LJ explained in *Rolled Steel Products (Holdings) Ltd v British Steel Corp*,[34] the 'power[s]' to sell, mortgage or invest property do not 'flow'[35] from the applicable set of terms, but from the trustee or company having legal personality and title to specific property. 'Power' is being used to refer to when the exercise of some pre-existing legal power is authorised.[36]

The distinction between power and authority can be hard to perceive for those legal powers that depend on authority. This dependency occurs when the power-generating rules condition an effective exercise of power on it being lawful and authorised, in addition to other requirements, such as the power-holder's manifestation of her intention and satisfaction of various formality requirements. The power-generating rules incorporate the applicable power-controlling rules and the effectiveness or validity

[33] *Re Hastings-Bass* [1975] Ch 25 (CA) 41 (Buckley LJ). See also *Pitt v Holt* [2011] EWCA Civ 197, [2012] Ch 132 [126].

[34] [1986] Ch 246 (CA) 303–04.

[35] ibid.

[36] See also *Wellington Capital Ltd v Australian Securities and Investments Commission* [2014] HCA 43, (2014) 254 CLR 288 [38], [40] (French CJ, Crennan, Kiefel and Bell JJ), [60] (Gageler J).

of an exercise of power depends on the power-holder's authority in the sense of her compliance with the relevant power-controlling rules. An example is a power to vary the terms of an express trust, which can only be effectively exercised within the scope of authority defined by the applicable power-controlling rules. This is in distinction to a trustee's power to transfer her title to trust property which, as discussed above, is not limited by the trustee's authority. The power-generating rules providing for the assignment of the trustee's title do not condition an effective execution on the trustee's adherence with the trust terms, for example.

The dependency of some legal powers on authority is a complex and important phenomenon and the reasons why some power-generating rules incorporate or overlap with power-controlling rules are considered in section III.A.i below. What matters for now is that the dependency of some legal powers on authority explains the interchangeable use of the labels of power and authority in some cases and that this use does not negate the fundamental distinction between these concepts and legal rules that define them.

'Power' is also used in the wider Hohfeldian sense of A's ability to effect a legal change to her own and/or B's legal status via A's volitional actions[37] irrespective of whether A's actions manifest her intention to effect that change. An example of this wider sense of power is an express trustee's 'power' to overreach a beneficiary's interest under the trust[38] such that a third party acquires title clear of any equitable proprietary claim. Overreaching is not, however, a legal power in the narrower sense of a person's freedom to effect change by manifesting her intention to do so. It is the legal consequence of an authorised exercise of the trustee's legal power as titleholder and occurs irrespective of whether the trustee manifested an intention to overreach.

Finally, 'power' is also used to refer to terms conditioning the parties' legal relations on one party's formation of an opinion or evaluative judgment as to some state of affairs. For example, in *Braganza v BP Shipping Ltd*,[39] the terms of an employment contract conditioning an employer's duty to pay a death benefit on the employer's (or insurer's) formation of an opinion as to the circumstances of the employee's death were described as a 'contractual discretion' or 'power'. In *Braganza*, 'power' is not describing the employer's freedom to change the parties' contractual relations and the employer did not have a choice to undertake an obligation to pay.[40] It can be hard to distinguish the situation where the parties' legal relations depend on one party's formation of an opinion as to some factual matter, as in *Braganza v BP Shipping Ltd*, from that where the parties' legal relations depend upon a party's actions in manifesting her intention as to what those relations are. Nonetheless, it matters as there may be differences in the reasons for control, and the nature of control. There may be good reasons why the law should control how opinions are formed when the

[37] W Hohfeld, 'Fundamental Legal Conceptions as Applied in Judicial Reasoning' (1913) 23 *Yale Law Journal* 16, 44–46.

[38] *Akers v Samba Financial Group* [2017] UKSC 6, [2017] AC 424 [51]–[52], approving *Independent Trustee Services Ltd v GP Noble Trustees Ltd* [2012] EWCA Civ 195, [2013] Ch 91 [106]; *Ali v Dinc* [2020] EWHC 3055 (Ch), [2021] 2 P & CR 19 [318]; C Harpum, 'Overreaching, Trustees' Powers and the Reform of the 1925 Legislation' (1990) 49 *CLJ* 277.

[39] *Braganza* (n 7) [1].

[40] See further *Finch v Telstra Super Pty Ltd* [2010] HCA 36, (2010) 242 CLR 254 [29]–[30], [64]–[66].

parties' legal relations depend upon them as this effectively arrogates to one party the court's role in evaluating the facts according to which the parties' legal relations will be determined. It is beyond this chapter to explore these reasons, save to point out that they may be different to why law should control the exercise of legal power. A legal power does not give a party the ability to determine the facts according to which their legal relations are determined, and rather allows a party to choose what those legal relations are.

B. Preserving the Guidance Function of Power-Generating Rules

Whatever law's ends in generating legal powers, their pursuit all depends on the guidance function of power-generating rules.[41] This depends, in part, on these rules being such that people can take advantage of them, and understand and respect the consequences of execution. If power-generating rules do not provide reliable guides for action, or if power-holders and objects of their powers are not clear about the consequences of execution, then people may be less disposed to use legal powers, or to respect the consequences of execution. Thus, a legal system's choice to recognise a legal power demands a commitment to ensuring the power-generating rules are accessible and provide clear, certain and predictable guidance to the power-holder and the object of the power whose legal status is liable to change. These qualities help to secure legal powers as a form of freedom understood as a temporal horizon for action. They also help ensure legal powers supply part of the necessary legal framework for a range of legal relationships and institutions.

There is, however, a further pre-condition to the normative force of power-generating rules, which is that people have a disposition to be guided by law. This will depend on a range of conditions, which relevantly includes rules that prevent people abusing the law, and the legal entitlements law provides them. No matter how clear and reliable power-generating rules are, people will be less likely to be guided by them if there are not some other rules that prevent, and, if not, respond to, the arbitrary, unfair or unconscientious abuse of legal powers. If abuse goes unchecked, this may undermine the conditions in which people are disposed to use legal powers and respect the legal entitlements effected as a consequence of execution, and ultimately the ends to which those powers were generated.

C. Preventing the Abuse of Legal Power

What is an abuse of power? There are different types of power that may be abused. In addition to powers generated by legal rules, there are powers generated by other social or physical phenomena that might be abused in ways that matter for different reasons. Equity controls some of these other powers, including powers arising from social facts such as a party's ascendency or influence. Much can be said about

[41] MacCormick and Raz (n 17) 80–81; Austin, 'The Power of the Rule of Law' (n 23) 276–81.

equity's control of factual or informal powers although they are beyond the scope of this paper, which just asks how equity defines and controls the abuse of legal power.

Equity does not control all legal powers. Absent other factors, such as an express trust, a titleholder is free to do as she pleases with her title and incidental powers.[42] The difference between the express trustee and non-trustee titleholder, and the trigger for equity's control is that the trustee holds her legal power on terms, and an abuse occurs when power is exercised in a manner contrary to the applicable set of terms.[43] Essentially, 'the terms according to which a power is held' is a generic descriptor for the instructions or mandate for how a power-holder should and should not exercise power. They may be expressed in different ways, including as permissions, prohibitions and/or directives. A power-holder may be permitted to exercise a power to achieve some effects, and that permission might be conditional upon certain social phenomena, including the formation of an opinion. Sometimes the terms may require a power-holder to exercise a power, and sometimes they may expressly prohibit the exercise of power.

Sometimes, the terms are (mis)understood as the terms of (the scope of) a legal power. This, however, confuses the power-generating rules that define the existence and scope of a legal power, such as the rules for the assignment of title to property, with the terms providing for how that power may lawfully be exercised, such as the parties' choices for how an express trustee should hold and use her title, or a principal's intention for how an agent may and may not act, or parliament's intention for how a public official should use a power of title to publicly owned land, for example. The terms according to which a power is held are (just) the meanings attributed to the relevant party's actions in expressing their intention for how that power should be exercised. These terms give content to, and thereby derive legal effect from, equity's power-controlling rules that require power to be exercised in accordance with them. Explained another way, the difference is between 'validity conditions' for whether a power has been effectively exercised and 'authority conditions' for the lawfulness of an exercise of power. Albeit, there can be an overlap in these different sets of terms when the terms according to which a power is held themselves generate a power to vary those terms, and the reasons for the overlap and implications are discussed in section III.A.i below.

The terms according to which a power is held are the instructions or mandate for the lawful exercise of power. The questions as to *whose* instructions they are, and why they should be obeyed, will vary across contexts. The terms may be derived from the meaning(s) attributed to the parties' actions in manifesting their intentions for how power should and should not be exercised, such as for express trusts, deceased estates, partnerships, and agencies, for example. The terms might also be derived from the meaning of a legal rule that provides for how a power should and should not be exercised. Examples include equitable and statutory rules that supply terms,

[42] This makes the definition of abuse, as well as the justification of the legal power in the first place, more challenging: see further Austin, 'The Power of the Rule of Law' (n 23).

[43] Another trigger is the power-holder's action in inducing B to believe that A will exercise (or not) her power in certain ways, upon which B relies in such a way as to raise a promissory or proprietary estoppel.

in the absence of the parties' modification or exclusion, permitting trustees to sell, mortgage or invest trust property, and indemnify themselves for properly incurred expenses.[44] More examples can be added from across a range of contexts, including companies, statutory trusts, and public office-holders. In these and other situations, the terms are derived from the parties' choices and/or some legal rule, be it sourced in statute, common law or equity.

The terms are sometimes misunderstood as being literally the provisions of a written document.[45] However, this confuses any document that might be produced by the parties' actions in manifesting their choices, and the terms understood as the meaning of those actions. The instrument or document could be destroyed, for example, but the terms understood as the meaning of the parties' actions in creating the documents and the legal (including equitable) rules that give effect to them would not cease to exist and apply.

Irrespective of how they are derived and evidenced, the terms matter because they express the law's ends in recognising the specific power-holding arrangement, and an abuse of a legal power is one that undermines any or all of law's ends in recognising that arrangement. Those ends might differ across contexts, such as to give effect to the parties' choices. Take for example an agency relationship, the 'primary object' of which is to 'enable the attorney to act in the management of his principal's affairs.'[46] The actual or apparent[47] terms are the meanings of the principal and agent's actions in manifesting their expressions of intention and consent for how the agent may use her power.[48] The law's ends in recognising an agency relationship are to give effect to the parties' choices for how the agent will hold and use her power to act for the principal. Likewise, the terms of an express trust are the meanings attributed to the parties' actions in expressing their intentions and consent for how the trustee should and should not exercise her power(s) as titleholder.[49] The law's ends in recognising and enforcing various rules for trust creation and operation are to give effect to the parties' choices for how the trustee may lawfully hold and use her title to trust property.[50]

[44] In the express trust context see, eg, Trustee Act 2000, s 3 (permits a trustee to make certain investments); Trustee Act 2000, s 31(1) (permits a trustee to use trust funds either to recoup trust expenses or to discharge trust liabilities); *Investec Trust (Guernsey) Ltd v Glenalla Properties Ltd* [2018] UKPC 7, [2019] AC 271 [59]; *Carter Holt Harvey Woodproducts Australia Pty Ltd v Commonwealth* [2019] HCA 20, (2019) 268 CLR 524 [29]–[33], [80]–[84].

[45] See, eg, *Space Investments Ltd v Canadian Imperial Bank of Commerce Trust Co (Bahamas) Ltd* [1986] 1 WLR 1072 (PC) 1073–74. A similar point is made in relation to contractual terms in F Wilmot-Smith, 'Term Limits' (2019) 39 *OJLS* 705.

[46] *Reckitt v Barnett, Pembroke & Slater Ltd* [1928] 2 KB 244 (CA) 268.

[47] Apparent authority is derived from the meaning of the principal's actions in manifesting her intention to a third party, see generally *Freeman & Lockyer v Buckhurst Park Properties (Mangal) Ltd* [1964] 2 QB 480 (CA); *Hely-Hutchinson v Brayhead Ltd* [1968] 1 QB 549 (CA).

[48] *Pole v Leask* (1863) 33 LJ Ch 155, 161; *Garmac Grain Co Inc v HMF Faure & Fairclough Ltd* [1968] AC 1130 (HL) 1137; Reynolds, Watts and Bowstead (n 32) art 1, excepting agency by necessity where the terms are supplied by law.

[49] See n 27 and accompanying text above.

[50] The essentiality of this feature is recognised in *Countess of Bective v Federal Commissioner of Taxation* (1932) 47 CLR 417 (HCA) 418–22; *DKLR Holding Co (No 2) Pty Ltd v Commissioner of Stamp Duties* [1980] 1 NSWLR 510 (NSWCA) 518–29.

Similar comments can be made as to the terms for other power-holding arrangements, and where the terms might be the meanings attributed to the parties' choices and/or express some other of the law's ends. A company, for example, is conferred a legal personality and incidental powers and further powers as provided by statute. The terms on which a power to issue, vary and cancel shares, for example, may be exercised will in part be derived from the meanings attributed to the relevant parties' actions, such as company promoters, directors, corporate officers or individual members. In addition, some may be sourced in statute or general law, including, for example, statutory provisions in relation to related party transactions, conferral of related party benefits, or the issue and variation of shares. The terms express the mandate or reason for the existence of the company, and its powers as such. Further, the exercise of the company's powers must necessarily be allocated to one or more individuals, the allocation of which is again subject to terms that express the reason for the generation and allocation of power.

No matter the source of the terms, they derive from the law's reasons or ends for recognising the particular power-holding arrangement, any or all of which would be undermined by an abuse of that power. Regardless of whether the rule of law is understood as an ideal for law as a source of normative guidance, or as requiring the prevention of the arbitrary exercise of power, the law's generation of legal powers demands a further commitment to ensuring power is exercised in accordance with the applicable terms. Without such a commitment, the normative force of power-generating rules and the legal relationships and institutions that depend upon power will all be undermined.

D. An Inherent Tension

In principle, it could have been possible for a legal system to implement a commitment to the terms by conditioning the existence and scope of any legal power on the power-holder's adherence with the applicable set of terms, and indeed this was the case for companies under the old doctrine of corporate *ultra vires*. However, as explained by Browne-Wilkinson LJ in *Rolled Steel Products (Holdings) Ltd v British Steel Corporation*, 'such ruthless logic has not been pursued'[51] for those legal powers for which the power-generating rules do not condition an effective execution on adherence with the applicable set of terms. Were such logic pursued, the guidance function of legal powers would be undermined, as the existence and scope of a legal power would depend upon complicated factors that may be difficult to ascertain, such as a power-holder's subjective intentions and her compliance with the parties' objective intentions for how the power should be exercised.

As explained above, the terms according to which a power is held are not 'validity conditions', they are not the same as the power-generating rules also referred to as 'terms' that define the existence and scope of power. The terms according to which a power is held do not limit or disable power, and there is thus the potential for

[51] *Rolled Steel Products* (n 34) 303.

legal powers to be exercised contrary to them. Agents and company directors with a power to transfer the principal's or company's title to property, can, for example, exercise their power if they comply with the relevant power-generating rules. These rules invariably operate upon the powerholder's external manifestation of her intention and compliance with applicable formality requirements, and sometimes, a third party's actions in registration. As discussed, there are good reasons why the power-generating rules operate upon these relatively simple and objective factors, allowing for the powerholder and those with whom she deals, and other third parties, to understand and have faith in the legal consequences of execution. This also means, however, that the consequences of execution are dependent upon the power-holder's compliance with the different power-generating rules alone, and which may or may not condition an effective execution on it being authorised in accordance with any applicable power-controlling rules. Similar comments can be made in relation to express trustees, partners, mortgagees and public officials. All hold powers that are not disabled by and can be exercised contrary to the relevant terms because the relevant power-generating rules do not condition an effective execution on it being authorised.

Pausing here, it is important to observe that in relation to some legal powers, such as a power to vary the trust terms, the power-generating rules do condition an effective execution on it being authorised according to the terms, as discussed above in section II.A.ii. These powers are thus indirectly limited by the terms. Outside of these powers are a range of other legal powers that are held subject to terms, yet the power-generating rules do not condition an effective execution on it being authorised according to the terms, such as some legal powers held by express trustees, personal representatives, agents and directors. These other legal powers are not limited by the terms according to which they are held, or the applicable power-controlling rules and thus create an inherent tension between inconsistent commitments to the rule of law. Law's commitment to ensuring that power-generating rules operate so that they provide clear, reliable, and stable reasons for individual action means that it is not possible to prevent or disable the abuse of power from the outset. This other commitment must be implemented another way, and the question is how, if at all, are law's ends served when control of the (ab)use of legal power is outsourced to equity?

III. WHY EQUITY?

What is special about equity's control is its modality as a discretionary gloss on authority. Equity's rules do not directly limit or disable power and thus do not undermine the guidance function of the *ex ante* power-generating rules. Equity's power-controlling rules implement a commitment to the relevant terms by setting standards or requirements for the lawful exercise of power.[52] Like some other

[52] *Netglory Pty Ltd v Caratti* [2013] WASC 364 [346]–[349] (Edelman J); L Smith 'Fiduciary Relationships: Ensuring the Loyal Exercise of Judgment on Behalf of Another' (2014) 130 *LQR* 608.

equitable rules, equity's two rules requiring a power-holder's adherence with the terms operate as 'meta'[53] or 'secondary'[54] rules to control when a legal power may be lawfully exercised and determine when equitable relief is available to reverse the consequences of an unauthorised execution so that it is *as if* the power-holder were disabled from exercising power in an unauthorised manner. They define a sphere for lawful, that is, authorised execution and conversely demarcate a sphere of unlawful or unauthorised execution, the effects of which are susceptible to equitable relief as necessary to prevent or reverse the consequences of an unauthorised execution so that it is *as if* the power-holder were disabled from exercising power in an unauthorised manner. Without such rules, legal powers that generate legal powers may be (ab)used in ways that undermine any or all of law's ends in recognising the specific power-holding arrangement. To explain this further it is necessary to pinpoint the equitable rules that condition a power's holder's authority on her adherence with the terms, and to address some different (mis)conceptions about their operation and effect(s).

A. Two Rules Conditioning Authority on a Power-Holder's Objective and Subjective Adherence to the Terms

Across a range of relationships and institutions, a power-holder's authority always expresses the 'fundamental juristic principle' of 'general application' according to which 'any form of authority may only be exercised for the purposes conferred, and in accordance with its terms'.[55] For fiduciary and non-fiduciary power-holders, including express trustees,[56] agents,[57] partners,[58] mortgagees[59] and personal representatives,[60] the lawfulness of an exercise of power (ie *authority*) depends on the power-holder's compliance with the applicable set of terms where compliance is determined by two equitable rules. These rules are sometimes referred to as the excessive execution rule and fraud on a power.

Even where a power is 'unfettered' or 'uncontrolled',[61] such as some powers of variation held by a trustee or a third-party donee,[62] the power-holder's authority

[53] Smith, 'Equity as Meta-Law' (n 10).

[54] McFarlane, 'Form and Substance in Equity' (n 10).

[55] *Wong* (n 31) [27].

[56] *Pitt v Holt* [2013] UKSC 26, [2013] 2 AC 108 [93]; *Youyang Pty Ltd v Minter Ellison Morris Fletcher* [2003] HCA 15, (2003) 212 CLR 484 [30]–[38].

[57] *Re David Payne & Co Ltd* [1904] 2 Ch 608 (CA); *John v Dodwell & Co Ltd* [1918] AC 563 (PC); *Reckitt* (n 46); *Great Investments* (n 30) [71].

[58] *National Commercial Banking Corp of Australia Ltd v Batty* (1986) 160 CLR 251 (HCA) 275.

[59] *Yorkshire Bank plc v Hall* [1999] 1 WLR 1713 (CA) 1728; *Downsview Nominees Ltd v First City Corpn Ltd* [1993] AC 295 (PC) 315; *Barns v Queensland National Bank Ltd* (1906) 3 CLR 925 (HCA) 943.

[60] *Comr Stamp Duties (Qld) v Livingston* [1965] AC 694 (PC) 707.

[61] As in *Gisborne v Gisborne* (1877) 2 App Cas 300 (HL) 309; *Duke of Portland* (n 26) 54; *Re Hay's ST* [1982] 1 WLR 202 (Ch) 209–10; *Scaffidi v Montevento Holdings Pty Ltd* [2011] WASCA 146, (2011) 6 ASTLR 446 [149]; *Mercanti v Mercanti* [2016] WASCA 206, (2016) 50 WAR 495 [315]. Even a general power of appointment is subject to these principles, although these principles will usually be satisfied owing to the terms.

[62] Sometimes referred to as a 'guardian', 'appointor', 'consultant' or 'enforcer', for example.

still depends on the same two rules. Further, equity's other power-controlling rules accommodate themselves to the terms, which may exclude or modify the scope of a power-holder's duty of care,[63] duty to segregate,[64] or duty of fiduciary loyalty.[65] Even a power-holder who is typically considered to be a fiduciary by virtue of status, will *not* owe fiduciary duties if the terms provide otherwise; agents,[66] solicitors[67] and express trustees[68] may all act self-interestedly when permitted by the terms.

i. The Rule Against Excessive Execution

The first rule requires the immediate legal effect of the power-holder's actions in execution to be permitted by the applicable set of terms. The immediate legal effect is the change(s) to parties' legal statuses that the power-holder objectively manifested an intention to achieve and the achievement of which depends on satisfaction of the relevant set of power-generating rules, such as the rules for assignment of title to specific property. This first rule just asks whether the immediate legal effect of execution is permitted by the terms. It does not ask about any downstream effects, some of which may or may not be permitted by the terms. Further, this rule does not ask about the power-holder's subjective intention, the effect(s) she actually intends to achieve via execution: this is instead the concern of fraud on a power.

If the immediate effect of the power-holder's actions, such as a third-party's receipt of title to property, is not permitted by the applicable set of terms, then one or more forms of equitable relief are available which, in one way or another, either prevent or reverse the unauthorised effect(s) of execution. An example is if a trustee plans to grant a mortgage over trust property in X's favour when this is not permitted by the trust terms. A beneficiary or co-trustee may commence litigation prior to the trustee's unauthorised exercise of power to seek an injunction to prevent execution.[69] However, the trustee may exercise her power and create a mortgage over trust property in X's favour prior to the award of injunctive relief, or in contempt of any court order prohibiting execution.[70] Other equitable remedies

[63] *Armitage v Nurse* [1998] Ch 241 (CA) 251–54.

[64] *Associated Alloys Pty Ltd v ACN 001 452 106 Pty Ltd* [2000] HCA 25, (2000) 202 CLR 588; *Space Investments* (n 45) 1073–74.

[65] *Lord Vesty's Executors v IRC* [1949] 1 All ER 1108 (HL) 1115, 1132; *Re Skeats' Settlement* (1889) 42 Ch D 522 (Ch) 527; *Re Wills Trusts Deeds* [1964] Ch 219 (Ch) 228; *Basel Trust Corporation v Ghirlandina* [2008] JLR 1 (Jersey Royal Court); *Mercanti* (n 61) [397]–[398].

[66] *Kelly v Cooper* [1993] AC 205 (PC) 214; *New Zealand Netherlands Society 'Oranje' Inc v Kuys* [1973] 1 WLR 1126 (PC) 1129–30; *Wood v Commercial First Business Ltd* [2021] EWCA Civ 471, [2022] Ch 123 [26]; M Conaglen, 'The Fiduciary Status of Agents' in P Davies (ed), *Intermediaries in Commercial Law* (Oxford, Hart, 2022) ch 2.

[67] *Beach Petroleum v Kennedy* (1999) 48 NSWLR 1 (NSWCA) 188; *Canadian National Railway Co v McKercher LLP* [2013] SCC 39, [2013] 2 SCR 649 [37].

[68] *Space Investments* (n 45) 1075. See also *New Zealand 'Oranje'* (n 66) 1129–30.

[69] See, eg, *Crossman v PILT Nominees Pty Ltd* [2008] NSWSC 557 (injunction awarded to prevent unauthorised grant of mortgage). See also *Yorkshire Miners' Associations v Howden* [1905] AC 256 (HL) (injunction awarded to prevent unauthorised payment of trust funds).

[70] See, eg, *Crossman v PILT Nominees* [2009] NSWSC 393 (orders in response to trustee's contempt of orders made in *Crossman v PILT Nominees Pty Ltd* (n 69) and equitable relief to address the unauthorised execution).

are needed to respond to the consequences of the unauthorised execution. These include equitable money remedies against the trustee[71] and/or third parties,[72] or various proprietary remedies against the power-holder and/or third parties.[73] All these remedies prevent or address the consequences of an unauthorised execution so that it is *as if* the unauthorised exercise of power had not occurred.[74]

This first rule is sometimes labelled as the 'excessive execution rule', and the power-holder's non-compliance is said to result in the exercise of power being 'void', 'null' and/or ineffective.[75] The difficulty with these labels is that they also describe the different imperative that a power-holder's action will be ineffective to produce the intended legal effect when that action is beyond the scope of, or in excess of the power. This other sense of excessive execution arises when the power-holder has not complied with the relevant power-generating rules, such as the rules of assignment, for example. The one label of excessive execution has thus been used to express different imperatives. The equitable rule requiring a power-holder's adherence to the terms has been elided with the logical imperative that a power-holder's actions are ineffective, void or null if she does not follow the applicable power-generating rules.

No matter the label for the first rule requiring adherence with the terms, it is important to be clear that it does not define the scope of a legal power in the sense of prescribing what a power-holder must do to effect the change she wants. It rather defines a power-holder's authority by conditioning the lawfulness of execution on the immediate effect of execution being permitted by the terms.

The use of the label of excessive execution to refer to a lack of authority can in part be explained by the fact that some legal powers depend on authority, such as powers to vary the terms of an express trust, as discussed in section II.A.ii above. For such powers, the power-generating rules condition an effective execution on it being authorised so that actions that do not comply with the applicable terms and are in excess of authority are necessarily in excess of the power, and void

[71] As in *Re Pauling's Settlement Trusts* [1964] Ch 303 (CA); *Target Holdings Ltd v Redferns* [1996] AC 421 (HL); *AIB Group (UK) plc v Mark Redler & Co Solicitors* [2014] UKSC 58, [2015] AC 1503. In relation to other power-holders, such as company directors and agents, see, eg, *Re Lands Allotment Co* [1894] 1 Ch 616 (CA) 638; *O'Halloran v R T Thomas & Family Pty Ltd* (1998) 45 NSWLR 262 (NSWCA). Some uncertainties attend the assessment of some of these money remedies, see further S Elliott, 'Personal Monetary Claims' in J McGhee (ed), *Snell's Equity*, 34th edn (London, Sweet & Maxwell, 2020) ch 20; C Mitchell et al, *Underhill and Hayton: Law of Trusts and Trustees*, 20th edn (London, LexisNexis, 2022) paras [91.32]–[91.46].

[72] *El Ajou v Dollar Land Holdings plc* [1993] BCC 698 (Ch) 715–16; *Bank of Credit and Commerce International (Overseas) Ltd v Akindele* [2001] Ch 437 (CA).

[73] For express trusts, see *Foskett v McKeown* [2001] 1 AC 102 (HL); *Independent Trustee Services* (n 38); agency and companies, see *Re David* (n 57); *John* (n 57); *Reckitt* (n 46); deceased estates see *Hill v Simpson* (1802) 7 Ves Jun 153; *Nelson v Larholt* [1948] 1 KB 339 (KBD); C Mitchell, '*Commissioner of Stamp Duties (Queensland) v Livingston* (1964)' in B Sloan (ed), *Landmark Cases in Succession Law* (Oxford, Hart, 2019) 273; partnerships, see *Sharp v Union Trustee Co of Australia Ltd* (1944) 69 CLR 539 (HCA); *Gordon v Gonda* [1955] 1 WLR 885 (CA).

[74] See Hudson, 'One Thicket' (n 4) for discussion of why the priority of a claim for equitable proprietary relief differs across these situations. See too, Smith's chapter in this volume for discussion of the functional benefits of recognising rights which are protected against specific third parties without having full *in rem* effect.

[75] See, eg, *Pitt v Holt* (n 56) [60], [93]; *Grand View Private Trust Company Ltd v Wong* Civil Appeal No 5A of 2019, 20 April 2020 [48], [92], [312]–[317] this issue was not raised on appeal, [2022] UKPC 47 [122].

or null.[76] These powers depend on authority because they are an expression of the same fundamental principle as authority: that a trustee must hold and use her title to trust property in accordance with the terms understood as the parties' choices. When the parties choose to defer definition of the ways in which it will be lawful for the trustee to exercise her power to the future choices of a trustee or third party this generates a legal power of variation. These powers give effect to the parties' choices and are necessarily limited by those choices.

Not all powers, however, are limited in this way and the relevant power-generating rules do not condition an effective execution on it being authorised by the applicable power-controlling rules. This is shown by the unauthorised transfer cases where there is an *effective* exercise of power, such as by an agent[77] or express trustee[78] who has satisfied relevant power-generating rules.[79] In these cases, the problem and reason for equitable relief is not that the power-holder's actions are ineffective, 'void' or 'null'.[80] The power-holder has exercised a legal power to produce the effect she manifested an intention to achieve but which is not permitted by the applicable set of terms. There is an excess of authority, not power. Equity's remedies are needed precisely because the first rule requiring the power-holder's objective adherence to the terms does not limit or disable an unauthorised execution. The next best thing is for equitable relief to reverse the effects of the unauthorised execution.

ii. Fraud on a Power

It is tempting to think that the first rule exhaustively defines authority. However, leaving aside the situation where the terms require the power-holder to exercise her power to produce a specific effect(s), a power-holder may have a discretion or choice to exercise a power. This choice means that a power-holder may exercise her legal power to produce an immediate legal effect that is permitted by the terms, but which is subjectively intended to have some other impermissible effect(s). Some further rule is therefore required to ensure that the power-holder cannot pursue an unauthorised effect. That rule is fraud on a power.

The rule against fraud on a power (also known as the proper purposes rule),[81] protects against the subversion of the relevant terms[82] by imposing the additional requirement that when the terms permit the power-holder a choice, that choice is made '… with an entire and single view to the real purpose and object of the power, and not for the purpose of accomplishing or carrying into effect any bye or

[76] See further J Hudson and C Mitchell, 'Legal Consequences of the Flawed Exercise of Pension Scheme Powers' in S Agnew, P Davies and C Mitchell (eds), *Pensions: Law, Policy and Practice* (Oxford, Hart, 2020) ch 7.

[77] *Re David* (n 57); *John* (n 57); *Reckitt* (n 46); *Great Investments* (n 30) [71].

[78] As in *Foskett* (n 73); *Independent Trustee Services* (n 38); *Wellington Capital* (n 36) [60].

[79] See further *Rolled Steel Products* (n 34) 303–04; *Akers* (n 38) [51]; Hudson and Mitchell, 'Legal Consequences' (n 76); S Agnew and B McFarlane, 'The Paradox of the Equitable Proprietary Claim' in S Agnew and B McFarlane (eds), *Modern Studies in Property Law*, vol 10 (Oxford, Hart, 2019) 307.

[80] See further Hudson, 'One Thicket' (n 4).

[81] *Eclairs Group Ltd v JKX Oil & Gas plc* [2015] UKSC 71, [2016] 3 All ER 641 [15]–[22].

[82] This rationale is discussed in *Topham v Duke of Portland* (1869) LR 5 Ch App 40 (CA) 59; *Duke of Portland* (n 26) 54; *Re Greaves* [1954] Ch 434 (CA) 446–47.

sinister object …'.[83] There is a body of cases defining and categorising improper purposes.[84] Extrapolating from these cases, 'purpose' means the effect(s) the power-holder subjectively intends to achieve via her exercise of power. The rule against fraud on a power conditions a proper and lawful execution on the power-holder subjectively intending to achieve an effect that is permitted by the terms, objectively understood.[85] Subjective and objective inquiries are therefore involved in determining whether a power has been exercised properly or whether there is a fraud on the power. The power-holder must form a view as to the effect(s) she intends to achieve, believe the terms permit her to pursue that intended effect or purpose,[86] and the terms, objectively understood, must permit the pursuit of that purpose. An improper exercise of power is treated in the same way as one where the immediate effect(s) are not permitted.[87] The same forms of equitable relief are available either to prevent execution or to reverse the consequences of execution.

A source of confusion over the rule against fraud on a power is its operation, and its relationship with the first rule: the rule against excessive execution. Opposing views have been expressed on whether a fraud on a power renders execution ineffective and void and is part of, or separate to, excessive execution.[88] On this chapter's analysis, the premise for debate is flawed as it elides legal power and the rules that generate it with authority and the equitable rules that define it. The logical imperative that a power-holder's actions are ineffective if she does not follow the applicable power-generating rules is different to whether a power-holder has acted within the scope of her authority as defined by the power-holder's objective and subjective adherence with the terms. The rule against fraud on a power is not a power-generating rule. It does not generate a freedom to act by prescribing the actions a power-holder must take to effect some intended change; it rather restricts the power-holder's freedom to act by narrowing the types of purposes the power-holder can lawfully pursue via the exercise of power.

As with the rule against excessive execution, the operation and effect of fraud on a power can be difficult to assess for those legal powers that depend on authority, such as a power to vary the terms of an express trust. For such powers, an improper purpose will render execution ineffective and void because the applicable power-generating

[83] *Duke of Portland* (n 26) 54. See also *Vatcher v Paull* [1915] AC 372 (PC) 379–80; *Topham* (n 82) 59.

[84] See that outlined in G Farwell, CJW Farwell and FK Archer, *A Concise Treatise on Powers*, 3rd edn (London, Stevens & Sons, 1916) ch 10; *Eclairs* (n 81) [15]–[22].

[85] *Hindle v John Cotton Ltd* (1919) 56 Sc LR 625 (HL) 630; *Mills* (n 30) 158–86; *Eclairs* (n 81) [15].

[86] To this extent, fraud on a power encompasses good faith as a conscious and sincere commitment and as required in *Dowager Duchess of Sutherland v Duke of Sutherland* [1893] 3 Ch 169 (Ch) 191–93; as well as *Turner v Turner* [1984] Ch 100 (Ch) 111 albeit not under the label of 'good faith'. Other instantiations of good faith depend on the terms, see further C Mitchell, 'Good Faith, Self-Denial and Mandatory Trustee Duties' (2018) 32 *Trust Law International* 92.

[87] See, eg, *Topham v Duke of Portland* (1863) 1 De GJ & S 517, 568–69 where 'unauthorised' was used in relation to an improper exercise of power. See also *Redman v Permanent Trustee Company of New South Wales Ltd* (1916) 22 CLR 84 (HCA); *Re Pauling's ST* (n 71) 335, 341.

[88] Fraud on a power is excessive execution in Y Grbich, 'Fraud on a Power' (1977) 3 *Monash University Law Review* 210, 212–14; R Grantham, 'The Powers of Company Directors and the Proper Purpose Doctrine' (1994–95) 5 *King's College Law Journal* 16, 32–34; although is understood as being separate to 'the excessive execution doctrine', in *Eclairs* (n 81) [15]; *Grand View* (n 75) [92].

rules condition an effective execution on it being authorised.[89] However, this is not the case for all powers. Fraud on a power does not render an improper exercise of power 'void', 'null' or ineffective[90] in cases where an express trustee transfers title to a third party;[91] a board of directors varies the terms of shares, or issues new shares;[92] or an agent transfers the principal's title to a third party.[93] Fraud on a power does not disable or prevent the abuse of power, it (just) determines the lawfulness of an exercise of power, and thus when equitable relief is available.

The rule against fraud on a power has also been understood as an implied term.[94] This, however, elides the terms understood as the meanings attributed to the parties' actions in manifesting their intentions with the legal rules (equitable or otherwise) that give legal effect to those intentions. The rule does derive some of its content from the terms, as the propriety of the power-holder's purpose is assessed by reference to them. However, this does not mean that the rule forms part of the meanings (express or implied) attributed to the parties' actions and as explained by Briggs' LJ 'formidable dissent'[95] in *JKX Oil & Gas plc v Eclairs Group Ltd*,[96] fraud on a power is a 'restriction imposed by law … [and] … [i]t is not a question of implied terms at all.'

IV. CONCLUSION

Equity's rules are (just) a gloss on authority and do not change the underlying legal power, or the rules that define it. Equity's gloss can be hard to perceive given the interchangeable use of the labels of power and authority in trust instruments, legislation, cases and commentaries, and when the equitable rules defining authority are (mis)understood as defining the scope of legal power.[97] Further, equity's modality can be hard to make out when applied to those powers that depend on authority, such as a power to vary the trust terms. As explained in section III.A.ii above, this dependency helps to explain why some cases have understood equity's power-controlling rules as limiting or defining the scope of some powers. However, equity's two rules do not limit or disable legal powers generally. The parties to an agency relationship or express trust, for example, can (only) determine the content of equity's controls, which themselves are just a gloss on the lawfulness of execution. The parties cannot re-write the law of property or law of contract, for example, to change the rules that provide for how a titleholder can effect an intended change to another's legal status in manifesting her intention to do so. Nor can the parties redefine the various rules of

[89] See, eg, *Cloutte* (n 26) 30–32; *Redman* (n 87).
[90] See further, Hudson, 'One Thicket' (n 4).
[91] See, eg, *Hillsdown Holdings plc v Pensions Ombudsman* [1997] 1 All ER 862 (QB) [139]; *Roadchef (Employee Benefits Trustees Limited) v Ingram Hill* [2014] EWHC 109 [122], [126]–[131]; *Wong* (n 31).
[92] See, eg, *Howard Smith Ltd v Ampol Petroleum Ltd* [1974] AC 821 (PC); *Eclairs* (n 81).
[93] See eg: *John* (n 57); *Reckitt* (n 46).
[94] *General Assembly of Free Church of Scotland v Overtoun* [1904] AC 515 (HL) 695.
[95] *Eclairs* (n 81) [29] (Lord Sumption). See also Sales, 'Use of Powers' (n 25).
[96] *JKX Oil & Gas plc v Eclairs Group Ltd* [2014] EWCA Civ 640, [2014] 4 All ER 463 [99].
[97] See section II.A.ii above.

property and tort law that determine a titleholder's legal entitlements as such. Equity thus respects the overall legal system's choice not to delimit or disable legal power according to the applicable set of terms, thereby preserving the guidance function of the *ex ante* power-generating rules.[98]

If the distinction between the equitable rules defining authority and those defining power is not maintained, then the law's ends in generating legal powers would be undermined owing to the complexity and instability with which power would be defined if limited by authority. Across any given situation, the terms could be the meanings attributed to the parties' choices, the construction of which may not be easy. Further, one of equity's controls, the rule against fraud on a power, depends on subjective matters that look to the broader legal and social effect(s) the power-holder intends to achieve, and her subjective understanding of the terms, which may be difficult for anyone else to be sure about. If a power-holder's ability to effect an intended change depended on her adherence with the applicable set of terms, then in many instances the power-holder would not be able to know what she needs to do to effect the result she wants.

In addition, there are significant third-party concerns, such as a party contracting with a principal via an agent, or a recipient of property transferred by a trustee or agent with a power over a principal's property. The third party's ability to understand and predict how the law applies to determine her legal entitlements, and her ability to be guided thereby are undermined when power is dependent on authority. A third party cannot know, for example, whether a titleholder is a trustee, and the terms of the trust, let alone form a conclusive view as to the meaning of the terms and the authority they define. Similarly, a third party cannot know the inner or subjective intentions of the power-holder as to the effect the power-holder intends to achieve, and upon which her authority depends. In those situations where equity does respond to an effective, yet unauthorised, execution to reverse the consequences of execution and produce an outcome that is different to that produced by the underlying power-generating rules, this is an individualised prioritisation of equity's commitment to the terms and whatever value(s) they express. This priority does come at the expense of the stability, certainty and predictability of the legal power and rules that define it, and sometimes does have an impact on an innocent third party, who, for example, may have to return property or may not have the equitable interest they thought they did, and for which they may have even paid value.

Ultimately, however, a balance must be struck somewhere between commitments to affording freedom in the form of legal power and preventing its abuse. Equity's modality as a gloss on authority means this balance is struck via a targeted and situation specific intervention, applying *in personam* between the parties, and not effecting any broader change to the underlying legal power. Further, the discretionary nature of equitable relief means that intervention occurs only after application of one or more defences and the equitable discretionary factors that provide final checkpoints.[99]

[98] See section III.C above.

[99] The role of equitable discretion has sometimes been denied (see, eg, *Foskett* (n 73) 109 (Lord Browne-Wilkinson), 128 (Lord Millett)) nonetheless, there are cases, including in the context of express trusts, in which equitable discretionary factors have either applied or been considered applicable to bar

These checkpoints are critical to mediating the interconnections between the underlying legal power, and equity's rules that re-define the power-holder's authority. Discretionary factors such as unclean hands, hardship, laches and acquiescence, for example, in one way or another, prevent equitable relief being awarded in circumstances where it would be unfair to do so. They show how equity is a self-reflexive body of rules that looks inward to prevent the unconscientious assertion of an entitlement to equitable relief, preserving the guidance function of equity itself.[100]

The discretionary nature of equitable relief has been criticised as undermining the rule of law owing to its indeterminacy and unpredictability.[101] However, and noted by Joe Campbell, the discretionary nature of equitable relief 'does not involve deserting the firm ground of sure principles for a trackless sea of uncertainty'.[102] Equitable discretion is bound by defined equitable rules, which themselves are largely consistent with rule of law demands.[103] In addition, the formal separation or distinctiveness of equity marks a clear and certain line around those instances where equity's remedial discretion is applicable, and when it is not. This means that it is at least clear and predictable as to when a claim for relief is subject to discretion and the rules that guide it, even if the content of those rules that guide the discretion are relatively qualitative and open-textured.

Equity's discretionary gloss on authority reconciles inconsistent commitments to the rule of law that arise from a legal system's choice to generate legal powers. Equity's role is not pejorative of the common law and does not presuppose problems or inadequacies with it. The relationship between the two sets of rules is better understood as that of symbiosis: equity allows the common law power-generating rules to work as they should, while providing a set of rules to identify and respond to abuses of power that would ultimately undermine the common law's ends, and that of the legal system overall.

one or more forms of relief in response to an unauthorised exercise of power, see, eg, *Hourigan v Trustees, Executors and Agency Co Ltd* (1934) 51 CLR 619 (HCA) 629, 651; *Orr v Ford* (1989) 167 CLR 316 (HCA) 323, 329–32, 337–46.

[100] See further, H Smith, 'Equitable Defences as Meta Law' in P Davies, S Douglas and J Goudkamp (eds), *Defences in Equity* (Oxford, Hart, 2018); Smith, 'Equity as Meta-Law' (n 10) 1110.

[101] See eg: P Birks, 'Three Kinds of Objection to Discretionary Remedialism' (2000) 29 *University of Western Australia Law Review* 1, 2 and 15–17.

[102] J Campbell, 'Access by Trust Beneficiaries to Trustees' Documents, Information and Reasons' (2009) 3 *Journal of Equity* 97, 145.

[103] Harding, 'Equity and the Rule of Law' (n 10) 293–95.

3

Section 25(6) of the Judicature Act 1873: A 'Procedural' Approach

C.H. THAM*

I. INTRODUCTION

THE COURT OF Chancery has facilitated assignments of legal choses in action from at least the seventeenth century,[1] although the common law was more reluctant.[2] Even so, *Snell's Equity* tells us that:[3]

> The old common law rule against the assignment of chose[s] in action was gradually relaxed. … Ultimately, by the Judicature Act 1873 [, section 25(6)[4]], and now by the Law of Property Act 1925[, section 136(1)[5]], 'any debt or other legal thing in action' was made assignable at law.

Section 25(6) was re-enacted[6] as section 136(1), replacing the law French 'chose in action' with the more Anglo-Saxon 'thing in action',[7] together with other minor differences, but to no substantial effect.[8] Largely unchanged, the construct now found in section 136(1) has been part of English law for 150 years. However, understanding what section 136(1) does, and how it does it, remains muddled.

* Professor of Law, Yong Pung How School of Law, Singapore Management University.

[1] See, eg, *Meechett v Bradshaw* (1633) Nels 22, 21 ER 779; *Hurst v Goddard* (1670) 1 Ch Cas 169, 22 ER 746; *Corderoy's Case* (1675) 1 Freem 312, 22 ER 1233.

[2] *Lampet's Case* (1613) 10 Co Rep 46b, 48a; 77 ER 994, 997.

[3] J McGhee (ed), *Snell's Equity*, 34th edn (London, Sweet & Maxwell, 2021) para [3-003].

[4] Hereafter, 'section 25(6)'.

[5] Hereafter, 'section 136(1)'. For ease of reference, both provisions have been set out in the Appendix at the end of this chapter.

[6] *Raiffeisen Zentralbank Österreich AG v Five Star General Trading LLC* [2001] EWCA Civ 68, [2001] 1 QB 825 [59].

[7] The Bankruptcy Act 1914, ss 38(c) and 167, had also replaced 'chose in action' with 'thing in action'.

[8] An assignment falling within section 136(1) is, 'effectual in law (subject to equities having priority over the right of the assignee)', whereas under section 25(6), it would have been 'effectual in law (subject to all equities which would have been entitled to priority over the right of the assignee if this Act had not been passed)'. The proposition that these changes meant they operated differently was rejected in *Glencore Grain Ltd v Agros Trading Co Ltd* [1999] 2 All ER (Comm) 288 (CA) [30].

The High Court of Australia takes the view that Australian equivalents[9] to sections 25(6) and 136(1) set out substantive formality requirements which *must* be complied with, else the non-conforming assignment becomes invalid (unless value had been given in exchange). However, the position in England is less clear.

On the one hand, given Lord Macnaghten's pointed observation in *William Brandt's Sons v Dunlop Rubber* that, '[section 25(6)] does not forbid or destroy equitable assignments or impair their efficacy in the slightest degree',[10] *Smith & Leslie* takes the view that English law does *not* follow the Australian position, suggesting that *Olsson v Dyson*, the leading Australian decision, was wrongly decided.[11] On the other, *Guest on Assignment* suggests that '[t]he position to be adopted in English law awaits resolution by the courts'.[12] *Snell's Equity* is also equivocal.[13]

This chapter agrees with *Smith & Leslie* that English law justifiably takes a different view of sections 25(6) and 136(1) from their Australian equivalents. This chapter explains how section 136(1), like section 25(6), operates at what may be termed a 'non-substantive' or 'procedural' level to effect a slightly non-obvious manner of 'transfer' whereby:

(i) the assignee is invested with *copies* of the assignor's entitlements arising from the chose in action assigned that the assignee can effectively invoke *as though* it were the creditor/obligee of the chose assigned, *even though it is not*; and
(ii) the assignor is thereafter *barred* from effectively invoking these replicated entitlements for her own benefit such that it will seem *as though* the assignor was no longer the creditor/obligee, *even though it remains so*.

These provisions make it seem as though the assignee had replaced the assignor as creditor/obligee, without that being so as a matter of substantive principle.

II. 'TO TRANSFER' AND 'TO PASS': MULTIPLE MODES

A. Ordinary Language Usage

The verb 'to transfer' operates differently in different contexts. For example: in the sentence, 'Cristiano Ronaldo has been transferred from Juventus to Manchester United', the word 'transferred' connotes that Juventus has no call on the services of Ronaldo on the football pitch post-transfer, whereas only Manchester United will be

[9] Currently, these comprise the Conveyancing Act 1919 (NSW), s 12 (which is *in pari materia* with s 25(6)) on the one hand, and on the other: Civil Law (Property) Act 2006) (ACT), s 205; Law of Property At 2000 (NT), s 182; Property Law Act 1974 (Qld), s 199(1)–(2); Law of Property Act 1936 (SA), s 15; Conveyancing and Law of Property Act 1884 (Tas), s 86(1)–(2); Property Law Act 1958 (Vic), s 135; Property Law Act 1979 (WA), s 20 (which are largely *in pari materia* with s 136(1)).

[10] *William Brandt's Sons & Co v Dunlop Rubber Co Ltd* [1905] AC 454 (HL) 462.

[11] M Smith and N Leslie, *The Law of Assignment*, 3rd edn (Oxford, OUP, 2018) para [11.179]. See also CH Tham, *Understanding the Law of Assignment* (Cambridge, CUP, 2019) 434–36.

[12] YK Liew, *Guest on the Law of Assignment*, 4th edn (London, Sweet & Maxwell, 2021) para [3-65].

[13] McGhee (n 3) para [3-019].

so entitled. By contrast, in the sentence, '[t]he data in the hard disk in John's laptop has been transferred to Mary's USB drive', 'transferred' does not entail extinction or erasure of the transferred data post-transfer. Such transfer entails *copying* the data in the hard disk to the USB drive. But erasure from the source hard disk does not necessarily follow.[14] To an extent, this is because data is information. 'Transfers' of information do not extinguish that information; nor do they entail the transferor deleting such information from its memory. But they do entail the transferor having increased the number of entities who know it. So 'transfers' of information are *replicative* without necessarily being *extinctive* (though additional steps may certainly be taken to achieve that).

The verb 'to pass' is similar. Where the subject matter that has been passed is 'rivalrous',[15] for example, A's possession of a particular soccer ball, the 'passing' of possession by A to B entails A losing it to B. But where the subject matter is *not* rivalrous, this 'extinctive' entailment does not arise. Suppose a professor asked a student of hers to 'pass' the message to the other members of the tutorial group that the following week's tutorial will be postponed, and the student does so. As the message is information, the 'passing' of the message does not extinguish it. Nor does its 'passing' entail that it be forgotten by the professor and the student who had passed it along.

B. Technical Legal Usage

As Holmes observed:[16]

> If A, being the possessor of a horse or a field, gives up the possession to B, the rights which B acquires stand on the same ground as A's did before. The facts from which A's rights sprang have ceased to be true of A, and are now true of B. The consequences attached by the law to those facts now exist for B, as they did for A before. The situation of fact from which the facts spring is a continuing one, and any one who occupies it, no matter how, has the right attached to it.

The 'transfer' or 'passing' of legal title in an estate in land is similar. Transfers of legal title of this kind extinguish the transferor's entitlements arising from its status as 'title-holder' because legal titles to estates in land are transferred via substitutions of *status*. As the entitlements (and obligations) of title-holding are specified by reference to an individual's status – whether one is/is not the title-holder at the relevant point in time – when the status of title-holder is 'transferred' from one holder to a successor,

[14] Technically, the source data will not be 'erased' until it is overwritten by other data. For example, where the MS-DOS operating system is used: 'In MS-DOS, one can use the undelete command. In MS-DOS the "deleted" files are not really deleted, but only marked as deleted – so they could be undeleted during [sic] some time, until the disk blocks they used are eventually taken up by other files.': Wikipedia entry, 'File deletion' https://en.wikipedia.org/wiki/File_deletion.

[15] *Lloyd v Google LLC* [2019] EWCA Civ 1599, [2020] QB 747 [68]; *Thaler v Comptroller General of Patents Trade Marks and Designs* [2021] EWCA Civ 1374, [2022] Bus LR 375 [133].

[16] OW Holmes, *The Common Law*, M De Wolfe Howe's edn (London, Macmillan, 1968) 265.

so, too, the associated entitlements and obligations.[17] However, not all transfers work like this.

Section 2 of the Carriage of Goods by Sea Act 1992 effects a 'transfer' differently:

> **2.** (1) Subject to the following provisions of this section, a person who becomes—
>
> (a) the lawful holder of a bill of lading;
>
> (b) the person who (without being an original party to the contract of carriage) is the person to whom delivery of the goods to which a sea waybill relates is to be made by the carrier in accordance with that contract; or
>
> (c) the person to whom delivery of the goods to which a ship's delivery order relates is to be made in accordance with the undertaking contained in the order,
>
> shall (by virtue of becoming the holder of the bill or, as the case may be, the person to whom delivery is to be made) have transferred to and vested in him all rights of suit under the contract of carriage *as if he had been a party to that contract.* (emphasis added)

Unlike the Bills of Lading Act 1855 which it replaced, the subject matter of the 'transfer' in section 2(1) of the 1992 Act comprises the 'rights of suit' of the 'contract of carriage'[18] to which the shipping documents in question relate. However, like the 1855 Act, the technique used to 'transfer' these entitlements from the original shipper to indorsees or consignees is similar: section 2(1) renders it '*as if* he [the indorsee or consignee] had been party to the contract of carriage.'

The indorsee/consignee's entitlement-acquisition via section 2(1) cannot entail status-substitution: if the indorsee/consignee acquired the shipper's status as a contract-party, the indorsee/consignee would *have* that status, and it would not be *as if* it had been a party. To make it *as if* the indorsee/consignee were a party, section 2(1) has to operate by duplicating or copying the shipper's entitlement to sue the carrier (given its status as a contract-party), before enabling the indorsee/consignee to invoke the copied entitlement *even though* it remains a non-contract-party.

Like the 1855 Act, the 1992 Act effects a 'transfer' through *copying* or *replication*. But it goes further: section 2(5) provides that the entitlements of the shipper arising from its contract of carriage with the carrier as might pre-date the creation of the bill of lading setting out distinct entitlements are extinguished when section 2(1) is triggered for subsequent holders of bills of lading, though not sea waybills or ship's delivery orders. So, the 'transfer' effected by section 2(1) operates 'extinctively' in some cases, but not all. Still, how are such 'extinctive' effects, where present, achieved?

As with entitlement-acquisition, entitlement-extinction through status-substitution is inapplicable: if section 2(1) substituted the indorsee/consignee for the shipper as party to the contract of carriage, it would not be *as if* the indorsee/consignee were a party: the indorsee/consignee *would* be a party. Therefore, the 'extinctive' effect of these section 2(1) 'transfers' as modified by section 2(5) must arise otherwise. Perhaps, if the consignees/indorsees are to be treated *as if* they were party to those

[17] Tham (n 11) 51–52.

[18] And not the '[c]ontract contained in the Bill of Lading' as had been provided in the Bills of Lading Act 1855, s 1.

contracts, even though they are not, by parity of reasoning, the original shipper should be treated *as if* it was no longer party to those contracts, *even though it still is*?

Treating it 'as if' the shipper was no longer party to those contracts leaves intact the substantive legal rules by which the shipper is recognised by the substantive law as having the status of being a contract party. Since it leaves substantive rules unchanged, this mode of operation can be termed 'non-substantive', or 'procedural'. In other words, although the shipper still *has* those entitlements, it is *disabled* from effectively invoking them. As the following shows, such techniques are no stranger to English law.

III. THE 'PROCEDURAL BAR' ARISING FROM ENGLISH STATUTES OF LIMITATION

In *Ketteman v Hansel Properties Ltd*, in a dispute which came within the Limitation Act 1939 (which the Limitation Act 1980 repealed and replaced),[19] Lord Griffiths held that:[20]

> A defence of limitation raises a procedural bar which prevents the plaintiff from pursuing the action against him. It has nothing to do with the [substantive] merits of the claim which may all lie with the plaintiff, but as a matter of public policy Parliament has provided that a defendant should have the opportunity to meet a stale claim. The choice lies with the defendant and if he wishes to avail himself of the statutory defence it must be pleaded.

The Limitation Act 1939 was repealed and re-enacted by the Limitation Act 1980. However, the latter still operates by way of a 'procedural bar': generally, unless that limitation period be extended or excluded in accordance with the provisions in Part II of the Act, where the limitation period for a cause of action set out in Part I of the Act has elapsed, no action may be brought in respect of it.[21] Read together with section 38(1),[22] this means that no proceeding in a court of law may be brought by a claimant on a cause of action whose limitation period has fully elapsed. Since the 1980 Act leaves intact the substantive law which generates the substantive *rights* whose (alleged) breach gives rise to the claimant's cause of action, as the Law Commission observed, 'as a general rule the expiry of the limitation period under the 1980 Act operates to bar the claimant's remedy,[23] rather than extinguish his or her rights'.[24] Hence, section 2 of the 1980 Act does not result in extinction of the claimant's entitlement to sue arising from the substantive law – it is just that although the claimant still *has* it, its effective *use* is barred. Consequently, it is *as though* the claimant no longer has those entitlements so far as access to judicial remedies is concerned.

[19] Although there are significant differences in the operation of the 1980 as opposed to the 1939 Act, those differences do not impact the manner of operation of the time-bar in either Act.

[20] *Ketteman v Hansel Properties Ltd* [1987] AC 189 (HL) 219.

[21] Limitation Act 1980, s 5.

[22] Limitation Act 1980, s 38(1) provides: 'In this Act, unless the context otherwise requires – "action" includes any proceeding in a court of law, including an ecclesiastical court.'

[23] But see text following n 25.

[24] Law Commission, *Limitation of Actions* (Law Com No 270, 2001) para [5.20]. See also *Royal Norwegian Government v Constant & Constant* [1960] 2 Lloyd's Rep 431 (QB) 442.

IV. CONSTRUING SECTIONS 25(6) AND 136(1): THE POWER OF 'AS THOUGH'

Like the Limitation Act 1980, sections 25(6) and 136(1) also cover a wide range of entitlements arising from different areas of substantive law. The matters which are passed and transferred by sections 25(6) or 136(1) may arise from any form of debt or other legal chose/thing in action. Hence, sections 25(6) and 136(1) may be applied to assignments of entitlements arising from contractual choses in action, choses in action arising in equity,[25] or choses in action generated from *causes* of action say, from a breach of contractual or statutory duties, or even a 'tortious duty' (ie, a duty not to commit a tort). And when they *are* applied, sections 25(6) and 136(1) 'pass and transfer' certain entitlements from assignor to assignee, namely:

(a) the legal to the subject-matter as had been assigned;
(b) all legal and other remedies for the same; and
(c) the power to give a good discharge for the same without the concurrence of the assignor.

But the *manner* by which these particular entitlements 'pass' and 'transfer' by reason of the statutory provisions is not immediately obvious. Fortunately, the manner of their operation was explained in connection with the assignment of a contract debt, in *Read v Brown*.[26]

As Lord Esher MR held in *Read v Brown*:[27]

> In construing s 25, sub-s 6, we must adopt the ordinary rule as to the construction of Acts of Parliament, that of giving, if possible, a meaning to each word. ... Now the defendant's argument comes to this, that the 'legal right' to a debt is the same thing as the 'legal and other remedies' for it ... That is a wrong rule of construction; the words mean what they say; they transfer the legal right to the debt as well as the legal remedies for its recovery. The debt is transferred to the assignee and becomes *as though it had been his from the* beginning; it is *no longer to be the debt of the assignor at all*, who cannot sue for it, the right to sue being taken from him ... (emphasis added)

These observations have two aspects: a positive *enabling* aspect; and a less obvious, negative *disabling* aspect. Both will be explored below.

[25] More properly, a 'chose in equity'. Although some academic doubts persist as to whether choses in equity can come within s 25(6), the case law accepts that they do: *Harding v Harding* (1886) 17 QBD 442 (QB); *Manchester Brewery Co v Coombs* [1901] 2 Ch 608 (Ch) 619; *Re Pain* [1919] 1 Ch 38 (Ch) 44; *Torkington v Magee* [1902] 2 KB 427 (KBD) 430–31. Since s 136(1) and s 25(6) are *in pari materia*, it seems likely that the same holds for s 136(1). McGhee (n 3) paras [3-003] and [3-009] accepts this. However, Smith and Leslie (n 11) paras [16.11]–[16.16] suggest that these cases have been incorrectly decided or are at least doubtful. Liew (n 12) para [2-09] takes a more ambivalent position. None of these works addresses the point that ss 25(6) and 136(1) have disabling effects which are also relevant where equitable choses have been assigned: see Tham (n 11) 380–83, and also section IV.B below.

[26] *Read v Brown* (1888) 22 QBD 128 (CA).

[27] ibid 132; Lopes LJ agreed (at 133).

A. The Enabling Aspect of Sections 25(6) and 136(1)

i. '[T]he Right to the Debt or Other Legal Chose[/Thing] in Action'

In *Read v Brown*, Brown & Co contracted to sell and deliver goods for just under £17 to the defendant, Brown. The contract was formed, and the goods delivered, in Sussex. At Read's premises in Fleet Street, Brown & Co equitably assigned to Read the benefit of Brown's contract debt absolutely, 'in writing under the hand of the assignor', and Brown received written notice. Hence, the assignment to Read 'became' statutory pursuant to section 25(6). When Brown failed to pay, Read sued him in the Mayor's Court of the City of London, relying on section 25(6).

Brown applied to the Divisional Court for a writ of prohibition directing the cessation of Read's Mayor's Court proceedings for want of jurisdiction. The Mayor's Court had common law and equity jurisdiction where the entirety of the claimant's cause of action arose within the City's geographical limits. However, its common law jurisdiction was extended by Mayor's Court Procedure Act 1857, section 12. In particular, where the plaintiff's action in debt did not exceed £50, and if the plaintiff's cause of action arose within the City or the liberties thereof, 'either wholly or in part', no plea to the Court's jurisdiction would be allowed.

The Divisional Court declined to issue the writ of prohibition, holding that Read had showed cause.[28] On appeal, it was held that part of Read's 'cause of action' against Brown *had* arisen within the City of London since Read's cause of action had to include pleadings setting out the written assignment in the assignee's premises in Fleet Street. As less than £50 was claimed, section 12 applied.

Anticipating the two 'classic definitions'[29] of a cause of action in *Letang v Cooper*[30] and *Cooke v Gill*,[31] Lord Esher MR,[32] Lopes and Fry LJJ[33] explained that a 'cause of action' is that set of facts which a claimant before a court must plead and prove successfully to obtain judgment in his/her favour.[34] To commence an action at law in the High Court in his own name against Brown as 'statutory assignee' of a debt owed by Brown to the assignor (Brown & Co), Read had to plead as part of *his* cause of action against Brown:

(i) facts concerning the cause of action arising between the assignor-vendor, Brown & Co, and the debtor-purchaser, Brown (meaning, facts about the formation of the contract of sale between Brown & Co, and Brown (in Sussex);

[28] It is for the party resisting the writ of prohibition to show cause why it should not be issued: *The Mayor & Aldermen of the City of London v Cox* (1867) LR 2 HL 239, 280 (Willes J, in argument).
[29] *Roberts v Gill & Co* [2011] UKSC 22, [2011] 1 AC 240 [41] (Lord Collins); [107] (Lord Walker).
[30] [1965] 1 QB 232 (CA) 242–43.
[31] (1872–73) LR 8 CP 107 (Court of Common Pleas) 116.
[32] *Read v Brown* (n 26) 131.
[33] ibid 133.
[34] One often encounters statements like, 'the claimant's *cause of action* is time-barred'. So used, 'cause of action' seems to refer to the claimant's legal standing to bring a claim. Such usage is endemic: see, eg, *Berezovsky v Abramovich* [2011] EWCA Civ 153, [2011] 1 WLR 290 [56]; *Ballinger v Mercer Ltd* [2014] EWCA Civ 996, [2014] 1 WLR 3597 [9]. Though confusing, such usage is not improper, since one's

(ii) the due performance by Brown & Co of its obligation to deliver the said goods to Brown (also in Sussex)); *as well as*

(iii) facts concerning execution of the equitable assignment of the debt owed by Brown to the assignor-vendor at Read's premises in Fleet Street, the assignment being absolute, under the hand of the assignor, and written notice having been given to the debtor, so making the equitable assignment statutory.

Obviously, if Brown & Co had commenced an action on the contract between it and Brown, it would have been prolix to plead the facts in (iii) pertaining to the assignment to Read. Hence, Read's cause of action as 'statutory assignee' of Brown & Co was not the same as Brown & Co's cause of action in its own right. Accordingly, section 25(6) did not 'transfer' Brown & Co's cause of action to Read. What, then, did it do?

Read v Brown tells us that the 'passing' and 'transferring' of the entitlements specified in section 25(6) did not substitute Read in place of Brown & Co as a contract-party. Rather, section 25(6) *replicated* Brown & Co's 'right to the debt or legal chose in action', 'legal and other remedies for the same', and 'power to give a good discharge, without concurrence of the assignor', and impressed them in Read. Through such replication, matters became, in Lord Esher MR's judgment,[35] *as though* the debt arising from the contract between Brown and Brown & Co had been owed to Read 'all along' – meaning, this would be so, *even though* Read remained a stranger to that contract. Consequently, by employing the power of 'as though', Read was enabled by section 25(6) to sue Brown in a way analogous to the technique of 'as if' employed in the Bills of Lading Act 1855, and which has been retained in the Carriage of Goods by Sea Act 1992.[36]

Confirmation that section 25(6) does not work by status-substitution may be found in *Bennett v White*,[37] where the Court of Appeal concluded that the defendant in an action in debt was entitled to rely on the Statutes of Set-off as statutory assignee of the benefit of a debt which had been owed by the plaintiff to the assignor. Echoing Lord Esher's analysis, Cozens-Hardy MR concluded in *Bennett v White* that section 25(6) made it such that '... [t]he debt [was] for all purposes [including the purposes of the Statutes of Set-off] in the same position *as if* it had been the original debt of the assignee' (emphasis added).[38] And the same would be true of section 136(1) today.

legal standing to sue depends on the facts which make up a 'cause of action'. In the present analysis, it is suggested that the usage set out in the main text (focussing on the root sense of 'cause of action' as being 'a set of facts' upon which one's standing to sue depends) is more appropriate within the context of ss 25(6) and 136(1).

[35] See text accompanying n 27.

[36] See section II above.

[37] [1910] 2 KB 643 (CA).

[38] ibid 646. Farwell and Kennedy LJJ agreed.

ii. '[A]ll Legal and Other Remedies'

In *Read v Brown*, Lord Esher MR also said:[39]

> Sect 25, sub-s 6, of the Judicature Act, 1873, gives to the assignee of a debt ... more than the mere right to sue for it; it gives him the debt and *the legal right to the debt*, and it follows from that that he would have a legal right to sue for and recover it, *even had the section not contained the words, 'and all legal and other remedies for the same.'* (emphasis added)

Fry LJ, whose judgment immediately followed Lord Esher's, was 'of the same opinion',[40] and Lopes LJ concurred with Lord Esher MR's interpretation.[41] The Court of Appeal in *Read v Brown* thus located the assignor's power to sue (ie, to bring an action) within the words, 'the legal right to the debt' in section 25(6) (and now, in section 136(1)(a)).

Certain observations set out in *Camdex International v Bank of Zambia (No 1)* suggest a different construction:[42]

> By section 25 of the Supreme Court of Judicature Act 1873, now section 136 Law of Property Act 1925, debts were made assignable at law. If the statutory conditions are satisfied, such an assignment passes to the assignee 'all legal and other remedies for the same.' It is thus apparent from the wording of the statute that Parliament sanctioned not only the assignment of a debt, an item of property, but also the transfer of the concomitant right to sue for it.

Peter Gibson LJ seems to have located the 'transfer' of a statutory assignor's right to sue for a debt as had been assigned in the language of section 136(1)(b), ('all legal and other remedies for the same'), instead of section 136(1)(a) ('the right to the debt or other legal thing in action'). But having accepted that sections 25(6) and 136(1) were equivalents to each other, it is regrettable that the interpretation of section 25(6) in *Read v Brown* was not drawn to his attention.[43] Had it been, Peter Gibson LJ might well have followed suit, instead of charting a different course. Nor would the outcome in *Camdex International* have been altered had he followed *Read v Brown*.

As Lord Esher noted, where possible, every word in a statute should be given meaning.[44] If the transfer of the assignor's right to sue is located in section 136(1)(b) as a form of 'remedy', what would the 'debt or other legal thing in action' specified in section 136(1)(a) refer to? Peter Gibson LJ's construction may tend towards rendering section 136(1)(a) redundant, and that would be a 'wrong rule of construction'.[45]

One's right to sue another in a court of competent jurisdiction is distinct from the outcomes or results of those proceedings. Judicial remedies like damages certainly follow from judicial proceedings that conclude favourably for the claimant. But if not,

[39] (n 26) 132.
[40] ibid.
[41] ibid 133.
[42] *Camdex International Ltd v Bank of Zambia (No 1)* [1998] QB 22 (CA) 40 (Gibson LJ).
[43] It was not cited in argument, nor was it referred to in any of the judgments.
[44] *Read v Brown* (n 26) 132.
[45] ibid.

no such remedies would be ordered – instead, judicial orders might be made in the defendant's favour (eg, for costs). So, while terming one's right to sue to be a form of judicial remedy is not incorrect, conceiving this right to be a *step* towards obtaining judicial remedies may be more accurate.

In light of *Read v Brown*, it seems that the reference in section 136(1)(b) to 'all … legal remedies' may well denote remedies by way of judicial orders. Hence, where section 136(1) was satisfied, judicial orders as might otherwise have been made in favour of the assignor had the action been brought by the assignor may now be made in favour of the 'statutory' assignee bringing the action in his own name.

This is practically significant. For example, an action in debt gives rise to a specific remedy whereby the debtor is ordered to perform his *primary obligation* to pay the fixed sum of money *to his creditor*. Suppose A had sold B goods for a price of £10,000. Because of substantive contract principles, B would become indebted to A given the A–B sale contract between them. B's primary obligation under that contract is to make payment *to A*. Hence, if A successfully sued B on the debt arising from *that A–B contract*, B (as debtor) could only be ordered to perform his primary obligation to make payment of the sums owed *to his creditor*, that is, *to A*.[46]

Suppose A equitably assigned the benefit of the A–B contract absolutely to C, and the section 136(1) writing and notice requirements were met. If section 136(1) operates identically to section 25(6), following *Read v Brown*, C would be enabled to sue B in his own name despite (still) being a stranger to the A–B contract given section 136(1)(a). However, merely enabling C to sue B at law in his own name would *not* mean that B could be ordered to make payment to C because the *primary obligations* under the contract (*inter alia*, to make payment *to A*) would remain unchanged, and C is enabled by section 136(1)(a) to sue only *as if* he were the creditor, even though he is not. But if C were permitted to bring an action in debt in his own name, only for B to be ordered to make payment to *A*, there would still be unfinished business.

Although sums paid to A pursuant to the A–B contract would probably be held by A on trust for C (given the trust-like relationship as arises between equitable assignor and assignee),[47] if A failed to hand them over to C, C would have to sue A in equity to compel A to do so. Since the Judicature Act 1873 was aimed at reducing multiplicity of proceedings, particularly the need for litigants to commence proceedings at

[46] At common law, 'every creditor has a right to insist on payment to himself, or to such person as he thinks fit': *Hodgson v Anderson* (1825) 3 B & C 842, 853–54; 107 ER 945, 949–50 (Bayley J). As noted in SJ Bailey, 'Assignments of Debts in England from the Twelfth to the Twentieth Century, Part III' (1932) 46 *LQR* 547, 550, 'this rule [in *Hodgson v Anderson*] … merely enabled the creditor to choose whom the debtor was to pay'. This may be conceived as a case where a creditor ('A') having the power to discharge the debt by accepting payment from the debtor ('B') had delegated its exercise to another ('X'). Alternatively, as a matter of construction or implication, the A–B contract could be one where B was duty-bound to A to make payment 'to A *or A's nominee*'. In either case, even if A had delegated to/nominated X, X does not become B's creditor since X did not sell B the goods which gave rise to the debt: A did. Hence, notwithstanding these possibilities, it remains the case that B's obligation *as a debtor* under the A–B contract is to pay A, his *creditor*.

[47] *Gorringe v Irwell India Rubber and Gutta Percha Works* (1886) 34 Ch D 128 (CA) 136; *Warner Bros Records Inc v Rollgreen Ltd* [1976] 1 QB 430 (CA) 443–44.

law and in equity to completely resolve their legal difficulties,[48] it is arguable that Parliament incorporated the wording 'all legal … remedies' in section 25(6) in 1873 to address this problem. If so, this position would be preserved in section 136(1) given the equivalent wording in section 136(1)(b). That is, the courts would be permitted to make an order compelling B to make payment to C in respect of the debt arising from the A–B contract, *as if* C was a party thereto, *even though he was and is not a party.*

As for the 'other remedies' mentioned in section 137(1)(b), these arguably refer to self-help remedies, for example, the 'self-help remedy' of a contractual promisor to discharge a contract following an anticipatory repudiatory breach of contract by the contractual promisee. Suppose X contracts to buy 1,000 widgets from Y at a price of £10 per widget for delivery in six months' time. One month later, Y renounces the contract. If X 'accepts' Y's renunciation, that discharges the contract and generates in X an 'immediate right of action'[49] against Y. Hence, X may immediately sue Y for damages for the consequential losses from the renunciation. If there be an available market for the widgets, those losses would be quantified to be the difference between the contract and the market price.[50]

Suppose X had transferred the entirety of her business undertaking to Z. As part of this, X had equitably assigned the benefit of the X–Y contract to Z absolutely in a duly-signed writing, and written notice was given to Y thereby making the assignment 'statutory'. If not for section 136(1)(b), as a non-party to the X–Y contract, Z would have no entitlement to discharge it by 'accepting' Y's anticipatory repudiatory breach. But section 136(1)(b) allows Z to be treated as though he was a party to the X–Y contract for purposes of accessing 'other remedies' (even though he is not) – so Z may accept Y's renunciation, discharge the contract, and acquire 'an immediate right of action'. This dovetails with section 136(1)(a) such that Z may sue on that 'immediate right of action' in his own name, as though he were party to the X–Y contract.

iii. '[T]he Power to Give a Good Discharge for the Same without the Concurrence of the Assignor'

Turning to section 136(1)(c) ('the power to give a good discharge …', re-enacting the same words in section 25(6)): it does not follow from the 'statutory' assignee being entitled to sue the debtor/obligor in his own name (because of section 136(1)(a)) that he can also 'give' the debtor/obligor a 'good discharge, without concurrence of the assignor'.

Through the 1800s, it had become common practice for the prudent equitable assignee of a legal debt or chose in action to also insist that the assignor provide further authorisations for the assignee to deal with the assigned subject matter without further assignor involvement. For example, in an 1859 precedent for the

[48] See Tham (n 11) 329–39.
[49] *Johnstone v Milling* (1886) 16 QBD 460 (CA) 467 (Lord Esher MR). See also *Yukong Line Ltd of Korea v Rendsburg Investments Corp of Liberia (The Rialto)* [1996] 2 Lloyd's Rep 604 (CA) 697.
[50] Sale of Goods Act 1979, s 51(3).

assignment of a bond, we find the following language for a suggested power of attorney to be embedded within the indenture of assignment:[51]

> *And* for the considerations aforesaid the said (*assignor*) doth hereby constitute and appoint the said (*assignee*) his executors administrators and assigns his true and lawful attorney and attornies in the name or names of the said (*assignor*) his executors administrators or assigns to ask demand and receive all and every the sum and sums of money now due or hereafter to become due upon the said bond or obligation and on nonpayment thereof or any part thereof in the name or names of the said (*assignor*) his executors or administrators but at the proper costs and charges of the said (*assignee*) his executors administrators or assigns to commence and prosecute with effect any actions or suits against the said (*obligor*) his executors administrators or assigns until full satisfaction and payment of the said sum of £ ***And on receipt thereof to cancel or deliver up the said bond or obligation or to make and give good and sufficient releases and discharges for the sum or sums of money so received*** ... (emphasis in bold italics added)

Similar language remained current in the period preceding the Judicature Act 1873 reforms. For example, in the 1871 edition of his *Practical Guide to Conveyancing*, Sir Howard Elphinstone warned that:[52]

> Bearing in mind the importance, where a legal chose in action is assigned, of being able to sue the debtor at law in the name of the original creditor, a power called a power of attorney is *always* inserted in the assignment of a legal chose in action, enabling the assignee 'to demand, sue for, recover, receive, *and give effectual discharges for the debt, in the name of the assignor*.' (emphasis added)

Furthermore, in an 1873 compendium prepared by Frederick Prideaux[53] and John Whitcombe, the following precedent for the assignment of a bond debt was suggested:[54]

> ... AND THE SAID [assignor] doth hereby absolutely and irrevocably appoint the said [assignee], his executors, administrators, and assigns, the true and lawful attorney and attorneys of the said [assignor], his executors, or administrators, for him or them, and in his or their name or names, or otherwise, *to receive and give effectual discharges for*, and to sue for and recover the monies hereby assigned, or expressed so to be, ... (emphasis added)

Lawyers of that period understood that the assignee had to be specifically authorised in relation to both the bringing of actions, as well as the giving of discharges: the one

[51] L Shelford, *Crabb's Complete Series of Precedents in Conveyancing and of Common and Commercial Forms in Alphabetical Order*, 5th edn (London, Butterworths, 1859) vol I, 361. For earlier examples, see G Horseman, *Precedents in Conveyancing* (London, His Majesty's Law Printers, 1785) vol I, 132–34; W West, *Symbolæography* (London, Charles Yetsweirt Esq, 1594) precedent for 'A letter of attorney to recover and retaine a debt' (Sect 521).

[52] HW Elphinstone, *A Practical Introduction to Conveyancing: Containing the Substance of Two Lectures Delivered Before the Incorporated Law Society in 1869, 1870 and 1871* (London, W Maxwell, 1871) 201–02.

[53] Frederick Prideaux was appointed reader in real and personal property to the Inns of Court in 1866: JM Rigg (revised E Metcalfe), 'Prideaux, Frederick (1817–1891)' in *Oxford Dictionary of National Biography Online* (Oxford, OUP).

[54] F Prideaux and J Whitcombe, *Prideaux's Precedents of Conveyancing*, 7th edn (London, Stevens & Sons, 1873), vol I, 375.

did not entail the other. Consequently, if words pertaining to the latter were absent, the giving of a discharge by an assignee might only be effective with the assignor's further concurrence.

Just as how the assignor's right to sue was replicated such that the assignee would, pursuant to the wording in that part of section 25(6) now re-enacted in section 136(1)(a), be impressed with a similar right *as though* the assignee was the creditor/obligee to the debt/chose as had been assigned, the wording in that part of section 25(6) now re-enacted in section 136(1)(c) also replicated the assignor's power to give a good discharge and impressed that on the assignee, thereby enabling the assignee to *also* give a good discharge, likewise. By enacting section 25(6), powers of attorney that had been *de riguer* in earlier times became unnecessary.[55] So long as section 25(6) (or, today, section 136(1)) applied, the assignee would be enabled to give a good discharge in its own right, without needing further assignor-concurrence.

B. The Disabling Aspect of Sections 25(6) and 136(1)

The discussion thus far has focussed on the enabling aspect of sections 25(6) and 136(1). However, they also have a disabling aspect.

In relation to the right to sue at law, the Court of Appeal's judgment in *Hughes v Pump House Hotel Co Ltd (No 1)*[56] suggests that, where section 25(6) applies, the 'statutory' assignor will become unable to sue on the chose as had been assigned. In that case, the plaintiff, Hughes, sued the defendant company for non-payment of the balance of the contract price for construction services which the defendant company had engaged Hughes to provide. However, Hughes had assigned such sums as would be due to him to Lloyd's Bank Ltd, to secure a loan. Relying on this, the defendants raised a preliminary issue that this was an absolute assignment within the meaning of section 25(6), and that Hughes was no longer able to sue on the construction contracts in question.

Although this submission was rejected by Wright J in the court below (who ruled that section 25(6) did not apply as Hughes's assignment had not been 'absolute'), the Court of Appeal held otherwise.[57] Consequently, the Court of Appeal dismissed Hughes's action because Hughes, 'had no right of action'.[58] This could be taken as authority for the notion that section 25(6) extinguishes the assignor's entitlement to sue. But there is no such express language in section 25(6) (or section 136(1)). So, the 'extinctive' effect rests in the verbs 'to pass' and 'to transfer' employed therein.

[55] See, eg, F Prideaux and J Whitcombe, *Prideaux's Precedents of Conveyancing*, 8th edn (London, Stevens & Sons, 1876) vol I, 398–99, where the elaborately-worded power of attorney of earlier editions has been expunged. However, old habits die hard, and powers of attorney are still often used in conjunction with assignments: see H Beale, L Gullifer and S Paterson, 'A Case for Interfering with Freedom of Contract? An Empirically Informed Study of Bans on Assignment' [2016] *JBL* 203, 223.

[56] [1902] 2 KB 190 (CA).

[57] ibid 194 (Mathew LJ); 198 (Cozens-Hardy LJ).

[58] ibid 198 (Cozens-Hardy LJ).

Once again, Lord Esher MR's judgment in *Read v Brown* helpfully reminds us that, '[t]he debt is transferred to the assignee and becomes *as though* it had been his from the beginning; it is no longer to be the debt of the assignor at all, who cannot sue for it, the right to sue being taken from him …'.[59] Though the latter phrase might suggest that the assignor's right to sue had been extinguished, that would be incoherent.

Lord Esher tells us that the assignee is to be treated *as though* it were the creditor. So, the assignee is *still* not the creditor. For consistency, the sentence 'it is no longer to be the debt of the assignor …' must mean that the assignor is to be treated *as though* it was not the creditor, *even though it still is* (based on the substantive law giving rise to the debt/chose as had been assigned).

To give effect to this, the 'procedural' approach employed in statutes like the Limitation Act 1980 seems apt. Adopting that approach, where a debt/chose in action has been assigned in a manner which triggers section 136(1), although the 'statutory' assignor remains creditor/obligee, in relation to the entitlements spelt out in section 136(1)(a), (b) and (c) (and which were formerly set out in section 25(6)), the statute *disables* the assignor from effectively invoking them by directing the court to view invocations of these entitlements by the assignor to be ineffective. Hence it becomes *as though* the assignor no longer has them.

V. THE EFFECT OF NOT FULFILLING SECTION 25(6) OR SECTION 136(1) REQUIREMENTS

For Lord Macnaghten, although the assignment before their Lordships in *Brandt's* might not have been 'absolute' as to bring it within section 25(6), that did not mean that the assignment could not continue to operate as an equitable assignment.[60] This could be taken as authority for the proposition that an equitable assignee who fails to bring itself within the ambit of section 25(6) (or, today, section 136(1)), is still entitled to rely on its entitlements as an equitable assignee. Though some commentators have taken the position that that is indeed the case in English law,[61] other works, including the current edition of *Snell's Equity*, have been more circumspect[62] given the approach taken by the High Court of Australia to Australian equivalents to sections 25(6) and 136(1).

A. The Australian Position

The High Court of Australia has construed Australian equivalents to sections 25(6) and 136(1) as having created requirements which, if unfulfilled, invalidate the assignment. The key Australian authority seems to be *Olsson v Dyson*.[63]

In that case, just prior to his death, a husband in South Australia purported to make his wife a parol gift of the chose in action arising from a loan of money. The

[59] *Read v Brown* (n 26) 132.
[60] *Brandt's* (n 10) and the text accompanying n 69.
[61] See n 11.
[62] McGhee (n 3); Liew (n 12).
[63] (1968) 120 CLR 365 (HCA), on appeal from the Supreme Court of Southern Australia.

High Court of Australia held that the parol gift failed for non-compliance with section 15 of the Law of Property Act 1936 (SA).[64] As Kitto J explained, there being no equity to perfect an incomplete gift, where the assignment was made parol and the husband having died without making a duly signed assignment in writing, he had failed to do all that he had to do to comply with section 15. Hence, the gift was still incomplete as at his death for want of writing under his hand.[65]

Windeyer J concluded likewise. He also reasoned that section 15 had to be followed for this gift to be complete at law, and that there was no equity to complete an incomplete gift.[66] This echoed points he had previously made in *Norman v Federal Commissioner of Taxation*:[67]

> [T]he law now provides a means whereby the legal owner of a chose in action may make a complete and perfect gift of it. That being so, and as equity does not perfect an imperfect gift, can there ever now be an effectual voluntary assignment unless all the statutory requirements are met? ... Equity intervened to assist the assignments of choses in action because they were not assignable at law. Now that they are, why, it may be asked, should equity aid imperfect attempts at voluntary assignments of them. On the other hand, it can be urged that the statute provides a method or machinery whereby assignment may be effected, but that it does not detract from the validity of any transaction that would have been effective in equity if it had occurred before the statute came into operation. There is some authority for the latter proposition: see eg *German v Yates*.[68] And Lord Macnaghten's well-known words in *William Brandts' Sons & Co v Dunlop Rubber Co*, are sometimes invoked in support of it: 'Why that which would have been a good equitable assignment before the statute should now be invalid and inoperative because it fails to come up to the requirements of the statute, I confess I do not understand. The statute does not forbid or destroy equitable assignments or impair their efficacy in the slightest degree'.[69] But this was said in reference to an assignment for value. I do not think that his Lordship's remarks should be read as qualifying the principle that equity does not perfect imperfect voluntary assignments. If an attempt is made to assign, by way of gift, a chose in action assignable under the statute, ... the requirements of the statute cannot be ignored; for the general rule of equity is that an effective assignment occurs only if the donor does all that, according to the nature of the property, he must do to transfer the property to the donee.

Here, Windeyer J attempted to distinguish *Brandt's* on grounds that it involved an assignment for value. But English judges have declined to follow suit.

B. The English Position

English judges have taken Lord Macnaghten's views in *Brandt's*[70] to be generally applicable, even to voluntary assignments unsupported by consideration. This can be seen in *German v Yates*.[71]

[64] Which is *in pari materia* with section 136(1).
[65] *Olsson* (n 63) 375. Barwick CJ and Menzies J agreed with Kitto J.
[66] ibid 385.
[67] (1963) 109 CLR 9 (HCA) 28.
[68] (1915) 32 TLR 52 (KBD).
[69] *Brandt's* (n 10) 461.
[70] Reproduced above, see the text accompanying nn 10 and 69.
[71] (n 68).

In that case, Sophia Yates gave Mrs German an IOU for a loan of £100. Later, Mrs German told Sophia Yates to pay the £100 when due to Maria Yates. Sophia Yates agreed, and gave Maria Yates a new IOU after Mrs German had destroyed the original one. No consideration was given by Maria Yates to Mrs German in relation to this transaction. Mrs German then passed away.

Mrs German's widower (acting as administrator of Mrs Gernan's estate) contended that if there had been an assignment of the benefit of the £100 debt to Maria Yates, it was ineffective; consequently, the debt remained part of Mrs German's estate. The report states:[72]

> [T]he subject matter here was a simple chose in action which could be transferred so as to give the transferee a right to sue under the Judicature Act *and could also be transferred by equitable assignment*. No form of words was required for an equitable assignment; the only thing that was necessary was to make the reasoning plain (*Brandt's v Dunlop* [1995] AC, at p 462 ...).
>
> [Counsel for the administrator] had contended that since the Judicature Act the creditor could make a good legal assignment under the Act, and that if he purported to make an equitable assignment without consideration he was trying to do what could be quite well done in another way and the transaction failed. But he (Mr Justice Lush) could not accept that view. *Brandt's v Dunlop* (*supra*, at p 461) showed that the Act had not destroyed equitable assignments or impaired their efficiency in any way, and they still existed alongside of the new kind of assignment under section 25. Nor could he accept that the assignment here was invalid because it was incomplete; it was perfectly good and complete.

Plainly, Lush J did *not* take Lord Macnaghten's observation in *Brandt's* to apply only to assignments for value since he applied it to Mrs Green's absolute assignment to a volunteer. Nor was Lush J alone, for Atkinson J adopted the same position in *Holt v Heatherfield Trust Ltd*,[73] a case involving section 136(1) of the Law of Property Act 1925.

In *Holt*, the plaintiff, Holt ('C'), had been equitably assigned the benefit of a judgment debt which was owed to the assignor, Samuel Partington ('A'), by the judgment debtor, the Chloride Electrical Storage Co Ltd ('B'). A obtained judgment on 14 June 1940, and the benefit of the judgment was assigned in writing to C the same day, C receiving the written assignment on 15 June 1940. But written notice of the assignment was only sent to B on 17 June, B receiving the notice on 18 June.

In other proceedings, A owed a judgment debt to the defendant, Heatherfield Trust Ltd ('G'). To enforce the judgment it had obtained against A, G obtained a garnishee order nisi and served it on B on 17 June, after A had assigned the benefit of B's judgment debt to C, but before B received written notice of the assignment on 18 June. The issue was whether the garnishee order nisi on the judgment debt which B owed A ought to be discharged or made absolute given A's assignment to C.

[72] ibid 52–53.
[73] [1942] 2 KB 1 (KBD) 14.

Atkinson J concluded that C had the better claim to B's judgment debt, even though written notice of the assignment was only received by B on 18 June:[74]

> Bearing in mind these two results, first, that the assignment was a perfectly good equitable assignment, which could be turned into a legal assignment [pursuant to section 136(1)] at any moment by giving [written] notice, and which without notice, the assignee could have sued upon so long as he joined the assignor as defendant, and secondly, that a judgment creditor is in no better position than the assignor and cannot garnishee anything which the assignor could not honestly deal with, it seems to me perfectly clear that the plaintiff's [C's] title is a good one …

Having rejected G's contention that A's assignment to C was fraudulent,[75] Atkinson J observed that the purported assignment by A to C had been in consideration of loans which C had made to A previously.[76] But, this was irrelevant as Atkinson J followed *Glegg v Bromley*[77] and held that the issue of consideration was only pertinent where a future debt (ie, a debt which was not in existence at the time of the assignment, but which might come into existence at some future time) had been assigned.[78] Since the assignment by A to C was of a presently extant judgment debt, and not a future debt,[79] the presence or absence of consideration was inconsequential. That is, *even if* there had been no consideration from C for the assignment, A would *still* have validly equitably assigned the benefit of the judgment debt owed by B to C once the written assignment was executed, and *before* written notice was received by B: 'the assignment [from A] was a perfectly good equitable assignment, which could be turned into a legal assignment at any moment by giving notice …'.[80] This is completely at odds with the reasoning of the High Court of Australia in *Olsson v Dyson*, which was decided a few years later.

Closer to the present day, the disinclination of English courts to adopt the Australian line of reasoning persists. For example, the unreported cases of *Sycamore Sandpits Developments Ltd v Phoenix Assurance Co Ltd*[81] and *Technocrats International Inc v Fredic Ltd*[82] both tell us that assignments of a legal chose in action which fall outside the ambit of section 136(1) may still take effect as an equitable assignment.

[74] ibid.

[75] ibid 2.

[76] ibid 2–3.

[77] [1912] 3 KB 474 (CA).

[78] The position is different in Australia: see *Commissioner of Taxation of the Commonwealth of Australia v Everett* (1980) 143 CLR 440 (HCA) 450.

[79] *Holt* (n 73) 5.

[80] ibid 14 (Atkinson J).

[81] (QBD, 23 May 1986) in which Tudor Evans J accepted that an oral assignment of a legal chose in action arising from a policy of insurance was effective as an equitable assignment. Although the oral assignment was to have been in consideration for a nominal sum of £100, the £100 was never paid. Tudor Evans J held that the payment of the £100 was 'not necessary' for the oral assignment to be effective in equity.

[82] [2004] EWHC 692 (QB) [57] in which Field J held that a written assignment of the benefit of a contract to pay sums by way of commission which was signed by an agent of the assignor was not 'under the hand of the assignor' (at [53]), but could still take effect as an equitable assignment; Field J also doubted that consideration was required for the equitable assignment to be effective, but it would in any event have been present in light of a promise by the assignee to pay the assignor £350,000 for the assignment.

Furthermore, although *Sycamore Sandpits* and *Technocrats International* were also cases in which the assignments were arguably supported by some form of consideration, this did not appear to the court in either case to be critical.[83]

VI. CONCLUSION

These English cases tell us that sections 25(6) and 136(1) operate quite differently from their Australian cousins. Strong arguments can be made in support of the English proposition that immediate and absolute gifts of presently extant legal choses in action made with neither writing under the assignor's hand, nor *written* notice to the debtor/obligor, are effective.

First, in *Hockin v Royal Bank of Scotland plc*, Asplin J agreed with the proposition that 'section 136 Law of Property Act 1925 does not create a statutory right of assignment in itself as much as regulates the effects of assignments which have taken place'.[84] This necessarily denotes that assignments which would have been effective and valid independently of section 136 will continue to be effective and valid whether the requirements of section 136 are met, or not: *their* validity does not depend on section 136 – although the availability of the effects mandated by section 136 certainly do.

Neither section 25(6) nor section 136(1) defines what counts as an 'assignment' for the legislative effects spelt out therein to arise. Each states that, when there has been an absolute assignment of a debt or legal chose/thing in action, and if that assignment had been in 'writing under the hand of the assignor', when written notice of such assignment is also received by the debtor/obligor of the chose assigned, certain entitlements of the assignor would *then* 'pass' and 'transfer'.[85] Thus, satisfaction of the requirements of a duly signed writing and written notice to the debtor/obligor are pre-requisites for the passing and transfer of the stipulated entitlements: they are not pre-requisites for the validity of the *assignment* of the debt or legal chose in action. Consequently, if these pre-requisites are *not* met, all that follows is that the 'passing' and 'transferring' of these stipulated entitlements as effected by the statute will not occur, but the 'assignment' of the debt or legal chose in action would still take effect so far as the general law apart from the statute would permit. Sections 25(6) and 136(1) merely build upon pre-existing institutions of assignments of debts or choses/things in action such as the institution of *equitable* assignment: they do not modify the substantive law of such institutions, but merely set out a statutory superstructure.[86]

[83] See nn 81–82.

[84] *Hockin v Royal Bank of Scotland plc* [2016] EWHC 925 (Ch) [44].

[85] Hence, in *Curran v Newpark Cinemas* [1951] 1 All ER 295 (CA) 299H, the Court of Appeal concluded that where a debt or thing in action had not been effectively equitably assigned in the first place, and where none of the mechanisms permitting assignment at law apart from s 136(1) had been validly invoked, s 136(1) could not be relied on because there would have been no 'assignment' for it to be applied to.

[86] Tham (n 11) 435–36.

Second, as Sargant J observed in *Re Westerton*, 'the aim of the sub-section [ie, section 25(6)] was to inform procedure …'.[87] As explained in section IV above, given what was held in *Read v Brown*, the modifications effected by section 25(6) and its legislative successor, section 136(1), operate *despite* the substantive law giving rise to the debt/chose assigned stipulating otherwise. That is how an assignee of a debt or chose in action can be treated *as though* the debt or obligation(s) relating to the chose assigned was/were owed to the assignee, *even though* the debt/obligation(s) is/are not. Correspondingly, where these provisions apply, the assignor can be treated *as though* the debt/obligation(s) was/were *not* owed to it even though they still are.

Obviously, *Olsson v Dyson* has no binding force on an English court. But, as explained above, there are good conceptual reasons why the path trodden by the High Court of Australia need not be followed in England.[88] Notwithstanding the esteem in which the High Court of Australia is held, the hesitancy in the current edition of *Snell's Equity* on the point is, perhaps, ripe for review, 150 years after the publication of the first.

APPENDIX

Judicature Act 1873

> **25.** And whereas it is expedient to take occasion of the union of the several Courts whose jurisdiction is hereby transferred to the said High Court of Justice to amend and declare the Law to be hereafter administered in England as to the matters next hereinafter mentioned: Be it enacted as follows:
>
> …
>
> (6) Any absolute assignment, by writing under the hand of the assignor (not purporting to be by way of charge only), of any debt or other legal chose in action, of which express notice in writing shall have been given to the debtor, trustee, or other person from whom the assignor would have been entitled to receive or claim such debt or chose in action, shall be, and be deemed to have been effectual in law (subject to all equities which would have been entitled to priority over the right of the assignee if this Act had not been passed), to pass and transfer the legal right to such debt or chose in action from the date of such notice, and all legal and other remedies for the same, and the power to give a good discharge for the same, without the concurrence of the assignor: Provided always, that if the debtor, trustee, or other person liable in respect of such debt or chose in action shall have had notice that such assignment is disputed by the assignor or any one claiming under him, or of any other opposing or conflicting claims to such debt or chose in action, he shall be entitled, if he think fit, to call upon the several persons making claim thereto to interplead concerning the same, or he may, if he think fit, pay the same into the High Court of Justice under and in conformity with the provisions of the Acts for the relief of trustees.
>
> …

[87] *Re Westerton* [1919] 2 Ch 104 (Ch) 133. See also *Marchant v Morton Down & Co* [1901] 2 KB 829 (KBD) 832; and *Torkington* (n 25) 435.

[88] Or, by jurisdictions employing similar legislation: see, eg, Civil Law Act 1909 (Singapore), s 4(8).

Law of Property Act 1925

136. Legal assignments of things in action.

(1) Any absolute assignment by writing under the hand of the assignor (not purporting to be by way of charge only) of any debt or other legal thing in action, of which express notice in writing has been given to the debtor, trustee or other person from whom the assignor would have been entitled to claim such debt or thing in action, is effectual in law (subject to equities having priority over the right of the assignee) to pass and transfer from the date of such notice—

(a) the legal right to such debt or thing in action;
(b) all legal and other remedies for the same; and
(c) the power to give a good discharge for the same without the concurrence of the assignor:

Provided that, if the debtor, trustee or other person liable in respect of such debt or thing in action has notice—

(a) that the assignment is disputed by the assignor or any person claiming under him; or
(b) of any other opposing or conflicting claims to such debt or thing in action; he may interplead concerning the same, or pay the debt or other thing in action into court under the provisions of the Trustee Act 1925.

…

4

Equity and the Land Registration Act 2002: Form, Conscience, and the Judiciary

ARUNA NAIR*

I. INTRODUCTION

MOST LAND IN England and Wales is now 'registered land',[1] meaning that the creation, transfer, and priority of rights affecting that land are governed by the Land Registration Act 2002 ('LRA 2002'). As a result, any descriptive account of a historically important[2] domain of equity – the law governing the creation, transfer and priority of rights affecting land in England and Wales – must take account of the difference that the statute has made to its operation in that domain. However, in addition to the descriptive relevance of the statute to our understanding of the law of one jurisdiction, the role played by equity in this context can also contribute to our general understanding of what is special, or not, about equity – both as a source of rights that differ in important ways from property rights recognised at law[3] and as a mode of reasoning that differs in important ways from the common law.[4]

* Tutorial Fellow, Hertford College, Oxford; Associate Professor, Faculty of Law, University of Oxford.
I am grateful to participants in the Equity conference and to the editors of the volume for helpful comments on previous drafts of this chapter.

[1] According to Land Registry, as of 2017, almost 85 per cent of the land mass of England and Wales was registered: see HM Land Registry, *Business Strategy 2017–2022* (29 November 2017), https://www.gov.uk/government/publications/hm-land-registry-business-strategy-2017-to-2022. This means that title to some estate in that land has been registered, so that dealings with that estate are governed by the provisions of the LRA 2002: LRA 2002, s 132.

[2] J Baker, *Introduction to English Legal History*, 5th edn (Oxford, OUP, 2019) 113.

[3] For different views on this question, see R Nolan, 'Equitable Property' (2006) 122 *LQR* 232; B McFarlane and R Stevens, 'The Nature of Equitable Property' (2010) 4 *Journal of Equity* 1; T Cutts, 'The Nature of Equitable Property: A Functional Analysis' (2012) 6 *Journal of Equity* 44; J Penner, 'The (True) Nature of a Beneficiary's Equitable Proprietary Interest Under a Trust' (2014) 27 *Canadian Journal of Law & Jurisprudence* 473; B McFarlane and R Stevens, 'What's Special About Equity? Rights About Rights' in D Klimchuk, I Samet and H Smith (eds), *Philosophical Foundations of the Law of Equity* (Oxford, OUP, 2020).

[4] For different views on this question, see P Birks, 'Equity in the Modern Law: An Exercise in Taxonomy' [1996] 22 *University of Western Australia Law Review* 1; A Burrows, 'We Do This at Common Law

This is because it is generally accepted that the English title registration system is the product of an avowedly reformist project intended to tilt the balance of English land law towards greater certainty and predictability and so to lower the costs of conveyancing.[5] As such, one aim of the system is to reduce the role played by open-textured and unpredictable standards in the creation and enforceability of interests capable of binding purchasers of land, and to increase the role of formal and predictable rules on which such purchasers can rely without undue expense.[6] To the extent that equity is primarily distinctive because of its reliance on such standards,[7] therefore, we might expect the legislation to downplay the significance of the law/equity distinction, either by getting rid of equitable interests or by taming them under the rubric of a rule-based order that assimilates them to legal interests. Conversely, if the role of equity is precisely to ameliorate the injustices that arise from the generality of legal rules,[8] we might expect the generality of the land registration legislation to generate frequent injustices of precisely this type, which might then tempt the judges to 'do equity'. In this way, both the land registration legislation and the case law interpreting that legislation – what the LRA 2002 has done with equity, and what equity has done with the LRA 2002 and its predecessors – can provide us with insights into the character of the law/equity distinction.

In this chapter, I argue that the LRA 2002 demonstrates the continuing importance of the law/equity distinction, but also shows that there is only limited overlap between that distinction and the distinction between rules and standards. Section II looks at how the legislative framework deploys the distinction between law and equity, while section III looks at how the judiciary have deployed equitable concepts in interpreting the legislation. In both contexts, the distinction between law and equity does sometimes reflect the distinction between rules and standards but it sometimes has a purely formal character and sometimes it is equity's own formalism that is opposed to the substantive standards embodied by the legislation.

II. WHAT LAND REGISTRATION HAS DONE WITH EQUITY: MODES OF REGISTRATION AT LAW AND IN EQUITY

It has been suggested that, under the LRA 2002, the traditional dichotomy between legal and equitable interests in land has become otiose, so that it is more important to classify property rights in land on the basis of whether they are registrable

but That in Equity' (2002) 22 *OJLS* 1; D Klimchuk, 'Equity and the Rule of Law' in LM Austin and D Klimchuk (eds), *Private Law and the Rule of Law* (Oxford, OUP, 2014) 21; C Webb, 'Discretionary Justice' in D Klimchuk, I Samet and H Smith (eds), *Philosophical Foundations of the Law of Equity* (Oxford, OUP, 2020) 12; I Samet, *Equity: Conscience Goes to Market* (Oxford, OUP, 2019); H Smith, 'Equity as Meta-Law' (2021) 130 *Yale Law Journal* 1050, 1071–90; S Bray and P Miller, 'Getting Into Equity' (2022) 97 *Notre Dame Law Review* 1763.

[5] See, generally, S Anderson, *Lawyers and the Making of English Land Law 1832–1940* (Oxford, Clarendon Press, 1992).

[6] For the distinction between rules and standards, see D Kennedy, 'Form and Substance in Private Law Adjudication' (1976) 89 *Harvard Law Review* 1685; and Samet, *Equity* (n 4) 25.

[7] As argued by Samet (n 4); Smith 'Equity as Meta-Law' (n 4).

[8] ibid.

or non-registrable.[9] However, this binary distinction between the 'registrable' and 'non-registrable' cannot account for the complexities of a title registration system like that created by the LRA 2002. Unlike a title recording system,[10] a title registration system does not simply require parties to deposit evidence of their transactions and then preserve that evidence in a publicly accessible repository. Rather, it involves the registrar in the task of interpreting the documents submitted by private parties and then constructing an authoritative account of the rights now affecting the land as a result of the transactions evidenced by those documents.[11] Such a system must determine not only *which* rights affecting land are to be reflected on the register but also *how* they are to be reflected. Each mode of registration may have different legal consequences, so that a given property right may be registrable in one sense and under one mode and yet non-registrable in some other sense and under some other mode.

The LRA 2002 recognises three distinct types of registration, each of which has different consequences. First, there are '*registrable estates*': these are rights that are independently registrable, with each 'estate' being given a title number and described on the 'property register'; the 'proprietorship register' states the name of the 'registered proprietor' who holds that estate and certifies the quality of their title as either 'absolute', 'qualified' or 'possessory'.[12] Only some property rights in land can be registered in this way appearing on the property register associated with a title number and with the name of the right-holder then appearing on the proprietorship register. Secondly, there are '*notices*':[13] these are entries which appear on the 'charges register' associated with a registered estate, and which disclose the content of certain rights that burden that estate. Finally, there are '*restrictions*':[14] these are entries on the proprietorship register that regulate 'the circumstances in which a disposition [of the registered estate] ... may be the subject of an entry in the register.'[15] Some rights burdening a registered estate in land can only be reflected on the register by the entry of a restriction, since they cannot be entered as a notice.

Thus, a functional classification of rights, based on their treatment under the LRA 2002, must first distinguish between rights that are independently registrable ('registrable estates') and rights that are not. Next, among the rights that cannot be independently registered but that can only appear on the register as burdens on registered estates, we must further distinguish between rights that may be disclosed in full on the register (by the entry of 'notices') and rights that can only be indirectly reflected on the register (by the entry of 'restrictions'). I argue below that the formal difference between law and equity is vital to the first of these distinctions, while the second turns on the substantive difference between trusts and other (legal and equitable) interests in land.

[9] E Cooke, *The Modern Law of Land Registration* (Oxford, Hart, 2003) 35.

[10] B Arruñada and N Garoupa, 'The Choice of Titling System in Land' (2005) 48 *Journal of Law and Economics* 709.

[11] See A Pottage, 'The Measure of Land' (1994) 3 *MLR* 361, 377–84, distinguishing the 'tabular' account of title presented by such a register from the 'genealogical' accounts constructed by traditional conveyancing practice.

[12] LRA 2002, s 9.

[13] LRA 2002, ss 32–39.

[14] LRA 2002, ss 40–47.

[15] LRA 2002, s 40(1).

A. Registrable Estates: Rights to Land and Incumbrances on Rights to Land

Under the LRA 2002, registration as '*proprietor*' of a '*registered estate*' in land confers several benefits. First, where a person is registered with an 'absolute title'[16] to a registered estate, the state will guarantee her title. This means that the estate will be vested by statute in the new proprietor,[17] even if she would not otherwise be entitled to it under the general law (as where the underlying transaction is void or non-existent); an indemnity may be available[18] if the register is subsequently changed[19] to correct a mistaken registration of this type. Secondly, under section 29, completion by registration of a 'registrable disposition'[20] for value of a registered estate will give the disponee priority over many interests that would otherwise bind her: the only exceptions are interests that appear on the register as notices and 'overriding interests' under Schedule 3.[21] This priority will often depend on registration as proprietor of a registered estate, since many dispositions will only be 'completed by registration' for the purposes of section 29 once such an entry is made.[22] Finally, the registered proprietor of a registered estate, or any person entitled to be so registered,[23] is vested with 'owner's powers' in relation to the registered estate. This means that the registered proprietor is entitled to 'make a disposition of any kind permitted by the general law';[24] under section 26, any disponee from her will take a title unaffected by any limits on her powers of disposition, unless there is a restriction on the register reflecting those limits.

This mode of registration, with its attendant benefits, is available only to those entitled to *legal* estates and interests in land. These include rights to possession, such as freeholds and (some) leaseholds, but also lesser rights like rentcharges,[25] franchises,[26] and profits à prendre in gross.[27] However, not all legal estates and interests in land can be independently registered in this way. Some short leases cannot be registered because it would be an undue administrative burden, both on the parties and on the state, for such short-lived rights to be added and then removed from the register as they arise and terminate. These leases are excluded from the state guarantee of title, but not from the priority conferred by section 29: section 29(4) expressly

[16] LRA 2002, s 9(2): 'A person may be registered with absolute title if the registrar is of the opinion that the person's title to the estate is such as a willing purchaser could properly be advised by a competent professional adviser to accept'.

[17] LRA 2002, s 11(3) (first registration); LRA 2002, s 58 (subsequent registration).

[18] Under LRA 2002, Sch 8.

[19] Under LRA 2002, Sch 4.

[20] LRA 2002, s 29(1).

[21] LRA 2002, s 29(2).

[22] LRA 2002, Sch 2.

[23] LRA 2002, s 24.

[24] LRA 2002, s 23(1)(a).

[25] A right to be paid a sum of money by the holder of an estate in land, where the right does not arise under a tenancy: Rentcharges Act 1977, s 1.

[26] A right to do something, such as hold a fair or a market, that would otherwise be a prerogative of the Crown: *Spook Erection Ltd v Secretary of State for the Environment* [1989] QB 300 (CA) 303.

[27] A right to take something from the land of another person, such as a right to fish, hunt, cut turf, or pasture animals. Such a right exists 'in gross' (as opposed to as an 'appurtenant' right) where it is held by a person in her own right rather than in her capacity as the owner of an estate in land.

provides that the grant of such a lease is to be treated *as if* it is a registered disposition for the purposes of the section. Meanwhile, all easements and some profits can only exist as rights appurtenant to benefitted estates, so that a person can only be registered as proprietor of such an interest where the benefitted estate is itself registered. Where the benefitted estate is not registered, the appurtenant right can only appear as a notice on the charges register of the burdened estate;[28] in such a case, the right will not attract the state guarantee of title but will qualify for the favourable priority rules under section 29, if value has been given.[29] If the benefitted estate is registered, the easement or profit will be noted on the property register of that estate, and will then be guaranteed by the state.[30] Finally, it is not possible to register a charge by way of legal mortgage as a freestanding right, without registration of the mortgaged estate. Instead, the mortgagee may apply in the name of the mortgagor for the registration of the mortgagor's title to the charged estate, if that title is not already registered.[31] Once the mortgagor's title to the charged estate is registered, the mortgagee will be entered on the charges register as '*proprietor*' of the registered charge;[32] this registration also qualifies for favourable priority rules,[33] confers owner's powers in relation to the charge,[34] and engages the state guarantee of title.[35] Thus, under the LRA 2002, most holders of legal estates or interests in land can be entered as registered proprietors, with the benefits of possible priority over earlier unprotected interests, owners' powers of disposition, and the state guarantee of title. Where they do not have the option of such registration, the statute gives them equivalent priority protection.

By contrast, holders of equitable interests are wholly excluded from registration in this mode. The only circumstance where the holder of an equitable interest can apply for registration as proprietor of a property right is where he is entitled to require that a *legal* estate be vested in him.[36] In such a case, he will be registered as proprietor of that legal estate, not as proprietor of the equitable interest; in so far as he has owner's powers before such registration,[37] these will relate to the legal estate rather than to his equitable interest. Meanwhile, the special rules that apply to property rights that cannot be registered with separate titles – short leases, appurtenant rights, and mortgages – apply only at law. For example, section 29(4) applies on 'the grant of a leasehold estate in land out of a registered estate'; it is well-established that the language of 'grant', in this type of context, captures the grant of *legal* leases and not

[28] LRA 2002, Sch 2, para 7(2).

[29] LRA 2002, s 29(1), providing that 'completion by registration' of a registrable disposition for value attracts the defence and Sch 2, para 7(2), defining completion by registration of an appurtenant right as requiring only the entry of a notice, except where the interest is created for the benefit of a registered estate.

[30] LRA 2002, s 58; *Smith v Muller* [2008] EWCA Civ 1425 [28].

[31] LRA 2002, s 4(1)(g); Land Registration Rules 2003 (SI 2003/1417) ('LRR 2003'), r 21.

[32] LRA 2002, Sch 2, para 8; LRR 2003, r 22(2), r 34.

[33] LRA 2002, s 30.

[34] LRA 2002, s 23(2).

[35] LRA 2002, s 58; *Swift 1st Ltd v Chief Land Registrar* [2015] EWCA Civ 330, [2015] Ch 602.

[36] LRA 2002, s 3(2)(b).

[37] Under LRA 2002, s 24(b). The precise scope of the powers conferred by the section on a person 'entitled to be registered as the proprietor' is contested: see *Skelwith (Leisure) Ltd v Armstrong* [2015] EWHC 2830 (Ch), [2016] Ch 345 criticised by E Lees, 'Powers of the Beneficiary of a Trust of a Charge' [2016] *Conveyancer and Property Lawyer* 157.

the creation of equitable leases.[38] The holder of an equitable easement can apply for entry of her easement as a notice on the charges register of the burdened estate, but cannot apply for entry of her interest on the property register of the benefitted estate, whether or not the benefitted estate is registered;[39] meanwhile, the creation of the easement in her favour will not count as a registrable disposition[40] capable of conferring priority under section 29, even if she has given value. The holder of an equitable charge cannot compel the registration of the charged estate, and the notice on the charges register that reflects the existence of his charge will not attract the state guarantee of title;[41] nor is the grant of an equitable charge a registrable disposition for the purposes of section 29.[42] Thus, the purchaser of an equitable interest who enters her interest on the register of title in the only way facilitated by the LRA 2002 – by the entry of a notice or restriction on the register of title of someone else's estate – will not thereby gain anything except protection from a loss of priority[43] to a later disponee of the registered estate, under either section 29 (in the case of a notice) or section 26 (in the case of a restriction).[44]

On the face of it, this is odd. Why should purchasers of relatively marginal rights like rentcharges, franchises and profits in gross enjoy these advantages, while purchasers of such standard and commercially significant rights as equitable leases and options do not? In justifying the independent registration of franchises and profits, which first became possible under the LRA 2002, the Law Commission described both as 'valuable' rights which are often 'bought and sold'[45] or 'sold and leased'.[46] But many equitable interests are also valuable rights which are capable of being assigned and often are assigned for money. The existence of a market for a right that is somehow connected to land does not, therefore, seem to be the sole criterion which explains when that right will be independently registrable, in the sense that attracts the privileges of priority over certain earlier interests and the state guarantee of title. In its most recent work on land registration, the Law Commission did raise the possibility that registration of an equitable interest, as a notice, should confer priority over earlier unregistered interests.[47] These proposals were eventually abandoned on

[38] *City Permanent Building Society v Miller* [1952] Ch 840 (CA); *Mortgage Business plc v O'Shaughnessy* [2012] EWCA Civ 17, [2012] 1 WLR 1521 [21], [57]–[64].

[39] LRR 2003, rr 33(1) and 73A(2).

[40] LRA 2002, s 27(2)(d).

[41] LRA 2002, s 32(3).

[42] LRA 2002, s 27(2)(f).

[43] See B McFarlane, *The Structure of Property Law* (Oxford, Hart, 2008) 87–88, distinguishing between the positive operation of registration (conferral of rights) and its negative operation (protection from loss of priority) and noting that only the latter mode is relevant to equitable interests.

[44] It has been argued that s 26, unlike s 29, applies in favour of a disponee of an equitable interest: S Watterson and A Goymour, 'A Tale of Three Promises (3): The Empowerment Promise' in A Goymour, S Watterson and M Dixon (eds), *New Perspectives on Land Registration: Contemporary Problems and Solutions* (Oxford, Hart, 2018) 387–88. As Goymour and Watterson note, if this is correct, s 26 protection will apply in favour of a disponee whose interest is not reflected on the register in any way and thus this is not a benefit that flows from registration of the equitable interest.

[45] Law Commission, *Land Registration for the Twenty-First Century: A Conveyancing Revolution* (Law Com No 271, 2001) para [3.19].

[46] ibid para [3.20].

[47] Law Commission, *Updating the Land Registration Act 2002: A Consultation Paper* (Law Com CP No 227, 2016) paras [6.7]–[6.30].

the basis that they might potentially make a wider class of already existing equitable interests – themselves unlikely to be registered, because arising informally – vulnerable to destruction in favour of the narrow class of persons likely to acquire and register equitable interests in the future, such as property developers taking options to purchase.[48] However, this argument only raises the question why a property developer who buys and then registers an option to purchase land should be in a weaker position than the purchaser of a legal estate in the same land who completes his acquisition of the estate by registration. Many unregistered interests are unregistered because they have arisen informally, and it is one of the aims of the title registration system to allow a purchaser to avoid being bound by such unregistered interests where they are not overriding interests (and thus readily discoverable by inspection of the land). Why should the purchaser of an option not be given the same protection, subject to the same qualification in favour of holders of overriding interests?

One possible answer is that the property developer who acquires, and then registers, an option to purchase is not a person who has (yet) acquired *land*: the option does not entitle its holder to possess or use the land itself, it merely entitles him to compel a transfer of such rights of possession and use in the future.[49] It is only when the option is exercised that the developer will be in a position to take control of the land itself; at that stage, he will become entitled to a legal estate and entitled to apply for registration as its proprietor. This analysis echoes the 'rights against rights' model of equitable interests, developed and advanced by McFarlane and Stevens.[50] On this view, the key feature of an equitable interest is that it is not a property right in a thing; it is, instead, a right governing the exercise of someone else's rights, which may or may not relate to a thing. In the case of land, a legal estate or interest will normally[51] impose duties on the world at large rather than on one person or class of persons in particular; the duty governs the actions of the duty-bearer in relation to the physical land that is the subject matter of the estate or interest.[52] By contrast, an equitable interest 'in land' imposes a duty on a specific right-holder – the holder of some estate or interest in land – and/or those who derive rights from her. The duty governs the actions of the right-holder in relation to her own rights or powers as the holder of a title to the land. The register reflects this precise structure. A person who has a right to possess or benefit from land itself[53] can be registered as proprietor of

[48] Law Commission, *Updating the Land Registration Act 2002* (Law Com No 380, 2018) paras [6.72]–[6.80].

[49] L Katz, 'Equitable Remedies: Protecting "What We Have Coming to Us"' (2021) 96 *Notre Dame Law Review* 1116.

[50] McFarlane and Stevens, 'The Nature of Equitable Property' (n 3). For the application of this model in the land registration context, see McFarlane, *The Structure of Property Law* (n 43) 81–99 and 477–501.

[51] For the more complicated case of the rentcharge, see n 53 below.

[52] B McFarlane and S Douglas, 'Defining Property Rights' in J Penner and H Smith (eds), *Philosophical Foundations of Property Law* (Oxford, OUP, 2013) 219; B McFarlane and S Douglas, 'Property, Analogy and Variety' (2022) 42 *OJLS* 161, 165–69.

[53] This characterisation of a rentcharge may be doubted, on the basis that it imposes a duty on the holders of a freehold estate (not the world at large) and only remotely concerns the physical land. However, a legal rentcharge is not a 'right against a right' in the sense that it imposes a duty on a freeholder governing his use of the rights that he has as a freeholder. Rather, it is a freestanding right to be paid money by anyone who takes a freehold title to the land and is thus traditionally conceived of as a right 'issuing out of land': see Rentcharges Act 1977, s 1. Most modern rentcharges are linked to the enjoyment of land itself,

that right, ensuring that all those who wish to make use of the land or take possession of it can identify the appropriate person to negotiate with and insuring them against the risk of negotiating with someone who turns out not to have such rights under the general law. Meanwhile, equitable interests appear on the register as incumbrances on legal rights – informing those who wish to buy those rights of potential burdens that they may come under if they go ahead with the transaction – but not as freestanding marketable interests in the land itself.

Thus, the distinction between registrable estates and rights that cannot be registered in this mode precisely mirrors the distinction between legal and equitable interests and indicates an important functional difference between legal and equitable interests. However, that difference does not overlap with the distinction between form and substance. The registrar is directed to treat legal estates and interests differently from equitable interests, but not to rely on standards in one case and not in the other. A person who applies to be registered as proprietor of an equitable interest will fail to obtain such registration because rules say so; a person who applies to be registered as proprietor of a legal estate will succeed if the registrar is willing to certify his title to that estate, a question that turns on a combination on rules and relatively open-textured standards (such as whether the title is such that a 'competent' professional could 'properly' advise a willing purchaser to accept it).[54] It is difficult to relate the differential treatment of law and equity, in this context, to the idea that the duties imposed by equitable interests are specially dependent on standards, whereas legal interests require compliance with rules. Rather, the distinction reflects a difference in subject matter: equitable interests are rights against rights, not rights in relation to land.

B. Notices, Restrictions, and Overreaching: Trusts and Other Incumbrances

By contrast, the distinction between notices and restrictions can more readily be linked to the difference between rules and standards. A notice on the register discloses 'details of the interest protected':[55] for example, the terms of a restrictive covenant or of an easement may be quoted in full or incorporated by reference to the copy of the underlying deed, which is then provided on application. Where an interest appears on the register as a notice, it will bind a purchaser under a registered disposition,[56] unless the purchaser can avoid liability in some other way, such as obtaining the consent of the holder of the notice to a postponement of priority.[57] Thus, purchasers relying on the register must duly interpret the terms of any notices and decide whether they are willing to take the estate subject to the interests disclosed. A 'restriction', on the other hand, prescribes conditions that must be satisfied in order for the register to be

since they are linked to the performance of covenants or services for the benefit of the burdened land by the person with the benefit of the rentcharge: see Rentcharges Act 1977, s 2.

[54] LRA 2002, s 9(2).

[55] LRR 2003, r 84.

[56] LRA 2002, s 29(2)(a)(i).

[57] *Ali v Dinc* [2020] EWHC 3055 (Ch), [2021] 2 P & CR 19.

changed, without disclosing the terms of any underlying interest that explains why those conditions are relevant. Its effect is that the registrar may not make an entry in the register that is inconsistent with its conditions,[58] except where an order disapplying or modifying those conditions has been successfully applied for by an interested party.[59] Purchasers relying on the register must therefore either ensure compliance with the terms of any restrictions or apply for their discharge or modification; if they succeed, they will take free of any adverse interest underlying the restriction under section 29(1), unless that interest is overriding under schedule 3.[60]

Some interests cannot be entered on the register as notices and can be reflected on the register, if at all, only in the form of restrictions.[61] Unlike the distinction between registrable estates and other interests in land, this distinction between interests that can be entered as notices and interests that are excluded from such registration does not track the distinction between law and equity. Notices may reflect the existence of legal interests – easements, profits, mortgages – but they can equally include such equitable interests as equitable easements, equitable leases, restrictive covenants, options to purchase land, and equitable charges. Rights that cannot be entered as notices, meanwhile, include legal interests like short leases,[62] rights of common registered under the Commons Act 2006,[63] and interests in coal mines.[64] They also include restrictive leasehold covenants[65] and interests under trusts of land and strict settlements.[66] However, all the legal property rights that cannot be registered as notices are rights that will necessarily bind a purchaser, as overriding interests, even without such registration;[67] the motive for excluding them from the register is that they are readily discoverable by other means and their presence on the register would unduly clutter the title. Equitable interests, by contrast, are never overriding, except when their holders are in actual occupation of the land.[68] Trusts, therefore, represent a particular sub-category of equitable interest marked out for special treatment. Like other equitable interests, they will not bind a purchaser in the absence of a notice on the register, unless their holder is in actual occupation of the land. Unlike the holders of other equitable interests, however, the beneficiary under a trust does not have the option of protection from the priority-postponing effect of section 29 by entry of a notice. Instead, the only mechanism that is available is entry of a restriction.

According to the Law Commission, this is because 'a buyer wishes to take free of such interests',[69] which should 'be overreached and bind the proceeds of sale'.[70] Of course, a purchaser might well wish to take free of *every* adverse interest affecting

[58] LRA 2002, s 41(1).
[59] LRA 2002, s 41(2).
[60] LRA 2002, s 29(1).
[61] LRA 2002, s 33.
[62] LRA 2002, s 33(b).
[63] LRA 2002, s 33(d).
[64] LRA 2002, s 33(e).
[65] LRA 2002, s 33(c).
[66] LRA 2002, s 33(a).
[67] LRA 2002, Sch 3, para 1 (short leases), para 3 (registered rights of common) and para 7 (coal mines).
[68] LRA 2002, Sch 3.
[69] Law Commission, *Land Registration for the Twenty-First Century* (n 45) para [6.9].
[70] ibid.

the registered title; this does not in itself give us a reason to prefer the interests of the purchaser over the interests of the beneficiary, who may wish the purchaser *not* to take free of her interest. The point is rather that this is not considered to be a legitimate goal for the beneficiary under a trust of land to pursue and therefore it is not one that the legislation will facilitate. Instead, the option of registering a restriction facilitates a different outcome, the overreaching of the beneficial interest. This is the mechanism by which an authorised disposition by trustees will properly terminate the beneficiaries' interest in the trust asset and give them, instead, an interest in any substitute assets obtained by the trustees.[71] Under the Law of Property Act 1925, statutory overreaching of equitable interests will occur where there has been a conveyance to a purchaser of a legal estate,[72] the equitable interest is of a type capable of being overreached by a transaction of that type,[73] and – in the case of an interest under a trust – any funds generated by the transaction are paid to two trustees or a trust corporation.[74] Where these conditions are satisfied, the purchaser under an overreaching transaction will take free of the overreached equitable interest even where the interest-holder is in actual occupation of the trust land.[75] The standard restrictions that reflect the existence of a trust are designed to produce this outcome.[76] Meanwhile, various classes of equitable interest – restrictive covenants, equitable easements, certain equitable charges, and 'estate contracts' – are exempt from statutory overreaching by court-appointed trustees;[77] many of these are intrinsically incapable of being overreached, apart from the statute, because the duties they impose on right-holders do not encompass the power to make authorised substitutions.

This illuminates a general point of difference between trusts and other equitable interests. In the case of a trust, the core right of a beneficiary is that the trustees will properly exercise their powers of disposition[78] in accordance with a set of open-textured standards that include duties of good faith[79] and propriety as to motive.[80] Trustees' failure to comply with these standards could affect a disponee in the sense that, before 1926, a transaction would not overreach beneficial interests if the trustees did not meet these standards:[81] disponees who took under a transaction that was an improper exercise of the trustees' powers, even if they were unaware of the fact, might then become liable to the beneficiaries in the sense that the beneficiaries could compel them to re-convey the trust asset to the original trustees or at the direction of the court.[82] However, overreaching was not the only mechanism whereby disponees

[71] See, generally, D Fox, 'Overreaching' in P Birks and A Pretto-Sakmann (eds), *Breach of Trust* (Oxford, OUP, 2002) 95.

[72] Law of Property Act 1925 ('LPA 1925'), s 2(1).

[73] LPA 1925, s 2(1), (5).

[74] LPA 1925, ss 2(1)(ii), 27.

[75] *City of London Building Society v Flegg* [1988] AC 54 (HL).

[76] LRA 2002, s 44(1); LRR 2003, Sch 4, Form A and Form B.

[77] LPA 1925, s 2(5).

[78] Penner (n 3).

[79] J Hudson, 'One Thicket in Fraud on a Power' (2019) 39 *OJLS* 557, 579–83.

[80] L Smith, 'The Motive, not the Deed' in J Getzler (ed), *Rationalising Property, Equity and Trusts: Essays in Honour of Edward Burn* (Oxford, OUP, 2003) 53.

[81] Hudson (n 79) 590–92. This remains the case in the modern law for assets other than land.

[82] See B McFarlane and S Agnew, 'The Paradox of the Equitable Proprietary Claim' in B McFarlane and S Agnew (eds), *Modern Studies in Property Law: Volume 10* (Oxford, Hart, 2019) 303, 304–06.

could avoid this liability. The 'equity's darling' defence would come to the aid of a bona fide purchaser for value of a legal estate, if he could show that he lacked notice of the breach of trust.[83] Purchasers who failed to take certain positive steps to monitor trustees' compliance with the standards imposed on them by equity might be fixed with 'constructive notice' of a breach of trust and lose the protection of the defence; for example, they were expected to obtain a receipt from the trustees declaring that they had properly applied the purchase money paid to them.[84] In this way, the law made purchasers from trustees to some degree responsible for monitoring whether the trustees had met the standards governing their exercise of powers, by placing purchasers under a liability to re-convey the legal estate if they failed to take the relevant steps and the trustees were in fact in breach.

The precise relationship between these traditional rules, statutory overreaching under the Law of Property Act 1925, and section 26 of the LRA 2002 is contested.[85] However, the basic structure is clear. While many equitable interests impose defined and rule-like duties on the holders of a legal title – duties which are capable of direct transmission to successors in title – trusts impose standards of performance on trustees that are *not* capable of such direct transmission. It is not a purchaser's responsibility to take on the role of the trustee or to investigate whether the trustees have actually met the standards governing their exercise of powers;[86] it is only his responsibility to obtain some basic and well-defined evidence that the trustees have met those standards, a responsibility that cashes out in the modern law as a responsibility to make sure that the terms of a restriction are complied with. This explains why the terms of trusts are hidden behind the 'curtain'[87] of the register, while the terms of other equitable interests are visible.

The idea of the register as a curtain, concealing information that purchasers do not need, can be explained by reference to the distinction, drawn for example by McFarlane and Televantos, between 'internal' features of an arrangement between private parties and the 'external' effect of that arrangement on third parties.[88] The argument is that third parties do not have to worry about idiosyncratic features of the internal relationship between the holder of a legal title and the holder of an equitable interest affecting that legal title, since the external effects of any such relationship

[83] *Pilcher v Rawlins* (1871–72) LR 7 Ch App 259 (CA).

[84] See C Harpum, 'Overreaching, Trustees' Powers and the Reform of the 1925 Legislation' (1990) 49 *CLJ* 277, 283–87 and authorities cited there.

[85] G Ferris and G Battersby, 'The General Principles of Overreaching and the Reforms of 1925' (2002) 118 *LQR* 270; N Jackson, 'Overreaching and Unauthorised Disposition of Registered Land' [2007] *Conveyancer and Property Lawyer* 120; P Sparkes, 'Overreaching, Trust Breaking and Underreaching' [2019] *Conveyancer and Property Lawyer* 14; J Roche, 'Historiography and the Law of Property Act 1925: The Return of Frankenstein' (2018) 77 *CLJ* 600.

[86] For a recent case emphasising the purchaser's lack of responsibility to investigate such matters beyond ensuring compliance with the terms of a restriction, see *N3 Living Ltd v Burgess Property Investments Ltd* [2020] EWHC 1117 (Ch).

[87] T Ruoff, *An Englishman Looks at the Torrens System* (Sydney, The Law Book Co of Australia Pty Ltd, 1957) para [8-15].

[88] B McFarlane and A Televantos, 'Third Party Effects in English Law: Form and Function' in P Miller and J Oberdiek (eds), *Oxford Studies in Private Law Theory: Volume 1* (Oxford, OUP, 2020) 107, 120, drawing on F Maitland, 'Trust and Corporation' in D Runciman and M Ryan (eds), *Maitland: State, Trust and Corporation* (Cambridge, CUP, 2003) 75.

are simpler and more predictable than its internal effects.[89] The LRA 2002 indicates that this argument is most persuasive in relation to trusts in particular rather than equitable interests in general. The refusal to disclose the idiosyncratic terms of trusts to third parties, on the face of the register, can be explained on the basis that those terms, and the standards that are intrinsically associated with them, are 'internal' to the trustee–beneficiary relationship, while restrictions reflect the simpler 'external' effects of the trust. By contrast, a purchaser who takes land subject to a restrictive covenant, an equitable easement, or an estate contract, is expected – subject to defences – to perform the very same obligation as his predecessor in title and must know the terms of that obligation, which is cast in rule-like terms that make it suitable for assumption by a stranger.

It is arguable that this analysis, while proper to some trusts, cannot apply to bare trusts, since such trustees also owe a simple rule-like duty that anyone may perform, ie, to convey the title to the beneficiary. However, the usual terms of a bare trust are that the trustee must hold to the direction of the beneficiary, rather than simply being under an obligation to convey.[90] The propriety of the trustee's exercise of this power may involve a multi-faceted inquiry into the terms of any direction given to the trustees by the beneficiary, and their motives in carrying out the direction,[91] of the precise kind that the curtain of the register is designed to conceal from purchasers. Some 'constructive trusts', like the so-called 'vendor–purchaser constructive trust', may indeed involve a simpler duty to convey without the need to comply with the standards that normally govern trustee decision-making.[92] If so, this implies that the principles that govern the overreaching of beneficial interests under trusts should not apply to 'trusts' of this type, which should be treated as a *sui generis* category.[93] Although there is first-instance authority suggesting that the interest of a purchaser under a vendor–purchaser constructive trust *is* capable of being overreached by a transaction of two vendors,[94] it is difficult to make sense of such a rule in policy terms. It is clear that an 'estate contract', the equitable interest of a purchaser of land that arises after contracts are exchanged, is capable of being entered on the register as a notice[95] and is incapable of being overreached by a transaction of the vendor or vendors.[96] If this is correct, a purchaser of registered land is in a weaker position *after* execution of a conveyance in his favour, as, at this point, his interest is no longer an 'estate contract' but instead arises under a trust;[97] such a purchaser has less security of title than a

[89] See too, Smith's chapter in this volume, noting limits to the effects of different equitable property rights on third parties.

[90] *Christie v Ovington* (1875) 1 Ch D 279 (Ch) 281. Statute also confers broad powers of disposition on *all* trustees of land and requires such trustees to meet the usual standards in exercising those powers: Trusts of Land and Appointment of Trustees Act 1996, ss 1(2)(a), 6.

[91] For the duty of trustees to make an independent judgment as to whether to follow directions of the beneficiary, even in the case of a bare trust, see *Re Brockbank* [1948] Ch 206 (Ch).

[92] *Shaw v Foster* (1871–72) LR 5 HL 321, 457 (Lord Hatherley LC).

[93] W Swadling, 'The Fiction of the Constructive Trust' (2011) 64 *Current Legal Problems* 399.

[94] *Baker v Craggs* [2016] EWHC 3250 (Ch), [2017] Ch 295, overruled on a different point, [2018] EWCA Civ 1126, [2018] Ch 617, but followed on this point in *Knight v Fernley* [2021] EWHC 1343.

[95] As, for example, in *Williams v Broadoak Private Finance Ltd* [2018] EWHC 1107 (Ch).

[96] *Baker v Craggs* [2016] EWHC 3250 (Ch), [2017] Ch 295, [41] (Newey J).

[97] See *Baker v Craggs* [2016] EWHC 3250 (Ch), [2017] Ch 295 [40], adopting the obiter view of Lady Hale in *Scott v Southern Pacific Mortgages Ltd* [2014] UKSC 52, [2015] AC 385 [113]. The decision was

purchaser of unregistered land, who obtains a legal title as soon as the conveyance in his favour is executed and does not need to rely on a trust in the 'registration gap'.[98] Neither result can reflect the likely intentions of the legislator. An analysis that distinguishes the so-called 'vendor–purchaser constructive trust' from a true trust on the basis of the distinction between rules and standards, and which relates overreaching to this feature of the true trust, allows us to avoid this unsatisfactory outcome.

III. WHAT EQUITY HAS DONE WITH LAND REGISTRATION: NOTICE, UNCONSCIONABILITY AND REASONING ABOUT RIGHTS

In England and Wales, each legislative experiment with land registration has been accompanied by anxiety about the risk of judicial subversion of its policy. For example, local deeds registration was introduced in Yorkshire and Middlesex in the early eighteenth century;[99] by the early nineteenth, it was a commonplace[100] that the judiciary had effectively frustrated the functioning of this legislation, with Jeffrey complaining in the *Edinburgh Review* that judicial interpretations of the legislation were better 'considered rather a repeal or abrogation of them altogether'.[101] In a similar vein, the 1857 Royal Commissioners appointed to consider the creation of a system of title registration in England and Wales pre-emptively raised the question whether their recommendations would be futile even if accepted by Parliament, noting the possibility that 'the judges would, *notwithstanding any law to the contrary*, in the course of time contrive some means of neutralizing any enactment which went to exclude the doctrine of notice'.[102] The same concern appears in writing on the Land Registration Act 1925 ('LRA 1925'),[103] and remains a theme of current scholarship on the LRA 2002.[104]

overruled on a different point and Henderson LJ took care to say that he had expressed 'no view on the question' of when the estate contract ceases to exist: [2018] EWCA Civ 1126, [2018] Ch 627 [21].

[98] Provided that he applies for first registration of the title in his name within the period stipulated by the legislation: LRA 2002, s 6. If an application for registration is not made in time, the legal title reverts to the vendor who will then hold it on trust for the purchaser: LRA 2002, s 7(2)(a).

[99] Statute 1703 (2 & 3 Anne c 4) (West Riding of Yorkshire); Statute 1707 (5 Anne c 18) (East Riding of Yorkshire); Statute 1708 (7 Anne c 20) (Middlesex); Statute 1735 (8 Geo 2 c 6) (North Riding of Yorkshire).

[100] eg, F Jeffrey, 'A Series of Letters to a Man of Property, on the Sale, Purchase, Lease, Settlement and Devise of Estates' (1821) 35 *Edinburgh Review* 190; J Humphreys, *Observations on the Actual State of the English Laws of Real Property: With Outlines for a Systematic Reform*, 2nd edn (London, John Murray, 1827) 354; C Ker, *The Question of Registry or No Registry Considered* (London, Colburn & Bentley, 1830) 41.

[101] Jeffrey (n 100) 211.

[102] *Report of the Commissioners Appointed to Consider the Subject of the Registration of Title with Reference to the Sale and Transfer of Land* (1857) 39 (emphasis added).

[103] eg, J Martin, 'Constructive Trusts of Registered Land' [1978] *Conveyancer and Property Lawyer* 52; M Thompson, 'Registration, Fraud and Notice' (1985) 44 *CLJ* 280; N Jackson, 'Title by Registration and Concealed Overriding Interests: The Cause and Effect of Antipathy to Documentary Proof' (2003) 119 *LQR* 660.

[104] eg, A Goymour, 'Mistaken Registrations of Land: Exploding the Myth of "Title by Registration"' (2013) 72 *CLJ* 617; E Lees, 'Title by Registration: Rectification, Indemnity and Mistake and the Land Registration Act 2002' (2013) 76 *MLR* 62, 82.

There have been two situations where judicial interpretations of the legislation have been argued to be subversive of its ends: in both contexts, it is equity that has been the source of the contested interpretation. First, a purchaser for value of a legal estate, under a registration system, will normally have a defence against an earlier unregistered interest, except in certain limited situations defined by the legislation. Courts have sometimes been reluctant to give effect to these defences in situations where the purchaser has actual knowledge of the unregistered interest, despite the want of registration and even though the statutory exceptions to the defence do not seem to be engaged.[105] Secondly, the title registration legislation vests a legal estate in a registered proprietor, now by means of section 58 of the LRA 2002,[106] even where that registered proprietor has obtained title under circumstances that would prevent title from passing to him under the general law (eg, fraud, forgery, mistake on the part of the registrar). In these cases, courts have sometimes responded by turning the registered proprietor into a trustee for the former registered proprietor,[107] with far-reaching consequences for the legislative framework that sets out the consequences of mistaken registration.[108]

In both instances, it is possible to explain equity's intervention on the basis that it is operating as a body of second-order standards that is meant to prevent opportunistic exploitation of first-order rules. However, neither set of cases in fact bears out this conclusion. The story of the interaction between the successive land registration statutes and the doctrine of notice cannot easily be turned into a story about the clash of rules and standards; it is better understood as a clash between different sets of standards, with one set of very stringent standards being replaced by another set of standards more favourable to purchasers, and a separate doctrine being evolved to address cases of genuine opportunism on the part of a purchaser. Meanwhile, to the extent that the imposition of a trust in section 58 cases can be understood as implicating the opposition between rules and standards, the opposition goes in the other direction: it is the formalism of the equitable reasoning that subverts the substantive standards that we find in the letter of the legislation.

A. Actual Knowledge of an Unregistered Right: Notice, Actual Occupation, and Unconscionability

In *Le Neve v Le Neve*, Lord Hardwicke LC held that a purchaser with notice of an unregistered deed ought to be bound by the interests under that deed, despite the apparently absolute defence conferred on the purchaser by statute.[109] He argued that any other interpretation 'would give an opportunity to take advantage of having the

[105] *Le Neve v Le Neve* (1747) 27 ER 893; *Peffer v Rigg* [1977] 1 WLR 285 (Ch).

[106] Formerly by LRA 1925, s 69.

[107] *Malory Enterprises Ltd v Cheshire Homes (UK) Ltd* [2002] EWCA Civ 151, [2002] Ch 216 (LRA 1925); *Nasrullah v Rashid* [2018] EWCA Civ 2685, [2020] Ch 37 (LRA 2002).

[108] LRA 2002, Sch 4 (alteration or rectification of the register), Sch 8 (indemnities).

[109] Statute 1708 (7 Anne c 20), s 1: 'every such [unregistered] deed or conveyance … shall be adjudged fraudulent and void against *any* subsequent purchaser or mortgagee for valuable consideration' (my emphasis): there is no reference in the legislation to notice, knowledge or good faith.

legal estate to commit fraud'.[110] This obviously echoes the traditional language of equity as a safeguard against opportunism: the legal rule is designed to protect a purchaser who is genuinely unaware of an unregistered interest, while a purchaser who *is* aware of an unregistered interest would be opportunistically exploiting the generality of the legal rule in order to obtain an advantage that it was never intended to confer.[111] A similar argument was accepted in *Peffer v Rigg*,[112] where it was held that a purchaser with actual knowledge of an earlier unregistered interest was not in good faith and so could not take advantage of the defence under the LRA 1925. These cases might be read to mean that equitable interests will bind any disponee whose conscience is affected by knowledge of the interest, and the courts will insist on applying this conscience-based standard as between an equitable interest-holder and a purchaser, even where the legislation does not seem to make room for this reasoning.

However, these decisions have not been followed in relation to the 2002 Act. Instead, the courts have held that the purchaser's actual knowledge of an unregistered adverse interest does *not* disqualify him from the registration defence.[113] In itself, this might simply mean that the post-2003 judiciary are less aware of their function, when sitting as a court of equity, than judges of earlier generations: modern judges are more willing than their predecessors to allow unscrupulous purchasers to get away with opportunistic conduct, for the sake of preserving the predictability and certainty of the general rules. However, the language of conscience has not vanished in this context: it is accepted that there might be 'rare'[114] cases where the purchaser's conduct is so 'unconscionable' that she will become liable to the unregistered interest-holder.[115] This will be the case where 'he has undertaken a new obligation, not otherwise existing, to give effect to the relevant incumbrance or prior interest'.[116] To show that the purchaser has come under such an obligation, it is not sufficient to show that he had notice of the prior interest, or even that he has agreed with the vendor to take 'subject to' that interest;[117] his conscience will only be affected if he has agreed to come under an obligation to the interest-holder, which might be evidenced by having paid a lower price in consideration for undertaking that obligation.[118] Recent authority has suggested that the principle can only operate in favour of an interest-holder who could not, in the circumstances, have protected her interest by registration.[119]

The doctrine of notice and the concept of unconscionability have thus come apart, in relation to the 2002 Act: the judges remain willing to enforce some conception

[110] *Le Neve* (n 105) 895.

[111] For the link between opportunism and notice, see section II of Smith's chapter in this volume.

[112] (n 105).

[113] *Lloyd v Dugdale* [2001] EWCA Civ 1754, [2002] 2 P & CR 13; *Chaudhary v Yavuz* [2011] EWCA Civ 1314, [2013] Ch 249.

[114] *Chaudhary* (n 112) [68].

[115] *Lyus v Prowsa Developments Ltd* [1982] 1 WLR 1044 (Ch).

[116] *Lloyd v Dugdale* (n 112) [52].

[117] *Ashburn Anstalt v Arnold* [1989] Ch 1 (CA) 26; *Chattey v Farndale Holdings Inc* (1998) 75 P & CR 298 (CA).

[118] *Lloyd v Dugdale* (n 112) [52]; *Melbury Road Properties 1995 Ltd v Kreidi* [1999] 43 EG 157 (West London County Court).

[119] *Chaudhary* (n 112); *Graveholt Ltd v Hughes* [2012] EWHC 3351 (Ch).

of unconscionability against a genuinely opportunistic purchaser, while refusing to find that his conscience is affected by mere notice of an unregistered interest. This parallels Agnew's distinction between the use of the term 'conscience' to describe 'the moral significance of factual knowledge as a prerequisite to … recognition and enforcement'[120] of equitable interests and the use of the term 'unconscionability' to describe the imposition of a primary liability on a defendant who has breached a moral obligation in acquiring a legal right. The moral significance of factual knowledge of a pre-existing interest is now mediated by the express provisions of the LRA 2002, which treat such knowledge as relevant only in some limited contexts. For example, where the holder of an interest affecting the legal estate is in actual occupation of the physical land, the normal rule is that the interest in question will only bind a purchaser for value of a registered estate if the occupation would have been obvious on 'a reasonably careful inspection of the land at the time of the disposition.'[121] However, this requirement of discoverability on a reasonably careful inspection is disapplied in a case where the purchaser has actual knowledge of the interest of the person in actual occupation at the date of the disposition.[122] Similarly, a legal easement that has arisen by prescription or implication – and thus has not needed to be registered in order to take effect at law – will normally only be overriding if it has been exercised in the past year or is obvious on a reasonably careful inspection of the land. Again, however, both these requirements are superseded where the easement is within the actual knowledge of the purchaser.[123] It is conventionally thought that the legislation preserves overriding status for certain interests in land only where a failure to protect them by registration is reasonable,[124] as where they have arisen informally and the interest-holder is unaware of her rights; it is only in these situations that the statute makes a purchaser liable where she could reasonably have discovered the existence of the interest or where she has actual knowledge of its existence. By contrast, there is no moral obligation to attend in this way to the interests of a person who has failed to register her rights when she could and should have done so; the purchaser's self-interested disregard for the interests of the unregistered interest-holder, in such a case, is no longer considered to be morally problematic opportunism of the kind that warrants equity's intervention. This also explains why, where loss of priority occurs because of a mistake made by Land Registry rather than because of an omission on the part of the right-holder, the purchaser is vulnerable to a claim for rectification that has the potential to deprive him of the priority gained under section 29.[125]

In this way, the statute expressly incorporates standards resembling those imposed by the doctrine of notice, while reducing the stringency of those standards to take account of the options for self-protection that the title registration scheme makes available to the holders of adverse interests. Unlike in the general law, these standards affect the enforceability of legal interests as well as equitable interests. The interplay

[120] S Agnew, 'The Meaning and Significance of Conscience in Private Law' (2018) 77 *CLJ* 479.
[121] LRA 2002, Sch 3, para 2(c)(i).
[122] LRA 2002, Sch 3, para 2(c)(ii).
[123] LRA 2002, Sch 3, para 3.
[124] Law Commission, *Land Registration for the Twenty-First Century* (n 45) para [2.25].
[125] *Gold Harp Properties Ltd v MacLeod* [2014] EWCA Civ 1084, [2015] 1 WLR 1249.

between the statute and equity, therefore, cannot be reduced to a straightforward opposition between (legal) rules and (equitable) standards. The strict standards of the old doctrine of notice have been replaced by a less-stringent set of statutory standards, both at law and in equity, with a separate doctrine of liability for unconscionable conduct capturing cases of genuine opportunism.

B. Registration Pursuant to a Flawed Transaction: 'Reasoning about Rights'

Under the LRA 2002, the state guarantee of title is governed by a structured but quite open-textured discretion. Title vests in a registered proprietor under section 58, regardless of the reasons for his registration, but it is open to anyone to apply for the alteration or rectification of the register under Schedule 4. Schedule 4 allows the register to be altered to correct a mistake, in circumstances where correction of the mistake would prejudice the present registered proprietor ('rectification'),[126] in accordance with a set of broad criteria that include whether the registered proprietor is in possession of the land, whether he has caused the mistake by his own fraud or lack of proper care, and whether it would for any other reason be unjust to refuse the order.[127] Loss caused by rectification, or by a refusal of rectification, will be covered by the state indemnity provided that the person suffering loss has not caused the mistake by their own fraud or lack of proper care.[128]

As Cooper has noted, it is one of the ironies of the modern law on the interpretation of these provisions that 'residual principles of equity'[129] have been invoked to exclude rather than engage this discretion. Where a person obtains a legal estate purely by the operation of section 58, it has been suggested that he comes under an immediate moral duty to restore the title to the original proprietor; this duty then, as a duty governing the exercise of a right in relation to land, gives rise to an immediate trust of the title in favour of the de-registered proprietor.[130] The outcome, within the statutory framework, is that the former registered proprietor is not obliged to ask for the register to be altered to correct a mistake but can instead exercise *Saunders v Vautier* powers to compel an immediate conveyance of the title to himself, short-circuiting the statutory discretion. If he is in actual occupation, he can bring a similar claim against a successor in title who has relied on the register. No indemnity will be available to the losing party in such a case because they will not be considered to have suffered loss by reason of the correction of a mistake.[131] These consequences flow from the rule-like character of the 'institutional' constructive trust,[132] recognised by English law as automatically imposing certain consequences on third parties from

[126] LRA 2002, Sch 4, para 1.
[127] LRA 2002, Sch 4, para 3(2).
[128] LRA 2002, Sch 8, para 1(a)–(b).
[129] S Cooper, 'Discretion in Property Law: A Study of Judicial Correction of Registered Title' (2018) 38 *Legal Studies* 1, 3.
[130] *Nasrullah* (n 106); *Malory Enterprises* (n 106).
[131] *Re Chowood's Registered Land* [1933] Ch 574 (Ch).
[132] *Bailey v Angove's Pty Ltd* [2016] UKSC 47, [2016] 1 WLR 3179 [27]–[28].

the date of its arising, without room for a broad discretionary inquiry into merits or proportionality of the kind that (absent equity's intervention) would occur under the statute. The decision to treat a person who gains title under section 58 as a trustee thus avoids precisely the kind of open-textured inquiry into the merits that is sometimes thought to be the special province of equity.

IV. CONCLUSIONS

I have argued that the use that the LRA 2002 makes of the law/equity distinction illustrates the continuing potency of that distinction: the legislation reflects deep structural differences between legal and equitable interests, and the substantive difference between trusts and other interests. At the same time, the story of the interaction between the land registration legislation and equity is, in some measure, the story of judicial temptations to 'do equity' in the face of a first-order body of legal rules that does not always offer an explicit opening for them to do so. As such, it provides a powerful illustration that 'doing equity' does not always mean doing discretionary justice and that, sometimes, it means quite the reverse.

Part II

Maxims and Doctrines

5

The Mischief of Maxims

WILLIAM SWADLING*

I. INTRODUCTION

THERE IS A book to be written on 'Equitable Legal Method', if that is not an oxymoron, concerned with how judges wearing their equity hats decide cases. The essential question would be whether, and if so, how, judicial reasoning in equity differs from that at common law. Such a book would have to concern itself with a number of matters. One would be the relationship between law and equity. Another would be the so-called 'good man' theory of equity.[1] Others still would be the differences, if any, concerning the criteria for the award of remedies, the use of precedent, the various uses of analogy, the effect of the Judicature Acts 1873–75, and the use of fictions. There would also be a chapter on maxims.

At common law, the use of maxims in judicial reasoning is generally eschewed. Thus, towards the end of the nineteenth century, Lord Esher MR said he detested attempts to 'fetter the law by maxims',[2] a sentiment endorsed many times since.[3] Yet in equity, the maxims are alive and well – thriving, in fact. Indeed, in recent years, two new maxims have been coined, that '[e]quity does not strive officiously to defeat a gift',[4] and '[e]quity tempers the wind to the shorn lamb'.[5] In contrast to the common law, judges in equity reason from maxims without compunction, and practitioner works such as *Snell* devote considerable space discussing them.[6] Though we have

* Professor of Law, University of Oxford, Fellow of Brasenose College. My thanks to Paul Matthews, James Penner, Steven Smith and Frederick Wilmot-Smith.

[1] Relied on, eg, by Sir Peter Millett, as the basis of an argument for trusts of bribes in P Millett, 'Bribes and Secret Commissions' (1993) 1 *Restitution Law Review* 7, 19. For a full discussion, see A Mackley, 'A Challenge to the Utility and Distinctiveness of the Good Man Theory of Equity' (2021) 27 *Trusts and Trustees* 376. One assumes Equity takes a similar view of the behaviour of women.

[2] *Yarmouth v France* (1887) 19 QBD 647 (QBD) 653.

[3] See the text to nn 18–29.

[4] *T Choithram International SA v Pagarani* [2001] 1 WLR 1 (PC) 11 (Lord Browne-Wilkinson).

[5] *Pennington v Waine* [2002] EWCA Civ 227, [2002] 1 WLR 2075 [54] (Arden LJ).

[6] J McGhee (ed), *Snell's Equity*, 34th edn (London, Sweet & Maxwell, 2021) devotes a whole chapter to maxims (ch 5). J Heydon, M Leeming and P Turner, *Meagher, Gummow and Lehane: Equity Doctrines and Remedies*, 5th edn (Chatswood NSW, LexisNexis Butterworths, 2015) paras [3-005]–[3-260] has a long and difficult discussion. There is a shorter treatment in the standard student work, J Glister and J Lee, *Hanbury and Martin: Modern Equity*, 22nd edn (London, Sweet & Maxwell, 2021) paras [1-024]–[1-036]. Interestingly, D Browne, *Ashburner's Principles of Equity*, 2nd edn (London, Butterworth & Co,

no equivalent texts for common law[7] or statute,[8] books on legal method contain no discussion of maxims, with the last edition of the leading common law work on maxims, *Broom's Legal Maxims*, published over 80 years ago, before the outbreak of the Second World War.[9]

The purpose of this chapter is to question the continued use of maxims in equity. In that respect, it is interesting to compare the approach of two recent editions of *Snell*. In the 32nd, published in 2010 (where the discussion is that of James Edelman),[10] their use is deprecated and the recommendation made that they be abolished altogether.[11] In the latest and 34th edition, published in 2021, Ben McFarlane is in charge,[12] and, though still critical, the argument is made that the maxims continue in some circumstances to be useful. This chapter urges that the approach of the 32nd edition be followed, and that courts stop reasoning from maxims altogether. However, it goes further. Edelman largely rejected the use of maxims because he thought judges could get to the same results without them. They were innocuous: mere rhetorical devices. This chapter argues that the position is worse than that, that maxims can lead judges into errors of reasoning or provide an excuse to give no reasons at all.

II. MAXIMS GENERALLY

The word 'maxim' is often used in common parlance to describe simple and memorable rules or guides for living. They are usually pedagogical and involve specific actions. The following definition of a proverb can also be applied to maxims: a 'short, generally known sentence of the folk which contains wisdom, truth, morals and traditional views in a metaphorical, fixed and memorisable form and which is handed down from generation to generation',[13] 'an aphoristic expression of an ostensible general rule of science'.[14] Proverbs in everyday speech include 'look before you leap', 'a stitch in time saves nine', 'marry in haste, repent at leisure' and 'ignorance is bliss'. There are hundreds, if not thousands of maxims, and they appear in most language systems.

More rarely, the word is used to describe general rules (for example about language or morality). Perhaps the best-known maxim is Kant's 'formula of the universal law'.[15] However, a philosopher would not (or, at least, should not) invoke a maxim to

1933) has no separate treatment. In fact, the word does not even appear in the index. This, as we shall see, is how it should be.

[7] Such books did once exist, eg, J Indemaur, *Principles of the Common Law: An Elementary Work Intended for the Use of Students and the Profession*, 5th edn (London, Stevens & Haynes, 1888). They died out in the 19th century with the rise of textbooks on substantive topics.

[8] At least not ones where the whole of the content of statutory law is discussed, rather than simply statutory interpretation.

[9] RH Kersley, *Broom's Legal Maxims*, 10th edn (London, Sweet & Maxwell, 1939).

[10] Then a professor of law at the University of Oxford, now a justice of the High Court of Australia.

[11] McGhee (n 6) para [5-001].

[12] Professor of English Law, University of Oxford.

[13] W Mieder, 'Proverbs' in JH Brunvand (ed), *American Folklore: An Encyclopaedia* (New York, Garland Publishing, 1996) 597–621.

[14] *The Compact Edition of the Oxford English Dictionary* (Oxford, Clarendon Press, 1971) 1748.

[15] Viz, 'act only according to that maxim through which you can at the same time will that it become a universal law': I Kant, *Groundwork of the Metaphysics of Morals* (M Gregor and J Timmermann tr, Cambridge, CUP, 2012) para [4:421].

put a stop to analysis. A maxim cannot be raised in answer to the question 'why do this?' without it being left open to question whether that maxim is a good approach to the question at hand (be it morality or language or whatever).[16] Reasoning from maxims alone, it has been said, is 'appropriate only for the obsessive, the lazy – or the simple-minded'.[17]

III. MAXIMS AT COMMON LAW

As we have seen, the use of maxims at common law, generally rendered in Latin, is deprecated. The reason Lord Esher MR gave in *Yarmouth v France*, speaking of the maxim *volenti non fit injuria*,[18] was that they are 'almost invariably misleading: they are for the most part so large and general in their language that they always include something which really is not intended to be included in them'.[19] Lord Wright later added: 'these general formulae are found in experience often to distract the court's mind from the actual exigencies of the case, and to induce the court to quote them as offering a ready made solution.'[20]

The problem, of course, is that maxims are conclusory, providing no reasons. Take as an example the maxim *in pari delicto potior est conditio defendentis*: 'where the fault of the parties is equal, the position of the defendant is the stronger'. What we are not told, however, is *why* the defendant's position is the stronger; if that is unknown, we have no guidance on the rule's application.[21] Thus, in *Patel v Mirza*,[22] where both the dicta of Lord Esher and Lord Wright were rehearsed,[23] it was rightly held by all nine members of the Supreme Court that the use of maxims was an unsatisfactory way to adjudicate on the consequences of illegality in private law.[24] We see similar problems with the maxim *sic utere tuo ut alieno non laedas*[25] in the law of nuisance, where its application is notoriously difficult, many harmful uses being perfectly lawful. As Lord Goff said of yet another common law maxim, that 'no-one should profit from his own wrong', it is 'in very general terms, and does not of itself provide any sure guidance to the solution of a problem in any particular case'.[26] Maxims at common law thus do no useful work and are often only incorporated for rhetorical effect.[27]

[16] I thank Frederick Wilmot-Smith for this insight.

[17] P Kitcher, 'What is a Maxim?' (2003) 31 *Philosophical Topics* 215.

[18] 'To a willing person, no injury is done.'

[19] *Yarmouth* (n 2) 653.

[20] *Lissenden v Bosch* [1940] AC 412 (HL) 440–41, in connection with the 'principle, rule, or maxim' that one 'cannot both approbate and reprobate'.

[21] The position is made more complex still by the interaction of this maxim with another, *ex turpi causa non oritur actio* (no action arises from a disgraceful cause).

[22] [2016] UKSC 42, [2017] AC 467.

[23] ibid [95] (Lord Toulson, with whom Lady Hale and Lords Kerr, Wilson and Hodge agreed).

[24] Though the court was then split on whether the solution was the formulation of a rule or the application of a balancing exercise of various factors. Somewhat unhelpfully, the latter approach was endorsed by the majority.

[25] So to use your own that you do not harm another.

[26] *Attorney General v Guardian Newspapers (No 2)* [1990] 1 AC 109 (HL) 286.

[27] A point forcefully made by P Jackson, 'The Maxims of Equity Revisited' in S Goldstein (ed), *Equity and Contemporary Legal Developments* (Jerusalem, International Conference on Equity – Sacher Institute for Legislative Research and Comparative Law, 1992) 72.

Moreover, as Lord Esher's statement makes clear, in that they are so generally stated, maxims have a tendency to snare things never intended to be caught, much as fishermen sometimes catch dolphins when fishing for cod. A well-known example is the maxim *ignorantia juris non excusat*, that ignorance of the law is no excuse, which for over two centuries was used to deny recovery to claimants paying money under mistakes of law.[28] Only recently have courts woken up to the fact that such claimants are not asking to be excused for their actions, as with criminal defendants, but are instead explaining why the transfer was made and giving a reason for recovery.[29]

IV. EQUITABLE MAXIMS

Equity knows its fair share of maxims which, unlike the common law's, are always rendered in English, though this helps little in their understanding. *Snell*, said to be canonical in this matter,[30] lists 12:

(i) Equity will not suffer a wrong to be without a remedy;
(ii) Equity follows the law;
(iii) Where there is equal equity, the law shall prevail;
(iv) Where the equities are equal, the first in time shall prevail;
(v) He who seeks equity must do equity;
(vi) He who comes into equity must come with clean hands;
(vii) Delay defeats equity;
(viii) Equity is equality;
(ix) Equity looks to intent rather than to form;
(x) Equity looks on that as done which ought to be done;
(xi) Equity imputes an intention to fulfil an obligation; and
(xii) Equity acts *in personam*.[31]

The equitable maxims are no better than their common law counterparts. As Gardner notes, 'they possess a particularly Delphic quality, wrapped as they are in metaphor, grandly unqualified, and acknowledging no authority but transcendent wisdom'.[32] Their use, he says, makes the law the 'subject of oracular pronouncements, as though it were a mystery of which the judges were priests'.[33] As to their source, Pound[34] demonstrated that many are traceable back to the *Digest*, attaining the status of

[28] A position once endorsed in *Snell* itself: 'money paid under a mistake of law cannot be recovered, this being perhaps the only type of relief where it can be regarded as absolutely clearly established by way of general rule that ignorantia legis non excusat': H Gibson Rivington, *Snell's Equity*, 21st edn (London, Sweet & Maxwell, 1934) 439–40.

[29] *Kleinwort Benson Ltd v Lincoln City Council* [1999] 2 AC 349 (HL).

[30] R Pound, 'On Certain Maxims in Equity' in P Winfield and A McNair (eds), *Cambridge Legal Essays* (Cambridge, W Heffer & Sons, 1926) 259.

[31] McGhee (n 6) para [5-000].

[32] S Gardner, 'Two Maxims of Equity' (1995) 54 *CLJ* 60, 60.

[33] ibid 67.

[34] (n 30).

maxims, not by judicial decision, but in a book written in 1728.[35] He also noted that they often have common law equivalents, so are not peculiarly equitable, start out as specific rules,[36] only later being elevated to the status of maxims, and, as with those at common law, can be taken as authority for many different propositions. A good example is the 'first in time' maxim, the common law equivalent of *qui prior est in tempore potior est in jure*, which was used at one point by Coke to justify primogeniture.[37]

Moreover, the list is unstable. We noted two recent judicial additions at the outset.[38] As will be seen, *Snell* originally listed only 11 maxims, the missing candidate being 'equity acts *in personam*'.[39] One modern student text lists 14, two of which, 'equity is cynical' and 'equity is imaginative',[40] are the invention of the author. And as anyone who studies the law of resulting trusts will know, yet another academic invention is the supposed maxim that 'equity is suspicious of gifts'.[41] At the same time, there are many equitable maxims which do not appear in the standard lists, including that 'equity leans against joint tenancies',[42] 'equity will not allow a trust to fail for want of a trustee', 'equity does not act in vain',[43] 'equity will not perfect an imperfect gift',[44] 'equity will not allow a statute to be used as an instrument of fraud',[45] and 'equity does not assist a volunteer'. Our focus, however, will be on those which make *Snell's* list.

V. MAXIMS MISUSED

Sometimes, the use of equitable maxims by judges is harmless; like their common law counterparts, their incorporation adds only a rhetorical flourish to a result which

[35] R Francis, *Maxims of Equity, Collected and Proved by Cases, Out of the Books of the Best Authority, in the High Court of Chancery* (London, E and R Nutt and R Gosling, 1728).

[36] An example is the usage of Lord Eldon in *Morice v Bishop of Durham* (1805) 10 Ves Jnr 522, 539: 'As it is a maxim, that the execution of a trust shall be under the control of the court, it must be of such a nature, that it can be under that control; so that the administration of it can be reviewed by the court …'.

[37] Pound (n 30) 272.

[38] See the text to nn 4–5.

[39] This seems to make its first appearance in the seventh edition of *Snell* (see EHT Snell and A Brown, *The Principles of Equity*, 7th edn (London, WH Stevenson, 1884) 17, where it is rightly described as 'relating to the procedure in a court of equity, and not to the principles themselves of equity'. After that, however, it is listed alongside the other maxims.

[40] G Virgo, *The Principles of Equity and Trusts*, 4th edn (Oxford, OUP, 2020) ch 2.

[41] P Birks, 'Restitution and Resulting Trusts' in S Goldstein (ed), *Equity and Contemporary Legal Developments* (Jerusalem, International Conference on Equity – Sacher Institute for Legislative Research and Comparative Law, 1992) 343–45; R Chambers, *Resulting Trusts* (Oxford, Clarendon Press, 1997) 11. The existence of such 'suspicion' is refuted in W Swadling, 'Explaining Resulting Trusts' (2008) 124 *LQR* 72. The confusion is probably caused by a failure properly to distinguish between matters of substance and procedure. In the same area, the supposed maxim that 'equity abhors a vacuum' was rightly rejected in *Vandervell v IRC* [1967] 2 AC 291 (HL).

[42] *Burgess v Rawnsley* [1975] Ch 429 (CA).

[43] *Attorney General v Guardian Newspapers Ltd (No 1)* [1987] 1 WLR 1248 (HL) 1270 (Sir Nicolas Browne-Wilkinson V-C); *Pitt v Holt* [2013] UKSC 26, [2013] 2 AC 108 [136]–[141] (Lord Walker).

[44] *Milroy v Lord* (1862) 4 De G F & J 264.

[45] *Rochefoucauld v Boustead* [1897] 1 Ch 196 (CA).

could have been reached through orthodox doctrinal reasoning. Moreover, judges in equity are sometimes likewise alive to their dangers. Thus, in speaking of the maxim 'equity does not assist a volunteer', Mason CJ and McHugh J in the High Court of Australia said:

> it would be a mistake to set too much store by the maxim. Like other maxims of equity, it is not a specific rule or principle of law. It is a summary statement of a broad theme which underlies equitable concepts and principles. Its precise scope is necessarily ill-defined and somewhat uncertain.[46]

Sometimes, however, their use is more pernicious. They obscure weak or non-existent reasoning; worse, they lead to wrong results. To demonstrate this, three maxims will be considered: 'equity looks upon as done that which ought to be done'; 'equity follows the law'; and 'equity acts *in personam*'.[47]

A. 'Equity Looks Upon as Done that which Ought to be Done'

There are three stages in the life of the maxim 'equity looks upon as done that which ought to be done'. It began as a perfectly sensible rule concerned with the performance of substantive duties affecting the devolution of estates. It then became a maxim and applied so that the availability of a specific remedy for failure to perform a substantive duty, a procedural issue, had the illogical effect of altering substantive rights. Finally, it became divorced from those primary duties altogether.[48]

(i) A Rule as to the Devolution of Estates

The rule that equity looks upon as done that which ought to be done originally applied to those cases where a trustee was obliged to convert a title to land into money or vice versa but failed in their duty. For the purposes of devolution, the trustee would be fictitiously treated as having performed such duty. The rights of those entitled were correctly held not to depend on the exact moment at which the duty was performed. Otherwise, said Chitty J:

> the property would shift from time to time as the trustees in the execution of their duty thought fit to sell; and there is this extraordinary result, that if the trustees, being bound by the imperative directions to make a sale, should omit, for good or bad reasons, to sell, and

[46] *Corin v Patton* (1990) 169 CLR 540 (HCA) 557, cited with approval by Lord Walker in *Pitt v Holt* (n 43) [136].

[47] There are no doubt others we might consider, as witness Gardner's critique (n 32) 63–68 of Lord Templeman's invocation in *Rhone v Stephens* [1994] 2 AC 310 (HL) of the maxim 'equity supplements but does not contradict the common law' to reject any doctrine of positive covenants between freeholders. The obvious difficulty is then to explain how the enforceability of negative covenants does not also fall foul of the maxim.

[48] Somewhat confusingly, this maxim appears twice in *Snell*, both in the list of maxims and later, as a 'doctrine': McGhee (n 6) ch 6 ('The Equitable Doctrines'). No explanation for this double treatment is, however, supplied.

> commit that which would be a breach of trust on their part, the result would be that the rights of the persons claiming under the heir would be altered.[49]

The conversion, of course, was purely notional. It did not 'turn sovereigns into acres, or *vice versa*', working a conversion only 'for the purpose of devolution.'[50]

(ii) From Rule to Maxim: Availability of a Specific Remedy to Enforce the Duty

While a 'rule' concerning the devolution of estates, 'equity looks upon as done' was both sensible and manageable. However, it later achieved the status of a maxim, at which point it became partially uncoupled from the duty. Attention now turned to the remedies available to enforce the duty, with everything turning on the availability of specific performance as opposed to damages. For that reason, as a maxim, it does not operate in favour of volunteers.[51] Nor will it be engaged where a damages award is adequate.

When applied to contracts for the sale of certain rights, most notably titles to land, the maxim is said to produce a trust. According to Sir George Jessel MR, 'the moment you have a valid contract for sale the vendor becomes in equity a trustee for the purchaser of the estate sold',[52] though as Lord Parker later added, this was 'only true if and so far as a Court of Equity would … grant specific performance of the contract'.[53] However, despite everything turning on the availability of a specific remedy, what is being considered as done is the performance of the substantive duty, not compliance with the court order, for the trust is said to arise on the making of the contract.[54]

There are a number of problems with this use of the maxim. First, why should substantive rights turn on the availability of a specific rather than a monetary remedy? The decision to award a specific remedy turns on issues having nothing to do with the substantive position of the parties. In deciding on remedies, courts look to practical issues concerning the administration of justice.[55] We would never say that a claimant's substantive rights were affected by the fact that a court declines specific performance on supervision grounds. Why then do the very opposite here? Moreover, as already

[49] *Re Richerson* [1892] 1 Ch 379 (Ch) 383. See also *Lechmere v Earl of Carlisle* (1733) 3 P Wms 211, 215.

[50] *Chandler v Pocock* (1880) 15 Ch D 491 (Ch) 496 (Sir George Jessel MR in argument). The importance of the rule today has diminished: McGhee (n 6) paras [6-003]–[6-005].

[51] *Re Ellenborough* [1903] 1 Ch 697 (Ch). This may be the difference between the rule as 'doctrine' (operating in favour of volunteers) and 'maxim' (which does not operate in favour of volunteers).

[52] *Lysaght v Edwards* (1876) 2 Ch D 499 (Ch). There is sometimes said to be a different doctrine operating to generate a trust where the purchase money has been paid in full, which does not depend on the availability of specific performance: D Waters, L Smith and M Gillen, *Waters' Law of Trusts in Canada*, 5th edn (Toronto, Thomson Reuters, 2021) 636.

[53] *Howard v Miller* [1915] AC 318 (PC) 326. See also *Ezair v Conn* [2020] EWCA Civ 687, [2020] BCC 865 [47] (Patten LJ); *Momin v February Point Resort Estates Ltd (Bahamas)* [2022] UKPC 3 [24] (Lord Burrows).

[54] This is an extremely contentious area. It is sometimes said that the trust only arises on payment of the purchase price, though it is then backdated to the date of the contract. There is no space to explore that issue here.

[55] See the excellent discussion by S Smith, *Rights, Wrongs, and Injustices: The Structure of Remedial Law* (Oxford, OUP, 2020) 167–68, 301–03. I am grateful to him for the point made in the text.

seen, the fiction attaches not to the remedy, but to the duty, yet all contracts of sale ought to be performed. It accordingly leads to arbitrary results. Take the example of two purchasers from the same vendor, the first of a specific parcel of shares in a private company, the second of the same in a public one. In the case of breach, the vendor in the first case will be ordered to perform, while in the second, the purchaser will only have a judgment for damages.[56] There will only be a trust in the first case, so that should the vendor become insolvent before performance, the second purchaser will be left to prove in the vendor's bankruptcy, along with the other creditors, while the first will obtain performance in full. Yet the merits of both are indistinguishable.

A second objection is that there is no explanation why the availability of specific performance (rather than the duty to convey) generates a trust. The thinking seems to be that by the application of the maxim, the duty to convey is treated as performed; however, since the fiction only applies in equity, there is a conflict: while the right contracted to be sold may be in the purchaser's hands so far as equity is concerned, the reality is that it remains with the vendor; to 'resolve' that conflict, courts interpose a trust. The explanation is, however, flawed, for trusts do not involve contradictions as to the location of rights. As Maitland famously explained:

> Equity did not say that the *cestui que trust* was the owner of the land, it said that the trustee was the owner of the land, but added that he was bound to hold the land for the benefit of the *cestui que trust*. There was no conflict here. Had there been a conflict here [section 25] of the Judicature Act [1873] would have abolished the whole law of trusts. Common law says that A is the owner, equity says that B is the owner, but equity is to prevail, therefore B is the owner and A has no right or duty of any sort or kind in or about the land. Of course the Judicature Act has not acted in this way; it has left the law of trusts just where it stood, because it found no conflict, no variance even, between the rules of the common law and the rules of equity.[57]

Third, the doctrine assumes that an order of specific performance will be made should the matter reach court. However, circumstances may change between the date of contract and court proceedings,[58] so that though specific performance might have been ordered on Day 1, it may not be on Day 2.[59] Moreover, the vendor might not be able to make out title. The courts have therefore qualified this 'trust' by saying that the vendor is not a full-blown trustee, merely 'in progress towards it',[60] a trustee *sub modo*.[61] On other occasions, they go further and say that the vendor is not a trustee at all, merely someone liable to be ordered to perform their contract. Lord Westbury

[56] *Duncuft v Albrecht* (1841) 12 Sim 189.

[57] FW Maitland, *Equity* (Cambridge, CUP, 1909) 17.

[58] As noted by the Court of Appeal in *Rayner v Preston* (1881) 18 Ch D 1 (CA).

[59] A well-known example is *Patel v Ali* [1984] Ch 283 (Ch), where Goulding J refused an order for specific performance of a contract of sale of a title to land because of illness after the contract was signed and the hardship it would thereby cause the vendor.

[60] *Wall v Bright* (1820) 1 Jac & W 494, 503 (Sir Thomas Plumer MR). See also *Jerome v Kelly* [2004] UKHL 25, [2004] 1 WLR 1409 [30].

[61] 'Subject to a condition'. The language is that of Stamp LJ in *Berkley v Poulett* [1977] 1 ECLR 86 (CA) 93.

said that 'the vendor is called a trustee only by a metaphor, and by an improper use of the term,'[62] while Deane J said that it was:

> inaccurate and misleading to speak of the unpaid vendor under an uncompleted contract as a trustee for the purchaser … [T]he ordinary unpaid vendor of land is not a trustee of the land for the purchaser. Nor is it accurate to refer to such a vendor as a 'trustee sub modo' unless the disarming mystique of the added Latin is treated as a warrant for essential misdescription.[63]

(iii) From Rule to Maxim: Extension Beyond Enforcement of the Duty

Though it may be too late to remove the vendor purchaser constructive trust,[64] we should certainly not expand it. Some recent cases, however, do that very thing, forgetting that the doctrine, however illogically, requires a substantive executory duty to convey, albeit one which equity will specifically enforce.

The first misuse of the doctrine is illustrated by *Bristol Airports plc v Powdrill*,[65] where an airline company was the lessee of a number of aircraft. It was indebted in respect of unpaid airport charges to Bristol Airport, which by statute was entitled to seize and sell aircraft of which the airline was the operator to recover such charges. The airline was insolvent. To enable it to continue trading, it had been placed under an administration order pursuant to section 8 of the Insolvency Act 1986. Section 11(3) of the same Act provided that no steps could be taken to 'enforce any security over the company's property … except with the consent of the administrator or the leave of the court'. The question was whether the airport authority required leave to exercise its statutory power of detention. They argued that the aircraft, being held under leases, were not the 'property' of the insolvent company, it being accepted on both sides that a lease of goods had no proprietary effect at law. The Court of Appeal held that even if a lease of goods did not amount to a legal property right, the aircraft were still the company's 'property' because of the specific enforceability of the contract of lease. Sir Nicolas Browne-Wilkinson V-C said:

> Although a chattel lease is a contract, it does not follow that no property interest is created in the chattel. The basic equitable principle is that if, under a contract, A has certain rights over property as against the legal owner, which rights are specifically enforceable in equity, A has an equitable interest in such property. I have no doubt that a court would order specific performance of a contract to lease an aircraft, since each aircraft has unique features peculiar to itself. Accordingly in my judgment the 'lessee' has at least an equitable

[62] *Knox v Gye* (1871–72) LR 5 HL 656, 675–76 (Lord Westbury). See also *Rayner* (n 58) 11 (Brett LJ): 'I doubt whether it is a true description of the relation between the parties to say that from the time of the making of the contract, or at any time, one is ever trustee for the other'; *Berkley* (n 61) 93 (Stamp LJ): 'the duties do not arise because he is a trustee but because he has agreed to sell the land to the purchaser and the purchaser on tendering the price is entitled to have the contract specifically performed according to its terms'.

[63] *Kern Corpn Ltd v Walter Reid Trading Pty Ltd* (1987) 163 CLR 164 (HCA) 192.

[64] Which has its defenders: P Turner, 'Understanding the Constructive Trust Between Vendor and Purchaser' (2012) 128 *LQR* 582; C McClure, 'Specific Performance and the Constructive Trust' in E Bant and M Bryan (eds), *Principles of Proprietary Remedies* (Pyrmont NSW, Thomson Reuters, 2013) ch 8.

[65] [1990] Ch 744 (CA).

> right of some kind in that aircraft which falls within the statutory definition as being some 'description of interest ... arising out of, or incidental to' that aircraft.[66]

Though the conclusion that a chattel lease is a property right may well be correct in the specific context of the Insolvency Act 1986, particularly in view of the extremely wide definition of 'property' contained therein,[67] it cannot be because of the maxim 'equity looks upon as done that which ought to be done'.

First, this was a case of an executed, not an executory, contract, to which the doctrine has no application. As Lord Selbourne LC explained in *Wolverhampton & Walsall Rly Co v London & North Western Rly Co*, the equitable remedy of specific performance 'presupposes an executory as distinct from an executed agreement, something remaining to be done, such as the execution of a deed or a conveyance, in order to put the parties in the position relative to each other in which by the preliminary agreement they were intended to be placed'.[68] Here, possession of the aircraft had been delivered by the lessor to the lessee; nothing remained to be done on the lessor's part.[69]

Second, a lease of land is a property right at common law, and an application of the maxim 'equity looks upon as done that which ought to be done' anticipates, albeit only in equity, the final result. But a lease of a chattel was assumed by Sir Nicolas Browne-Wilkinson V-C to create no property right at law; indeed, if it did, there would have been no need to resort to the equitable doctrine.[70] Since in his view actual performance could not create property rights, anticipated performance could not do so either. Indeed, if it did, equity would not simply be jumping the gun, but destroying altogether the division between personal and proprietary rights, for now the question whether a right was personal or proprietary would turn, not on the *numerus clausus* rule we see in *Hill v Tupper*[71] and *King v David Allen (Billposting)*,[72] but on the availability of specific performance; yet given that contractual licences to occupy land are both specifically enforceable[73] and not property rights,[74] we know this cannot be true.

A second illegitimate application of the maxim occurred in *Attorney General for Hong Kong v Reid*.[75] As is well known, the Court of Appeal in *Lister v Stubbs*[76] had

[66] ibid 759.

[67] Section 436 of the Insolvency Act 1986 defines 'property' as including 'money, goods, things in action, land and every description of property wherever situated and also obligations and every description of interest, whether present or future or vested or contingent, arising out, or incidental to, property'. As Sir Nicolas Browne-Wilkinson V-C remarked in *Powdrill* (n 65) 759, '[i]t is hard to think of a wider definition of property'.

[68] (1873) LR 16 Eq 433 (Court of Equity) 439.

[69] Even if it were a property right at law, there are no formalities prescribed for its 'grant', so nothing left to be done.

[70] For a full discussion, see W Swadling, 'The Proprietary Effect of a Hire of Goods' in N Palmer and E McKendrick (eds), *Interests in Goods*, 2nd edn (London, LLP, 1998) 491–526.

[71] (1863) 2 H & C 121.

[72] [1916] 2 AC 54 (HL).

[73] *Verrall v Great Yarmouth BC* [1981] QB 202 (CA).

[74] *National Provincial Bank v Ainsworth* [1965] AC 1175 (HL) 1253 (Lord Wilberforce); *Ashburn Anstalt v Arnold* [1989] Ch 1 (CA).

[75] [1994] 1 AC 324 (PC).

[76] (1890) 45 Ch D 1 (CA).

previously held that fiduciaries receiving bribes did not hold them on trust for their principal, that only a debtor–creditor relationship was generated. However, Lord Templeman in *Reid* used the 'equity looks upon as done' maxim, along with another, that equity acts *in personam*,[77] to produce a trust. He said of a public prosecutor who took a bribe, that when

> offered and accepted in money or in kind, the money or property constituting the bribe belongs in law to the recipient. … Equity, however, which acts in personam, insists that it is unconscionable for a fiduciary to obtain and retain a benefit in breach of duty. … The false fiduciary who received the bribe in breach of duty must pay and account for the bribe to the person to whom that duty was owed. In the present case, as soon as Mr Reid received a bribe in breach of the duties he owed to the Government of Hong Kong, he became a debtor in equity to the Crown for the amount of that bribe. … As soon as the bribe was received it should have been paid or transferred instanter to the person who suffered from the breach of duty. Equity considers as done that which ought to have been done. As soon as the bribe was received, whether in cash or in kind, the false fiduciary held the bribe on a constructive trust for the person injured.[78]

This is an incorrect application of the maxim for two reasons.

First, the prosecutor's duty was not to take any bribes at all.[79] However, were we to deem him never to have taken the bribes, there would not even be a personal claim to his gain. As we have seen, the vendor–purchaser constructive trust arises because of the fictional performance of the substantive duty of the vendor to perform their promise. In that sense, it is not a doctrine which can ever apply to wrongdoing, and *Reid*, at least in the view of Lord Templeman, who uses the phrase 'breach of duty' four times in the passage set out above, was a case concerning a wrong, breach of fiduciary duty.[80] Second, the argument mistakes the nature of the fiduciary's duty to account when ordered to do so by a court. The duty entails the making of an account and the payment of the debt found due at the end of the accounting process. But the debt, should there be one, can be satisfied by the payment of money from any source belonging to the person liable to account. Differently to an agreement to convey a title to a particular plot of land, it is not an obligation to transfer rights *in specie*.

B. Equity Follows the Law

The second maxim to be discussed is 'equity follows the law'. As was pointed out by Pound, what was operating here initially was once again a rule, not a maxim, one which provided that the rights of beneficiaries of bare trusts devolved in the same way as those forming the subject matter of the trust.[81] Thus in *Hopkins v Hopkins*, Lord Hardwicke said: 'It is the maxim of this court that trust estates, which are the

[77] Presumably on the basis that two maxims, as with two heads, are better than one. This second maxim is discussed below, text to nn 95–118.
[78] *Reid* (n 75) 331.
[79] A point also made by Gardner (n 32) 62.
[80] Though it is difficult to see how Reid was a fiduciary at all.
[81] Detail in Browne (n 6) 74.

creatures of equity, shall be governed by the same rules as legal estates in order to preserve the uniform rule of property'.[82]

The same thinking was applied to the equity of redemption.[83] It also applied so that the common law rule against limitations to successive unborn generations (now abolished) also governed equitable estates.[84]

As a rule, it made perfect sense and was easy to apply. However, as with the previously discussed maxim, once elevated to the status of a maxim, it lost its context and became nonsensical, for if literally true, there could be no equity at all: in the vast majority of cases where equity does have something to say, it most certainly does not follow the law. If it did, we would have no trusts, no fiduciary duties, nothing to fill books such as *Snell*. For that reason, Cardozo CJ famously said that the maxim should be reformulated to read: 'Equity follows the law but not slavishly nor always'.[85] On that basis, one would have thought that no judge would ever use it again. Yet use it they do, at the very least obscuring what they are trying to say.

A notorious example is *Stack v Dowden*,[86] where the issue was whether a title to land held by a man and woman as joint tenants was vested in them beneficially or whether, as the woman alleged, on trust for them both in unequal shares. In answering that question, Lord Walker said:

> In the ordinary domestic case where there are joint legal owners there will be a heavy burden in establishing to the court's satisfaction that an intention to keep a sort of balance-sheet of contributions actually existed, or should be inferred, or imputed to the parties. The presumption will be that equity follows the law. In such cases the court should not readily embark on the sort of detailed examination of the parties' relationship and finances that was attempted (with limited success) in this case.[87]

Likewise, Lady Hale said:

> At first blush, the answer appears obvious. It should only be expected that joint transferees would have spelt out their beneficial interests when they intended them to be different from their legal interests. Otherwise, it should be assumed that equity follows the law and that the beneficial interests reflect the legal interests in the property ….[88]

These statements are difficult to follow. It may be that both judges were doing nothing more than describing the location of the burden of proof in this type of civil proceeding.[89] But even so, given that equity does not slavishly follow the law elsewhere, why should it do so here? Maxims, as we have seen, allow judges to reach decisions without giving reasons, and this is a prime example of that vice. The only

[82] (1738) West t Hard 606, 619.
[83] *Casburne v Inglis* (1737) West t Hard 221.
[84] *Re Nash* [1910] 1 Ch 1 (CA).
[85] *Graf v Hope Building Corp* (1930) 254 NY 1 (New York Court of Appeals) 9.
[86] [2007] UKHL 17, [2007] 2 AC 432. McGhee (n 6) para [5-006] also notes that the 'potential for confusion in applying the maxim can be seen in *Stack v Dowden*'.
[87] *Stack* (n 86) [33].
[88] ibid [54].
[89] Or is it the standard of proof which is being referred to? If so, how do such statements square with that of Lord Hoffmann in *Re B (Children)* [2008] UKHL 35, [2009] 1 AC 11 [13] that there is only one standard of civil proof?

function it seems to play is to dispense with legal analysis. But it is worse than that. Both common law and equity, through the operation of presumptions, know situations in which the burden of proof shifts mid-trial.[90] If equity really did follow the law, then what Lord Walker and Lady Hale would be saying is that only in those situations in which presumptions operate at law will they likewise operate in equity. If so, by a sidewind, they will have abolished entirely the presumptions which operate to create resulting trusts, those operating in cases of undue influence,[91] and the so-called *Lake v Craddock*[92] presumption of tenancy in common arising where there are conveyances to joint tenants who are either business partners, unequal contributors to the purchase price, or mortgagees.[93] What has happened to these presumptions? The problem, as was we saw in relation to the common law, is that maxims tend to be expressed in such wide terms that they catch unintended material. Although there is a nod to some of the aforementioned presumptions in Lady Hale's speech, we are left with uncertainty as to their continued existence. It might be said that *Stack v Dowden* was not concerned with the question in *Lake v Craddock*, viz, whether there was a tenancy in common in equity or joint tenancy, but merely the quantification of the shares of tenants in common.[94] But the expression of the rule in terms of a maxim only muddies these already murky waters.

C. Equity Acts *in Personam*

The third maxim, that 'equity acts *in personam*', usually juxtaposed with the statement that 'the common law acts *in rem*',[95] is something of a latecomer. It was not listed by Hohfeld in his 1913 article on the relationship between law and equity,[96] and, as seen, only appeared in *Snell* in its seventh edition. Its inclusion, however, was a mistake, for it does not qualify as a maxim, laying down no rule, offering no words of wisdom. Properly understood, it does no more than describe an historical difference between common law and equity in matters of procedure.

We saw the use of the phrase as a rhetorical device in Lord Templeman's opinion in *Reid* discussed above.[97] A similar usage occurs in Lord Browne-Wilkinson's speech in *Target Holdings Ltd v Redferns*:

> a trustee in breach of trust must restore or pay to the trust estate either the assets which have been lost to the estate by reason of the breach or compensation for such loss. Courts of Equity did not award damages but, acting *in personam*, ordered the defaulting trustee to restore the trust estate. If specific restitution of the trust property is not possible, then the

[90] This perhaps explains Lord Walker's mysterious description of the maxim as a 'presumption'.

[91] Assuming there really is a presumption in such cases: W Swadling, 'Undue Influence: Lessons from America?' in C Mitchell and W Swadling (eds), *The Restatement Third: Restitution and Unjust Enrichment: Critical and Comparative Essays* (Oxford, Hart, 2013) 111.

[92] (1732) 3 P Wms 158 (assuming, of course, that a presumption really was involved in that case).

[93] As *Malayan Credit v Jack* [1986] AC 549 (PC) illustrates, the list is not closed.

[94] Though how the erstwhile joint tenants became tenants in common is an abiding mystery: A Briggs, 'Co-Ownership and an Equitable Non Sequitur' (2012) 128 *LQR* 183.

[95] See, eg, *Ewing v Orr Ewing (No 1)* (1883) LR 9 App Cas 34 (HL) 40 (Lord Selbourne LC).

[96] WN Hohfeld, 'The Relations Between Equity and Law' (1913) 11 *Michigam Law Review* 537, 550.

[97] See the text to n 77.

> liability of the trustee is to pay sufficient compensation to the trust estate to put it back to what it would have been had the breach not been committed.[98]

The maxim is clearly doing no work in these cases and could easily have been dispensed with. Indeed, in *Target* itself, Lord Browne-Wilkinson controversially adopted the common law rules of causation in a claim for equitable compensation for breach of trust, a case of equity following the law, it might be thought.

So what exactly does the phrase mean? The clue is in the word 'acts' – it is concerned with the *form* which equitable court orders take. By a judgment at common law, the defendant was not ordered to do anything. Instead, the Court ordered that 'the plaintiff shall have and recover of the defendant the sum of £xxx'. Not being an order against the defendant personally, he could not be jailed for contempt for non-compliance. Instead, his goods were seized and sold to meet the judgment. It was in this sense, therefore, that the common law traditionally acted *in rem.*[99] By contrast, orders of courts of equity were directed to the defendant personally, ordering him to do or refrain from doing something. A failure to comply was a contempt of court, which could lead to imprisonment. A court of equity thus went after the defendant's body, while the common law went after his goods, and it was in this sense that equity acted *in personam* and the common law *in rem*. As Scott explained:

> By a judgment at law the plaintiff is usually declared to have a certain right; by a decree in equity the defendant is usually ordered to act, or to refrain from acting in a certain way. A judgment at law is usually enforced without the co-operation of the defendant; if by the terms of the judgment the plaintiff is declared entitled to specific property the sheriff puts him in possession of that property; if by the terms of the judgment the plaintiff is entitled to recover a certain sum of money the sheriff seizes the defendant's property and sells it and out of the proceeds pays the plaintiff the amount to which he is entitled. On the other hand, a decree in equity is usually enforced by imprisoning the defendant and thereby making things so disagreeable for him that he will generally choose ultimately to obey rather than continue to suffer the disagreeable consequences of his disobedience.[100]

What the phrase describes, therefore, is not a maxim, not even a rule, just the process by which equity works.

This particular aspect of the 'maxim', however, is no longer literally true; indeed, it has not been so for centuries. Merely locking the defendant up, even when the windows of his cell were boarded up, or he was put in irons,[101] did not necessarily result in compliance with the order, and so was not particularly attractive to

[98] [1996] AC 421 (HL) 434. Another example from the same judge, then as a justice of the High Court, occurs in *Swiss Bank Corpn v Lloyds Bank Ltd* [1979] Ch 548 (Ch) 565–66. The phrase was more recently invoked by Lord Sumption to describe the 'proprietary' nature of the rights of a beneficiary of a trust: *Akers v Samba* [2017] UKSC 6, [2017] AC 424 [83].

[99] See the excellent account in N Oman, 'Why There is no Duty to Pay Damages: Powers, Duties, and Private Law' (2011) 39 *Florida State University Law Review* 137, 152–53.

[100] AW Scott, 'The Nature of the Rights of the *Cestui Que Trust*' (1917) 17 *Columbia Law Review* 269, 277. To be fair, McGhee (n 6) does not propose any wider use than this. So, eg, at para [5-017] he says that the maxim has a precise, technical meaning (explained at para [5-018] as a procedural distinction about the means of execution) and has been misused when divorced from that historical context.

[101] *Clerke v Waller* (1598) Monro 718: 'His lordship mindeth … to lay as many irons on him as he may bear'.

plaintiffs. As a consequence, equity very early on began to act in the same way as the common law, and by the end of the sixteenth century, principally through orders of sequestration, acted '*in rem*'. Under the process of sequestration, 'sequestrators were entitled to possession of the property over which the sequestration was granted, and, if possession was denied them, the court awarded a writ of assistance to put them in possession'.[102] It is important to understand that the fact that equity acts *in personam*, and the common law *in rem*, even when literally true, said nothing about the nature of the substantive rights there recognised. It was not saying that equity recognised only personal rights,[103] and the common law only property rights. As Hackney explained:

> 'The *in personam* phrase is not descriptive of X's rights, but simply describes the mode of execution of the court in protecting them – property rights protected by imprisoning contumacious violators. One can protect rights *in rem* by judgments *in personam*'.[104]

Unfortunately, judges using the 'maxim' do not always appreciate this point, the most egregious modern example being that of Lord Neuberger in *FHR European Ventures LLP v Cedar Capital*.[105]

We already encountered the misapplication of the maxim that 'equity looks upon as done that which ought to be done' by Lord Templeman in *Attorney General for Hong Kong v Reid*[106] in holding that a bribe was held on trust for the victim of the breach of fiduciary duty, invoking the *in personam* maxim for good measure. In *Sinclair Investments v Versailles*,[107] Lord Neuberger MR, then sitting in the Court of Appeal, refused to apply *Reid*, going so far as to predict that the Supreme Court would not follow it either.[108] However, in a complete *volte face* just two years later, and with only the occasional reference to *Sinclair*, his Lordship, now as President of the Supreme Court, wholeheartedly embraced *Reid*, using little by way of argument other than the *in personam* maxim. He said it was

> ... not possible to identify any plainly right or plainly wrong answer to the issue of the extent of the rule [that bribes are held on trust], as a matter of pure legal authority. There can clearly be different views as to what requirements have to be satisfied before a proprietary interest is created. More broadly, it is fair to say that the concept of equitable proprietary rights is in some respects somewhat paradoxical. Equity, unlike the common law, classically acts in personam ...; yet equity is far more ready to accord proprietary claims than common law. Further, two general rules which law students learn early on are that common law legal rights prevail over equitable rights, and that where there are

[102] Details in Browne (n 6) para [30-34]. It was also possible for plaintiffs to be put into possession of land and chattels.

[103] Many people make this mistake. An example is F de Londras, *Principles of Irish Property Law*, 2nd edn (Dublin, Clarus Press, 2011) paras [3-75]–[3-76].

[104] J Hackney, *Understanding Equity and Trusts* (London, Fontana Press, 1987) 26. McGhee (n 6) para [5-018] makes the same point about the maxim referring to execution and does not use the maxim to draw conclusions about the nature of equitable rights However, the point does not seem to be appreciated by Heydon, Leeming and Turner (n 6) paras [3-220]–[3-260], where the bulk of the discussion of the maxim comprises an exposition on the nature of equitable rights, whether *in rem* or *in personam*.

[105] [2014] UKSC 45, [2015] AC 250.

[106] (n 75).

[107] [2011] EWCA Civ 347, [2012] Ch 453.

[108] ibid [76].

> competing equitable rights the first in time prevails; yet, given that equity is far more ready to recognise proprietary rights than common law, the effect of having an equitable right is often to give priority over common law claims – sometimes even those which may have preceded the equitable right. Given that equity developed at least in part to mitigate the rigours of the common law, this is perhaps scarcely surprising. However, it underlines the point that it would be unrealistic to expect complete consistency from the cases over the past 300 years. It is therefore appropriate to turn to the arguments based on principle and practicality, and then to address the issue, in the light of those arguments as well as the judicial decisions discussed above.[109]

Seizing on the supposed confusion, his Lordship felt able to rise above the case law and lay down a bright line rule, viz, that bribes are held on trust.[110] The confusion, however, was purely of Lord Neuberger's own making. Had he understood the 'maxim' correctly, he would have been forced to engage with the prior law.

A final point concerns the relationship of this 'maxim' with the notion that 'equity is a court of conscience', fortunately not yet a maxim. The two are often run together, as seen in the famous statement of Lord Selbourne LC that the 'courts of Equity in England are, and always have been, courts of conscience, operating *in personam* and not *in rem* …'.[111] However, in the same way that 'equity acts *in personam*' is not a rule, so too is the notion of equity being a 'court of conscience'. Although often lost sight of, and being thought to give courts of equity the power to dispense justice on vague notions of fairness,[112] it describes nothing more than the relationship between law and equity, between competing legal systems.[113] More specifically, it describes the fact that courts of equity do not sit on appeal from common law courts,[114] do not overturn common law judgments, but instead direct defendants not to enforce them. As Lord Hardwicke explained two centuries ago:

> Though this court cannot set aside a judgment of a common law court obtained against conscience, yet will it decree the party to acknowledge satisfaction on that judgment, though he has received nothing; because obtained where nothing was due. So it cannot set aside a fine for being obtained by fraud and imposition … yet, on a conveyance so obtained, this court never sent the plaintiff to the Common Bench to set it aside, but considers the person obtaining the estate, even by fine, as a trustee, and decrees him to reconvey on the general ground of laying hold of the ill-conscience of the party, to make him do what is necessary to restore matters as before.[115]

[109] *FHR* (n 105) [32].

[110] Unfortunately, the equally bright line rule, that there should never be a trust – the approach taken in *Lister v Stubbs* itself – was nowhere considered.

[111] *Ewing* (n 95) 40.

[112] Famously criticised by Selden, F Pollock (ed), *Table Talk of John Selden* (London, Selden Society, 1927) 43 in the following terms: 'Equity is according to the conscience of him who is Chancellor, and as that is larger or narrower, so is equity. It is all one as if they should make the standard for the measure we call a *foot* "a chancellor's foot"'. Though subsequently refuted on many occasions, some judges still purport to decide cases on this basis, see, eg, Arden LJ's judgment in *Pennington* (n 5).

[113] According to Birks, it was the *in personam* rule which did this: P Birks, 'In Rem or In Personam?' (1994) 8 *Trusts Law International* 99, 100.

[114] See too, McFarlane's and Hudson's chapters in this volume.

[115] *Barnesly v Powel* (1749) 1 Ves Snr 284, 289. Today, it would be only in comparatively rare cases where a party would go to equity only after a common law judgment. Equitable intervention would normally be sought before that point.

Maitland said much the same thing at the turn of the last century:

> In fraud or in breach of trust you obtain a judgment against me in a court of law; I complain to the Chancellor, and he after hearing what you have to say enjoins you not to put in force your judgment, says in effect that if you do put your judgment in force you will be sent to prison. Understand well that the Court of Chancery never asserted that it was superior to the courts of law; it never presumed to send to them such mandates as the Court of King's Bench habitually sent to the inferior courts, telling them that they must do this or must not do that or quashing their proceedings – the Chancellor's injunction was in theory a very different thing from a mandamus, a prohibition, a certiorari, or the like. It was addressed not to the judges, but to the party. You in breach of trust have obtained a judgment – the Chancellor does not say that this judgment was wrongly granted, he does not annul it, he tells you that for reasons personal to yourself it will be inequitable for you to enforce that judgment, and that you are not to enforce it.[116]

Unfortunately, this fact is also often lost sight of.

A prime example is in some discussions of the nature of the rights of beneficiaries of trusts. Since equity both acts on the defendant's conscience and operates *in personam*, it is sometimes said that because trusts are the product of equity, the rights of trust beneficiaries can only be personal.[117] However, that is immediately contradicted by the empirical evidence for, as is well known, trusts have certain third-party effects, as witness the fact that a transferee from a trustee in breach of trust can be ordered to retransfer the rights unless a bona fide purchaser of a legal right without notice of the dissipation in breach of trust.[118] Indeed, as noted above, it was this very confusion which Lord Neuberger seized upon in *FHR* to draw a line under the existing law. The problem is that the protagonists in this debate have lost sight of the fact that, as we have seen, neither 'maxim' says anything about the substantive nature of the beneficiary's rights, is concerned only with matters of procedure. But that is the problem with maxims, and why their use, at least at common law, is rightly deprecated.

VI. CONCLUSION

We have examined three equitable maxims: 'equity looks upon as done that which ought to be done'; 'equity follows the law'; and, 'equity acts *in personam*'. As to the first two, though both were accurate statements of the law when merely rules, wrong turns were made on their elevation to the status of maxims. With the 'equity looks upon as done that which ought to be done' maxim, the mistake was to divorce the rule from the substantive duty and link it instead to the remedy; it led to arbitrary trusts and an illegitimate extension to contracts of hire and gains made in breach of fiduciary duty. In the case of the maxim 'equity follows the law', the immediate problem

[116] Maitland (n 57) 9.

[117] See, eg, the debate concerning Case C-294/92 *Webb v Webb* [1994] ECR I-1717: for discussion see, eg, Birks, 'In Rem or In Personam?' (n 113); A Briggs, *The Conflict of Laws*, 4th edn (Oxford, OUP, 2019) 59.

[118] *Pilcher v Rawlins* (1871–72) LR 7 Ch App 259 (CA).

is that it is patently false, for there are countless instances of equity *not* doing so. All the maxim does is cause confusion, as witness the speeches of Lord Walker and Lady Hale in *Stack v Dowden*. Finally, we saw that the maxim 'equity acts *in personam*' was no maxim at all, not even a rule. The phrase instead described how equity works, in the form of its orders and the method of their enforcement. Although frequently lost sight of, the 'maxim' says nothing of the nature of substantive rights in equity. Nor is this contradicted by the fact that equity acts on the defendant's 'conscience'.

Hohfeld told his students that the equitable maxims were 'mere "guide-posts"' and not to be taken literally.[119] Unfortunately, many judges in equity fail to heed this warning, and are led into error. On the sesquicentenary of the Judicature Acts, is it not time that equity followed the law and eschewed the use of maxims altogether?

[119] Hohfeld (n 96) 550.

Part III

Equitable Protection

6

Loose Ends in Accounting for Profits

LORD BRIGGS OF WESTBOURNE

THE LATE, GREAT, Peter (Lord) Millett described the topic of this chapter, accounts of profits, as 'the most controversial remedy of all'.[1] For someone who was, to put it mildly, no stranger to controversies when it came to equitable remedies, that is high praise indeed. Many are the references in the older cases to judges advising parties to settle, where an account of profits had been ordered because the process, largely conducted safely away from the eyes of law reporters and posterity in Masters' chambers, was simply too difficult and uncertain to bear thinking about.[2]

There is however nothing esoteric about accounts of profits. We are all familiar with the long-established principle running from *Keech v Sandford*[3] to *Regal (Hastings) Ltd v Gulliver*[4] and *Boardman v Phipps*[5] that a fiduciary who makes secret or otherwise unauthorised profits from their position is obliged to disgorge them via an account of profits. What is surprising is that the antiquity of the remedy belies a number of questions of fundamental importance which remain battlegrounds before the appellate courts both in England and throughout the common law world, sometimes with divergent outcomes.

The normative role of equity, in most of its enduring manifestations, is to remedy deficiencies in the common law. It does so by recognising and protecting types of property (mainly equitable interests) to which the common law is blind, and by tempering the harshness of rigid common law rules by reference to the dictates of conscience. But we have in recent years seen those roles reversed in the field of equitable accounts. In the famous case of *Target Holdings Ltd v Redferns*[6] the application by the Court of Appeal of rigid rules of equitable accounting was perceived by many (me included) to produce manifest injustice, indeed absurdity, and aspects of the

[1] P Millett, 'Account of Profits' (2014) 130 *LQR* 681 (review).

[2] I am grateful to Professor Matthew Conaglen for highlighting what he describes as the 'scant source material' for accounts of profits from an historical perspective in his excellent article 'Identifying the Profits for Which a Fiduciary Must Account' (2020) 79 *CLJ* 38.

[3] Sel Cas Temp King 61, [1726] 25 ER 223.

[4] [1967] 2 AC 134 (HL).

[5] [1967] 2 AC 46 (HL).

[6] [1996] AC 421 (HL).

common law rules about causation, already finely honed in the field of contract and tort, were invoked to produce a fair – I would say equitable – result. More recently, in *AIB Group (UK) plc v Mark Redler & Co Solicitors*,[7] that earlier intrusion was recognised as having amounted almost to a take-over in which, at least where putting right a loss is concerned, equitable compensation along common law lines has, or is in the midst of, ousting the process of surcharging or falsifying the account. This is at least so in the minds of most academic commentators, even if not perhaps fully in the Court of Appeal, or in Australia or Hong Kong, and even if this development would leave Lord Millett turning in his grave.[8]

But the equitable remedy of an account for profits has, save in a few places (such as Singapore),[9] remained something of a traditional redoubt against the inroads of the common law. I am referring to that remedy as against a defaulting trustee or fiduciary who is alleged to have made a secret profit, rather than the elective remedy of the owner of intellectual property, such as a patent, against someone who has infringed their property right, or the victim of a breach of confidence. There are obvious reasons why that may be so. There will often be no need to conduct a causation-based analysis of the link between the breach and the profit. The making of the profit may be the very breach itself. There are policy reasons (mainly *pour encourager les autres*) for the preservation of a bit of healthy rigour in the discipling of errant trustees. And equity has its own more flexible and discretionary tools for tempering the wind to the shorn lamb, such as relief for honest and reasonable trustees and other fiduciaries who ought fairly to be excused (now statutory) and the award of a just allowance for the trustee's care and skill.

In this chapter, I want to look at four areas of controversy and where we stand on them throughout the common law world at present. I hope to offer some thoughts on how progress might be made in them so as to put accounts of profits on a more certain footing, no longer to bedevil practitioners, and, just occasionally, judges.[10]

The first topic I address is the strict nature of the disgorgement required of profiting fiduciaries, particularly honest ones, via an account of profits. In particular, I will consider whether the time has come to take up the invitation laid down by Lady Arden (now recently retired) in the Court of Appeal in *Murad v Al Saraj*,[11] which remains the leading English case on accounts of profits in recent times, to reconsider

[7] [2014] UKSC 58, [2015] AC 1503.

[8] Although he has left us with a potent testament to his views on the subject in his brilliantly pithy judgment in the Hong Kong case of *Libertarian Investments Ltd v Hall* [2013] HKCFA 93, [2014] 1 HKC 368 [166]–[175].

[9] Notably in *UVJ v UVH* [2020] SGCA 49, which I will come on to discuss.

[10] I certainly do not suggest that these are the only loose ends in accounting for profits. For example, one further matter which may merit future attention is the relationship between accounts of profits and potentially co-extensive (or not) proprietary remedies against profits made by a defaulting fiduciary where they constitute the traceable proceeds of trust property. Notably, in the Hong Kong case of *Tang v Tang* [2017] HKCFA 3, Lord Millett doubted that an account of profits would be available if the profits constituted the traceable proceeds of trust property. I would respectfully question that view in light of the critique advanced by Professors L Ho and R Lee, 'The Beneficiaries' Right to Elect Remedies for Misapplied Funds' (2017) 133 *LQR* 565.

[11] [2005] EWCA Civ 959, [2005] WTLR 1573 [82]–[83].

the strictness of the rule in *Keech v Sandford* and whether the explanation that it serves as a deterrent is fully justified.

Second, I want to consider the role of causation in accounts of profits against defaulting fiduciaries. In the UK, the Supreme Court recently refused permission to appeal from the decision of the Court of Appeal in *Gray v Global Energy Horizons Corp.*[12] In that case, the Court of Appeal held that the extent of an account of profits was to be determined by reference to the scope of the fiduciary's duty rather than 'but for' causation or the notion of a 'sufficient causal connection' as had been the approach at first instance with the agreement of the parties. By contrast the Singapore Court of Appeal recently forthrightly adopted a causation-based approach in *UVJ v UVH*. The issue therefore remains very much alive and ripe, in an appropriate case, to be examined at the highest level in England.

Third is the treatment of accounts of profits ordered against those with accessory liability in a breach of fiduciary duty rather than defaulting fiduciaries themselves. In England, the Court of Appeal took the view in 2014 in *Novoship (UK) Ltd v Mikhaylyuk* that where knowing recipients and dishonest assisters are concerned, accounts of profits are available.[13] However, those equitable wrongdoers will be required only to disgorge profits which satisfy the common law rules on causation in relation to their wrongdoing which apply by analogy as they do on claims for equitable compensation. In 2018, the High Court of Australia declined to follow this approach in *Ancient Order of Foresters in Victoria Friendly Society Ltd v Lifeplan Australia Friendly Society Ltd*, instead holding that accounts of profits against fiduciaries and those with accessory liability in a breach of trust ought to be determined by reference to the same principles.[14]

Finally, I consider equitable allowances. This involves examining the justification for their use, particularly where dishonest fiduciaries are concerned, and the overall role they play in the fashioning of the account of profits as an equitable remedy fit for the modern world.

I. OUTMODED RIGOUR OF THE REMEDY

The supposed severity of the rule that a trustee is strictly accountable for secret profits has its typical manifestation in a requirement for disgorgement even where the trustee's conduct has been honest and in good faith, has caused no loss (or sometimes a positive benefit) to the beneficiaries and where, if offered the relevant business opportunity, the beneficiaries would have been unable to reap the benefit for themselves, or would have chosen not to do so, or would even have authorised the trustee to do so for his own account. As Lady Arden observed in *Murad v Al-Saraj*, it has sometimes been justified on the practical basis that the investigation of the counterfactual world in which the trustee had offered the opportunity to the beneficiaries is just too difficult

[12] [2020] EWCA Civ 1668, [2021] 1 WLR 2264.
[13] [2014] EWCA Civ 908, [2015] QB 499.
[14] [2018] HCA 43, (2018) 265 CLR 1.

and unreliable.[15] As she said, however, the courts are now better equipped to do this than maybe they used to be. In common law claims for negligence the courts regularly investigate such counterfactuals, and have developed sophisticated tools for doing so, such as the scope of duty limitation and the evaluation of a lost chance.

The other justification is often labelled *pour encourager les autres*, or deterrence. But although frequently invoked, I think it is a misnomer. No doubt the law always seeks to encourage law-abiding conduct, and not just by trustees (see the magisterial account in *The Rule of Laws*, by Fernanda Pirie).[16] The liability to account for secret profits without regard to such counterfactuals derives principally from the nature of the duty itself, which is that the trustee must discharge his office with single-minded or undivided loyalty to the beneficiaries. He must avoid even bringing himself into a situation where his own interest may conflict with that of the beneficiary. If the relevant business opportunity comes the way of the fiduciary in the course of his office as fiduciary, then he cannot, without the beneficiary's fully informed consent, either take it for his own benefit, or even share it with the beneficiary.[17]

In *Murad*, Lady Arden suggested that the rule might in some cases (although not the case actually before her, which was one of dishonesty) be incompatible 'with the desire of modern courts to ensure that remedies are proportionate to the justice of the case'.[18] I respectfully doubt whether this is, at heart, a problem about disproportionate remedies. The remedy of an account of secret profits is naturally appropriate to the relevant breach of fiduciary duty, because it transfers to the beneficiaries the profit which, acting loyally, the trustees should have made (if at all) for the beneficiaries rather than for themselves. This is the concept which underlies the persuasive analysis of Professor Lusina Ho in her chapter on 'Deemed Performance in Account of Profits' in *The Impact of Equity and Restitution in Commerce*.[19]

No-one has yet, so far as I am aware, taken up Lady Arden's challenge. But if they do, I think they will need to grapple more with the rigour of the underlying duty than with the proportionality of the remedy for its breach. I acknowledge that the concept of the trust and of fiduciary duty is so widespread and deeply embedded in modern business and commerce that many will find that they have undertaken duties of undivided loyalty without fully appreciating the consequences. There will be cases where pure nomineeship (the holding of a bare legal title without any of the powers and discretions typical of the true trustee) does not attract the loyalty duty in a sense which meaningfully limits what the nominee may do in the rest of their business life. The duty may be limited by contract, and its performance improved by good education. But to start afresh with a suggested downgrading of the essential core of the fiduciary duty of loyalty would to my mind be a large undertaking indeed, and I cannot see what public policy would thereby be served. The existence of the duty

[15] *Murad* (n 11) [76]–[88].

[16] F Pirie, *The Rule of Laws* (London, Profile Books, 2021).

[17] One clear example of the strict operation of the rule was the company case of *Bhullar v Bhullar* [2003] EWCA Civ 424, [2003] BCC 711.

[18] *Murad* (n 11) [83].

[19] L Ho, 'Deemed Performance in Account of Profits' in P Devonshire and R Havelock (eds), *The Impact of Equity and Restitution in Commerce* (Oxford, Hart, 2019) 183.

of loyalty is one of those foundation stones which separates business life from the jungle. It is a valuable contribution which equity makes to civilised life. The fact that it has ancient origins and, in principle, operates strictly even in cases where this may seem harsh does not seem to me, at the moment at least, to mean that it has passed its shelf-life. Indeed, it would be odd to dial down the fiduciary duty of loyalty even as the common law may be becoming more muscular in its approach to duties of good faith between contracting parties.

II. THE ROLE OF CAUSATION, IF ANY

Here at least the battle lines are already drawn, although the resolution lies in the future. A trustee or fiduciary (such as a company director) engages in profitable business in breach of the duty of loyalty and makes a secret profit. He defends the beneficiaries' claim by saying that, but for the breach, the beneficiary would have made no profit and that the breach caused the beneficiary no loss which would not have been suffered but for the breach. Or he may say that, if he had disclosed the opportunity at the outset, the risk-averse beneficiary would have declined to participate, and consented to the trustee making the profit for his own account. All these defences seek to include an element of 'but-for' causation into the accounting in a way which is the everyday bread and butter of the common lawyer.

The battle lines may be more easily identified if some peripheral smoke is first cleared away. First, it is well settled that the question whether, on a but-for basis, the trustee's breach of duty caused the beneficiaries any *loss* is irrelevant. An account of profits is an independent alternative to compensation for loss, not a form of substitute for it. Secondly, it is not the case that causation in the broader sense is entirely irrelevant. Equity judges commonly speak of profits being accountable because they were made 'as the result of' the breach of duty.[20] But thirdly, causation even in this limited sense may have very little work to do, either because the making of the profit by the trustee was itself the breach, or because it is plain and obvious that the profit was derived from the prohibited activity.

What remains may be summarised thus by reference to the broader debates in the field of equitable remedies. On the one hand, those who might be described as accounting traditionalists say that all that need be established for profits to be subject to disgorgement by a defaulting fiduciary is that the profitable activity fell within the scope of the fiduciary duty. On the other, the *Target*- and *Redler*-inspired common law invaders say that there must be a sufficient causative link between the breach and the profit, and that the common law techniques of causation analysis, including the 'but-for' test, are at least part of the toolkit by which that link must be established.

[20] eg, *Gwembe Valley v Koshy* [2003] EWCA Civ 1048, [2004] 1 BCLC 131 [6] (Mummery LJ).

The issue came to the fore in *Gray v Global Energy Horizons Corp*.[21] GEHC obtained an order for an account of profits made by Mr Gray in breach of fiduciary duty. His breach of duty had been to place himself in a position of conflict through his involvement in the exploitation of ultrasound technology for maximising the yield from depleted oil wells, technology which GEHC already wished to exploit. The order for an account was expressed as applicable to all monies and other benefits received by Mr Gray '*directly or indirectly arising from*' or '*as a result of*' the breaches.[22] It had been common ground at the trial before Asplin J that GEHC needed to show a sufficient causal link between the offending conduct of Mr Gray and his receipt of accountable benefits. This remained common ground between counsel in the Court of Appeal, although one of Mr Gray's grounds of appeal was that the judge had been wrong to identify a sufficient causal link in relation to some of the benefits for which she held him liable to account. In particular, Mr Gray alleged that the link had been too remote and that he would have made the profits anyway if he had not breached his duties.[23]

The Court of Appeal (David Richards, Henderson and Rose LJJ) were having none of this causation analysis. They said that while there needed to be some link or nexus between the breach and the profit: 'the link or nexus does not need to be of a causal character. It will normally be sufficient if the profit arose within the scope of a defaulting fiduciary's conduct in breach of duty'.[24] They approved the following dictum of Morritt LJ in *United Pan Europe Communications NV v Deutsche Bank AG*:

> If there is a fiduciary duty of loyalty and if the conduct complained of falls within the scope of that fiduciary duty … then I see no justification for any further requirement that the profit shall have been obtained by the fiduciary 'by virtue of his position'. Such a condition suggests an element of causation which neither principle nor the authorities require.[25]

It does not appear that this judicial dislike of the parties' agreed test made any difference to the outcome of the appeal. Permission to appeal to the Supreme Court was accordingly refused.

There is no civil war in England about this. The 'scope of duty' approach was for example applied by the Court of Appeal in *Parr v Keystone Healthcare Ltd*.[26] The battle is an international one, and was joined by the contrary decision of the Court of Appeal of Singapore, earlier in 2020, in *UVJ v UVH*. The litigation arose between the children (two sisters and three brothers) of a deceased Singaporean businessman. All were beneficiaries in his estate. The brothers were also executors and directors of several family companies part-owned by the estate. They failed as executors to distribute the shares forming part of the estate or reveal their existence to the

[21] (n 12).
[22] ibid [112]–[113] (Vos J) (emphasis added).
[23] ibid [157].
[24] ibid [128].
[25] [2000] 2 BCLC 461 (CA) [47].
[26] [2019] EWCA Civ 1246, [2019] 4 WLR 99.

sisters. The sisters obtained orders that the brothers account (as secret profits) for directors' remuneration and associated benefits received by them during the 19 years since their father's death. The brothers appealed. The judgment of the court contains much interesting procedural learning about the difference between an account on the basis of wilful default (a process) and an account of profits (a remedy), but for present purposes what matters is the way in which the Court of Appeal dealt with the brothers' case that, even if they had not voted the estate's shares in support of their remuneration and benefits, they would still have received it because of the affirmative votes of other (non-fiduciary) shareholders.

After a very full citation of English and Commonwealth authority, and a conventional affirmation that an account of profits does not depend in any way upon the beneficiaries having suffered a loss,[27] the Court of Appeal concluded as follows:

> For the above reasons, it is our opinion that the profits sought to be disgorged via an account of profits must be caused by the breaches of fiduciary duty, whether this be that the trustee acted in conflict of interest or was guilty of some other breach. To find otherwise would be for equity to become an unruly horse where any breach by a fiduciary can be used to recover a profit however unconnected the two may be, *and even if the profits would have been earned by the fiduciary in the absence of the breach*.[28] (emphasis added)

Shorn of the last line, that conclusion may go little further than established authority on similar facts, such as *Re Gee*,[29] where the fact that the defendant director held a small minority of shares on trust did not make him accountable for directors' fees after the other shareholders had appointed him as a director. But it is well apparent that, in including 'but-for' causation within the requirement that the profits be caused by the breach, the Court of Appeal was quite deliberately stepping outside established English authority, including *Murad*, on the footing that they did not bind a court in Singapore.[30]

We have thus far been examining the 'but-for' causation test as a defensive weapon, where the fiduciary claims that he would still have made the relevant profit if he had committed no breach of duty: for example, where he seeks to prove that, after full disclosure, the beneficiary would have consented. But a series of Australian cases show that it may also be relied on by the beneficiary, as a lesser hurdle than having to prove effective cause, or *causa causans*. They include *Warman v Dwyer*[31] and the *Foresters* case.[32] The need to prove some kind of causation is said to arise where a fiduciary employee of company A misappropriates confidential information or an opportunity for the purpose of deploying it, with others, in a competing business run by their newly formed company B, which goes on to make profits. A sues the former employee for breach of fiduciary duty and B for dishonest assistance, in both cases seeking an account of profits. How does A identify the profits for which

[27] *UVJ* (n 9) [73]–[97].
[28] ibid [98].
[29] [1948] Ch 284 (Ch).
[30] *UVJ* (n 9) [87]–[89].
[31] (1995) 182 CLR 544 (HCA).
[32] (n 14).

the defendants must account? The employee's business partners may bring their own information, skill and goodwill to promote B's success. And A's business may have been on the slide anyway, precipitating the employee's departure.

In *Foresters* the appellant was in the position of company B, and argued unsuccessfully for a steep causation hurdle, as between its acts of assistance and the profits made. In a joint judgment, in which they proceeded on the basis that there was no difference for this purpose between the defaulting fiduciary and the dishonest accessory, a subject to which I will return, Kiefel CJ, Keane and Edelman JJ said:

> Whether a benefit can be said to be obtained 'as a result of' knowing participation in a breach of fiduciary duty by another contrary to the principles of equity is a question of causation or contribution that depends on 'a precise examination of the particular facts' of the case, rather than upon attempts to refine the expression 'as a result of', as if that phrase has some determinate operation of its own that may be discerned and applied independently of the equitable principle of which it is part. The equitable disgorgement principle with which we are concerned is a 'prophylactic rather than a restitutionary principle'. It is sufficient to show that the profit would not have been made but for dishonest wrongdoing.[33]

I am not even going to begin to try and reconcile those three different dicta in *Gray*, *UVJ* and *Foresters* about the role of causation in an account of profits. But I venture to suggest that it is not a cop-out to say that their weight, in any particular context, is likely to be very fact-sensitive. There are cases, at one end of the scale, where it was so obviously a breach of trust for the trustee to make and keep the relevant profit without full disclosure, that causation has little if any role to play. But there will be others, where there is an identifiable profit, but it is in part derived from activities, including those of third parties, that are apparently legitimate in themselves, where isolating that part of the profit which truly is within the scope of the duty broken cannot sensibly be undertaken without some element of causation analysis.

III. ACCOUNTING FOR PROFITS BY ACCESSORIES

The *Foresters* case was, as already noted, about the liability of an accessory: someone whom in England we now call a dishonest assistant, but who in Australia appears still to be called a knowing assistant in a dishonest breach. The premise for the dictum about causation in account of profits, that there was no difference between the liability of the fiduciary and the accessory for this purpose had, in 2014, been denied in the most careful terms by the English Court of Appeal in *Novoship (UK) Ltd v Mikhaylyuk*. A Mr Nikitin had, through the use of bribes, dishonestly assisted the general manager of the claimant Novoship, a Mr Mikhaylyuk, in the corrupt chartering of ships to companies owned by Mr Nikitin. The ships were found in fact to have been chartered at market rates, following which Mr Nikitin's companies had made profits due to an unexpected rise in the charter market. But for Mr Mikhaylyuk's

[33] ibid [9].

breach of fiduciary duty and Mr Nikitin's dishonest assistance, however, the charters would not have occurred and the profits would not have been made.

The Court of Appeal decided as a matter of principle that the remedy of an account of profits was indeed available against a party with accessory liability in a breach of fiduciary duty.[34] But they denied *Novoship* an account of those profits as against Mr Nikitin and his companies, on three grounds.[35] First, since they were only dishonest assistants and not fiduciaries, it had to be shown that their dishonest assistance, rather than Mr Mikhaylyuk's breach of fiduciary duty, caused the profits to be made. Second, mere 'but-for' causation, as against a dishonest assistant, was insufficient. The full panoply of the common law tests for causation had to be satisfied, including effective cause. Thirdly, an account of profits against a dishonest assistant was discretionary, and might be refused if it produced a disproportionate result, measured against the nature and extent of the wrongdoing. Since the effective cause of the profits in question was the movement of the market after the charters had been entered into, none of these conditions was satisfied.

The Court of Appeal's decision in *Novoship* appears to have been underpinned, though on the face of the judgment largely tacitly,[36] by the Supreme Court's decision in *Williams v Central Bank of Nigeria*,[37] given a few months before *Novoship* was heard. Though mainly a case about limitation, the underlying reasoning in *Williams* was concerned with distinguishing between, on the one hand, 'true' constructive trustees who have voluntarily assumed the obligations of trusteeship and owe the fiduciary duty of loyalty and, on the other, those who are sometimes, perhaps inaccurately, labelled 'constructive trustees' because they are deemed to assume trustee-like liabilities as a result of being an accessory to a breach of trust. The Supreme Court made clear however that the latter class of persons are not fiduciaries. They have never undertaken a duty of loyalty to the beneficiary.[38]

The applicability of this distinction in a *Novoship*-type situation would seem to be that because an accessory has never undertaken a duty of loyalty pursuant to which he must single-mindedly subordinate his interests to those of the beneficiary, there is no bar to him retaining profits which he would have made in any event or which have no causal connection to the breach and which have not been made, in any sense, at the expense of the beneficiary. Indeed, in one sense, it is hard to see how a scope of duty test of the type adopted by the English Court of Appeal in *Gray* could ever be applicable to an accessory, when the guiding principle in *Williams* suggests that he never owes any fiduciary duty in the first place. The Australian approach of applying a causation-based test to all accounts of profits neatly avoids this difficulty. But in England, the Court of Appeal may have been correct to treat an accessory's liability to account for profits differently from that of a fiduciary.

I must however admit to a feeling of considerable disquiet about each of the supposed points of distinction in *Novoship* between an account of profits against a

[34] *Novoship* (n 13) [93].
[35] ibid [94]–[120].
[36] In the sense that it attracts relatively few citations in the judgment.
[37] [2014] UKSC 10, [2014] AC 1189.
[38] ibid [9] (Lord Sumption), [118] (Lord Neuberger PSC).

fiduciary and against an accessory. As to the Court of Appeal's view that the accessory is only liable for the consequences of their acts of assistance, this is contrary to earlier English Court of Appeal dicta, for example in *Grupo Torras SA v Al-Sabah (No 5)*[39] and *Casio Computer Co Ltd v Sayo (No 3)*, that 'loss caused by the fiduciary is recoverable from the accessory'.[40] If that is true of loss, why not of profit? Secondly, the proposition that a more stringent causation test applies to accounts against an accessory than against a fiduciary is directly contrary to the ratio of the *Foresters* case, in which reference is made to *Novoship* in a footnote as being contrary to their view. Thirdly, while every equitable remedy is in a sense discretionary (so that, for example, an applicant who causes prejudice by delay or who does not come with clean hands may be denied relief) the general rule is that an account of profits is a remedy for which the beneficiary may elect, as of right, regardless of whether it gives him a recovery which is disproportionate to any loss suffered by him.

Now is not the time to examine the authorities which led the Court of Appeal to enunciate these three principles in relation to accounts of profits by accessories. But two considerations lead me to think that this is fertile ground for a visit to the Supreme Court. The first is the simple strength of the principle applied in *Foresters* that the accessory is liable as if he were a trustee. Gageler J put it this way:

> The reasons for holding the dishonest and fraudulent fiduciary to account and the reasons for holding the knowing participant to account being the same, there is no reason why the principles by which the knowing participant's liability to account is assessed should be different from those by which the dishonest and fraudulent fiduciary's liability to account is assessed.[41]

The point is even stronger if the current English phraseology of dishonest assistant is used, in place of knowing participant, to describe the accessory. There is no reason for a dishonest accessory to be treated more gently than, for example, a fiduciary who has committed an honest and technical breach of trust.

The second is what one may describe as the gut feeling that may be derived from a common example of this problem, where the 'accessory' is the payer of a bribe to the fiduciary. True it may be that there exists no prior fiduciary relationship between the accessory and the beneficiary, but if the whole purpose of the bribe is to procure a breach of fiduciary duty by the fiduciary, why should the profit made by the briber be identified by the use of more stringent hurdles than against the bribee? Or as Gageler J put it in *Foresters*,[42] why should the accessory be treated more leniently? That does not of course mean that the profits will be the same. The bribed fiduciary's profit is usually the bribe, whereas the profit of the briber will derive from the advantageous transaction made with the beneficiary (or principal) as the result of the bribe and may well be exponentially greater than the size of the bribe itself.

[39] [2001] Lloyd's Rep Bank 36 (CA).
[40] [2001] EWCA Civ 661, [2001] ILPr 43 [15] (Tuckey LJ).
[41] *Foresters* (n 14) [80].
[42] ibid [81].

IV. EQUITABLE ALLOWANCES

It is commonplace (despite warnings to the contrary in *Guinness plc v Saunders*)[43] for a court of equity to temper the rigour of an account of profits by making an allowance for the contribution made to the profits by the care, labour and skill of the defaulting fiduciary, even sometimes when the fiduciary has been found to have been dishonest. But neither the cases nor academic commentaries disclose a single unifying principle as the basis for doing so, other than the pursuit of justice and equity in the broadest sense. A most impressive essay by Professor Matthew Harding[44] suggests that the candidates for an underpinning principle may include the following:

(a) A perception that it may facilitate the re-introduction or effective replacement of principles of common-law causation and remoteness by the back door, by judges who lament the apparent exclusion of those principles by binding authority.
(b) A safety valve which prevents the rigour of the account of profits from causing disproportionate or unjust results.
(c) An application of Professor Ho's concept of deemed performance.[45]
(d) A reflection of Professor Harding's own proposed unifying principle of desert.
(e) No more or less that what it says on the tin: ie, a discretionary allowance for the contribution made to the accountable profits by the time, care and skill of the fiduciary: a sort of non-cash disbursement.

Before looking at the candidates in detail, it is worth defining our subject matter. We are not concerned here with the fiduciary's actual expenditure of money, or with monetary liabilities properly incurred, in earning the profit. They are always deductible, as Wilberforce J said in *Boardman v Phipps*, as disbursements.[46] Their deduction is necessary for identifying the amount of the profit in the first place. Rather, we are concerned with the intangible contribution made by the deployment of the fiduciary's personal time, care and skill to the profitable activity, for which, if acting properly as a trustee, the fiduciary would not generally be entitled to be paid, in the absence of express provision for remuneration in the trust instrument. Furthermore, in the case of typically remunerated fiduciaries like company directors, their remuneration will already have been contracted for, and is most unlikely to be variable in amount by reference to the amount of extra time and skill applied to a particular project, even if authorised. The contribution actually made to the profit by the application of the fiduciary's own care and skill may be infinitely variable, from critical (in the sense of being the effective cause) at one end, to negligible, where for example the profit is fruit ripe for the picking, or where the fiduciary buys in all the necessary skill from third parties, who may or may not be accessories.

We are also concerned, at least arguably, with the fiduciary's assumption of commercial risk in undertaking the activity which proves later to be profitable. Although not 'named on the tin', risk was treated as relevant in some of the most

[43] [1990] 2 AC 663 (HL) 693–94 (Lord Templeman), 700–01 (Lord Goff).
[44] M Harding, 'Justifying Fiduciary Allowances' in A Robertson and TH Wu (eds), *The Goals of Private Law* (Oxford, Hart, 2009).
[45] See the text accompanying nn 18–19.
[46] *Boardman v Phipps* [1964] 1 WLR 993 (Ch) 1017–18.

famous cases, such as *Warman v Dwyer*.[47] A feature of the account of profits is that, subject perhaps to laches, the beneficiary can, in principle, wait and see whether the unauthorised activity proves to be profitable before electing for a risk-free account instead of equitable compensation for loss, whereas the defaulting fiduciary has to take those risks personally, upfront, always assuming of course that he does not expose trust property to the relevant risks by his unauthorised use of it. Typically the defaulting fiduciary risks his own or his partners' money in the exploitation of the relevant business opportunity. Although the opportunity may itself be regarded as trust property, it is not something which risks being invested and lost at the expense of the beneficiaries in the same sense.

Finally, by way of prelude, we must acknowledge an element of potential conflict between judges and academics when undertaking this exercise. Puisne judges prefer that the principles which are meant to govern the exercise of their discretionary powers are as broad and flexible as possible. That gives them the freedom to provide bespoke solutions to the fact-sets before them which accord with their perception of the justice of the case, while protecting them from being unduly disturbed on appeal. Appellate judges are meant to respect the breadth of the discretion given to the first instance judge. Appellate judges who give lectures or write articles always face the risk that the very issue about which they are asked to declaim in public will land on their plate for decision in the unopened papers awaiting their return to real work. For academics, all this consequential wooliness is what they are there to sort out, and to re-order into nice, neat patterns (like iron filings above a magnet) which contribute to a properly principled and therefore coherent and predictable state of the law.

Thus forewarned, or forearmed, I turn to the competing candidates for a unifying principle behind just allowances for care and skill. As to the first (getting causation and remoteness in by the back door) it cannot be doubted that the application of care and skill by the defaulting fiduciary (and his accessories) is relevant to both causation and remoteness. *Warman v Dwyer* is a good example. There, the business model of the principal (ie, the company) was, in the court's view, doomed to eventual failure, whereas the defendants' competing business was, because of their more skilled approach to its development, a considerable long-term success. Accordingly, the court limited the accountable profits to the first two years of the competing business, treating the remainder as too remote.[48] In a post-*Gray v Global Energy Horizons Corp* environment in England, in which it seems likely that all the profits made would have been regarded as within the scope of the fiduciary duty which the defendants had breached, the same result could be achieved by raising the discretionary allowance to 100 per cent of the profits after the second year.

But I am uncomfortable, to say the least, in elevating what some would say is an elegant dodge around inconvenient authority into a unifying principle. The application of principles of causation and remoteness to an equitable account of profits should stand or fall on their own merits. And there is a risk of double-counting. If the causative effect of the defaulting fiduciary's care and skill is effective in reducing the

[47] (n 30) [32]–[33].
[48] ibid [46], [52].

scope of the account, then there can be no room for the same input to be used as the basis for a just allowance thereafter.

The notion that a generous allowance for care and skill is a safety valve against the rigour of the account producing injustice is a familiar way of looking at cases about 'deserving' fiduciaries, as in *Boardman v Phipps*. That may be saying no more than that the existence of the discretion contributes to a conclusion that account of profits is an equitable remedy that generally does equity. The problem is that the allowance is too narrow a tool for that general purpose. There will be cases where the fiduciary has contributed no significant care and skill to the making of the unauthorised profit, but yet the rigour of the account is perceived by some as disproportionate and unjust. For accessories there is apparently an unqualified discretion to avoid that outcome, but not for fiduciaries.[49] My preference (at least for fiduciaries) is, as already noted, to recognise that the apparent severity of the remedy is no more or less than a just and equitable reflection of the rigour of the duty which has been broken.

The concept of deemed performance advanced by Professor Ho strikes me as coming much closer to qualifying as a unifying principle, but for one problem. The concept requires the account, including the just allowance, to be moulded by reference to what would have happened if the profit had been legitimately generated for the benefit of the beneficiary. Although trustees are, in default of express provision, expected to act gratuitously (and many fiduciaries such as directors will already have been paid), there is nothing wrong with a hypothetical which, in a case where the profit actually was the result of the fiduciary's special care and skill, contemplates the fiduciary saying to the principal: 'Here is a valuable opportunity, but it is beyond the confines of what I have agreed to undertake on my current pay (if any). But I will do it if you agree that I should be rewarded for my contribution of care and skill.' The same could be said for any exposure of the fiduciary's money to commercial risk.

The problem is that the hypothetical which underlies the concept of deemed performance is blind to the question whether the defaulting fiduciary has, in the real world, acted bona fide or dishonestly. While there have been a few cases where a dishonest fiduciary has received a just allowance,[50] few would be able to say, with a straight face, that dishonesty has nothing to do with the exercise of the equitable discretion. True it is that equity is not a penal jurisdiction, but it is not blind to dishonesty. That is, for example, the very bedrock of the equitable liability of an accessory.[51] And a conclusion that a thoroughly dishonest fiduciary ought not to receive a discretionary allowance may be justified on much wider grounds than mere penalty, or even deterrence.

Professor Harding's preferred principle of 'desert' focuses the court on the question what, if anything, does the defaulting fiduciary deserve to receive in all the circumstances. Those circumstances readily include any dishonesty by the fiduciary, not because withholding an allowance is a desirable penalty, but because a dishonest

[49] See *Novoship* (n 13) [116]–[120].
[50] eg, *Murad* (n 11).
[51] See *Royal Brunei Airlines Sdn Bhd v Tan* [1995] 2 AC 378 (PC).

fiduciary does not deserve an allowance in the first place. This formulation certainly deals with the problem about the 'deemed performance' principle, but I wonder if asking what a defendant deserves would add anything very specific to the thinking of a judge seeking to exercise the discretion than simply asking what would be just and equitable in all the circumstances. Nice for judges, but it might leave the academics feeling a bit short-changed.

There remains much to be said, as a unifying principle, for just doing what it says on the tin: ie, deciding what if any compensation the defaulting fiduciary should receive on account of his time, care and skill. But as already noted the trouble with that is that the label on the tin misses out the risking of the fiduciary's own money.

V. CONCLUSION

The moving of the previously mysterious process of equitable accounting for profits from the privacy of the master's room to the glare of open court, law reporting and academic scrutiny, and to the comparative analysis of the development of the common law in jurisdictions around the world, has certainly revealed loose ends in the principles by which the process is, or should be, regulated. So has the ever-increasing role of trusts and fiduciaries in the world of business and commerce. Now that essentially the same process is routinely applied in a variety of eminent but entirely independent common law jurisdictions, there is no reason to suppose that the divergences revealed by this brief overview are all going to be reconciled by one decision in any particular top court. Nor is it to be taken for granted that the issues which continue to separate us will necessarily be regarded as being of sufficient general public importance to warrant being made the subject of permission to appeal, either here or abroad.

But we should not think that the existence of these loose ends significantly weakens the role of the account of profits as a means of redress for breach of the core fiduciary duty of loyalty, or *pour encourager les autres*. The execution of Admiral Byng on his own quarterdeck in 1757 was almost certainly a travesty of justice, but the history of the Royal Navy over the following 50 years strongly suggests that it served what Voltaire thought was its purpose. The very fact that the extent of a liability to account for profits, being enforced by a galloping chancery judge, may look like an 'unruly horse'[52] in the eyes of the fiduciary toying with the temptation to breach his duty may increase rather than reduce the deterrent effect of the remedy. But what really matters is that the duty itself is not accidentally watered down by reason of sympathy for the occasional fiduciary who may be thought to be harshly treated for its breach.

[52] As the Singapore Court of Appeal put it in *UVJ* (n 9) [98].

7

Judicature and Accounts

MATTHEW CONAGLEN*

THIS CHAPTER IS concerned with identifying some of the effects of the Judicature reforms in the realm of accounts. The first is one lingering consequence of the Judicature reforms for the application of fiduciary principles to agents. The second concerns the recognition of a claim for equitable compensation for breach of trust without any need for an account to be taken. The third is whether that separate claim for equitable compensation should operate on principles different from those that would otherwise govern the taking of accounts in equity. Those topics appear somewhat disparate at first glance, but they are related in the sense that the Judicature reforms have caused us to forget important aspects of the history of equitable accounting. While that history does not necessarily provide the only available answers to questions that arise nowadays, it is in the nature of a common law system that its principles are anchored by reference to what our forebears did and so it is, at the very least, useful to understand that history.

I. ACCOUNTS, AGENTS AND FIDUCIARIES

Prior to the Judicature reforms, common law courts and courts of equity exercised a concurrent jurisdiction to take accounts. Without delving too deeply into the history of accounting,[1] by the nineteenth century it was relatively uncommon for an account to be ordered at common law.[2] Accounts were more commonly taken in the equitable jurisdiction 'because, in certain cases, it has better means of ascertaining the rights of the parties'.[3] That concurrent jurisdiction meant the courts exercising equitable

* Professor of Equity and Trusts, Sydney Law School. I am grateful, with the normal disclaimers, to Michael Crawford, Jamie Glister, Jeff Gordon and Bill Gummow for comments on an earlier draft.

[1] For a 930-year history, see J Watson, *The Duty to Account* (Sydney, Federation Press, 2016).

[2] This was not, however, completely unknown: eg, in *Baxter v Hozier* (1839) 5 Bing (NC) 288, 300; 132 ER 1115, 1117, Tindal CJ gave judgment in the Court of Common Pleas against the defendant '*quòd computet*' (which was an order requiring the defendant to account: see Watson (n 1) paras [169] and [173]) – the defendant was a co-owner of linen, which he sold in the Caribbean as a bailiff or agent for all of the co-owners; the plaintiff (another of the co-owners) was successful in forcing the defendant to account at law.

[3] *North-Eastern Railway Co v Martin* (1848) 2 Ph 758, 762; 41 ER 1136, 1138 (Cottenham LC).

jurisdiction had to develop principles to determine whether a particular account should be taken in equity or the parties left to their remedies at common law. It is those principles which generate the point noted here, as they apparently assert that some agents do not owe fiduciary duties, which seems inconsistent with the modern view that 'every agent owes fiduciary duties to his principal'.[4]

It is suggested here that we misunderstand these nineteenth-century dicta if we divorce them from the context in which they were decided, and that the Judicature reforms are part of the reason for us now misunderstanding them because those reforms removed that context. From 1 November 1875, when the Judicature Acts 1873 and 1875 came into force,[5] '[a]ll causes and matters for … the taking of … accounts'[6] were assigned to the Chancery Division of the High Court of Justice. Also from that date, Rules of Court provided that where an account was sought, if no preliminary questions needed to be tried, the court should forthwith make 'an order for the account claimed, with all directions now usual in the Court of Chancery in similar cases'.[7] The combined effect of these changes was that common law accounting had received its final *coup de grâce*, replaced by equitable accounting principles.[8]

That might suggest the topic is no longer noteworthy. Somewhat counter-intuitively, however, that is not the case because the equitable cases prior to the Judicature reforms have left a lasting legacy in the form of rather cryptic references to non-fiduciary agents, which do not sit easily with the widespread modern view of agency as a recognised category of fiduciary relationship. Indeed, the inconsistency between these nineteenth-century dicta and the modern view of agency as a fiduciary relationship has led one commentator to argue that the dicta are mere 'misconceived [and] unsupported assertion'[9] which should be confined to the dustbin of history. It is a small misfortune of the Judicature reforms that they led to this case law being forgotten for a considerable period, in a way that left it poorly explained in modern terms and thus potentially confusing to modern readers. It is suggested here that these dicta can be explained in a way that makes sense of the approach the equitable courts were taking to accounts before the Judicature reforms, and in a way that leaves modern principles regarding the fiduciary status of agents intact.

A. Case Law

The key question in the cases which generate the confusing dicta regarding non-fiduciary agency was whether a defendant's role as agent was sufficient reason to

[4] *Paragon Finance plc v DB Thakerar & Co* [1999] 1 All ER 400 (CA) 416 (Millett LJ). See also *Hospital Products Ltd v United States Surgical Corp* (1984) 156 CLR 41 (HCA) 96.

[5] Judicature Act 1875, s 2.

[6] Judicature Act 1873, s 34(3). See now Senior Courts Act 1981, Sch 1, para 1(f).

[7] Judicature Act 1875, Sch 1, order XV, r 1. See also Supreme Court of Judicature Act 1873, Sch 1, para 8, but this was replaced by the 1875 Act provisions before the 1873 Act came into force: see 1875 Act, s 16. See also Rules of the Supreme Court ('RSC') 1883 (SI 1983/1181) order XV, r 1.

[8] J Story and AE Randall, *Commentaries on Equity Jurisprudence*, 3rd edn (London, Sweet & Maxwell, 1920) 184.

[9] R Flannigan, 'Fiduciary Agency Denied' [2021] *Journal of Business Law* 50, 51.

justify an account being taken in equity, or whether the parties should instead be left to their remedies at common law. There were cases where the defendant's role as an agent for the plaintiff justified an account being taken in equity, particularly where the defendant was a 'confidential agent and steward',[10] whose obligation was to receive rents and manage the estates owned by his principal. And an agency relationship was considered sufficient to justify an equitable accounting in other cases: in *Mackenzie v Johnston*, Leach VC said, 'wherever such a relation exists, a bill will lie [in equity] for an account.'[11]

However, other cases indicate that the mere fact that the case concerned an agency relationship did not necessarily mean that an equitable account would be ordered. In *Hirst v Peirse*, for example, an agent was sued at law on a promissory note, and filed a bill seeking to restrain the legal action and have an account taken in equity, arguing that he was owed a considerable sum for work he had done as agent. Richards CB rejected this bill because it did not involve a mutual account (one where both parties to the arrangement made and received payments on behalf of the other),[12] adding: 'I never yet heard that agency merely was matter of account.'[13] This decision could potentially be explained on the basis that the agent sought the equitable account, rather than the principal: as Turner VC said in *Padwick v Stanley*, '[t]he right of the principal rests upon the trust and confidence reposed in the agent, but the agent reposes no such trust or confidence in the principal',[14] so one can understand why an agent might be refused an equitable accounting, whereas the principal in the agency relationship could perhaps expect one. However, less than four months earlier, in *Phillips v Phillips*,[15] Turner VC had himself refused an equitable accounting where it was the principal who sought it, and who relied on that very status as justification for the account being taken in equity.

The equity courts would also take the account where it was complicated.[16] But where a case was relatively straightforward, so the liabilities could be dealt with adequately at law, a demurrer would be allowed against a bill seeking to have the account taken in equity, including in cases involving agency.[17] Indeed, in *Fluker v Taylor*[18] Kindersley VC indicated that even a mutual account would not necessarily justify an equitable accounting if it was not complicated; although in *Padwick v Hurst*, Romilly MR seemed to consider mutuality as an *alternative* justification to complexity for an equitable accounting.[19]

[10] *Beaumont v Boultbee* (1800) 5 Ves 485, 492; 31 ER 695, 698 (Lord Loughborough LC); affirmed on re-hearing: (1802) 7 Ves 599, 32 ER 241.

[11] *Mackenzie v Johnston* (1819) 4 Madd 373, 375; 56 ER 742, 743 (Sir John Leach VC). See also *Lord Hardwicke v Vernon* (1798) 4 Ves 411, 31 ER 209 and (1808) 14 Ves 504, 33 ER 614; *Massey v Banner* (1819) 4 Madd 413, 417; 56 ER 757, 759; *Smith v Pococke* (1854) 2 Drew 197, 203; 61 ER 694, 696.

[12] *Padwick v Hurst* (1854) 18 Beav 575, 579–80, 52 ER 225, 227.

[13] *Hirst v Peirse* (1817) 4 Price 339, 345; 146 ER 483, 485. Similarly, see *Dinwiddie v Bailey* (1801) 6 Ves 136, 31 ER 979.

[14] *Padwick v Stanley* (1852) 9 Hare 627, 628; 68 ER 664, 664.

[15] *Phillips v Phillips* (1852) 9 Hare 471, 68 ER 596.

[16] *Taff Vale Railway Co v Nixon* (1847) 1 HLC 111, 121–22; 9 ER 695, 699; *O'Connor v Spaight* (1804) 1 Sch & Lef 305, 309.

[17] See, eg, *Freitas v Dos Santos* (1827) 1 Y & J 574, 148 ER 800; *Mare v Lewis* (1869) 4 IR Eq 219, 239.

[18] (1855) 3 Drew 183, 192; 61 ER 873, 876.

[19] *Padwick v Hurst* (n 12) 579, 227. See also *Smith v Leveaux* (1863) 2 De GJ & S 1, 5; 46 ER 274, 275.

The case law contained inconsistent indications as to whether the fiduciary status of an agent could provide a different basis – separate from mutuality and complexity – for ordering an equitable accounting. In *King v Rossett*,[20] for example, a principal sought to have its agent account in equity, relying on what would now be termed the fiduciary nature of the relationship: 'This bill is filed by the principal against his agents, which distinguishes it from the cases cited, which were those of agents against their principal: in the one case, a confidence is reposed; in the other, all the circumstances must be within the knowledge of the party.'[21] Consistently with the approach that Turner VC would later take in *Phillips v Phillips*,[22] Alexander LCB expressly rejected that argument:

> Undoubtedly, a principal is entitled to an account from his agent, and may apply to a Court of Equity for that purpose; but, as I conceive, before that Court will interfere, a ground for its interposition must be laid, by showing an account which cannot fairly be investigated by a Court of Law.[23]

Similarly, in *Navulshaw v Brownrigg*, Lord Cranworth VC rejected an argument that the mere fact of a relationship of agency was sufficient justification for an account being taken in equity:

> [I]n a case in which there is no fraud, not only all the authorities but all the text-books shew that this Court will not decree an agent to account to his principal, unless the case is one which is not capable of being conveniently inquired into in a Court of law.[24]

But there were indications elsewhere in the cases that the fiduciary status of an agent would justify an account being taken in equity. In *Foley v Hill*,[25] for example, in explaining that a customer is not entitled to an equitable account against his banker, Lord Cottenham LC referred to the fact that the banker

> does not hold [a] fiduciary character, and therefore there is no such original jurisdiction; and if there be no such original jurisdiction growing out of the relative situations of the parties, then, to see if the account is of such a nature that it cannot be taken at law, we are to look to the account itself […] We find no complicated account at all here.[26]

The banker's relationship with his client was contrasted with that of an agent or factor,[27] suggesting that the fiduciary character of the latter types of relationships could justify an account being taken in equity. Similarly, in *Padwick v Hurst*, having referred to mutuality and complexity as bases for accounts being taken in equity, Romilly MR separated these from 'the fiduciary relation and the trust reposed by the

[20] *King v Rossett* (1827) 2 Y & J 33, 148 ER 820.
[21] ibid 35, 820.
[22] See n 15 above.
[23] *King v Rossett* (n 20) 35, 821.
[24] *Navulshaw v Brownrigg* (1851) 1 Sim NS 573, 584–85; 61 ER 221, 226. Affirmed on appeal: (1852) 2 De GM & G 441, 42 ER 943. See also *Barry v Stevens* (1862) 31 Beav 258, 268–69; 54 ER 1137, 1141; *Blyth v Whiffin* (1872) 27 LT (NS) 330 (VC) 334.
[25] *Foley v Hill* (1848) 2 HL Cas 28, 9 ER 1002.
[26] ibid 39–40, 1007.
[27] ibid 35–36, 37 and 43; 1005 and 1008.

principal in the agent' as different justifications for 'bills for an account by a principal against his agent'.[28]

In other cases, decided at around the same time, the courts continued to recognise the fiduciary status of the agent as a separate basis for an account being taken in equity, but did so in a way that suggested that agents are not always fiduciaries and so the agency relationship would not always justify an equitable accounting. These cases further embed the suggestion that an agent was not necessarily a fiduciary. In *Hemings v Pugh*,[29] for example, Stuart VC allowed a demurrer against a bill seeking an equitable account, but emphasised that mutuality was not the only justification for an equitable accounting:

> *[W]henever an agency partakes of a fiduciary character this Court has jurisdiction*, and will direct an account, although the receipts and payments are all on one side, and there are no mutual payments between the parties. That rule has not been shaken by the decision in *Phillips v Phillips*.[30] (emphasis added)

Importantly for present purposes, the demurrer was allowed because Stuart VC considered that 'there is no allegation of any mutual dealings, or of *anything fiduciary* in the relation of the parties, who on the bill are stated as *mere principal and agent*.'[31] (emphasis added)

Consistently with *Hemings v Pugh*, in *Makepeace v Rogers*,[32] in the Court of Appeal in Chancery, Knight Bruce LJ said that he did not think Turner VC had intended, in *Phillips v Phillips*, to suggest that a bill for an account in equity could lie only where there were mutual accounts:

> The existence of a fiduciary relation between the parties, as, for example (as was the case here) that of principal and agent, was sufficient to confer jurisdiction on this Court, and allegations of fraud or special circumstances were unnecessary.[33]

Turner LJ himself explained in *Makepeace v Rogers* that he had decided *Phillips v Phillips* as he did because 'the bill made no case of general agency, alleging only an isolated agency transaction connected with the sale by the Defendant of some railway shares belonging to the Plaintiff'.[34] This again suggested that the fiduciary nature of an agency relationship could justify an account being taken in equity, as a separate basis from mutuality or complexity, but at the same time these cases suggest that not all agencies involve a fiduciary relationship of the relevant kind.

B. Explanations

These dicta are confusing, but they can be understood if one bears in mind that 'vocabulary can stay the same over hundreds of years, even as its meaning

[28] *Padwick v Hurst* (n 12) 579, 227.
[29] (1863) 4 Giff 456, 66 ER 785.
[30] ibid 459, 787.
[31] ibid.
[32] (1865) 4 De GJ & S 649, 46 ER 1070.
[33] ibid 653, 1072.
[34] ibid 654, 1072.

changes'.[35] That is definitely so for the 'fiduciary' concept, which had a range of meanings, particularly in the Victorian period.[36] In the present context, the cases seem to deploy the fiduciary descriptor in two subtly different senses, each of which links to different aspects of the equitable jurisdiction. Understood in this way, these dicta from the pre-Judicature agency cases can be squared with modern principles regarding the fiduciary status of agents.

i. General Agency

First, the fiduciary label was sometimes used, as Turner LJ did in *Makepeace v Rogers*, to reflect the idea of a general agency, contrasting with a special or isolated agency transaction.[37] The concept of general agency was used in the nineteenth century to refer

> not merely [to] a person substituted in the place of another for transacting all manner of business (since there are few instances in common use of an agency of that description), but a person whom a man puts in his place to transact all his business of a particular kind. [In contrast,] a special agent [is] employed about one specific act, or certain specific acts only.[38]

The Court of Chancery did not have a large judicial manpower,[39] and so it is understandable that it would restrict access to its accounting processes in the concurrent jurisdiction – where other remedies were available at common law – to cases where it could offer advantages over the common law. A 'special' agency would not normally be as complicated as a general agency, and so might not justify deploying equity's machinery. To describe that distinction using fiduciary terminology is somewhat confusing to modern readers, but it seems this was one sense in which the nineteenth-century judges used the fiduciary label when identifying whether an account would be taken in equity.

ii. Trust-Like Arrangements

A second, more central, sense in which the fiduciary descriptor was used in these cases referred to the defendant's management of *property* for the plaintiff. As Jeremy said, describing the circumstances in which an account would be taken in equity:

> The relation of principal and agent generally is one of great extent. It seems to comprise all cases in which one is authorized to act for another; but *with reference to the subject*

[35] A Televantos, 'Losing the Fiduciary Requirement for Equitable Tracing Claims' (2017) 133 *LQR* 492, 492.

[36] LS Sealy, 'Fiduciary Relationships' [1962] *CLJ* 69, 70–72; LS Sealy, 'The Director as Trustee' [1967] *CLJ* 83, 85–86; Televantos (n 35) 493, 513.

[37] See also *Mare v Lewis* (n 17) 240.

[38] W Paley, *The Law of Principal and Agent* (London, Butterworth, 1812) 139–40. See also, eg, J Story, *Law of Agency*, 5th edn (Boston, Little Brown & Co, 1857) 18, 146; JW Smith and GM Dowdeswell, *A Compendium of Mercantile Law*, 6th edn (London, Stevens & Norton, 1859) 134–35; CM Smith, *Master and Servant*, 2nd edn (London, H Sweet, 1860) 165, 168.

[39] JH Baker, *An Introduction to English Legal History*, 5th edn (Oxford, OUP, 2019) 122.

> *now before us, it is limited to those in which the control or management of property is so confided.*[40] (emphasis added)

A defendant's management or control of the plaintiff's property meant the defendant was operating in a way which bore similarities to the role of a trustee. It was clear that a trustee would be compelled to render an account in equity, in its exclusive jurisdiction, 'upon the mere fact of the relation which subsists between him and his *cestui que trust*'.[41] It is thus understandable that someone who controlled property of another could sensibly be subjected to a similar accounting regime, notwithstanding that the agency relationship meant that common law procedures and remedies could also apply. The words 'trust' and 'fiduciary' were much more fluid in their meanings in this period: this sort of fiduciary control of another's property was often described as a trust.[42] As that language became more precise, the fiduciary label came to be used to refer to relationships that, while not strictly trusts, were sufficiently trust-like to justify similar judicial treatment.

In other words, this approach reflects the function that the fiduciary concept served, particularly historically, in exporting the legal incidents of one form of relationship to other similar relationships; and the paradigm fiduciary relationship from which fiduciary duties were exported in this fashion is the relationship between trustee and beneficiary.[43] The 'fiduciary relationship has developed by analogy from the trust relationship.'[44] That analogical reasoning process can be seen at work in numerous cases.[45] In *Foley v Hill*, for example, in explaining why an equitable account would not be ordered against a banker, Lord Cottenham LC differentiated the banker's position from that of a factor or agent in the following way:

> [A]s between principal and factor, there is no question whatever that that description of case … has always been held to be within the jurisdiction of a Court of Equity, because the party *partakes of the character of a trustee*. … So it is with regard to *an agent dealing with any property*; … though he is not a trustee according to the strict technical meaning of the word, he is *quasi* a trustee for that particular transaction for which he is engaged; and therefore in these cases the Courts of Equity have assumed jurisdiction. But the *analogy* entirely fails, as it seems to me, when you come to consider the relative situation of a banker and his customer.[46] (emphasis added)

[40] G Jeremy, *A Treatise on the Equity Jurisdiction of the High Court of Chancery* (London, J & WT Clarke, 1828) 513. See also IP Cory, *A Practical Treatise on Accounts*, 2nd edn (London, W Pickering, 1839) 246–48.

[41] Jeremy (n 40) 523.

[42] Televantos (n 35) 497–98. See, eg, *Burdett v Willett* (1708) 2 Vern 638, 23 ER 1017; *Charitable Corp v Sutton* (1742) 2 Atk 400, 405–06; 26 ER 642, 644–45; and *Charitable Corp v Sutton* (1742) 9 Mod 349, 355; 88 ER 500, 503.

[43] *Re West of England & South Wales District Bank, ex p Dale & Co* (1879) 11 Ch D 772 (Ch) 778.

[44] *Gwembe Valley Devt Co Ltd v Koshy (No 3)* [2003] EWCA Civ 1048, [2004] 1 BCLC 131 [89] (Mummery LJ).

[45] In addition to the cases discussed in the text, see also *Spackman v Evans* (1868) LR 3 HL 171, 189–90; *Re Gresham Life Assurance Society* (1872) LR 8 Ch App 446 (CA) 449; *Re Lands Allotment Co* [1894] 1 Ch 616 (CA) 631, 638; *New Lambton Land and Coal Co Ltd v London Bank of Australia Ltd* (1904) 1 CLR 524 (HCA) 541–42; *Selangor United Rubber Estates Ltd v Cradock (No 3)* [1968] 1 WLR 1555 (Ch) 1575; *Wallersteiner v Moir (No 2)* [1975] 1 QB 373 (CA) 397–98.

[46] *Foley v Hill* (n 25) 35–36, 1005.

It made sense to assert accounting control over relationships that were similar to those involved in trusts, while refusing to make those processes available in other agency cases where a remedy was available at law and where the facts were neither complicated nor similar to a trust arrangement. It is suggested that this is the core meaning of the statements in the cases that an agent would not be held to account in equity if he were not a fiduciary.

This explains Lord Hatherley LC's observation in *Moxon v Bright* that '[i]t was not every agent who held a fiduciary position'.[47] Immediately preceding that observation, he had noted that there

> were numerous cases shewing that where the relation of principal and agent had imposed a trust upon the agent, the Court would entertain a bill for an account, and the only difficulty was in determining what constituted this species of trust. … *Foley v Hill* shewed that though a banker was the agent of the customer for many purposes, they were not such as would constitute a trust. … [T]he sole point in this suit was whether there existed between them an agency in which a fiduciary position was created.[48]

Similarly, in *Hemings v Pugh*, Stuart VC indicated that an account could be obtained against an agent in equity *if* the agent were a fiduciary, even if the payments and receipts were not mutual; he gave the instance of a steward or land agent as an example of 'an agency [that] partakes of a fiduciary character'.[49] And in *Makepeace v Rogers* – which Knight Bruce and Turner LJJ both considered a clear case of 'fiduciary relation between the parties',[50] justifying an account in equity – the defendant had for many years been employed as the plaintiff's 'agent and manager of his estates'.[51]

The nineteenth-century dicta which suggest that agents are not necessarily fiduciary are best understood as reflecting the availability of an accounting in equity in the Court of Chancery's concurrent jurisdiction. Relief would be available against an agent at law, but an account could be taken in equity if (a) this was necessary because the common law process was not sufficiently nuanced to the case, as where the accounts were mutual or otherwise complicated (including in cases involving a general agency); or (b) the relationship between the principal and agent bore characteristics similar to those involved in a trust (in the form of control or management of the plaintiff's property). If there was no reason for the account to be taken in equity, the parties would be left to their remedies at law.

While this is a counter-intuitive example of the lasting impact of the Judicature reforms, what it illustrates is the importance of a recognition of the changes that those reforms wrought which are not so well noticed in modern times – in this case

[47] *Moxon v Bright* (1869) LR 4 Ch App 292 (CA) 294.

[48] ibid 294–95. Similarly, see *Massey v Banner* (n 11) 417, 759; *Burdick v Garrick* (1870) LR 5 Ch App 233 (CA) 240, 243; *Ex parte Cooke* (1876) 4 Ch D 123 (CA) 128; *Marris v Ingram* (1879) 13 Ch D 338 (Ch) 344, 345; *New Zealand and Australian Land Co v Watson* (1881) 7 QBD 374 (CA) 382, 383–84; *Piddocke v Burt* [1894] 1 Ch 343 (Ch) 346; *John v Dodwell & Co Ltd* [1918] AC 563 (PC) 569.

[49] *Hemings v Pugh* (n 29) 459, 787.

[50] *Makepeace v Rogers* (n 32) 653, 1072.

[51] ibid 652, 1072.

removing the distinction between the principles governing accounting at common law and in equity – and an appreciation of the context of the case law preceding those changes. Failure to appreciate that context runs the risk of dicta in those cases being misunderstood in modern times. Despite the terminology used in these cases, these dicta were not concerned with whether the defendant agents owed duties of the kind that would, in modern legal parlance, be referred to as fiduciary duties.

II. ORIGINS OF DIRECT CLAIM FOR EQUITABLE COMPENSATION

The second and third aspects of the Judicature reforms addressed here are more directly concerned with the effect of those reforms on the state of the modern law. Both are also concerned with the way in which accounts were taken in equity, particularly against trustees, but they raise questions as to whether the modern claim for equitable compensation for breach of trust – without any account being taken – is or should be governed by different principles from those applied to the taking of trust accounts. The Judicature reforms are again part of that picture, albeit not the entire landscape.

In recent years, claims seeking a monetary remedy against trustees following a breach of trust have often been pleaded and considered as claims for equitable compensation for breach of trust, rather than as claims seeking an account and consequential remedies. The traditional accounting approach involved two steps, as Lord Millett NPJ explained in *Libertarian Investments v Hall*:

> an account does not in itself provide the plaintiff with a remedy; it is merely the first step in a process which enables him to identify and quantify any deficit in the trust fund and seek the appropriate means by which it may be made good. Once the plaintiff has been provided with an account he can falsify and surcharge it.[52] If the account discloses an unauthorised disbursement the plaintiff may falsify it, that is to say ask for the disbursement to be disallowed. This will produce a deficit which the defendant must make good, either in specie or in money. Where the defendant is ordered to make good the deficit by the payment of money, the award is sometimes described as the payment of equitable compensation; but it is not compensation for loss but restitutionary or restorative.[53]

[52] As Dr Turner has pointed out, these labels were strictly associated with challenges to settled (or stated) accounts: PG Turner, 'Want of Causation as a Defence to Liability for Misapplication of Trust Assets' in PS Davies, S Douglas and J Goudkamp (eds), *Defences in Equity* (Oxford, Hart, 2018) 155, 159–60. In an open account (one which had not yet been finalised and agreed, and so was not settled), the labels of 'charge' and 'discharge' were more appropriate. The trustee was charged with (the value of) assets that he had, or should have, received; and discharged where assets were legitimately transferred away or otherwise lost without a breach of duty: see also SB Elliott, *Compensation Claims Against Trustees* (Oxford DPhil, 2002) 107–15. However, as Turner also recognised, the labels of falsification and surcharge have become so prevalent in explaining the taking of accounts (largely because of the influence of Lord Millett: see PJ Millett, 'Equity's Place in the Law of Commerce' (1998) 114 *LQR* 214, 225–26) that it is perhaps easier just to use those: see, eg, *AIB Group (UK) plc v Mark Redler & Co Solicitors* [2014] UKSC 58, [2015] AC 1503 [52]. Falsification is the equivalent of disputing a discharge, and surcharge involves an argument that the trustee either received something for which he did not account, or should have received an asset if he had been acting consistently with his duty.

[53] *Libertarian Investments Ltd v Hall* [2013] HKCFA 93, (2013) 16 HKCFAR 681 [168]. See also *Barnett v Creggy* [2016] EWCA Civ 1004, [2017] Ch 273 [22].

One question which the modern claim for equitable compensation generates is whether that different form of claim requires or justifies any difference in the principles which the court applies to calculate the quantum of compensation payable by the trustee. The genesis of the direct claim to equitable compensation could potentially provide part of – albeit not the whole – the answer to that question, but that genesis remains elusive. The discussion here identifies indicators in the case law of the genesis of the separate claim and the role that the Judicature reforms had in it.

As Heydon, Leeming and Turner say, it seems that '[i]n the nineteenth century a more direct means of recovering loss came about when it became possible to sue for particular breaches of trust in isolation without using the equity courts' accounting procedures at all'.[54] They cite *Coppard v Allen*, where Turner LJ explained that a claim could be brought against a trustee to establish a breach of trust without necessarily joining the other trustees, which contrasts with the situation where an accounting was sought, where all trustees would need to be joined.[55]

But there are other indications in the case law of the courts developing an ability to focus directly on the award necessary to rectify a breach of trust, and the Judicature reforms contributed to this development.

One example of this can be seen in the Judicature reforms loosening the previously sharp distinction between common accounts and accounts taken on the basis of wilful default: prior to the Judicature Acts, if a common accounting identified instances of wilful default, the trustees could not be charged with wilful default without a separate suit, which required leave from the court, unless the court's original order had reserved power to make further directions for a wilful default accounting.[56] 'But since the Judicature Act, the stringency of the rule has been somewhat relaxed',[57] to the point where 'under the new practice an order charging him with wilful default may be made at any time on a proper case being made'.[58] The ability to provide a remedy which directly addressed an identified breach of trust, without unnecessary procedural obstacles being thrown in the way, seems consistent with the development of the court's ability to provide a remedy for identified breaches directly without a full account needing to be taken.

At around the same time, the courts were given the ability to provide judicial advice on specific questions concerning the administration of a trust, without needing to take over the entire execution of the trust in order to resolve the particular point, as had previously been the case with an order for general administration of the trust.[59]

[54] JD Heydon, MJ Leeming and PG Turner, *Meagher, Gummow and Lehane's Equity: Doctrines and Remedies*, 5th edn (Chatswood, LexisNexis, 2015) para [23-030].

[55] *Coppard v Allen* (1864) 2 De G J & S 173, 180–81; 46 ER 341, 344.

[56] *Hodson v Ball* (1842) 1 Ph 177, 41 ER 599; *Jones v Morrall* (1852) 2 Sim NS 241, 249–50; 61 ER 333, 336; *Partington v Reynolds* (1858) 4 Drew 253, 258–59; 62 ER 98, 100. For the difference between wilful default and common accounts, see M Conaglen, 'Equitable Compensation for Breach of Trust: Off *Target*' (2016) 40 *Melbourne University Law Review* 126, 129–35.

[57] HG Hanbury, 'Forms of Account Against Executors and Trustees' (1936) 52 *LQR* 365, 366.

[58] *Job v Job* (1877) 6 Ch D 562 (Ch) 564. An adequate pleading of wilful default was still necessary: *Mayer v Murray* (1878) 8 Ch D 424 (Ch) 426–27. See also *Re Symons* (1882) 21 Ch D 757 (Ch) 761; *Smith v Armitage* (1883) 24 Ch D 727 (Ch) 728–29; *Re Youngs* (1885) 30 Ch D 421 (CA) 431–32; HW Seton and others, *Forms of Judgments and Orders*, 7th edn (London, Stevens & Sons, 1912) 1121.

[59] *McLean v Burns Philp Trustee Co Pty Ltd* (1985) 2 NSWLR 623 (NSWSC) 635.

This development began before the 1873–1875 Judicature reforms, with the enactment of section 30 of the Law of Property Amendment Act 1859,[60] which enabled a trustee to apply by petition or summons to a judge of the Court of Chancery 'for the opinion, advice, or direction of such judge on any question respecting the management or administration of the trust property'. However, this procedure could only be used where the question was not difficult and required no factual inquiries, and it was not available for questions of construction.[61] The ability to focus on particular questions was enhanced by the Rules of the Supreme Court 1883, promulgated in the wake of the 1873–1875 reforms. The 1883 rules included detailed rules regarding the work of the Chancery Division in Chambers, which had not been present in the initial rules in Schedule 1 to the Judicature Act 1875. Importantly, the new Rules included Order LV, rule 3 which enabled trustees or beneficiaries to take out an originating summons returnable in the chambers of a Chancery Division judge to determine questions without an administration; and they emphasised in Order LV, rule 10 that '[i]t shall not be obligatory on the Court or a judge to pronounce or make a judgment or order … for the administration of any trust … if the questions between the parties can be properly determined without such judgment or order'.

Three decisions in the first half of 1885 demonstrate that the courts quickly appreciated the flexibility that the new Rules afforded them.[62] In *Re Wilson*, some of the beneficiaries and one trustee applied for a general administration order, which was opposed by the other trustees and beneficiaries. Pearson J made the order, as a number of the beneficiaries were 'infants who cannot examine [the] accounts for themselves',[63] but he observed that the new power to resolve questions without administration was 'very useful',[64] commenting that '[t]here were no means, according to the old practice, of bringing isolated questions under a will before the Court for its determination except by an administration suit',[65] which could involve unnecessary expense.

As Fry LJ said in *Re Blake*, '[t]he object of the orders is to prevent the general administration of the estate when the questions in controversy can otherwise be properly determined',[66] and if an application for general administration turned out to have been unnecessary because the questions could have been resolved by that more direct route then the party seeking the administration order could be made to pay costs. Further, as Cotton LJ observed:

> Where there are questions which cannot properly be determined without some accounts and inquiries or directions which would form part of an ordinary administration decree, then the right of the party to have the decree is not taken away, but the Court may direct

[60] 22 & 23 Vict, c 35. See also Law of Property Amendment Act 1860, s 9.

[61] *Re Mockett's Will* (1860) Johns 628, 630; 70 ER 571, 571; GO Morgan and EA Wurtzburg, *Morgan's Chancery Acts and Orders*, 6th edn (London, Stevens & Sons, 1885) 103.

[62] The Rules were also applied to administration actions commenced before, but tried after, they came into operation: *Re Llewellyn* (1883) 25 Ch D 66 (Ch).

[63] *Re Wilson* (1885) 28 Ch D 457 (Ch) 463.

[64] ibid 460.

[65] ibid.

[66] *Re Blake* (1885) 29 Ch D 913 (CA) 919.

> the order simply to those points which will enable the question which requires to be adjudicated upon to be settled.[67]

In *Re Gyhon*, the plaintiff had brought a claim for breach of trust against trustees of a deceased estate, alleging the trustees had sold part of the estate but not accounted for the proceeds of sale, and that one trustee had mortgaged part of the estate in breach of trust and applied the loan moneys to his own purposes. The plaintiff then took out a summons for an order for ordinary accounts and inquiries regarding the estate, as well as an inquiry into the mortgages. The Court of Appeal refused to make these orders because the specific inquiries turned on whether there had been a breach of trust, which could not yet be known, and the ordinary accounts may turn out to be unnecessary once the result of the claims for breach of trust was known.[68]

Campbell v Gillespie[69] provides an illustration of the court's use of the new Rules to provide direct relief for specific breaches. A debtor created a trust to pay creditors and later assigned his interest in the trust (essentially an interest in the surplus) to his wife for value. Three years after that, the trustee transferred the surplus trust assets to the wife, certifying that the trusts were fully executed. A further two years later, the trustee sent the trust account books away for destruction, unwisely but honestly believing them no longer to be needed. The wife filed proceedings the following month, claiming an account of all the trustee's dealings as trustee, on a wilful default footing. The trustee resisted that claim, but admitted three particular transactions that could be criticised. Cozens-Hardy J rejected the wilful default plea, but then turned to the question of what relief was justified. His approach again reflects the impact, and his approval, of the Judicature reforms:

> Under the old law I think it is plain that the [plaintiff[70]] would have been entitled, as a matter of right, to a common account against the defendant. There has been no release; there has been no settled account; there has been nothing upon which the defendant could rely by way of defence. But happily, under Order LV, r10, I have now a discretion, and I am not bound to give the plaintiff a decree for a common account if the questions between the parties can be properly determined without such a decree.[71]

Cozens-Hardy J noted that the trustee had kept proper accounts, had had them audited by accountants around the time of the transfer to the plaintiff, and the plaintiff had not asked for any further accounts until she instituted her suit. While he could not acquit the defendant trustee of all misconduct in respect of the three transactions, Cozens-Hardy J refused to order a full account of the entire period that the trust had operated, as 'I think I can properly determine the questions between the

[67] ibid 916. Similarly, even where an instance of wilful default was proven, the courts could order that an account be taken on a wilful default footing in respect of that breach *alone*, leaving the rest of the account to be taken on the usual basis, where there was nothing to suggest that other breaches of trust had occurred: *Re Tebbs (deceased)* [1976] 1 WLR 924 (Ch) 930.

[68] *Re Gyhon* (1885) 29 Ch D 834 (CA) 837–38.

[69] [1900] 1 Ch 225 (Ch).

[70] The report reads 'defendant' here, but that is clearly an error.

[71] *Campbell v Gillespie* (n 69) 228.

parties without giving the plaintiff a full decree.'[72] In each of the three improper transactions, the sums were clear and so judgment was given directly.

These cases are consistent with a judicial willingness – and, indeed, a growing desire and insistence – to focus attention on the issues that would resolve the dispute at hand. That attitude cannot be attributed solely to the Judicature reforms, as there is also evidence of the courts wanting to avoid unnecessary procedural complexity before those reforms came about.[73] But the Judicature reforms – particularly the changes to the procedural rules – provided the courts with a further string to that bow, which they grasped with both hands.

By the turn of the twentieth century,[74] Warrington J was able to say, in *Re Wrightson*, that '[i]n cases of breach of trust relief is given in respect of those specific breaches of trust which are proved, and in respect of those only.'[75] He also said that

> if wilful default is alleged and if an instance is proved, then the trustees are not in a position to claim to have against them the ordinary account only, but the account must be directed on the footing of wilful default. In my judgment that rule does not apply to cases of breach of trust.[76]

However, while these statements appear to indicate a separate claim for breach of trust, what Warrington J was referring to was the difference between the two traditional forms of account (common accounting and wilful default accounting), rather than between accounts and claims for equitable compensation. His point was to reject the proposition that proof of any breach of trust would necessarily lead to the 'roving inquiry' that a wilful default accounting entails,[77] rather than to show a difference between claims for equitable compensation for breach of trust and claims for accounts following a breach. Indeed, he said that 'in the case of a breach of trust there is no general form of account which is substituted for the common account'.[78]

The precise genesis of the distinct claim for equitable compensation for breach of trust, absent an accounting, is thus difficult to pinpoint, but it seems likely that it originated in cases where a specific breach of trust was proved and where it was sufficiently clear to the court what remedy was needed to repair that breach without

[72] ibid 229.

[73] See, eg, in the context of an account of profits argument, *Parker v McKenna* (1874–75) LR 10 Ch App 96 (Divisional Court) 122. See also TH Haddan, *The Administrative Jurisdiction of the Court of Chancery* (London, W Maxwell, 1862) 54.

[74] A provision equivalent to RSC 1883, Order LV, r 10 continued into the 20th century in RSC 1965 (SI 1965/1776), Order 85, r 5(1). That rule was, in turn, carried over into the Civil Procedure Rules 1998 by Pt 50 and Sch 1. However, RSC 1965, Order 85 was removed from the CPR when Pt 64 was introduced by the Civil Procedure (Amendment) Rules 2002, SI 2002/2058. Neither Pt 64 nor PDs 64A and 64B replicate the substance of r 5(1) of Order 85. Presumably it was thought that a statutory provision was no longer required to guide the courts' decision as to whether a general administration order was appropriate, given such orders had generally been considered unnecessary for so long.

[75] *Re Wrightson* [1908] 1 Ch 789 (Ch) 799–800.

[76] ibid 800.

[77] ibid 799.

[78] ibid. See also *Re Stevens* [1898] 1 Ch 162 (CA) 176–77.

needing to send the case off for an account to be taken of the trustee's management of the entire trust fund.[79] As Patten LJ said more recently:

> From the 19th century onwards one finds an increasing use of the Court of Chancery's power to entertain actions based on particular breaches of trust for which compensation would be awarded without going through the cumbersome and often extremely lengthy process of taking an account. The modern term for this is equitable compensation but it has its roots in a much older jurisdiction and practice.[80]

III. PRINCIPLES FOR CALCULATING EQUITABLE COMPENSATION

The third impact of the Judicature reforms to be noticed here links with the second: it concerns the degree to which those reforms might have altered the principles for calculating the sum of equitable compensation that a trustee or other fiduciary steward must pay following a breach of their stewardship duties. In particular, a question arises as to whether equitable compensation for breach of trust should be calculated by reference to the principles commonly applied in assessing damages for breaches of contract or for torts, or instead should be calculated in accordance with traditional accounting principles that were designed to restore the trust estate without considering issues such as causation, foreseeability and remoteness.[81]

As the previous section indicates, the recognition and development of a direct claim for equitable compensation – without seeking an account and consequential remedies – does not appear to have been intended to alter the outcome in individual cases. The difficulty in pinpointing the genesis of the separate claim for equitable compensation makes it hard to be categorical, but if the claim for equitable compensation was simply a more direct and focused way of redressing a breach of trust, without needing to go through the process of accounting because that was thought unnecessary in the instant case, the quantum of the remedy ought not to differ from what would have been ordered following an account being taken.[82] Further, insofar as the development of the separate equitable compensation remedy was assisted by the Judicature reforms, that further supports the view that a substantive change to the quantum of equitable compensation payable by a breaching trustee was not – at that stage, at least – intended. As Jessel MR said of the Judicature reforms:

> It is stated very plainly that the main object of the Act was to assimilate the transaction of Equity business and Common Law business by different Courts of Judicature. It has been

[79] See, eg, *Libertarian v Hall* (n 53) [130]–[140], [174].

[80] *Barnett v Creggy* (n 53) [22].

[81] *Re Dawson (deceased); Union Fidelity Trustee Co Ltd v Perpetual Trustee Co Ltd* [1966] 2 NSWR 211 (NSWSC) 214–16.

[82] See, in a related context, *Conway v Fenton* (1888) 40 Ch D 512 (Ch) 515–16; *Re Medland* (1889) 41 Ch D 476 (CA) 480, 492. See also R Chambers, 'Liability' in PBH Birks & A Pretto (eds), *Breach of Trust* (Oxford, Hart, 2002) 1, 22; PG Turner, 'Measuring Equitable Compensation for Breach of Fiduciary Duty' [2014] *CLJ* 257, 257.

> sometimes inaccurately called 'the fusion of Law and Equity'; but it was not any fusion, or anything of the kind; it was the vesting in one tribunal the administration of Law and Equity in every cause, action, or dispute which should come before that tribunal. That was the meaning of the Act. Then, as to that very small number of cases in which there is an actual conflict, it was decided that in all cases where the rules of Equity and Law were in conflict the rules of Equity should prevail.[83]

The last sentence of that passage refers to section 25(11) of the Judicature Act 1873, which effectively codified the outcome of the *Earl of Oxford's Case*.[84] 'In principle, the outcome of a dispute would be no different after the Judicature Acts from the result under the old divided jurisdictions of courts of common law and equity.'[85] Consistently with that, one would expect that the outcome of a claim for equitable compensation would not be substantively different from what the court would have ordered if an accounting process had been gone through before remedial orders were made. As Lord Reed JSC put it in *AIB Group (UK) plc v Mark Redler & Co Solicitors*, '[t]he measure of compensation is therefore the same as would be payable on an accounting, although the procedure is different'.[86]

It was, therefore, somewhat surprising to find Lord Toulson JSC open his judgment in that same case with the sentence: '140 years after the Judicature Act 1873 (36 & 37 Vict c 66), the stitching together of equity and the common law continues to cause problems at the seams.'[87] In *AIB*, the claimants had brought their claim as a suit for equitable compensation for breach of trust.[88] It is difficult to see how common law considerations arise in such a claim, as it would previously have been dealt with in the exclusively equitable jurisdiction, and so the Judicature Act 1873 should not have affected the case.

Despite that perhaps unfortunate choice of rhetorical flourish at the beginning of his judgment, the tenor of Lord Toulson's judgment suggests that what he had in mind was not so much the impact of the Judicature Act 1873 directly, but rather the development of legal and equitable principles over time. As Jessel MR said in *Re Hallett's Estate*:

> it must not be forgotten that the rules of Courts of Equity are not, like the rules of the Common Law, supposed to have been established from time immemorial. It is perfectly

[83] *Salt v Cooper* (1880) 16 Ch D 544 (CA) 549. See also *Britain v Rossiter* (1879) 11 QBD 123 (CA) 129; *Joseph v Lyons* (1884) 15 QBD 280 (CA) 285–86, 287; R Evershed, 'Reflections on the Fusion of Law and Equity After 75 Years' (1954) 70 *LQR* 326, 327 and 329; MJ Leeming, 'Equity, the Judicature Acts and Restitution' (2011) 5 *Journal for Equity* 199, 213–15; MJW Lobban, 'What Did the Makers of the Judicature Acts Understand by "Fusion"?' in JCP Goldberg, HE Smith and PG Turner (eds), *Equity and Law: Fusion and Fission* (Cambridge, CUP, 2019) 70. Jessel MR's apparently contradictory dicta, two years later in *Walsh v Lonsdale* (1882) 21 Ch D 9 (CA) 14, can be explained in a way that does not require treating the Judicature Acts as having eradicated the distinction between common law and equity: see *Chan v Cresdon Pty Ltd* (1989) 168 CLR 242 (HCA) 250–55.

[84] See (1615) 1 Ch Rep 1, 6–7, 10; 21 ER 485, 487; and see James I's proclamation of 18 July 1616: Cary 133–35, 21 ER 65.

[85] J McGhee and S Elliott (eds), *Snell's Equity*, 34th edn (London, Sweet & Maxwell, 2020) para [1-017]; and see paras [1-009]–[1-010], [1-021].

[86] *AIB Group* (n 52) [91]; see also [108].

[87] ibid [1].

[88] The preliminary issues dealt with in the case *solely* concerned breach of trust: see *AIB Group (UK) plc v Mark Redler & Co* [2012] EWHC 35 (Ch), [2012] PNLR 16 [4].

> well known that they have been established from time to time – altered, improved, and refined from time to time.[89]

Lord Toulson did not favour the traditional accounting principles that would have been used to determine the quantum of equitable compensation payable by a trustee, saying that '[t]here is something wrong with a state of the law which makes it necessary to create fairy tales'.[90] Instead, he preferred to apply causation concepts from contract law, calculating the compensation by reference to the position that would have been achieved had the trust been properly performed, rather than the traditional approach of restoring assets which were wrongfully disbursed from the trust fund.[91]

The point here is not to quibble with that policy decision, but to recognise that it is a policy decision to develop the law, and that it is one which was neither generated nor required by the Judicature Acts and their allied procedural reforms. The development has taken place because the traditional principles by which equity determined the quantum of equitable compensation payable by a trustee are considered unsuited to the modern dynamics of a trust that is used as part of a commercial transaction.[92] Lord Toulson made clear that he thought that equitable compensation should be calculated, in this sort of case at least, by the application of the same principles that would be applied if the claimant had sought damages for breach of contract at common law. That was, he said, not because of the Judicature Acts – which he recognised would have required the equitable rules to be applied if there was any conflict – but rather because the trust was created as part of the machinery for the performance of a contract, and it would be artificial to consider the trust as a distinct legal relationship, separate from the contractual context in which it arose.[93] In other words, the 'seam' between common law and equity that Lord Toulson had in mind in his opening sentence, arose from the fact that the trust was created in the context of performance of a contract, and the outcome of the claim needed to reflect that fact.

It has long been recognised that there is 'no dichotomy between [trust and contract because a] contractual relationship provides one of the most common bases for the establishment or implication and for the definition of a trust'.[94] However, it does not follow that the doctrines applicable to trusts necessarily need to change to match contract law. A trustee is holding property subject to onerous duties to devote that property to the benefit of another. That arrangement leaves the beneficiary vulnerable

[89] *Re Hallett's Estate* (1880) 13 Ch D 696 (CA) 710. See also *Andrews v Australia and New Zealand Banking Group Ltd* [2012] HCA 30, (2012) 247 CLR 205 [62].

[90] *AIB Group* (n 52) [69].

[91] For examples of the traditional approach, see *Re Dawson (deceased)* (n 81); *Youyang Pty Ltd v Minter Ellison Morris Fletcher* [2003] HCA 15, (2003) 212 CLR 484.

[92] *AIB Group* (n 52) [70]–[71].

[93] ibid [71].

[94] *Gosper v Sawyer* (1985) 160 CLR 548 (HCA) 568–69 (Mason and Deane JJ). See also FW Maitland, *Equity*, 2nd edn rev by J Brunyate (Cambridge, CUP, 1936) 54; *Associated Alloys Pty Ltd v ACN 001 452 106 Pty Ltd* [2000] HCA 25, (2000) 202 CLR 588 [27]–[28]; *Byrnes v Kendle* [2011] HCA 26, (2011) 243 CLR 253 [59], [103]; *Prickly Bay Waterside Ltd v British American Insurance Co Ltd* [2022] UKPC 8, [2022] 1 WLR 2087 [47].

to misapplication of the property by the trustee. The duties of trustees (and other fiduciary stewards) were traditionally crafted with that vulnerability in mind, and were strictly enforced by remedies which refused to allow a trustee to be discharged from his responsibility to hold the trust assets safe unless there had been strict compliance with the trustee's duties. When the trust is created, the parties are free to alter that strictness, by extending the powers that the trustee has,[95] by abridging the duties that the trustee owes, or by providing the trustee with an exemption from liability for breaches of trust.[96] But if the parties have chosen not to take those routes, then their (contractual) choice to use a trust mechanism without modification appears a choice to protect the beneficiary by adopting the strictness of the traditional liability regime.

This view of the situation seems to underpin the Court of Appeal's decision in *Main v Giambrone & Law*, where a law firm released investment funds from its client account without having received the required documentation for release, and the funds could not now be recovered. Jackson LJ differentiated the case from *AIB* and *Target Holdings v Redferns*, on the basis that the solicitors' role in relation to the clients' funds in *Giambrone* was 'an obligation to act as custodians of the deposit monies indefinitely'.[97] That is the traditional view of a trustee's role, and the liability to replace wrongfully disbursed funds – as opposed to identifying what would have happened if the trust had been properly performed – is consistent with traditional trust principles. But the solicitors in *AIB* and *Target Holdings* had the same role – they also were to act as custodians for their client's money unless and until particular conditions had been satisfied.[98]

The traditional accounting process captures well the concern that the Court of Appeal had in *Giambrone* as it focuses attention on the trust property and the appropriateness of what the trustee did with it, rather than on what might have happened if the trustee had acted properly. If the trustee acted improperly by disbursing assets from the trust to persons who should not have them, or on terms that ought not to have been agreed to, the trustee was required to return to the trust the assets which were wrongfully disposed so that the trust could be properly administered. In *White v Baugh*, for example, the House of Lords held that a receiver who had paid money into a bank which failed was liable for the sum lost because he had placed improper restrictions on how the money could be withdrawn from the bank. Lord Lyndhurst considered it was 'altogether immaterial'[99] that it had not been shown that those restrictions caused the loss to be suffered. The receiver's attempt to avoid his liability to account, on the basis that the loss had been occasioned without any fault on his part, failed because his deposit of the funds on those terms was itself improper,[100]

[95] This was more important historically than it is now, given the wide powers that are included in trusts as default rules under statutory provisions: see, eg, Trustee Act 2000, s 3; Trustee Act 1925 (NSW), s 14.

[96] See *Armitage v Nurse* [1998] Ch 241 (CA).

[97] *Main v Giambrone & Law* [2017] EWCA Civ 1193, [2018] PNLR 2 [62].

[98] Similarly, see *Jessup v Lawyers Private Mortgages Ltd* [2006] QCA 432 [47]–[48].

[99] *White v Baugh* (1835) 3 Cl & Fin 44, 65; 6 ER 1354, 1362.

[100] ibid 63, 65–66; 1361–62. See also *Salway v Salway* (1831) 2 Russ & M 215, 220; 39 ER 376, 378; Cory (n 40) 278.

irrespective of whether those terms had caused the loss of the funds. The trustee had to be able to point to a relevant power, or other justification,[101] if he sought to justify a disposal of trust property:[102] the trustee was expected to have the trust property in his control unless it was disposed of in an authorised fashion and in accordance with any relevant duties. If the trustee disposed of an asset without authority, the beneficiaries could falsify the unauthorised entry and hold the trustee to his fundamental duty to produce the trust property.

> A trustee ... can only discharge himself by showing that he has paid the trust fund to the right person. ... [W]hen an account is taken at the instance of the beneficiary, he will be charged, as still being in his hands, with any trust money which he cannot prove to have been properly disbursed by him.[103]

As Stebbings said:

> Whatever the reason underlying the breach, the law held transgressing trustees liable to replace any money lost. *This position reflected the paramount safety of the trust fund.* ... The orthodox uncompromising attitude of the law was ... and always had been, promoted with the object of ensuring the highest standards of behaviour by trustees to emphasise that anything falling short in relation to the administration of trusts would not be tolerated and thereby to discourage breaches of trust.[104] (emphasis added)

The focus was on restoring to the trust fund the assets which were wrongfully removed from it, in order then to give effect to the trustee's fundamental duty to hold those assets and deal with them in accordance with the terms of the trust; it was not on attempting to determine what would have happened if the trustee had not acted in breach of trust. As the Privy Council's decision in *British American Elevator Co Ltd v Bank of British North America* demonstrates, a failure to appreciate that difference can lead courts into error. The defendant bank had knowingly allowed the plaintiff's agent improperly to withdraw funds from the plaintiff's bank account for the agent's personal use. At first instance, Galt J required the defendant to return the misapplied money, but the Manitoba Court of Appeal varied that order, directing a reference to ascertain what loss the plaintiffs had suffered by reason of the wrongful withdrawals. The Privy Council reinstated Galt J's judgment. Viscount Haldane explained that the Court of Appeal appeared to have treated the action as one for damages for breach of the agreement between the plaintiffs and the defendant bank, an approach that was 'quite inadequate'.[105] He surmised that the Court of Appeal may have been led into error by the fact that the claim was pleaded as one for specific sums, rather than for an account of the sums misapplied in breach of trust.[106] 'The Court of Appeal

[101] eg, a trustee can justify the loss of the trust property if he or she proves it was stolen without fault on the part of the trustee: *Morley v Morley* (1678) 2 Ch Cas 2, 22 ER 817; *Jones v Lewis* (1751) 2 Ves Sen 240, 241; 28 ER 155, 155; Cory (n 40) 277. The trustee is not an insurer: *Re Chapman* [1896] 2 Ch 763 (CA) 775.

[102] *Pickering v Pickering* (1839) 4 My & Cr 289, 298–99; 41 ER 113, 116.

[103] *Re Windsor Steam Coal Co (1901) Ltd* [1929] 1 Ch 151 (CA) 166. See also *Re Anglo-French Co-operative Society, Ex parte Pelly* (1882) 21 Ch D 492 (CA) 506; *Re Hulkes* (1886) 33 Ch D 552 (Ch) 557.

[104] C Stebbings, *The Private Trustee in Victorian England* (Cambridge, CUP, 2002) 169, 172.

[105] *British America Elevator Co Ltd v Bank of British North America* [1919] AC 658 (PC) 663.

[106] ibid 663–64.

should have treated the claim as one for replacement of trust funds, and not for damages';[107] their failure to do so led them into error as it was misleading to think about a trustee's liability to restore misapplied funds in terms of causation.[108] As the New South Wales Court of Appeal put it more recently, 'what is called "equitable compensation" is a shorthand for requiring a fiduciary to account … This is quite different from the liability to pay common law damages'.[109]

The position in England appears to be set by the Supreme Court's decision in *AIB*, in favour of a shift towards aligning the claim for breach of trust with claims for damages for breach of contract, at least where the trust is a commercial trust created in the performance of a contractual agreement. The precise contours of that shift are still being worked out, as the decision in *Giambrone* highlights – as the Court of Appeal said in another case, this is 'a developing area of the law'.[110] But the Court of Appeal's attempt in *Giambrone* to distinguish *AIB*, in order to justify its decision, is not compelling. The supposed distinction between (i) a trustee who released trust funds without receiving the appropriate documentation to justify release (as in *Giambrone*); and (ii) a trustee who was obliged actively to seek out particular documentation but released the trust funds without receiving the appropriate documentation to justify release (as in *Target* and *AIB*),[111] is a distinction without a difference: in each situation, the breach of trust lies in disbursing trust assets without authority, and the trust fund suffers loss as soon as that wrongful disbursement takes place.[112]

In circumstances where leading exponents of nineteenth-century Chancery doctrine regarding accounts stand accused of having been fabulists, engaged in creating 'fairy tales', it is appropriate to recall the point Lord Simonds LC made in a different context: 'It is even possible that we are not wiser than our ancestors.'[113] It remains to be seen whether *AIB* will be followed in other jurisdictions. In Australia, for example, the High Court's decision in *Youyang v Minter Ellison*[114] includes statements which appear to endorse the approach in *Target Holdings*, but the result appears more consistent with the outcome one would expect from a traditional accounting. The facts in *Youyang* were closer to those in *AIB* and *Giambrone* than *Target Holdings*, as the trustees never received the documentation that was required before

[107] ibid 666 (Viscount Haldane).

[108] See also *Magnus v Queensland National Bank* (1888) 37 Ch D 466 (CA) 472, 477–78 and 479–80; Millett (n 52) 225.

[109] *Cassaniti v RCG CBD Pty Ltd* [2022] NSWCA 161 [117].

[110] *Auden McKenzie (Pharma Division) Ltd v Patel* [2019] EWCA Civ 2291, [2020] BCC 316 [64]. Other points include: (1) whether the causal counterfactual can only consider the position that the trustee was *duty-bound* to reach, or whether it can also include options that the trustee *could* have chosen to take: as to which, see, eg, *Auden v Patel* [47], [49] and [59]; and *Hynes v Redington* (1844) 1 Jo & Lat 589, 600–01; 68 RR 349, 350; and (2) whether the causal rules for other fiduciary custodians of property – like company directors – will follow the same approach as *AIB* requires for trusts: as to which, see, eg, *Re Lands Allotment Co* (n 45) 638; *O'Halloran v RT Thomas & Family Pty Ltd* (1998) 45 NSWLR 262 (NSWCA) 277–78; *Bairstow v Queens Moat Houses plc* [2001] EWCA Civ 712, [2001] 2 BCLC 531 [53]–[54]; *Interactive Technology Corp Ltd v Ferster* [2018] EWCA Civ 1594, [2021] WTLR 561 [30]; *Auden v Patel* [57]–[58].

[111] *Giambrone* (n 97) [60]–[61].

[112] *Magnus* (n 108) 472–73, 477–78 and 480.

[113] *Chapman v Chapman* [1954] AC 429 (HL) 444.

[114] *Youyang* (n 91).

the investment funds could be released from the trust, whereas the relevant documents were received in *Target Holdings* at a later date. The decision in *Youyang* was reached before *AIB* was decided, and so without being able to consider the Supreme Court's reasoning in that case. It is always difficult to predict – and perhaps foolish to do so – but there are indications in Australia that *Youyang* does not herald a causal analysis of the sort adopted in *AIB*. In *Crossman v Sheahan*, for example, Ward JA treated (albeit in obiter) the High Court's decision in *Youyang* as adopting the view that the remedy of equitable compensation following an unauthorised disbursement of trust funds 'is not dependent on any "loss" being established beyond the fact of the unauthorised disbursement'.[115] That is more consistent with the claim for equitable compensation being analysed in accordance with traditional equitable accounting principles than with the principles that govern common law claims for damages for breach of contract. Whether that continues to hold true when the High Court is faced with a case like *AIB* remains to be seen. What is clear is that any shift in that view will not be attributable to the Judicature Acts – at least, not directly.

IV. CONCLUSION

This chapter has been concerned with identifying some of the lasting impacts of the Judicature reforms in the context of accounts, particularly equitable accounts. Somewhat counter-intuitively, those lasting impacts lie in aspects of equitable accounting which have largely been forgotten because of the success of the Judicature reforms in removing procedural obstacles to sensible outcomes in particular cases, but which ought to be remembered if we are to make sound decisions about the direction of modern equitable jurisprudence.

One is the meaning of dicta in nineteenth-century cases prior to the Judicature reforms which suggested that agents were not always in a fiduciary position. The meaning of these dicta came to be confusing, at least to modern ears, as the fiduciary concept developed into its modern shape and as the reason for the dicta being uttered in the first place disappeared with the advent of the Judicature reforms. These judges were, I suggest, using the fiduciary label in a way that was more common in that era, to refer to the question whether an agent occupied a position like that of a trustee, as if that were the case then an account could sensibly be taken in equity, but if it were not then the parties would be left to their accounting and other remedies at law. That distinction evaporated after the Judicature reforms because thereafter all claims for accounts were sent to the Chancery Division, which was instructed by the new procedural Rules to conduct that account in accordance with the practices of the Court of Chancery. So, the reason for making the point about non-fiduciary agency disappeared, and its explanation became confused over the years; but it is important to recall the history in order to understand that eminent Chancery judges who referred to agents who do not owe fiduciary duties were referring to something

[115] *Crossman v Sheahan* [2016] NSWCA 200, (2016) 115 ACSR 130 [313]; see also [316]. And see *Jessup v Lawyers Private Mortgages Ltd* [2006] QSC 3 [79]–[84] and [2006] QCA 432 [56]–[64].

quite different from what we would mean today if we were to say that someone does not owe fiduciary duties.

The second impact of the Judicature reforms which this chapter has considered is the effect those reforms had on the claim for equitable compensation for breach of trust. Although the precise genesis of that claim is difficult to pinpoint, it seems clear from the case law that the procedural reforms associated with the Judicature Acts provided a considerable impetus for the recognition of an ability in the court to award a direct remedy of equitable compensation for a particular breach of trust without the matter needing to be sent for an account to be taken as would have happened in the past. That in turn suggests, when coupled with recognition that the Judicature Acts were only intended (at the time, at least) to achieve a 'fusion' of procedure in the one court, that the new remedy of equitable compensation for breach of trust was not intended to provide a different outcome from that which would have obtained pre-Judicature, but merely a more streamlined procedure to achieve that outcome. However, case law in England in the last 25 years or so indicates a shift in the jurisprudence, caused not so much by the fusion of the Judicature reforms as by a belief that, where commercial parties adopt a trust as part of the mechanism for their transaction, the concerns of those parties are more appropriately reflected in a remedy for a breach of that trust which applies concepts of causation more commonly associated with the assessment of damages for breach of contract. While questions remain regarding how that more recent view will be applied in practice, the position appears set in England now; but it has been suggested that there are legitimate reasons why other common law jurisdictions may not follow this particular development in English equitable jurisprudence.

Part IV

Equitable Remedies

8

Equitable Damages

THE HONOURABLE JUSTICE EDELMAN

IN A LEGAL world that is 150 years post-Judicature, the primary point of this chapter is simple. Lawyers should abandon their nervous reluctance to describe money awards for equitable wrongs as 'damages'. That reluctance continues to frustrate the coherent development of the law of damages. The secondary point is to explain two matters. First, like common law damages, there are different species of damages in equity. Secondly, also like the common law, some money awards in equity are more properly described as equitable debt rather than as damages.

I. THE OLD LANGUAGE: EQUITABLE ACCOUNTING

Historically, it was legal heresy for 'equitable' to be used as an adjective to qualify 'damages'. In 1998, Millett LJ spoke of this historical attitude, saying extrajudicially: 'Woe betide a Chancery Junior who spoke of "damages for breach of trust" or "damages for breach of fiduciary duty"'.[1] A reason for this attitude was that historically the jury was seen as the proper mechanism for assessing and awarding damages but judges in Chancery sat without juries. So the procedures and the language developed by the Court of Chancery, borrowed from the common law account against receivers which had fallen into desuetude, were the procedures and language of 'accounting'.

In 1868, Edmund Snell spoke of account in equity in the classic terms of asking whether the parties were in a relationship that permitted equity to order an account. The relationships included: those that were fiduciary, such as a principal seeking an account from an agent or a beneficiary from a trustee; relationships where each of two parties has paid money on the other's account; or where an account is too complicated for the cumbersome procedures of the common law courts.[2] There were three types of account.[3] As Kindersley VC put the first two:[4] the first was an account of

[1] P Millett, 'Equity's Place in the Law of Commerce' (1998) 114 *LQR* 214, 225.

[2] E Snell, *The Principles of Equity* (London, Stevens and Haynes, 1868) 411–12.

[3] See the discussion in *Agricultural Land Management Ltd v Jackson (No 2)* [2014] WASC 102, (2014) 48 WAR 1 [334]–[349].

[4] *Partington v Reynolds* (1858) Drew 253, 255–56; (1858) 62 ER 98, 98–99 (Kindersley VC).

administration, 'a decree compelling [the accounting party] to account only for what he has received'; the second, which was 'entirely grounded on misconduct', was an account on the basis of wilful default 'for what he might, without his wilful neglect or default, have received, although he has not received it'. The liability for 'wilful default' required only a 'lack of ordinary prudence or due diligence'.[5] Upon showing a lack of prudence, the court would surcharge the account by the amount that should have been received or it would falsify the account to remove a claimed expense.[6] The third type of account was the account of profits. As the Lord Chancellor said in *Jegon v Vivian (No 2)*,[7] the Court of Chancery considered that it never allowed a person 'to make profit by a wrong'. Most commonly, where the person was in a relationship in which they had expressly or impliedly undertaken to act in the interests of another then the court would order that an account of any profits be made by the principal from the relationship.[8]

The problem with the language and procedure of account, however, was that it concealed the reason that the accounting party was required to make the payment after the taking of the account. In the case of a common account of administration the focus was only upon the suitor's need to prove the existence of the relationship that gave rise to the duty to account. Once that relationship was proved the accounting party was liable to account for the value of the rights for which the other party was a custodian. In instances where there had been no unauthorised dispositions from the trust the accounting would simply require recognition or payment of that which was held. In that sense the common account was thought to be what James and Bagallay LJJ called 'an equitable debt or liability in the nature of debt'.[9] But the common account went further than that. If a deficiency was found on the accounting the accounting party was required to reconstitute the trust fund. As Dr Lushington said in *Doss v Doss*,[10] the decree ordering the defendant to account was made on the basis that they are liable to pay anything that is found to be due. The reason why an amount was due – because the accounting party had failed to establish that a disbursement was authorised – was seen only as part of the mechanism of the accounting process.

In cases of an accounting on the basis of wilful default or an accounting for profits, the accounts, respectively, of the compensation required to be paid to the claimant and of the profit required to be paid to the defendant were not of the amounts which had been unauthorised payments. The language of account in these two cases concealed the wrongdoing which was the basis for that liability to compensate or disgorge profits. The law of accounting 'went far beyond the mere quantification of profit and loss'.[11] But the account was presented by equity as a *fait accompli* without

[5] See *Pit v Cholmondeley* (1754) 2 Ves Sen 565, 566; 28 ER 360, 360–61.
[6] Millett (n 1) 225–26. See *Re Chapman* [1896] 2 Ch 763 (CA) 776 (Lindley LJ).
[7] (1871) LR 6 Ch App 742 (CA) 761.
[8] *Keech v Sandford* (1726) Sel Cas Temp King 61, 62; 25 ER 223, 223–24; *The Governor and Company of Undertakers for Raising Thames Water in York Buildings v MacKenzie* (1795) 8 Bro PC 42, 66; 3 ER 432, 447.
[9] *Ex parte Adamson* (1878) 8 Ch D 807 (CA) 819.
[10] (1843) 3 Moo Ind App 175, 196–97; 18 ER 464, 472.
[11] P Birks, *Unjust Enrichment*, 2nd edn (Oxford, Clarendon Press, 2005) 294.

any analysis into why the accounting party was required to disgorge the profits or compensate for the losses found on the account.

For a long time, neither equitable accounting nor the order for payment upon the taking of the account was thought of as comparable to 'damages'. The primary reason for this was that at common law the calculation of damages was generally a matter for the jury, subject to control by the judge only in cases of gross excess or gross inadequacy.[12] But in Chancery the judges sat without juries. The perception of difference between the order following the account and the common law jury award began to break down following the introduction of Lord Cairns' Act and the Judicature reforms.

II. SHIFTING UNDERSTANDINGS

A. Lord Cairns' Act and the Judicature Reforms

The first explicit recognition that money awards in equity could be described as damages came in the Chancery Amendment Act 1858, promoted by Sir Hugh Cairns, later Lord Cairns, as Solicitor-General. The Act became known as Lord Cairns' Act. If the Court of Chancery had power to order specific performance or to grant an injunction 'for breach of any covenant, contract, or agreement, or against the commission or continuance of any wrongful act', Lord Cairns' Act provided, in section 2, an additional power for the Court of Chancery, with a purpose of doing 'complete justice',[13] to 'award damages to the party injured either in addition to or in substitution for such injunction or specific performance, and such damages may be assessed in such manner as the court shall direct'. Despite some contrary views,[14] it came to be accepted that equitable damages could be awarded even where equity would not have awarded a remedy of specific performance or injunction, provided that it had the *power* to do so or, on a slightly different approach, that there was a real possibility that it might have done so.[15] Lord Cairns' Act was thus used from an early stage to avoid the extreme consequences of a mandatory injunction, such as requiring waste by demolition of valuable buildings.[16]

Prior to Lord Cairns' Act, the Common Law Procedure Act 1854[17] had provided for a power for the common law courts to make an order for an injunction.

[12] *Ash v Ash* (1697) Comb 357, 90 ER 526; *Chambers v Robinson* (1726) 2 Stra 691, 93 ER 787; *Sharpe v Brice* (1774) 2 Black W 942, 96 ER 557. Compare F Buller, *An Introduction to the Law Relative to Trials at Nisi Prius* (London, Strahan and Woodfall, 1806) 327: 'the jury are the sole judges of the damages'.

[13] JA Jolowicz, 'Damages in Equity – A Study of Lord Cairns' Act' (1975) 34 *CLJ* 224, 225.

[14] *Aynsley v Glover* (1875) LR 18 Eq 544 (Ch) 558; *Smith v Smith* (1875) LR 20 Eq 500 (Ch) 505; *Holland v Worley* (1884) 26 Ch D 578 (Ch) 584. Discussed in Jolowicz (n 13) 240–41.

[15] *City of London Brewery Co v Tennant* (1873) LR 9 Ch App 212 (CA); *Hooper v Rogers* [1975] Ch 43 (CA). Discussed in Jololwicz (n 13) 240–41. See also *Lavery v Pursell* (1888) 39 Ch D 508 (Ch) 519; *Jaggard v Sawyer* [1995] 1 WLR 269 (CA) 285.

[16] *Isenberg v East India House Estate Co* (1863) 3 De G J & S 263, 273; 46 ER 637, 641; *Wrotham Park Estate Co Ltd v Parkside Homes Ltd* [1974] 1 WLR 798 (Ch). *cf Krehl v Burrell* (1878) 7 Ch D 551 (Ch) 554 (Jessel MR): 'the Court in every case, at the instance of the rich man, is to compel the poor man to sell him his property at a valuation'.

[17] s 79.

Lord Brougham thought the new Chancery power to order damages was merely 'the converse' of that common law power.[18] In other words, if the common law could make a specific award like an injunction to avoid a litigant having to commence a separate action in Chancery then equity should have the power to make a money award like damages to avoid a separate action at common law.

On this view of Lord Cairns' Act, the Act was really just designed to avoid circuity of action.[19] As the Commissioners, chaired by Romilly MR, explained in the Report that was the instigator for Lord Cairns' Act the goal was to extend the jurisdiction of equity to allow the Court of Chancery to provide a final settlement of the parties' dispute. The example they gave was where a person injured by a wrongful act was entitled to damages at common law and an injunction in equity. The Court of Equity, they recommended, should have the power to award damages to avoid the claimant having to return to common law.[20] This included cases where the claimant had been entitled to equitable relief, such as specific performance, at the time the Bill was commenced although some later change in circumstances meant that specific performance was no longer available but damages remained available.[21] In that respect, Lord Cairns' Act was a limited forerunner to the Judicature reforms by aiming to 'put into one hand the remedies theretofore held in two'.[22] But in two respects it made significant changes to the procedures for an award of damages at common law.

The first significant departure was from the assessment of damages by a jury. The money award of damages under Lord Cairns' Act could be assessed by a judge, or arguably in some cases a Master or Chief Clerk.[23] Although the Court of Chancery had the power, by section 3, to call for the assessment of damages by a jury (and the Commissioners' Report thought that in many cases it would be expedient to do so),[24] it was not required to do so. This significant change led Lord St Leonards, a man who generally opposed any sweeping legal innovation,[25] to object to the power in the Act for damages to be assessed by a judge. But as Chelmsford LC observed, on this point Lord St Leonards 'stood alone' in the House of Lords.[26]

The second significant departure from the common law model of damages was in the jurisdiction that it was held to confer upon the Court of Chancery to award damages in cases where no damages would have been available at common law. Two extensions can be noted. First, Lord Cairns' Act damages were available in lieu of an injunction to restrain an anticipated wrong that had not yet occurred.[27] But at

[18] HL Deb, 8 June 1858, vol 150, col 1690.

[19] See K Barnett and M Bryan, 'Lord Cairns' Act: A Case Study in the Unintended Consequences of Legislation' (2015) 9 *Journal of Equity* 150, 153.

[20] Chancery Commission, *Third Report of the Commissioners Appointed to Inquire into the Practice of Chancery* (London, Houses of Parliament, 1856) 3.

[21] For instance, *Cory v Thames Ironworks & Shipbuilding Co Ltd* (1863) 8 LT 237, decided by Wood VC who had been one of the Chancery Commissioners that produced the Third Report.

[22] *Slack v Leeds Industrial Co-operative Society Ltd* [1924] AC 851 (HL) 872.

[23] The possibility of a non-judge assessing the damages was a matter about which Lord Brougham objected: HL Deb, 8 June 1858, vol 150, cols 1690–91.

[24] Chancery Commission (n 20) 4.

[25] See J Getzler, 'Sugden, Edward Burtenshaw, Baron St Leonards (1781–1875)' in B Harrison, L Goldman and D Cannadine (eds), *Oxford Dictionary of National Biography* (Oxford, OUP, 2004).

[26] HL Deb, 8 June 1858, vol 150, col 1690.

[27] *Slack* (n 22) 863; *Johnson v Agnew* [1980] AC 367 (HL) 400.

common law, damages were not available for future wrongs. Secondly, by what was described as a 'beneficient interpretation',[28] Lord Cairns' Act damages were available for wrongdoing that was purely equitable such as the breach of a restrictive covenant by a subsequent purchaser[29] or breach of confidence.[30] This extension was controversial. It plainly took Lord Cairns' Act beyond any purpose of merely avoiding circuity of action by providing for damages in Chancery for a common law wrong. The words 'any wrongful act' in section 2 of Lord Cairns' Act, were an expression used in section 83 of the Common Law Procedure Act 1854 to refer only to torts.[31]

If the effect of Lord Cairns' Act had only been to avoid circuity of action then the introduction of the Judicature Acts from 1873, which fused the administration of the common law and equity, would have made Lord Cairns' Act redundant. Indeed, in 1883, Lord Cairns' Act was repealed[32] apparently on the footing that 'the Judicature Acts re-enacted the powers, and therefore that Lord Cairns' Act had become obsolete'.[33] But as Viscount Findlay, with whom Lord Birkenhead and Lord Dunedin agreed, later explained, the repeal on this basis had involved a 'misapprehension' that Lord Cairns' Act gave jurisdiction only for the award of common law damages.[34]

The repeal of Lord Cairns' Act did not, however, have the effect of removing the equitable jurisdiction to award damages that the Act had created. The repealing Act contained a saving clause preserving any jurisdiction conferred under a repealed Act.[35] The effect of the saving clause was that the only consequence of the repeal was the omission of Lord Cairns' Act from the formal statute book.[36] The jurisdiction that was originally conferred by Lord Cairns' Act is now back in the statute book and contained in section 50 of the Senior Courts Act 1981. That provision is still commonly described as Lord Cairns' Act and the damages are still called Lord Cairns' Act damages. Section 50 provides that '[w]here the Court of Appeal or High Court has jurisdiction to entertain an application for an injunction or specific performance, it may award damages in addition to, or in substitution for, an injunction or specific performance'.

B. Lord Cairns' Act Provided a New Way of Thinking

In fact, the innovation was not as radical as Lord St Leonards had supposed. It just provided the possibility of a new way of thinking about Chancery awards. As for the awarding of damages by judges rather than juries, Chancery judges already assessed and awarded damages, describing them as such, upon an undertaking to

[28] *Attorney General v Guardian Newspapers Ltd (No 2)* [1990] 1 AC 109 (HL) 286.

[29] See *Eastwood v Lever* (1863) 4 De G J & S 114, 128; 46 ER 859, 865; *Johnson v Agnew* (n 27) 400.

[30] *Malone v Commissioner of Police of the Metropolis (No 2)* [1979] 2 All ER 620 (Ch) 633; *Talbot v General Television Corp Ltd* [1980] VR 224 (Supreme Court of Victoria) 242–44; *Attorney General v Guardian Newspapers Ltd (No 2)* (n 28) 286.

[31] See the discussion in Barnett and Bryan (n 19) 160–63.

[32] Statute Law Revision and Civil Procedure Act 1883, s 5(b).

[33] *Chapman, Morson & Co v Guardians of Auckland Union* (1889) 23 QBD 294 (CA) 299.

[34] *Slack* (n 22) 863.

[35] Statute Law Revision and Civil Procedure Act 1883, s 5(b).

[36] *Slack* (n 22) 863.

pay damages in circumstances in which the claimant was not ultimately entitled to relief.[37] And even prior to the amendments to jury trials in the County Courts Act 1846 and the Common Law Procedure Act 1854, common law judges had sometimes assessed damages without a jury in exceptional cases such as upon a writ of inquiry of damages where a jury had omitted to do so or where judgment was given in default, on demurrer or by confession.[38]

As for the possibility of damages for purely equitable wrongs or in other circumstances where common law would not have recognised damages, the change provided a potential lens through which to view many of the existing money awards in equity. The language of 'damages' used in relation to Lord Cairns' Act led some to start thinking about whether requirements to pay money after an accounting should be thought of as substantive matters of liability rather than a merely formal accounting. As Gummow J said, 'long before the birth of Lord Cairns, delinquent trustees were brought to book in Chancery and … were obliged to make up from their own pockets the value of trust funds which had been lost'.[39] An early observation was by Washington who noticed that in the accounting process to ascertain loss, 'the auditors see to what extent the party is damaged, and place all in the arrearages, so that in effect he recovers damages'.[40] Much later, Brightman J in *Bartlett v Barclays Bank Trust Co Ltd (No 2)*,[41] responded to a submission that it was 'heretical' to treat a bank's liability to compensate for a breach of trust as damages, saying that an account based on wilful default was 'not readily distinguishable from damages except with the aid of a powerful legal microscope'.[42]

In *Johnson v Agnew*, after recognising that Lord Cairns' Act damages applied to causes of action that were purely equitable, Lord Wilberforce said that the assessment of damages under Lord Cairns' Act is no different in substance from the assessment of common law damages.[43] Lord Reed has more recently cautioned that these remarks must be treated with care since Lord Cairns' Act damages are available on a different basis, in different circumstances, and in respect of different types of wrong.[44] That may be so but those differences may rarely affect methods of assessment of damages. For instance, as Lord Wilberforce recognised in relation to the date of assessment of damages – the issue in *Johnson v Agnew* – neither the common law nor equity inflexibly insists upon either the date of breach or the date of judgment. Lord Wilberforce's central point is that the difference between a money awards for loss caused by wrongdoing at common law and a money awards for loss for the same wrongdoing in equity is not a difference of principle.

Although a claim can still be brought in the form of an account in equity, since Lord Cairns' Act and the Judicature reforms there has been a slow development of

[37] A point made in Chancery Commission (n 20).

[38] eg, *East v Eastington* (1702) 3 Salk 400, 91 ER 896.

[39] *Smith Kline & French Laboratories (Aust) Ltd v Secretary, Department of Community Services and Health* (1990) 22 FCR 73 (FCA) 83.

[40] G Washington, 'Damages in Contract at Common Law: Part 1' (1931) 47 *LQR* 345, 370.

[41] [1980] Ch 515 (Ch).

[42] ibid 545.

[43] *Johnson v Agnew* (n 27) 400. Thus the possibility of aggravated damages in equity under Lord Cairns' Act is canvassed in *Cardwell v Walker* [2003] EWHC 3117 (Ch), [2004] 2 P & CR 9 [66]ff.

[44] *One Step (Support) Ltd v Morris-Garner* [2018] UKSC 20, [2019] AC 649 [47].

understanding that equity can perform a role that is functionally identical to the awarding of damages at common law. English courts now refer sporadically to equitable 'damages' as a synonym for compensation for loss in equity.[45] For example, in *Swindle v Harrison*,[46] where Hobhouse LJ described the claim for breach of fiduciary duty as one that sought 'damages or "equitable compensation" of the character of damages for breach of duty'. Further, more and more often cases are presented by counsel on all sides on the assumption that the rules such as those of causation, scope of duty and remoteness that govern recovery for equitable and common law compensation for loss were to be treated in the same manner.[47] Such language and approach is to be applauded, with the proviso that equitable damages must be separated from the distinct concept of debt.

III. EQUITABLE DEBT IS NOT EQUITABLE DAMAGES

In *AIB Group (UK) Plc v Mark Redler & Co Solicitors*,[48] Lord Toulson observed that in *Bank of New Zealand v New Zealand Guardian Trust Co Ltd*,[49] Tipping J had:

> … rightly observed that while historically the law has tended to place emphasis on the legal characterisation of the relationship between the parties in delineating the remedies available for breach of an obligation, the nature of the duty which has been breached can often be more important, when considering issues of causation and remoteness, than the classification or historical source of the obligation.

Relevantly, an order to pay a sum of money in response to a duty which is in the nature of a voluntarily undertaken debt is not damages and is not governed by the rules concerning damages. But claims for a debt in equity and claims that can properly be described as equitable damages are not always separated. A decision from each of the House of Lords and the Supreme Court of the United Kingdom illustrate the difference even though the cases were not argued in a manner that clearly demarcated debt from damages.

The first case is the decision of the House of Lords in *Target Holdings Ltd v Redferns*.[50] On the assumed facts for the purposes of the summary judgment application, Target Holdings lent £1.5 million to a purchaser of property and paid the money to the purchasers' solicitors, Redferns. Redferns agreed to hold the money on trust and not to distribute it until Redferns had obtained a mortgage over

[45] *ABCI v Banque Franco-Tunisienne* [2003] EWCA Civ 205, [2003] 2 Lloyds' Rep 146 [16]–[17]; *P & O Nedlloyd BV v Arab Metals Co* [2006] EWCA Civ 1717, [2007] 1 WLR 2288 [39]; *Danilina v Chernukhin* [2018] EWHC 39 (Comm) [87]; *Gresport Finance Ltd v Battaglia* [2018] EWCA Civ 540 [25]; *Davies v Ford* [2021] EWHC 2550 (Ch); *Umbrella Care Ltd v Nisa* [2022] EWHC 86 (Ch) [144].

[46] [1997] 4 All ER 705 (CA) 722.

[47] See, for instance, *Sharp v Blank* [2019] EWHC 3096 (Ch) [891] (causation and remoteness); *LIV Bridging Finance Ltd v EAD Solicitors LLP (In Administration)* [2020] EWHC 1590 (Ch), [2020] PNLR 24 [35] (scope of duty).

[48] [2014] UKSC 58, [2015] AC 1503 [59]. *cf* Lord Reed SPJ at [136]–[137]. See also *Daniel v Tee* [2016] EWHC 1538 (Ch), [2016] 4 WLR 115.

[49] [1999] 1 NZLR 664 (NZCA).

[50] [1996] AC 421 (HL).

the property. In breach of the terms of the trust agreement, Redferns disbursed most of the money before the mortgage was executed. After the purchaser defaulted, Target sold the property for £450,000 and claimed the difference from Redferns. Redferns defended the claim on the basis that the property had been overvalued as a result of fraud, alleging that Target Holdings would have lost the difference in any event. On these facts, Target Holdings should have succeeded against Redferns in a simple claim for debt. Whether the claim was expressed as a debt arising at common law from the agreement or in equity from the undertaking in the trust deed, the result would be the same. Redferns had promised to hold the money for Target Holdings and to repay it to Target Holdings unless a mortgage over the property was obtained. It is no answer to a claim for debt at common law for the debtor to claim that, on a counterfactual analysis, if some unfulfilled condition had been fulfilled then the debtor would not have been required to repay. If a debt is subject to defeasance by a condition and the condition is not fulfilled then the debt does not disappear. The same is true in equity.

But the assumed facts of *Target Holdings* were a little more complex. Although Redferns disbursed the trust money without first having obtained a mortgage, the mortgage was later obtained by Redferns. The simple answer to the claim for common law or equitable debt may have been that on the proper construction of the agreement by which the money was paid on trust to the solicitors, the debt that the solicitors owed to Redferns was defeasible by the solicitors obtaining the mortgage, even if they obtained the mortgage after disbursing the money. This was perhaps why Target Holdings never pleaded a claim for debt. But we will never know because the claim brought by Target Holdings against Redferns for the full amount of the money wrongfully disbursed was not brought as a claim for debt.

Another case that might have been brought as a claim for debt is the decision of the Supreme Court of the United Kingdom in *AIB Group (UK) plc v Redler*.[51] In that case, AIB lent £3.3 million to borrowers to remortgage their property. AIB paid the £3.3 million to its solicitors to hold on trust pending completion of settlement. AIB intended the solicitors to take, for AIB, the security of a first charge over the property to be re-mortgaged before the solicitors released the funds. The solicitors should have paid out £1.5 million to discharge the existing legal charge held by Barclays. But, by mistake, they only paid out around £1.2 million and paid the rest to the borrowers. So Barclays kept the first charge. As the Court of Appeal held, on a point that was not challenged in the Supreme Court, the transaction between AIB and the borrowers did not complete.[52] The borrowers later defaulted and Barclays sold the property for £1.2 million, taking the remainder which it was owed and leaving the rest to AIB (£867,697). If the solicitors had completed the transaction by paying £1.5 million to Barclays then AIB would have had a first charge and, on the sale of the property, AIB would have received around £300,000 more than the proceeds it received.

The claim for debt would have been a very simple claim that AIB could have brought against its solicitors. There was no doubt that AIB and its solicitors had

[51] (n 48).

[52] *AIB Group (UK) Plc v Mark Redler & Co Solicitors* [2013] EWCA Civ 45, [2013] PNLR 19 [43]. The Supreme Court spoke loosely of completion as a 'commercial' matter but recognised that there was no completion according to legal requirements: see *AIB Group* (n 48) [74].

entered an enforceable contract as well as having created a trust. Under that contract, the solicitors owed a common law debt of £2,432,303 (being the £3.3 million less £867,697 that AIB had accepted in discharge of that debt, which included the proceeds of the sale of the property). The contract between AIB and its solicitors provided: 'You [the solicitors] must hold the loan on trust for us [AIB] until completion. If completion is delayed, you must return it to us when and how we tell you.'[53] A delay in completion must include a delay that arises when it is known that completion will not occur. If the borrowers had terminated their contract with AIB prior to settlement then after the proposed date of completion the solicitors could not have kept the £3.3 million that they held on trust for AIB. The clause concerning return of the funds therefore contemplated that if completion did not or could not occur the solicitors would be required to return the £3.3 million when and how they were told to do so by AIB. So why were they not required to do so?

The answer is that AIB brought four claims: breach of trust, breach of fiduciary duty, breach of contract and negligence. Breach of contract and negligence were admitted by the solicitors.[54] But AIB never brought a claim for a common law debt, a claim which was of the form 'repay the money which you promised to repay under the conditions which occurred'. The obvious advantage of a claim in AIB for debt is that matters concerning causation, loss and remoteness would have been irrelevant. As Millett LJ (Otton LJ and Sir Stephen Brown P agreeing) said in *Jervis v Harris*,[55] there is a clear distinction between a claim for payment of a debt and a claim for damages for breach of contract. A plaintiff 'who claims payment of a debt need not prove anything beyond the occurrence of the event or condition on the occurrence of which the debt became due. He need prove no loss; the rules as to remoteness of damage and mitigation of loss are irrelevant'.

AIB made two errors. It tried to litigate a common law debt claim as an equitable claim. There was no room left for an equitable debt if a common law debt existed. Such an equitable debt would be functionally identical to the unpleaded common law debt claim. The second error was that AIB tried to make this equitable debt argument as a claim based on breach of trust. AIB argued that the solicitors held the money on trust and were under a duty maintain the funds, for which they were required to account in a common form accounting process. But AIB's case was pleaded and presented at trial as one involving compensation for the wrong of breach of contract or breach of trust. 'By focusing on the wrong' it can be said, AIB 'took their eyes off the right'.[56] The Supreme Court therefore, correctly, held that Mark Redler was not required to pay £2,432,303 to AIB. Lord Toulson JSC said that to have ordered payment of that new amount would involve:[57]

> effectively treating the unauthorised application of trust funds as creating an immediate debt between the trustee and the beneficiary, rather than conduct meriting equitable compensation for any loss thereby caused.

[53] *AIB Group* (n 48) [4].
[54] ibid [9].
[55] [1996] Ch 195 (CA) 202.
[56] See *Smethurst v Commissioner of Police* [2020] HCA 14, (2020) 376 ALR 575 [245] (Edelman J).
[57] AIB Group (n 48) [61].

IV. TWO TYPES OF DAMAGES TO COMPENSATE IN EQUITY

A. The Two Types of Compensation at Common Law Revisited

Whether compensation in equity is described as 'equitable compensation' or as 'equitable damages', as is observed in *Snell's Equity*,[58] it is necessary to distinguish between two different forms of compensation. These two forms of compensation in equity follow the same underlying premises as the two purposes of compensation at common law. At common law the two types of damages to compensate are sometimes described as normal loss and consequential loss.[59] The distinction is between what Lord Dunedin in *Admiralty Commissioners v SS Susquehanna*[60] described as damages to compensate 'for the wrongful act' and damages to compensate for the 'consequences of the wrongful act'.[61] The normal loss is that which is required to rectify or undo the wrongful act. Further, consequential losses arising from the wrong can be recovered separately. In *Lewis v Australian Capital Territory*,[62] I distinguished between court orders that aim to rectify or correct a wrongful act and those that respond to its consequences.

Common law damages can aim to rectify a wrongful act, independently of its consequences. Since these orders are not concerned with consequences, issues such as causation of consequences, remoteness of consequences or the scope of duty concerning the consequences are irrelevant. The damages aim only to rectify the wrongful act by providing a substitute. Orders of this nature can appear to be similar to claims for debt because of their lack of concern with consequences. But unlike debt they do not require the (late) performance of the duty. Rather, they are concerned with substituting for the primary duty, by rectifying the failure to perform the duty. By contrast, damages for consequential loss, which are the most commonly understood at common law, are concerned with repairing losses suffered as a consequence of the wrong. They are subject to well-known rules for recovery based on principles such as causation and remoteness of damage which are designed to establish the extent to which a defendant is responsible for adverse consequences suffered by a claimant.

An example of the common law aiming to rectify a wrongful act rather than its consequences is the wrong of conversion of goods by a bailee. If damages are inadequate, such as because the goods are unique[63] or because they are needed urgently and there is not a ready market,[64] the most perfect means of rectifying that wrongful

[58] J McGhee and S Elliott (eds), *Snell's Equity*, 34th edn (London, Sweet & Maxwell, 2020) 613–15 paras [20-028]–[20-035].

[59] J Edelman, *McGregor on Damages*, 21st edn (London, Sweet & Maxwell, 2021) para 3-008.

[60] [1926] AC 655 (HL) 661. Compare, as to 'natural and direct', *Overseas Tankship (UK) Ltd v The Miller Steamship Co Pty ("The Wagon Mound (No 2)")* [1967] 1 AC 617 (PC).

[61] See also *Lewis v The Australian Capital Territory* [2020] HCA 26, (2020) 271 CLR 192 [140]–[152].

[62] ibid [140]–[152].

[63] *Pusey v Pusey* (1684) 1 Vern 273, 23 ER 465; *Duke of Somerset v Cookson* (1735) 3 P Wms 390, 24 ER 1114; *Saville v Tankred* (1748) 1 Ves Sen 101, 27 ER 918; *Fells v Read* (1796) 3 Ves 70, 30 ER 899; *Lloyd v Loaring* (1802) 6 Ves 773, 31 ER 1302; *Lowther v Lowther* (1806) 13 Ves 95, 33 ER 230.

[64] *Aristoc Industries Pty Ltd v R A Wenham (Builders) Pty Ltd* [1965] NSWR 581 (NSWSC) 589; *Doulton Potteries Ltd v Bronotte* [1971] 1 NSWLR 591 (NSWSC) 598–99.

act, the 'complete remedy',[65] would be a specific order in equity for delivery up of the goods. But common law courts could also rectify that wrongful act by recognising that the claimant is entitled to payment of the objective value of the goods as a substitute being an alternative way to undo the wrong. In the sixteenth century, the bailee at common law could be made liable in this way through the action for an account.[66] Until the eighteenth century, the bailee was strictly liable for the value of the goods bailed to them even if the goods had been lost or stolen without the fault of the bailee, unless there was an express stipulation against such liability.[67] But even as the strict liability was ameliorated and the remedy of account disappeared at common law, the bailor was still entitled in a claim of detinue (now absorbed into conversion)[68] to the value of the goods carelessly lost by the bailee even if, for example, the bailor suffered no loss because the goods would have been lost in any event. Thus it was said that detinue is

> a continuing cause of action which accrues at the date of the wrongful refusal to deliver up the goods and continues until delivery up of the goods or judgment in the action for detinue … [the defendant] was estopped from asserting that he had wrongfully delivered the chattel to a third person or had negligently lost it before demand for delivery up.[69]

It will not, however, always be possible for an award of money damages at common law to be made in order to rectify a wrongful act. In *Lewis v Australian Capital Territory*, Mr Lewis effectively sought such an award for a period of his false imprisonment. The High Court of Australia considered cases where a defendant was required to pay the amount that would have represented a licence fee in order to rectify the wrongful taking of an opportunity to use. But those cases did not apply in circumstances of false imprisonment where the claimant's liberty was not a commodity that could be licensed. There was simply no manner in which the wrong could be undone or rectified. Only its consequences and effect on Mr Lewis could be compensated.

B. The Same Two Types of Compensation in Equity

Compensation in equity, whether under Lord Cairns' Act or in equity's inherent jurisdiction, is also best understood as divided into the same two species. In equity these two forms of compensation have been described by Dr Elliott as substitutive compensation and reparative compensation.[70]

[65] J Mitford and JW Smith, *A Treatise on the Pleadings in Suits in The Court of Chancery, by English Bill*, 5th edn (London, V & R Stevens and GS Norton, 1847) 138–39; *North v Great Northern Railway Co* (1860) 2 Giff 64, 68; 66 ER 28, 30.

[66] *Woodlife's Case* (1597) Moo 462, 72 ER 696.

[67] See OW Holmes, *The Common Law* (Boston, Little, Brown, 1881) 179.

[68] Torts (Interference with Goods) Act 1977, s 3.

[69] *General & Finance Facilities v Cooks Cars (Romford)* [1963] 1 WLR 644 (CA) 648–49.

[70] See S Elliott and C Mitchell, 'Remedies for Dishonest Assistance' (2004) 67 *MLR* 16 approved in *Agricultural Land Management Ltd* (n 3) [348]. See also C Mitchell, 'Equitable Compensation for Breach of Fiduciary Duty' (2013) 66 *Current Legal Problems* 307, 322.

i. Substitutive Compensation

Substitutive compensation seeks to repair or substitute as a way of undoing the wrongdoing itself. In the common accounting process, if no unauthorised dispositions are found then the rights of the beneficiaries are, as we have seen, akin to a debt. There is nothing to substitute or rectify. But where there is an unauthorised disposition the trustee has always been required to reconstitute the trust fund by a 'substitute' unless the unauthorised transaction can be excused. The rules concerning causation, remoteness of consequences or scope of duty that are concerned with consequential loss do not apply to the rectification of this unauthorised transaction. But substitutive compensation is not a claim for a debt. To simplify the facts of *AIB Group (UK) Plc v Mark Redler & Co*,[71] consider a solicitor trustee who holds money on trust for a financier beneficiary, with a promise in the contractual trust deed between them to pay the money to the financier beneficiary if completion of a transaction does not occur. If the completion does not occur but the solicitor trustee pays the money to the wrong party then the financier beneficiary can bring a claim for the debt. The unauthorised payment to the wrong party is irrelevant.

In a claim for substitutive compensation based on an unauthorised disposition the claimant does not need to establish a promise by the defendant to pay the amount. Rather, it is a claim for the payment in money of a substitute for, or to rectify, the unauthorised payment. It is therefore assessed at the date at which the unauthorised event occurred. For instance, in a judgment on a strike-out claim in *Rahman v Rahman*,[72] Master Clark held that Lord Cairns' Act damages for a claim for breach of an oral agreement to allot shares were to be assessed at the date of judgment since that was the date at which the claimant's 'entitlement to the shares is treated as coming to an end and being replaced by financial compensation'. And in his judgment in *Brooke Homes (Bicester) Ltd v Portfolio Property Partners Ltd*,[73] Mr Hugh Sims QC, referring to *Snell's Equity*,[74] described the two types of award of equitable compensation as making good a loss and compelling a defendant 'to perform an equitable duty substantively by paying an equivalent amount of money instead'.

The most common instance of substitutive compensation awards arises in relation to an unauthorised payment contrary to the duty of a trustee, as Lindley LJ put it, 'properly to preserve the trust fund'.[75] Just as a bailee at common law was historically required to account for the value of goods that had been lost or given away without authority, the order for payment following a deficiency on a common account required the trustee to pay for any deficiency in the trust assets that had been disbursed without authority. Although some older authorities held that it was not necessary to plead or prove a 'breach of duty', in cases where the claim is for a money substitute for the asset, it is not performance of a duty that is sought but rectification of a wrongful disposition; there must still be a 'wrongful payment' or

[71] (n 48).
[72] [2020] EWHC 2392 (Ch).
[73] [2021] EWHC 3015 (Ch) [299].
[74] McGhee and Elliott (n 58) 613–15 paras [20-028]–[20-035].
[75] *Low v Bouverie* [1891] 3 Ch 82 (CA) 99. See also *CGU Insurance Ltd v One.Tel Ltd (In Liq)* [2010] HCA 26, (2010) 242 CLR 174 [36].

'unlawful payments'.[76] A trustee was only required to make payments following the common account for dispositions that could not be shown to be authorised. The underlying reason for the order for payment was the breach of duty. And like the rule that developed for bailees, it would not be a wrongful payment, and thus there would be sufficient discharge, if the trustee could show that the money had been stolen without the fault of the trustee.[77]

Again, like damages for 'normal loss' against a bailee, the order for substitutive compensation did not compensate for loss. Rather, it compensated to rectify the failure of the trustee to perform as promised. For that reason, unlike reparative compensation or damages for consequential loss, notions of causation of loss or remoteness of loss are irrelevant. As Lord Millett explained in *Libertarian Investments Ltd v Hall*,[78] '[w]here the defendant is ordered to make good the deficit by the payment of money, the award is sometimes described as the payment of equitable compensation; but it is not compensation for loss but restitutionary or restorative'. The cost of performing the trust duty is usually calculated by the value of the notional trust assets at the date of trial because the trustee's undertaking usually continues until trial.[79] Hence, in *Main v Giambrone & Law (A Firm)*,[80] where solicitors released deposits paid by their clients, and held on trust, without fulfilling the requirement of receiving guarantees the solicitors were liable for equitable compensation. The equitable compensation was described as running in tandem with contractual damages to perform a promise for a 'breach of contract [that] consisted of wrongfully paying out deposit moneys which it had undertaken to keep safe'.[81]

A simple example is *Magnus v Queensland National Bank*.[82] In breach of trust, a bank transferred to a fraudulent beneficiary the purchase money that it held on trust for two other beneficiaries. The other beneficiaries claimed that the bank must account to them for the money. Lord Halsbury LC observed that the two other beneficiaries trusted the fraudster so much that 'he might have defrauded the trust in some other way',[83] an example of which might be if he had obtained the authority of the other beneficiaries for the money to be paid to him for the purposes of further investment. But whether or not the money would have been lost in any event did not matter. As Cotton LJ said, the bank 'must be held answerable to the trustees just as if the money was still in [the bank's] hands'.[84]

In *Bairstow v Queens Moat Houses plc*,[85] the Court of Appeal held that a director who had knowingly and wrongfully distributed dividends without authority was

[76] *Re Stevens* [1898] 1 Ch 162 (CA) 170; *Ahmed Angullia bin Hadjee Mohamed Salleh Angullia v Estate and Trust Agencies* (1927) Ltd [1938] AC 624 (PC) 637.

[77] *Jones v Lewis* (1750) 2 Ves Sen 240, 241; (1750) 28 ER 155, 155.

[78] [2013] HKCFA 93, [2014] 1 HKC 368 [168].

[79] *Re Dawson (deceased)*; *Union Fidelity Trustee Co Ltd v Perpetual Trustee Co Ltd* [1966] 2 NSWR 211 (NSWSC); *Hagan v Waterhouse (No 2)* (1991) 34 NSWLR 308 (NSWSC) 345–46; *Canson Enterprises Ltd v Boughton & Co* [1991] 3 SCR 534; *Target Holdings* (n 50) 437; *Youyang Pty Ltd v Minter Ellison Morris Fletcher* [2003] HCA 15, (2003) 212 CLR 484 [35].

[80] [2017] EWCA Civ 1193, [2018] PNLR 2. Applied in *LIV Bridging Finance* (n 47) [26]–[29].

[81] *Main* (n 80) [63] (Jackson LJ).

[82] (1888) 37 Ch D 466 (CA) 471–72 (Halsbury LC), 477 (Cotton LJ) and 480 (Bowen LJ).

[83] ibid 473. See also 477 (Cotton LJ) and 480 (Bowen LJ).

[84] ibid 477.

[85] [2001] EWCA Civ 712, [2002] BCC 91.

required to make compensation to the company of the value of the dividend payments. It did not matter that 'lawful dividends could and would have been paid'.[86] In the leading judgment, Robert Walker LJ said that the same principles should apply to directors as those that apply to trustees: custodial directors 'were not strictly speaking trustees, as title to the assets was not vested in them; but they had trustee-like responsibilities, because they had the power and the duty to manage the company's business in the interests of all its members'.[87]

Another example is the decision of the House of Lords in *Revenue and Customs Commissioners v Holland, In Re Paycheck Services 3 Ltd*.[88] In that case, in the course of discussing the liability of a director for the unlawful payment of a dividend, Rimer LJ (with whom Elias and Ward LJJ agreed on this point) described the liability to compensate as 'restitution', saying that 'directors of a company, if not trustees in the strict sense (because its assets are not vested in them), owe a like duty as a trustee not to misapply the company's assets and a like duty to make restitution to the company if they do'.[89] In the Supreme Court, the approach of Rimer LJ was endorsed by Lord Clarke[90] and Lord Walker.[91] Lord Hope also said that 'where dividends have been paid unlawfully, the directors' obligation is to account to the company for the full amount of those dividends'.[92]

Again, in *Interactive Technology Corp v Ferster*,[93] the substitutive compensation approach was taken when the respondent director dishonestly withdrew more than £4 million from the appellant company in unauthorised remuneration. The director argued that his services were worth the full value withdrawn. Before the Court of Appeal, the company sought to avoid any argument by the director that if the remuneration had not been unlawfully paid then it would have been lawfully paid. The company argued that only one species of equitable compensation, described as 'reparative compensation', was concerned with compensation for losses. David Richards LJ (with whom Newey LJ agreed) accepted this submission, concluding that the other species, 'substitutive compensation', akin to a claim for debt in equity, was not concerned with causation of loss but with 'claims for a money payment as a substitute for performance of the trustee's obligation'.[94]

Like compensation for normal loss that seeks to rectify a wrongful act at common law, it will not always be possible to rectify an act that is a breach in equity. In *Davies v Ford*,[95] the claimant sought equitable compensation for losses suffered from two directors who had breached their fiduciary duties including by diversion of business from the principal company in which they were directors to a new company in which they were the directors and shareholders. The judge of the trial as to quantum, David Holland QC, held that apart from funds from the principal company the claim

[86] ibid [54] (Robert Walker LJ).
[87] ibid [53].
[88] [2010] UKSC 51, [2010] 1 WLR 2793.
[89] *Re Paycheck Services 3 Ltd* [2009] EWCA Civ 625, [2010] Bus LR 259.
[90] *Re Paycheck Services 3 Ltd* (n 89) [146].
[91] ibid [124].
[92] ibid [49].
[93] [2018] EWCA Civ 1594, [2018] 2 P & CR DG22.
[94] ibid [17]–[21].
[95] (n 45).

did not involve any misapplication of pre-existing corporate assets.[96] The judge held that substitutive compensation applies to such cases of misapplication of existing company or trust property and that in such cases it is not open to the trustee or fiduciary in breach to 'argue the counterfactual, that is that the trust property would have been lost or paid away even if he or she had not been in breach'.[97] But since the central claim was not for misappropriation of existing company property, the equitable compensation fell to be assessed on 'the reparative basis', for which questions of causation of loss are relevant, and the directors succeeded in part by establishing that some of the loss suffered by the principal company would have been suffered in any event.[98]

ii. Reparative Compensation

Reparative compensation for loss in equity should follow the same principles for compensation for consequential loss as the common law. To return to the point made above that Lord Wilberforce recognised in relation to the date of assessment of damages in equity under Lord Cairns' Act: the principles for compensation for loss should not differ solely according to whether the origins of the wrong were in the Court of Chancery or a court of common law.

The point can be illustrated outside Lord Cairns' Act in the context of fraud. As Snell observed from the first edition of his work, even in cases where 'the common law affords complete and adequate relief' there was a 'general and perhaps a universal concurrent jurisdiction' in Chancery in relation to fraud.[99] In 1873, in *Peek v Gurney*,[100] by a Bill in equity the claimant had sought orders including declarations that various directors were 'jointly and severally liable to make good to the Plaintiff or indemnify him against the loss which he had sustained and might sustain'.[101] Lord Chelmsford remarked that a suit in Chancery based on actual fraud was 'precisely analogous to the common law action for deceit' and that it was 'a suit instituted to recover damages'.[102] It is hard to see why the common law and equity should differ in their application of the rules for the calculation of the same loss, based on the same fraud, with the same cause of action. The same point can be made about negligence of a company director causing loss to the company. Although such an action was traditionally brought in the Court of Chancery rather than at common law, it is now well recognised that the same principles apply as those for negligence at common law when assessing whether the director was negligent and whether loss is recoverable.[103] Directors are not in a different legal position as regards negligent behaviour from, for example, an accountant or a bailee at common law.[104]

[96] ibid [109].
[97] ibid [100], [103], [106].
[98] ibid [109]–[110], [272].
[99] *Snell* (n 2) 359.
[100] (1873) LR 6 HL 377.
[101] *Peek v Gurney* (1871) LR 13 Eq 79 (Ch) 88 (Lord Romilly MR).
[102] *Peek v Gurney* (n 101) 390, 393. And, more recently, see the endorsement of this in *Talacko v Talacko* [2021] HCA 15, (2021) 389 ALR 178 [27].
[103] *Bristol and West Building Society v Mothew* [1998] Ch 1 (CA) 17.
[104] *Henderson v Merrett Syndicates Ltd* [1995] 2 AC 145 (HL) 205.

The same reparative compensation approach should apply where the loss arises from a fiduciary duty. The scope and terms of a fiduciary duty must conform to the terms of a contract where the fiduciary duty arises in the contractual context. Even outside that contractual context, where the same express or implied undertaking to act in the interests of another exists, but unilaterally rather than contractually, the fiduciary duty has been described as 'equivalent to contract'.[105] Hence, it has been said that principles of damages in contract such as those concerning 'transferred loss'[106] should be applied to the breach of the equitable obligation in the same way. And the order for compensation against a director in breach of fiduciary duty has thus been referred to interchangeably as equitable compensation and damages.[107]

iii. Difficult Cases

We have seen above that in the House of Lords and Supreme Court decisions of *Target Holdings Ltd v Redferns*[108] and *AIB Group (UK) Plc v Mark Redler & Co*,[109] it was held that the only compensation available was reparative compensation for the losses that had been caused by the solicitor's negligence. In the leading speech in *Target Holdings Ltd*, Lord Browne-Wilkinson acknowledged that the traditional substitutive (or rectifying) equitable approach required the trustee to account for the money that it held and that 'the common law rules of remoteness and causation do not apply'.[110] But Lord Browne-Wilkinson sought to distinguish the traditional equitable approach of the common account on the basis that it should not usually apply in a commercial situation such as a bare trust where the beneficiary is absolutely entitled to the trust fund.[111]

Lord Browne-Wilkinson's basis for distinguishing traditional trust accounting principles has not been met with subsequent favour. Lower courts have sometimes applied the restrictive approach taken in *Target Holdings* without emphasis on this rationale[112] but in some cases discussed below, *Target Holdings* has been distinguished entirely, again without reference to Lord Browne-Wilkinson's distinction.[113] In *Bairstow v Queens Moat Houses plc*,[114] Robert Walker LJ suggested that a more satisfactory dividing line might not be between the traditional trust and the commercial trust but between 'a breach of fiduciary duty in the wrongful disbursement of funds of which the fiduciary has this sort of trustee-like stewardship and a breach of fiduciary duty of a different character'. In *AIB Group (UK) plc v Mark Redler & Co*,[115] in the leading

[105] *Nocton v Lord Ashburton* [1914] AC 932 (HL) 972 (Lord Shaw).

[106] *Argos Pereira Espana SL v Athenian Marine Ltd* [2021] EWHC 554 (Comm), [2022] 1 All ER (Comm) 345 [24] (Sir Michael Burton CBE).

[107] *Umbrella Care* (n 45) [144].

[108] (n 50).

[109] (n 48).

[110] *Target Holdings* (n 50) 434.

[111] ibid 435–36.

[112] See, for instance *Wessely v White* [2018] EWHC 1499 (Ch), [2019] BCC 289 [45]–[46]; *LIV Bridging Finance Ltd* (n 47).

[113] For other jurisdictions see in Australia, *Agricultural Land Management* (n 3), and in the Singapore Court of Appeal, *Ping v Winsta Holding Pte Ltd* [2020] SGCA 35.

[114] (n 85) [53].

[115] (n 48) [71].

judgment, Lord Toulson rejected the notion that the principles of equity could vary according to the nature of the trust, and said that 'the fact that the trust was part of the machinery for the performance of a contract is relevant as a fact in looking at what loss the bank suffered by reason of the breach of trust because it would be artificial and unreal to look at the trust in isolation from the obligations for which it was brought into being'.

Nevertheless, the result in *Target Holdings* is justified. It was explained on traditional principles by Sir Peter Millett who argued that 'the acquisition of the mortgage or the disbursement by which it was obtained ... was an authorised application of what must be treated as trust money notionally restored to the trust estate'.[116] Sir Peter Millett's reasoning appears to involve a fiction; the trust money was not restored to the estate so why treat it as having been so restored? The Supreme Court later described this as a 'fairy tale'.[117] The better approach, without resort to fiction, is to say that on a common accounting, or substitutive compensation approach, Target Holdings could not claim that the money had been disbursed without authority at the same time as accepting the benefit of the mortgage obtained from the disbursement of the money. The disbursement was a wrongful act requiring the solicitors to compensate for the loss suffered. But the solicitors could not be asked by Target Holdings to perform their duty of repaying the money to the trust fund when Target Holdings had accepted the benefits from the solicitors' wrongful disbursement. As Lord Reed put this point in *AIB Group (UK) plc v Mark Redler & Co*,[118] a claim for substitutive compensation was unavailable because '[t]he assets under the control of the trustee were then exactly what they ought to have been. There was nothing missing from the trust fund, and therefore no basis for a claim for restoration'. All that was left was a claim for reparative compensation for consequential loss. Thus, as Lord Toulson also said in the Supreme Court in *AIB Group (UK) plc v Mark Redler & Co*,[119] in circumstances such as those in *Target Holdings*, the measure of equitable compensation 'should be the same as if damages for breach of contract were sought at common law'.

More difficult is the rejection of a claim for substitutive compensation in *AIB Group (UK) plc v Mark Redler & Co*.[120] As we have seen, no debt claim was brought for the amount of £2,432,303 (£3.3 million, less amounts received in partial discharge after sale). That is why AIB's claim for that amount failed. Any claim for £2,432,303 would be a claim based on debt, not upon an unauthorised disposition. A claim for substitutive compensation, to rectify an unauthorised disposition could only ever have recovered the amount of the unauthorised disposition, around £300,000. As Lord Reed observed, it was a fallacy to assume that Redler had misapplied the entire £3.3 million rather than approximately £300,000 which had been paid to the borrowers rather than to Barclays.[121]

[116] Millett (n 1) 227.
[117] *AIB Group* (n 48) [69] (Lord Toulson).
[118] ibid [14].
[119] ibid [71].
[120] ibid.
[121] ibid [140].

The decisions in *Target Holdings* and *AIB Group* have thus been correctly distinguished by the Court of Appeal in other cases where substitutive compensation is sought. They have been described as concerned with the particular circumstances of obligations of solicitors that were defined by express and implied instructions and where 'the beneficiary obtained the full benefit for which it bargained' or was placed in the same position as if performance had occurred.[122]

Another difficult decision is the leading Australian case on the subject in *Youyang Pty Ltd v Minter Ellison Morris Fletcher*.[123] In that case, an investment company agreed with solicitors to pay money to the solicitors, the first half of which was only to be released for investment by the solicitors after they obtained a bearer deposit certificate. The other half of the money was then subsequently to be invested in speculative activities on the international money market. In breach of the contractual terms that established the trust on which the solicitors held the money, the solicitors released all the money without obtaining a certificate. The solicitors later reinvested the money but still no bearer deposit certificate was obtained. The investments were poor and the money was all lost. A majority of the New South Wales Court of Appeal held that Youyang's claim should fail because at the time of reinvestment of the money if the director who acted on behalf of Youyang 'had been told about the form of the certificate he would not have been concerned and would have proceeded with the investment'.[124]

The difficulty with the appeal to the High Court of Australia is that it was argued by counsel for the solicitors as a case of reparative compensation for loss[125] but argued by counsel for Youyang as a case of substitutive compensation to restore the value of the trust fund.[126] Neither party explained that the measures were both legitimate. The High Court dealt with both measures but without expressly recognising that they were different. As to reparative compensation, the High Court dealt with the objection as to causation by endorsing the comments of Hodgson JA who dissented in the New South Wales Court of Appeal that there was, at least, an evidentiary onus upon the trustee to establish that the beneficiary would have authorised the action if asked.[127] On the other hand, the High Court also made a number of remarks that appeared to endorse substitutive compensation, such as by referring to Lord Millett's explanation of *Target Holdings* as a case in which the trust money had been 'notionally restored to the trust estate on the taking of the account'.[128] Critically, to the point that I have made above, one ground upon which the High Court distinguished *Target Holdings* was that the proposed commercial transaction was never completed.[129] In short, the duty for which substitutive compensation was sought had not been, belatedly, performed.

[122] *Auden McKenzie (Pharma Division) Ltd v Patel* [2019] EWCA Civ 2291, [2020] BCC 316 [49] (David Richards LJ).
[123] (n 79).
[124] ibid [60] (the Court).
[125] ibid 488–89.
[126] ibid.
[127] ibid [60].
[128] ibid [45] (the Court).
[129] ibid [48].

V. CONCLUSION

The purpose of this chapter has been to foreshadow a coherent twenty-first century understanding of money awards for equitable wrongs. The starting point for that coherence is to complete a development that began with the nineteenth century English procedural reforms. That requires the recognition that money awards for wrongdoing in equity should be recognised as damages. Difficult questions can then be tackled as a matter of principle. One is to recognise when a money award in equity is a claim for debt, seeking to enforce a right, rather than a claim for damages. Another is to recognise that, as with the common law, there are different species of damages for which different principles apply. One species (substitutive compensation) is concerned with rectifying wrongful acts. Another (reparative compensation) is concerned with compensation for loss.

9

The Basic Structure of Rescission

STEVEN ELLIOTT KC[1]

I. INTRODUCTION

IN AN INAUGURAL lecture delivered in 2001, Professor Burrows argued that judges, legislators and practising lawyers were not doing enough to eradicate substantive inconsistencies between the common law and equity.[2] Over the past 20 years, however, his call to arms has led to only qualified progress. Indeed, in 2015 the editors of the fifth edition of *Equity: Doctrines and Remedies* effectively claimed victory in that book's campaign against 'casual or uninformed judicial reasoning based on a misconception of the Judicature legislation'.[3] This chapter responds to Professor Burrows' call, arguing that there is room for progress in relation to the basic structure of rescission.

The rescission of contracts is not uniquely indigenous to either the common law or equity. Before the Judicature Act 1873, courts of each type gave relief in different classes of case. There was overlap in the central instances of fraud and grounds affecting insurance contracts so that the appropriate court would depend on the particular circumstances of the case. The distinctions were byzantine. The complexity was compounded by the fact that those courts administered justice in different ways, which contributed to the development of distinct models of rescission.

These dualities have left a legacy of complexity and confusion. For example, some modern judges proceed on the basis that rescission always occurs by the act of the party,[4] an old common law idea, where others proceed on the basis that the operative step is always the order of the court, an idea developed in equity.[5] In other cases the

[1] I am grateful to Dominic O'Sullivan KC and to Matthew Hoyle for discussing with me some of the points developed in this paper, as well as for comments from Professor Birke Häcker, Professor Ben McFarlane and Professor Charles Mitchell.

[2] A Burrows, 'We Do This at Common Law but That in Equity' (2002) 22 *OJLS* 1. Academic lawyers are notably absent from the list. For discussion of this lecture, see too, McFarlane's chapter in this volume.

[3] JD Heydon, MJ Leeming and PG Turner, *Meagher, Gummow and Lehane's Equity: Doctrines and Remedies*, 5th edn (Chatswood NSW, LexisNexis Butterworths, 2015) paras [2-365], [2-340], [2-370].

[4] This is sometimes referred to as self-help rescission, but it is not true self-help relief any more than is any other exercise of a power. Rescinding to recover legal title can help to justify recaption of goods, which is a self-help remedy in the normal sense.

[5] Compare, eg, *Shalson v Russo* [2003] EWHC 1637 (Ch), [2005] Ch 281 [122] with *Islington London Borough Council v Uckac* [2006] EWCA Civ 340, [2006] 1 WLR 1303 [26].

courts posit a continuing distinction between those circumstances in which rescission occurs by the election of the rescinding party and those in which the court must exercise a discretionary power. The distinction depends on the grounds on which rescission is sought. For example, the line has most recently been drawn between fully secret commissions, where rescission occurs by election, and half-secret commissions (the agent discloses that there is an inducement but not its amount or nature) where the power to rescind belongs to the court.[6] Speaking of rescission in equity for fraud, Henderson LJ has concluded that the authorities are in such a state of disarray that only the Supreme Court can reconcile them.[7]

The proprietary consequences of rescission have also been shaped by history in ways which are difficult to explain on any principled basis. An aggrieved party who is able to rescind in circumstances that would have been recognised by the common law courts may immediately recover legal title to goods transferred under the contract.[8] But where rescission would only have been recognised in Chancery, upon election the rescinding party can only acquire equitable rights,[9] with quite different consequences.

The basic structure of rescission is unfinished business. In *The Law of Rescission* we endeavour to state the law as we find it, identifying those categories of case that are governed by the rules developed in the common law courts and those governed by equity, distinguishing within the second category as best we can between cases in which equity gives effect to party election and those where the power to rescind lies with the court, and offering such justifications as can be given.[10] We conclude, however, by noting that this topic needs reappraisal.[11] That is the purpose of this chapter: to reconsider the basic structure of rescission. Instead of working upward from the authorities binding on intermediate appellate courts, this chapter steps back to consider the law by reference to foundational authorities and deeper principles. The purpose is to identify a practical reconciliation, open to the Supreme Court and apex courts elsewhere in the Commonwealth, which places the law on a simpler footing which is more defensible.

The conclusion will be that, when the opportunity arises,[12] apex courts should recognise and affirm, consistently with dominant authorities, that rescission is *always* the act of the aggrieved party exercising a power to rescind, the consequences of

[6] *Hurstanger Ltd v Wilson* [2007] EWCA Civ 299, [2008] Bus LR 216 [46]–[47]; *Conway v Prince Eze* [2018] EWHC 29 (Ch) [148], [154], [156] (appeal dismissed [2019] EWCA Civ 88); *Wood v Commercial First Business Ltd* [2021] EWCA Civ 471, [2022] Ch 123 [8], [98]–[101], [128].

[7] *HMRC v IGE USA Investments Ltd* [2021] EWCA Civ 534, [2021] Ch 423 [91].

[8] *Load v Green* (1846) 15 M & W 216, 221; 153 ER 828, 830; *Clough v London and North Western Railway* (1871–72) LR 7 Ex 26 (Court of Exchequer Chamber) 32; *Car and Universal Finance Co Ltd v Caldwell* [1965] 1 QB 525 (CA) 532.

[9] Judges have taken to calling this a 'rescission trust': eg, *National Crime Agency v Robb* [2014] EWHC 4384 (Ch), [2015] Ch 520.

[10] D O'Sullivan, S Elliott and R Zakrzewski, *The Law of Rescission*, 3rd edn (Oxford, OUP, 2023) esp chs 10 and 11.

[11] ibid para [11.111]. Even allowing for this explanation, attentive readers may detect discrepancies between this chapter and the book. Different parts of the book are primarily written by different authors and the authors do not necessarily agree on all points.

[12] The task apex courts will face in such case will be comparable to that which the Supreme Court confronted in *FHR European Partners LLP v Cedar Capital* [2014] UKSC 45, [2015] AC 250.

which flow immediately and automatically.[13] The court may be required to exercise judgement in working out what those consequences have been but it does not enjoy a strong discretion whether to grant relief at all. If rescission is not barred then the aggrieved party may rescind as a matter of right. In addition, the courts should transcend the jurisdictional duality by assimilating the proprietary consequences of rescission, whatever the grounds on which the power to rescind arises, to those that obtain where party election is given effect in equity, as those consequences better balance competing interests than the old common law rules. These two steps would go some distance toward shaping a unified doctrine of rescission and ensuring that substantive outcomes do not merely depend on the jurisdictional provenance of the different grounds.

II. THE LAW WE HAVE

A. The Position before 1875

It is difficult to state the law in this area without beginning with the different ways in which relief relating to rescission could be sought and granted before the Judicature reforms.[14] The common law did not have an action for rescission. What it had was actions for consequential relief of various kinds. In each case the role of the common law court was to adjudicate, in the context of a claim for consequential relief, a contention that the contract already had been extinguished by the aggrieved party's election. This model only crystallised in the decades preceding the Judicature reforms. Most importantly, Parke B's landmark decision in *Load v Green* in 1846 reconciled earlier threads on the basis that a contract induced by fraud was capable of conferring a title but the title was defeasible on the election of the innocent party.[15] Accordingly, the contract was properly described not as void, as had often been thought, but as voidable. This aligned with earlier decisions which had established that claims for personal restitution were only available where it was proved that the contract had been rescinded by manifesting an election to treat the contract as at an end, as by demanding the return of money paid or by tendering back goods purchased.[16]

[13] Disagreeing on this particular point with J O'Sullivan, 'Rescission as a Self-Help Remedy: A Critical Analysis' (2000) 59 *CLJ* 509 (although there is much agreement on wider points); A Reilly, 'Is the "Mere Equity" to Rescind a Legal Power? Unpacking Hohfeld's Concept of "Volitional Control"' (2019) 39 *OJLS* 779; and N Andrews, A Tettenborn and G Virgo, *Contractual Duties: Performance, Breach, Termination and Remedies*, 3rd edn (London, Sweet & Maxwell, 2020) para [1-029]. The position taken is broadly aligned with A Burrows, *A Restatement of the English Law of Contract*, 2nd edn (Oxford, OUP, 2020) para [34.4] and S Zogg, *Proprietary Consequences in Defective Transfers of Ownership* (Cambridge, Intersentia, 2020) ch 4, para [2.1.2]. Häcker does not specifically address this point but her legal and equitable power *in rem* theory implies that she would also reject the court order model: B Häcker, *Consequences of Impaired Consent Transfers* (Oxford, Hart, 2013) ch 4.

[14] See generally O'Sullivan, Elliott and Zakrzewski (n 10) ch 3, on which the next few paragraphs are based.

[15] *Load v Green* (n 8).

[16] *Weston v Downes* (1778) 1 Doug 23, 99 ER 19; *Towers v Barrett* (1786) 1 TR 133, 99 ER 1014; and subsequent cases.

Where the relief granted by the common law courts was unavailable or unsatisfactory, a suitor was sometimes able to obtain relief in Chancery. Here rescission was considered directly in that the bill itself prayed that the contract be set aside and consequential relief granted. The function of the court was to weigh all the evidence placed before it, and to determine whether the contract should be set aside and if so on what terms, rather than to enforce rights arising on a prior election. Chancery might give effect to its determination by granting a common injunction to prevent the defendant from proceeding at law or by cancelling the instrument so it could not be proven at law. This may be all the Chancery judges meant when they spoke of a contract being set aside, on the basis that equity did not extinguish common law rights. Thus in *Clark v Malpas* the Lords Justices clarified that where a deed conveying land was rescinded, it should not be declared void 'for the deed is not legally but only equitably void', but the order should instead be 'in the usual way that [the deed] be set aside'.[17]

A plaintiff was only entitled to proceed at law if the ground for rescission fell within a short list of recognised possibilities including fraud (meaning actual fraud and also bribery); duress; and non-disclosure and misrepresentation relating to insurance contracts and guarantees.[18] Historically, relief in Chancery was usually framed by reference to fraud but, as is well known, that concept was given an extremely broad ambit. Chancery exercised a concurrent jurisdiction at least in cases of actual fraud and the grounds relating to insurance contracts.[19] In addition, Chancery would also rescind contracts on grounds not recognised by the common law courts including undue influence, abuse of confidence by those occupying fiduciary roles, unconscionable conduct, in certain cases of unilateral mistake, and, as the law later developed, in cases of non-fraudulent misrepresentation generally.

That is more or less how matters stood in the years immediately preceding the Judicature reforms. The compartmentalisation of English private law was such that the discrepancy in the approaches was not much remarked upon. A principled synthesis was attempted, however, right on the eve of the reforms in the shape of the Indian Contract Act 1872. Crystallising analytic advances on both sides of the English jurisdictional divide, the 1872 Act systematically distinguished between void agreements and voidable contracts, the latter being enforceable at the outset but becoming void at the option of one or more of the parties.[20] The Indian Law Commissioners did not consider that they needed to introduce any distinction between rescission at law and in equity where that jurisdictional divide did not already exist in India.

[17] *Clark v Malpas* (1862) 4 De GF & J 401, 405; 45 ER 1238, 1240 (Knight-Bruce LJ).

[18] Authorities are identified at O'Sullivan, Elliott and Zakrzewski (n 10) para [10.23], also addressing mental infirmity and intoxication.

[19] *Newbigging v Adam* (1886) 34 Ch D 582 (CA) 592; *Hoare v Bremridge* (1872–73) 8 Ch App 22 (CA).

[20] Indian Contract Act 1872, ss 2(i) and (j), 10 and 56. Title to assets may pass to the responsible party under a voidable contract, albeit it is a title defeasible by rescission, and third parties who do not have notice of the vitiating factor may acquire indefeasible rights in those assets from the responsible party: *Central National Bank Ltd v United Industrial Bank Ltd* 1954 AIR 181 (Supreme Court of India); *Ningawwa v Byrappa* 1968 AIR 956 (Supreme Court of India); Sale of Goods Act 1930 (India), s 29.

B. Developments Since 1875

Soon after the Judicature reforms, important steps were taken toward the formulation of a unified doctrine of rescission. In 1886, Bowen LJ was able to state comprehensively that '[a] contract obtained by fraud, being voidable and not void, remains until it is set aside, and when it is set aside it is treated both at law and in equity as non-existing'.[21] There are two important ideas here: first that such contracts are generically voidable, and second that the general effect of avoiding such a contract is that it ceases to exist. Another famous example of a unifying step is found in *Erlanger*, where Lord Blackburn was able to draw on authorities decided both at common law and in equity to find a generic rule that there should be *restitutio in integrum* as a condition of rescission, albeit he noticed a considerable difference in the mode by which that principle was applied in those different courts.[22]

The achievement was not complete and the differences Lord Blackburn noticed are one example of a distinction that is usually thought to have continued: common law rescission remains more closely circumscribed by the *restitutio in integrum* impossible bar. In many cases where rescission is barred at law it will nonetheless be possible in equity, which only requires substantial *restitutio in integrum* and which often permits counter-restitution by pecuniary substitute.[23] The distinction between rescission at law and in equity still matters, however, not least for its proprietary consequences. Legal title in assets transferred will only revest at the point of election where rescission is effective at common law. Where instead rescission by election takes effect in equity, equitable rights vest instead,[24] with quite different consequences, identified further below.

C. The Position Today

Focussing on the location of the power to rescind a contract, recent authorities recognise that there continues to be a category of case governed by common law principles in which rescission occurs by the communication of an election.[25] This has been said to be so in relation to fraudulent misrepresentation, bribery and duress.[26] There is also a category of case, which includes at least fraud, where rescission is also possible in equity and equity recognises the rescinding party's election.[27] Finally, recent cases have identified a category of case, governed by equitable principles, in which the

[21] *Newbigging* (n 19) 592.

[22] *Erlanger v The New Sombrero Phosphate Co* (1878) 3 App Cas 1218 (HL) 1277–79.

[23] *Compagnie Française des Chemins de Fer Paris-Orleans v Leeston Shipping Co Ltd* [1919] 1 Lloyd's Rep 235 (KBD) 238; O'Sullivan, Elliott and Zakrzewski (n 10) paras [18.54]–[18.61].

[24] *Alati v Kruger* (1955) 94 CLR 216 (HCA) 223.

[25] In some cases even an uncommunicated announcement: *Car & Universal Finance* (n 8).

[26] *Halpern v Halpern (No 2)* [2006] EWHC 1728 (Comm), [2007] QB 88 (duress); *IGE USA* (n 7) [20] (fraudulent misrepresentation); *Ceviz v Frawley* [2021] EWHC 8 (Ch) [120] (fraud); *UBS AG v Kommunale Wasserwerke Leipzig GmbH* [2017] EWCA Civ 1567, [2017] 2 Lloyd's Rep 621 [371] (bribery); *Wood* (n 6) (bribery).

[27] *Alati* (n 24) 233.

court is said to exercise a discretionary power whether to grant relief. The principal authorities concern fiduciary misconduct and the specialised example of half-secret commissions.[28] For example, in concluding that Patten J had been entitled to refuse to rescind a surety contract, Dyson LJ said in *Johnson v EBS Pensioner Trustees Ltd*:

> [W]hatever the position in relation to a claim to rescind based on misrepresentation, the right to rescission on grounds of undue influence, abuse of confidence or breach of fiduciary duty depends on the exercise of the discretion by the court to intervene in the enforcement of legal rights. … When exercising its equitable jurisdiction, the court considers what fairness requires not only when addressing the question of the precise form of relief, but also when considering whether the remedy should be granted at all.[29]

In recent restatements, Australian courts have also affirmed the continuing vitality of the distinction between those cases in which the power to rescind lies with the aggrieved party and those in which it lies with the court.[30]

Against this, however, important authorities assert that rescission has now been generalised such that it *always* occurs by the exercise of the aggrieved party's power, without the need for an order of the court. This idea is sometimes traced back before the Judicature reforms to Lord Hatherley LC's speech in *Reese River Silver Mining Co v Smith*,[31] but that case actually concerned a statutory power to amend a company's register.[32] However, the same idea has been formulated and applied in other cases down the years, and whilst it is possible to dispute the standing of some of these as precedents supporting the general proposition,[33] together they form an impressive body of opinion.[34]

Innocent misrepresentation has caused a degree of confusion. The ground finds its roots in equity and at least one judge has concluded that rescission lies in the power of the court.[35] The Court of Appeal was not prepared to endorse that view, saying that the point was highly controversial and noting that the Misrepresentation Act 1967 presupposes that, in some cases at least, rescission does not depend on obtaining a court order.[36] To this it may be replied that the legislature seems to have hedged its

[28] *Johnson v EBS Pensioner Trustees Ltd* [2002] EWCA Civ 164, [2002] Lloyd's Rep PN 309 [57], [78]–[79] (fiduciary misconduct); *Hurstanger* (n 6) [46]–[47] (half secret commission); *UBS AG* (n 26) [162] (half-secret commissions, 'undoubted discretion').

[29] *Johnson* (n 28) [78]–[79]; Mummery LJ said much the same thing at [57].

[30] *Nadinic v Drinkwater* [2017] NSWCA 114, (2017) 94 NSWLR 518 [28]–[29]; *Jonval Builders Pty Ltd v Commissioner for Fair Trading* [2020] NSWCA 233, (2020) 383 ALR 334 [29]–[34]; *Harvard Nominees Pty Ltd v Tiller* [2020] FCAFC 229, (2020) 282 FCR 530 [96].

[31] (1869–70) LR 4 HL 64.

[32] O'Sullivan, Elliott and Zakrzewski (n 10) paras [11.68]–[11.74]; J O'Sullivan (n 13) 533–36.

[33] O'Sullivan, Elliott and Zakrzewski (n 10) paras [11.75]–[11.84].

[34] *Horsler v Zorro* [1975] Ch 302 (Ch) 310; *Society of Lloyd's v Leighs* [1997] CLC 1398 (CA); *Drake Insurance plc v Provident Insurance plc* [2003] EWHC 109 (Comm), [2003] Lloyd's Rep IR 781 [31]–[32]; *Brotherton v Aseguradora Colseguros SA* [2003] EWCA Civ 705, [2003] 2 All ER (Comm) 298 [27], [44]–[48]; and *Shalson* (n 5) [122]. In Australia, *Alati* (n 24) 223.

[35] *SK Shipping Europe Ltd v Capital VLCC 3 Corp (The C Challenger)* [2020] EWHC 3448 (Comm), [2021] 2 Lloyd's Rep 109 [241]. In *Peak Hotels and Resorts Ltd v Tarek Investments Ltd* [2015] EWHC 1997 (Ch), Barling J noted at [131] that the point is controversial but his conclusion at [136] presupposes that the court order model applies.

[36] *SK Shipping Europe Ltd v Capital VLCC 3 Corp (The C Challenger)* [2022] EWCA Civ 231 [89] (Males LJ), referring to the statutory words 'if it is claimed … that the contract ought to be or has been rescinded'.

bets by accommodating both possibilities and that the statutory power to declare a contract subsisting operates with less difficulty where the power to rescind is itself a power of the court.[37] However, as is discussed below, the point is in fact determined by the authority of *Abram Steamship Co Ltd v Westville Shipping Co Ltd* in favour of the view that the power to rescind for innocent misrepresentation lies with the representee.[38]

III. THE MECHANICAL DUALITY

A. The Problem

This state of the law is evidently imperfect. That it is shaped by the old jurisdictional duality is not itself an objection, but it does have the consequence that the law is much more complicated than seems necessary. At one level the choice of mechanism expresses a preference as between, on the one hand, simplicity and certainty, and, on the other hand, the capacity for nuanced justice. Views may differ and reasonable arguments can be made in support of both the party election model and the court order model. However, a special case is needed to support a system that blends the two, for this brings with it enhanced complexity and differential if not inconsistent treatment.

The party election model often favours the aggrieved party because there is less scope for judicial control of the remedy. The discretionary power the court order model entails is, necessarily, only used either to refuse to give effect to an election to rescind or to impose terms conditioning the availability of rescission. It might, therefore, be thought that the common law's commitment to the party election model is explained by the wickedness of fraud and duress. However, this idea quickly fails as a general explanation for the pattern of the current law. This is because the party election model also applies in relation to grounds which are not necessarily wicked, such as non-disclosure in the context of insurance.[39] Equally, the courts have made clear that rescission for fiduciary misconduct lies in the discretion of the court, unless the circumstances are such that the common law would have found fraud or bribery, but the betrayal of trust can make fiduciary misconduct at least as morally wrong as fraud perpetrated at arm's length. It is therefore difficult to explain why the law stipulates a different mechanism for these different categories of case on anything other than historical grounds.

Moreover, the co-existence of the two models can produce divergent outcomes in relation to grounds which may overlap or be suggested by the same facts. A dishonest fiduciary's alleged misconduct may also be said to constitute fraud of a kind recognised at common law. One characterisation entitles the principal to end the contract by communicating their election, the other requires proceedings to be prosecuted to

[37] O'Sullivan, Elliott and Zakrzewski (n 10) para [28.05].

[38] *Abram Steamship Co Ltd v Westville Shipping Co Ltd* [1923] AC 773 (HL). This was also the premise of Roch LJ's opinion in *TSB Bank plc v Camfield* [1995] 1 WLR 430 (CA) 438–39.

[39] *Brotherton* (n 34).

a conclusion. Grounds that shade into one another should not be treated so very differently.

B. *Abram Steamship*

There are, therefore, good reasons why the law should settle on a single model to be applied in all cases. In 1923, in *Abram Steamship*, the House of Lords chose the party election model, at least for fraud and misrepresentation, in a case where the competition between the alternatives was the very point in issue.[40] The appellant had assigned a contract for the building of a steamer to the respondent on the basis of innocent misrepresentations that the steamer had reached a certain stage of construction. The respondent then assigned its contract to a third party, repeating the misrepresentations. The third party discovered the true state of affairs and sued the respondent in the Welsh courts to rescind the assignment. The respondent conceded that action but, crucially, before doing so it brought separate proceedings against the appellant in Scotland to rescind the original assignment. The appellant argued that those Scottish proceedings were premature and should fail because at the time they were instituted the sub-sale still survived so that the respondent was not in a position to effect *restitutio in integrum*. This defence failed essentially on the basis that the sub-sale was extinguished upon the election of the third party, not the later order of the court.

Lord Atkinson explained the point most fully in a speech which has been cited many times:

> Where one party to a contract expresses by word or act in an unequivocal manner that by reason of fraud or essential error of a material kind inducing him to enter into the contract he has resolved to rescind it, and refuses to be bound by it, the expression of his election, if justified by the facts, terminates the contract, puts the parties in statu quo ante and restores things, as between them, to the position in which they stood before the contract was entered into.[41]

Lord Atkinson went on to explain that this was the case even where the issue was disputed in court: 'The verdict is merely the judicial determination of the fact that the expression by the plaintiff of his election to rescind was justified, was effective, and put an end to the contract.'[42]

The appeal was from Scotland but the case has been rightly treated as stating the law of England and Wales. It concerned the rescission of a contract between two companies both of which were in Cardiff,[43] which is also where the rescission of the sub-sale had been litigated. Choice of law was not mentioned but the contract and its rescission must have been governed by the law of England and Wales; at least that is how we would look at it today. In any event, the judges who heard the subsequent dispute that ended in the House of Lords seem to have proceeded on the basis that English and Scots law were in relevant respects identical. The Scottish judges

[40] *Abram Steamship* (n 34).
[41] *Abram Steamship* (n 34) 781.
[42] ibid 781 and see 785.
[43] *The Westville Shipping Co Ltd v Abram Steamship Co Ltd* 1922 SC 571 (CSIH) 572, 575.

cited Scots authorities and the English judges, including Lord Atkinson, cited English authorities, all to the same effect. A few years later Lord Wright remarked in *Spence v Crawford*, another Scots case, that the principles governing rescission are the same in Scotland as in England.[44]

Lord Atkinson did not mention the division between law and equity, preferring half a century after the Judicature reforms to express himself generically. He might have, however, for the ground in question was innocent misrepresentation, which only ever supported proceedings in Chancery. The jurisdictional relationship was later explained in *Alati v Kruger*,[45] a fraud case. On this account, rescission is more readily available in equity because of its broader powers to do what is practically just between the parties, and so to restore them substantially to the *status quo ante*, but rescission for misrepresentation is always the act of the party rather than that of the court.

In retrospect we can see that *Abram Shipping* marked an important development in the law. The election model Lord Atkinson explained originally developed in the common law courts and had not, before that time, been applied in a contract case with its jurisdictional roots in equity, at least by an appellate court.[46] By holding that the mechanism of rescission is the same in cases on both sides of the jurisdictional divide, their Lordships took an important step toward the recognition of the simpler, unified understanding of rescission to which the courts have been progressing since the nineteenth century.

In circumstances where this step was not explained in the speeches, the decision has been said to have involved a confusion of law and equity. But we should be slow to assume that such eminent Law Lords, including two who had served as Lord Chancellor, did not appreciate the distinctions formerly drawn in the area.[47] As noted above, there is particular good sense in taking a consistent approach to the mechanism of rescission where alternative grounds sit closely together, and fraud was indeed an alternative at first instance in *Abrams Shipping*.[48] We should not regret a decision which simplifies the law such that the mechanism of rescission does not differ based on accidents of jurisdictional birth occurring in the distant past. Reconciling discordant authorities was part of the function of the House of Lords.

Lord Atkinson spoke of cases involving fraud or essential error, meaning innocent misrepresentation, and did not say whether the same analysis would apply in cases concerning other grounds. It is in relation to grounds formerly recognised only in equity – especially cases involving fiduciaries and undue influence – that the Court of Appeal continues to insist on the pre-Judicature court order model. However, in circumstances in which the House of Lords has applied the election model to innocent misrepresentation, it is no longer possible to draw a line according to whether the ground was recognised in equity. In *Abram Shipping* the election model penetrated that

[44] *Spence v Crawford* [1939] 3 All ER 271 (HL) 288.

[45] *Alati* (n 24) 223.

[46] In *Re Glubb* [1900] 1 Ch 354 (CA) gifts procured by innocent misrepresentation were held to have been avoidable at the election of the donors.

[47] In addition to Lord Atkinson, the appeal was heard by the Earl of Birkenhead, Viscount Finlay, Lord Dunedin and Lord Shaw of Dunfermline.

[48] *Westville Shipping* (n 43) 576.

boundary and has now occupied part of the territory of equity for nearly a century. In *Brotherton v Aseguradora Colseguros SA* Mance and Buxton LJJ each expressed the view that following *Abram Shipping* rescission occurs by party election in all cases, specifically deciding that this was true where the ground was non-disclosure by a proposing reinsured.[49] Reinsurers in that case had rescinded reinsurances for non-disclosure of certain rumours; the reinsured was not allowed to challenge that on the basis that the rumours later proved groundless, for the rescission had already occurred. That case would, before the Judicature reforms, have been brought in Chancery.[50]

C. Substantive Arguments

The Court of Appeal has emphasised in this area that arguments based on historic jurisdictional distinctions should rarely justify differential treatment.[51] If the continuation of the court order model is to be justified in some defined categories of case, the reasons for this will need to be substantive. As argued above, however, the starting point should be a preference for simplicity and consistency of treatment, which favours the general application of only one of the two models. Moreover, whatever considerations can be advanced in favour of the court order model considered in the abstract, the House of Lords (and the High Court of Australia) long ago opted for the election model in cases of fraud and misrepresentation,[52] and this has been extended to non-disclosure by a proposing insured. At this stage a powerful case would be needed to support the general adoption of the court order model. It may be observed that the party election model also applies to the doctrine of termination for breach or repudiation, a close parallel which was only decisively separated from rescission less than 50 years ago.[53]

Two points of substance favour the election model. First, the election model is more satisfactory so far as claims against accessories are concerned. It is generally understood that where a contract is rescinded in equity, the rescinding party's equity to rescind is replaced by equitable rights in relation to assets transferred pursuant to the contract or their traceable product. These rights are said to vest retrospectively for the purposes of tracing, but this does not create retrospective personal liability.[54] From the point of election, however, a person knowingly holding an asset subject

[49] *Brotherton* (n 34) [27], [44]–[48]; and see *Drake Insurance* (n 34) [27], [44]–[48], which was reversed on appeal but this point was not challenged: [2003] EWCA Civ 1834, [2004] QB 601 [81].

[50] While the common law courts and Chancery exercised a concurrent jurisdiction in relation to non-disclosure by a proposing insured, a claim like this one by the insurer seeking a declaration that the policy had been rescinded could only have been brought in Chancery: *Hoare v Bremridge* (n 19) 26–27.

[51] *Halpern v Halpern (Nos 1 and 2)* [2007] EWCA Civ 291, [2008] QB 195 [70].

[52] The Supreme Court of India has reached the same conclusion albeit Indian contract law is not affected by a historical jurisdictional divide as ours is: *Hungerford Investment Trust v Haridas Mundra* 1972 AIR 1826 (Supreme Court of India); *Ganga Retreat & Towers Ltd v State of Rajasthan* (2003) 12 SCC 91 (Supreme Court of India).

[53] *Johnson v Agnew* [1980] AC 367 (HL).

[54] *Lonrho plc v al Fayed (No 2)* [1992] 1 WLR 1 (Ch) 11–12; *El Ajou v Dollar Land Holdings plc* [1993] 3 All ER 717 (Ch) 735; *Bristol and West Building Society v Mothew* [1998] Ch 1 (CA).

to the rescinding party's equitable title will be liable if they misdirect the asset. Moreover, while there is a surprising paucity of authority, it would seem to follow that a third party who knows of the fraud cannot be liable for assisting in the movement of such an asset before the contract is rescinded, for at that time there was no trust.[55] Similarly, third parties who know of the fraud but who receive and transmit the asset before the contract is rescinded would seem to avoid liability on the basis of knowing receipt.[56] In other words, a mere equity to rescind is not a sufficient interest to support a claim against an accessory. These propositions are a function of the contracts in question being voidable rather than void.

If all of that is correct, it would appear to follow that the court order model leaves an unfortunate lacuna between the point at which the rescinding party announces their intention and the point at which the court ultimately rescinds the contract, which may in practice be years later. During that period third parties may assist in transactions concerning the assets or receive and transmit those assets without liability even though they know the contract was induced by fraud and know of the claim to rescind. It is only when the court finally rescinds the contract that sufficient rights crystallise to support third-party liability. The election model is more satisfactory in that rights vest at that earlier time. It might be suggested that the court order can be given retrospective effect for this purpose, but that substantially concedes the argument in favour of election being the critical moment.

Second, it seems wrong that a party who elects to rescind their contract must seek judicial relief. Imagine that A quickly discovers B's misconduct and calls off the contract between them at a time when it remains wholly executory. B does not respond. No agreement to cancel the contract could be implied, but A should be entitled to proceed on the basis that they are free from their obligations. A should not be required, on pain of remaining bound, to take legal proceedings, which would entail cost and complexity even if B does not contest them.

Arguments in support of the court order model generally focus on the discretion that model accords the court when deciding whether to grant relief. The argument is that the complexity and potential range of contractual relationships is such that comparatively unstructured judicial powers are needed to effectively regulate the consequences of misconduct. It is certainly the case that the election model leaves no room for an open-textured judicial evaluation of the fairness of the overall relief. Where rescission takes effect by the communication of a complaining party's election, it has immediate and final effect. The contract is extinguished, property rights revert, and the parties are automatically entitled to such unconditional relief as is necessary to restore them to their original positions. In determining what that relief is, the court may need to consider complex questions and make subtle judgments. But the court must necessarily apply definite rules and principles to give effect to changes in the legal relations between the parties which have already, and finally, occurred.

[55] This appears to have been a premise of the reasoning in *Nolan v Minerva Trust Co Ltd* [2014] 2 JLR 117 (Royal Court of Jersey) especially [147]. A third party may be liable for dishonest assistance if their pre-rescission conduct assists in the misdirection of the asset after the point of rescission.

[56] *E D & F Man Capital Markets Ltd v Come Harvest Holdings Ltd* [2022] EWHC 229 (Comm) [610]–[642], which is consistent with *Byers v Saudi National Bank* [2022] EWCA Civ 43, [2022] 4 WLR 22.

These consequences are not, however, shortcomings of the election model. Whilst rescission is often said to be discretionary,[57] that discretion is usually understood to be guided by settled principles which have been articulated over the years in the definition of the circumstances in which rescission will be barred on one ground or another. These are the equitable defences and their common law cognates.[58] If rescission has become barred then the court will exercise its discretion to refuse rescission. By contrast, it is well established that if *restitutio in integrum* is possible, and if rescission is not otherwise barred, then the innocent party is entitled to have the contract rescinded as a matter of right.[59] Similarly, the discretion a court enjoys in working out the consequences of rescission in complex cases is guided by the principle of achieving the practically just result of substantial *restitutio in integrum*.[60] A rich body of authority indicates how this should be done in particular classes of case.[61]

That the courts exercise a judgment of this limited kind is not logically or practically inconsistent with the election model. If the court considers, for example, that in all of the circumstances the aggrieved party affirmed the contract, or that in all the circumstances, *restitutio in integrum* was impossible, then the conclusion will be that the election was ineffective. If the court considers that financial adjustments of one kind or another are necessary to achieve substantial *restitutio in integrum*, these define the entitlements of the parties immediately following the election to rescind.

It is hardly surprising that English judges should approach their task in this way. A stronger form of discretion would sit uneasily with the importance of commercial certainty, which the Court of Appeal has emphasised in this area,[62] if not the rule of law. 'On the whole', Rix LJ observed in *Drake Insurance plc v Provident Insurance plc*, 'English commercial law has not favoured the process of balancing rights and wrongs under a species of what I suppose would now be called a doctrine of proportionality. Instead it has sought for stricter and for simpler tests and for certainty.'[63] As cases have come before the courts, as well as through the work of commentators, it has over the past century been possible to gradually define and refine the circumstances in which rescission is possible, and with what consequences, so that well advised parties can know with reasonable confidence where they stand. There are of course novel and complex cases in which care may be needed in applying recognised rules and principles. But the courts should not cloud analytic progress in this area by encouraging a concept of justice unmediated by principle.

Johnson is the first of the recent decisions in which the Court of Appeal has marked out a continuing field of operation for the court order model.[64] The case

[57] *Spence* (n 44) 288 is a well-known example.

[58] The effect of delay is a special case where equity and the common law have followed very different paths. See most recently *IGE USA* (n 7).

[59] *Lagunas Nitrate Co v Lagunas Syndicate* [1899] 2 Ch 392 (CA) 456 (Rigby LJ). Although he was dissenting in that case, Rigby LJ's remark has been specifically approved both in the House of Lords and in the High Court of Australia: *Spence* (n 44) 280; *Brown v Smitt* (1924) 34 CLR 160 (HCA) 165.

[60] *Erlanger* (n 22) 1278–79; *Spence* (n 44) 288.

[61] O'Sullivan, Elliott and Zakrzewski (n 10) ch 17.

[62] *The C Challenger* (n 36) [88].

[63] *Drake Insurance plc v Provident Insurance plc* [2003] EWCA Civ 1834, [2004] QB 601 [88]. For the importance of certainty in relation to commercial law, and its implications for equitable doctrines see too, Newbury's and Yip's chapters in this volume.

[64] *Johnson* (n 28).

concerned loans which Mr Johnson, a solicitor, had arranged in favour of a '£100 company' named Dufose, repayment of which its owner Mr O'Shea had guaranteed. Mr O'Shea was a client of Mr Johnson with the consequence that Mr Johnson acted in a dual capacity. He failed to disclose that his firm levied a 1.5 per cent service charge on the lenders. Dufose defaulted and Mr O'Shea sought to avoid liability under his guarantee.

The Lords Justices considered that the service charge should have been disclosed and (by a majority) that it was material to the transaction, but they were unwilling to permit Mr O'Shea to rescind his guarantee, instead requiring that Mr Johnson disgorge the service charge. Echoing the views of Patten J at first instance, Mummery and Dyson LJJ each reasoned that the remedy is equitable and therefore discretionary. Mummery LJ emphasised that the loans to Dufose were made on the basis of the guarantee and that those loans enabled Dufose to continue what was in reality Mr O'Shea's business. He concluded that '[w]here counter-restitution is not given, fairness requires an order for an account of the service charge, rather than rescission of the surety by reason of non-disclosure of the service charge'.[65]

It is not controversial that where counter-restitution is not given, rescission is not possible,[66] and that proposition does not require that the court should exercise a strong form of discretion as to whether rescission should be granted. The application of that proposition in favour of a surety is, however, controversial. A surety does not receive the loan money other than incidentally and so counter-restitution is inapt. It might be argued that *restitutio in integrum* is nonetheless impossible because, the lender having in good faith advanced money to the borrower on the strength of the guarantee, they would be unjustifiably prejudiced if the guarantee was now set aside.[67] That argument, however, has usually been thought to be precluded by *MacKenzie v Royal Bank of Canada*, in which Lord Atkin said that '[t]he mere fact that the party making the representation has treated the contract as binding and has acted on it does not preclude relief'.[68] It may be that Lord Atkin's dictum can be confined to cases involving vulnerable sureties, which Mr O'Shea was not. This was the real issue in *Johnson's* case but unfortunately *MacKenzie* was not mentioned. The question whether rescission occurs by party election or by the order of the court was a red herring.

The defendants in the second case, *Hurstanger v Wilson*, applied through a broker for an £8,000 loan from the claimant lenders. They were told that '[i]n certain circumstances this company does pay commission to brokers', but not that on this occasion a commission of £240 was in fact being paid to the fiduciary broker. Tuckey LJ reasoned that the statement negated secrecy, so that the law of bribery was not engaged, but that the borrowers' informed consent was nonetheless not obtained. Citing *Johnson*, he considered that the Court had a discretion whether or not to rescind the contract, and concluded that the Court should instead award to the borrowers £240 plus

[65] ibid [58].
[66] *Erlanger* (n 22).
[67] As to this aspect of the *restitutio in integrum* bar, see O'Sullivan, Elliott and Zakrzewski (n 10) paras [18.106]ff.
[68] *MacKenzie v Royal Bank of Canada* [1934] AC 468 (PC) 476.

interest. Tuckey LJ considered that to rescind the transaction would be unfair and disproportionate.

One should be slow to gainsay Tuckey LJ's judgment as to the fairness of the outcome the Court of Appeal achieved, although it is worth noting that upon rescission the borrowers would have been required to repay the loan with interest.[69] Be that as it may, rescission can sometimes have consequences that seem disproportionate. For this reason, by section 2(2) of the Misrepresentation Act 1967 Parliament conferred on the courts a power to uphold contracts and award damages instead. But it only created that power in cases of innocent misrepresentation. The decision in *Hurstanger v Wilson* effectively extends that statutory power to other grounds recognised in equity in respect of which Parliament did not act. This judicial innovation seems to go further than our constitution allows.

In addition to precluding the possibility of a broad discretion to refuse relief, the party election model has other consequences that must be taken into account in an evaluation of its merits and demerits. One consequence is that events after the election cannot undo rescission or give a basis for refusing relief. Janet O'Sullivan is right to criticise the decision in *Alati v Kruger* for the majority's assertion, at one and the same time, that rescission occurs by the act of the party *and* that the remedy is discretionary and may be refused if the rescinding party acts unconscientiously during the pendency of the proceedings.[70] However, it is difficult to identify cases in which developments after the point of election have had a decisive impact on the outcome. To the contrary, in *Brotherton* the Court of Appeal considered that it would be wrong to take into account the discovery, after the date of election, that undisclosed rumours were in fact untrue.[71]

In principle, there is no reason why the date at which the line is drawn should be the date of judgment as opposed to the earlier date of election, as it is where a contract is terminated for breach or repudiation. An election to rescind is like the exercise of any other power that changes the relations between parties. If the election proves to have been valid, relief must be given on the basis of those changed relations, and the impact of intervening events must be assessed on that basis. If, for example, a party resisting rescission mistakenly stands on their supposed rights and refuses to accept the return of goods which are then lost or damaged, that party risks finding that their remedies are limited to those available against an involuntary bailee.

Another consequence of the election model is that if prices or other circumstances change so that rescission now favours the party whose conduct caused the ground for rescission, after election it is too late to change course. By contrast, where rescission occurs by the order of the court, it is at least possible to argue that the complaining party may withdraw up until the order is made, subject to estoppels and the sanction of costs.[72] Indeed, where rescission is ordered conditionally on the complaining party

[69] *Maguire v Makaronis* (1998) 188 CLR 449 (HCA).

[70] *Alati* (n 24) 223 and 225. J O'Sullivan (n 13) 541.

[71] *Brotherton* (n 34).

[72] O'Sullivan, Elliott and Zakrzewski (n 10) paras [11.113]–[11.116]. The Indian Contract Act 1872, s 66 permits revocation of an election to rescind, and the same idea is found in two of the United States Restatements: Restatement (First) of Restitution, s 68(2) and Reporter's Note at 282; Restatement (Second) of Contract, vol 3, s 382 and Reporter's Note at 242–43. The point was not taken up in the Restatement (Third) of Restitution, s 54.

making counter-restitution,[73] it appears to be possible to withdraw by simply declining to fulfil the condition. In general, however, certainty favours holding a rescinding party to their choice, even if circumstances change so that the other party benefits. Otherwise, the rescinding party could speculate at the other party's expense.[74] To the extent the law permits a party who has previously announced rescission to withdraw and enforce the contract, that leaves the other party in a position of radical uncertainty until the matter can be brought to a judicial determination. The practice of granting rescission conditionally on terms is objectionable for these reasons.

In summary, while there is much to be said in favour of each of the alternative mechanisms, it is difficult to defend a system in which the two operate side-by-side in cases so similar that they often overlap. While the Court of Appeal insists that the court order model continues to apply in cases of fiduciary misconduct and undue influence, it is over a century since the House of Lords broke down the jurisdictional divide by applying the part election model in a case of innocent misrepresentation. That decision should not be regretted including because the broad and unstructured discretion sometimes claimed as the cardinal advantage of the court order model sits uncomfortably with the emphasis English commercial law rightly places on simplicity and certainty.

IV. THE PROPRIETARY DUALITY

The prime continuing importance of the distinction between rescission at law and in equity lies in their differing proprietary consequences. The argument here is that these differences are anomalous and should be synthesised in favour of the position originally developed in equity in relation to all grounds.

As noted above, in the central case of fraud Chancery exercised a concurrent jurisdiction with the common law courts.[75] If the case is one in which the common law courts would have recognised the rescission and given relief on that basis, then we say the rescission takes effect at law. At least where the case involves a sale of goods to a fraudulent purchaser, relief in those cases is given on the basis that, by their election, the rescinding vendor extinguishes the contract and revests legal title in the goods to themselves.[76] This presupposes that the wrongdoer did not previously sell the goods to someone who bought in good faith and without notice of the seller's defect in title.[77] If the case is instead one in which only the courts of equity would have recognised the rescission and given relief, then we say that the rescission takes effect in equity. In such cases, by their election the rescinding party extinguishes the

[73] *Peak Hotels* (n 35) [135]; O'Sullivan, Elliott and Zakrzewski (n 10) para [15.52].

[74] *Erlanger* (n 22) 1281 (Lord Blackburn): 'If no steps to repudiate a purchase of a lottery ticket were taken till after the ticket came up a blank, so that the purchaser, if it came up a prize, might have kept it, it would surely be inequitable to set aside the contract then.'

[75] *Newbigging* (n 19) 592. For simplicity the discussion focusses on fraud, but the position seems to be the same in relation to the other grounds for rescission recognised at common law: O'Sullivan, Elliott and Zakrzewski (n 10) para [10.25]. Albeit there may not be authorities addressing each of those grounds, there is no reason why a different analysis should apply. In relation to duress, see *Halpern v Halpern* (n 26) [11].

[76] See the authorities cited at n 8 above.

[77] Sale of Goods Act 1979, s 23.

contract and acquires equitable rights in relation to assets they transferred pursuant to it, again assuming the assets have not already passed into the hands of a bona fide purchaser for value, including in this case the purchaser of an equitable interest.

It is important to note that both at common law and in equity it is the rescinding party's election that extinguishes the contract and automatically confers on them rights in relation to assets previously transferred pursuant to that contract. Whatever the position in equity may have been before or immediately after the Judicature reforms, this is certainly the law now in all cases of fraud.[78] The process is therefore the same: the only difference is the nature of the resulting rights, sometimes legal and sometimes equitable.

Each of these types of right has its own strengths and weaknesses. Legal title is stronger in that it will often trump the claims of third parties who, after the point of rescission, purchase assets from wrongdoers, regardless of the state of the third party's knowledge.[79] That was what happened in *Car & Universal Finance Co Ltd v Caldwell*.[80] Equitable rights, by contrast, are vulnerable to the claims of bona fide purchasers for value of the legal title.[81] Legal title is weaker in that it does not confer a right to specific restitution of the asset where equitable rights do. A holder of legal title who wants specific restitution can only ask the court to exercise the discretionary power under section 3 of the Torts (Interference with Goods) Act 1977, which it will generally only do where damages would be inadequate because the asset is rare or unique. Finally, a particular strength of equitable rights is that they can, at least under the law as it is presently understood, more readily form the basis of a claim to substitute assets.[82] *El Ajou v Dollar Land Holdings plc* is a well-known example, for the fraud would have supported a claim for common law remedies but tracing was not possible on that basis.[83]

It can therefore matter a great deal whether the rights the rescinding party gains are legal or equitable and so it is important to know in what circumstances rescission occurs at law and in equity. This was explained by the High Court of Australia in *Alati v Kruger* in terms that have been said to represent English law as well:

> The difference between the legal and the equitable rules on the subject simply was that equity, having means which the common law lacked to ascertain and provide for the

[78] *Newbigging* (n 19) 592; *Abram Steamship* (n 34) 781; *Alati* (n 24) 233.

[79] There are limited common law and statutory exceptions. As to the common law exceptions, see O'Sullivan, Elliott and Zakrzewski (n 10) para [21.53] (cash and negotiable instruments). As to the statutory exceptions, see Sale of Goods Act 1979, s 24 (seller remaining in possession following sale), s 25 (buyer in possession with the consent of the seller), s 21(1) (estoppel); and Factors Act 1889, ss 8 and 9 (unauthorised sale by mercantile agent).

[80] *Car & Universal Finance* (n 8).

[81] *Pilcher v Rawlins* (1871–72) LR 7 Ch App 259 (CA) and other cases cited in O'Sullivan, Elliott and Zakrzewski (n 10) para [21.58]. Good faith purchasers of equitable titles, on the other hand, are bound by pre-existing legal and equitable property rights: *Phillips v Phillips* (1862) 4 De GF & J 208, 45 ER 1164; *Cave v Cave* (1880) 15 Ch D 639 (Ch); *Latec Investments Ltd v Hotel Terrigal Pty Ltd* (1965) 113 CLR 265 (HCA).

[82] Whether the rules of tracing applied at common law and in equity should be assimilated is itself an important question, as to which see *Foskett v McKeown* [2001] 1 AC 102 (HL) 128–29 (Lord Millett) and also 113 (Lord Steyn). To the extent we are moving towards a unified doctrine of tracing, as it seems we are, that is consistent with the thesis here advanced that there should also be convergence in the proprietary consequences of rescission.

[83] *El Ajou* (n 54) 733–34.

> adjustments necessary to be made between the parties in cases where a simple handing back of property or repayment of money would not put them in as good a position as before they entered into their transaction, was able to see the possibility of restitutio in integrum, and therefore to concede the right of a defrauded party to rescind, in a much wider variety of cases than those which the common law could recognize as admitting of rescission. Of course, a rescission which the common law courts would not accept as valid cannot of its own force revest the legal title to property which had passed, but if a court of equity would treat it as effectual the equitable title to such property revests upon the rescission.[84]

The distinction is therefore entirely a product of historical circumstances that ceased to obtain 150 years ago. It is at least odd that the proprietary consequences of rescission should depend on the former capabilities of different courts where those courts have long since been merged into one.

Case law contains little discussion of how the alternatives interact where rescission is possible at common law. *Alati v Kruger* seems to suggest that rescission takes effect at common law where possible and otherwise in equity. But a claimant might want to recover assets, legal title to which cannot automatically revest, such as shares or land. A claimant might also prefer to have the more flexible tracing remedies available in equity, and this was permitted in *El Ajou*.[85] This possibility has led one commentator to conclude that there is a free choice and that a rescinding party should make clear whether their election takes effect at law or in equity.[86] This unrealistic conclusion suggests that a wrong turn has been taken somewhere along the way.

The real problem here is the idea that the common law and equity continue to operate in the overlapping fashion described in *Alati v Kruger*. This state of the law is illogical for two related reasons. First, the explanation why an election to rescind revests legal title in some cases and vests equitable rights in others is not rationally related to the choice between these different outcomes. The explanation is that before the merger of the courts, the common law courts had less flexible procedures so that *restitutio in integrum* was only possible in those courts in a more limited class of cases. That helps us to understand how the law developed as a matter of history, but it does not explain why, following the merger of the courts, a rescinding party should get legal title in some cases and equitable rights in others.[87] It is not a normative explanation at all. The most that can be said is that the courts continue to follow old precedents, but those precedents were shaped by practical constraints that no longer obtain.

Second, the law is answering the same question in two different ways. The question asks what interest a rescinding party gains, upon electing to rescind, in assets previously transferred pursuant to the contract. The common law and equity each give this question a different answer in circumstances that are essentially the same in relevant respects. The one says legal title and the other says equitable rights where the

[84] *Alati* (n 24) 224 (Dixon CJ, Webb, Kitto and Taylor JJ); *O'Sullivan v Management Agency and Music Ltd* [1985] QB 428 (CA) 457 (Dunn LJ).

[85] *El Ajou* (n 54) 733–34.

[86] Zogg (n 13) ch 4 para [2.2.3.1(b)].

[87] In explaining the reason for the distinction he observed between rescission at law and in equity, Lord Blackburn was careful not to comment on the effect of the Judicature Acts 1873 and 1875: *Erlanger* (n 22) 1277–79.

difference can be important. That there is a rule for deciding which answer applies does not change the fact that different answers are given to the same question, and as noted that decision rule itself has no normative force.

It is tempting to risk the smirks and scorn of the editors of *Equity: Doctrine and Remedies* by invoking section 49 of the Senior Courts Act 1981, which provides that the rules of equity shall prevail wherever 'there is any conflict or variance between the rules of equity and the rules of the common law with reference to the same matter'. Here there is evidently variance between the rules, for their consequences can differ sharply; and that variance refers to the same matter, being the nature of the rights a rescinding party gains upon election. That there is no conflict is only because of a senseless decision rule. The framers of the Judicature Act 1873 seem to have anticipated that the merger of the courts would bring into focus situations of this general type, and whatever they may have actually had in mind, the words of the provision apply easily and naturally. The Court of Appeal has encouraged us to consider using section 49 to resolve inconsistencies between the legal and equitable rules relating to rescission and this seems a reasonable place to start.[88]

If one prefers a narrow interpretation of section 49, convergence in this instance is in any event appropriate because the law we have is illogical and anomalous. An advantage of the statute is that it decides for us which system should prevail. But it is anyhow right that the rules of equity should prevail because they balance competing interests better in this context. On the one hand, the greater reach of the equitable tracing rules offers more effective relief for the victims of fraud, as in *El Ajou*.[89] On the other hand, Janet O'Sullivan is right to observe that the common law's application of the *nemo dat quod non habet* rule gives a rescinding party too strong a position in relation to innocent third parties who may purchase assets from the wrongdoer after the point of election.[90] With limited exceptions, the rescinding party's title will prevail. But as between the two of them the innocent third party's title will usually have greater merit because it was the rescinding party who was duped. Equity would favour the third party in such a competition, provided they are a bona fide purchaser. Swadling is similarly right to criticise the common law rules on the basis that '[t]here is no logical reason why a good faith purchaser who intervenes after the act of rescission should be treated any differently from one who has the good fortune to come along before'.[91]

V. CONCLUSION

The basic structure of rescission is more complicated than it needs to be. This is a legacy of the topic having straddled the jurisdictional boundary between the common law and equity. One hundred and 50 years after the Judicature reforms, no reason can be given for important divisions within the topic except that before those reforms we did one thing in the common law courts and another thing in Chancery.

[88] *Halpern v Halpern* (n 51) [70].
[89] *El Ajou* (n 54) 733–34.
[90] J O'Sullivan (n 13) 532.
[91] W Swadling, 'Rescission, Property and the Common Law' (2005) 121 *LQR* 123, 131.

When the topic next reaches the Supreme Court,[92] it should take the opportunity to further develop the simple, unified understanding of rescission towards which we have been progressing since the middle of the nineteenth century. Specifically, the Supreme Court should hold that rescission is effected in every case by the election of the rescinding party, rather than the eventual order of the court, and that the proprietary consequences of rescission are in every case those originating in equity. The position to which the courts should ultimately aim is one in which it is neither necessary nor meaningful to say that a contract is rescinded at law or in equity. This unified understanding would be a shared achievement, drawing on innovations of both equity and the common law, rather than a victory for either one.

[92] The general proposal here is that the law should be synthesised by the Supreme Court, but it might be argued that this development is open to the Court of Appeal on the basis that cases such as *Caldwell* in which the continuing vitality of the common law rules has been recognised were decided *per incuriam* s 49 of the Senior Courts Act 1981. I am grateful to John McGhee KC for this point.

10

When are Negotiating Damages Available?

JOHN McGHEE KC*

I. INTRODUCTION

DAMAGES FOR CIVIL wrongs (that is for torts, breaches of contract and equitable wrongs) are usually assessed on the basis of the sum required to put the claimant[1] in the financial position it would have been in had the wrong not occurred.[2] But sometimes damages are assessed not on that basis but as the sum which the claimant might reasonably have demanded as a *quid pro quo* for the relaxation of the obligation in question,[3] and even though the wrong has not adversely affected the claimant's financial position at all. In the leading case of *One Step (Support) Ltd v Morris-Garner*[4] Lord Reed (with whose judgment Baroness Hale, Lord Wilson and Lord Carnwath agreed) used the expression 'negotiating damages' to describe damages awarded on this basis.

Negotiating damages have been awarded in cases of trespass to land,[5] interference with goods,[6] patent infringement,[7] interference with easements[8] and for breaches of restrictive covenants.[9] They have also been awarded for breach of a licence agreement governing the use of music recordings,[10] for breaches of both landlord[11] and tenant[12] covenants in leases and for breaches of equitable and contractual duties

* KC, Wilberforce Chambers, London. I am grateful to Andrew McLeod of One Essex Court, London for his valuable comments on an earlier draft.

[1] The expression 'claimant' and 'defendant' are used for convenience to describe the person with the right and subject to the duty in question respectively. The discussion which follows is obviously not limited to cases where court proceedings are brought by the right-holder against the duty-holder.

[2] *One Step (Support) Ltd v Morris-Garner* [2018] UKSC 20, [2019] AC 649 [1].

[3] ibid [95(4)].

[4] ibid.

[5] *Whitwham v Westminster Brymbo Coal & Coke Co* [1896] 2 Ch 538 (CA).

[6] *Strand Electric & Engineering Co Ltd v Brisford Entertainments Ltd* [1952] 2 QB 246 (CA).

[7] *Watson Laidlaw & Co v Pott Cassels & Williamson* 1914 SC (HL) 18.

[8] *Carr-Saunders v Dick McNeil Associates Ltd* [1986] 1 WLR 922 (Ch).

[9] *Wrotham Park Estate Co Ltd v Parkside Homes Ltd* [1974] 1 WLR 798 (Ch).

[10] *Experience Hendrix LLC v PPX Enterprises Inc* [2003] EWCA Civ 323, [2003] 1 All ER (Comm) 830.

[11] *Lunn Poly Ltd v Liverpool & Lancashire Properties Ltd* [2006] EWCA Civ 430, [2006] 2 EGLR 29.

[12] *Crestfort Ltd v Tesco Stores Ltd* [2005] EWHC 805 (Ch), [2005] 3 EGLR 25.

of confidence.[13] But they have been refused for breach of non-compete and non-solicitation covenants in contracts,[14] for breaches of European competition law[15] and for false imprisonment.[16]

It is not easy to discern why negotiating damages are awarded in some cases but not others. Why are they awarded for nuisance in the case of interference with easements but not in all cases of nuisance? Why are they available for breach of a restrictive covenant relating to land (even where the original parties own the land and the claim is in contract) but not for breach of all negative covenants in contracts? Why are they available where a defendant sells his former employer's confidential information but not for breach of non-compete and non-solicitation covenants where the covenants similarly serve to protect the claimant's business?

In seeking to answer these questions I consider first the academic and judicial discussion of the basis of negotiating damages which I conclude is inadequate to explain those circumstances in which such damages are and are not available. I then identify the cause of the problem as the methodology conventionally used, which concentrates on the different remedies imposed on the defendant for breach of duty rather than on the different interests of the claimant which give rise to that duty. I proceed to identify the relevant interest of the claimant which alone justifies the award of negotiating damages and then explain how the presence or absence of that interest successfully predicts the result in those cases in which negotiating damages are awarded and those cases in which they are not awarded.

II. *ONE STEP (SUPPORT) LTD* v *MORRIS-GARNER*

In *One Step* Lord Reed set out to identify the circumstances in which negotiating damages are available and highlighted three different categories of case. First, he said they are available 'for the invasion of rights to tangible moveable or immoveable property (by detinue, conversion or trespass)' and 'on a similar basis for patent infringement and breaches of other intellectual property rights'.[17]

Secondly, he said they are available in some cases where damages are awarded under Lord Cairns' Act in substitution for specific performance or an injunction. But he made it clear that they were not available in all such cases: 'It is for the court to judge what method of quantification, in the circumstances of the case before it, will give a fair equivalent for what is lost by the refusal of the injunction.'[18]

Thirdly, he said that negotiating damages are available in some but not all cases of breach of contract, that is 'where the loss suffered by the claimant is appropriately measured by reference to the economic value of the right which has been breached, considered as an asset.'[19]

[13] *Pell Frischmann v Bow Valley Iran Ltd* [2009] UKPC 45, [2011] 1 WLR 2370; *Vercoe v Rutland Fund Management Ltd* [2010] EWHC 424 (Ch), [2010] Bus LR D141.

[14] *One Step* (n 2).

[15] *Devenish Nutrition Ltd v Sanofi-Aventis SA* [2008] EWCA Civ 1086, [2009] Ch 390.

[16] *Lewis v The Australian Capital Territory* [2020] HCA 26, (2020) 271 CLR 192.

[17] *One Step* (n 2) [95(1)–(2)].

[18] ibid [95(5)].

[19] ibid [95(10)].

The first category is reasonably straightforward. But it is not immediately clear why it should be limited to tangible (that is corporeal) moveable or immoveable property. Why does it not extend to other interests in property such as security interests and in the case of land to proprietary rights by way of easements, profits or restrictive covenants? Why as a matter of principle should there be a distinction between rights of this sort which apparently do not fall within this category and intellectual property rights which are expressly included?

There are three difficulties with the second category. First, it overlaps with the first and third categories. Thus, as to the first category, the court will generally be prepared to grant specific relief to protect rights to land and to goods which are unique and not generic; and as to the third category, specific performance is granted as of course for contracts for the sale of land, and injunctive relief is generally available to enforce negative covenants in contracts. The second difficulty is that it gives rise to the question of what, if any, prospect there need to be of specific relief being granted. If there does need to be some prospect of such relief being granted it does not seem right that whether or not negotiating damages are awarded should depend, for example, on whether as a matter of practice the court has decided that it will not enforce a certain category of covenants because of the difficulties of supervision.[20] And if there does not need to be any such prospect then the second category means no more than that such damages can be awarded in any case where the court thinks that it is right to do so. The third difficulty is that it is not at all clear in what circumstances a judge should consider that negotiating damages are a 'fair equivalent' for what is lost by refusal of an injunction and in what circumstances they are not.

The third category faces its own difficulties. It is not clear in what circumstances a case will fall within this category. The word 'asset' is not a legal term of art. Any contractual right which is assignable for value might be treated as an asset. But this would open up the scope of negotiating damages enormously. It seems that Lord Reed's reference to the loss suffered by the claimant as being 'appropriately' measured as the economic value of the right is intended to circumscribe the circumstances in which breach of assignable rights are to be treated as giving rise to negotiating damages. But it also seems plain that this third category is not intended to be limited to those contractual rights (such as restrictive covenants or options) which give rise to proprietary rights as if so, he would have referred to property rights as he did in the first category.

III. THE DEBATE ABOUT THE BASIS OF NEGOTIATING DAMAGES

There has been a prolonged judicial[21] and academic[22] debate about whether negotiating damages are to be regarded as compensatory or restitutionary. But on the

[20] *Co-operative Insurance Society Ltd v Argyll Stores (Holdings) Ltd* [1998] AC 1 (HL).

[21] See, eg, *World Wide Fund for Nature v World Wrestling Federation* [2007] EWCA Civ 286, [2008] 1 WLR 445.

[22] See, eg, A Burrows, 'Are Damages on the Wrotham Park Basis Compensatory, Restitutionary or Neither' in D Saidov and R Cunnington (eds), *Contract Damages: Domestic and International Perspectives* (Oxford, Hart, 2008).

face of it neither explanation satisfactorily explains in what circumstances damages on this basis are available. Justice Sharpe and Professor Waddams[23] suggested that negotiating damages are awarded for the loss which the claimant suffers from the loss of opportunity to bargain away its rights. But that does not explain cases such as *Wrotham Park Estate Co Ltd v Parkside Homes Ltd*[24] where negotiating damages were awarded but the claimant was not willing to give up its rights at all. Justice Edelman[25] suggested that damages are awarded to reverse a transfer of value from the claimant to the defendant. This suffers from the opposite problem: it cannot explain why negotiating damages are awarded only in some but not in all cases where the defendant makes a profit by reason of its breach of duty.

Other explanations of the basis of negotiating damages have been suggested.[26] Professor Stevens[27] has suggested that negotiating damages are to be regarded as the next best substitute for performance. Professor Varuhas[28] has suggested that they serve to vindicate a claimant's rights. Josias Senu has suggested that they compensate for the loss of the ability to choose whether or not to enforce the obligation in question.[29] But, again, none of these suggestions successfully explains why they are not available in all cases. Professor McInnes[30] has suggested that negotiating damages are awarded for the value of the lost right to control access and use. But this suggestion is either too narrow (being confined to property rights) or too wide in applying to all rights.

A different approach is to seek a connection between the availability of negotiating damages and the availability of injunctive relief. Professor Barker[31] has suggested that what a claimant has lost is its right to seek an injunction to prevent the breach. But if that were so negotiating damages would be unavailable where the court would not grant injunctive relief either in principle (eg, because of the difficulties of supervision) or on the particular facts of the case (eg, where the claimant has delayed in seeking relief) whereas the availability of negotiating damages does not appear to depend on these considerations.

Nicholas McBride and Daryl Xu have recognised the problem with other explanations in being either under-inclusive or over-inclusive and have sought to categorise rights into those which do and those which do not give rise to negotiating damages. McBride[32] has suggested that a distinction is to be drawn between rights which

[23] RJ Sharpe and SM Waddams, 'Damages for Lost Opportunity to Bargain' (1982) 2 *OJLS* 290.

[24] (n 9).

[25] See, eg, J Edelman, *Gain Based Damages* (Oxford, Hart, 2002).

[26] See generally PS Davies, 'One Step Backwards: Restricting Negotiating Damages for Breach of Contract' [2018] *Lloyd's Maritime and Commercial Law Quarterly* 433; A Burrows, 'One Step Forward?' (2018) 134 *LQR* 515. For a useful review see K Barnett, *Accounting for Breach of Contract* (Oxford, Hart, 2012) ch 2.

[27] R Stevens, 'Damages and the Right to Performance: A Golden Victory or Not?' in J Neyers, R Bronaugh and S Pitel (eds), *Exploring Contract Law* (Oxford, Hart, 2009); R Stevens, *Torts and Rights* (Oxford, OUP, 2007) ch 4.

[28] J Varuhas, 'The Concept of Vindication in the Law of Torts, Rights, Interests and Damages' (2014) 34 *OJLS* 253.

[29] J Senu, 'Negotiating Damages and the Compensatory Principle' (2020) 40 *OJLS* 110.

[30] M McInnes, 'Gain, Loss and the User Principle' (2006) 14 *Restitution Law Review* 76.

[31] K Barker, 'Damages Without Loss: Can Hohfeld Help?' (2014) 34 *OJLS* 631.

[32] N McBride, 'Restitution for Wrongs' in C Mitchell and W Swadling (eds), *The Restatement Third: Restitution and Unjust Enrichment* (Oxford, Hart, 2013).

protect liberty (where negotiating damages are available) and rights which protect welfare (where they are not available). But it is not easy to see how this distinction will be made in practice, nor why negotiating damages should be available in one category and not the other. Xu[33] has suggested that, so far as contractual rights are concerned, a distinction is to be drawn between contractual obligations made in furtherance of some broader financial or economic purpose (where negotiating damages are not available) and contractual obligations which are made as ends in themselves and serve no such broader purpose (where negotiating damages are available). But in practice all contractual obligations are likely to be part of some broader purpose and, even if this distinction can be made, it is not easy to see why it should be the test for whether negotiating damages are available. Neither explanation seems to map accurately with the case law in which awards of negotiating damages have been granted or refused.

Another way of seeking to delineate the availability of negotiating damages is to treat it as a remedy of last resort. This is the approach taken by the Court of Appeal in Singapore in *Turf Club Emporium Pte Ltd v Yeo Boong Hua*[34] in a decision delivered shortly after the decision of the Supreme Court in *One Step*. The court said that three requirements must be satisfied for negotiating damages to be awarded. First, on a conventional basis the claimant is entitled to no or only nominal damages; secondly, the covenant which has been breached is a negative covenant; and thirdly the case must not be one 'where it would be irrational or totally unrealistic to expect the parties to bargain for the release of the relevant covenant, even on a hypothetical basis'.[35]

The first requirement is one way of limiting negotiating damages. But it is neither rationally justified nor consistent with the case law. Assume a case where a developer has infringed an adjoining owner's rights of light and the adjoining owner seeks negotiating damages.[36] Say that if the court were able to award negotiating damages it would make an order for £1 million, being one third of the estimated increased profit which the developer will make by being able to interfere with the adjoining owner's rights of light and thus build higher. Why should the question of whether or not the court makes this order depend on whether the diminution in the value of the adjoining owner's property by reason of the interference with its rights of light is £1 or £10,000? As a matter of fact, in both cases the court awards negotiating damages.[37]

As to the second requirement, it is difficult to see why in principle negotiating damages should be limited to breach of negative covenants. Consider a breach by the tenant of a user covenant in a lease. Assume that the covenant is a negative covenant in which the tenant covenants not to use the property otherwise than as a newsagent but in breach of covenant it uses it as a supermarket. Assume that the covenant is instead a positive covenant requiring the tenant to keep the property open during

[33] D Xu: 'Negotiating Damages: Rationalising the Compensatory View' [2020] *Journal of Business Law* 561.

[34] [2018] SGCA 44, [2018] 2 SLR 655.

[35] ibid [217] (Phang Boon Leong JA).

[36] *Tamares (Vincent Square) Ltd v Fairpoint Properties (Vincent Square) Ltd (No 2)* [2007] EWHC 212 (Ch), [2007] 1 WLR 2167; *Beaumont Business Centres Ltd v Florala Properties Ltd* [2020] EWHC 550 (Ch).

[37] See *Carr-Saunders* (n 8) where the claimant's property was diminished in value by £3,000 but negotiating damages of £10,000 were awarded.

normal trading hours trading as a newsagent and again assume that in breach of covenant it uses it as a supermarket. It is difficult to see why the availability of negotiating damages against the tenant should depend on whether or not the covenant is in positive or negative form.

There is obvious sense in the third requirement: it is difficult to see how the court could conduct the hypothetical negotiating exercise to determine the appropriate quantum of negotiating damages if such a negotiation is not something which can sensibly be conceived as having occurred. But this requirement is merely a practical reason for the limit on the availability of the negotiating damages. It does not provide an insight into the reasons why it is not available in a range of cases where a bargaining between the parties is something which could be contemplated.

There is a further difficulty with the test propounded by the Singapore Court of Appeal. The Court seemed to take the view that negotiating damages would be awarded provided only that the three tests were satisfied. But that would mean that negotiating damages would be available for the breach of almost all negative contractual covenants provided only that the claimant has suffered no loss suffered on a conventional basis. The proposed test is therefore both too narrow (in that some cases are wrongly excluded) and too wide (in that some are wrongly included).

IV. THE IMPORTANCE OF METHODOLOGY

The lack of any convincing explanation of the circumstances in which negotiating damages are and are not available is a function of the methodology that is conventionally adopted. Simply by way of illustration and because it is typically clear and concise it is useful to consider the approach adopted by McGregor on Damages[38] edited by Justice Edelman and adopted in his judgment in *Lewis v The Australian Capital Territory*[39] (although other illustrations could readily have been used instead). Edelman J takes as the starting point the wrong (that is, the breach of the duty by the defendant in committing the breach of contract, tort or equitable wrong in question). Then he considers what right to damages the claimant has where that breach of duty occurs. A distinction is made between two different rights: a right to damages for so called 'normal loss' (that is, the compensation required to rectify the wrongful act) and a right to damages for 'consequential loss' (that is, compensation for the adverse consequences suffered by the claimant). So for example on a failure to deliver goods the buyer obtains damages for normal loss measured as the difference between the market price and the contract price. Any expenditure incurred by the buyer is recoverable in addition as damages for 'consequential loss'. Next he regards the right to damages for 'normal loss' as responding to the claimant's interest in performance by the defendant of its duty to the claimant and accordingly that the claimant's right to damages for 'normal loss' is a remedy which is 'generally' available.[40] Finally he

[38] J Edelman, *McGregor on Damages*, 21st edn (London, Sweet & Maxwell, 2021) paras [3-008]–[3-010].
[39] (n 16) [140].
[40] *Moore v Scenic Tours Pty Ltd* [2020] HCA 17, (2020) 268 CLR 326 [64].

identifies negotiating damages as damages for 'normal loss'.[41] The conclusion would thus appear to be that negotiating damages, being damages for 'normal loss', are generally available. The difficulty of course is that they are not generally available but only available in restricted circumstances. The terminology which he uses is thus confusing. It is compensation for the adverse consequences suffered by a claimant which is normally available. Compensation required to rectify the wrongful act insofar as it exceeds that is only available exceptionally.

The problem with this methodology is that it seeks to determine the availability of negotiating damages by concentrating on the different remedies imposed for breach of duty and by seeking to deduce from such remedies in turn: first, the scope of the defendant' duty; secondly, the scope of the claimant's right; and thirdly, the interest which the right exists to protect.

There are three points which it is important to note. The first is that the remedy which the law imposes on a defendant does not necessarily fully describe the scope of the defendant's duty. To say that someone has a legal duty is not just a prediction about what sanction the law will impose.[42] So the fact that the consequence of a breach of contract is an order for damages rather than an order for specific performance does not mean that a party to a contract has a duty either to perform the contract or to pay damages. Rather it has a duty to perform but in certain circumstances the remedy which the court will impose for breach of that duty is damages rather than specific performance.[43]

The second point is that, just as the remedy which the law imposes does not necessarily fully describe the scope of the defendant's duty, neither is it useful to regard rights and duties as, in a Hohfeldian sense, simply two sides of the same coin.[44] As Professor Raz has pointed out: 'A right of one person is not a duty on another. It is the ground of a duty, ground which, if not counteracted by conflicting considerations, justifies holding that other person to have the duty.'[45]

There are two things which follow from these first two points. First, the fact that the court sometimes awards by way of damages compensation required to rectify the wrongful act rather than simply compensation for the adverse consequences suffered by the claimant does not necessarily mean that that the nature of the defendant's duty is different depending on the nature of the award. In both cases the defendant's duty in a case of breach of contract is to comply with its contractual obligation. It is just that the law responds to breach of that duty in different ways. Secondly, even if the defendant's duty were different in these two cases, it does not necessarily follow that the claimant's right is limited to a right to require the defendant to comply with its duty although it clearly includes that.

[41] Edelman, *McGregor on Damages* (n 38) paras [3-012A], [14-003]; *Lewis* (n 16) [143]–[145].

[42] HLA Hart, *The Concept of Law* (Oxford, OUP, 2012) 38–42; and see D Friedmann, 'Rights and Remedies' in N Cohen and E McKendrick (eds), *Comparative Remedies for Breach of Contract* (Oxford, Hart, 2005).

[43] C Webb, 'Performance Damages' in G Virgo and S Worthington (eds), *Commercial Remedies: Resolving Controversies* (Cambridge, CUP, 2017).

[44] For this view see, eg, J Finnis, 'Natural Law: The Classical Tradition' in J Coleman and S Shapiro (eds), *The Oxford Handbook of Jurisprudence* (Oxford, OUP, 2002) 24 describing duties and rights as 'interdefined'.

[45] J Raz, *The Morality of Freedom* (Oxford, OUP, 1986) 171.

The third point which it is important to understand is the relationship between rights and interests. Again, as Raz has pointed out:[46]

> Rights ground requirements for action in the interest of other beings … The interests are part of the justification of the rights which are part of the justification of the duties. Assertions of rights are typically intermediate conclusions in arguments from ultimate values to duties. They are, so to speak, points in the argument where many considerations intersect and where the results of their conflicts are summarized to be used with additional premisses when need be. Such intermediate conclusions are used and referred to as if they are themselves complete reasons.

So in conclusion it is a mistake to say that because damages amounting to the compensation required to rectify the wrongful act are a sanction imposed for the defendant's breach of duty to perform its contract, the claimant's right is to be regarded as merely a right to performance of that duty and that its interest is limited to an interest in the performance of that duty. It is valuable to consider the interests which form part of the justification for regarding the claimant as having particular rights but, as with rights and duties, interests and rights do not necessarily precisely correlate.

In practice, the courts do seek to address the question of the claimant's interests directly. In *Experience Hendrix LLC v PPX Enterprises Inc*[47] in which negotiating damages were awarded for breach of the terms of a settlement agreement which imposed restrictions on the right of the defendant to licence certain recordings, Gibson LJ noted that the intention underlying the restriction 'was to protect the claimant's interests' in those recordings. In *Marathon Asset Management LLP v Seddon*,[48] in which negotiating damages were refused amongst other things for a breach of contract by an employee in failing to report the wrongful copying of the claimant's files, Leggatt J said that the claimant did not have a 'legitimate interest in performance of such duty' which went beyond the avoidance of loss and that the 'purposes' of such duty were limited to enabling the employer to take steps to protect itself from harm.

Similarly in *Lewis v The Australian Capital Territory*, Edelman J said that negotiating damages were not available 'where the plaintiff's only interest is to rectify the adverse consequences, or damage, caused by the wrong'.[49] In rejecting the contention that the claimant should have negotiating damages for false imprisonment he examined the nature of the claimant's interest in the following passage:[50]

> A user fee award is not appropriate as a means of rectifying wrongdoing unless the defendant has obtained an opportunity from the plaintiff by a wrongful act which the plaintiff would have licensed. As a matter principle, a user fee award could not be available for the false imprisonment of Mr Lewis for which the Australian Capital Territory was responsible. It would be incoherent for Mr Lewis to be awarded damages as a means to attempt to rectify the wrongful act of his imprisonment by requiring payment of a user fee when his consent was irrelevant to the lawfulness of the act and his imprisonment by statute would never have been a matter the subject of monetary payment for permission.

[46] ibid 180–81.
[47] (n 10) [54].
[48] [2017] EWHC 300 (Comm), [2017] 2 CLC 182 [218].
[49] *Lewis* (n 16) [150].
[50] ibid [155].

The task therefore is to identify the interest of the claimant which gives rise to a right to negotiating damages.[51] It is not sufficient to say that it arises where the claimant's interest is in performance rather than in the avoidance of harm for two reasons: first because the claimant always has an interest in the performance by the defendant of its duties, however arising, even in cases where on the breach of those duties it is only awarded damages to compensate for the adverse consequences suffered by reason of the defendant's breach of duty; and secondly because this does not explain why negotiating damages are awarded only in some but not all cases of breaches of duty. Neither is it sufficient to say that it arises where the claimant has an interest in preventing the defendant making a profit from its breach of duty, again for two reasons: first, it does not distinguish the conceptually distinct claim for disgorgement of the whole of the profit in fact made by the defendant from its breach of duty from the claim for negotiating damages by way of a reasonable licence fee;[52] and secondly, a formulation in terms of an interest in preventing the defendant making a profit restates rather than illuminates the reasons why the defendant should not be entitled to retain that profit.

A. Identifying the Relevant Interest

I suggest that there are two possible interests which a claimant may have and which justify the remedies imposed by the court for a breach of duty. The first is an interest in performance of the duty. The second is an interest in choosing whether or not and in what circumstances and on what terms to release the duty. A claimant always has an interest in the performance of the duty. That interest in performance is a justification for the remedies of injunctive relief, specific performance and damages for loss suffered as a result of the breach. In some but not all cases the claimant will, in addition to having an interest in performance, have an interest in choosing whether or not and in what circumstances and on what terms to release the duty. That interest is a justification for the award of negotiating damages.

Three points should be noted at the outset. First, a claimant has an interest in performance of the duty even if, on breach of that duty by the defendant, specific performance and injunctive relief is refused (for example, because of the difficulties of supervision)[53] and the only remedy granted is damages to compensate for the adverse consequences suffered by the claimant as a result of the defendant's breach of duty. As Adam Kramer notes in the context of contractual duties, negotiating parties typically have in mind the interests which the contract serves to promote not the losses which would result from breach.[54]

[51] W Day, 'Restitution for Wrongs: One Step Forwards, Two Steps Back?' (2018) 26 *Restitution Law Review* 60, 62 is illuminating: '… it is necessary to look at the underlying interest being protected by the cause of action and assess whether restitution would adequately uphold that interest'.

[52] *One Step* (n 2) [90].

[53] See, eg, *Argyll Stores* (n 20).

[54] A Kramer, *The Law of Contract Damages*, 2nd edn (Oxford, Hart, 2017) para [14-06].

Secondly, the nature of the interest in choosing whether to release the duty is not to be confused with the right to do so. Many tortious duties and all contractual duties can, in principle, be released. But a claimant only has an interest in choosing whether to release the duty if the law treats that as part of the justification for the imposition of the duty in the first place.

Thirdly, although negotiating damages are awarded where the claimant's interest extends to choosing whether or not to release the duty, there are other cases where the same measure of damages is adopted even though the claimant only has an interest in performance of the duty. Thus where a seller fails to complete on a sale of land or goods the buyer may be awarded the difference between the market price and the contract price notwithstanding that it has arranged a subsale of the property at more than the market price.[55] This may be because the buyer has an interest in choosing whether or not to release the seller from the duty. But alternatively it may be because the buyer only has an interest in performance but the court, for pragmatic reasons, decides that it should award nevertheless damages on the basis of the market price.[56] It is not always easy (nor necessary) to determine whether or not the claimant's interest is merely in the performance of the duty or is also in choosing whether to release the duty because the measure of damages in the same in either case.[57] Similarly damages for failure to provide a promised service may be valued on the basis of the price for obtaining a substitute service irrespective of whether the failure has caused any financial loss to the claimant.[58] In such a case the court recognises that losses are not always purely financial and it seeks to value that non-financial loss as the cost of obtaining a suitable substitute.

B. Application of the Interest Test: Torts and Equitable Wrongs

There are duties recognised at common law where the claimant's interest is clearly confined to the duty being performed rather than in being able to choose whether or not to release the duty. Thus duties of care are imposed in order to protect a claimant from the harm that would result if care was not exercised. A barrister who cuts corners in his research in order to be able to produce five opinions in a week and thus make more money when, had he carried out proper research, he would only have been able to produce three opinions, is liable for loss caused to his client when in one of these opinions he gives wrong advice. But he is not liable to pay by way of compensation a share of the extra profit which he might have been anticipated to make by cutting corners in this way. That is because his client's interest is confined to having an accurate opinion rather than in being able to control what other work the

[55] See, eg, *William Bros Ltd v Agius Ltd* [1914] AC 510 (HL).

[56] A Burrows, *Remedies for Torts, Breach of Contract and Equitable Wrongs*, 4th edn (Oxford, OUP, 2019) 192. For a different view see S Smith, 'Substitutionary Damages' in C Rickett (ed), *Justifying Private Law Remedies* (Oxford, Hart, 2008).

[57] *cf* D Winterton, 'Claims for the Value of the Lost Contractual Performance' (2019) 45 *University of Western Australia Law Review* 75, 80.

[58] *Giedo Van der Garde BV v Force India Formula One Team Ltd* [2010] EWHC 2373 (QB). See also Webb (n 43). But see Kramer (n 54) para [2-42] for cogent criticism of the rule.

barrister takes on. Similarly a person who writes a salacious book about a celebrity containing known untruths is liable in defamation for the loss caused to the celebrity. But she is not liable for a proportion of the profit which she might have been expected to make from writing such a salacious book. The purpose of the law of defamation is to protect a person's reputation not to protect a person's right to licence another to write untruths about that person.

There are other cases where as a matter of policy the duty in question is not regarded as one which a claimant should be entitled to exploit for money. Thus although a person is entitled to sell for profit his goods or his land the law will not enforce an agreement by him with another for profit to cause him personal injury since, otherwise than as part of a lawful sport or where he has agreed to surgery, a person cannot effectively consent where bodily harm is intended or caused.[59] For these reasons negotiating damages are not available for false imprisonment,[60] assault[61] or failure to get informed consent to surgery.[62]

There are other tortious acts where it is clear that negotiating damages are available. These are cases where the tort interferes with an interest which the law regards as property or as closely analogous to property. Although the concept of property has no precise definition,[63] its core case is one in which the owner has a right, which the law protects by imposing duties on others, to enjoy that property to the exclusion of others and to dispose of the property or otherwise exploit it for value. In exploiting property for value the owner releases duties which would otherwise be owed by others, for example by giving a licence to a person to enter land who would, but for that licence, commit the tort of trespass. Accordingly, it is clear that an owner of property is regarded as having an interest in choosing whether to release the duties owed to it as owner and is entitled to negotiating damages for breach of those duties.

The same applies to other duties such as the equitable duty of confidence. As Lord Leggatt explained in *Lloyd v Google LLC*,[64] the basis of a right to privacy is 'the protection of a person's freedom to choose and right to control whether and when others have access to his or her private affairs' and accordingly negotiating damages are available if that right is infringed.

Not all torts or equitable wrongs can so easily be divided into categories in which negotiating damages are and are not available, however. A particular problem arises with the tort of private nuisance. The essence of a nuisance is an interference with, disturbance of or annoyance to a person in the exercise of enjoyment of his ownership or occupation of land. A nuisance is committed where a person encroaches upon or causes physical damage to his neighbour's land or where, without encroaching, he interferes with the enjoyment of that land.[65] Given the requirement that the

[59] *R v Brown* [1994] 1 AC 212 (HL).
[60] *Lewis* (n 16).
[61] ibid [149] (Edelman J).
[62] *cf Shaw v Kovac* [2017] EWCA Civ 1028, [2017] 1 WLR 4773.
[63] AM Honoré, 'Ownership' in AG Guest (ed), *Oxford Essays in Jurisprudence* (Oxford, Clarendon Press, 1961); J McGhee, 'Boundaries of Personal Property: Shares and Sub-Shares' (2006) 122 *LQR* 525.
[64] [2021] UKSC 50, [2021] 3 WLR 1268 [142].
[65] MA Jones, *Clerk & Lindsell on Torts*, 23rd edn (London, Sweet & Maxwell, 2020) paras [19-001], [19-006].

enjoyment of land is affected it might be thought that nuisance was a clear case for the award of negotiating damages. However, in *Coventry v Lawrence*[66] the Supreme Court left the question open.

There are cases of nuisance where negotiating damages have been awarded. The cause of action for interference with an easement is nuisance and it has been held that negotiating damages are available in nuisance for interference with a right of light[67] and it seems clear that they would also be awarded for interference with a right of way.[68] Those decisions are undoubtedly correct. Easements are important property rights and are the subject of express grants and reservations. Rights of light in particular are frequently released in return for significant sums of money in order to allow neighbouring land to be developed. Accordingly, a person with an easement over other land has an interest not just in ensuring that its easement is not interfered with but in choosing whether or not to release it.

But negotiating damages are not awarded in all cases of nuisance. In *Stoke-on-Trent City Council v W & J Wass Ltd*[69] a claim for negotiating damages for nuisance was refused against the defendant who held a market in breach of the council's exclusive right to hold a market in the area. Nourse LJ's attempts to distinguish the trespass cases and the decision in *Wrotham Park* are unconvincing.[70] But Nicholls LJ correctly addressed the question of the nature of the council's interest protected by the right and concluded[71] that it lay only in being protected from disturbance. As he noted, that explained why, if an unauthorised market was held without disturbing a lawful market, the owner had no remedy at all. Given the nature of the claimant's interest negotiating damages were rightly regarded as not available.[72]

I suggest that negotiating damages would also usually be refused for noise nuisance. A person who suffers from noisy neighbours so as to make living in his house intolerable is entitled to damages for loss of amenity.[73] But his interest is clearly confined to ensuring that he is not disturbed by noise. It cannot sensibly be suggested that he has an interest in being able to require his neighbours to pay for permission to cause such a noise.

Accordingly, it would be wrong to conclude that every person with a claim in nuisance has the same interest which the duty of the neighbour not to cause a nuisance is designed to protect. There is no direct correspondence between the cause of action and the interest which it protects. So in some cases of nuisance that interest will be confined to ensuring that the neighbour complies with his duty not to interfere with the enjoyment of his property. But in other cases it will extend to his interest in choosing whether or not to release the neighbour from that duty.

[66] [2014] UKSC 13, [2014] AC 822 [128]–[131] (Lord Neuberger).

[67] *Carr-Saunders* (n 8); *Tamares* (n 36); *cf Coventry v Lawrence* (n 66) [248] (Lord Carnwath).

[68] In *Bracewell v Appleby* [1975] Ch 408 (Ch) and *Jaggard v Sawyer* [1995] 1 WLR 269 (CA) damages for trespass were awarded on the basis of the sum that could have reasonably been demanded for the grant of a right of way over the land.

[69] [1988] 1 WLR 1406 (CA).

[70] ibid 1414–15.

[71] ibid 1418.

[72] See too Leggatt J's analysis in *Marathon Asset Management* (n 48) [175]–[180].

[73] *Hunter v Canary Wharf Ltd* [1997] AC 655 (HL).

It would also be wrong to conclude that whether negotiating damages are available depends simply on the manner in which a claimant's enjoyment of his property is impaired. So it does necessarily follow so far as noise nuisance is concerned that because an owner of a terraced house only has an interest in ensuring that her neighbour does not cause excessive noise rather than in choosing whether to release that duty, no person could ever have an interest in choosing whether or not to release the duty of a neighbouring owner not to cause a noise nuisance. It seems that the right to cause what would otherwise be a noise nuisance can be the subject matter of an easement[74] and it might well be argued that a person does have an interest in choosing whether or not to grant such an easement in favour of a neighbour proposing to carry out a commercial activity for profit such as an electricity substation[75] or a racing track.[76]

In summary, it seems that two different approaches are taken depending on the context. In some cases, such as trespass to land or goods, whatever the nature of the property and whatever the nature of the interference, it appears that negotiating damages are always available. In other cases, the availability of such relief, and accordingly the nature of the claimant's interest, will vary with the circumstances. However, it is important to note that the question of whether or not the claimant has an interest in choosing whether or not to release the duty is never a subjective inquiry into the claimant's relevant state of mind. Thus negotiating damages may be awarded even if the claimant would have chosen not to release the duty at all.[77]

C. Application of the Test: Breach of Contract

Where the wrong takes the form of a breach of contract, the question of whether the claimant has an interest in choosing whether or not to release the duty does not depend on its subjective intentions in entering into the contract. Rather the nature of the inquiry has some similarities with what is involved in determining whether a party is to be treated as having assumed responsibility for a particular loss or whether that loss is to be regarded as too remote.[78]

There is at least one clear case in which a person has a claim in negotiating damages for breach of contract, that is where in selling land it imposes a restrictive covenant on the subsequent use of the land. Such an award was made in *Wrotham Park Estate Co Ltd v Parkside Homes Ltd*[79] where the claim was made under the doctrine of *Tulk v Moxhay*[80] by and against successors of the original parties. But the claim would

[74] *Coventry v Lawrence* [2012] EWCA Civ 26, [2012] 1 WLR 2127 [89]–[91] (Lewison LJ).

[75] See the facts of *Re State Electricity Commission of Victoria and Joshua's Contract* [1939] VR 121 (Supreme Court of Victoria).

[76] See the facts of *One Step* (n 2).

[77] *Lloyd v Google* (n 64) [142]. See, eg, *Wrotham Park* (n 9) 815D.

[78] *Transfield Shipping Inc v Mercator Shipping Inc (The Achilleas)* [2008] UKHL 48, [2009] 1 AC 61. See Burrows, *Remedies for Torts, Breach of Contract and Equitable Wrongs* (n 56) 103 on the extent to which this depends on the 'objective' intention of the parties or is an externally imposed default rule.

[79] (n 9).

[80] (1848) 2 Ph 774, 41 ER 1143.

clearly have succeeded too if it had been a claim in contract between the original parties. There are two reasons for this. First, a restrictive covenant is recognised as a form of property interest and an important feature of property rights is that the property owner has the right to exploit them for value.

The second reason is that the imposition of the covenant on sale was something which might have reduced the price that the purchaser would otherwise have paid for the property and therefore the release of it was something which the parties would have regarded as being of value. Thus in *Burrows Investments Ltd v Ward Homes Ltd*[81] a breach of a covenant restricting the disposal of land by the purchaser which was designed to protect the vendor's right to overage on resale of parts of the land was held to give rise to negotiating damages. Such a covenant restricting the disposal of an interest in land does not fall within the doctrine of *Tulk v Moxhay* and gives rise only to contractual rights. But Henderson LJ said: 'The benefit of the contractual restriction was a potentially valuable piece of property in its own right, and Burrows was deprived of the opportunity to exploit it, for what it was worth, by Ward's unilateral action.'[82]

This second reason (that the covenant might have reduced the sale price) would still apply if the land was sold to a purchaser without the vendor having any retained land benefitting from the covenant, in which case the doctrine of *Tulk v Moxhay* would not apply and the covenant would not be regarded as a property interest. Negotiating damages ought therefore to be available in this case too. *Surrey County Council v Bredero Homes Ltd*[83] is authority to the contrary in which nominal damages were awarded where the claimant sold land to the defendant subject to a covenant that it would only build 72 houses on the land and, in breach of covenant, it built 77. But it was regarded as wrongly decided in *Attorney General v Blake*[84] and is unlikely to be followed. For the same reasons, the breach by a tenant of a user covenant in a lease (whether a negative covenant or a positive 'keep open' covenant for which the court will not grant specific relief[85]) ought to give rise to a claim for negotiating damages. There is no relevant distinction between a user covenant imposed on the sale of land and one imposed on a lease of land.

Whether or not negotiating damages are available for breach of other landlord or tenant covenants in leases depends on the interest which those covenants are designed to protect. In *Crestfort Ltd v Tesco Stores Ltd*[86] negotiating damages were awarded when the tenant underlet premises without the landlord's consent in breach of an alienation covenant which provided that it was a pre-condition of any underletting that the sublease contained a full tenant's repairing covenant. It is easy to see why the court awarded negotiating damages given that it was common ground between the experts instructed on both sides that the tenant would have agreed to pay the landlord a sum of money for the release of that condition. However, the better view is

[81] [2017] EWCA Civ 1577, [2018] 1 P & CR 13.
[82] ibid [61].
[83] [1993] 1 WLR 1361 (CA).
[84] [2001] 1 AC 268 (HL) 283 (Lord Nicholls) and 298 (Lord Hobhouse).
[85] *Argyll Stores* (n 20).
[86] [2005] EWHC 805 (Ch), [2005] 3 EGLR 25.

that the purpose of the pre-conditions was, as with the requirement that the landlord was to be entitled reasonably to withhold its consent,[87] merely to protect the landlord from harm to its reversionary interest. Accordingly negotiating damages ought to have been refused.

Lunn Poly Ltd v Liverpool & Lancashire Properties Ltd[88] was another case where negotiating damages were awarded for breach of a covenant in a lease, in this case for breach of the landlord's covenant for quiet enjoyment. On the face of it the tenant's interest might appear to be limited to performance of the covenant. However, the nature of the breach of the covenant in that case was the blocking up of a fire door through which the tenant clearly had a right of way. The decision was therefore correct. Whether a breach of a covenant for quiet enjoyment gives rise to a claim in negotiating damages is similar to the question of whether or not a claim in nuisance does so. Just as a claim in nuisance based on interference with an easement can be the basis of a claim in negotiating damages so can a claim for breach of a covenant for quiet enjoyment based on the interference with an easement. The tenant's right of way through the fire door was a property interest which it acquired on the grant of the lease and for the release of which it could reasonably be expected to be paid.

The justification for the grant of negotiating damages that, as in *Wrotham Park*, the contractual provision in question itself gives rise to a property interest would apply in other circumstances such as in the case of a specifically enforceable contract for sale which creates in favour of the purchaser an equitable interest in the property to be sold.[89] However, in that case, as mentioned above,[90] the fact that damages are awarded on the basis of the difference between the market price and the contract price has an alternative explanation.

Although negotiating damages are awarded in the case of breach of restrictive covenants on sale they are not available for the breach of all negative covenants in contracts. In another landlord and tenant case, *Zinc Cobham 1 Ltd v Adda Hotels*,[91] the court refused to award negotiating damages for breach of a covenant by the tenant of 10 hotels to maintain them in accordance with standards prescribed for hotels run under the Hilton brand. This seems correct. The purpose of the covenant was to maintain the value of the Hilton brand, not to be able to make money by authorising tenants to operate on terms which did not conform to that brand. The position is akin to non-compete covenants and non-solicitation covenants whose purpose is limited to the protection of the business from harm and which accordingly do not give rise to negotiating damages.[92]

Breach of non-compete or non-solicitation covenants are to be distinguished from covenants to keep information confidential.[93] Breach of those covenants do give rise to

[87] *cf International Drilling Fluids Ltd v Louisville Investments (Uxbridge) Ltd* [1986] Ch 513 (CA).
[88] (n 11).
[89] *Lysaght v Edwards* (1876) 2 Ch D 499 (Ch).
[90] See text accompanying nn 55–57.
[91] [2018] EWHC 1025 (Ch), [2018] L & TR 36.
[92] *One Step* (n 2).
[93] *Pell Frischmann* (n 13); *Vercoe* (n 13); *Force India Formula One Team Ltd v 1 Malaysia Racing Team Sdn Bhd* [2012] EWHC 616 (Ch), [2012] RPC 29 (the measure of damages was not considered on appeal: [2013] EWCA Civ 780, [2013] RPC 36 [97]).

negotiating damages since the claimant has an interest in choosing whether or not to release the information for value.[94] A distinction was therefore rightly made between the breach of covenant to report that another employee had copied the claimant's files (the purpose of which was to enable the claimant to take steps to protect itself from harm) and the breach of the duty not to use confidential information contained in those files (the purpose of which included the ability to licence the use of such information for value).[95]

Other cases where negotiating damages were either granted or refused for breach of contract are also explained by this analysis. It explains the result in *Experience Hendrix LLC v PPX Enterprises Inc*[96] which concerned an agreement between Jimi Hendrix's estate and PPX, limiting PPX's right to use its copyright in recordings by requiring it to pay royalties for licensing certain recordings and prohibiting it from licensing others. Negotiating damages were awarded when, in breach of that agreement, PPX granted licences in respect of those recordings whose licensing was prohibited. As Lord Reed explained in *One Step*:[97]

> The agreement gave the claimant a valuable right to control the use made of PPX's copyright. When the copyright was wrongfully used, the claimant was prevented from exercising that right, and consequently suffered a loss equivalent to the amount which could have been obtained by exercising it.

Similarly, in *Mahmood v Big Bus Co*[98] it was held that the claimant's right to participate in a joint venture with the defendant should the defendant pursue that venture was one breach of which gave rise to negotiating damages. Eady J rejected the contention that the claimant's right was to be treated as akin to a non-compete covenant. As she explained:

> Critically, the anti-circumvention obligation created by clause 7 protected the Claimant's idea for a Dubai-based tourist bus business and his initial contacts and information; it provided that protection by effectively affording the Claimant a right of veto over the Defendant entering into a tourist bus business in Dubai without his involvement. That was a valuable asset lost by the Defendant's breach of clause 7 …

On the other hand, negotiating damages were rightly refused in *Priyanka Shipping Ltd v Glory Bulk Carriers Pte Ltd*[99] where the claimant bought a ship from the defendant on terms that it would be sold only for the purposes of demolition, but then in breach of that covenant concluded trading fixtures for it. Although the reasons are not set out very clearly in the judgment, it appears to have been contemplated that the ship would be scrapped more or less immediately so it seems unlikely that the parties would have thought that the defendant might release the benefit of the covenant at a future date. Furthermore, it appears that the defendant's concerns in imposing the

[94] Note that although in *One Step* there were breaches of both contractual and equitable duties of confidence, those duties were not treated separately and the thrust of the complaint was for breach of the non-compete and non-solicitation covenants: see *One Step* (n 2) [17].
[95] *Marathon Asset Management* (n 48) especially at [218], [222].
[96] (n 10).
[97] (n 2) [89].
[98] [2021] EWHC 3395 (QB) [153].
[99] [2019] EWHC 2804 (Comm), [2019] 1 WLR 6677.

covenant were to reduce the oversupply of vessels and thus to protect its own business by reducing competition. The Court was therefore correct to regard the covenant in question as analogous to the non-compete obligation in *One Step*.[100]

V. THE RELATIONSHIP BETWEEN NEGOTIATING DAMAGES AND SPECIFIC RELIEF

It follows from this analysis that the availability of negotiating damages does not depend on the question of whether the court had 'jurisdiction' to grant injunctive relief or specific performance at the date proceedings were commenced,[101] still less on whether there was a realistic prospect of that relief being granted.[102] There is however a degree of overlap between the circumstances in which such specific relief is in principle available and the circumstances in which negotiating damages are awarded. The court will not award specific relief where it regards compensation for the adverse consequences suffered by the claimant as an adequate remedy. Compensation for such loss is justified by the claimant's interest in performance of the duty. Negotiating damages are justified by the claimant's interest in being able to choose whether, on what terms and in what circumstances to release the duty. Accordingly, in those categories of case where the court refuses specific relief on the basis that damages amounting to compensation for the adverse consequences of the defendant's wrongful act are an adequate remedy the claimant does not have an interest in choosing whether or not to release the duty which would justify an award of negotiating damages.

But it does not follow that where specific relief is in principle available that the claimant always has an interest in choosing whether or not to release the duty. This is because there are other reasons which may justify the court awarding such relief. Thus it will award injunctive relief to restrain a threatened personal injury not because the claimant has an interest in choosing whether or not to be injured but simply because he has an interest in not being injured, that is in the defendant performing her duty not to injure him. So also, and perhaps surprisingly, negative covenants in contracts are ordinarily enforced by way of prohibitory injunctive relief without the claimant being required to have an interest which extends beyond performance of the obligation.[103]

Conversely, where negotiating damages are available, it will often be the case that specific relief is also in principle available. The reason is that if negotiating damages are available then it follows that the claimant's interest extends beyond the performance of the duty to an interest in choosing whether or not to release the duty. Compensation for financial loss will therefore be regarded as inadequate because it serves only to protect the claimant's interest in performance. But there are exceptions where specific relief may be refused even if the claimant's interest extends to choosing whether or not to enforce the duty. Thus a record label might have entered into

[100] ibid [13]–[14], [199].
[101] *Jaggard* (n 68) 285, 290; *One Step* (n 2) [45].
[102] Burrows, *Remedies for Torts, Breach of Contract and Equitable Wrongs* (n 56) 315; *One Step* (n 2) [113] (Lord Sumption).
[103] For a recent example see *Priyanka Shipping* (n 99).

an arrangement with an artist requiring it to make a specified number of recordings. If, in breach of that agreement, the artist records with a rival label, the court would refuse to grant specific relief requiring the artist to make the recordings on the basis that the court does not generally specifically enforce a contract of personal service.[104] But it is possible that the contract might be characterised as one giving rise to negotiating damages.

VI. CONCLUSION

I have sought to demonstrate that the academic and judicial discussion to date has failed to provide a satisfactory test determining those circumstances in which negotiating damages are available and those in which they are not available. The tests which have been suggested are either too vague to be useful or are under-inclusive or over-inclusive (and sometimes both). The problem arises from the methodology adopted which concentrates on the remedies imposed for breach of duty rather than on the justification for the rights which give rise to that duty and which wrongly assumes a precise correspondence between interests, rights, duties and remedies.

The solution is to identify two relevant interests: first, the claimant's interest in the performance by the defendant of its duty; and secondly, the claimant's interest in choosing whether or not and in what circumstances and on what terms to release that duty. Only the latter gives rise to an award of negotiating damages. Having identified the relevant interest which gives rise to negotiating damages, an examination of the case law shows that where negotiating damages have been awarded, this has been because the claimant has an interest which extends beyond the performance of the duty to choosing whether or not to release that duty; and where negotiating damages have been refused, this has been because the claimant only has an interest in performance of the duty. This analysis also predicts when negotiating damages will be granted or refused in future cases, and enables an explanation to be given of the relationship between the availability of negotiating damages and of specific relief.

Finally, an incidental effect of this analysis is to explain why it is correct to regard negotiating damages as compensatory rather than restitutionary. It is correct to regard them as compensatory because the reason that negotiating damages are awarded is not because the defendant has made a gain at the claimant's expense nor even because the defendant had an opportunity to do so, but rather in order to protect the claimant's interest in being able to choose whether or not and in what circumstances and on what terms to release the duty in question. It is thus a claimant-centred, not a defendant-centred, remedy which is awarded to 'compensate' the claimant for the injury to its interest.

[104] *CH Giles & Co Ltd v Morris* [1972] 1 WLR 307 (Ch).

11

Specific Performance and the Reflective Loss Rule

JANET O'SULLIVAN*

I. INTRODUCTION

JUST ONE YEAR after the Judicature Act 1873, Lord Selbourne said that 'the Court gives specific performance instead of damages, only when it can by that means do more perfect and complete justice'.[1] The discretionary, equitable jurisdiction to award specific performance remains exceptional, but vitally important, in the twenty-first century. This chapter will focus on a current, and practically significant, conflict between a relentlessly commercial, common law rule of company law which prohibits shareholders from recovering damages for breach of contract where their loss is merely 'reflective' of the company's loss, and the court's power to decree specific performance, 'part of the discretionary jurisdiction of the Court of Chancery to do justice in cases in which the remedies available at common law were inadequate'.[2]

The reflective loss rule is a spin-off from the fundamental principle of company law known as the rule in *Foss v Harbottle*,[3] or the 'proper plaintiff' rule, which states that the only person who can seek relief for an injury done to a company, where the company has a cause of action, is the company itself.[4] The rule centrally applies where

* Associate Professor, Faculty of Law, University of Cambridge. I am very grateful to Will Swainson and Finn Callow for invaluable research assistance, and to Julius Grower for very helpful comments on the draft chapter – all errors and infelicities that remain are my own.

[1] *Wilson v Northampton and Banbury Junction Railway Co* (1873–74) LR 9 Ch App 279 (CA).

[2] *Co-operative Insurance Society Ltd v Argyll Stores (Holdings) Ltd* [1998] AC 1 (HL) 11 (Lord Hoffmann).

[3] (1843) 2 Hare 461, 67 ER 189.

[4] The major exception is where a shareholder is able to bring a 'derivative action', the detail of which is outside the scope of this chapter. At common law a derivative action was only available, in summary, in cases of a fraud on the minority by the controllers of the company that could not be ratified (the academic literature is vast, see, eg, BAK Rider, 'Amiable Lunatics and the Rule in *Foss v Harbottle*' (1978) 37 *CLJ* 270). Implementing the recommendations of the Law Commission, *Shareholder Remedies* (Law Com No 246, 1997), the Companies Act 2006, pt 11 introduced a statutory procedure for derivative actions: a claimant must seek the permission of the court to pursue a derivative action, which 'must arise from an actual or proposed act or omission involving negligence, default, breach of duty or breach of trust by a

an individual shareholder attempts to pursue, on the company's behalf, a wrong done only to the company, but its logic has been extended to prevent a shareholder with a *personal* right of action from pursuing that personal right, where the shareholder's loss 'reflects' the company's loss and the company has its own cause of action.

The extension derives from the Court of Appeal's decision in *Prudential Assurance Co Ltd v Newman Industries Ltd (No 2)*,[5] in which directors of a company were alleged to have made a fraudulent misrepresentation in a circular distributed to its shareholders, so as to induce them to approve in general meeting the purchase of assets at an overvalue from another company in which the directors were interested. Prudential, which was a minority shareholder in the company, brought both a personal and a derivative action[6] against the directors, relying on the same facts for both and claiming that the directors had committed the tort of conspiracy[7] against the company and its members. For the purposes of this chapter it is the personal claim that is of interest. The Court of Appeal concluded that, where a company and its shareholders had suffered wrongs which resulted in a loss to the company and a fall in the value of its shares, a shareholder could not bring a personal action against the wrongdoer:

> But what he [the shareholder] cannot do is to recover damages merely because the company in which he is interested has suffered damage. He cannot recover a sum equal to the diminution in the market value of his shares, or equal to the likely diminution in dividend, because such a 'loss' is merely a reflection of the loss suffered by the company. The shareholder does not suffer any personal loss. His only 'loss' is through the company, in the diminution in the value of the net assets of the company … The plaintiff's shares are merely a right of participation in the company on the terms of the articles of association.[8]

This rule was applied, re-explained and extended in several cases thereafter, but in 2020 the Supreme Court in *Marex Financial Ltd v Sevilleja*[9] definitively restored the reasoning in *Prudential*, undoing much of the intervening jurisprudence. The detailed decision in *Marex* will be considered in the next section, but it is first worth pausing to consider how this principle might intersect with the availability of specific performance.

director of the company', a wide definition including breaches of duty in respect of which the derivative action was not available at common law. For an argument that the statutory procedure does not replace the underlying common law requirements for a derivative action, see D Kershaw, 'The Rule in *Foss v Harbottle* Is Dead: Long Live the Rule in *Foss v Harbottle*' (2015) 3 *Journal of Business Law* 274.

[5] [1982] Ch 204 (CA).

[6] The Court of Appeal differed from Vinelott J at first instance on the procedural question of whether the claimant's standing to bring a derivative action should have been litigated first. The Court of Appeal also rejected Vinelott J's view that such an action should be more broadly available where the 'interests of justice' demand it.

[7] The Court of Appeal held that, on the facts, the serious allegation of fraudulent conspiracy was not made out, but that the directors did mislead the general meeting.

[8] *Prudential* (n 5) 222–23 (the Court).

[9] [2020] UKSC 31, [2021] AC 39. Commentary includes A Tettenborn, 'Less Law is Good Law? The Taming of Reflective Loss' (2021) 137 *LQR* 16; S Laing, 'Reflective Loss in the UK Supreme Court' (2020) 79 *CLJ* 411; I Sin, 'The "No Reflective Loss" Principle in *Marex v Sevilleja*: One Step Forward, One Step Back' (2021) 4 *JBL* 285.

Most of the reported cases involving the reflective loss rule are claims by the shareholder for damages for tortious wrongdoing[10] – negligence or one of the intentional economic torts – or for breach of fiduciary duty. Some, however, involve breaches of contract, where specific performance[11] might exceptionally be available. It should be emphasized that this chapter's concern is *not* to argue that specific performance should be available where it would not otherwise be, to evade or defeat the reflective loss rule. Rather, it will consider whether, if the reflective loss rule prevents the shareholder recovering damages, it should *also* bar an action for specific performance, in circumstances where specific performance would otherwise normally be to enforce the relevant contractual right. Simple examples might include (i) a shareholders' agreement in which one shareholder agrees to transfer real property to the company but in breach does not make the transfer, and where the company is itself also a party to the agreement; and (ii) a joint venture agreement made between shareholders of a newly formed joint venture company, which is itself party to the agreement, whereby one shareholder agrees to transfer shares in another company to the joint venture company, but in breach does not do so.[12]

This chapter will argue that the justification for the reflective loss rule, rooted in *Foss v Harbottle*, does not extend to claims by shareholders for specific performance of an obligation that will benefit the company.[13] The rationale for the reflective loss rule is that a wrong done to the company primarily causes loss to the company, which is then reflected in a reduction in the value of the shareholder's shares. This means that the proper claimant is the company; the shareholder does not suffer a separate, distinct loss recognised by the law. This chapter will argue that this rationale has no application to claims for specific performance, a remedy which is not dependent on the claimant having suffered a loss (or indeed there having been a breach of contract), but instead ensures performance of a promised obligation. Detailed analysis of this issue must, however, begin with the Supreme Court's recent exposition of the reflective loss rule.

[10] While a shareholder's derivative action is only available where the defendant is a director, the reflective loss problem can arise where the defendant is external to the company, such as the allegedly negligent solicitors representing the company in *Johnson v Gore Wood & Co* [2002] 2 AC 1 (HL).

[11] Or other specific remedies having, in practice, an equivalent effect.

[12] This second example reflects the fact pattern of *Broadcasting Investment Group Ltd v Smith* [2021] EWCA Civ 912, [2022] 1 WLR 1, save that in *Broadcasting* the joint venture company had not been incorporated at the time of the contract and so was not a party to it, though on incorporation acquired the right to enforce the contract under s 1 of the Contracts (Rights of Third Parties) Act 1999. See further the text accompanying n 39.

[13] This chapter focusses on the fact pattern of an obligation owed both to the company and the shareholder as promisees, but for the benefit of the company alone, where the shareholder seeks specific performance (thus increasing the value of the shares), as this is the pattern in which it has been suggested that the shareholders' claim for specific performance would be barred under the reflective loss rule. Where both the company and a shareholder will benefit directly from the obligation, there is no 'reflection' involved: either party has a separate right to enforce the obligation, but such enforcement can *ex hypothesi* happen only once. Where a shareholder has an independent, specifically enforceable right that is owed only to it, not to the company, there is no problem of reflective loss, because there is no 'reflection' involved, a fact pattern seen in *Cavendish Square Holdings BV v Makdessi* [2015] UKSC 67, [2016] AC 1172 considered in n 37.

II. THE REFLECTIVE LOSS RULE AS EXPLAINED IN *MAREX*

In *Marex Financial Ltd v Sevilleja*, Carlos Sevilleja owned two companies in the BVI, which he used for trading in foreign exchange. Marex had contracted with these companies and obtained judgment against them for breach of contract amounting to US$5.5m (plus costs of £1.65m). As judgment was handed down, Sevilleja procured that more than US$9.5m of the companies' funds was transferred offshore to his personal accounts to defeat payment of the judgment debt. The companies were placed into liquidation, but Sevilleja took steps to hinder the liquidator. Marex sought damages from Sevilleja for intentional economic torts. It obtained an order for permission to serve proceedings outside the jurisdiction and Sevilleja sought to set that order aside. His argument was that Marex (a creditor) did not have a good claim against him, because Marex's losses were simply reflective of the companies' losses. The Court of Appeal held that the reflective loss rule barred nearly all of Marex's claim, so Marex appealed to the Supreme Court.

The Supreme Court unanimously allowed Marex's appeal, but the reasoning was not unanimous. The minority view articulated by Lord Sales, with whom Lady Hale and Lord Kitchin agreed, favoured abolition of the reflective loss rule. In its place, Lord Sales advocated a case-by-case approach that would deal with potential double recovery problems by case management and expert evidence.[14] The majority, by contrast, favoured retaining a bright-line rule, but restricting its scope, so that it would no longer preclude claims by creditors such as Marex.

Lord Reed gave the majority judgment with the support of Lady Black, Lord Lloyd-Jones and Lord Hodge, the latter in a short concurring judgment. Lord Reed began by emphasising the origin of the reflective loss rule in *Prudential* as a logical consequence of fundamental company law principles:

> … its rationale is that, where it applies, the shareholder does not suffer a loss which is recognised in law as having an existence distinct from the company's loss. On that basis, a claim by the shareholder is barred by the principle of company law known as the rule in *Foss v Harbottle* …[15]

He went on to explain that what the court in *Prudential* meant was that where a company suffers actionable loss, and that loss results in a fall in the value of its shares (or in its distributions), the fall in share value (or in distributions) is not a loss which the law recognises as being separate and distinct from the loss sustained by the company, which is the reason that it does not give rise to an independent claim to damages on the part of the shareholders.[16]

[14] This echoes C Mitchell, 'Shareholders' Claims for Reflective Loss' (2004) 120 *LQR* 457, 465: 'There is much to be said for the view that the courts should have a discretion to resolve claims of this kind in a more nuanced way, both by ensuring that all the interested parties are given a voice in any proceedings against the defendant, and by expressly considering whether any of them would be disadvantaged if the shareholder's claim for reflective loss were allowed.'

[15] *Marex* (n 9) [10].

[16] ibid [28].

Lord Reed approved the approach of Lord Bingham in *Johnson v Gore Wood & Co*,[17] which he regarded as consistent with the origins of the reflective loss rule in the rule in *Foss v Harbottle*. In particular, Lord Bingham set the boundary of the reflective loss rule as follows:

> Where a company suffers loss caused by a breach of duty to it, and a shareholder suffers a loss separate and distinct from that suffered by the company caused by breach of a duty independently owed to the shareholder, each may sue to recover the loss caused to it by breach of duty owed to it but neither may recover loss caused to the other by breach of the duty owed to that other.[18]

Lord Reed approved this proposition, noting that it 'reflects the fact that the shareholder's loss, where it does not consist merely of a fall in the value of his shareholding, or in the distributions which he receives by virtue of his shareholding, does not fall within the ambit of the rule in *Prudential*'.[19]

For Lord Reed, confusion had arisen because caselaw after *Prudential* had tended to justify the reflective loss rule in a different way, specifically as a means of preventing double recovery where the company suffers loss which is reflected in the diminution of the value of the claimant's shares. That explanation derived from the speech of Lord Millett in *Johnson*.[20] The problem with the explanation, according to Lord Reed, was that it did not of itself confine the reflective loss rule to shareholders suing *in that capacity*, which meant the courts extended the application of the rule to claims made by other claimants such as creditors (as in *Marex*) or employees, wherever there was a risk of double recovery. As Lord Reed put it, '[t]he supposed "reflective loss" principle has been treated as being based primarily on the avoidance of double recovery and the protection of a company's unsecured creditors, and as being applicable in all situations where there are concurrent claims and one of the claimants is a company'.[21] This was not correct, so Lord Millett's explanation 'departs from the reasoning in *Prudential* and should not be followed'.[22] The true role of the reflective loss principle was narrower, as Lord Reed explained by drawing a distinction between (1) cases where claims are brought by a shareholder in respect of loss which he has suffered in that capacity, in the form of a diminution in share value or in distributions, which is

[17] (n 10).

[18] ibid 35. This dictum was recently interpreted by HHJ Matthews (sitting as a Judge of the High Court) in *Burnford v Automobile Association Developments Ltd* [2022] EWHC 368 (Ch). Here the defendant addressed misrepresentations to the company and to the claimant shareholders; similarly, the company and the shareholders were party to a contract, alleged to have been breached by the defendant. The shareholders sought to defeat the defendant's reflective loss plea by relying on Lord Bingham's dictum, on the basis that they had their own independent breach and misrepresentation claims, but this argument was rejected (at [87]): 'It is not enough to say that the shareholders have their own independent cause of action. It is not enough to say that they have suffered loss as a result of a wrong done by the defendant. It is necessary to go on and show that the company has not suffered the same loss, in respect of which it is (or would otherwise be) entitled to make a claim.'

[19] *Marex* (n 9) [47].

[20] *Johnson* (n 10) 56–68.

[21] *Marex* (n 9) [77].

[22] ibid [67] (Lord Reed). In contrast, as has been said, Lord Bingham's reasoning in *Johnson* accorded with Lord Reed's in *Marex* and was followed.

the consequence of loss sustained by the company, in respect of which the company has a cause of action against the same wrongdoer, and (2) cases where claims are brought, whether by a shareholder or by anyone else, in respect of loss which does not fall within that description, but where the company has a right of action in respect of substantially the same loss.[23] He concluded:

> The critical point is that [in cases of the first kind] the shareholder has not suffered a loss which is regarded by the law as being separate and distinct from the company's loss, and therefore has no claim to recover it. As a shareholder (and unlike a creditor or an employee), he does, however, have a variety of other rights which may be relevant in a context of this kind, including the right to bring a derivative claim to enforce the company's rights if the relevant conditions are met, and the right to seek relief in respect of unfairly prejudicial conduct of the company's affairs.
>
> The position is different in cases of the second kind. One can take as an example cases where claims are brought in respect of loss suffered in the capacity of a creditor of the company. The arguments which arise in the case of a shareholder have no application. There is no analogous relationship between a creditor and the company. There is no correlation between the value of the company's assets or profits and the 'value' of the creditor's debt, analogous to the relationship on which a shareholder bases his claim for a fall in share value. The inverted commas around the word 'value', when applied to a debt, reflect the fact that it is a different kind of entity from a share.[24]

The majority's decision was therefore to narrow the ambit of the rule, overruling cases in which it had been applied to claimants other than shareholders suing in that capacity, hence the allowing of the appeal in Marex's favour.

The direction of travel in *Marex* was not, however, entirely in favour of claimants. The expansion of the rule from *Johnson* onwards, and its justification as a means of avoiding double recovery, had led to the carving of exceptions where double recovery was not a risk. For example, in *Giles v Rhind*,[25] Roderick Rhind (a former shareholder) used confidential information to divert a lucrative contract to a third party, in breach of a shareholders' agreement with Edward Giles (also a shareholder). Rhind's contractual obligations were owed both to the company and to Giles. The company became insolvent and, in the light of its insolvency, discontinued its action against Rhind. Giles sought to pursue personal claims for damages against Rhind, alleging breaches of the shareholders' agreement so far as there were covenants in his favour, and claiming damages for the loss of value of his shares in the company.[26] The Court of Appeal held that the reflective loss rule did not apply where the company was unable to pursue the wrongdoing,[27] and thus Giles's personal claim against Rhind was not barred. This exception was applied, for example, in *Perry v Day*[28] where the defendant shareholder had breached his obligations to the company by insisting on

[23] ibid [79].
[24] ibid [83]–[84].
[25] [2002] EWCA Civ 1428, [2003] Ch 618.
[26] Giles also claimed for loss of remuneration he would otherwise have earned.
[27] In *Kazakhstan Kagazy plc v Arip* [2014] EWCA Civ 381, [2014] 1 CLC 451 [31]–[33] Longmore LJ held that *Giles v Rhind* was a 'very limited' doctrine, expressing the test as whether it would be 'impossible' for the company to bring the claim.
[28] [2004] EWHC 3372 (Ch), [2005] 2 BCLC 405.

the company giving up its claim on terms generous to him, thus triggering the *Giles v Rhind* exception to the normal rules regarding the irrecoverability of reflective loss.

Lord Reed expressed sympathy 'with the Court of Appeal's sense of the unattractiveness of the defendant's position' in *Giles v Rhind*, but nonetheless disapproved of the exception it created:

> … the fact that a wrongdoer has unmeritoriously avoided his liability in damages to A is not a reason for requiring him to pay damages to B. The basis of the decisions in *Prudential* and *Johnson* is that a shareholder, whose shares have fallen in value as the consequence of loss suffered by the company for the recovery of which it has a cause of action, has not suffered a recoverable loss. That conclusion does not depend on whether the company is financially able to bring proceedings or not. If the shareholder has not suffered a recoverable loss, he has no claim for damages, regardless of whether, or why, the company may have failed to pursue its own cause of action.[29]

So the *Foss v Harbottle* theory that the shareholder-claimant suffers no recoverable loss is to be applied relentlessly to deny a claim for damages, even where, in practice, the claimant has been the victim of a personal wrong and has suffered a real loss.[30] For the purposes of this chapter, of more relevance is Lord Reed's obiter suggestion that the same theory also rules out specific equitable remedies on the part of a shareholder-claimant, despite existing authority to the contrary.

III. JUDICIAL DISCUSSION OF SPECIFIC PERFORMANCE AND THE REFLECTIVE LOSS RULE

A. Lord Reed's Obiter Discussion of Specific Remedies and the Reflective Loss Rule

Specific remedies were not in issue in *Marex*, but Lord Reed dealt with them in passing, in the context of his critique of Lord Millett's reasoning in *Johnson*. For Lord Reed, the problem with justifying the reflective loss rule as a means of avoiding double recovery is that the double recovery principle 'is one of the law of *damages*. It does not deny the existence of the shareholder's loss, as the rule in *Prudential* does, where the loss falls within its ambit, but on the contrary is premised on the recognition of that loss'.[31] He further pointed out that Lord Millett's approach has been used to 'circumvent the rule in *Foss v Harbottle*: a rule which is not confined to actions for damages

[29] *Marex* (n 9) [70].

[30] The thesis of this chapter is that the reflective loss rule is inapplicable, as a matter of principle, wherever a shareholder seeks specific performance of an obligation for the benefit of the company. It will therefore not explore a lesser, compromise argument that specific performance should at least be allowed in cases which previously attracted the *Giles v Rhind* exception. Suffice it to say that all the cases which previously benefitted from the exception were damages claims, but what if there had been a possibility of specific performance? If the company had been disabled by the actions of the defendant from seeking specific performance itself, this would seem an overwhelming reason for the exercise of the court's discretion to allow the remedy.

[31] *Marex* (n 9) [52] (emphasis added).

but also applies to other remedies'.[32] Immediately thereafter Lord Reed raised the following authorities involving specific remedies,[33] thus strongly implying that they should be regarded as wrongly decided:

> For example, in *Peak Hotels and Resorts Ltd v Tarek Investments Ltd*,[34] the judge considered it arguable that the 'reflective loss' principle, as explained by Lord Millett in *Johnson*, did not bar proceedings by a shareholder, who complained of a fall in the value of his shares resulting from loss suffered by the company in respect of which the company had its own cause of action, where the relief that he sought was not damages but a mandatory injunction requiring the defendant to restore property to the company. A similar view was taken in *Latin American Investments Ltd v Maroil Trading Inc*,[35] where the shareholder complained of a fall in the value of its shares resulting from a breach of obligations owed to the company, which also involved a breach of contractual obligations owed to itself. It responded to the argument that its claim was for 'reflective loss' by seeking an order for the payment of the contractual damages not to itself but to the company.[36]

For now, it is worth noting that, in both authorities, the effect of the specific remedy was to benefit the *company* directly.[37] This is a long way removed from Lord Reed's

[32] ibid [52]. See also *Prudential* (n 5) 201 (the Court): 'A cannot, as a general rule, bring an action against B to recover damages or *secure other relief* on behalf of C for an injury done by B to C. C is the proper plaintiff because C is the party injured, and, therefore, the person in whom the cause of action is vested. This is sometimes referred to as the rule in *Foss v Harbottle* (1843) 2 Hare 461 when applied to corporations, but it has a wider scope and is fundamental to any rational system of jurisprudence' (emphasis added).

[33] Though not specific performance per se.

[34] [2015] EWHC 3048 (Ch), where the claimant's personal damages claim was struck out, but a claim for an injunction for fraudulent conspiracy and causing loss by unlawful means to compel the defendants to re-transfer of shares (in the holding group) to the company was allowed to proceed. Birss J said at [73]: 'it seems to me that a claim for an injunction raises different considerations to a claim for damages. If the defendant owes a duty to claimant and has breached that duty, and it is otherwise appropriate, I cannot see why an injunction is not capable of being an appropriate remedy.'

[35] [2017] EWHC 1254 (Comm), [2017] 2 CLC 45.

[36] *Marex* (n 9) [53]. Lord Reed went on to reference (at [53]) '*Xie Zhikun v Xio GP Ltd*, Cayman Islands Court of Appeal, unreported, 14 November 2018. Summarising complex facts, in that case the shareholder applied for a quia timet injunction to prevent the breach of fiduciary duties owed both to the company and to himself, which would cause the company to suffer loss, and would consequently affect the value of his interest in it. Sir Bernard Rix JA observed at para 66 that he did not see "how, other than perhaps in terms of pure formalism … the present case differs from … a derivative action".'

[37] This is a possible basis for explaining a possible inconsistency between Lord Reed's disapproving view of *Peak Hotels* and the result in *Makdessi* (n 13), where specific performance was granted of the purchasers' favourable call option for the vendor's remaining shares, triggered by the vendor's breach of a non-competition covenant in the share sale agreement. Notably, specific performance was granted even though it was common ground that a claim for *damages* for that same breach would have been barred by the reflective loss rule, because the company had its own claim against the vendor for breach of fiduciary duty triggered by his competitive activities. It is unclear whether, under Lord Reed's reasoning in *Marex*, specific performance of the disputed clause would be treated as having the effect of evading *Foss v Harbottle*, and thus just as unenforceable as a claim for damages at common law. Intuitively it seems not, since the purchasers' rights under their option were (unlike in *Peak Hotels*) independent and unique to them, ie not shared by the company, but nonetheless the mechanism by which competition by the vendor would cause loss to the purchasers would be by diminishing the value of their shareholding, which is the nub of the reflective loss rule (see the dictum from *Burnford* (n 18)). The fact that specific performance of the option benefitted the purchasers, not the company, serves to distinguish *Peak Hotels*, but does not tell us anything about why the claim in *Peak Hotels* should not succeed as well. If anything, its merits seem stronger, as the company would have been benefitted by the injunction.

summary of the reflective loss rule that, in cases where it applies, 'the shareholder has not suffered a loss which is regarded by the law as being separate and distinct from the company's loss, and therefore has no claim to recover it'.[38]

B. *Broadcasting Investment Group v Smith*

The case concerned an oral joint venture agreement entered into by Broadcasting Investment Group ('BIG'), Mr Adam Smith and various others. Under the agreement, the parties agreed to incorporate a joint venture vehicle company named Simplestream Group plc (not incorporated until after the agreement was made), whose shares they would hold. Smith agreed to transfer his shares in other companies to the plc, but in breach of contract he did not. BIG sued in respect of this breach, seeking specific performance of Smith's obligation to transfer the shares, or damages in lieu; alternatively, it claimed damages at common law for breach of Smith's obligation. Smith sought to strike out all BIG's claims, on the basis that they were barred by the rule against reflective loss. Andrew Simmonds QC struck out all BIG's claims, finding them firmly within the rule on reflective loss.[39] For him, the reflective loss rule was relevant because, on incorporation, Simplestream Group plc acquired its own right under section1(1)(b) of the Contracts (Rights of Third Parties) Act 1999 to enforce the joint venture agreement, whereupon BIG's claim fell within the *Prudential* rule. Section 4 of the 1999 Act, stating that the Act does not affect any right of the promisee (BIG) to enforce the contract, was held to be subject to generally applicable legal principles, such as the reflective loss principle.

Andrew Simmonds QC therefore had to deal squarely with Lord Reed's obiter comment in *Marex* that the reflective loss rule barred specific remedies as well as claims for damages. Counsel for BIG valiantly urged the judge to disagree with Lord Reed. He argued that the rule in *Prudential* should not apply to a claim for specific performance because it is not a claim directly or indirectly for compensation, but instead a claim to vindicate the rights of a promisee. The judge, however, disagreed:

> … The principal difficulty for [counsel] here is that his argument would appear to conflict both with the Court of Appeal judgment in *Prudential* itself and with … Lord Reed's judgment in *Marex*… Pausing there, each of these references in *Prudential* itself and in *Marex* to 'other relief' and 'other remedies' is in general terms. There is no suggestion that any specific remedy, such as specific performance, is exempt from the rule.
>
> … [Counsel] submitted that Lord Reed's disapproval of the *Latin American* decision was limited to the claim for the payment of contractual damages to the company and that he made no adverse comment about the claim for specific performance. I cannot accept that. It is clear from the judgment of Teare J in *Latin American* that the claim for 'specific performance' referred to in his paragraphs [4] and [6] *was* the claim for an order that the defendants pay the relevant sums to the company … (emphasis added)[40]

[38] *Marex* (n 9) [83].
[39] *Broadcasting Investment Group Ltd v Smith* [2020] EWHC 2501 (Ch).
[40] ibid [57]–[58].

The Court of Appeal allowed BIG's appeal, because it adopted a different interpretation of section 4.[41] This meant that it was unnecessary to address in detail the 'difficult questions' of whether specific performance falls within the reflective loss rule, but Asplin LJ's brief comments were not a ringing endorsement of Lord Reed's approach in *Marex*. She noted that, although Lord Reed's reference to a shareholder being unable to bring an action to recover damages 'or secure other relief for an injury done to the company' and his treatment of authorities on specific relief, together with the application of the principle in *Foss v Harbottle* 'might on superficial consideration lead one to the conclusion that claims for specific performance ... also fall within the rule in *Prudential*, the matter is complex. It is best left to a case in which it is essential to determine the issue'.[42]

IV. THE ROLE OF SPECIFIC PERFORMANCE

The reflective loss rule is no longer rationalised as a device for avoiding double recovery, but it assumes, in contrast, that the claimant-shareholder does not suffer a recoverable loss at all, that is, a loss recognised at common law. The discussion of specific performance in *Marex* and in *Broadcasting Investment Group* has tended to treat equitable remedies as subsidiary and as being similarly unavailable, so as not to allow evasion of the common law rule. It is interesting to consider whether, if focus is shifted to the equitable principles and criteria that determine whether specific performance should be available, the same outcome is reached. In short, is the reflective loss rule a reason not to award specific performance, or an irrelevance whose rationale does not apply to a performance-vindicating specific remedy?

Specific performance is said to be available where damages are an inadequate remedy[43] (or, the occasionally used, and potentially slightly broader formulation,

[41] *Broadcasting Investment Group* (n 12). The Court of Appeal held that, on the proper construction of the Act, rights conferred by s 1 are additional to any right of the promisee to enforce the contract. The 1999 Act gives a limited inroad into the privity rule by giving a right of enforcement to the third party, but it has no ability to take a right away from a promisee. BIG's right to enforce the joint venture agreement was not extinguished by the reflective loss rule, because that rule was only engaged once SS plc gained a right to enforce the contract, and this right was only generated by section 1. *Prudential* had no life independent of s 1, and to suggest otherwise was artificial and sidestepped s 4.

[42] *Broadcasting Investment Group* (n 12) [62].

[43] See for example *Adderley v Dixon* (1824) 1 S&S 607, 610; 57 ER 239, 240 (Sir John Leech): 'Courts of Equity decree the specific performance of contracts, not upon any distinction between realty and personalty, but because damages at law may not, in the particular case, afford a complete remedy'; *Hutton v Watling* [1948] Ch 26 (Ch) 36 (Jenkins J): 'I understand the jurisdiction to grant specific performance of a contract for the sale of land to be founded not on the equitable interest in the land which the contract is regarded as conferring upon the purchaser, but on the simple ground that damages will not afford an adequate remedy'; *Argyll Stores* (n 2) 11 (Lord Hoffmann): 'There may have been some element of later rationalisation of an untidier history, but by the nineteenth century it was orthodox doctrine that the power to decree specific performance was part of the discretionary jurisdiction of the Court of Chancery to do justice in cases in which the remedies available at common law were inadequate. This is the basis of the general principle that specific performance will not be ordered when damages are an adequate remedy.'

whether it would be just to confine the claimant to a claim in damages).[44] But what does 'inadequacy of damages' mean? After all, as Schwarz observes, arguing for broader availability of specific performance, '[t]he very fact that a promisee requests specific performance thus implies that damages are an inadequate remedy'.[45]

In some respects, specific performance defers to the common law's notion of loss and calculation of damages. Damages for breaches of commercial contracts where there is a ready market are based on the difference in economic value caused by the breach,[46] importantly subject to the claimant's 'duty' to mitigate their loss. Specific performance is given on the basis that such a measure is 'inadequate' and is therefore not available where substitute performance is readily available in the market.[47] A related point is that a claimant cannot be heard to say that damages are inadequate because they involve a requirement of mitigation. More than a century before the Judicature Acts, the Earl of Hardwicke LC held in *Buxton v Lister* that

> in general this court will not entertain a bill for a specific performance of contracts of stock, corn, hops, &c. … for as those are contracts which relate to merchandise, that vary according to different times and circumstances, if a court of equity should admit such bills, it might drive on parties to the execution of a contract, to the ruin of one side, when upon an action, that party might not have paid, perhaps, above a shilling damage.[48]

Nor are damages regarded as inadequate so as to justify specific performance where the common law's quantum does not fully capture the claimant's expectation from performance, as where cost of cure damages are not awarded because they are regarded as 'disproportionate' to the claimant's loss.[49]

There are, however, a limited number of situations in which equity does regard damages as inadequate and thus where specific performance is potentially[50] available. The first and most obvious involves contracts for unique items,[51] where money cannot buy substitute performance. Damages are in such cases an inadequate remedy because of the nature of the subject matter.

[44] See Lord Selbourne's quote from *Wilson* (n 1). G Jones and W Goodhart, *Specific Performance*, 2nd edn (London, Butterworths, 1996) 5 describes 'inadequacy of damages' as the 'chameleon formula', preferring a test of the 'propriety of specific performance'.

[45] A Schwarz, 'The Case for Specific Performance' (1979) 89 *Yale Law Journal* 271, 277.

[46] See, eg, *Golden Strait Corp v Nippon Yusen Kubishika Kaisha (The Golden Victory)* [2007] UKHL 12, [2007] 2 AC 353 [37] (Lord Scott): 'the overriding compensatory principle that the injured party is entitled to such damages as will put him in the same financial position as if the contract had been performed.'

[47] *Re Schwabacher* (1907) 98 LT 127 (Ch). See too the earlier case of *Cud v Rutter* (1719) 1 P Wms 570, 571; 24 ER 521, 522 where Parker LC held 'that a court of equity ought not to execute any of these contracts, but to leave them to law, where the party is to recover damages, and with the money may if he pleases buy the quantity of stock agreed to be transferred to him; for there can be no difference between one man's stock and another's.'

[48] *Buxton v Lister* (1746) 3 Atkyns 383, 384; 26 ER 1020, 1021.

[49] *Tito v Waddell* [1977] Ch 106 (Ch), discussed in B Coote, 'Contract Damages, *Ruxley*, and the Performance Interest' (1997) 56 *CLJ* 537, 567.

[50] Specific performance, as a discretionary remedy, might nonetheless be denied for second tier reasons, such as the claimant's conduct, great hardship to the defendant, or the difficulty of policing specific performance of ongoing obligations.

[51] Most obviously land and antique chattels, but also shares that cannot readily be bought in the market, as in *Makdessi* (n 13) (also discussed in n 37).

Secondly, damages can be inadequate in a different sense, where it is impossible or excessively difficult to prove or quantify the claimant's loss because the counterfactual is too speculative.[52] In *Evans Marshall & Co Ltd v Bertola SA (No 1)*[53] Sachs LJ said: 'The courts have repeatedly recognised that there can be claims under contracts in which, as here, it is unjust to confine a plaintiff to his damages for their breach. Great difficulty in estimating these damages is one factor that can be and has been taken into account.'

Sachs LJ went on to state a third[54] reason why damages may not be regarded as an adequate remedy, of most interest in the context of this chapter, namely because there are 'certain areas of damage which cannot be taken into monetary account in a common law action for breach of contract: loss of goodwill and trade reputation[55] are examples.' In other words, there are heads of loss suffered in practice by a claimant, which the common law does not recognise or regard as actionable. In this category, damages are inadequate because of restrictions in the common law rules of recoverability. This brings the reflective loss rule back into focus. Lord Reed might seek to distinguish this category, on the basis that there is a difference between heads of loss which the common law acknowledges but does not compensate, compared to the shareholder's position in a reflective loss case, where 'the shareholder has not suffered a loss which is regarded by the law as being separate and distinct from the company's loss'.[56] But this is not convincing.

It is not convincing because specific performance is not primarily concerned with, or dependent on, loss to the claimant, but with vindication of the claimant's contractual right to performance.[57] In *Broadcasting Investment Group*, and in the simple fact patterns set out in the introduction above,[58] an order for specific performance would vindicate the claimant's right to contractual performance, but would

[52] A recent example, *AB v University of XYZ* [2020] EWHC 2978 (QB), [2021] ELR 1 involved a student disciplinary process, where the university denied the student legal representation. The hearing took place and the committee upheld the complaint and decided to expel the student. Having been denied legal representation, student successfully sought a mandatory order (effectively specific performance) compelling reinstatement. Hugh Southey QC said (at [102]): 'In principle it appears to me there is good reason why specific performance should be ordered in this case. There is no realistic way to assess damages because it is impossible to know whether the same outcome would have been reached if the Defendant had complied with its contractual obligations and permitted the claimant to be legally represented.'

[53] [1973] 1 WLR 349 (CA).

[54] A controversial hint that there might be a fourth category can be found in *B v D* [2014] EWCA Civ 229, [2015] 1 WLR 771 where an interim injunction was granted where the applicant argued that damages would be an inadequate remedy for a threatened breach of contract, because recoverable damages were limited by an exclusion/limitation clause in the parties' contract. It is unclear whether this reasoning would extend to an order for specific performance where the parties have agreed a restricted level of damages.

[55] At the time (now see *Malik v BCCI SA (in liq)* [1998] AC 20 (HL)) an injury to a claimant's employment prospects and reputation was not recoverable in damages at common law, and this it was suggested might be a potential justification for the award of specific performance, even for a contract for personal services where it is generally unavailable.

[56] *Marex* (n 9) [83].

[57] This gains support from Coote's analysis of exceptional remedies that protect a promisee's performance interest even where no 'market value loss' has been suffered, such as specific performance, damages on the 'cost of cure' measure, and Lord Griffiths' 'broad ground' analysis of damages for the promisee from *Linden Gardens Trust Ltd v Lenesta Sludge Disposal Ltd* [1994] 1 AC 85 (HL) – see B Coote, 'The Performance Interest, *Panatown* and the Problem of Loss' (2001) 117 *LQR* 81.

[58] See the text accompanying n 12.

primarily benefit *the company*. Far from being a reason to deny specific performance, this pattern is generally a justification for it. The most famous example is *Beswick v Beswick*,[59] where Lord Hodson explained why specific performance was available in circumstances where no loss was suffered by the promisee's estate:

> The remedy at law is plainly inadequate, as was pointed out by the Court of Appeal, as (1) only nominal damages can be recovered; (2) in order to enforce a continuing obligation it may be necessary to bring a series of actions whereas specific performance avoids multiplicity of action.[60]

Lord Guest's explanation is also instructive:

> Why should the estate be barred from exercising its full contractual rights merely because in doing so it secures justice for the widow who, by a mechanical defect of our law, is unable to assert her own rights? Such a principle would be repugnant to justice and fulfil no other object than that of aiding the wrongdoer.[61]

For Jones and Goodhart, commenting on *Beswick*, '[i]t was because damages were nominal that it was just that specific performance should be granted',[62] while the editors of *Chitty on Contracts* assert that 'as a general principle, the promisee should be able to obtain specific performance in favour of the third party whenever that is the most appropriate method of enforcing the contract that was actually made'.[63] Thus specific performance is available to enforce a promise for the benefit of a third party to the contract where the promisee has suffered *no* loss. Why, then, should specific performance be *unavailable* where it is primarily to enforce a promise for the benefit of a third party, but where that will also indirectly benefit the promisee? In both cases the action is directed at enforcing the promisee's contractual right, not compensating its loss on breach. Indeed, there is (pre-Judicature Acts) authority that an order for specific performance may be granted where there is no *breach* by the other party. In *Bass v Clivley (widow)*[64] the plaintiff sought specific performance of a term in a loan agreement. The court held that term was not in fact part of the agreement, so he could only have specific performance of the agreement as proved, which he elected to take. The defendant then objected that she had 'always been anxious to perform' the agreement as proved. The court granted specific performance anyway, but with costs in favour of the defendant. If breach is not essential for specific performance, the remedy can only be explained as vindicating the right to performance, not as concerned with compensating loss on breach. Specific performance does not depend on the claimant having suffered a loss.[65]

[59] [1968] AC 58 (HL).
[60] ibid 81.
[61] ibid 89.
[62] Jones and Goodhart (n 44) 36.
[63] H Beale (ed), *Chitty on Contracts*, 33rd edn (London, Sweet & Maxwell, 2018) para [27-056].
[64] (1829) Taml 80, 48 ER 33.
[65] See also *Hasham v Zenab* [1960] AC 316 (PC) where a vendor repudiated a contract for the sale of land, but the repudiation was not accepted by the purchaser – the Privy Council granted an order for specific performance before the due date for performance (not to take effect until the due date), approving (at 330) Lord Tucker's statement that '[t]he court has no jurisdiction to award damages at law except in case of a breach of the contract; while the equitable jurisdiction to order an agreement to be specifically performed is not limited to the cases in which at law damages could be recoverable'.

It is now appropriate to address the Court of Appeal's influential dictum in *Prudential*, relied on by Lord Reed in *Marex*: 'A derivative action is an exception to the elementary principle that A cannot, as a general rule, bring an action against B to recover damages *or secure other relief* on behalf of C for an injury done by B to C. C is the proper plaintiff because C is the party injured, and, therefore, the person in whom the cause of action is vested.'[66] Lord Reed took the phrase 'or secure other relief' to refer to specific remedies, but if that is what was intended, the inconsistency with *Beswick v Beswick* is striking. A more plausible explanation, it is suggested, is that the qualifier 'as a general rule' was intended to leave specific remedies outside the Court of Appeal's 'elementary principle'. In their pleaded derivative claim, the *Prudential* claimants initially sought rescission of the relevant company contracts, as well as damages, and the Court of Appeal was clear that the *Foss v Harbottle* rule applied equally to rescission – this may account for the reference to 'other relief'. There was, however, no mention of specific performance or any other specific remedy in the judgment.

It is therefore suggested that, focussing on principle and the nature of the remedy, specific performance should be available to a shareholder to enforce a contractual promise for the benefit of the company. Nonetheless it is also important to consider whether the policy reasons offered to support the common law's stance on reflective loss apply with equal weight to specific performance. As a discretionary, equitable remedy, the courts would likely bar it if there were compelling, contrary policy arguments.

V. WOULD THE AVAILABILITY OF SPECIFIC PERFORMANCE SUBVERT THE POLICY BEHIND THE REFLECTIVE LOSS RULE?

A number of policy arguments were offered in *Prudential* and in *Marex* to support the reflective loss rule as an aspect of the broader rule in *Foss v Harbottle*. On examination, most have no application if the claimant shareholder is seeking a specific remedy.

Some justifications are explicitly only relevant to damages claims, such as 'ensuring that a party does not recover compensation for a loss which another party has suffered', and 'ensuring that the company's creditors are not prejudiced by the action of individual shareholders'.[67] Similarly, it is suggested that the same applies to the policy articulated in *Gray v Lewis*,[68] explaining that *Foss v Harbottle* operates

> *to avoid oppressive litigation … [and] to avoid the multiplicity of suits…* the shareholder who first filed a bill might dismiss it, and if he was a poor man the Defendant would be unable to obtain his costs, then another shareholder might file a bill, and so on.[69]

This is a significant concern in practice, for example where a fund is set up as a company, with large numbers of investors holding shares. This fact pattern was in

[66] *Prudential* (n 5) 210 (the Court) (emphasis added). The judgment of the Court of Appeal was delivered by Cumming-Bruce, Templeman and Brightman LJJ.
[67] *Marex* (n 9) [48] (Lord Reed) citing Lord Bingham in *Johnson* (n 10) 36.
[68] (1872–73) LR 8 Ch App 1035 (CA).
[69] ibid 1050–51 (James LJ) (emphasis added).

issue in *Allianz Global Investors Gmbh v Barclays Bank plc*,[70] where Phillips LJ noted the 'pragmatic advantages of a clear rule that only the company can pursue a right of action',[71] citing Lord Reed's warning of a 'proliferation of claims, possibly in different proceedings, at different times, and in different jurisdictions'.[72] But it is suggested that this concern applies to successive damages claims by individual shareholders, each of whom has suffered a diminution in share value, not to a once-and-for all claim to specific performance, brought by the promisee, to benefit the company.

Finally, Lord Reed in *Marex* offered a justification based on the difficulties of quantification of damages in a reflective loss pattern,[73] which is of no relevance to a claim for specific performance, indeed it would normally be regarded as a factor *supporting* specific performance.

In contrast, there is one policy rationale for the reflective loss rule that might have some relevance to specific performance, derived from the fundamental principle of company autonomy[74] at the heart of *Foss v Harbottle*. As Lord Reed put it in *Marex*

> … The existence of concurrent claims could also result in the shareholder's preventing the company's management from dealing with its claim in the way they considered appropriate in the best interests of the company, thereby undermining the rule in *Foss v Harbottle*. That could occur, for example, where the company's management wanted to compromise the company's claim but were prevented from doing so by the shareholder's refusal to enter into a settlement with the wrongdoer. One can envisage other situations where the existence of concurrent claims could result in the shareholder's acting contrary to the company's interests, for example where the wrongdoer's assets were inadequate to satisfy both claims.[75]

Although the example in Lord Reed's final sentence envisages concurrent damages claims, the broader fear of shareholder action prejudicing the company's freedom to settle with the wrongdoer may have some relevance to specific performance. The Court of Appeal in *Prudential* noted that counsel for the company had made a 'forceful statement on day 1 to the effect that, although the action was brought for the benefit of [the company], "it is the concern of the board that the company shall not be *killed by kindness*" …'.[76] This comment related to the derivative action (for damages and/or rescission) which the claimant sought to pursue on the company's behalf, where the officious 'help' of a minority shareholder is a clear challenge to the

[70] [2022] EWCA Civ 353.

[71] ibid [43].

[72] *Marex* (n 9) [38].

[73] ibid: 'Even without the complications arising from the existence of concurrent claims it would not be straightforward to establish the extent, if any, to which a fall in the value of a company's shares was attributable to a loss that it had suffered as a consequence of the defendant's wrongdoing. But the existence of a concurrent claim by the company would add another dimension to the difficulties. It would be necessary, for example, to take account of the fact that the wrongdoing had resulted in the company's acquiring an asset, namely its right of action against the defendant, which might have offset any detrimental effect of the wrongdoing on the value of his shares.'

[74] See Lord Bingham in *Johnson* (n 10) 36, cited by Lord Reed in *Marex* (n 9) [48]. Lord Bingham described the rule in *Foss v Harbottle* as 'the consequence of the fact that a corporation is a separate legal entity'.

[75] *Marex* (n 9) [37].

[76] *Prudential* (n 5) 211 (the Court) (emphasis added). Counsel for the company added that not only was it the view of the board that the action was one which they did not wish to pursue on behalf of the company but that it was quite contrary to the interests of the company that the transaction should now be the subject of any rescission or criticism.

company's autonomy. It is, however, conceivable that those controlling the company might prefer not to take the benefit of an order for specific performance, but instead accept a repudiatory breach by the wrongdoer and sue for damages. Another iteration that might apply to a claim for specific performance is mentioned in *Gray v Lewis*: '[I]f the company sued in its corporate character, the defendant might allege a release or a compromise by the company in its corporate character – a defence which would not be open in a suit where a plaintiff is suing on behalf of himself and other shareholders.'[77] It is, however, unnecessary to treat the risk of these exceptional[78] fact patterns as enough on its own to rule out *in limine* a shareholder's claim for specific performance, in favour of the company, in reflective loss cases. The court can use the discretionary powers available to it where specific performance is sought, in order to distinguish cases of this kind and to deal with them appropriately. For example, where the shareholder is pursuing specific performance knowingly contrary to the will or interests of the company, the 'clean hands' principle might apply to rule out relief.[79] The company should be joined as a party to the claim, so that its objections can be weighed by the court in deciding whether to grant specific relief.

The conclusion is therefore that there is no compelling reason of policy to extend the reflective loss rule to block shareholder claims for specific performance.

VI. CONCLUSION

This chapter has argued that the principled rationale for the reflective loss rule does not extend to actions for specific performance brought by shareholders in order to benefit the company, and that dicta to that effect should not be followed (or, in the case of the first such dictum in *Prudential*, should not be read as suggesting a general rule to that effect). No longer rationalised as a means of avoiding double recovery, the reflective loss rule is a substantive[80] common law rule that treats shareholders' loss that reflects that of the company,[81] being loss that consists in the diminution of the value of their shareholding, as irrecoverable. There is no reason of principle for this common law rule to render specific performance unavailable, being a remedy focused on vindicating the claimant's right to performance for which loss to the claimant is not an essential element, as *Beswick v Beswick* demonstrates. Most arguments of policy justifying the common law rule have no application to specific performance, while any residual policy concerns can be addressed by the use of the court's discretionary powers.

[77] *Gray* (n 68) 1051 (James LJ).

[78] In truth it is not clear how exceptional they would be – these sorts of conflicts between shareholder and company may be the principal situations in which the shareholder would be seeking specific performance on behalf of the company.

[79] See eg, *Shell UK Ltd v Lostock Garage Ltd* [1976] 1 WLR 1187 (CA).

[80] The decision of the Privy Council in *Primeo Fund (in liq) v Bank of Bermuda (Cayman) Ltd* [2021] UKPC 22, [2022] 1 All ER (Comm) 1219 confirms that it is a substantive rule of law, tested at the date the loss is suffered, not a procedural or pleading rule tested at the date of trial, so a shareholder does not avoid the rule by disposing of their shares and crystallising their loss pre-trial.

[81] As the Court of Appeal put it in *Prudential* (n 5) 224 'when the shareholder acquires a share he accepts the fact that the value of his investment follows the fortunes of the company'.

12

Freezing Orders: Casting Off the Shackles of The Siskina?

PAUL S DAVIES*

I. INTRODUCTION

INJUNCTIONS MAY BE granted 'in all cases in which it appears to the court to be just and convenient to do so'.[1] This flexible formulation has been consistently invoked to allow the courts scope to develop the law to reflect modern advancements. But although the power to grant an injunction can now be found in statute, it is important to note that it is not 'a solecism to refer to the power deriving from the inherent jurisdiction of the court'.[2] As Lord Scott put it in *Fourie v Le Roux*, '[t]he power of a judge sitting in the High Court to grant an injunction against a party to proceedings properly served is confirmed by, but does not derive from, section 37 of the Supreme Court Act 1981 and its statutory predecessors. It derives from the pre-Judicature Act 1873 powers of the Chancery courts, and other courts, to grant injunctions'.[3]

Despite some initial confusion,[4] the law was not ossified by the Judicature Acts.[5] On the contrary, the law on injunctions has continued to evolve, and is an important weapon in the armoury of commercial litigators. All injunctions are powerful equitable remedies, not least since their breach is sanctioned by contempt of court, but one of the most eye-catching recent developments concerns the growth of freezing

* Professor of Commercial Law, UCL; Barrister, Essex Court Chambers. I was instructed by the appellants in the appeal to the Privy Council in *Broad Idea v Convoy Collateral Ltd*, but all views expressed, and any errors, can only be attributed to me. I am grateful to those who participated at the conference for their comments and questions, and in particular Paul McGrath KC and Ryan Turner. I am also very thankful for the generous support of the Leverhulme Trust through a Philip Leverhulme Prize.

[1] Senior Courts Act 1981, s 37(1).

[2] *UL v BK* [2013] EWHC 1735 (Fam), [2014] Fam 35 [14] (Mostyn J).

[3] *Fourie v Le Roux* [2007] UKHL 1, [2007] 1 WLR 320 [25].

[4] *Holmes v Millage* [1893] 1 QB 551 (CA) 557 (Lindley LJ); *Morgan v Hart* [1914] 2 KB 183 (CA) 191 (Buckley LJ). cp *Malmesbury Railway Co v Budd* (1876) 2 Ch D 113 (Ch); *Beddow v Beddow* (1878) 9 Ch D 89 (Ch).

[5] *Masri v Consolidated Contractors International (UK) Ltd (No 2)* [2008] EWCA Civ 303, [2009] QB 450 [141]–[147] (Lawrence Collins LJ).

injunctions over the past 50 years.[6] The modern law on freezing injunctions shows how creative and flexible the equitable jurisdiction can be in response to the challenges posed in the context of large-scale international fraud, and this has been illustrated by the recent decision of the Privy Council in *Broad Idea v Convoy Collateral Ltd*.[7] That decision is the focus of study in this chapter. The background to the dispute will first be outlined, before analysing the judgments and their wider ramifications in both England and Wales and offshore jurisdictions. Freezing orders continue to be an increasingly potent weapon in commercial litigation.

II. FREEZING INJUNCTIONS IN THE PRIVY COUNCIL

In *Mercedes Benz AG v Leiduck*,[8] the Privy Council refused to grant a freezing order to restrain a defendant in Monaco from dissipating his assets in Hong Kong. Lord Nicholls began his judgment by saying: 'The first defendant's argument comes to this: his assets are in Hong Kong, so the Monaco court cannot reach them; he is in Monaco, so the Hong Kong court cannot reach him. That cannot be right. That is not acceptable today. A person operating internationally cannot so easily defeat the judicial process. There is not a black hole into which a defendant can escape out of sight and become unreachable.'[9] Unfortunately, the majority of the Board disagreed with Lord Nicholls.

A quarter of a century later, the Privy Council re-visited this problem of 'black holes' in *Broad Idea v Convoy Collateral Ltd*.[10] The Board unanimously held that, on the facts, no freezing orders should be granted, but a bare majority (four:three) held that Lord Nicholls' dissenting judgment should be (partly) adopted and that the court does have the power, at common law, to grant a freezing order even where there is no pre-existing cause of action against the defendant within the jurisdiction of the court. Lord Leggatt, who gave the leading judgment,[11] thought that the contrary view which had been favoured by the House of Lords in *Siskina (Owners of Cargo Lately Laden on Board) v Distos Cia Naviera SA*[12] should no longer be followed, and concluded that '[t]he shades of *The Siskina* have haunted this area of the law for far too long and they should now finally be laid to rest'.[13]

This enlightened approach of the majority is welcome. In the context of sophisticated international fraud, it is increasingly common for the substantive dispute to be heard in one jurisdiction, whilst the defendant's assets are located in another.[14] It is important that freezing orders be available to support claimants and frustrate

[6] The first case to recognise this injunction was *Nippon Yusen Kaisha v Karageorgis* [1975] 1 WLR 1093 (CA) although for some time they were known as '*Mareva* injunctions' after one of the early cases that first recognised it, involving a ship of that name: *Mareva Compania Naviera SA v International Bulkcarriers SA* [1975] 2 Lloyd's Rep 509 (CA).

[7] [2021] UKPC 24, [2022] 2 WLR 703.

[8] [1996] AC 284 (PC).

[9] ibid 305.

[10] (n 7).

[11] With which Lord Briggs, Lord Sales and Lord Hamblen agreed.

[12] [1979] AC 210 (HL).

[13] *Broad Idea* (n 7) [120].

[14] See, eg, Lord Neuberger's Foreword to S Gee, *Commercial Injunctions*, 6th edn (London, Sweet & Maxwell, 2016) xiii–xv.

fraudsters. Even the minority judgment in *Broad Idea*, given by Sir Geoffrey Vos,[15] recognised that Lord Leggatt provided an 'erudite and compelling exposition of how, rationally, the common law affecting the grant of freezing and other interlocutory injunctions ought to have developed had *The Siskina* been decided differently'.[16] Lord Leggatt's judgment is likely to become a central reference point when considering the juridical foundation of freezing orders. However, further litigation may be required to establish that the majority approach in *Broad Idea* represents the law in England and Wales.

A. The Appeals

Convoy Collateral Ltd ('CCL') appealed two decisions of the Eastern Caribbean Court of Appeal ('ECCA') of 2020. Both emerged from the so-called 'Enigma Network' of companies, said to be part of a massive fraud carried out in Hong Kong. CCL is alleged to be one of the largest victims of the fraud.

CCL sought a freezing order in the BVI against Dr Cho, a resident of Hong Kong. Dr Cho was a director of Broad Idea International Ltd ('Broad Idea'), owning 50.1 per cent of the company. Broad Idea's only asset was a shareholding in Town Health International Medical Group Ltd ('Town Health'), a company originally incorporated in the Cayman Islands, continued into Bermuda, and listed on the Hong Kong Stock Exchange. Dr Cho was a director of both Town Health and CCL's parent company, Convoy Global Holdings. Both these companies were named as members of the Enigma Network, and, following the allegations of fraud, Dr Cho was removed as director of the former and resigned as a director of the latter.

CCL successfully obtained an ex parte freezing injunction to restrain Dr Cho from disposing of, dealing with or diminishing the value of his shares in Broad Idea.[17] CCL also obtained permission to serve its application on Dr Cho in Hong Kong. This decision was subsequently set aside upon Dr Cho's application, and the ECCA dismissed CCL's appeal.[18]

A freezing order was also sought to restrain Broad Idea from disposing of, dealing with or diminishing the value of its shareholding in Town Health.[19] Although CCL did not have a cause of action against Broad Idea itself, it is well established that a freezing order may be granted under the *Chabra* jurisdiction[20] against a 'non-cause of action defendant' where the person injuncted holds or controls assets against which a judgment against the primary defendant could potentially be enforced. The freezing order was granted against Broad Idea at first instance, but set aside by the ECCA.[21]

[15] With which Lord Reed and Lord Hodge agreed.

[16] *Broad Idea* (n 7) [220].

[17] Dr Cho was also enjoined from disposing of, dealing with or diminishing the value of his assets within the BVI up to US$75.5m, and from effecting any changes, variations or amendments to any agreement or trust in relation to which his shares in Broad Idea were held: *Broad Idea* (n 7) [131(ii)].

[18] *Broad Idea International Ltd v Convoy Collateral Ltd* BVIHCMAP2016/0030 (30 March 2020).

[19] Up to a value of some US$75.5m; Broad Idea was also enjoined from registering, or causing to be registered, any change in the ownership of Dr Cho's shares in Broad Idea: *Broad Idea* (n 7) [131(i)].

[20] So-called after the leading case: *TSB Private Bank International SA v Chabra* [1992] 1 WLR 231 (Ch).

[21] *Broad Idea International Ltd v Convoy Collateral Ltd* BVIHCMAP 26/2019 (29 May 2020).

B. The Decision of the Privy Council

The ECCA insisted that the Court had no power to grant an injunction in situations where CCL did not have a pre-existing cause of action in the BVI against either Dr Cho or Broad Idea. This 'power issue' is at the heart of the decision of the Privy Council, and the reason why an enlarged panel of seven judges was convened. The majority disagreed with the approach of the ECCA in principle, but on the facts both appeals were unanimously dismissed.

CCL could not obtain a freezing order against Dr Cho because CCL could not serve Dr Cho out of the jurisdiction. The relevant provisions of the procedural rules concerning service out were drafted in materially similar terms to those which were applicable in *The Siskina* and *Mercedes Benz*, in which the House of Lords and Privy Council, respectively, had held that the injunction gateway did not allow a free-standing claim for a freezing injunction to be served out of the jurisdiction. Lord Leggatt declined an invitation to interpret the rules more broadly, memorably saying that '[t]he common law does not operate on a principle of third time lucky'.[22]

Broad Idea could also not be injuncted because there was no proper evidence to support the judge's finding that there was a good arguable case that the shares in Town Health held by Broad Idea are beneficially owned by Dr Cho. Indeed, at the time the freezing order against Broad Idea was originally granted, there was no freezing order against Dr Cho restraining him from dealing in any way he chose with his controlling shareholding in Broad Idea.[23] As Lord Leggatt observed, '[i]n circumstances where Dr Cho remained free to dispose of or deal in any other way with his shares in Broad Idea, there was no justification for seeking to prevent conduct which would indirectly diminish the value of those shares. There was therefore no justification for granting a freezing injunction against Broad Idea which was designed to maintain the value of Dr Cho's shares in Broad Idea'.[24]

C. The 'Power Issue'

The Board was split on the question of whether the court has the power to grant free-standing freezing orders. The controversy surrounding this 'power issue' stems from *The Siskina*. That case involved a dispute between the owners of *The Siskina* and the owners of cargo which had been carried on board. *The Siskina* sank, and the only asset against which a judgment in favour of the cargo owners could potentially be enforced was the proceeds of the ship's insurance policy with London underwriters. The cargo owners feared, quite reasonably, that the insurance monies would be paid to the shipowners and deposited in another jurisdiction, depriving the cargo owners of an effective remedy. They therefore sought a freezing order, but first had

[22] *Broad Idea* (n 7) [67].
[23] Such an injunction has now been granted by the Hong Kong Court: see ibid [113].
[24] ibid [112].

to establish that they could serve a writ outside the jurisdiction. The Rules of the Supreme Court ('RSC') 1962, Order 11, rule 1(1)(i), permitted service of a writ out of the jurisdiction with leave of the court 'if in the action begun by the writ an injunction is sought ordering the defendant to do or refrain from doing anything within the jurisdiction'. The House of Lords, allowing the shipowners' appeal,[25] interpreted this provision narrowly. Lord Diplock famously said:[26]

> The words used in sub-rule (i) are terms of legal art. The sub-rule speaks of 'the action' in which a particular kind of relief, 'an injunction' is sought. This pre-supposes the existence of a cause of action on which to found 'the action'. A right to obtain an interlocutory injunction is not a cause of action. It cannot stand on its own. It is dependent upon there being a pre-existing cause of action against the defendant arising out of an invasion, actual or threatened by him, of a legal or equitable right of the plaintiff for the enforcement of which the defendant is amenable to the jurisdiction of the court.

These remarks have been regularly cited, but their significance has been exaggerated and divorced from the context of the decision. The *ratio* of *The Siskina* was limited to the service out issue – in respect of which it was followed in both *Mercedes Benz* and *Broad Idea*. Lord Diplock himself admitted that it was not necessary to consider 'the wider question of what restrictions, whether discretional or jurisdictional, there may be' upon the court's power to grant injunctions.[27] In *Broad Idea*, the Board rightly recognised that *The Siskina* did not decide, as part of its *ratio decidendi*, that a pre-existing cause of action was required for a freezing order to be granted. As a result, the majority was free to conclude that no such bar to equitable relief existed.

Indeed, *The Siskina* itself was grounded upon unsteady foundations. For instance, Lord Diplock relied upon the decision of the Court of Appeal in *North London Railway Co v Great Northern Railway Co*[28] for the proposition that the High Court, since the Judicature Acts, 'has no power to grant an interlocutory injunction except in protection or assertion of some legal or equitable right which it has jurisdiction to enforce by final judgment'.[29] But that is not what *North London Railway* decided. As Lord Collins has forcefully pointed out, *North London Railway* placed no substantive restrictions on a court's ability to grant injunctive relief.[30] The jurisdiction to grant equitable relief remains very broad.

[25] Lord Denning had given the leading judgment in the Court of Appeal, and 'although well used to reversals by the House of Lords' (as Lord Leggatt put it: *Broad Idea* (n 7) [7]) he later wrote that 'they were never so disappointing as this one', since the decision was unjust to the cargo owners: AT Denning, *The Due Process of Law* (Oxford, OUP, 1980) 141.

[26] *The Siskina* (n 12) 256. Lord Diplock also thought that s 45(1) of the Supreme Court of Judicature (Consolidation) Act 1925 (see now s 37(1) of the Senior Courts Act 1981) which put on a statutory footing the court's ability to grant an injunction, should also be interpreted restrictively, since '[t]hat subsection, speaking as it does of interlocutory orders, presupposes the existence of an action, actual or potential, claiming substantive relief which the High Court has jurisdiction to grant and to which the interlocutory orders referred to are but ancillary': *The Siskina* (n 12) 254.

[27] *The Siskina* (n 12) 254.

[28] (1883) 11 QBD 30 (CA).

[29] *The Siskina* (n 12) 256.

[30] *Masri v Consolidated Contractors International (UK) Ltd (No 2)* (n 5) [141]–[147]; *Tasarruf Mevduati Sigorta Fonu v Merrill Lynch Bank & Trust Co (Cayman) Ltd* [2011] UKPC 17, [2012] 1 WLR 1721 [56]. See too *Broad Idea* (n 7) [43]–[47] and [143]–[147].

It should also be remembered that *The Siskina* was decided by the House of Lords at an early stage in the development of freezing orders.[31] The very first decisions of the commercial court granting *Mareva* injunctions (as they were then called) had only been decided a few years previously,[32] and there was a sense that this 'nuclear weapon'[33] should be treated with caution. Yet freezing orders are now regularly granted and are crucial in ongoing attempts to defeat increasingly sophisticated fraudsters. Lord Leggatt pointed out four major developments since *The Siskina*:[34] i) freezing orders can be granted in aid of a judgment already given against the defendant (which cannot be seen as ancillary to a cause of action); ii) freezing orders can be granted against non-cause of action defendants;[35] iii) section 25(1) of the Civil Jurisdiction and Judgments Act 1982 was enacted to provide that the High Court 'shall have power to grant interim relief … where proceedings have been or are to be commenced';[36] iv) worldwide freezing orders have become commonplace.

As the law has developed, individual Law Lords have expressed doubts about 'whether the law as laid down by *The Siskina* (as subsequently modified) was correct in restricting the power to grant injunctions to certain exclusive categories',[37] and the House of Lords has on multiple occasions softened the impact of *The Siskina*.[38] For example, in *Castanho v Brown & Root (UK) Ltd* Lord Scarman held that 'the width and flexibility of equity are not to be undermined by categorisation'.[39] Interestingly, Lord Diplock agreed with Lord Scarman, and emphasised 'our principles of a "wide and flexible" equity' in *British Airways Board v Laker Airways Ltd*.[40] A decade later, in *Channel Tunnel Group Ltd v Balfour Beatty Construction Ltd*,[41] the House of Lords granted an interim injunction to restrain the defendants from suspending work on the Channel Tunnel, even though the injunction was not sought in aid of a claim for substantive relief which the court had jurisdiction to grant since the substantive dispute was to be resolved by arbitrators. Lord Browne-Wilkinson astutely observed that '[g]iven the international character of much contemporary litigation and the need to promote mutual assistance between the courts of the various jurisdictions which such litigation straddles, it would be a serious matter if the English courts were unable to grant interlocutory relief in cases where the substantive trial and the ultimate decision of the case might ultimately take place in a court outside England'.[42]

[31] *Mercedes Benz* (n 8) 308; *Fourie* (n 3) [30]; *Broad Idea* (n 7) [11].

[32] *Nippon Yusen Kaisha* (n 6) 1095; *Mareva Cia Naviera SA* (n 6); *Rasu Maritima SA v Perusahaan Pertambangan Minyak Dan Gas Bumi Negara (Government of the Republic of Indonesia intervening) (The Pertamina)* [1978] QB 644 (CA).

[33] *Bank Mellat v Nikpour* [1985] FSR 87 (CA) 92 (Donaldson LJ).

[34] *Broad Idea* (n 7) [13]–[21].

[35] *Chabra* (n 20).

[36] This was originally limited to the Contracting States to the Brussels Convention, but was expanded in 1997 to proceedings commenced or about to be commenced anywhere in the world: Civil Jurisdiction and Judgments Act 1982 (Interim Relief) Order 1997 (SI 1997/302).

[37] *Channel Tunnel Group Ltd v Balfour Beatty Construction Ltd* [1993] AC 334 (HL) 343 (Lord Browne-Wilkinson) echoing the doubts previously expressed by Lords Goff and Mackay in *South Carolina Insurance Co v Assurantie Maatschappij "De Zeven Provincien" NV* [1987] AC 24 (HL) 44.

[38] Compare the decision of the Court of Appeal in *The Veracruz I* [1992] 1 Lloyd's Rep 353 (CA): see section III.C below.

[39] [1981] AC 557 (HL) 573. See too *South Carolina Insurance* (n 37); *Channel Tunnel Group* (n 37).

[40] [1985] AC 58 (HL) 95.

[41] (n 37).

[42] ibid 341, cited in *Broad Idea* (n 7) [28]. See too *Fourie* (n 3).

The narrow approach adopted in *The Siskina* has largely been circumvented in subsequent cases and is inconsistent with the equitable roots of the injunction. What is now section 37 of the Senior Courts Act 1981 has always been cast in very broad terms; since 1873 Parliament has consistently passed legislation that the court has power to grant injunctions when it is 'just and convenient' to do so.[43] The development of freezing orders,[44] search orders,[45] website-blocking orders,[46] third-party disclosure orders,[47] and injunctions to restrain the presentation or advertising of a winding-up petition where this would be an abuse of the process of the court,[48] for example, demonstrates that the law can continue to develop incrementally to grant injunctions in novel situations which are not necessarily based on a distinct underlying right the claimant enjoys against the defendant. However, care must be taken before suggesting that the 'jurisdiction' to grant injunctions has expanded. As Lord Scott pointed out in *Fourie v Le Roux*, 'jurisdiction is a word of some ambiguity'.[49] In the strict sense, jurisdiction to grant an injunction exists whenever the court has personal jurisdiction over the party against whom the injunction is sought. But jurisdiction is, confusingly, often also used in a looser sense simply to mean that the court's power to grant an injunction must be exercised in accordance with principle and rules of precedent. This latter usage of 'jurisdiction' is best avoided.[50]

In the context of freezing orders, the approach of the majority in *Broad Idea* is particularly welcome since '[i]n the increasingly sophisticated world of international

[43] See the predecessors to Senior Courts Act 1981, s 37(1): Judicature Act 1873, s 25(8); Supreme Court of Judicature (Consolidation) Act 1925, s 45.

[44] And see too the development of 'notification injunctions' which require the respondent to give notice of any dealings with or disposal of assets or other transactions that fall within the scope of the order: *Candy v Holyoake* [2017] EWCA Civ 92, [2017] 2 All ER (Comm) 513.

[45] *Anton Piller KG v Manufacturing Processes Ltd* [1976] Ch 55 (CA).

[46] *Cartier International AG v British Sky Broadcasting Ltd* [2016] EWCA Civ 658, [2017] 1 All ER 700 (appealed solely on the issue of costs: [2018] UKSC 28, [2018] 1 WLR 3259); *Google Inc v Equustek Solutions Inc* 2017 SCC 34, [2017] 1 SCR 824.

[47] *Norwich Pharmacal Co v Customs and Excise Comrs* [1974] AC 133 (HL); *Ashworth Hospital Authority v MGN Ltd* [2002] UKHL 29, [2002] 1 WLR 2033; see too the 'closely-related' (per *Broad Idea* (n 7) [49]) *Bankers Trust* orders: *Bankers Trust Co v Shapira* [1980] 1 WLR 1274 (CA).

[48] *Bryanston Finance Ltd v De Vries (No 2)* [1976] Ch 63 (CA).

[49] *Fourie* (n 3) [25]. Lord Scott quoted the following remarks of Pickford LJ in *Guaranty Trust Co of New York v Hannay & Co* [1915] 2 KB 536 (CA) 563: 'The first and, in my opinion, the only really correct sense of the expression that the court has no jurisdiction is that it has no power to deal with and decide the dispute as to the subject matter before it, no matter in what form or by whom it is raised. But there is another sense in which it is often used, ie, that although the court has power to decide the question it will not according to its settled practice do so except in a certain way and under certain circumstances.'

[50] In *Broad Idea* (n 7) [57], Lord Leggatt thought 'it would be difficult to improve on the following passage in Spry, *Equitable Remedies*, 9th edn (Sydney, Thomson Reuters Australia, 2014), at 333: 'The powers of courts with equitable jurisdiction to grant injunctions are, subject to any relevant statutory restrictions, unlimited. Injunctions are granted only when to do so accords with equitable principles, but this restriction involves, not a defect of powers, but an adoption of doctrines and practices that change in their application from time to time. Unfortunately there have sometimes been made observations by judges that tend to confuse questions of jurisdiction or of powers with questions of discretions or of practice. The preferable analysis involves a recognition of the great width of equitable powers, an historical appraisal of the categories of injunctions that have been established and an acceptance that pursuant to general equitable principles injunctions may issue in new categories when this course appears appropriate.' This passage from Spry was also quoted with approval in *Broadmoor Special Health Authority v Robinson* [2000] QB 775 (CA) [20] (Lord Woolf MR); *Cartier* (n 46) [47] (Kitchin LJ); see too *Samsung Electronics (UK) Ltd v Apple Inc* [2012] EWCA Civ 1339, [2013] FSR 9 [72] (Sir Robin Jacob).

movement of goods, assets and money, and the formation of companies and the hiding of assets, the courts have to be astute to ensure that the law keeps pace with modern developments and is not flouted'.[51] Lord Leggatt noted that '[t]he situation in *The Siskina* where a defendant's assets are situated in a country other than that in which the substantive proceedings are taking place was comparatively uncommon in commercial litigation in 1977 but is now normal';[52] the facts of *Broad Idea* are a good example of this.

III. THE IMPACT OF *BROAD IDEA*

A. The Basis of Freezing Orders

The majority sensibly based the award of freezing orders[53] upon the 'enforcement principle': 'the essential purpose of a freezing injunction is to facilitate the enforcement of a judgment or order for the payment of a sum of money by preventing assets against which such a judgment could potentially be enforced from being dealt with in such a way that insufficient assets are available to meet the judgment'.[54] This explains why there is no need (*contra* Lord Diplock in *The Siskina*) to try to assimilate freezing orders with 'ordinary' interlocutory injunctions which are awarded according to the *American Cyanamid* principles.[55] The claimant's right which is protected is not the right on which the substantive cause of action is based. Rather, the claimant's right is one to have a (usually prospective) judgment or order (from whatever jurisdiction) enforced through the court's process.

The minority seemed unwilling to engage in this debate about the rationale of freezing orders.[56] Sir Geoffrey Vos instead chose to 'echo'[57] the comments of Lord Millett in *Mercedes Benz* that '[i]deally … the first step would be to ascertain, not only what a *Mareva* injunction does, but also how, juristically speaking, it does it. This should be straightforward, but is not. After only a few years the development of a settled rationale was truncated by the enactment of [section 37(3)].[58] This did not, as is sometimes said, turn the common law *Mareva* injunction into a statutory remedy, but it assumed that the remedy existed, and tacitly endorsed its validity'.[59]

[51] *Linsen International Ltd v Humpuss Transportasi Kimia* [2011] EWCA Civ 1042 [17] (Lord Neuberger MR).

[52] *Broad Idea* (n 7) [60].

[53] The judgments in *Broad Idea* refer to both 'freezing orders' and 'freezing injunctions'; whether freezing orders are best characterised as a (sui generis) injunction requires further consideration beyond the scope of this chapter, but see generally P Devonshire, 'Freezing Orders, Disappearing Assets and the Problem of Enjoining Non-Parties' (2002) 118 *LQR* 124.

[54] *Broad Idea* (n 7) [85].

[55] *American Cyanamid Co v Ethicon Ltd* [1975] AC 396 (HL).

[56] *Broad Idea* (n 7) [213].

[57] ibid.

[58] 'The power of the High Court under subsection (1) to grant an interlocutory injunction restraining a party to any proceedings from removing from the jurisdiction of the High Court, or otherwise dealing with, assets located within that jurisdiction shall be exercisable in cases where that party is, as well as in cases where he is not, domiciled, resident or present within that jurisdiction.'

[59] *Mercedes Benz* (n 8) 299.

It is undoubtedly true that the quick enactment of section 37(3) meant that the courts could simply rely upon the statute rather than elucidate the principles underpinning relief through incremental developments in case law. But it remains important to be clear about the basis of freezing orders, since that helps to establish the appropriate parameters of the power to grant relief – including the *Chabra* jurisdiction, and what assets can be the subject of freezing orders. The majority's explanation is clear, compelling, and consistent with earlier authorities both in this jurisdiction[60] and Australia,[61] for example. The minority appeared to think that revisiting the basis for freezing orders could 'throw the common law into uncertainty',[62] but this is highly unlikely. Rather than sowing the seeds for uncertainty, the majority's persuasive explanation of the law ensures that freezing orders are grounded upon a stable juridical basis, which can only make the law more predictable.

B. The Ratio of Broad Idea

The minority suggested that 'the majority's ground-breaking exposition of the law of injunctions will not, as a matter of precedent, be binding on lower courts, but will be powerful obiter dicta'.[63] By contrast, Lord Leggatt insisted that '[t]he majority of the Board considers that it is both necessary and important on this appeal to confront and decide the power issue'.[64] Of course, the Board itself cannot determine what constitutes *ratio decidendi* or *obiter dicta*;[65] this must be worked out through subsequent cases.

The minority approach rests upon the basis that both appeals could be dismissed on their facts without deciding the 'power issue', discussion of which was therefore not necessary for the outcome of the case. However, the majority of the Board considered that it was first necessary to decide whether a free-standing injunction could, in principle, be granted, since that issue is logically prior to consideration of the *Chabra* jurisdiction, for example. The majority drew an analogy with *Hedley Byrne & Co Ltd v Heller & Partners Ltd*,[66] where the conclusion that, on the facts, the defendant had successfully disclaimed responsibility for its misrepresentation did not prevent

[60] eg, *Fourie* (n 3) [2] (Lord Bingham); *JSC BTA Bank v Ablyazov (No 10)* [2015] UKSC 64, [2015] 1 WLR 4754 [13] (Lord Clarke), adopting the language of Beatson LJ in the Court of Appeal: [2013] EWCA Civ 928, [2014] 1 WLR 1414 [34]. See too Lord Nicholls in *Mercedes Benz* (n 8).

[61] *Cardile v LED Builder Pty Ltd* (1999) 198 CLR 380 (HCA); *PT Bayan Resources TBK v BCBC Singapore Pte Ltd* [2015] HCA 36, (2015) 258 CLR 1.

[62] *Broad Idea* (n 7) [213] (Sir Geoffrey Vos MR who also expressed the concern that the majority would 'seek to unwind its development back to 1996', but this is unconvincing: see section V below).

[63] *Broad Idea* (n 7) [221] (Sir Geoffrey Vos MR).

[64] ibid [120].

[65] Interestingly, in *Bremer Vulkan Schiffbau und Maschinenfabrik v South India Shipping Corpn Ltd* [1981] AC 909 (HL) 979 Lord Diplock said that in *The Siskina* the House of Lords 'had occasion to confirm as a matter of ratio decidendi the well-established law that the jurisdiction of the High Court to grant injunctions, whether interlocutory or final, was confined to injunctions granted for the enforcement or protection of some legal or equitable right', but the suggestion that this was part of the ratio is obviously difficult to support: see *Broad Idea* (n 7) [23].

[66] [1964] AC 465 (HL).

the House of Lords from deciding the important point of principle that there can be liability in tort for a negligent misrepresentation in the absence of a contract between the parties.

The narrow view of the minority may leave the law in an unsatisfactory state. In the BVI, free-standing injunctive relief had been granted over a decade earlier in *Black Swan Investment ISA v Harvest View Ltd*.[67] Bannister J explicitly preferred the reasoning of Lord Nicholls in *Mercedes Benz*, and granted a freezing order against BVI companies said to be controlled by an individual against whom proceedings had been brought in South Africa. *Black Swan* was supported by the ECCA in *Yukos CIS Investments Ltd v Yukos Hydrocarbons Investments Ltd*.[68] Yet in *Broad Idea* the ECCA held that *Black Swan* and *Yukos* (and the numerous decisions applying their approach) were wrong: following *The Siskina* and the majority in *Mercedes Benz*, Pereira CJ held that, 'as undesirable as it may be perceived in modern day international commerce',[69] the BVI court had no 'subject matter jurisdiction' to grant a freezing injunction otherwise than in aid of proceedings claiming substantive relief in the BVI. If the comments on the 'power issue' in the Privy Council are truly obiter dicta only, it would be very unfortunate if the comments in the ECCA were to mean that the *Black Swan* jurisdiction was killed off. But perhaps, if the treatment of the 'power issue' in the Privy Council was obiter, then so too were the comments in the Court of Appeal. As a result, *Black Swan* and *Yukos* should remain good law. And the guidance of the Privy Council should still be followed to establish that (i) the comments of the *The Siskina* on the 'power issue' were themselves obiter and should not be followed; and (ii) courts have the power to grant injunctive relief whenever it is 'just and convenient', which may well involve granting freezing orders where there is no pre-existing cause of action.

However, since the majority viewed these elements as necessary steps in their reasoning as regards the appeal against Broad Idea, it may be better to consider them to be part of the *ratio*,[70] and it is suggested that courts are likely to adopt this view. In practice, this difference between obiter dicta and *ratio decidendi* is only likely to matter for other jurisdictions which are bound by the Judicial Committee of the Privy Council as their apex court: it is not likely to be of great importance in the BVI itself, since legislation was brought into force at the start of 2021 to put free-standing freezing orders on a statutory footing.[71] Unless there is a binding appellate decision which clearly states that free-standing freezing orders cannot be granted,[72] courts will be free to follow the interpretation of the Privy Council in *Broad Idea* that the 'power issue' was not part of the *ratio* in either *The Siskina* or *Mercedes Benz*.

[67] BVIHCV 2009/399 (23 March 2010).

[68] HCVAP 2010/028 (26 September 2011).

[69] *Broad Idea* (n 7) [50].

[70] See, eg, *R (Youngsam) v Parole Board* [2019] EWCA Civ 229, [2019] 3 WLR 33 [48]–[59] (Leggatt LJ).

[71] Section 3 of the Eastern Caribbean Supreme Court (Virgin Islands) (Amendment) Act 2020 inserted a new s 24A into the Eastern Caribbean Supreme Court Act 1969 which provides that '[t]he High Court or a judge thereof may grant interim relief where proceedings have been or are about to be commenced in a foreign jurisdiction'.

[72] *cf The Veracruz I* (n 38) in England, considered in section IV below. In *VTB Capital plc v Universal Telecom Management* [2013] 2 CILR 94, the Cayman Islands Court of Appeal essentially supported the approach already taken in *Black Swan*.

C. The Impact in England and Wales

The guidance of the Privy Council will naturally be considered to be persuasive in England and Wales. The interpretation of *The Siskina* in particular is likely to prove influential. Any perceived need to circumvent the supposed restrictions laid down in *The Siskina* regarding the 'power issue' was without proper foundation and should not be repeated.[73]

However, the decision in *Veracruz Transportation Inc v VC Shipping Co Inc (The Veracruz I)*[74] renders the law in England and Wales more uncertain. A ship was about to be delivered in a defective condition to the buyer. The purchase price would be the only asset of the seller against which the buyer's claim for damages could be enforced, and the risk of that asset being dissipated was high. Nevertheless, the Court of Appeal held that it could not grant a freezing order as a result of *The Siskina*: the claimant's cause of action had not yet arisen.

The Veracruz I is generally seen as problematic. As Sir John Megaw recognised in the case itself, 'I see no valid reason, in logic or practical convenience in the interest of justice, why jurisdiction should not exist … But we are precluded by authority from so deciding …'.[75] Once *The Siskina* is properly understood not to mandate such a conclusion, it is understandable why Lord Leggatt concluded in *Broad Idea* that 'the time has long since come to state unequivocally that the practice followed in *The Veracruz I* is likewise unsound in principle, unfit for modern commerce and should no longer be adopted'.[76]

But does this decision of the Privy Council trump the earlier decision of the Court of Appeal? Until recently, this question would have been summarily answered in the negative: *Broad Idea* concerns the law of the BVI, and cannot alter the law of England and Wales. However, in *Willers v Joyce*[77] the Privy Council, for apparently pragmatic reasons,[78] held that 'provided that the point at issue is one of English law, the members of that panel can, if they think it appropriate, not only decide that the earlier decision of the House of Lords or Supreme Court, or of the Court of Appeal, was wrong, but also can expressly direct that domestic courts should treat the decision of the JCPC as representing the law of England and Wales'.[79] This was, in itself, remarkable and it remains to be seen how it will be applied.[80] It is suggested that the majority in *Broad Idea* stopped a little short of 'expressly directing' English courts to follow *Broad Idea* rather than *The Veracruz I*: saying it 'should no longer be adopted' is not quite a direction 'not to follow' the Court of Appeal.

[73] *cf Fourie* (n 3).

[74] (n 38).

[75] ibid 361, cited by Lord Leggatt in *Broad Idea* (n 7) [98]; see too 360 (Nourse LJ); L Collins, 'The Legacy of the Siskina' (1992) 108 *LQR* 175.

[76] *Broad Idea* (n 7) [100]. Leggatt J had previously expressed the same view at first instance in *Kazakhstan Kagazy plc v Zhunus* [2016] EWHC 1048 (Comm), [2016] 4 WLR 86 [56]–[58], although he recognised that he was bound by the appellate decisions (overturned on appeal, since the right to institute proceedings had already arisen on the facts: [2016] EWCA Civ 1036, [2017] 1 WLR 1360).

[77] [2016] UKSC 44, [2018] AC 843.

[78] ibid [19].

[79] ibid [21] (Lord Neuberger).

[80] P Mirfield, 'A Novel Theory of Privy Council Precedent' (2017) 133 *LQR* 1.

As a result, it would appear that *The Veracruz I* remains good law in England and Wales, although it undoubtedly rests upon shaky foundations. Its reasoning is wholly dependent upon an out-of-date reading of *The Siskina*, which pulls the rug out from under the decision. It is likely to be challenged soon enough,[81] and a leapfrog appeal to the Supreme Court may be possible.[82] No doubt some principled arguments may be made in favour of *The Veracruz I*; for instance, perhaps the defendant should remain free to deal with their property as they wish unless and until an obligation to pay the claimant arises.[83] But blanket rules such as those favoured in *The Siskina* and *The Veracruz I* take an unduly narrow view of the freezing order jurisdiction. The other checks on freezing order relief – most significantly, that the claimant has a good arguable case as to the merits of the substantive action and that there is a real risk, if no injunction is granted, that assets against which a judgment could be enforced will be removed or dissipated[84] – can ensure that injunctions are only granted when 'just and convenient' to do so. Artificial bars on the equitable jurisdiction are inappropriate.[85] It is to be hoped that *The Veracruz I* will soon be definitively jettisoned in this jurisdiction too.

IV. THE INJUNCTION GATEWAY

The decision of the Privy Council not to allow service out is understandable. Since the applicable procedural rules were introduced in materially similar terms to those at issue in *The Siskina* and *Mercedes Benz*, it may be inferred that they were intended to bear the meaning that the case law had already established.[86] As Sir Geoffrey Vos observed, '[t]he whole thrust of these rules is that service out is in respect of claim forms and statements of claim',[87] and CCL had not issued a claim form to serve out upon Dr Cho.

Nevertheless, as a matter of policy, it is unsatisfactory for the court to be able to award a free-standing freezing order, but not to be able to grant service out of the jurisdiction. It will often be the case that assets are located in offshore jurisdictions (such as the BVI) but the defendant is elsewhere. And given the speed at which assets can be moved around jurisdictions by increasingly sophisticated fraudsters,[88] it is important to be able to serve a claim form abroad. Any presumption against service out has substantially lessened in force since *The Siskina* and *Mercedes Benz* were

[81] *cf Mercedes Benz* (n 8) 314 (Lord Nicholls).

[82] Administration of Justice Act 1969, ss 12–16 (as amended by the Criminal Justice and Courts Act 2015).

[83] *cf* A Zuckerman '*Mareva* Injunctions and Security for Judgment in a Framework of Interlocutory Remedies' (1993) 109 *LQR* 432.

[84] *Broad Idea* (n 7) [101]. Note too that the claimant will normally have to give the usual undertaking in damages.

[85] Lord Leggatt explicitly rejected two further potential bars on freezing order relief: (i) that the judgment must be one of the domestic court; and (ii) that the judgment should be against the respondent: *Broad Idea* (n 7) [102].

[86] *Broad Idea* (n 7) [69].

[87] ibid [196], having analysed the relevant provisions in pts 7 and 8 of the Eastern Caribbean Supreme Court Civil Procedure Rules 2000.

[88] *Derby & Co Ltd v Weldon (Nos 3 and 4)* [1990] Ch 65 (CA) 92 (Neill LJ): 'The transfer of funds from one jurisdiction to another grows ever more speedy and the methods of transfer more sophisticated'.

decided;[89] as Briggs has observed, '[t]he world is much smaller than it used to be, and out of the jurisdiction is really not so far away as once it was'.[90]

The onus is therefore on offshore jurisdictions[91] to modify their civil procedure rules to permit the service out of free-standing freezing orders.[92] It is to be hoped that this will be achieved quickly. Yet not all rules committees move with great haste; this may be an area where different jurisdictions end up (through a combination of extraneous factors) with different rules.

V. CONCLUSION

The decision of the majority in *Broad Idea* will be welcomed in offshore jurisdictions. After all, the ECCA only departed from *Black Swan* with great reluctance. In the latter decision, Bannister J presciently observed that[93]

> … there are sound policy reasons why important offshore financial centres, such as Jersey and the BVI, should be in a position to grant such orders in aid where necessary. The business of companies registered within such jurisdictions is invariably transacted abroad and disputes between parties who own them and others are often resolved abroad. It seems to me that when a party to such a dispute is seeking a money judgment against someone with assets within this jurisdiction, it would be highly detrimental to its reputation if potential foreign judgment creditors were to be told that they could not, if successful, have resort to such assets unless they were to commence substantive proceedings here in circumstances where, in all probability, they would be unable to obtain permission to serve them abroad – thus presenting them with an effective brick wall or double bind of the sort so deplored by Lord Nicholls in *Mercedes Benz*.

Awarding free-standing freezing orders can therefore help to advance the reputation of a jurisdiction, and is in accordance with principles of comity.[94] The minority in *Broad Idea* was anxious not to 'put the clock back to 1977'[95] by departing from *The Siskina*, but that is the wrong way around:[96] sticking steadfastly to *The Siskina* when the law has moved on in important ways over the past 45 years would be to put the clock back. The majority's recognition of modern developments and the practical

[89] See, eg, *Abela v Baadarani* [2013] UKSC 44, [2013] 1 WLR 2043 [53] (Lord Sumption).

[90] A Briggs, 'Service Out in a Shrinking World' [2013] *Lloyd's Maritime and Commercial Law Quarterly* 415.

[91] In England and Wales, service out is clearly possible: CPR PD 6B, para 3.1(5).

[92] Interestingly, the Jersey courts had already expressly departed from *Mercedes Benz* as regards service out of the jurisdiction: *Solvalub Ltd v Match Investments Ltd* [1998] ILPr 419 (Jersey CA); *Krohn GmbH v Varna Shipyard (No 2)* (1997) 1 OFLR 482 (Royal Court of Jersey); *State of Qatar v Al Thani* [1999] JLR 118 (Royal Court of Jersey). The Privy Council did not follow the Jersey approach, but that does not necessarily mean that the Jersey courts need to change their approach given the different (Norman) influences upon their legal system: see, eg, *Broad Idea International Ltd v Convoy Collateral Ltd* BVIHCMAP2016/0030 (30 March 2020) [29].

[93] *Black Swan* (n 67) [15].

[94] See, eg, *Solvalub Ltd v Match Investments Ltd* (n 92) [30]–[31] (Sir Godfray Le Quesne QC); *Channel Tunnel Group* (n 37) 341 (Lord Browne-Wilkinson); *Crédit Suisse Fides Trust SA v Cuoghi* [1998] QB 818 (CA) 827 (Millett LJ).

[95] *Broad Idea* (n 7) [203] (Sir Geoffrey Vos MR).

[96] ibid [115].

utility of freezing orders in an increasingly international commercial context helps to keep the law up to date. The minority feared that the majority's approach could create uncertainty, but – beyond wrinkles such as the status of *The Veracruz I* in England and Wales – it is difficult to understand why this should be so, and no concrete examples are given. Any fraudster who has deliberately squirrelled away assets in an offshore jurisdiction might be disappointed to find that the courts in those jurisdictions can now freeze their assets, for instance, but that hardly seems a cause for concern.

Indeed, Sir Geoffrey Vos recognised that 'there could, in an appropriate case, be power at common law … to grant an interim or *Mareva* injunction against a defendant … where there was either (a) an actual or threatened substantive claim against that defendant in foreign proceedings or in arbitration … or (b) a sustainable claim on *Chabra* grounds that the defendant within the jurisdiction is the creature or money box of a defendant against whom there is an actual or threatened foreign claim or arbitration'.[97] His Lordship did not fundamentally disagree with the 'ground-breaking'[98] substantive conclusions of the majority, but rather insisted that they were not necessary for the resolution of appeals.[99] This should not deflect future courts from following the path taken by the majority. The equitable jurisdiction to grant injunctive relief is very broad and should not be 'straitjacketed'[100] by *The Siskina*. It is to be hoped that the majority in *Broad Idea* has sunk *The Siskina* on the 'power issue', and that the ability to serve out free-standing freezing orders will soon be available in all jurisdictions through amendments (if necessary) to civil procedure rules.

[97] ibid [218].

[98] ibid [221].

[99] This perhaps illustrates the conservative approach to incremental developments through the courts previously advocated by Sir Geoffrey Vos: see, eg, G Vos, 'Preserving the Integrity of the Common Law' (Lecture to the Chancery Bar Association, 16 April 2018).

[100] *Cartier* (n 46) [54] (Kitchin LJ).

Part V

Trusts

13

Bankruptcy Protection for Trusts before the Judicature Acts

DAVID FOX*

I. INTRODUCTION

THIS CHAPTER TAKES the Judicature Acts of 1873–75 as a vantage point for looking backwards at a defining characteristic of the English trust. It is nowadays taken as given that the right of a beneficiary under an English trust creates a proprietary interest in the trust assets.[1] Among others, two features of the beneficiary's interest are said to show its proprietary character. These are the preservation of the trust assets from the claims of the trustee's general creditors, and the priority of the beneficiary's claim to the trust assets if the trustee becomes insolvent.[2] In English law, it is property, rather than a theory of divided patrimony, which does the work of explaining why trust interests are treated differently from the claims of the trustee's personal creditors.[3] By the time of the Judicature reforms, the special

* School of Law, University of Edinburgh. I am grateful to Daniel Carr, Patrick Follan and Kenneth Reid for our conversations about the formation of the trust in early Scots law, which were the origin of this chapter. The usual disclaimers apply.

[1] eg, *Westdeutsche Landesbank Girozentrale v Islington LBC* [1996] AC 669 (HL) 705 (Lord Browne-Wilkinson); *Akers v Samba* [2017] UKSC 6, [2017] AC 424 [16] (Mance JSC). The general point stands even though the incidents of the beneficiary's interest and the way they are enforced may vary from one kind of trust to another. Thus, the rights of a beneficiary under a bare trust are markedly different from those of a potential object under a discretionary trust. Nonetheless, the essential proprietary incidents of the kind outlined in this chapter are common to both kinds of trust even if the nature of the rights enforced against the trustee may differ. See further R Nolan, 'Equitable Property' (2006) 122 *LQR* 232.

[2] For expressions of this view, see GL Gretton, 'Trusts Without Equity' (2000) 49 *ICLQ* 599, 606; P Jaffey, 'Explaining the Trust' (2015) 115 *LQR* 377, 380. The priority of the trust against the trustee's creditors and in bankruptcy are not the only indicators of the beneficiary's proprietary interest. Another is the persistence of the trust beneficiary's interest against third parties to whom trust assets are transferred in breach of the trustee's powers. Even this feature was originally explained without reference to a proprietary theory. Transferees of trust assets who took without good faith or for valuable consideration were presumed to undertake afresh the original trustee's obligations to the beneficiary: see further D Fox, 'Purchase for Value Without Notice' in PS Davies, S Douglas and J Goudkamp (eds), *Defences in Equity* (Oxford, Hart, 2018) 57–62.

[3] For the use of the patrimony explanation in Scotland, see Scottish Law Commission, *Liability of Trustees to Third Parties* (DP 138, 2008) ch 2.

status of trust interests was put beyond any doubt in England. Just a few years earlier, the Bankruptcy Act 1869 provided that '[p]roperty held by the bankrupt on trust for any other person' was excepted from the property of the bankrupt divisible among his creditors.[4] Statutory fiat confirmed an understanding that had first developed in the Court of Chancery almost 200 years earlier.

In investigating this feature of the trust, the chapter takes as its starting point Maitland's six historical stages in the development of the beneficiary's interest under a trust. Maitland outlined these stages in his classic *Lectures in Equity* (1909, 1936).[5] As is well known, Maitland was making a larger argument that the interest of a beneficiary under a trust remained essentially personal in character although its features were modelled on proprietary rights recognised at common law. The third stage of Maitland's explanation was the courts' recognition that the trust assets were not available to meet debts owed to the trustee's general creditors. He cited just one authority, *Finch v Earl of Winchelsea* (1715).[6] After a closer investigation, we find that this decision lies amidst a rich cluster of related case law. When read together, the cases show a consistent understanding of how trusts were enforced against the trustee's general creditors and in bankruptcy.

The chapter concentrates on a neglected formative period in the law of trusts after the Chancellorship of Lord Nottingham (1673–82).[7] This is the period extending from the late seventeenth century through to the tenure of Lord Hardwicke as Lord Chancellor (1737–56).[8] MacNair has shown how the post-Restoration law of trusts, while rich in technical doctrine, lacked overarching conceptual explanations. Such explanations as there were tended to give more weight to the obligational nature of trusteeship than any proprietary character of the beneficiary's interest. Writers used analogies with civil law institutions of contract or time-limited property-holding, such as *depositum*, *fideicommissum* or *usufructus*, to explain the trust.[9] Their explanations emphasised the Chancery's distinctive approach to the enforcement of obligations by granting specific relief against defendants who were subject to the court's jurisdiction.

The chapter shows how the early Court of Chancery recognised and explained these features of the beneficiary's interest without articulating them in terms of the modern distinction between rights *in personam* and rights *in rem*. Indeed, the whole scholarly controversy over the characterisation of the beneficiary's interest which

[4] Bankruptcy Act 1869, s 15(1).

[5] FW Maitland, *Equity: A Course of Lectures*, 2nd edn by J Brunyate (Cambridge, CUP, 1936) Lecture IX, 112–14.

[6] (1715) 1 P Wms 277, 24 ER 387. See generally the summary of the cases in DEC Yale, *Lord Nottingham's Chancery Cases* (London, B Quaritch, 1961) vol II, 79 SS, 93.

[7] Although Lord Nottingham explained the operation of uses and trusts in his extra-judicial 'Prolegomena', he did not there turn his attention to their interaction with the trustee's creditors. See DEC Yale (ed), *Lord Nottingham's 'Manual of Chancery Practice' and 'Prolegomena of Chancery and Equity'* (Cambridge, CUP, 1965) chs XII–XVIII.

[8] Fortunately, we now have A Televantos, *Capitalism Before Corporations* (Oxford, OUP, 2021). Although Televantos concentrates on equity's contribution to the commercial law of the later Georgian era, he shows how its origins lie in the Chancery practice of the early eighteenth century.

[9] M MacNair, 'The Conceptual Basis of Trusts in the Later 17th and Early 18th Centuries' in R Helmholz and R Zimmermann (eds), *Itinera Fiduciae* (Berlin, Duncker & Humblot, 1998).

was set running by Maitland's writings would have been foreign to the Chancery judges who did the actual work of fashioning the beneficiary's interest.[10] More recent iterations of that debate continue as the 'obligational', 'rights against rights' or 'persistent' rights theories of the trust.[11] As will be seen, however, the eighteenth-century judges had their own principled reasons for recognising the distinctive claim of a trust beneficiary to priority over the trustee's creditors. The controversy over the *in personam* or *in rem* character of the beneficiary's right might only have become relevant some 150 years later once English lawyers began recasting their existing institutions in terms of the categorisations of right articulated by John Austin in his *Lectures on Jurisprudence* (1863).[12] These categories framed Maitland's analysis.[13] Austin's categories were themselves rarefied abstractions developed by jurists of the civil law tradition working from the Middle Ages through to the Natural Law era. So far as there was ever a problem of explaining the nature of a beneficiary's interest under a trust, it was one was that came later. It arose from the need to accommodate trusts within the concerns of theorists and comparativists who sought to find similarities between trusts and institutions in the civil law tradition.[14]

The chapter proceeds by stages, and begins by setting some background. Section II explains the broad range of legal relations which eighteenth-century courts called 'trusts'. These were wider than our modern core notion of the trust. Many relations which eighteenth-century courts were content to call 'trusts' might nowadays be considered marginal or outlier cases. Sections III and IV move to the substance of the idea. They show how courts of equity and common law recognised the different capacities in which a person might owe debts. Debts owed by a trustee in his personal capacity were generically distinct from those owed in his capacity as trustee. True, all debts represented the benefit of rights *in personam* held by creditors, but that analytical characteristic was not a reason to ignore the different capacities in which the trustee might have incurred the debts. The Court of Chancery also recognised that certain of the trustee's obligations related to specific property, and that remedies to enforce them could bind successors of title. Moreover, the explanation for the priority of the trust in bankruptcy had its own special elements. The wording of the bankruptcy statutes and general principles of universal succession went some way to explain why the Chancery held that trusts took priority over general creditors. Chancery recognised other ways to make a beneficiary's interest bind third

[10] For the original controversy, see AW Scott, 'The Nature of the Rights of the "Cestui que Trust"' (1917) 17 *Columbia Law Review* 269; HG Hanbury, 'The Field of Modern Equity' (1929) 45 *LQR* 199; and D Waters, 'The Nature of the Trust Beneficiary's Interest' (1967) 45 *Canadian Bar Review* 219.

[11] See P Parkinson, 'Reconceptualising the Express Trust' (2002) 61 *CLJ* 657; B McFarlane and R Stevens, 'The Nature of Equitable Property' (2010) 4 *Journal of Equity* 1; T Cutts, 'The Nature of Equitable Property: A Functional Analysis' (2012) 6 *Journal of Equity* 44; JE Penner, 'The (True) Nature of a Beneficiary's Equitable Proprietary Interest under a Trust' (2014) 27 *CJLJ* 473; and from the different perspectives of comparative and remedial analysis, see L Smith, 'Trusts and Patrimony' (2008) 38 *Revue Générale de Droit* 379, and Nolan (n 1) 122 *LQR* 232.

[12] The relevant passages are found in J Austin, *Lectures on Jurisprudence*, 5th edn (London, J Murray, 1885) Lecture XIV.

[13] Maitland (n 5) Lectures IX, 111.

[14] Maitland himself attempted the comparative exercise in his essay on 'Trust and Corporation' in HD Hazeltine, G Lapsley and PH Winfield (eds), *Maitland Selected Essays* (Cambridge, CUP, 1936) ch IV.

parties, without necessarily supposing that it must be a right *in rem* as Austin or modern-day commentators might have understood that concept. Section V returns to the Judicature reforms of 1873–75. The chapter ends with some implications of this view from the early eighteenth century for understanding some of the modern commentators' debates about the nature of a beneficial interest under a trust.

Alongside this main historical narrative, the chapter introduces a second theme. From time to time, it refers to the Scottish law of trusts. A comprehensive comparative history of the law of trusts in Scotland and in England would be an illuminating exercise but one too vast to undertake here. Nonetheless, features of the evolution of the trust beneficiary's interest in Scotland show strong parallels to the history in England, although they happened about 100 years later.[15] In its day-to-day operation, the Scottish trust works rather like the trust in England.[16] This practical similarity is unsurprising. Some of the main features of the modern trust, such as the trustees' duties of care and fiduciary loyalty, were worked out late in the nineteenth century by the House of Lords as the final appellate court for England and Scotland. Authorities were shared back and forth between them.[17] Nonetheless, two great differences remain. Unlike in England, Scots law has never resorted to a separate notion of equity to explain its trust doctrine, and the interest of a beneficiary under a Scottish trust is undoubtedly a right *in personam*.[18] In this respect, the modern Scottish trust shows some parallels to the way English courts of the early eighteenth century explained the operation of the trust. The problems encountered by the Scottish courts in explaining the priority between trusts and general creditors throw into relief the distinctive approach taken in England during the eighteenth century.

II. PRELIMINARY: THE RANGE OF THE EIGHTEENTH-CENTURY TRUST

Before embarking on the rationale for protecting the trust from claims of the trustee's creditors, we must first sketch out the range of transactional forms that eighteenth-century English judges described as trusts. Their usage of the term was less specialised than we would nowadays expect. This preliminary stage is important not just for

[15] Fortunately, this part of the larger story of how trusts evolved in Great Britain has now been told: PJ Follan, *Trust Beneficiaries and Third Parties* (Edinburgh, Edinburgh Legal Education Trust) forthcoming.

[16] For the best modern summary, see Scottish Law Commission, *Report on Trust Law* (Scot Law Com No 239, 2014) and the discussion papers preceding it. There is some shared trust law legislation between England and Scotland, notably in relation to public and charitable trusts: Law Reform (Miscellaneous Provisions) Scotland Act 1990, ss 9–11; Charities and Trustee Investment (Scotland) Act 2005.

[17] eg, *Learoyd v Whiteley* (1887) 12 App Cas 727 (HL) and *Rae v Meek* (1889) 16 R (HL) 31 (on the duty of care); and *Aberdeen Railway Co v Blaikie* (1854) 17 D (HL) 20 and *Magistrates of Aberdeen v University of Aberdeen* (1877) 4 R (HL) 48 (on fiduciary duties).

[18] The beneficiary's interest under a Scottish trust is no more than 'a personal right to sue the trustees and compel them to administer the trust in accordance with the directions it contains': *Inland Revenue v Clark's Trustees* 1939 SC 11 (CSIH) 22 (Lord President Normand). This explanation of the content of a beneficiary's interest resonates with the dictum that the 'basic right of a beneficiary [under an English trust] is to have the trust duly administered in accordance with the provisions of the trust instrument, if any, and the general law': *Target Holdings Ltd v Redferns* [1996] AC 421 (HL) 434 (Lord Browne-Wilkinson).

marking out the range of our inquiry. What strikes a modern reader of the formative cases on protection against creditors is that few of them involved fully constituted trusts, duly created by settlement or declaration, as we might now expect.[19] Most of the cases seem to be outliers from this imagined core.

Writing about the eighteenth-century Court of Chancery, Professor Sealy observed nicely in 1962: 'Our ancestors did not mince words: many … matters of confidence were naturally called "trusts," whether there was any strict trust of property or not.'[20] Sealy's point was that many different relations of confidence, which would nowadays be called 'fiduciary' in character, were grouped under the general label of 'trust'. A person, A, was called a trustee not only where B had entrusted A with property to hold and deal with on behalf of himself or others – what Sealy called a 'trust strictly so-called' – but also where 'A undertook to exercise a power, to conduct a sale, to supervise an estate or business, or in some other way to become B's employee or agent'.[21] But even in Sealy's stricter usage of the term – where A held property for B – we find a greater variety of transactional forms than a modern reader would naturally think of as trusts.

The early reports on trust priority were more often concerned with personal property than real property. Most common were the cases of bankrupt factors who held merchandise on their principals' behalf.[22] A factor was 'in the nature of a trustee only; and although he has the right at law, yet he is in equity but a trustee'.[23] A factor was said to have 'no property' in the merchandise since he held it with only a bare authority to sell it for his principal.[24] These arrangements between factors and their principals generated a disproportionate amount of Chancery litigation. The reasons followed from the restricted scope of the early bankruptcy statutes. Commissions of bankruptcy only applied to defined types of debtor, and these tended to be drawn from the mercantile classes who made their living by trade rather than from the landed classes who might have become trustees of settled estates.[25]

In considering creditors' claims, the courts treated personal representatives of a deceased person as holding their legal interest in the assets on trust for the beneficiaries entitled to take on inheritance.[26] Personal property cases might also involve the equitable assignment of a debt.[27] The assignment created a relationship of trust, where the assignor held his legal right of action on the debt subject to equitable duties enforceable by the assignee.[28] In all, the impression is of the Chancery recognising

[19] Significantly, the one instance when a trust estate of land figures in the reports was raised *obiter* as a hypothetical example, as if to imply that the rule applying to it went without saying: *Scott v Surman* (1742) Willes 400, 403; 125 ER 1235, 1237 (Willes CJ).

[20] LS Sealy, 'Fiduciary Relationships' (1962) 20 *CLJ* 69, 70.

[21] ibid 69.

[22] See the cases in section IV.D below.

[23] *Burdett v Willett* (1708) 2 Vern 638, 638; 23 ER 1017, 1017 (Cowper LC).

[24] *Godfrey v Furzo* (1733) 3 P Wms 185, 186; 24 ER 1022, 1023 (King LC).

[25] Thus the Bankrupts Act 1571 (13 Eliz 1 c 7), s 1 applied to 'any Merchant or other person using or exercising the Trade of Merchandize by way of Bargaining, Exchange, Rechange, Barter, Chevisance or otherwise'.

[26] *Farr v Newman* (1792) 4 TR 621, 630; 100 ER 1209, 1214 (per Grose J); 645–46, 1222–23 (Ashhurst J).

[27] See *Peters v Soame* (1701) 2 Vern 428, 23 ER 874 discussed in section IV.A below.

[28] For discussion of the nature of such an assignment, see ch 3 in this volume by Chee Ho Tham.

certain special offices where one person held property in right of another, where the nature of the beneficiary's rights against the office-holder, as being personal or proprietary, was not a significant part of the analysis. Status rather than the analytical nature of legal rights determined the priority of creditors' claims.

Even the land cases do not involve fully constituted settlements of real estate of the kind usually seen as the paradigm instances in the historical evolution of the English trust.[29] They would nowadays be regarded as incomplete conveyances of real property or cases where the full formalities for constitution of a settlement remained incomplete. The courts of the time were content to call these 'trusts'.[30] They would nowadays be seen as akin to vendor–purchaser constructive trusts, mere interim arrangements by which a contract purchaser or an intended beneficiary of a settlement secured their position pending the completion of the intended transaction.

III. THE PRIORITY OF THE TRUST OVER THE TRUSTEE'S CREDITORS

The idea that a beneficiary's right to performance of the trust took priority over the trustee's general creditors figures in the 1670s, early in the judicial career of Finch LK, who went on to become the Lord Chancellor, Lord Nottingham. The Court of Chancery had no difficulty in recognising a distinction between the two kinds of right, and providing a principled reason to explain why the beneficiary should be preferred to the general creditors. We find no reference to the beneficiary's right having a proprietary character. The beneficiary's right against the trustee was, if anything, more readily characterised as *in personam* than *in rem*. What mattered was that it related to identified land and could be enforced by specific remedies. It created what was called a 'specific lien'. As we shall see, this same term figures in the bankruptcy cases from the same era.[31] Although the bankruptcy regime depended on some special considerations of its own, it too assumed that one person could owe obligations in different capacities.

One of the earliest cases from Finch LK's tenure was *Medley v Martin* (1673).[32] While the result is clear enough in the report, its rationale is less so. The plaintiff Medley contracted through a trustee, Rows, to purchase lands from Harrington. In simplified form, the effect of the transaction was that Rows held the lands as to one half for Medley, and as to the other half for himself in his own right. Separately, Rows was indebted to the defendant, Martin, on certain bonds and a promissory note.

[29] Even T Lewin, *Practical Treatise on the Law of Trusts and Trustees* (London, A Maxwell, 1837) ch 1 defines trusts in terms of Coke CJ's classic definition of a use of real estate from *Coke upon Littleton* (c 1628), para 272b. He leaves out the wider range of transactions to which the term 'trust' was applied at the time.

[30] A defendant bound by a decree to convey an estate was 'in the Nature of a Trustee' to the purchaser: *Burgh v Francis* (1673) R Temp Finch 28, 29; 23 ER 16, 16 (Finch LK). See also *Taylor v Wheeler* (1709) 2 Salk 449, 449; 91 ER 388, 388 (Lord Cowper LC): '*Et come moy semble*, he became a trustee for the purchaser [*mortgagee*]'.

[31] See *Bosvil v Brander* (1718) 1 P Wms 458, 24 ER 470, discussed in section IV.D below.

[32] (1673) R Temp Finch 63, 23 ER 33.

Finch LK decreed that only the half share held by Rows in his own right was to be available to Martin to satisfy the judgments obtained on his bonds. The half share held on trust for Medley was held clear of the debts.

The rationale for exempting the trust property from the trustee's debts becomes more obvious from the later decisions. The question seemed to arise most frequently in cases of incomplete conveyances, under what would now be analysed as estate contracts. A person in the position of a vendor would covenant to convey an estate in land to a person in the position of a purchaser for value.[33] The purchaser would pay at least part of the money price. But the conveyance of the legal estate would not in fact happen, or the full formalities required would not be completed. The legal estate remained with the vendor. Meanwhile, the vendor would incur unsecured debts under a bond or statute. The creditor would seek to enforce a lien against the vendor's land to enforce his or her judgment for the debts, which put the creditor in dispute with the purchaser. The question was whether the purchaser could get a decree for completion of the conveyance free from the creditor's lien.

As Maitland noted, the leading case was *Finch v Earl of Winchelsea* (1715).[34] Lord Harcourt LC and Lord Cowper LC applied the settled version of a doctrine that seems to have developed during Lord Nottingham's time. The late Earl of Wincheslea had made an agreement with his wife for the mortgage and settlement of property under which he was to take a residue of the mortgage term and the equity of redemption for himself for life, and then to his eldest son for life, with remainders over. The plaintiffs eventually claimed under these remainders. For whatever reason, the late Earl failed to execute the agreement for settlement. He then died leaving debts under bonds and judgments. In the first stage of the proceedings, Lord Harcourt LC had held that the plaintiffs were entitled to a decree to have the settlements executed. The judgment creditors then brought proceedings before Lord Cowper LC to enforce liens against the lands for their debts. Lord Cowper LC accepted that the Earl's agreement to convey the estate for valuable consideration made him a trustee for the use of the settlement.[35] As the plaintiffs' argument put it, the estate 'belonged' in equity to the beneficiaries, rather than the trustee.[36] All other things being equal, it would have been exempt from the judgment creditors' lien. But the trust beneficiaries' claim to priority failed on the facts since it was found that the consideration provided to the late Earl was inadequate. In the end, the creditors enforced their lien.

The general rationale for enforcing the trust interest against the creditors can only have rested on the specific enforceability of the plaintiff's bill to complete the

[33] *Burgh v Francis* (n 30) (mortgage defective for want of livery); *Baden v Countess of Pembroke* (1690) 2 Vern 213, 23 ER 739 (incomplete conveyance by way of sale).

[34] (n 6) cited in Maitland (n 5) Lecture IX, 117. See generally the summary of the cases in Yale, *Lord Nottingham's Chancery Cases* (n 6) 79 SS at 93. A late example of the same fact pattern is *Russel v Russel* (1783) 1 Bro CC 269, 28 ER 1121.

[35] It was accepted that a defendant bound by a decree to convey an estate was 'in the Nature of a Trustee' to the purchaser: *Burgh v Francis* (n 30) R Temp Finch 28, 29; 23 ER 16, 16 (Finch LK). See also *Taylor v Wheeler* (n 30) 2 Salk 449, 449; 91 ER 388, 389 (Lord Cowper LC).

[36] *Finch* (n 6) 1 P Wms 277, 278; 24 ER 387, 388.

conveyance of the estate. The trustee's obligation related to specific property. In *Burgh v Francis* (1673), a case of an incomplete conveyance by way of mortgage, Finch LK justified postponing the creditors on the ground that 'they are not put in a worse Condition than they ought to be, *viz*, to be postponed to the Mortgage'.[37] If the conveyance had been completed at law, the estate would not have been available for the creditors to attach. The reason assumes that the right of the mortgagee in that case (or of the settlement beneficiaries in *Finch v Earl of Winchelsea* (1715)) and the right of the judgment creditors were different in kind. The obligation of the trustee to convey certain land, specifically enforceable by decree, distinguished it from a purely personal debt incurred by the trustee, albeit one that might ultimately be enforced by a lien on the estate. The trustee's obligation created a 'specific lien' on the land.[38] While the cases of incomplete conveyances might seem like outliers from those of fully constituted trusts, the Court seems to have seen no relevant distinction between the two kinds of transaction. As we saw earlier, they were both 'trusts' by the lights of the time.[39] In both cases, the essential character of the beneficiary's interest consisted in compelling the trustee to perform an obligation. The trustee's obligation to the beneficiary bound third-party creditors because they were joined as parties to the suit. Joinder, rather than any theory of equitable property, could explain why third parties to the transaction between the trustee and beneficiary were bound by the obligations it created.

The default priority of the trust over the trustee's judgment creditors would apply even if they had no notice of the trust.[40] The rule did not depend on assessments of the relative fault of the parties. Personal creditors were assumed to lend on the general faith or credit of the borrower rather than on the strength of any specific property in his estate.[41] This distinction did not stand up to close scrutiny. It is early evidence for the general favour given by the Court of Chancery to trusts. It culminated in the view taken in the 1740s that the reputed ownership provisions in the bankruptcy statute did not apply to trusts. A trust beneficiary did not lose the trust assets in bankruptcy on the ground that he allowed them to remain in the apparent ownership and possession of the trustee.[42]

Notice might only have been relevant if the creditor had taken a legal mortgage of the estate for valuable consideration. The creditor would then have qualified as a purchaser for value without notice of the trust beneficiaries' equity. There was no good reason to interfere in the creditor's right to possession founded on the common law mortgage, and the Court of Chancery would have denied any jurisdiction over the creditor.[43]

[37] *Burgh v Francis* (n 30) R Temp Finch 28, 29; 23 ER 16, 16.
[38] *Finch* (n 6) 1 P Wms 277, 279; 24 ER 387, 388.
[39] See section II above.
[40] *Finch* (n 6) 1 P Wms 277, 278–79; 24 ER 387, 388.
[41] ibid; *cf Medley v Martin* (n 32) R Temp Finch 63, 64; 23 ER 33, 34; *Taylor v Wheeler* (1706) 2 Vern 564, 565–66; 23 ER 968, 968.
[42] See *Ryall v Rolle* (1750) 1 Ves Sen 348, 27 ER 1074, discussed in Televantos (n 8) ch 2.
[43] For the relevance of good faith purchase to the Chancery's jurisdiction to grant relief, see generally Fox (n 2) 65–67.

IV. THE PRIORITY OF THE TRUST IN BANKRUPTCY

Developing in parallel with the enforcement of the trust against the trustee's personal creditors was the protection given to the trust assets when the trustee fell bankrupt. In hindsight, it is easy to view this as a feature of the *in rem* character of the modern trust. The enforcement of the beneficiary's interest against the trustee in bankruptcy would seem to show its effect 'against persons generally or universally', as Austin explained rights *in rem*.[44] In the early eighteenth century, however, that character would have been equivocal. The protection for the trust could also be derived from the wording of the early bankruptcy statutes themselves and the distinctive character of the duties owed by the assignee in bankruptcy. If we look for reasons to explain the priority of the trust over the bankrupt trustee's creditors, then they are to be found as much outside the trust as they are to be found in any inherent characteristics of the trust itself. The combined effect of these reasons was to blunt any sharp analytical distinction between rights *in personam* and rights *in rem* under a trust.

A. The Early Modern Bankruptcy Statutes

The main parts of the eighteenth-century bankruptcy regime derived from a series of enactments, beginning with the statute of Henry VIII (1542–42), the statute of Elizabeth I (1571), and two statutes of James I of 1603–04 and 1623–24.[45] Each statute made incremental extensions to the bankruptcy regime then in force and attempted to close loopholes exploited by debtors. The degree to which later enactments wholly replaced, or merely qualified, earlier provisions was not always clear, and the meaning of key terms in the statutes was obscure. In a memorable phrase, Lord Hardwicke described the provisions of the Act of 1623–24 as 'darkly penned'.[46] The only advantage of this obscurity was that it left the legislative wording sufficiently open for courts to introduce their own nascent ideas of trust-like offices into the statutes. They could have an eye also to public policy and the usual commercial practice among people who handled goods or money on behalf of others. The courts attempted to read the series of statutes as a whole, which meant that the rationale of the earliest enactments coloured the court's reasoning when it applied the pertinent provisions of later enactments to the disputes actually before them. The statutes made an untidy pile of rules. That they worked as a system at all was due to the efforts of the courts and practitioners who developed their own practical understanding of what the statutes must mean and how they should apply.

[44] Austin (n 12) Lecture XIV, 369.

[45] Statute of Bankrupts 1542–43 (34 & 35 Henry 8 c 4); Bankrupts Act 1571 (13 Eliz 1 c 7); Statute 1603–04 (1 Jac 1 c 15); Bankrupts Act 1623 (21 Jac 1 c 19). See generally WJ Jones, 'The Foundations of English Bankruptcy: Statutes and Commissions in the Early Modern Period' (1979) 69 *Transactions of the American Philosophical Society* 1.

[46] *Ex parte Marsh* (1744) 1 Atk 158, 159; 26 ER 102, 103 (Hardwicke LC). If Atkyns' reports are to be believed, Hardwicke LC made this complaint about the drafting of the bankruptcy statutes more than once: *Ex parte Turner* (1742) 1 Atk 148, 149; 26 ER 96, 96; *Plunket v Penson* (1742) 2 Atk 290, 293; 26 ER 577, 579.

By the turn of the eighteenth century, the Court of Chancery had formed its view of the effect of trust-like rights in bankruptcy. Assets subject to these rights were exempted from bankruptcy and the claimant would recover them in priority to the bankrupt's general creditors. In *Peters v Soame* (1701),[47] one Darwin had assigned a bond for £300 to Peters. Peters' rights under the assignment were only enforceable in equity, a situation that was understood as creating a trust relationship between the assignor, Darwin, and the assignee, Peters.[48] Darwin became bankrupt, which put in issue Peters' claim to enforce payment of the bond in priority to Darwin's general creditors. The Lord Keeper held: 'The assignees [under the commission] can have no better right than the bankrupt himself; and as the bankrupt is bound by the assignment [to Peters], the assignee under the statute must be bound likewise, and stand in his place.'[49] The outcome was that Peters should have been entitled to recover the bond from the assignees in bankruptcy. The assignee was barred from enforcing payment on the bond to the general creditors.

There was some divergence of views about the technical mechanism that exempted the trust beneficiary's claim from the bankrupt's assets. The view which became the norm in the nineteenth century was first suggested by Willes CJ in *Scott v Surman* (1742):

> If therefore the bankrupt were seised of a trust estate in lands, for the reasons already mentioned I should think that it did not vest in the assignees at all, but that the legal estate as to that should still remain in the bankrupt for the benefit of the cestui que trust.[50]

Rather than have the assets pass to the assignee subject to any equitable duties previously assumed by the bankrupt trustee, Willes CJ's understanding was that it was simpler to leave them in the bankrupt. Otherwise, the trust claimants would then have to bring a bill in Chancery to require the assignees to restore them to the trustee, a process which would be circuitous and expensive. As we have seen, the nineteenth-century bankruptcy statutes confirmed this view, which remains the case today.[51]

Willes CJ acknowledged, however, that his own understanding was not the dominant one at the time and the other members of the court preferred not to endorse it.[52] The alternative view of the way the bankruptcy statutes affected trust-like arrangements was that all the bankrupt's assets passed to the assignees, even those that were subject to a trust obligation. But since the assignees stood in the same position as the bankrupt, they were bound by the trust, which barred them from applying the assets for the general creditors. There are some examples among the cases where this clearly happened.[53] Although, for the most part, this divergence of views made no great

[47] (n 27).

[48] *Winch v Keeley* (1787) 1 TR 619, 621–22; 99 ER 1284, 1285 (Ashhurst J).

[49] *Peters v Soame* (n 27) 2 Vern 428, 429; 23 ER 874, 874.

[50] *Scott v Surman* (n 19) Willes 400, 402–03; 125 ER 1235, 1237 (Willes CJ) applied in *Taylor v Plumer* (1815) 3 M & S 562, 105 ER 721.

[51] See Bankruptcy Act 1869, s 15(1); Bankruptcy Act 1883, s 44(1). Insolvency Act 1985, s 238(1), (3)(a) provides the modern rule.

[52] *Scott v Surman* (n 19) Willes 400, 403; 125 ER 1235, 1237 (Willes CJ). For a recent summary of the history, see *Carter Holt Harvey Wood Products Pty Ltd v Commonwealth* [2019] HCA 20, (2019) 268 CLR 524 [24]–[28].

[53] eg, *Bosvil* (n 31); *Bennet v Davis* (1725) 2 P Wms 316, 24 ER 746.

difference to the result as far as the Chancery was concerned, it helps to keep both views in mind when reading the cases. When we speak generally about the assignees being 'bound by the trust' or the trust being 'excepted from the bankruptcy', we need to recall that these results were explicable by different technical interpretations of the statutes.[54]

Returning to *Peters v Soame* (1701), references to the assignees 'standing in the place' of the bankrupt or being in 'no better case' than him were the usual ways of explaining the assignees' position against the bankrupt and any person claiming equitable rights against him.[55] But this simple rationalisation – pithy though it was – was not enough to explain the practical priority given to the beneficiary's right. It was one thing for the assignees to be bound by the trust, but another for the trust claim to be preferred to the claims of the bankrupt's general creditors. The assignees might have been bound by the trust, but allowed to apply the trust assets *pari passu* among all the bankrupt trustee's creditors. A combination of other elements, which were less obvious in the decisions, was necessary to explain the priority of the beneficiary's interest

B. The Statutory Definition of the Bankrupt's Estate

The first element of the explanation was the wording of the statutes that defined the bankrupt's estate. The statutes defined the types of assets to which the commission of bankruptcy applied. At the risk of stating the obvious, any assets not falling within the statutory definitions were excluded from the assignee's powers of distribution. When it came to trusts, the courts read the statutory words to ensure this effect.

The statute of Henry VIII applied the commission to property so far as 'the interest right and title of the [bankrupt] shall extende or be, and may then lawfully be departed with by the saide [bankrupt]'.[56] The statute of Elizabeth I referred variously to 'lands tenements hereditaments … which [the bankrupt] shall have in his or her own right before he or she became bankrupt … which he may lawfully depart withal'.[57]

The definition in the statute of Henry VIII operated on different features of the statutory transfer of the bankrupt's assets to the assignees. Under the first, the assignees took the same positive title to the assets as the bankrupt himself. Whatever 'interest, right and title' the bankrupt had in the assets vested in the assignees. The vesting of this positive title in the assignees was essential since it enabled them to realise the assets for the general creditors' benefit.

[54] The divergence of views only made a difference in the rare cases where the plaintiff sued on a common law title to the disputed asset: *Taylor v Plumer* (n 50). See S Khurshid and P Matthews, 'Tracing Confusion' (1979) 95 *LQR* 79; L Smith, 'Tracing in *Taylor v Plumer*: Equity in the Court of King's Bench' [1995] *Lloyd's Maritime and Commercial Law Quarterly* 240.

[55] *Jacobson v Williams* (1717) 1 P Wms 383, 383; 24 ER 435, 435 (Lord Cowper LC). See also *Bosvil* (n 31) 1 P Wms 458, 461, 24 ER 470, 471; *Bennet* (n 53); *Child v Pitt* (1725) Sel Cas T King 16, 25 ER 197; *Paul v Birch* (1743) 2 Atk 621, 622; 26 ER 771, 771 (Lord Hardwicke LC); *Brown v Heathcote* (1746) 1 Atk 160, 162; 26 ER 103, 105 (Lord Hardwicke LC).

[56] Statute of Bankrupts 1542–43 (34 & 35 Henry 8 c 4), s 1.

[57] Bankrupts Act 1571 (13 Eliz 1 c 7), s 2.

The second feature of the definition consisted in a limitation. The assignees took the assets subject to the same lawful restrictions on dealing as applied to the assets in the bankrupt's hands. Any limitation that would have affected the bankrupt's lawful authority to 'depart' with the assets also bound the assignees. The Chancery judges interpreted those limitations generously.[58] The limitations might have been of a proprietary character, as where a third party asserted what might nowadays be analysed as a right *in rem* in the bankrupt's assets. But they might also have been obligationary in nature. The bankrupt might owe a positive duty to perform some act for a third party in relation to the disputed asset. The assignees took the asset subject to the same duty.

The wording of the statutes of Elizabeth I had a similar influence on the court's definition of the bankrupt's estate. Unless the bankrupt held the assets 'in his or her own right' they were not available for distribution by the assignees.[59] The words afforded an opening to recognise that while a bankrupt might have had the legal property in assets, he nonetheless held them in right of another person (*en auter droit*). The obvious example was assets held by the executor or administrator of a deceased person's estate, but the understanding seemed to extend more generally and applied also to cases where the bankrupt held merchandise as a factor for a principal.[60] In *Ex parte Marsh* (1744),[61] a widow was in possession of a quantity of plate that once belonged to her deceased husband. As her late husband's administratrix, she was bound to deal with it for the heirs of the estate. She remarried and her second husband eventually fell bankrupt. Lord Hardwicke LC accepted that whatever title the second husband might have derived through his wife, he took the plate subject to her duties in right of the heirs. The commissioners under the second husband's bankruptcy had no claim to it.

The common law courts took the same view when reviewing a seizure of goods under a writ of *fieri facias*. When a widow held goods as executrix for her deceased husband then, if she re-married, they were not available to be seized by the judgment creditors of her second husband.[62] The legitimacy of the seizure did not depend on the simple question of whether the widow – and through her the second husband – had the legal property in the goods or whether they were in her apparent possession. Common law courts had no qualms about recognising the capacity in which she owned the goods (and by extension the capacity in which she might owe debts in respect of it). An executrix with legal property in goods did not own them in her own right but only as 'the distributor and dispenser of them for the benefit of the

[58] See section IV.C below.

[59] Willes CJ seems to have found similar authority for the priority of trusts of debts in the wording of Statute 1603–04 (1 Jac 1 c 15). Section 8 included in the bankrupt's estate 'such debts due or to be due to or for the benefit of the said bankrupt'. The words provided a foundation for distinguishing debts due to the bankrupt in his own right and debts due on behalf of the principal (*cf Burdett* (n 23) (debt due to deceased factor on principal's behalf). See Willes' note to *Scott v Surman* (n 19) Willes 400, 403; 125 ER 1235, 1237.

[60] eg, *Scott v Surman* (n 19) Willes 400, 404; 125 ER 1235, 1237 (Willes CJ). Peere Williams argued as counsel that the position of factors and personal representatives was equivalent under the bankruptcy statutes: *Copeman v Gallant* (1716) 1 P Wms 314, 24 ER 404.

[61] (n 46). Similarly *Ex parte Butler* (1749) 1 Atk 210, 213; 26 ER 136, 138 (Hardwicke LC).

[62] *Farr* (n 26).

[testator's] creditors'.[63] The executrix had only a 'qualified' property in the goods and they were treated differently from any goods she might have had in her own right.[64]

C. Universal Succession

The next element of the explanation for the beneficiary's priority follows from the capacity in which the assignees took the bankrupt's assets. This began to be articulated early in the nineteenth century, although it was probably understood in practice before then. It gave a more precise meaning to the general assertions that the assignees stood 'in the place' of the bankrupt or were in 'no better case' than him.[65]

In *Mitford v Mitford* (1803), Sir William Grant MR proceeded on the basis that assignees stood in the place of the bankrupt because they were 'general' assignees of the bankrupt in a similar position to personal representatives under a deceased person's estate.[66] The distinction was between what would be known in civil law systems and in Scotland as a universal successor, taking a title by representation by operation of law, and a singular successor, taking an assignment of a particular asset by an intentional transaction between the bankrupt and a third party.[67]

As universal successors, the assignees took the bankrupt's rights 'precisely in the same plight and condition as he possessed them'.[68] The assignees were bound by the same duties as would have bound the bankrupt himself. It was unnecessary to suppose that third parties' rights binding on the assignees were a proprietary qualification to the bankrupt's title. The notion of universal succession, as much as a proprietary interest, could explain why the assignees were bound by rights limiting the bankrupt's title to deal with assets in the estate. Consequently, even on the dominant interpretation of the bankruptcy statutes in the early eighteenth century – where the trust assets did in fact pass to the assignees – the assignees would have taken them subject to the beneficiary's claims.[69]

Developing the analogy, Grant MR distinguished the position of the bankrupt's assignees from that of singular successors who took an assignment of a specific asset in the bankrupt's estate. This analysis would have applied if, for example, the bankrupt had assigned an asset to a third person in breach of trust or in fraud of his

[63] ibid 4 TR 621, 629; 100 ER 1209, 1214 (Buller J).

[64] ibid, 4 TR 621, 645; 100 ER 1209, 1222 (Ashhurst J).

[65] See section IV.A above.

[66] *Mitford v Mitford* (1803) 9 Ves Jun 87, 100; 32 ER 534, 539 (Grant MR). See also the explanatory note of Peere Williams to his report of *Bosvil* (n 31) 1 P Wms 459, 461; 24 ER 470, 471: 'where the property is the subject of equitable cognisance, it is clear that the general assignees of the husband (whether by operation of law or otherwise), are subject to the same equity with the husband himself'.

[67] For the distinction in Scotland, see J Erskine, *An Institute of the Law of Scotland*, 1st edn (Edinburgh, John Bell, 1773) II, vii, 1. In the Scots law of the early nineteenth century, creditors attaching the heritable estate of a debtor by adjudication, sale or sequestration were treated as singular successors: see GJ Bell, *Principles of the Law of Scotland*, 4th edn (Edinburgh, Thomas Clark, 1839), paras 783ff. This view of the creditors' status might have contributed to the much later recognition in Scots law that trusts took priority over the creditors of a bankrupt trustee. The point was eventually resolved in *Heritable Reversionary Co Ltd v Millar* [1892] AC 598 (HL); 1892 19 R (HL) 43, discussed in section IV.E below.

[68] *Mitford* (n 66) 9 Ves Jun 87, 100; 32 ER 534, 539 (Grant MR).

[69] See section IV.A above.

creditors. For a singular successor, it was relevant to ask whether he had notice of the bankrupt's duty to the third party. If the successor lacked notice, then he might have taken free of the third party's claim by providing valuable consideration.[70] The general defence of good faith purchase for value without notice had taken shape during the middle of the sixteenth century, and it had a statutory equivalent in the legislation on fraudulent conveyances.[71] The situation of the bankrupt's assignees was generically different. They took an assignment of the bankrupt's entire estate by a representative title. Whatever tasks they undertook in distributing the bankrupt's assets to the creditors, the court would not recognise that they gave consideration for the assignment to them.[72] Notice or not, consideration or not, they were bound by the same rights as the bankrupt was – and importantly, as we shall see – the specific remedies which Chancery would have awarded to enforce them.

D. Specific Relief

The final element of the explanation turned on the availability of specific relief. The priority of the trust was not recognised merely in some abstract way but by a decree ordering the assignees to do a specific act with the trust asset or the documents evidencing it. Although the decree necessarily issued against the person of the bankrupt or the assignees, it always enforced the defendant's duty in relation to a specific asset or document – extant and identifiable – in the bankrupt's estate. As general representatives of the bankrupt, they were liable to the same remedial jurisdiction as would have applied to the bankrupt. It was easy enough to bind the assignees to the court's decree since the consistent practice in bankruptcy disputes was to make them party to the suit. The trustee's general creditors became bound by the decree through the assignees. As we saw earlier, the Chancery's rules on joinder of parties bound third parties to the trust, giving the beneficiary's interest something like a proprietary effect.[73]

When the beneficiary of the trust sued to enforce her claim to the trust asset against the assignee, she would be treated as having a 'specific lien' on it, which preserved it from the bankruptcy. The corollary was that the trust beneficiary lost her priority if the asset ceased to be identifiable. The court would not order the assignees to deal with an asset that could no longer be located or which had ceased to exist.

Thus in *Bennet v Davis*(1725), Mrs Bennet was the beneficiary of a devise of lands under her father's will.[74] The devise was clearly intended for her own separate and exclusive use, but the father failed to nominate trustees to hold the land for his daughter. A properly constituted settlement of this kind would have prevented the lands

[70] *Mitford* (n 66) 9 Ves Jun 87, 97, 100; 32 ER 534, 538–39 (Grant MR).

[71] Statute 1603–04 (1 Jac I c 15), s 3.

[72] The same point about a trustee in sequestration providing onerous consideration remained live and arguable in Scotland until the House of Lords decisively rejected it in *Heritable Reversionary Co Ltd* (n 67) 611 (Lord Watson).

[73] See section III above.

[74] *Bennet* (n 53).

from passing to her husband under the common law rules of coverture. With things left in this incomplete state, the daughter married. Her husband fell bankrupt so the legal estate in the lands intended for the wife passed to the husband and then, under the bankruptcy, to the assignees. The wife succeeded in her bill for a decree against the husband and the assignees to join in a conveyance of the lands to separate trustees. They would then hold the lands to her use, as the testator had intended. Jekyll MR recognised that the husband had become a trustee of lands by default for his wife. Her equity to complete the proper constitution of the trust against the husband bound his assignees in bankruptcy.

Similarly, in *Bosvil v Brander* (1718) a woman held a mortgage of an estate in fee for a debt of £800.[75] She married a tradesman who later became bankrupt. All the tradesman's assets passed to his assignees. Jekyll MR held that if the husband and wife had entered into a marriage settlement which created a trust of the mortgage for the wife, then the court would have enforced it against the husband and the assignees. The trust would create a 'specific lien' on the mortgage. The wife could have prevented the husband or the assignees claiming the money on the mortgage without allowing her share. She could have had an order for delivery up of the deeds relating to the mortgage to enforce the trust attaching to it. On the facts, however, the wife failed since the husband's duties under the marriage settlement could not be enforced by decree against him.[76]

Claims for specific relief in relation to identifiable assets characterise all the early cases where the beneficiary of a trust-like relationship sued to enforce her rights against the assignees in bankruptcy. As in *Bennet v Davies* (1725), the beneficiary might enforce her rights by obtaining a decree that the bankrupt and assignees join in a legal conveyance that would complete the beneficiary's title to lands.[77] Where the trust asset was a chattel, or a money claim under a bill of exchange, the beneficiary would have an order for delivery up, which removed the asset from the hands of the bankrupt's assignees.[78] Conversely, the Court of Chancery would deny any equitable relief to assignees in bankruptcy who sought to prevent merchants from diverting their goods away from the hands of their bankrupt factors.[79] The Court held that the merchants were not only acting lawfully in frustrating the assignees' attempts to get possession of their goods but their actions were described as 'very allowable in equity'. The assignees would not have so much as a decree for discovery of documentary evidence against the merchants.[80] The Court of Chancery saw an analogy between its own practice of enforcing the 'specific lien' and the practice of common law courts. Thus, the master of a ship who hired it by charterparty had a specific lien on the goods carried to cover the costs of the hire. It took priority over the claims of

[75] *Bosvil* (n 31) 1 P Wms 459, 461; 24 ER 470, 471.
[76] ibid 1 P Wms 459, 460; 24 ER 470, 470.
[77] *Taylor v Wheeler* (n 41); *Taylor v Wheeler* (n 30) (decree that plaintiff be admitted as copyhold tenant); similarly *Burgh v Francis* (n 30) Rep Temp Finch 28; 23 ER 16; *Boughton v Pierrepoint* (1673) 3 Swans 550, 36 ER 971 (decree that defendant complete conveyance by way of mortgage).
[78] *Ex parte Marsh* (n 46) (order for delivery up of plate); *Ex parte Dumas* (1754) 1 Atk 232, 26 ER 149 (order for delivery up of identified bills); similarly *Brown v Heathcote* (n 55).
[79] *Wiseman v Vandeputt* (1690) 2 Vern 203, 23 ER 732.
[80] ibid.

the assignees in bankruptcy for the general creditors.[81] Even the common law courts would recognise that if the beneficiary were entitled to specific relief in equity, the asset in question was exempted from the bankruptcy.[82]

Since the beneficiary's claim was analysed as a 'specific lien' on an asset, it was only good if the asset could still be located in the hands of the bankrupt or the assignees. Assets such as merchandise or money claims in undiscounted bills of exchange could therefore be exempted from the bankruptcy. If the asset or its proceeds ceased to be identifiable, then the beneficiary was relegated to the position of a general creditor. So it was that the cases involving the bankruptcy of a factor became some of the earliest equitable authorities on the following and tracing of moveable assets.

The original understanding of Chancery, as in the common law courts, was that money had 'no ear-mark'.[83] The leading Chancery authority on the application of this maxim to bankruptcies was *Whitecomb v Jacob* (1710).[84] The court is reported as holding that if the principal entrusted merchandise to a factor for sale which remained extant and identifiable when the factor fell bankrupt, then the principal would recover it from the bankrupt's assignees. The same would be true if the principal had an outstanding claim for payment of money under a bill of exchange or for delivery of goods under a bill of lading.[85] The document lent the necessary specificity to the claim. Even an unpaid debt due to the factor on the principal's behalf would be paid to the principal rather than to the assignees for the benefit of the general creditors.[86] While it remained undischarged, the debtor's obligation had the necessary specificity to be distinguishable among the bankrupt's assets.

By extension, if the factor sold the merchandise and reinvested the sale proceeds in other specific goods, then they too would be exempted from the bankruptcy. As Willes CJ explained in *Scott v Surman* (1742), 'in reason the thing produced ought to follow the nature of the thing out of which it is produced, if it can be distinguished'.[87] The rationale articulated, in an intuitive way, a principle of real subrogation recognised in civil law systems.[88] If, however, the factor kept the money loose, without applying it to buy other goods, then, as *Whitecomb v Jacob* (1710) explained, it would 'be looked upon as the factor's estate, and must first answer the debts of a superior creditor, etc for in regard that money has no ear-mark, equity cannot follow that in behalf of him that employed the factor'.[89]

[81] *Paul* (n 55) 2 Atk 621, 623; 26 ER 771, 772 (Lord Hardwicke LC).

[82] *Scott v Surman* (n 19) Willes 400, 404; 125 ER 1235, 1237 (Willes CJ); *Zinck v Walker* (1777) 2 Black W 1154, 96 ER 681.

[83] For the evolution of the rule at common law and its use in equity, see D Fox, '*Banks v Whetston* (1596)' in S Douglas, R Hickey, E Waring (eds), *Landmark Cases in Property Law* (Oxford, Hart, 2014).

[84] (1710) 1 Salk 160, 91 ER 149. See also *Kirk v Webb* (1698) 2 Freeman 229, 230; 22 ER 1177, 1177 (Lord Somers LC); *Ryall v Ryall* (1739) 1 Atk 59, 59; 26 ER 39, 39 (Lord Hardwicke LC).

[85] *Ex parte Dumas* (n 78); *Brown v Heathcote* (n 55).

[86] *Burdett* (n 23) (debt due to deceased factor).

[87] *Scott v Surman* (n 19) Willes 400, 404; 125 ER 1235, 1238 (Willes CJ). See also *Taylor v Plumer* (n 50) 3 M & S 562, 575; 105 ER 721, 726 (Ellenborough CJ). For a complex application, see *Ex parte Emery* (1755) 2 Ves Sen 674, 28 ER 430.

[88] See generally M Raczynska, 'Parallels Between the Civilian Separate Patrimony, Real Subrogation and the Idea of Property in a Trust Fund' in L Smith (ed), *The Worlds of the Trust* (Cambridge, CUP, 2013).

[89] *Whitecomb* (n 84) 1 Salk 160, 160–61; 91 ER 149, 149. If the principal's goods lost their specific identify by being mixed with the factor's then, by analogy with money, the principal seemingly lost his priority to recover them: *Paul* (n 55) 2 Atk 621, 623; 26 ER 771, 772 (Lord Hardwicke LC).

The emphasis on specific identification is revealing about the court's rationale for recognising the priority of the trust in bankruptcy. Specific individuation of an asset is a necessary condition to the creation of a proprietary interest in it.[90] But the early bankruptcy cases saw the matter from a different angle. For them, specific individuation was also a necessary condition to ordering equitable relief against a defendant who was alleged to hold the plaintiff's asset. It was futile to order the assignees to deal with an asset that no longer existed in identifiable form. If a maxim were needed, it would presumably be that 'lex non cogit impossibilia'.[91] The recognition of the principal's equitable property in the asset and the practical possibility of specific relief over it worked in a reflexive relation with each other.

E. Scottish Comparison

What stands out from the way the Court of Chancery explained the protection of trust assets from the trustee's general creditors is the irrelevance of Austin's distinction between rights *in rem* and rights *in personam*. Categories which we might think were fundamental to any modern ordering of private law did not determine the practical outcome of the cases. The singularity of the reasoning in Chancery becomes even stronger if we compare it with the approach in Scotland. In the nineteenth- and twentieth-century Scottish cases on trusts and trust-like relations, the distinction between real and personal rights not only figured in the courts' reasoning but was directly determinative of their outcomes. The occasions when the distinction was not observed tended to be decisions of the House of Lords where, rightly or wrongly, the court was influenced by reasoning borrowed from English equity.

Thus, in *Sharp v Thomson* (1995), where purchasers of land went into possession on the strength of an unregistered deed of disposition, the Inner House of the Court of Session held that they had no more than a right *ad rem* in relation to the land.[92] The purchasers' right was essentially personal in character.[93] Their right to be put in possession of specific property was only good against the vendors. They did not have a real right in the land. Therefore, they could not prevail against a bank that held a floating charge over the vendors' assets. Their right was limited to enforcement against the vendors, regardless of the remedies available or the specificity of the property to which the right related. As Lord President Hope explained, the legal answer to the dispute lay 'in the distinction between the law of property and the law of obligations. This is one of the most fundamental of all the divisions which exist in our law'.[94] The House of Lords took a different view, by interpreting the terms of the bank's floating charge to exclude heritable property which was subject to a

[90] This general principle explains the contrasting rules for passing of property in unascertained and specific goods under the Sale of Goods Act 1979, ss 16–18, explained in *Re Goldcorp Exchange Ltd (in receivership)* [1995] 1 AC 74 (PC) 89–90.

[91] The law does not compel someone to do something that cannot be performed: H Broom, *A Selection of Legal Maxims*, 1st edn (London, Sweet & Maxwell, 1845) 59.

[92] *Sharp v Thomson* 1995 SC 455 (CSIH).

[93] ibid 463–65.

[94] ibid 461.

binding contract to convey. The decision was widely criticised.[95] The House of Lords went some way towards reaffirming the orthodox view in *Burnett's Trustee v Grainger* (2004).[96] The House reaffirmed a long line of authority concerning uninfeft proprietors of land under deeds of disposition which they had failed to register before a competing real right in security or a bankruptcy supervened. The House held that the personal right of the purchasers to be put in possession of the land carried no special priority against the trustee in sequestration of the bankrupt vendors.

The taxonomical distinction between personal rights and real rights also proved a conceptual obstacle to recognising that a beneficiary's interest under a Scottish trust should take priority over the claims of the trustee's general creditors. As we have seen, a Scottish beneficiary's interest is undoubtedly personal in character.[97] Unlike in England, the Scottish bankruptcy legislation of the nineteenth century did not provide an explicit exception for trusts. On its face, the trustee in sequestration of the bankrupt took 'with all right, title and interest, the whole property of the debtor'.[98] Applying a formal distinction between personal rights and real rights, the Inner House of the Court of Session held in *Heritable Reversionary Co Ltd v Millar* (1891) that a beneficiary of a latent trust of land could not prevail over the general creditors of the bankrupt trustee.[99] The beneficiary ranked as a mere personal creditor. The House of Lords held otherwise on appeal.[100] The Lords achieved this result by taking a narrow, functional reading of the bankruptcy legislation. They held that it could not be read to include assets held on bare trust for another person and which the trustee could not dispose of without committing a criminal offence. Cutting through formal taxonomical distinctions, Lord Watson described the trust beneficiary as the 'true owner' and the trustee as mere 'apparent owner' possessed of a 'legal title'.[101] The obvious anomalies in his reasoning only faded from relevance once the Scottish bankruptcy legislation recognised a specific exception for property held by the bankrupt on trust for another. This happened as late as 1985.[102] The notion of dual patrimony has since provided a theoretical justification for this difference in treatment between the two classes of assets owned by the trustee.

Such was the distinctive step taken by the judges who fashioned the incidents of the beneficiary's trust interest in the early eighteenth century. Creditors' rights to enforce what we might nowadays analyse as personal rights were not all equal. The subject matter of the right – a specific asset – and the remedy for enforcing it justified taking that asset out of the pool available for distribution to the trustee's other

[95] It was the subject of a special 'Report on *Sharp* v *Thomson*' (Scot Law Comm No 208, 2007) para [2.10] of which argued that (had it not been limited by the later decision in *Burnett's Trustee*) the case would have subverted key principles of property law.

[96] 2004 SC (HL) 19.

[97] See section I above.

[98] Bankruptcy (Scotland) Act 1856, s 102.

[99] *Heritable Reversionary Co Ltd v Millar* (1891) 18 R 1166 (CSIH) 1174 (Lord M'Laren), 1180 (Lord Kinnear).

[100] *Heritable Reversionary Co Ltd* (n 67).

[101] ibid 609–10.

[102] Bankruptcy (Scotland) Act 1985, s 33. Previously, the Bankruptcy (Scotland) Act 1913, s 97 made no explicit reference to property held by the bankrupt on trust. The case law exception recognised by *Heritable Reversionary Co Ltd* (n 67) continued to be read into the definition of the bankrupt's estate.

creditors. Rules on joinder of parties to Chancery suits gave the beneficiary's interest a sort of proprietary effect. The result was consistent with two fundamental premises of Chancery practice: that equity acted *in personam* and that equity was essentially a remedial jurisdiction. Rights were created by the availability of remedies rather than remedies being determined by the existence of rights.

V. CONCLUSION AND IMPLICATIONS

By the time of the Judicature Acts of 1873–75, most of the judicial work of explaining why English trusts took priority over the trustee's personal creditors was done. As we have seen, the Bankruptcy Act 1869 excepted '[p]roperty held by the bankrupt on trust for any other person' from the general definition of the bankrupt's property that was divisible among his creditors.[103] The Act confirmed the same protection for trust assets that the Court of Chancery had managed to find in the obscure wording of the earliest bankruptcy statutes and which developed from its own distinctive approach to awarding specific remedies. After 1869, it no longer seemed necessary to find an analytical justification based on the beneficiary's property in the trust assets or the distinctive character of the trustee's duties in relation to them. Statutory fiat made claims arising under trusts generically different from the claims of the trustee's general creditors. The problem persisted in Scotland if only because the Scottish legislation did not provide a similar exception for trusts until 1985. Case law had to contrive the exception instead.

The Judicature Acts left this regime in England untouched. Indeed, the Acts preserved the special forms of equitable relief on which the beneficiary's interest depended. The new High Court of Justice and Court of Appeal were invested with powers to recognise 'any equitable estate and right', and to award 'relief upon any equitable ground against any deed, instrument, or contract, or against any right, title, or claim whatsoever' asserted by a party.[104] If anything had changed since the eighteenth century, it was perhaps that the legislation explicitly recognised that a person might have an equitable 'estate' or 'right' in property. From late in the eighteenth century, the beneficiary's interest in the trust assets gradually underwent a process of reification. It became possible to speak of a person being 'equitably and beneficially entitled to and interested in' trust assets.[105] That expression came to refer to a distinctive kind of proprietary interest rather than a practical state of beneficial enjoyment enforced by Chancery remedies. This was the transition in the beneficiary's interest that Maitland grappled with in his *Lectures in Equity*.[106]

What implications might the eighteenth-century view of the beneficiary's interest still have for modern understandings of the trust? For one thing, it shows that the debates of the twentieth and twenty-first centuries over the nature of a beneficiary's interest were bound to happen, and to be intractable. The very subject of the

[103] Bankruptcy Act 1869, s 15(1).
[104] Judicature Act 1873, s 24(1)–(2).
[105] See Statute 1796 (36 Geo 2 c 90).
[106] See section I above.

commentators' debates evolved without any regard to the criteria that were treated as the fundamental premises of the debates themselves. The categorisation of the beneficiary's interest as a right in *personam* or *in rem*, or as some combination of the two, did not figure in the reasoning of the early eighteenth-century judges. They worked from their own premises, which turned on the Chancery judges' distinctive approach to granting specific remedies over identified property. They were supported in this approach by the wording of the bankruptcy legislation they applied to the disputes before them.

So far as history tips the balance in any of the modern debates, it would support a 'relational view' of the beneficiary's interest. The history bears out Smith's observation that the notion of a beneficiary's equitable title to trust property would be misleading if it were understood to mean a direct link between the beneficiary and the trust property: 'All equitable proprietary rights require at least two people, in addition to the object of the right.'[107] The beneficiary's interest was constructed out of his right to compel the trustee or a third person to deal with specific property in a certain way. The similarities to the Scottish trust, where the beneficiary's interest is clearly a right *in personam*, may be closer than they first seem.

This is not to deny that an English beneficiary's interest is proprietary in character, as the modern case law accepts. Even rights *in personam* relating to a person's dealings with specific property can have proprietary effect. To call a right 'proprietary' only explains the range of persons against whom the beneficiary's rights in relation to a specific asset might be enforced. Unlike the Scottish notion of a real right in a thing, to say that the English beneficiary's interest is proprietary does not imply that he has a right directly in or against the thing itself.[108] Rights which are essentially *in personam* can affect third parties to the transactions in which they were created. And if the eighteenth-century history of the English trust shows that the distinction between rights *in personam* and rights *in rem* came late in the Court of Chancery's understanding of trusts, it also shows that we gain nothing by oversimplifying the distinction between them. The beneficiary's interest in the trust was explicable for its own good reasons of principle. A reductionist view of legal taxonomy does more to obscure our understanding of the trust than it does to cast light on it.

[107] Smith, 'Trusts and Patrimony' (n 11) 392.

[108] *cf* N MacCormick, *Institutions of the Law: An Essay in Legal Theory* (Oxford, OUP, 2007) ch 8, especially 139–40; Gretton (n 2) 608.

Part VI

Administration of Assets

14

Wasting Away: Devastavit and the Judicature Act 1873

SIMON DOUGLAS

I. INTRODUCTION

DEVASTAVIT, WHICH MEANS 'he has wasted', is an action available against the personal representative of a deceased person's estate. A personal representative, who can be either an executor (a person appointed by the deceased's will) or an administrator (a person appointed by the court), has duties to collect in, preserve and administer a deceased's estate. A failure to do this, in a way which causes loss to the estate, is a devastavit. In essence, devastavit is the wrong of 'maladministration'. Matthew Bacon's *Abridgment on Executors*, published in the eighteenth century and for long the leading text on estate administration, provides a definition that is still broadly correct today:

> A devastavit is mismanagement of the estate and the effects of the deceased, in squandering and misapplying the assets contrary to the trust and confidence reposed in them, for which executors and administrators shall answer out of their own pockets, as far as they had, or might have had, assets of the deceased.[1]

Common examples of devastavit include failing to insure the deceased's assets, allowing debts to become statute barred, failing to dispose of wasting assets or allowing interest repayments to accrue without good cause. Devastavit can also occur at the point at which the estate is distributed, such as where a residuary beneficiary is paid before all of the debts have been discharged, or where a common creditor is paid before a secured creditor.

Devastavit is a creation of both the common law and equity. It originated as a means of enforcing debts against a decedent's estate in the common law courts, but was eventually appropriated by legatees suing in the Chancery Court. Important differences emerged between the common law and equitable versions of the wrong, which were ultimately resolved by the Judicature Act 1873. The hybrid nature of the wrong, part equitable and part legal, still exerts an influence on its modern application.

[1] M Bacon (ed), *A New Abridgement of the Law* (London, A Strahan, 1832) 510.

II. COMMON LAW ORIGINS

The office of 'personal representative' is a distinctive feature of the common law with no direct equivalent in civil law systems.[2] It is the personal representative who collects in the deceased's estate, arranges the funeral, settles the inheritance tax account, pays other debts and then distributes the estate to the beneficiaries.[3] Importantly for present purposes, the office of personal representative was recognised by the common law. Unlike the trustee, whose recognition in the common law courts was oblique at best,[4] the personal representative could sue and be sued in that capacity in the common law courts.

The personal representative 'represents' the deceased person[5] because the deceased's estate – both their assets and liabilities – become vested in the personal representative.[6] It would not be inaccurate to speak of the personal representative as the continuation of the deceased person's legal personality, or *patrimony*,[7] as not only do the deceased's assets vest in them, but they stand in the deceased's shoes vis-à-vis creditors. For instance, a contractual debt will not be terminated on the death of the debtor as it continues to be enforceable against their personal representative.[8] The general rule was stated by Lord Mansfield in *Hambly v Trott*[9] as:

> [W]here the cause of action is money due, or a contract to be performed, gain or acquisition of the testator, by the work and labour, or property of another, or a promise of the testator express or implied; where these are the causes of action, the action survives against the executor.[10]

In one sense the death of a debtor is not legally significant as the debt continues to be enforceable against the personal representative, and limitation periods which began during the debtor's life continue to run after their death.[11] Defences that would have been available to the deceased are equally available to the personal representative.[12]

Although the personal representative is in the same position, legally speaking, as the deceased, there are limits to this principle. A personal representative may have

[2] The civil law 'heir' is perhaps the closest office to that of executor. See generally Dutta, 'Testamentary Execution' in J Basedow et al (eds), *Max Planck Encyclopedia of European Private Law* (Oxford, OUP, 2012).

[3] Administration of Estates Act 1925, s 25.

[4] JD Haydon, MJ Leeming and PG Turner (eds), *Meagher, Gummow and Lehane's Equity: Doctrines & Remedies* (Chatswood NSW, LexisNexis Butterworths, 2015) para [1-245].

[5] In *Phillips v Homfray (no 2)* (1883) 24 Ch D 439 (CA) 456 Bowen LJ said: 'By the English law an executor represents the debts and property, but not the person of the testator.'

[6] Law Reform (Miscellaneous Provision) Act 1934, s 1.

[7] L Smith, 'Trusts and Patrimony' in R Vaslan (ed), *Trust and Patrimonies* (Edinburgh, EUP, 2015) 44.

[8] The extent of this rule was a matter of debate, with personal liabilities and rights dying with the testator. The report on *Wheatley v Lane* (1667) 1 WMS Saunds 216 records the view (at n 1) that '… the better opinion is, that an action will not lie except in cases where the breach of contract is of such a nature as appears by the record to render the personal estate less beneficial to the executor; and accordingly, in 2 M. & S. 408, *Chamberlain v. Williamson*, it was held, that an administrator cannot have an action for breach of promise of marriage to his intestate where no special damage is alleged'.

[9] (1776) 1 Cowper 371.

[10] ibid 375 (Lord Mansfield).

[11] *Thorne v Kerr* (1855) 2 K&J 54, 69 ER 691.

[12] A Learmonth et al (eds), *Williams, Mortimer and Sunnucks on Executors, Administrators and Probate*, 21st edn (London, Sweet & Maxwell, 2018) para [60-17].

taken a grant of probate (the formal process by which the will is declared valid and their authority as executor confirmed) yet found that the deceased had no assets from which the debts could be satisfied. In these circumstances the personal representative, upon being sued by a creditor for the debt, could plead *plene administravit* (no goods)[13] and the court would then need to determine whether they had in fact received assets from the deceased's estate to pay the debts. A variation of this plea was *plene administravit praetor*, which meant that there were assets but they were insufficient to meet the liability. In such cases the personal representative was admitting liability but only to the extent of the assets.[14] If they had no assets then they were obviously discharged from liability.[15] On the other hand, if the plea failed because they had received sufficient assets, then a writ was issued for the seizure of those goods for the satisfaction of the debt. It is at this stage that an allegation of 'devastavit' might be made. If the sheriff returned the writ with *nulla bona testatoris* (no goods of the testator could be found) engrossed upon it, then the creditor would allege a devastavit.[16] The essence of the claim was that the personal representative, having received sufficient assets to pay the debt, had wasted the estate and therefore should be personally liable to pay the debt.[17]

The pleading rules admitted little flexibility and could result in substantive unfairness for the personal representative. A personal representative may have received assets from the deceased's estate yet still have a good reason for not paying a creditor. An example is the case of *Crosse v Smith*[18] where an executor had received the deceased's assets but passed them, in good faith, to a co-executor who subsequently absconded. When a creditor sued the executor it was not possible to set up the *plene administravit* defence as he had in fact received assets from the estate, with the court stating:

> As no case at law has yet decided, that an executor once become fully responsible by actual receipt of a part of his testator's property, for the due administration thereof, can his discharge in respect thereof, as against a creditor seeking satisfaction out of the testator's assets, either on the score of inevitable accident, as, destruction by fire, loss by robbery, or the like or reasonable confidence disappointed, or loss by any of the various means which afford excuse to ordinary agents and bailees in cases of loss without any negligence on their part; I say, as no such case in respect to executors has yet occurred in a Court of Law, we are not from the particular hardship of the present case authorised to make such a precedent in favour of this defendant.[19]

[13] Although this translates as 'administration complete', in terms of pleading it means 'no assets'. See R Turner et al (eds), *Atkins Court Forms* (London, LexisNexis, 2008) vol 2, para [52]: 'The defence of *plene administravit* is in effect, a denial that there are any assets in the hands of the personal representatives.' See also *Marsden v Regan* [1954] 1 WLR 423 (CA).

[14] See *Erving v Peteres* (1790) 3 Term Rep 685, 100 ER 803.

[15] *Wheatley v Lane* (n 8) 219–219h and 335–336b.

[16] *Governors of St Bartholomew's Hospital v Camden* [1914] 1 Ch 233 (CA) 250.

[17] *Levy v Kum Chah* (1936) 56 CLR 159 (HCA). The procedure is discussed in detail at note 8 in the reporter's notes upon *Wheatley v Lane* (n 8). See also *Lacons v Warmoll* [1907] 2 KB 350 (CA) 360: 'In the ordinary course of the old practice under a similar judgment in the Superior Courts, the question of a devastavit would not have arisen unless and until, upon the return to a fieri facias, the sheriff had returned nulla bona testatoris and a devastavit, or merely nulla bona testatoris, in which latter case the plaintiff could sue on the judgment against the defendant as executor, suggesting a devastavit.'

[18] (1806) 7 East 246, 103 ER 94.

[19] ibid 258, 99. See also *Jewsbury v Mummery* (1872–73) LR 8 CP 56 (Court of Exchequer Chamber).

In effect, once a personal representative received sufficient assets from the deceased's estate they became strictly liable to pay the debts to the creditors. It was not possible to escape liability by showing that the assets had been lost by robbery, accident or fraud, notwithstanding that the personal representative may have acted reasonably and in good faith. Despite the obvious unfairness this causes, there was an internal logic to the rule. If the deceased, during their lifetime, had lost goods through no fault of their own, this would not have relieved them from liability to their creditors; arguably the personal representative, who represents the legal continuation of the deceased's estate, should be in no better position. This form of common law devastavit has never formally been abolished, and the rule remains that a personal representative is legally liable for the deceased's debts. However, as we will see, equitable intervention has significantly altered the wrong by introducing a fault requirement.

III. DEVASTAVIT IN THE CHANCERY COURT[20]

Whereas the common law courts would enforce debts against a deceased's estate, the other aspect of administration – the payment of legacies, residuary gifts or interests arising under an intestacy – fell within the jurisdiction of the ecclesiastical courts.[21] Where a person died leaving a will, the normal procedure would be for the executor to prove the validity of the will in the court of the bishop of the diocese where the testator was domiciled.[22] This jurisdiction to declare the validity of a will, or to 'grant probate', included an examination of the will's formal validity as well as matters of capacity, fraud and duress.[23] Not only did the ecclesiastical courts have the jurisdiction to pronounce upon the validity of a will, but also to construe its terms and thereby determine beneficial entitlements to the estate. Moreover, if an executor had not distributed the estate to those entitled, a disappointed beneficiary could ask the court to make an order for account. Henry Swinburne, an ecclesiastical lawyer who worked at the Archbishop of York's court, wrote in his treatise on testaments:

> [I]f the Executor have well and faithfully executed his Office, and fully discharged the Trust reposed in him, what should move him that should not willingly make a due Account thereof, and thereby obtain an Acquittance, and be delivered from the Burthen laid upon him?[24]

In taking an account from an executor or administrator, the court could determine whether legacies had been paid, and how much was due to the residuary beneficiary.

[20] The development of the chancery jurisdiction over succession matters and devastavit is dealt with in detail in Justice Nye Perram's excellent article on the topic: N Perram, 'The Operations and Present Operation of the Action in Devastavit' (FCA) [2012] *Federal Judicial Scholarship* 23.

[21] See *Deeks v Strutt* (1794) 5 Term Rep 690, 101 ER 384, where the Court declined to treat a legacy as a debt enforceable in the common law courts. See also R Helmholz, *The Oxford History of the Laws of England: The Canon Law and Ecclesiastical Jurisdiction from 597 to the 1640s* (Oxford, OUP, 2004) 411–14.

[22] H Swinburne, *A Brief Treatise of Testaments and Last Wills* (London, the Stationers' Company, 1640) pt VI, ch XI.

[23] ibid pt 7.

[24] ibid pt 6, ch XVII.

Of course, as the succession of land was governed by fixed legal rules, the jurisdiction of the ecclesiastical courts only extended to legacies from the deceased's personal estate.[25]

The ability of the ecclesiastical courts to declare on the validity of wills and enforce legacies continued until this jurisdiction was abolished by the Court of Probate Act 1857.[26] However, even before the formal abolition of this jurisdiction, the ecclesiastical courts had lost much of this business to the Chancery Court. The Chancery Court had assumed a concurrent jurisdiction over succession matters since at least the seventeenth century.[27] Perhaps the main reason why the Chancery Court eventually grew to become the dominant jurisdiction in all matters related to succession and administration of estates was the ability of a party interested in an estate to seek an 'administration order'.[28]

An order for administration is still technically possible today, although they are seldom made.[29] The current civil procedure rules still capture the essence of the original action: it is an application for an order that the 'administration of the estate of a deceased person, or the execution of a trust, … be carried out under the direction of the court'.[30] If granted, the principal effect of an order is that it is not possible for the personal representative to exercise a power without the sanction of the court.[31] As Clarry explains, this means that the estate is paralysed, with both the estate's assets and the personal representative's powers being surrendered to the court:

> … control of the trust and of the actual trust property was seized by the Court and the trustee was disempowered from acting without the sanction (or 'privity') of the Court until those proceedings had been finalized and the Court transferred control of the trust back to the trustee.[32]

The main procedural benefit of proceedings for an administration order is that all parties interested in the estate – both creditors and legatees – could take part in the proceedings. This meant that instead of separate claims needing to be issued in the common law courts (for enforcement of debts) and the ecclesiastical courts (for payment of legacies), the Court of Chancery provided a single forum in which all disputes over a deceased person's estate could be resolved.[33]

Administration orders were also made by the Chancery Court in respect of trusts, where powerful tools of discovery and accounting could be used to protect

[25] The jurisdiction to grant probate in respect of real property was not fully incorporated into the probate jurisdiction until the Land Transfer Act 1897.

[26] The Court of Probate, which was subsequently subsumed into the Family Division, only had the power to declare the validity of the will. Matters of construction were dealt with in the chancery courts. See Learmonth et al (n 12) para [2-03].

[27] Lord Nottingham's decision in *Noel v Robinson* (1682) 1 Vern 90, 23 ER 334 is seen as an important early authority in the development of this jurisdiction, as it decided that executors would be indemnified against unknown creditors if they paid a legacy under the order of the court. See W Holdsworth, *A History of English Law*, 2nd edn (London, Sweet & Maxwell, 1937) vol VI, 652.

[28] See Perram (n 20).

[29] *Re Savile's Estate* [2014] EWCA Civ 1632, [2015] BPIR 450 [51].

[30] Civil Procedure Rules ('CPR') 1998, r 64.2(b).

[31] *Re Furness* [1943] Ch 415 (Ch).

[32] D Clarry, *The Supervisory Jurisdiction Over Trust Administration* (Oxford, OUP, 2018) para [2.04].

[33] For examples of the use of this procedure in succession cases, see *Blake v Gale* (1885) 31 Ch D 196 (Ch) and *Governors of St Bartholomew's Hospital* (n 16).

the interests of the beneficiaries.[34] The Court would normally order that accounts be taken from the trustee, which might expose wrongful distributions or omissions to get in or grow the value of the trust fund (called an 'account on the footing of a wilful default'[35]). Litigants found that these tools could also be applied to a personal representative who had mismanaged an estate. An example is the case of *Hall v Hallet*,[36] decided by Lord Thurlow in 1784. Hall died in 1748, owning several ships involved in the East India Company, most of which were subject to mortgages. Letters of administration were obtained by Hallet later that year, who was also a creditor of the deceased. It appears that Hallet sold off a large part of the estate, and from the proceeds re-paid his own debt, but left the mortgages on the ships outstanding (and accruing interest) for several years before they were finally settled. The residuary beneficiaries brought administration proceedings to determine how much was due to them from the estate. The Court was able to examine the estate accounts in detail and determine that interest should not have been paid on the ship mortgages as it had been possible to discharge those at an early stage of administration. In response to the argument that the defendant could only be liable if he had personally profited from his default, Lord Thurlow held that the gist of the claim was not disgorgement of gains but loss to the estate:

> It has been contended, that an executor is not to be charged with interest for any money in his hands, unless it appears that he has employed it to advantage; but he might mismanage his testator's estate from many other sinister views, without any idea of immediate profit to himself.[37]

In finding the personal representative liable, the effect of the order was that they had to replenish the estate from their own resources. Although couched in the language of 'accounts' and 'wilful default', the action was similar to common law devastavit as the administrator was personally liable for loss resulting from his maladministration of the estate. Indeed, in later administration proceedings the Chancery Court started to describe this as a 'devastavit',[38] and this is how claims of this nature are now described in chancery business.

As noted above, one of the effects of a party starting administration proceedings was that the estate was paralysed, as the Court took sole charge of its administration. This included litigation in other courts, and the Chancery Court would issue injunctions to prevent parallel claims in the common law or spiritual courts.[39] One effect of this is that devastavit increasingly became an equitable concept. Whilst it remained possible for a creditor to plead devastavit in a common law claim,[40] most succession disputes were subject to administration proceedings, so that an allegation of devastavit was normally made in the Chancery Court.

[34] See S Williams and F Gutherie-Smith (eds) *Daniell's Chancery Practice*, 8th edn (London, Stevens & Sons, 1914) 864.

[35] eg, *Lord Kensington v Bouverie* (1855) 7 De GM & G 134, 44 ER 53.

[36] (1784) 1 CCC 134, 29 ER 1096.

[37] ibid 137–38, 1097.

[38] eg, *Job v Job* (1877) 6 Ch D 562 (Ch).

[39] *Smith v Kempson* (1790) 2 Dick 769, 21 ER 470.

[40] eg, *Marsden* (n 13).

IV. DIVERGENCE AND THE JUDICATURE ACT 1873

As we have seen, where a personal representative caused loss to an estate by maladministration, an allegation of devastavit could be made either in the common law courts or in the Chancery Court (although, in practice, it was normally the latter). Over the eighteenth and nineteenth centuries clear differences between these two proceedings emerged, which created the prospect of inconsistent approaches being taken towards personal representatives. This was not resolved until the Judicature Act 1873.

A. Developing the 'Wrong' Element of Devastavit

When devastavit was alleged by a creditor in a common law claim, it is clear that the claim was not merely for the original debt; rather, the creditor was alleging that the personal representative had committed a distinct wrong which had caused loss.[41] This is apparent from cases where limitation was raised as a defence. The relevant period was not that which ran in respect of the original debt, but from the personal representative's wrongful act of waste. As the court held in *Lacons v Wormall*:[42]

> The creditor in such a case elects to treat the executor as his own debtor. If the plaintiff chooses to say: 'It is not the estate of the debtor that is liable, but it is you, the executor, who are personally liable,' the executor, being then Charged with his own personal wrong-doing or tort, is entitled to avail himself of the benefit of the Statute of Limitations.[43]

Although common law devastavit was a wrong, the type of conduct that constituted that wrong was largely obscured by rigid pleading rules. All that a creditor needed to show in order to succeed was (1) that the personal representative had initially received assets from the deceased's estate and (2) that they no longer had those assets. The implication of these allegations was that the personal representative, after coming into possession of the deceased's assets, subsequently lost them. The reason for the loss – whether it be through theft, accidental loss or deliberate disbursement – was unimportant. The only relevant fact, which constituted the wrong, was the actual loss of the deceased's assets from the personal representative's possession or control. The personal representative had no opportunity to explain or justify the loss. Whilst this aspect of common law devastavit tended towards strict liability, which would have made it popular with creditors, in other respects it offered very limited protection. The reason a personal representative may be unable to pay a creditor may have nothing to do with loss of an asset, but due to more indirect acts of maladministration, such as failing to collect in assets in the first place (eg, by failing to sue upon debts due to the estate). Although such conduct was just as prejudicial to the creditor, the traditional pleas of *plene adminstravit* and *devastavit*, which assumed receipt then loss, were not appropriate.

[41] *Thorne v Kerr* (n 11) 63, 694 (Page Wood VC): 'At law, if an executor committed a *devastavit*, the remedy was by action of trespass against him.'
[42] (n 17).
[43] ibid 361–62 (Lord Alverstone CJ).

When devastavit was developed in the Chancery Court there was a much more explicit focus on the nature of the wrong committed by the personal representative. In the 1806 case of *Dornford v Dornford*,[44] where an executor had failed to invest and accumulate income for an infant beneficiary, Grant MR described the wrong in the modern terminology of 'breach of duty':

> … for the question is, what is the obligation, which this Court attaches upon the breach of such a duty. That obligation is equivalent to the contract of the party. This Court says, 'if you neglect your duty, and keep the money yourself, your obligation is to put the infant in the same situation, as if you had not done so.' The Court does not inquire into the particular benefit, that has been made; but fastens upon the party an obligation to make good the situation of the Cestuis que Trust.[45]

Although the gist of equitable devastavit, like its common law counterpart, is the causing of loss to the estate, 'loss' was interpreted much more widely. If a personal representative physically lost possession of an estate asset that might well be a devastavit in equity. However, value might be lost in less obvious ways, such as erosion of value due to inflation,[46] failing to collect in assets, or the holding of wasting assets.[47] In these cases the wrongful act was not an actual loss of possession, but the failure to administer the estate prudently. This wider notion of 'loss to the estate' was noted in *Re Stevens*[48] where an executor failed to discharge a mortgage on a life insurance policy for seven years, meaning that interest was needlessly paid throughout this period. The loss to the estate in this case was not the actual loss of estate assets from the executor's possession, but the failure to maintain their value through proper management. Vaughan Williams LJ commented:

> I may observe here that none of the forms employed at law for charging an executor as on a devastavit seem to be so framed as to include a claim for damages for negligent administration, all the forms being framed in terms applicable only to the loss of assets received, or which might have been received; but assuming that there is no liability which could be enforced at law, he might still be made liable by an action or bill, as it used to be called in equity, to make good the loss to the estate arising from his negligent administration …[49]

This wider concept of 'loss by negligent administration' was most likely developed by analogy with breach of trust, where trustees have similar duties to preserve the value of the trust fund. Just as trustees are made to account for their dealings with trust property, so too are personal representatives. The accounting process shines a light on the personal representative's investment decisions (or lack thereof) and disbursements, and it is a short step from this process to the court determining that an estate has not been administered properly.

It is also relevant that equitable devastavit can be alleged by a beneficiary, unlike the position at law where only creditors could sue. A residuary beneficiary, in contrast

[44] (1806) 12 Ves Jun 127, 33 ER 49.
[45] ibid 129, 50 (Sir William Grant MR).
[46] *Franklin v Frith* (1792) 3 Bro CC 433, 29 ER 627.
[47] *Rowley v Adams* (1839) 4 M & Cr 534, 39 ER 786.
[48] [1898] 1 Ch 162 (CA).
[49] ibid 177.

to a creditor, is not entitled to a fixed sum from the estate. When a residuary beneficiary alleges devastavit it is necessary for the court to ask what value the estate would have had if the personal representative had invested and managed the estate prudently.[50] This type of inquiry is far removed from that conducted in the common law courts, where the only question was whether sufficient assets were received to cover the debt. The focus in equity was not just on the initial quantum of the estate, but on what value the estate should have had if it had been administered prudently by the personal representative.

B. The Mental Element

Where a devastavit was alleged in the Chancery Court it was necessary in most cases to show that the personal representative had acted in bad faith or negligently. As Vaughan Williams LJ stated in *Re Stevens*, to succeed in the claim it is necessary 'to establish both the negligence and the damage resulting to the estate thereby …'.[51] As we saw above, the position at common law was different. Once a personal representative received assets from the estate, they were strictly liable for the payment of debts. It was no defence that the personal representative had been robbed of the assets, or otherwise deprived of them through no fault of their own. That the Chancery Court did not adopt this strict approach to liability was likely due to the long-standing rule that a trustee who was deprived of trust property was not answerable to the beneficiaries provided that they had acted with reasonable care. This was made clear in Lord Nottingham's well-known judgment in *Morley v Morley*,[52] a case in which a trustee was held not to be liable to the beneficiaries for £40 worth of gold that had been stolen from him. Where a trustee has lost trust assets, the appropriate claim is normally an account on the basis of a wilful default, where it is necessary to prove fault.[53] Personal representatives, whilst not trustees,[54] are in an analogous position in that they hold a fund for the benefit of others. It naturally follows that the same procedure, and the requirement for fault, should be applied to them in the Chancery Court.[55] This was made clear in *Jones v Lewis*[56] where Lord Harwicke drew an express comparison between a trustee and executor:

> If a trustee is robbed, that robbery properly proved shall be a discharge, provided he keeps them (the goods) so as he would keep his own. So it is as to an executor or administrator, who is not to be chargeable further than goods come to his hands; and for these not to be

[50] *Hall v Hallet* (n 36).

[51] *Re Stevens* (n 48) 177. See also *Jones v Lewis* (1751) 2 Ves Snr 240, 28 ER 155 and *Rice v Gordon* (1848) 11 Beavan 265, 50 ER 818.

[52] (1678) 2 Ch Cas 2, 22 ER 817.

[53] *Bartlett v Barclays Bank Trust Co Ltd* [1980] Ch 515 (Ch).

[54] *Re Trollope's Will Trusts* [1927] 1 Ch 596 (Ch); *Re Spencer & Hauser's Contract* [1928] Ch 598 (Ch). See also C Mitchell, '*Commissioner of Stamp Duties (Queensland) v Livingston* (1964): Rights of Estate Beneficiaries and Trust Beneficiaries Compared' in B Sloan (ed), *Landmark Cases in Succession Law* (Oxford, Hart, 2019).

[55] *Massey v Banner* (1820) 1 Jac & Walk 241, 37 ER 367.

[56] *Jones v Lewis* (n 51).

> charged, unless guilty of a devastavit; and if robbed, and he could not avoid it, he is not to be charged, at least in this Court.[57]

The clear similarity between a breach of trust and devastavit means that these terms, and associated terminology such as 'wilful default', are often used interchangeably.[58] There are important differences between breach of trust and devastavit which will be commented on below, but the analogy between the claims meant that the fault requirement in trusts was imported to devastavit.

C. The Judicature Act 1873

The use of administration proceedings to resolve disputes over decedents' estates led to the development of an equitable version of devastavit which diverged from its common law counterpart in three ways. First, administration proceedings opened the plea of devastavit to beneficiaries as well as creditors. Second, the equitable version was based upon the much wider concept of loss by maladministration. Whilst the physical loss of an asset may be a devastavit both in chancery and at law, causing loss in more indirect ways, such as by failing to invest prudently, was only an equitable wrong. Finally, when a personal representative was charged with devastavit in equity, it was normally necessary to prove negligence, whereas liability at law was strict.

By section 25(11) of the Judicature Act 1873 the rule was set down that where there was 'conflict or variance between the Rules of Equity and the Rules of the Common Law with reference to the same matter, the Rules of Equity shall prevail'. The effect of this rule on devastavit can be seen in the case of *Job v Job*.[59] In this case the deceased's estate comprised stock in trade from the deceased's watch-making business. The executor, in order to sell the stock, passed it in good faith to the deceased's son (who was also a watch-maker), who then lost the stock when he was declared bankrupt. In a claim for devastavit, counsel argued for the common law rule that the executor should be strictly liable for the loss of the stock:

> An executor is chargeable for the goods of his testator if he fails properly to dispose of them, and if he has once received the goods and they are lost, he cannot escape liability unless he can shew he has properly discharged himself.[60]

Jessell MR rejected the argument, and referred to the equitable rule that negligence was required in order to prove a devastavit. Moreover, he asserted that this equitable rule also replaced the common law's strict liability, meaning that wherever devastavit is alleged it will be necessary to prove fault:

> The rule there laid down is, however, as I have already intimated, not the rule now, even at law, for the Judicature Act 1873 provides by sect. 25, sub-sect. 11, that where 'there is any conflict or variance between the rules of equity and the rules of the common law

[57] ibid 241, 155.
[58] *Job v Job* (n 38); and *Re Stevens* (n 48).
[59] (n 38).
[60] ibid 563.

> with reference to the same matter, the rules of equity shall prevail.' The rule, then, at law as well as in equity, now is that an executor or administrator is in the position of a gratuitous bailee, who cannot be charged with the loss of his testator's assets without wilful default ...[61]

Maitland referred to this decision as the best illustration of the operation of section 25(11) of the Judicature Act 1873.[62] It meant that henceforth, whenever an allegation of devastavit was made at law or in equity, a personal representative would not be strictly liable for the loss of an estate asset. Rather, it was incumbent upon a claimant to show loss by maladministration, which requires (in most cases) an element of fault.

V. MODERN DEVASTAVIT

A. Common Law Devastavit

The traditional distinction between common law and equitable devastavit is preserved in the modern rules of civil procedure. Where a creditor of a deceased person brings a claim to enforce a debt, there are effectively two options. First, the creditor can use the normal procedures[63] for the enforcement of a debt, save that the defendant is sued in their capacity as personal representative rather than personally.[64] A claim of this nature, which is normally heard in the County Court or High Court depending on its value, is largely indistinguishable from claims brought against living debtors. Second, the creditor may choose to bring a claim in the Chancery Division under Part 64 of the CPR. Such claims are for the 'administration of the estate' of a deceased person.[65] This is a more flexible procedure than the old-fashioned proceedings for an 'administration order', as rather than being a claim for the complete administration of the estate by the court, it is a claim 'for the court to determine any question arising in the administration of the estate'. That question may concern the personal representative's failure to pay a creditor. Which course a creditor chooses largely depends on the complexity of the matter. If the issues arise from the defendant's administration of the estate, the second option is preferable; whereas if it is a simple dispute over the existence of the debt, then the first procedure will be appropriate. It is in the context of the first type of claim that common law devastavit continues to be relevant.

The pleading rules for alleging devastavit at law are largely unchanged from their medieval origin. If a creditor proves that they were owed a debt from the deceased, the personal representative may still attempt to escape liability by pleading *plene administravit* or *plene administravit preator*, that is, that they received no or insufficient

[61] ibid 564.
[62] FW Maitland, *Equity: A Course of Lectures* (Cambridge, CUP, 2011) (reprint) 155.
[63] By 'normal' I refer to claims issued under pt 7 of the CPR, where a statement of case must plead the facts upon which the debt arose.
[64] CPR, r 19.8(2)(a).
[65] CPR, r 64.1.

goods to discharge the debt.[66] If the defence fails,[67] and the creditor obtains a judgment (which remains unsatisfied) then an order can be made for an enforcement officer (formerly the sheriff) to seize the deceased's goods from the possession of the personal representative (*de bonis testatoris*).[68] If the enforcement officer makes a return of the writ *nulla bona* (no goods),[69] then the creditor may at this point bring a second claim alleging devastavit.

Whilst the pleading rules are largely unchanged, the facts required to prove the devastavit are now different. As we saw above, before the Judicature Act 1873, a return of *nulla bona* by the sheriff would have led to automatic liability in common law devastavit. Following the reforms the requirement for fault, developed in equitable devastavit, prevails. As such, a return of *nulla bona* leads, at most, to a presumption of devastavit, and the personal representative has an opportunity to explain or justify it. This was made clear in the case of *Batchelar v Evans*[70] where Farewell J said:

> … the fact of the sheriff's return of *nulla bona* is not conclusive against the defendants, but that it is open to them, if they can, to show why there had been this alteration in the situation between the date of the judgment, when they admitted assets, and the date of the return of *nulla bona*, and to establish that it is not due to any devastavit committed by them.[71]

The decision shows that the rules established in the Chancery Court have come to govern the position at law. Creditors can no longer avoid the need to prove fault by bringing their claim at law.

Common law devastavit is rarely used by creditors. Where there is very clear evidence of receipt of an asset by a personal representative followed by a loss, proving common law devastavit may be relatively straightforward. In most other cases, where a personal representative seeks to justify their inability to pay on some other ground, such as by reference to the general costs of administration or higher-ranking debts, then it will be much harder to prove devastavit at law. What is needed in such cases is an inquiry into the personal representative's administration of the estate. This makes an administration action in the Chancery Division more attractive to the creditor, as accounts can be taken and other parties with an interest in the estate can be joined. It is in the context of these administration claims that allegations of devastavit – or *equitable* devastavit – are typically made.

B. Equitable Devastavit

As we have seen, equitable devastavit has developed from a limited claim brought by creditors for physical loss of an estate asset, to a more sophisticated action of

[66] eg, *Midland Bank Trust Co Ltd v Green (No 2)* [1979] 1 WLR 460 (Ch).

[67] The burden is on the creditor to prove receipt of assets: *Giles v Dyson* (1815) 1 Stark 32, 171 ER 393.

[68] This is now called a 'writ of control': CPR, r 83.2(3)(a).

[69] Tribunals, Courts and Enforcement Act 2007, s 62(4).

[70] [1939] Ch 1007 (Ch). See also *Marsden* (n 13) 429; and *Leonard v Simpson* (1835) 2 Bing NC 176.

[71] *Batchelar* (n 70) 1012–13. To similar effect see Turner et al (n 13) para [63]: '… in as much as the return of nulla bona only raises a presumption of a devastavit, it is … open to [the personal representative] to show that there is a satisfactory explanation for the disappearance of the assets, as for example, the appointment of a receiver in an administration action between the date of the judgment and the issue of the writ of control.'

causing loss by maladministration. To explain equitable devastavit therefore requires an exploration of 'maladministration'. Section 25(a) of the Administration of Estates Act 1925 describes the basic duty of a personal representative as the duty to 'collect and get in the real and personal estate of the deceased and administer it according to law'. Broadly speaking, a personal representative's duty has two components: first, to collect in and preserve the value of the estate; second, to distribute the estate according to law (ie, in the correct order). If equitable devastavit is to be equated with 'maladministration', then it might be said to be comprised of a breach of the duty to either (1) preserve the value of the estate or (2) to distribute the estate.

i. Duty to Preserve the Estate

The personal representative owes duties to both the creditors and beneficiaries to take reasonable steps to preserve the value of the deceased's estate.[72] A failure to do this will amount to an equitable devastavit. What amounts to reasonable steps depends upon the nature and extent of the estate, but the following general statements can be made.

First, the personal representative should normally take steps to collect in and secure the deceased's estate as soon as reasonably practical after the deceased's death.[73] The deceased's title to any personal or real property will vest in an executor upon the deceased's death and, in an administrator's case, immediately upon their obtaining letters of administration. The personal representative should normally reduce these assets to their physical possession or control so as to prevent others from depriving the estate of these assets. This means obtaining keys to the house and car, transferring the deceased's bank monies to estate accounts and suing upon debts due to the deceased. Where prompt steps are not taken, and the estate thereby loses value, the personal representative's omission may count as a devastavit.[74]

Second, it will usually be necessary to divest the estate of any wasting assets, unless there is a specific direction to hold onto the same.[75] For instance, in *Rowley v Adams*[76] the deceased's estate included a lease which made the estate liable for rent to the landlord. The rent due was greater than the rent received from a sub-tenant, and the deficit had to be met by other assets in the estate. This could have been avoided if the executor had sold the lease in a timely fashion and his failure to do this amounted to a devastavit. Where the estate includes assets subject to a charge, it may be a devastavit if the personal representative fails to release the security in a reasonable time and thereby incurs unnecessary interest charges.[77] Similarly, where the market value of an estate asset is falling, the personal representative will need to justify their failure to sell it when it had a higher value.[78]

[72] *Re Tankard* [1942] Ch 69 (Ch).
[73] Learmonth et al (n 12) para [52-14].
[74] eg, *Lowson v Copeland* (1787) 2 Bro CC 156, 29 ER 89.
[75] For instance, if an estate includes a lease, it would normally be prudent to sell the residue of the term and distribute the proceeds, otherwise its value will continue to fall. However, a testator may direct that their spouse or child should have the use of the lease for their occupation.
[76] (n 47).
[77] *Hall v Hallet* (n 36).
[78] *Re Tankard* (n 72).

Third, in some cases it will be a devastavit if the personal representative fails to invest estate assets, otherwise there is a risk that the value will be eroded by inflation. Where there is a simple estate that can be fully administered within a year or two, the normal practice will be to convert the assets into money and pay the proceeds to creditors and beneficiaries.[79] Where administration proves more complicated, and several years may pass before the estate can be distributed, the personal representative will commit devastavit if they do not invest estate monies. In *Franklin v Frirth*[80] the executor kept the sum of £400 in hand (ie not invested) for seven years, as he feared he might be sued by a potential creditor. Lord Thurlow, finding that his fear of being sued was unfounded, made him liable for three per cent interest, stating that he 'never could permit an executor to keep £400 of his testator's money dead in his hands'.[81] In appropriate cases where authorisation is given in a will, personal representatives may need to go further than investment and actively manage a deceased's business in order to preserve the value of the fund.[82]

Fourth, personal representatives should avoid unnecessary or unauthorised disbursements from the estate. One instance where this issue often arises is in respect of funeral expenses, as personal representatives have a power to expend reasonable funds on the deceased's funeral. In *National Westmister Bank Plc v Lucas*,[83] the executors of the estate of Jimmy Saville expended over £70,000 on his funeral and wake. Whilst this expenditure might be justifiable for a public figure with a large estate, it proved contentious as Saville had (unknown to the executors at the time) died insolvent, with significant liabilities to several of his victims. The court did not find the executors liable in devastavit as the expenses had been incurred in good faith and before they were aware of potential claims against the estate. However, the case shows that where personal representatives make payments that they are not legally obliged to make they need to be able to justify them.

What these examples show is that those with an interest in the estate – creditors and beneficiaries – have an entitlement that the personal representative take reasonable steps to preserve the value of the estate. A failure to do this is an example of 'maladministration' and, if it results in loss, a devastavit. There is an obvious similarity between these devastavit cases and breach of trust claims, where trustees owe similar stewardship duties in respect of the trust fund, and the terms might be used interchangeably. Yet there are important differences also. For instance, a claim in devastavit can be brought by both beneficiaries and creditors, whereas a claim for breach of trust can only be brought by beneficiaries. Trust creditors have no direct interest in the trust fund, but instead have a personal contractual claim against the trustee.[84] As such, a trust creditor has no access to the administration action under Part 64 of the CPR, but can only sue the trustee at law for the debt.[85] By contrast, an

[79] It is possible to assent an asset directly to a beneficiary, especially when there is a bequest of that asset and it is not needed to meet the estate liabilities: Administration of Estates Act 1925, s 36(1).

[80] (n 46) 434, 628.

[81] ibid. See also *Taylor v Gerst* (1729) Mos 98, 25 ER 293.

[82] See *Kirkman v Booth* (1848) 11 Beav 273, 50 ER 821.

[83] [2013] EWHC 770 (Ch).

[84] *Muir v City of Glasgow Bank* (1879) 4 App Cas 337 (HL).

[85] The trust creditor has an indirect claim against the estate, as they can be subrogated to the trustee's indemnity: *Re Johnson* (1880) 15 Ch D 548.

estate creditor does have a direct interest in the estate, and the personal representative's administration of the estate will affect their ability to discharge the debts. That devastavit is open to creditors as well as beneficiaries affects the nature of the wrong. Exemption clauses in a will, or other rights and powers granted to an executor by the will, seem to have no bearing on creditor's claim against the estate. In *Re Tankard*,[86] where the executor was dilatory converting shares into cash in order to pay creditors, it was wholly irrelevant that the will gave the executor a power to postpone sale of the shares, as the creditors did not derive their rights from the will. When a beneficiary of a trust alleges a breach, the question is often whether the trustee has transgressed their duties or exceeded their powers as contained in the trust deed. When a devastavit is alleged, the terms of a will (if there is one) are largely irrelevant. The breach in devastavit is of the 'duty of administration', which is an equitable and statutory duty, not a duty arising from the terms of a will.[87]

ii. Duty to Distribute the Estate

Once the value of the estate is secured, the next stage is to distribute the estate by paying creditors and beneficiaries. There are two aspects to this duty. First, the personal representative must only make payments to those with an interest in the estate. Second, the payments should be made in the correct order, as not all interests are equal.

Where a personal representative delays in paying creditors or beneficiaries, an administration action can be brought to compel payment. Mere delay is not in itself a devastavit (unless the delay has caused a separate loss), as the personal representative remains capable of complying with their primary duty to distribute. For a devastavit those with an interest in the estate must suffer a loss. This can occur where, for instance, a personal representative makes a payment to someone who they mistakenly believe is a creditor or beneficiary. An example is provided by the case of *Re Rownson*,[88] where the deceased had orally promised his daughter the sum of £500 on her engagement to her future husband. Under section 4 of the Statute of Frauds promises made in consideration of marriage were void unless made in writing, meaning that the deceased's promise was not binding. When the daughter was appointed administrator and paid the debt to herself, this was held to be a devastavit as it was an unauthorised distribution. A similar case is *Manning v Purcell*[89] where the executor of a betting agent paid out on several bets that had been resolved before his death. Gambling contracts were binding in honour only, meaning that there was no lawful authority to pay out. Knight Bruce LJ said:

> … as to the payments in respect of bets decided in the testator's lifetime, there appears to us neither justification, nor what in this Court can be considered as an excuse, for making

[86] (n 72).
[87] Conversely, it is unlikely that a creditor could complain that the personal representative has retained an 'unauthorised investment', as any limit on the scope of an executor's investment powers are contained in the will, which is irrelevant for the creditor.
[88] (1885) 29 Ch D 358 (CA).
[89] (1855) 7 De GM & G 55, 44 ER 21.

> the payments; however proper, and in a sense laudable on the part of the lady, the feeling under which they may have been made.[90]

Interestingly, the personal representatives in these two cases were liable in devastavit without any proof of negligence or bad faith. The same strict approach seems to apply where payment is made to the wrong beneficiaries. In *Hilliard v Fulford*[91] the executors wrongly believed that there were five residuary beneficiaries when there were actually six. There is no suggestion in the report that they had acted imprudently, but Jessel MR held them liable for devastavit, stating, '… they who have made the error will have to pay for it'.[92] The approach here seems to mirror that found in trusts, where a trustee's fault (or lack of) is irrelevant where they have acted ultra vires and without authorisation.[93] This might be contrasted with the case where a personal representative pays money to an estate creditor notwithstanding that the limitation period for the debt has expired. Such a payment is not automatically a devastavit as it is not ultra vires: unless the statute of limitations defence is pleaded, the debt remains valid and the creditor has a valid interest in the estate.[94]

The second aspect of the personal representative's dispositive duties is the duty to pay creditors and beneficiaries in the correct order. The rule can be stated in three parts. First, creditors should be paid before beneficiaries.[95] Second, as to the creditors, the order of priority is the same as that for a bankrupt's estate, so that preference must be given to secured creditors before the payment of ordinary debts.[96] Third, as to the beneficiaries, the order of payment is governed by the rules of abatement, so that specific bequests should be paid first, followed by demonstrative legacies, legacies and finally the payment of the residue.[97] Of course, personal representatives can, and frequently do, distribute the estate in the incorrect order but take care to preserve enough assets to pay those with a prior claim.[98] The risk in doing this is obvious, and personal representatives sometimes find that prior claims are greater than they had appreciated. Where this happens, the loss caused to the prior creditor or beneficiary is the devastavit.

Liability in devastavit for distribution in the wrong order does not appear to be strict. After all, the personal representative has not acted ultra vires, as payments are made to those with an interest in the estate, albeit in the wrong order. It is open to the personal representative to plead that they had no notice of the prior claim. An example is *Chelsea Waterworks v Cowper*[99] where a (still enforceable) debt came to light

[90] ibid 63, 25.
[91] (1876) 4 Ch D 389 (Ch).
[92] ibid 394.
[93] *Armitage v Nurse* [1998] Ch 241 (CA) 251. The trustee may have a statutory defence under the Trustee Act 1925, s 61.
[94] *Lowis v Rumeny* (1867) LR 4 Eq 451 (Ch).
[95] *Hawkins v Day* (1753) Amb 160, 27 ER 107.
[96] This is governed by the Administration of Insolvent Estates of Deceased Persons Order 1986 (SI 1986/1999).
[97] Administration of Estates Act 1925, Sch 1.
[98] For instance, it is common to assent specific chattels even before all debts have been paid off.
[99] (1795) 1 Esp 275, 170 ER 355. See also *Re Fludyer* [1898] 2 Ch 562 (Ch).

some twenty-two years after the deceased's death, and long after the executors had distributed the estate to the residuary beneficiary. Lord Kenyon is reported as saying:

> ... where an executor or administrator has satisfied the debts and legacies affecting the testator's or intestate's estate, and paid over the remainder to the residuary legatee; and has had no notice of any other subsisting demand, provided he had not done it too precipitately, that it was a good answer to an action, such as the present.[100]

Specific statutory defences have now been introduced to protect personal representatives from unknown debtors,[101] but the basic rule appears to remain that a personal representative can plead lack of notice as a defence.

VI. CONCLUSION

A personal representative's duties are not limited to preserving and administering the estate. They also include duties to account, arrange for the funeral, submit an inheritance tax return and to do several other acts. Yet equitable devastavit is not the breach of *any* duty attached to the office of personal representative. Rather, its focus is on the core aspects of administration: preservation and distribution. It is the personal representative's failure to do either of these acts, in such a way that causes loss to those with an interest in the estate, which constitutes a devastavit. Whilst devastavit has much in common with breach of trust, its common law origins have also left it with distinctive features. Prime among these is the fact that duties of administration are owed to both creditors and beneficiaries, whereas a trustee's duties of administration are owed just to beneficiaries.

[100] ibid 277.

[101] The main tool is the power to advertise for creditors under the Trustee Act 1925, s 27. If an unknown creditor does not give notice within a certain period following an advertisement, the personal representatives can normally distribute without risk of committing devastavit. There is also the general defence available under Trustee Act 1925, s 61.

Part VII

Securities

15

Equity in Codified Secured Transactions Law

MAGDA RACZYNSKA

I. INTRODUCTION

THE ROLE OF equity in codifications of commercial law is little understood. A codification here means a statute that comprehensively sets out legal principles that govern the major questions arising in connection with a particular type of transaction or legal activity.[1] In England, this limited understanding is unsurprising given that only a handful of areas of commercial law are codified.[2] By contrast, in the US, most commercial law is found in a single code, the Uniform Commercial Code ('UCC'), a project that was borne out of a realist desire to break clean with existing concepts. Other common law jurisdictions have been inspired by the UCC in the areas of securities transfer law and, in particular, secured transactions law. A Personal Property Security Act ('PPSA'), influenced by Article 9 of the UCC[3] on secured transactions, can now be found in each of the Canadian provinces,[4] as well as in New Zealand[5] and Australia.[6] Calls for a substantial

[1] *cf* RJ Wood, 'The Codification of Commercial Law' (2016) 79 *Saskatchewan Law Review* 179, 182; A Burrows, 'Legislative Reform of Remedies for Breach of Contract: The English Perspective' (1997) 1 *Edinburgh Law Review* 155, 156.

[2] See the law governing sale of goods (under the Sale of Goods Act 1979, and earlier the Sale of Goods Act 1893), bills of exchange (under the Bills of Exchange Act 1882), and insurance (Marine Insurance Act 1906 and Insurance Act 2015). The Partnership Act 1890, the Companies Act 2006, the Insolvency Act 1986 and the Arbitration Act 1996 codify activity that is relevant to commercial activity but not aspects of commercial law itself.

[3] For brevity, Art 9 UCC in this chapter is referred to as UCC.

[4] See, eg, the Personal Property Security Act 1990 in Ontario (referred to as OPPSA), the 1993 Act in Saskatchewan (SPPSA), the 2000 Act in Alberta (APPSA).

[5] Personal Property Securities Act 1999 (NZ).

[6] Personal Property Security Act 2009 (Cth) (referred to as AusPPSA).

reform of English secured transactions law have a long history[7] but a codification is yet to be accomplished.[8]

This chapter shows that a reflection on codification of secured transactions law offers insights into the role equity plays in codes of commercial law. There are good reasons to focus on the area of secured transactions. First, it is of considerable practical importance. Security interests facilitate performance of obligations: creditors, in addition to the promise to perform, obtain rights and powers exercisable against some property with the purpose of enforcing the debtor's obligation in priority to at least some other creditors of that debtor.[9] In practice, therefore, security rights reduce credit risk faced by the lender and sometimes even determine whether the lender is willing to lend at all.[10] The second motivation for examining secured transactions law is that it is conceptually interesting. In England, and in other common law jurisdictions prior to reforms, the law of security rights has been shaped by both common law and equitable principles, which resulted in unnecessary complexity. To simplify the law, UCC and PPSAs introduced a 'unitary notion' of a security interest.[11] Among other things,[12] this move abolishes the distinction between legal and equitable interests. Proposals for reform of English law also contemplate a single concept

[7] There have been numerous reports going back as far as the *Report of the Committee on Consumer Credit* (Cmnd 4596, 1971). For a summary of reform efforts, see, eg, L Gullifer and M Raczynska, 'The English Law of Personal Property Security: Under-reformed?' in L Gullifer and O Akseli (eds), *Secured Transactions Law Reform: Principles, Policies and Practice* (Oxford, Hart, 2016) 271. For arguments favouring codification in other areas, too, see R Goode, 'The Codification of Commercial Law' (1988) 14 *Monash University Law Review* 135; M Arden, 'Time for an English Commercial Code?' (1997) 56 *CLJ* 516 reproduced in M Arden, *Common Law and Modern Society: Keeping Pace with Change* (Oxford, OUP, 2015) ch 13, 191; *cf* FH Lawson, *The Rational Strength of English Law* (London, Stevens & Sons, 1951) 24; Burrows (n 1); M Clarke, 'Doubts from the Dark Side: The Case against Codes' [2001] *Journal of Business Law* 605.

[8] Led by the Secured Transactions Law Reform Project, and a working party of the Financial Law Committee of the City of London Law Society ('CLLS FLC').

[9] *cf Bristol Airports plc v Powdrill* [1990] Ch 744 (CA) (Sir Browne-Wilkinson VC).

[10] J Armour, 'The Law and Economics Debate About Secured Lending: Lessons for European Lawmaking?' in H Eidenmüller and E-M Kieninger (eds), *The Future of Secured Credit in Europe* (Berlin, De Gruyter Recht, 2008) 3, 28–29.

[11] *Warehouse Sales Pty Ltd & Lewis and Templeton v LG Electronics Australia Pty Ltd* [2014] VSC 644, (2014) 291 FLR 407 [27]–[32] (Sifris J); *Innovation Credit Union v Bank of Montreal* 2010 SCC 47, [2010] 3 SCR 3 [42] (Charron J for the Court), cited in *Stiassny v Commissioner of Inland Revenue* [2012] NZSC 106, [2013] 1 NZLR 453 [51] (Blanchard J); *Hamersley Iron Pty Ltd v Forge Group Power Pty Ltd (in liq)* [2017] WASC 152, (2017) 52 WAR 90 [358] (Tottle J); *Diversa Pty Ltd v Taiping Trustees Ltd* [2022] FCA 316, (2022) 401 ALR 161 [237] (Beach J); *Waller v Bloodstock Ltd* [2006] 3 NZLR 629 (NZCA) 633 [13] (Robertson and Baragwanath JJ); JS Ziegel, 'Canadian Perspectives on "How Far is Article 9 Exportable"?' (1996) 27 *Canadian Business Law Journal* 226, 232; RCC Cuming, C Walsh and RJ Wood, *Personal Property Security Law*, 2nd edn (Toronto, Irwin Law, 2012) 116–17; M Gedye, RCC Cuming and RJ Wood, *Personal Property Securities in New Zealand* (Wellington, Thomson Brookers, 2002) 4–5, 20–21; RCC Cuming, C Walsh and RJ Wood, 'Secured Transactions Law in Canada: Significant Achievements, Unfinished Business and Ongoing Challenges' (2011) 50 *Canadian Business Law Journal* 156, 166.

[12] These words are covering much ground here. It is one of the distinctive features of UCC and PPSAs to also replace the distinction between traditional forms of security interests (charge, mortgage, pledge and contractual lien) and functional equivalents such as title-based financing interests under a contract of sale with a retention-of-title clause, a financing lease or hire-purchase agreement (sometimes referred to as quasi-security). The fact that UCC and PPSAs do that is not important for the purposes of the argument developed in this chapter.

of a security interest that would, at the very least, do as much.[13] Yet, a removal of the distinction between legal and equitable interests is not the same as abolishing common law or equitable principles.

The question addressed in this chapter then is whether the principles and doctrines of equity are, and should be, reflected in the codified secured transaction laws. Surprisingly, the issue has so far not been examined, perhaps because equity lawyers tend not to focus on security rights while those writing about reform tend to concentrate on critiquing specific rules rather than looking at the role of equity generally. The answers contribute to our better understanding of the role played by equitable principles in modern secured transactions regimes, and in commercial law generally. Such understanding, in turn, has practical implications for the law reform debate in England, and for codifications – when examining the extent to which principles of equity should supplement the statutes.

The argument is in two parts. It is first shown that while some notions of equity are inconvenient in the law of security rights, and not imported into reformed secured transactions codifications (notably, equity's priority rules including the bona fide purchaser defence), in key aspects the genius of equity is preserved in the codifications. This in turn raises the question, addressed in the second part, whether a codified security interest could be equitable in character, or whether it is best understood as legal, for certain purposes when issues arise requiring such characterisation. It will be seen that when priority conflicts arise not governed by the codification, a codified security interest should be seen as a legal interest. Possible downsides to this view, and solutions, will be suggested.

In this chapter, the words 'equity' and 'equitable' are used to denote the system of legal principles derived from the Court of Chancery,[14] as opposed to broader ideas of 'equity'.[15] References to 'codes' are to the UCC and PPSAs. The words 'asset' and 'property' are used interchangeably.

II. INCONVENIENT CONCEPTS OF EQUITY

At one point in the history of codification of security interests equity earned a bad reputation owing to the restricted enforceability of equitable security interests. This led the drafters of Article 9 of the UCC to reject the concept of equitable security interests altogether, as we see below. English law does not share such concerns, but – as this section also shows – there are problems with equity's distinct solutions to priority conflicts.

[13] See Secured Transactions Law Reform Project, 'General Policy Paper' (2016) para [2.2], available at securedtransactionslawreformproject.org/draft-policy-paper; CLLS FLC, Draft Version of the Secured Transactions Code (2020), s 7 and Commentary, available at www.citysolicitors.org.uk/clls/committees/financial-law. There is a debate in English law whether a single concept of a security interest should follow the example of UCC and PPSAs, but this is not addressed here.

[14] See FW Maitland, *Equity: A Course of Lectures*, 2nd edn by J Brunyate (Cambridge, CUP, 1936) 12–22.

[15] For broader concepts of equity, see, eg, Aristotle, *Nichomachean Ethics*, Book V, T Taylor tr (London, Prometheus Trust, 2002) 1137b 7–10 and F Tudsbery, 'Equity and the Common Law' (1913) 29 *LQR* 154, 161.

A. Equitable Security Interests in Pre-UCC USA

The principal draftsman of Article 9 of the UCC, Professor Grant Gilmore, argued that 'the word "equitable" should, so far as possible, be avoided in legal writing (except as a useful device to obscure the issues)'.[16] He dismissed the term 'equitable' as unhelpful because the word carried a number of meanings, and deprecated the distinction between 'equitable' and 'legal' as obfuscating the discussion about proprietary interests.[17] Such criticisms are easily disregarded. First, the fact that a particular term has multiple meanings does not entail that no meaning is helpful.[18] Secondly, the dismissal of the use of the term 'equitable' is at odds with the fact that the UCC itself preserves the relevance of principles of law and equity as they continue to play a supplementary role.[19]

Nevertheless, such a spirited dismissal of the term 'equitable' is unsurprising considering that Article 9 UCC was based on the idea of functionalism, the core of which is to '[detach] the legal incidents associated with taking security from the parties' status and the formal label they place on their transaction'[20] and instead to draw distinctions along functional lines.

Gilmore's further issue with equitable interests is substantive and has more merit. He observed:

> In modern usage 'equitable', when attached to 'assignment', 'lien' and the like [meaning interests such as security interests], has come to have principally a pejorative meaning … nine times out of ten, to call an interest 'equitable' is a way of saying that, in this case, on these facts, it will not be enforced.[21]

It is easy to see why the enforceability of equitable interests in pre-code USA was problematic. Equitable security interests, like all equitable interests, are vulnerable to a bona fide purchaser defence. For example, where A grants a charge over an asset in favour of B, and A later transfers a legal interest in that asset to C, who is bona fide and unaware that the transfer is in breach of the terms of the charge with B, C – who would otherwise be bound by A's prior interest – may raise a defence against A's claim and hold the asset free of A's charge.[22] In practice, the availability of the defence turns on whether C has notice of B's interest, actual or constructive. Under pre-UCC law, the circumstances in which a person acquired notice of

[16] G Gilmore, *Security Interests in Personal Property* (London, Little, Brown, 1965) vol I, para [7.2], 200.

[17] ibid 199.

[18] See RS Summers, 'General Equitable Principles under Section 1–103 of the Uniform Commercial Code' (1978) 72 *Northwestern University Law Review* 906, 930.

[19] UCC, s 1–103. In his treatise, Gilmore makes a perfunctory mention of this section in the Preface, noting that UCC 'was not designed, as the European Codes may have been, to abolish the past, even on the level of semantics or vocabulary' (Gilmore (n 16) viii). However, he omits to consider this section entirely when discussing the relevance of equity (at para [7.2]).

[20] Cuming, Walsh and Wood (n 11) 6.

[21] Gilmore (n 16) 199. He also decried equitable interests as 'good only between the parties and against purchasers with notice'.

[22] For leading authority under English law, see *Pilcher v Rawlins* (1871–72) LR 7 Ch App 259 (CA) 266 and 269; *Akers v Samba* [2017] UKSC 6, [2017] AC 424 [65] (Lord Neuberger).

an equitable interest were limited.[23] Mortgages over after-acquired property (recognised by courts of equity, and not at law)[24] are a good example. Where a debtor agreed to mortgage goods to be acquired in the future (for example, wood once the mortgagor cuts timber into wood), the agreement could not create a mortgage at law until the asset was acquired but it was enforceable against the mortgagor and those claiming through him with actual notice such as execution creditors.[25] State laws made it possible to register such an agreement. However, registration did not constitute constructive notice to purchasers of the property.[26] Moreover, '[e]ven [actual] knowledge by the purchaser of the existence of such mortgage [did] not, in the absence of any fraudulent intent [on the part of the purchaser], prevent his holding the property as against the mortgagee not in possession'.[27]

Such a restrictive application of the bona fide purchaser defence must have been a deliberate policy levied against all non-possessory security interests that existed at the time in the USA. Until the early nineteenth century, the pledge and a mortgage with delivery of possession were the only types of security rights that could be taken over property other than land. Transfer or creation of an interest in personal property without delivery of possession was void as fraudulent conveyance[28] until state legislatures introduced registration as an alternative to delivery of possession.[29] But even then the distrust towards non-possessory security interests persisted.

Much of the concern about the enforceability of equitable interests seen in pre-code USA does not apply in England. One reason for this is the effect of registration on the doctrine of notice.[30] In English law, mortgages and charges created by companies[31] are registrable at Companies House.[32] Registration can be of relevance when determining whether a purchaser had constructive notice of such interests. In consequence, the circumstances in which such notice can be established, and therefore the circumstances in which equitable security interests bind purchasers, are wider than in pre-UCC USA. In addition, under English law, equitable mortgages and charges are enforceable against liquidators, administrators and against creditors who acquire property rights or interests in the encumbered assets such as execution creditors[33]

[23] J Long, 'Notice in Equity' (1921) 34 *Harvard Law Review* 137, 140–41, 151–60 (arguing that the cases of constructive notice are 'few and special', resting on 'own peculiar ground').

[24] See L Jones, *A Treatise on the Law of Mortgages on Personal Property*, 5th edn (Indianapolis, The Bobbs-Merrill Company, 1908) para [138].

[25] ibid para [156].

[26] The position was different under New York law: HF Stone, 'Equitable Mortgage in New York' (1920) 20 *Columbia Law Review* 519, 534.

[27] Jones (n 24) para [157].

[28] This was following the decision in *Twyne's Case* (1601) 3 Co Rep 80b, 76 ER 809.

[29] See, eg, the New York Lien Law, s 230 (repealed by UCC, Art 9).

[30] This point relates to registration under the Companies Act 2006. Registration at the High Court of security bills of sale under the Bills of Sale Acts 1878–82 is notice to those who actually search it but it is unlikely to be constructive notice because the register is paper-based, and is very difficult to search, see Law Commission, *Bills of Sale* (Law Com CP No 225, 2015) paras [1.35], [7.1], [10.1], and see, too, *Joseph v Lyons* (1884) 15 QBD 280 (CA) 286 (Cotton LJ).

[31] Or limited liability partnerships, but for simplicity, the discussion that follows is limited to companies.

[32] Companies Act 2006, s 859A.

[33] *Re Ashpurton Estates Ltd* [1983] Ch 110 (CA) 123 (Brightman LJ).

and lien holders[34] provided they are registered at Companies House.[35] This was not always the case in pre-UCC USA,[36] which further illustrates why Gilmore's criticisms levied against equitable interests might have been justified pre-UCC but are of limited relevance in England. Importantly, under English law, there is no difference on insolvency between equitable and legal security interests, subject to the separate regulation of the floating charge.[37] Yet, as shown immediately below, equitable security interests are problematic in English law in the sense that the application of equity's priority rules leaves much to be desired.

B. Is there a Need for Equity's Distinct Priority Rules?

There are a few issues with equitable security interests in English law, all relating to equity's solution to priority conflicts. The first, addressed in this section, is existential: it concerns the need for a distinct rule in equity to resolve priority conflicts. The second and third, discussed in the sections below, relate to the way in which the bona fide purchaser defence and the rule in *Dearle v Hall*[38] operate.

It is sometimes argued that common law and equitable rights differ fundamentally in terms of their publicity, and the ease with which their existence and content can be detected.[39] Equitable rights are said to be hidden, private arrangements, which may have idiosyncratic content that is hard for a purchaser to detect whereas legal property rights are thought to be public in the sense that the members of the public can expect their existence and can reasonably predict their shape thanks to the *numerus clausus* principle. One difficulty with this argument in the context of security rights is that legal security interests can be seen as just as hard to detect as equitable interests, and much harder than legal ownership. The point is illustrated by a comparison of

[34] RM Goode and L Gullifer, *Goode and Gullifer on Legal Problems of Credit and Security*, 6th edn (London, Sweet & Maxwell, 2018) para [2-23].

[35] This is the effect of section 859H of the Companies Act 2006, which invalidates security interests for want of registration. There is an argument that this section replaces equity's bona fide purchaser defence (A Nair and I Samet, 'What Can "Equity's Darling" Tell Us about Equity?' in D Klimchuk, I Samet and HE Smith (eds), *Philosophical Foundations of The Law of Equity* (Oxford, OUP, 2020) 264, 282) but this seems to overstate the matters because the defence would not have applied anyway: most parties mentioned in section 859H would not qualify as purchasers. For example, liquidators, administrators and execution creditors are not purchasers as they do not acquire any interest in the debtor's property: see *Maddell v Thomas & Co* [1891] 1 QB 230 (CA) 238 (Lopes LJ). The decision in *Maddell* related to trustees in bankruptcy and execution creditors but the same applies, a fortiori, to liquidators and administrators because, by contrast to trustees in bankruptcy (in whom the bankrupt's estate vests under the Insolvency Act 1986, s 306(1)), the company's assets do not automatically vest in the liquidator or an administrator. A liquidator becomes merely a custodian of the assets, although in compulsory winding up he or she can apply to the court for a vesting order: Insolvency Act 1986, s 145(1).

[36] See Gilmore (n 16) 445–49 and ch 45, especially 1311; see also G Glenn, 'The "Equitable Pledge", Creditors' Rights and the Chandler Act' (1939) 25 *Virginia Law Review* 422.

[37] The holder of a floating charge is subordinated to claims secured by a fixed security interest (whether legal or equitable), expenses of the insolvency proceedings and preferential creditors: Insolvency Act 1986, ss 175, 176A, 176ZA and Sch B1, paras 65(2), 99(3) and 116; see, too, *Re Nortel GmbH (in liq)* [2013] UKSC 52, [2014] AC 209 [39] per Lord Neuberger.

[38] (1828) 3 Russ 1, 38 ER 475.

[39] Nair and Samet (n 35) 264, 282.

legal mortgage and ownership. A person might be expected to know from observation alone that an item of property she comes across is owned but she cannot know that it is subject to a legal mortgage. This is because nearly all objects in the world are owned, so it is reasonable for her to expect that if she does not own the object, someone else will (ie, she knows if the property is not hers). By contrast, the incidence of legal mortgages is much lower, so it is not possible to tell, purely by looking at a piece of property, whether it is mortgaged in favour of another, especially since property does not generally bear markings indicating that it is encumbered.[40] In addition, creation of a legal mortgage can be just as hidden and private an arrangement as creation of an equitable security interest: in certain cases a mortgage can be created informally by agreement, without even a requirement for a deed (eg, legal mortgages over goods).[41]

It could perhaps be argued that a member of the public might be expected to know that a piece of property could be subject to any right on the closed list (*numerus clausus*) of property rights recognised in law. *Numerus clausus* captures the idea that a person can only create a property right if it corresponds in content to an established, recognised type of right.[42] The list includes legal property rights but not equitable interests,[43] at least in the sense that equitable interests are based on obligations and courts generally allow their incidents to be more freely shaped than those of legal property rights. Such an understanding of the list's content fits with the argument that a member of the public is expected to know of legal but not equitable interests, which in turn warrants equity's different priority solutions. It is not immediately obvious, however, why inclusion of rights on the list would mean that the public should expect their existence. Hansmann and Kraakman argue that such a general expectation, which they call a 'universal presumption', is a solution to the problem of publicising property rights to third parties (which they call a 'verification' problem).[44]

[40] There are exceptions. In the modern world this typically applies to assets which have their own registers. For example, a legal mortgage over uncertificated securities held through the CREST system requires transfer of the securities from the mortgagor's account to the mortgagee's account held with the CREST system.

[41] See, eg, *Flory v Denny* (1852) 7 Exch 581, 155 ER 1080. Legal mortgages of goods requiring formalities for the purpose of their creation are exceptional, eg those created by non-corporate debtors (under the Bills of Sale Acts 1878–82) and mortgages over registered ships (under the Merchant Shipping Act 1995). Note that while legal mortgages created by companies are registrable under the Companies Act 2006, s 859A, such registration is not part of their creation.

[42] See, eg, B Rudden, 'Economic Theory v Property Law: The *Numerus Clausus* Problem' in J Bell and J Eekelaar (eds), *Oxford Essays in Jurisprudence: Third Series* (Oxford, Clarendon Press, 1987) ch 11, 244–45, citing, among others, *Keppell v Bailey* (1834) 2 My & K 517, 535–36; 39 ER 1042, 1049 (Brougham LC); *Hill v Tupper* (1863) 2 H & C 121, 127–28; 159 ER 51, 53 (Pollock CB). See, too, M Heller, 'Boundaries of Property' (1999) 108 *Yale Law Journal* 1163; T Merrill and H Smith, 'Optimal Standardization in the Law of Property: The *Numerus Clausus* Principle' (2000) 110 *Yale Law Journal* 1; H Hansmann and R Kraakman, 'Property, Contract, and Verification: The *Numerus Clausus* Problem and the Divisibility of Rights' (2002) 31 *The Journal of Legal Studies* S373.

[43] See, eg, L Smith, 'Trust and Patrimony' (2008) 38 *Revue Générale de Droit* 379, 394; B McFarlane and R Stevens, 'The Nature of Equitable Property' (2010) 4 *Journal of Equity* 1, 2; *cf* S Gardner, '"Persistent Rights" Appraised' in N Hopkins (ed), *Modern Studies in Property Law* (Oxford, Hart, 2013) vol 7, 321, 331; R Nolan, 'Equitable Property' (2006) 122 *LQR* 232, 260–61.

[44] Hansmann and Kraakman (n 42).

Such a general expectation can work as an effective notice to the public presumably[45] because people are motivated to learn about rules that bind them. This in turn ensures that they are not misled about the rights of others, and make uses of assets and assert rights that are consistent with the right-holder's entitlement. But, as Hansmann and Kraakman note, such a general expectation is not the only way in which property rights on the *numerus clausus* list can be discovered by third parties. Other ways include registration and delivery of possession.[46] English law already makes provision for such means of publicising legal security interests: delivery of possession in relation to the pledge, and registration – for nearly all non-possessory security interests (legal as well as equitable).[47] It cannot, therefore, be the case that the reason a legal security interest is effective against third parties is because it is part of the *numerus clausus*. Lack of registration at Companies House invalidates legal and equitable security interests alike for certain purposes at least,[48] which undermines an argument that there is a fundamental difference between legal and equitable interests in this area.

C. The Bona Fide Purchaser Defence

The bona fide purchaser defence[49] comes at a hefty price of limited predictability and therefore, an inflated risk of litigation. Elsewhere in law there may be good reasons for preserving equity's distinct solutions to priority conflicts but in the context of security rights any benefits of the defence, it is argued, are outweighed by the costs. Let us see why.

Key to the operation of this defence is the concept of notice. Under the general law, a purchaser (C) has constructive notice of a right of another (B) and takes subject to it 'if [he] knows of certain facts which put him on inquiry as to the possible existence of the rights of that other and he fails to make such inquiry or take such other steps as are reasonable to verify whether such earlier right does or does not exist'.[50] The failure to make reasonable enquiries could be deliberate[51] or careless.[52] Carelessness includes situations where a reasonable person in the position of the purchaser would have a 'serious cause' to investigate but the purchaser fails to do so.[53] This means the

[45] Hansmann and Kraakman do not explain why a universal presumption would work as an effective notice.

[46] They also include labelling and explicit contracting among the 'verification' rules: Hansmann and Kraakman (n 42) S385.

[47] Companies Act 2006, s 859A. Security interests in goods granted by non-corporate debtors are registered at the High Court under the Bills of Sale Acts 1878–82.

[48] See text accompanying nn 31–35.

[49] An example of the defence is set out above: see the text accompanying n 22.

[50] *Barclays Banks plc v O'Brien* [1994] 1 AC 180 (HL) 195–96 (Lord Browne-Wilkinson). See, too, *Sinclair Investments (UK) Ltd v Versailles Trade Finance Ltd* [2011] EWCA Civ 347, [2012] Ch 453 [100] (Lord Neuberger MR); *Papadimitriou v Crédit Agricole Corp and Investment Bank* [2015] UKPC 13, [2015] 1 WLR 4265 [19]–[21] (Lord Clarke).

[51] See, eg, *Jones v Smith* (1841) 1 Hare 43, 55; 66 ER 943, 948.

[52] See, eg, *Oliver v Hinton* [1899] 2 Ch 264 (CA); *Hudson v Viney* [1921] 1 Ch 98 (Ch).

[53] *Papadimitriou* (n 50) [20] (Lord Clarke).

court considers the circumstances in which the purchaser finds herself, including her own attributes.[54]

Such an exercise comes at a cost of greater unpredictability of outcome, and increased likelihood of litigation and judicial mistake. But the costs are generally worth paying because the defence is desirable as a matter of justice (since it facilitates eg, detailed enquiries into the purchaser's mind)[55] and – it is submitted – because it is systemically efficient in the following sense.[56] The circumstances in which a purchaser might acquire rights in property can be varied and unpredictable, and it would be impracticable, if not impossible, for a legal system to provide priority rules for every occasion if the objective is to achieve a balance between the interests of the two innocents (B and C). It would simply be too costly for courts or the legislature to devise, and for the users of a legal system to use, a plethora of priority rules.

In the context of secured transactions, however, the circumstances in which priority conflicts between B and C arise are in many ways predictable. It is not unusual for a company to have multiple dealings in relation to its assets, for example, by creating multiple security interests in the same assets in favour of different parties over time (say, C, D, E etc). Such dealings are not surprising because a security interest in an asset generally confers on the creditor a right to benefit from the asset only in part, ie, only to the extent needed to enforce the discharge of the debtor's obligation to the creditor. Since security interests are generally registered, the issue that any judge would need to consider in a dispute where C raises equity's bona fide purchaser defence is whether C had actual or constructive notice of B's registered interest. The question in practice is, then, whether C had a 'serious cause' to check the register. The type of right that C acquires is a circumstance that the court needs to consider in every dispute. The key question is, however, when C's acquisition of the right alone gives her a serious cause to check the register. Unfortunately, there is a dearth of authority on this point. The view prevailing in the literature, based on first principles, is that a creditor taking a charge or mortgage registrable at Companies House would, in normal circumstances, be expected to search the Companies House register whereas a buyer purchasing an asset in the ordinary course of business from the debtor would not.[57] It is less clear whether a creditor taking a pledge[58] or a security financial collateral arrangement[59] ought reasonably to search the register: such

[54] ibid (Lord Clarke).

[55] Nair and Samet (n 35) 284–86.

[56] For other arguments favouring efficiency of the bona fide purchaser defence, see Nair and Samet (n 35) 287–89.

[57] Goode and Gullifer (n 34) para [2-31]; E Ferran and L Ho, *Principles of Corporate Finance Law*, 2nd edn (Oxford, OUP, 2014) 344; G McCormack, *Secured Credit under English and American Law* (Cambridge, CUP, 2004) 106–07; R Calnan, *Taking Security*, 4th edn (Bristol, Jordan Publishing, 2018) paras [8.290]–[8.304]. For a contrary view, see W Gough, *Company Charges*, 2nd edn (London, Butterworths, 1996) 836 and generally ch 32 (arguing that registration is notice to the world) and see rebuttal in H Beale, M Bridge, L Gullifer and E Lomnicka, *The Law of Security and Title-Based Financing*, 3rd edn (Oxford, OUP, 2018) paras [12.04]–[12.14].

[58] Pledges are not registrable because they are not charges or mortgages, to which the Companies Act 2006, s 859A applies.

[59] Companies Act 2006, s 859A(6)(c) *juncto* Financial Collateral Arrangements (No 2) Regulations 2003 (SI 2003/3226), Reg 4(4).

creditors engage in secured finance, much like chargees (pointing to an expectation to search), but unlike chargees, they take unregistrable security rights (which suggests, probably more strongly, that they are not expected to search). Nevertheless, even if case law existed telling us whether a purchaser (eg, a creditor) acquiring a particular right was expected to search the register, this would not give us the certainty needed because constructive notice cannot be established in the abstract. This lack of predictable outcomes is unfortunate. We should be able to know in advance whether a purchaser acquiring a right from the debtor is expected to search the register. Both the existence of a registered right and the purchaser's acquisition of a right from the debtor are circumstances that are knowable in advance and it is a missed opportunity not to have a priority rule telling us how to balance them.

In addition, this uncertainty generates unnecessary costs for individual lenders. The reason is that, in practice, cautious lenders and other financiers will search the register and, on discovery of a registered right, enter into a subordination agreement with the right-holder. This, in turn, comes at a cost, which might be avoided with more certain priority rules.

D. The Rule in *Dearle v Hall*

A further example of an undesirable priority rule stemming from equity is the rule in *Dearle v Hall*.[60] It governs the priority of successive assignments, including assignments by way of security, in the following way. Assume that X owes a contractual debt to A, who assigns that right to B and then to C. The priority between the assignees (B and C) depends on the order in which notice of the assignment is given to the debtor (X) provided that a subsequent assignee giving notice (eg, C) does not know of the earlier assignment (eg, that to B) at the time of taking its assignment or when it provides consideration. The rule stems from cases involving assignments of equitable interests under trusts where it was necessary to give notice to the trustee.[61] It has since been applied much more widely: to both equitable and statutory assignments,[62] absolute and by way of security,[63] and to assignments of legal choses in action[64] as well as equitable interests.

The problems with the rule in *Dearle v Hall* are well known[65] and the key issues can be stated here briefly. First, the rationale for the rule has never been clear.[66] It is

[60] *Dearle v Hall* (n 38); see also Law of Property Act 1925, s 137(1).

[61] *Dearle v Hall* (n 38); *Foster v Cockerell* (1835) 3 Cl & F 456, 6 ER 1508.

[62] *E Pfeiffer Weinkellerei-Weineinkauf GmbH & Co v Arbuthnot Factors Ltd* [1987] BCLC 522 (QB) 533 (obiter); *Compaq Computer Ltd v Abercorn Group Ltd* [1993] BCLC 602 (Ch) 621–22 (obiter). See also *Harding Carpets Ltd v Royal Bank of Canada* [1980] 4 WWR 149 (Manitoba QB).

[63] *Colonial Mutual General Insurance Co Ltd v ANZ Banking Group (New Zealand) Ltd* [1995] 1 WLR 1140 (PC) 1144; *Pfeiffer* (n 62); *Compaq* (n 62).

[64] *Marchant v Morton Down & Co* [1901] 2 KB 829 (KBD).

[65] For fuller discussion, see, eg, F Oditah, *Legal Aspects of Receivables Financing* (London, Sweet & Maxwell, 1991) 140–42; C Brown, 'Preserving Priority in Receivable Financing: Time to Revisit *Dearle v Hall*' [1995] *Journal of International Banking and Financial Law* 3; McCormack (n 57) 244–45; Goode and Gullifer (n 34) para [5-08]; Beale and others, *The Law of Security and Title-Based Financing* (n 57) para [14.10].

[66] *Ward v Duncombe* [1893] AC 369 (HL) 387, 394 (Lord Macnaghten).

said to be based on the principle that giving notice equates to taking possession of the debt.[67] This might have worked as an (anomalous[68]) extension of the reputed ownership doctrine, but the doctrine has since been applied narrowly and was eventually abolished.[69] In any case, taking possession is not needed to pass property in goods, nor to create a legal mortgage over goods. The analogy with possession is best understood as a means of protecting third parties (assignees such as C) from being misled by the appearance of (A's) ownership of the debt.[70] But this is surprising considering that the rule applies irrespective of whether C made any enquiries,[71] so C need not actually be misled. It also only protects C if C herself gives notice (and thus only if she ensures further third parties are not misled); C is not protected solely because B failed to give notice.[72]

Further concern is that *Dearle v Hall* does not always lead to just outcomes.[73] For example, where an assignee (C) makes an advance to A not knowing of an earlier assignment by B but learns about it subsequently, and then gives notice to the debtor, she is not barred from taking priority over B.[74] This means that the rule fails to prevent 'people jumping in and taking advantage of a technical failure to give notice', which is the very thing the second limb of *Dearle v Hall* sought to prevent.[75]

Another problem is that it can lead to circularity. For example, if A makes multiple successive assignments, eg assigns first to B, then to C, and finally to D, and D gives notice to the debtor (X) before B or C give notice, when D knows about the prior assignment to C but not to B, D takes priority over B but not over C, while B takes priority over C under the first-in-time rule which applies where neither assignee gave notice. In result, the order of priority is C, D, B, C.

Further, the rule is not suited to modern receivables financing because it is not practicable (too expensive and time-consuming), especially in bulk assignments and assignments of future receivables, for financiers to give notice to debtors. The problem is not easily solved. For example, X might agree in a contract with A to a waiver of notice. In doing so, X might be able to remove the protections safeguarded by notice that apply to him (eg, those relating to set-off) but not those that apply to other people. If notice is required under priority rules to protect assignees from being misled by the appearance of A's ownership,[76] a term in a contract between A and X waiving the need to notify X will not remove the protection that the law confers upon assignees (B, C, D etc). This would not, therefore, be an effective way to work around

[67] *Dearle v Hall* (n 38) 22 (Sir Thomas Plumer MR).

[68] Oditah (n 65) 130.

[69] Insolvency Act 1986, Sch 10. For an excellent discussion of the doctrine's development, see F Stolker, 'The Rise and Fall of the Reputed Ownership Clause' (MSt, University of Oxford, 2016).

[70] *Dearle v Hall* (n 38) 24 (Sir Thomas Plumer MR).

[71] *Ward* (n 66) 387, 390–91 (Lord Macnaghten); Beale and others, *The Law of Security and Title-Based Financing* (n 57) para [14.10].

[72] *cf* Sale of Goods Act 1979, s 21(1): in the context of transfer of property in goods, a defence based on apparent ownership is not dependent on the disponee taking herself possession of the goods.

[73] See *Ward* (n 66) 393 (Lord Macnaghten).

[74] *Mutual Life Assurance Society v Langley* (1886) 32 Ch D 460 (CA).

[75] *Rhodes v Allied Dunbar (Pension Services) Ltd* [1987] 1 WLR 1703 (Ch) 1708, reversed [1989] 1 All ER 1161 (CA) but not on this point, and see Oditah (n 65) 133.

[76] See text accompanying nn 67–70.

the rule in *Dearle v Hall*. Each financier-assignee might of course choose not to give notice (as tends to happen in invoice-discounting as opposed to factoring of receivables), or assignees might agree between themselves to contract out of *Dearle v Hall* as it applies to them, but this will not stop possible further assignees from relying on the rule.

Where the first assignment (the assignment to B) is by way of security, and A is a company, the impact of the rule may be abated if the assignment is registered at Companies House because C may then have constructive notice of the first assignment.[77] However, the operation of the doctrine of constructive notice in priority conflicts is problematic.[78]

E. Solution: The New Principles

In codified secured transaction regimes the problems caused by equity's priority rules are solved by a suite of new principles.[79] The general principle is that priority between creditors taking security with respect to the same asset depends on the order of perfection, not the order of the date of creation.[80] Since perfection often takes place by registration in the register of security rights, priority is usually determined by the date of registration,[81] but the same generally applies to perfection by other means. For example, if one security interest is perfected by registration and another by possession, the one to perfect earlier prevails.[82] Exceptions do exist. For example, a security interest perfected by control prevails in some systems over one perfected by registration.[83] This is because a creditor taking control over financial assets generally takes security specifically over financial assets whereas a creditor perfecting only by registration generally takes a security interest over all of the debtor's assets which happen to include financial assets.[84]

The departure from the principles established in equity is clear.[85] First, the distinction between legal and equitable interests is irrelevant when determining priority. Second, priority conflicts can now be determined by the application of a simple rule, rather than requiring an investigation into a creditor's mind. Some PPSAs even provide that registration is not constructive notice of the existence or content of the registered security interest.[86] In result, the application of new principles offers more predictability than equity's priority rules.

[77] Beale and others, *The Law of Security and Title-Based Financing* (n 57) para [14.10].
[78] See the text accompanying nn 50–59.
[79] The statutory rules also replace, and solve the difficulties presented by, priority rules developed in common law, but these are not discussed here.
[80] See, eg, SPPSA, s 35(1); OPPSA, s 30(1); Cuming, Walsh and Wood (n 11) 419.
[81] See, eg, UCC, s 9–322; SPPSA, s 35; draft Secured Transactions Code (n 13), s 38.4.
[82] SPPSA, s 35; UCC, s 9–322.
[83] UCC, s 9–328.
[84] H Beale, 'An Outline of a Typical PPSA Scheme' in L Gullifer and O Akseli (eds), *Secured Transactions Law Reform: Principles, Policies and Practice* (Oxford, Hart, 2016) 7, 14.
[85] See *Warehouse Sales* (n 11) [27]–[32] (Sifris J) (referring to a paradigm shift from established principles).
[86] See, eg, SPPSA, s 47.

Such a change of priority rules comes at a hefty price of legislative reform but, if the number of jurisdictions that have already reformed their priority rules in secured transactions along these lines is anything to go by,[87] it is a price worth paying.

III. THE CONTINUING RELEVANCE OF EQUITY'S DISTINCT SOLUTIONS

Having seen that secured transactions codes reject equity's solutions to priority conflicts, it is important to notice principles in those codes that preserve the genius of equity, even if they do not do so by preserving the exact concepts.[88] This analysis is important for at least two reasons. First, it matters in practice because the UCC and PPSAs generally provide expressly that common law and equitable principles supplement the statute and continue to apply unless they are inconsistent with the statute.[89] Identifying whether a codification preserves principles underpinning equitable doctrines helps inform the question of whether there is an inconsistency between an equitable principle and the codification. Where no such inconsistency exists, equitable principles may well apply to resolve an issue not governed by the codification. Secondly, as a matter of conceptual analysis, this section shows that it is an overstatement to claim, as some appear to,[90] that the statutory character of a codified security interest necessarily precludes equitable features of such an interest.

The central concept of a security interest in PPSAs has been characterised as having the following features of an equitable charge. Where the debtor has or will have rights in property, the debtor and the creditor may agree that the creditor acquires an interest in the property by way of security. The debtor's rights are 'charged or to be charged with or encumbered with an interest granted in favour of the creditor for the purpose of securing performance of an obligation'.[91] This means that creation of a codified security interest, similarly to a charge, involves creation of a new right in favour of the creditor.

Another example relates to securing interests in future assets. PPSAs state that where the parties provide for a security interest in after-acquired property, the security interest attaches to that property without specific appropriation by the debtor, once the debtor has acquired rights in the asset (or a power to transfer rights in the asset to

[87] The idea that priority of security rights depends in most cases on registration has been adopted in a number of civil law as well as common law jurisdictions, see generally, eg, M Dubovec, 'UCC Article 9 Registration System for Latin America' (2011) 28 *Arizona Journal of International and Comparative Law* 117; M Dubovec and L Gullifer, *Secured Transactions Law Reform in Africa* (Oxford, Hart, 2019) 28–29; L Gullifer, 'Conclusion' in L Gullifer and D Neo (eds), *Secured Transactions Law in Asia. Principles, Perspectives and Reform* (Oxford, Hart, 2021) 425, 462–64.

[88] The idea that equity's solutions are 'distinct' refers here to the uniqueness of equity's rules by comparison to those applied by common law courts, and not by comparison to other jurisdictions across the world. The solutions discussed in this section are also found in (reformed) civil law jurisdictions, but it is unlikely that equitable principles were an inspiration for them, at least not directly and not uniquely.

[89] UCC, s 1–103; SPPSA, s 65(2); APPSA, s 66(3); OPPSA, s 72; *cf* AusPPSA s 254.

[90] L Widdup, *Personal Property Securities Act: Concepts in Practice*, 4th edn (Wellington, LexisNexis, 2016) para [2.6], citing JS Ziegel and DL Denomme, *The Ontario Personal Property Security Act: Commentary and Analysis*, 1st edn (Toronto, LexisNexis, 1994) 44.

[91] Cuming, Walsh and Wood (n 11) 118.

the secured creditor) and value has been provided.[92] This tracks very closely the principles that developed in equity, which dispensed with the common law requirement of a further act once the debtor acquired the property.[93] In addition, the equitable principles in this area continue to play a supplementary role where the codified regime does not provide for a rule to regulate priority conflicts. Assume that debtor creates two successive security interests in a car it intends to buy in favour of two creditors: C on Monday, and D on Tuesday. On Wednesday, the debtor acquires the car. If the security interests are registered they will rank in order of registration. However, if neither security interest is perfected, the interests would rank in order of attachment[94] (here, both on Wednesday). Where attachment is simultaneous, one Canadian authority suggests that priority is determined with reference to the dates of creation of the security interests, ie, the dates of the security agreements.[95] This conclusion was based on principles of equity, which the court considered were 'not inconsistent with the express provision of [the PPSA]'.[96]

In some areas, the law may have been re-written, but achievements of equity are functionally preserved. PPSAs and the UCC do not contain a distinct idea of a floating charge in the way that English law does. However, PPSAs recognise that a debtor may have the 'right or ability' to dispose of goods or funds in the ordinary course of its business and the buyer, lessee or transferee may take free of the security interest.[97] In relation to assets not normally disposed of in the ordinary course of business, the security agreement may confer the 'right' to dispose of free of the security interest. This is similar to the debtor's authority to dispose free from a charge under a floating charge prior to crystallisation under English law.[98] Yet, despite the functional similarity equitable principles applicable to floating charges cannot generally apply to a codified security interest because they would be inconsistent with the deliberate abolition of the distinction between fixed and floating charges.[99]

IV. IS A CODIFIED SECURITY INTEREST LEGAL OR EQUITABLE?

Priority conflicts are some of the more difficult issues which are not governed by the codified regime and to which principles of common law or equity might apply. For example, codifications do not generally regulate priority conflicts between security interests and non-consensual proprietary interests[100] such as common law and

[92] SPPSA, s 13 *juncto* s 12.

[93] *Holroyd v Marshall* (1862) 10 HL Cas 191, 11 ER 999; *Tailby v Official Receiver* (1888) 13 App Cas 523 (HL).

[94] SPPSA, s 35(1), OPPSA, s 30(1).

[95] *National Bank of Canada v Merit Energy Ltd* [2001] 10 WWR 305 (Alberta QB) [47]. See, too, *Royal Bank of Canada v Radius Credit Union Ltd* 2010 SCC 48, [2010] 3 SCR 38.

[96] APPSA, s 66(3).

[97] UCC, ss 9–205 and 9-320; SPPSA, s 30 and note s 31(2); *cf* AusPPSA, s 340.

[98] Beale (n 84) 16–17.

[99] New Zealand Law Commission, *A Personal Property Securities Act for New Zealand* (Report No 8, Wellington, 1989) 80; *Royal Bank of Canada v Sparrow Electric Corp* [1997] 1 SCR 411.

[100] There are some exceptions: see, eg, APPSA, s 32; OPPSA, ss 20(1)(a)(i) and 31, AusPPSA, ss 73–74.

equitable liens, statutory liens, statutory trusts and constructive trusts. If a statute or body of law under which the non-consensual interest arises provides a rule resolving a conflict with a consensual security interest, that rule should apply.[101] But if neither the code nor the statute lay down a rule, a solution is sought by applying the rules of common law and equity, as directed by the provision stating their supplementary role.[102] This requires us to characterise the codified security interest as legal or equitable, thinking from first principles, for the purpose of applying the priority rules under the general law.[103] There are three possible characterisations: legal interest, equitable interest, or either legal or equitable depending on the context. This section considers these alternatives.

A. An Equitable Interest

The idea that a codified interest is to be deemed equitable for the purpose of priority conflicts is easily dismissed. It was seen earlier[104] that there are a number of difficulties with equity's distinct priority rules, making the priority of the security interest undesirably unpredictable and vulnerable.

B. Legal or Equitable Depending on General Law

There is a view, expressed in the context of the Australian PPSA, that for the purpose of resolving a priority conflict, a statutory security interest ought to be characterised as either legal or equitable, depending on whether as a matter of general law it would operate as a legal or equitable interest.[105] A similar approach was suggested at one point in the draft Secured Transactions Code proposal in England. The proposal has since been abandoned, but it is worth setting it out here to illustrate what this option might look like:

> A [security interest] is a legal interest in the … [encumbered] asset concerned if:
>
> (a) the … asset is an interest in registered land, and the charge is a registered charge at Her Majesty's Land Registry; or
>
> (b) the … asset is an interest in unregistered land, and the … [security interest] takes effect as a charge by way of legal mortgage; or
>
> (c) the … [secured creditor] holds legal title to the … asset; or
>
> (d) the charge is a possessory charge [ie the creditor takes possession of the asset].[106]

[101] RJ Wood, 'Supplementing PPSA Priorities: The Use and Abuse of Common Law and Equitable Principles' (2014) 56 *Canadian Business Law Journal* 31, 38.

[102] See text accompanying n 89.

[103] ibid 33.

[104] See the discussion in section II.D.

[105] A Waldman, 'Resolving Priority Competitions Between PPSA Security Interests and Non-PPS Interests' (2021) 44 *University of New South Wales Law Journal* 811, 834–35.

[106] Draft Secured Transactions Code (n 13) s 3.1.

In practice, the characterisation of a codified security interest as either legal or equitable seems simple enough where security agreements contain traditional (pre-PPSA) forms of charging clauses and such clauses are capable of giving rise to the intended form of security. However, a mere agreement is not always sufficient and a formality is needed. In such situations, parties would need to ensure they fulfil the requirements of two legal regimes: the pre-code and the code requirements. This would create a 'dual system for determining claims over shared collateral over personal property'[107] and would, therefore, add to the unsatisfactory complexity of the law. It should also be added that, in English law, priority rules under the Land Registration Act 2002, similarly, do not depend on the legal/equitable distinction: neither the basic rule under section 28 of the Act nor its qualifications under section 29 depend on legal and equitable rights. For these reasons it was abandoned in the debate on English secured transactions law reform.

In addition, for PPSA systems to import the legal/equitable distinction would contradict one of the key principles underpinning PPSAs: the unitary approach to security.[108] It is possible to apply the unitary approach more narrowly, by stipulating that where a priority conflict arises under the PPSA, the security interests are governed by the same rules, but that for purposes outside the Act the legal/equitable characterisation remains.[109] Such an approach is popular with some writers in Australia[110] considering the wording of the Australian PPSA but, it is suggested, it should not be followed elsewhere due to the complexities it is likely to generate.

C. A Legal Interest

The general view is that a codified security interest under a PPSA regime is a legal interest. A good illustration is the decision by the Supreme Court of Canada in two joint appeals, *Bank of Montreal v Innovation Credit Union*[111] and *Royal Bank of Canada v Radius Credit Union Ltd.*[112] The Court considered the nature of a security interest under the relevant PPSA in the context of a priority dispute between a prior security interest and a subsequently acquired statutory interest arising under the (Canadian) Bank Act.[113] The Court held:

> Two characteristics of the PPSA are relevant for the present case. First, it is clear that *PPSA* security interest, just as the Bank Act security interest, is a statutorily created interest and, as such, an interest recognized at law. While some of the historical forms of security created

[107] J Stumbles, 'The PPSA: The Extended Reach of the Definition of the PPSA Security Interest' (2011) 34 *University of New South Wales Law Journal* 448, 455 (in the context of PPSA).
[108] See the text accompanying nn 11–12.
[109] Waldman (n 106) 835.
[110] See, eg, D Loxton, S McCracken and A Boxall, 'PPSA Models: A Minimalist Approach' (2018) 32 *Commercial Law Quarterly* 3, 4–5; A McCracken, J Stumbles and GJ Tolhurst, 'Title Transfers Collateral Arrangements under the Personal Property Securities Act 2009 (Cth): Paper I, Setting the Scene' (2015) 33 *Journal of Contract Law* 1, 8.
[111] (n 11).
[112] (n 95).
[113] SC 1991, c 46.

> equitable rather than legal interests, the effect of the PPSA's functional approach, which covers all of these antecedent security interests, is to treat them all equally as 'security interests' under the PPSA.[114]

The dictum reveals two key reasons for characterising the security interest as legal in nature. One is formal: that prior to the Judicature Acts 1873–75 statutory rights were enforced by a common law court, so a statutory interest must be a legal interest.[115] This is an odd argument to make now that one set of courts administers both common law and equity. It also overlooks the fact that the Chancery could also, of course, enforce legislation in matters that came before it.[116] The Court's second reason is more convincing. It is premised on the idea that all security interests are to be treated the same;[117] such a unitary approach has the advantage of simplicity as pre-code distinctions become redundant.[118] And, given the choice between equitable or legal, treating them as legal avoids the unpredictability associated with priority of equitable interests.

Characterising a PPSA interest as a legal interest is not without its problems. It might produce some 'commercially absurd results'.[119] For example, an unregistered (and so, unperfected) security interest, which is created first, might win over a registered, but later-in-time, non-PPSA interest. The drawbacks of such characterisation could be ameliorated where the holder of an unperfected security interest can be said to have constructive notice of a registered non-PPSA interest. Resorting to constructive notice doctrine would depend, however, on the statute or body of law governing the effect of registration of the *non*-PPSA interest.

In other situations, characterisation of a PPSA interest as a legal interest in priority conflicts might produce odd results, too. There are two answers to this. One is that we ought to be prepared to question our assumptions to test why a particular result seems odd. This is illustrated below.[120] The second is that courts should be willing to resolve priority conflicts in alternative ways, for example through the notion of an implied consent. Consider the following example. A creates a security interest in favour of B in an asset on day 1. On day 2, a non-consensual statutory lien arises in favour of C over the same asset. Applying the *nemo dat* rule, B wins over C because B was first. However, if it can be argued that B's security interest is such that B expressly or impliedly consents to a lien (or some other interest) arising in favour

[114] *Innovation Credit Union* (n 11) [42] (Charron J for the Court), cited in *Diversa* (n 11) [237]; *Hamersley Iron* (n 11) [358].

[115] Surprisingly, the argument seems to have been adopted without criticism in the literature, see Cuming, Walsh and Wood (n 11) 515; D Loxton, 'New Bottle for Old Wine? The Characterisation of PPSA Security Interests' (2012) 23 *Journal of Banking and Finance Law and Practice* 163, 180–81 and S McCracken, 'The Personal Property Security Interest: Identifying Some Essential Attributes' (2014) 30 *Law in Context: A Socio-Legal Journal* 146, 165.

[116] See, eg, *Re Lake* (1872–73) LR 8 Ch App 51 (CA).

[117] See also Stumbles (n 108) 454.

[118] Note, for example, that Canadian courts made it clear they are reluctant to apply pre-code characterisations. See, eg, *Sparrow Electric* (n 99) [54]–[56] (Gonthier J), [110]–[111] (Iacobucci J, in the majority) (characterising the PPSA security interest as a fixed interest even though under pre-PPSA law it would be floating, with both the majority and the minority agreeing on this point).

[119] *Innovation Credit Union* (n 11) [4].

[120] See the discussion in section IV.D.

of C, C wins over B.[121] An implication of consent is likely to be rare as that clearly weakens B's secured position for which it bargained. However, this reasoning, while at times artificial, might help avoid unsatisfactory results in egregious cases.

D. Example: Secured Creditor v Trust Beneficiary

PPSAs do not generally contain rules for the resolution of disputes between a creditor holding a security interest and a beneficiary under a trust, whether express, constructive or resulting. An exception is where a trust is created for security purposes and so satisfies the (broad) definition of a security interest,[122] in which case the usual PPSA priority rules apply. Most trusts are not created for security purposes. Let us see what issues arise where a PPSA interest is characterised as a legal interest.[123]

Consider the following example:

> **Example 1:** On day 1, C becomes a trustee of certain shares for B. On day 2, in breach of trust, C creates a security interest in favour of A over the same shares. When A comes to enforce its security interest, B claims that A may not do so as the shares are trust property.

In the absence of a statutory rule, the dispute between A and B is resolved according to the general law. B might argue that prima facie A comes under a duty to B not to use its rights, as a secured creditor, inconsistently with the terms of the trust.[124] A might argue that B consented to the security interest, or that A does not come under a duty to B. For example, A might seek to raise a defence of bona fide purchaser of the legal interest if it had no notice of the breach of trust, and in so doing, escape the imposition of the duty not to use its rights inconsistently with the trust. Trusts are not registrable, and notice of a breach of trust will not always be easy to establish, so the bona fide purchaser defence may well be available to A.

The matters are less straightforward where a security interest relates to future assets. Consider the following:

> **Example 2:** On day 1, X transfers property in shares to Y on trust for C. On day 2, B creates in favour of A a security interest in present and future assets to secure a loan A makes to B. The interest is duly registered in a personal property security register. On day 3, B acquires shares from Y in a transaction which was not authorised by the terms of the trust. B defaults on the loan, and both A and C claim the shares.

C's beneficial interest in the shares is first in time, suggesting C wins. However, A could argue that, under a PPSA, it holds a legal interest in the after-acquired property,[125] enabling A to raise a bona fide purchaser defence. There is a question whether A might be said to have had constructive notice of C's equitable interest

[121] See *Fisk v Attorney General* [2016] NZHC 479, [2016] NZAR 551.
[122] Cuming, Walsh and Wood (n 11) 514.
[123] For further detail see ibid 514–16.
[124] See, eg, *Williams & Glyn's Bank Ltd v Boland* [1981] AC 487 (HL).
[125] In PPSAs, there is no difference in characterisation between a security interest in existing property and one in after-acquired property: Cuming, Walsh and Wood (n 11) 262.

but this is improbable for two reasons: first, making enquiries into the existence of (non-registrable) interests beyond the register is unlikely to be reasonable; second, the logic of PPSA is to do away with the doctrine of constructive notice. This means that unless A obtains actual knowledge of C's interest, for example, by conducting inquiries, A will not have notice of C's equitable interest. In result, A wins over C.

This result seems surprising. Under pre-code law, A's interest in after-acquired property is equitable,[126] so it would not generally be open to A to invoke a bona fide purchaser rule;[127] C would win over A. The different result under a PPSA prompts us to ask whether the nature of a codified security interest is sufficiently different to warrant A benefitting from a bona fide purchaser rule. Intuitively, the answer is 'no' because in a codified system A does not seem to be more worthy than she would have been under pre-code law. The only thing that has changed is the codification and characterisation of A's interest. In line with this intuition, there is a view that the scope of the bona fide purchaser rule ought to be limited, so it would not apply in circumstances of Example 2. The reasoning, suggested in passing by Cuming, Walsh and Wood, is based on a particular (and uncommon) rationale for the bona fide purchaser defence,[128] namely that it protects individuals against unfair prejudice they would suffer if they could not benefit from an interest in property for which they paid the price.[129] It might seem that A in Example 1 suffers such a prejudice whereas in Example 2 she does not because she does not specifically pay for *that* asset, or that she takes a risk that a future asset might never be acquired. This might perhaps work where a creditor takes a security interest over all present and future assets as a security that 'sweeps' any assets not subject to other people's interests. However, such reasoning is harder to justify in other cases of lending against future assets where the creditor may well be lending the money on the faith that a future asset will be acquired. Since an enquiry in each case into whether a creditor specifically pays for future assets would be too costly, it seems more desirable to assume she does so pay.

A better way to view this issue is to flip the question and ask why, in a pre-PPSA system, a creditor taking a security over after-acquired property (and therefore necessarily an equitable interest) should be in any worse position than a creditor taking a legal mortgage. We have already seen[130] that there are no fundamental differences

[126] See *Holroyd v Marshall* (n 93); *Tailby* (n 93) 545–49; in Canada: *Lloyd v European and North American Railway Co* (1878) 18 NBR 194 (New Brunswick CA) 206–07 (Allen CJ), cited in *Lite Enterprises Ltd v Atlantic Power Lines Ltd* (1978) 24 NBR (2d) 607 (New Brunswick QB) [8] (Stevenson J); *Vassie v Vassie* (1882) 22 NBR 76 (New Brunswick Supreme Court).

[127] *Story v Lord Windsor* (1743) 2 Atk 630, 631; 26 ER 776, 777 but see, eg, *Pinkett v Wright* (1842) 2 Hare 120, 165, 67 ER 50, 56; *Thorndike v Hunt* (1859) De G&J 563, 569; 44 ER 1386, 1388 (Knight Bruce LJ); *Dodd v Hills* (1865) 2 H&M 424, 71 ER 528; *Serious Fraud Office v Litigation Capital Ltd* [2021] EWHC 1272 (Comm) [138]–[142] (Foxton J).

[128] Cuming, Walsh, Wood (n 11) 516.

[129] See K Barker, 'After Change of Position: Good Faith Exchange in the Law of Restitution' in P Birks (ed), *Laundering and Tracing* (Oxford, Clarendon Press, 1995) 195–98; K Barker, 'Bona Fide Purchase as a Defence to Unjust Enrichment Claims: A Concise Restatement' (1999) 7 *Restitution Law Review* 75, 76 (discussing the defence in the context of restitutionary claims arising out of similar circumstances of involuntary transfer).

[130] See the discussion in section II.B.

between a legal mortgage and an equitable charge that would require a different set of priority rules. The issue can also be seen as an old problem of whether equity's bona fide purchaser defence should be available to purchasers of equitable as well legal interests.[131] Other than historical,[132] the reason is not obvious. One of the more convincing explanations of the rationale of the bona fide purchaser defence is that it protects security of transfers by shielding the purchaser from undisclosed liabilities on account of the purchase.[133] In normal circumstances (ie where equities are equal), such rationale supports the protection of purchasers of equitable as well as legal interests. It is possible that by characterising the codified security interest in after-acquired property as a legal interest, and giving priority to B in Example 2, we arrive at a better result. We might add that the beneficiary, while losing to the creditor, has a range of remedies available against a trustee who misappropriates trust assets and against third parties, for example for knowing receipt.

V. CONCLUSION

Commercial law and equity have always had a tempestuous relationship, reflecting the tensions between the legal policies that underpin them. The marketplace requires certainty, speed and respect for parties' autonomy while equity is generally seen as probing in detail into, and regulating, parties' conduct and motives. Lord Millett, writing extra-judicially in 1998,[134] said that these policies were not irreconcilable but that an unbounded application of equity in the regulation of commerce risked undermining both policies. Two decades later, Lord Briggs[135] echoed this concern, arguing extra-judicially that in order to address this risk it was necessary to understand the principles that justify a particular intervention of equity.

This chapter has shown that codifications enable us to reflect on, and to formulate, the principles underpinning equity's operation, and in so doing help balance the policies of equity and commercial law. Not all of equity's principles are convenient in modern commercial practice, and so not all of them are, or should be, preserved in a codification. In secured transactions law, equity's priority rules – the bona fide purchaser defence together with the doctrine of constructive notice, and the rule in *Dearle v Hall* – are too costly and too uncertain as solutions to the basic question of ranking of creditors holding security rights over the same asset. Where security rights are registered, we have seen, the law would be simpler and more certain if basic

[131] For an argument favouring the application of the defence to equitable interests, see J Ames, 'Purchase for Value without Notice' (1887–88) 1 *Harvard Law Review* 1, 3, 8–12, and see text accompanying n 128.

[132] D Fox, 'Purchase for Value without Notice' in PS Davies, S Douglas and J Goudkamp (eds), *Defences in Equity* (Oxford, Hart, 2018) 53.

[133] *Stanhope v Earl of Verney* (1761) 2 Eden 81, 85–86 (Lord Northington LC); A Bell, *Modern Law of Personal Property in England and Ireland* (London and Edinburgh, Butterworths, 1989) 524–25; C Webb, *Reason and Restitution. A Theory of Unjust Enrichment* (Oxford, OUP, 2016) 230; *cf* M Bridge, L Gullifer, G McMeel, K Low, *The Law of Personal Property*, 3rd edn (London, Sweet & Maxwell, 2021) para [31-101].

[134] P Millett, 'Equity's Place in the Law of Commerce' (1998) 114 *LQR* 214.

[135] Lord Briggs, 'Equity in Business' (2019) 135 *LQR* 567.

priority disputes among secured creditors were decided with reference to the date of registration of their respective security rights. Such a solution is found in the UCC and in PPSAs and it should also be adopted in English law.

The difficulties with equitable principles governing priority should not, however, overshadow the genius of equity's contributions in other areas of secured transactions law. Concepts such as the charge, the floating charge and the principle that the validity of equitable security interests in future assets relates back to the security agreement are all important legal achievements. They have played a key role in facilitating financing transactions as they enabled borrowers to grant security rights in circumstances in which the common law would make it harder or impossible. It is unsurprising that the principles underpinning the application of these concepts have been adopted in modern secured transactions codifications. They should also be preserved in a future secured transactions reform in England. These concepts of equity should also act as a pointed reminder that equity functions not only through regulating a person's conduct and examination of their motives but also by perfecting obligations that relate to property.[136] It cannot be a surprise to see this particular function of equity grow into crucial principles of modern secured transactions laws. After all, equity's capacity to convert personal obligations into proprietary interests is, at least in some areas, closely aligned with commercial needs.[137]

Thus, the analysis in this chapter tells us something new about codified security interests: namely that they do have some equitable features, and equitable principles might apply to them in some aspects. Nevertheless, they are not, and should not be, characterised as equitable for the purpose of priority conflicts that arise outside the codifications when a priority conflict needs to be resolved by resorting to general principles of common law and equity.

The foray into secured transactions codifications teaches us also something new about equity, which is that there is no necessary link between interests which have equitable features such as interests in future assets, and the bona fide purchaser defence, at least in the context of security interests. This in turn calls to question one of the basic truths about equitable interests posited by the don of equity, Maitland. He said that the fundamental difference between legal and equitable interests is determined by the way priority conflict is solved.[138] The normative force of this statement is weakened if an interest may have equitable features without being subject to equity's priority rules.

[136] For further discussion, see eg L Smith, 'Fusion and Tradition' in S Degeling and J Edelman (eds), *Equity in Commercial Law* (Sydney, Lawbook Co, 2005) 32–35.

[137] For discussion in relation to floating charges, see M Raczynska, 'The Species and Structure(s) of the Floating Charge: The English Law Perspective on the Scottish Floating Charge' in J Hardman and ADJ MacPherson (eds), *Floating Charges in Scotland: New Perspectives and Current Issues* (Edinburgh, EUP, 2022) 304, 312–14.

[138] Maitland (n 14) 130.

Part VIII

International Perspectives

16

equity is not Equity

ALEXANDRA POPOVICI[1] AND LIONEL SMITH[2]

> Ring the bells that still can ring
> Forget your perfect offering
> There is a crack, a crack in everything
> That's how the light gets in.
>
> Leonard Cohen, *Anthem*

I. INTRODUCTION

A CONFERENCE ON 'Equity 150 years after the Judicature Acts' opens space for a very wide range of reflections. The authors of this chapter are both comparative lawyers, one more of a civilian who also teaches common law and one more of a common lawyer who also teaches civil law. Rather than examining any particular doctrine or contribution of Equity, we aim to bring a comparative perspective to the conference theme seen broadly. Like many before us, we will use 'Equity' to refer to Maitland's Equity:

> ... Equity now is that body of rules administered by our English courts of justice which, were it not for the operation of the Judicature Acts, would be administered only by those courts which would be known as Courts of Equity.[3]

By contrast, we will use 'equity' to refer to ... something else.[4] We will say more about equity below, but for the purposes of introduction we borrow a definition from the *Oxford English Dictionary:*

> The recourse to general principles of justice ... to correct or supplement the provisions of the law.[5]

[1] Professeure Agrégée, Université de Sherbrooke.
[2] Downing Professor of the Laws of England at the University of Cambridge and a Fellow of Gonville and Caius College.
[3] FW Maitland, *Equity; also, The Forms of Action at Common Law: Two Courses of Lectures*, edn by A Chaytor and W Whittaker (Cambridge, CUP, 1909) 1. *cf* J Bentham, *Rationale of Judicial Evidence, Specially Applied to English Practice*, V vols (London, Hunt and Clarke, 1827) vol IV, 330: 'What then is equity? Answer: – whatever has ever been done by a court of equity.'
[4] Hence the orthographical choice in the first word of the title of this chapter.
[5] *Oxford English Dictionary*, available at www.oed.com, sv 'equity', sense 3.

We note three things in relation to this working definition. First, 'correcting or supplementing' the law may, but does not necessarily, involve changing the law; we will return to this. Secondly, the definition does not distinguish between the *doing* of what it describes; the *authority* to do that; and the *justification* for such an authority. Our focus will be on justifications. Thirdly, we leave aside different and wider senses of 'equity', one of which captures fairness, in particular the fairness of treating like cases alike.[6] Another wide sense effectively means 'justice'.[7] These wide senses of 'equity' are extremely important, and one of them is usually the relevant sense of the word when it is used outside of the law; but they are different from the equity which is our concern.

Our motivation for making the present contribution is this. Many jurists in the common law tradition equate Equity with equity: they may unconsciously assume that all equity comes from Equity, that everything that comes from Equity is equity, or both. On that view, the Judicature Act reform could have serious and possibly grievous effects on equity. We do not hold that view.[8] equity is well known in the civilian tradition and this helps us to see what should be plain even within the common law tradition: that Equity and equity are different. We believe that the Judicature reforms helps us to see this more clearly. Our aim is to understand an equity that is not exclusively tied to Equity (although it is certainly related to it): it is found in the common law and in the civil law. And 150 years after the Judicature Acts, this is an equity that we should celebrate.

The structure of our chapter is this. We begin with a few words about the effects of the Judicature Acts, and about why we might still be asking about the fusion of common law and Equity 150 years after those statutes.[9] In the main part of the chapter, we look at some different meanings that are ascribed to equity, including in the civilian tradition that lacks Equity. We clarify what we understand by equity, and, since some readers may find our understanding to be an unusual one, we defend that understanding. In our conclusion, we ask what the future might hold in relation to the effects of the Judicature Act reforms.

II. FUSION OF COMMON LAW AND EQUITY: WHY HAVE CONFERENCES ABOUT IT?

On one view, fusion should not be such a big deal. *R v Gyngall*[10] concerned a dispute about whether a mother could recover custody of her child, who was still a minor

[6] ibid sv 'equity', sense 1: '[t]he quality of being equal or fair; fairness, impartiality; even-handed dealing.'

[7] J Baker, '1483–1558' in J Baker (ed), *The Oxford History of the Laws of England* (Oxford, OUP, 2003) vol VI, 40: '... the source and spirit of all law, an abstract concept of justice.'

[8] See also L Smith, 'Equity is Not a Single Thing' in D Klimchuk, I Samet, and H Smith (eds), *Philosophical Foundations of the Law of Equity* (Oxford, OUP, 2020) 144.

[9] In some common law jurisdictions, comparable reforms took place earlier, and in others, more recently; see chs 2–3 and 5–7 in JC Goldberg, HE Smith, and P Turner (eds), *Equity and Law: Fusion and Fission* (Cambridge, CUP, 2019).

[10] [1893] 2 QB 232 (CA).

of 15 years but who wished to remain with those who were caring for her. The mother brought the proceeding by applying for *habeas corpus* in the Queen's Bench Division. Lord Esher MR noted that prior to the Judicature Acts the matter might have been resolved through *habeas corpus* at common law, or in Chancery through the Court's parental jurisdiction, which did not involve determining the rights between the litigants but rather put the court in the place of a parent to act in the best interests of the child.

> The present case arises after the Judicature Act, and the proceedings are in the Queen's Bench Division. The effect of that Act is, as I have often said, not to invent a new jurisdiction or to create new rights, but to alter the mode of procedure, and, there having been before two independent jurisdictions, one common law and the other equity, the Act in effect provides that, if a person proceeds in the Queen's Bench Division under the common law jurisdiction, and it turns out that the case raises questions to which the Chancery jurisdiction is applicable, the Queen's Bench Division judges are not to send the suitor to a Chancery Court, but are to exercise the Chancery jurisdiction themselves.[11]

In relation to fusion, debates tend to focus on the fusion of common law and Equity (or, taking Lord Esher MR's view of the matter, on the fusion of the administration of common law and Equity). But there have been and are other legal systems in English law, including for example the law of admiralty, the local customary law of one manor or another, the law merchant and ecclesiastical law. The church courts used to hear and resolve disputes about the validity of wills, the administration of estates testate and intestate, about blasphemy and brawling, marital causes and defamation. Like Equity and the common law, those courts had their own judges, their own lawyers, their own procedures and their own law. Some of that law is no more, some passed to Chancery, some passed to courts of common law (and in England and Wales, some few matters still belong to the courts of the Church of England).[12] Very little hand-wringing seems to have been occasioned by these pre-Judicature fusions.[13]

So what is going on in fusion resistance? At an earlier conference on fusion, one of us speculated that some jurists might feel that their identity as such is threatened by fusion, at least if it goes in any measure beyond the purely procedural.[14] But the paradox of this attitude is that both common law and Equity are self-evidently in constant substantive evolution, and it would be very strange indeed if the only

[11] ibid 239 (Lord Esher MR).

[12] *Halsbury's Laws of England*, 5th edn (2011) vol 34, sv 'Ecclesiastical Law', section 8. For a recent example, see *In the matter of the Rustat Memorial, Jesus College, Cambridge* [2022] ECC Ely 2 (Consistory Court of the Diocese Ely).

[13] Even though it remains true that the law governing probate of wills, for example, is neither common law nor Equity but ecclesiastical law: AH Oosterhoff, 'The Discrete Functions of Courts of Probate and Construction' (2017) 46 *Advocates' Q* 316, esp 336–42.

[14] L Smith, 'Fusion and Tradition' in S Degeling and J Edelman (eds), *Equity in Commercial Law* (Sydney, Thomson/Law Book Co, 2005) 19. Some contemporary opponents of the Judicature Act reforms argued that Equity had 'a mystical quality which the common law judges could not aspire to apprehend': S Gardner, 'Equity, Estate Contracts and the Judicature Acts: *Walsh v Lonsdale* Revisited' (1987) 7 *OJLS* 60, 94.

direction in which they could not substantively evolve were towards one another.[15] Others may be uncomfortable with the possible effects of fusion on the basis that they believe that Equity makes a unique contribution to legal reasoning. This unique contribution may be seen to be reasoning that takes a certain form;[16] or, it may be seen as reasoning that has a certain goal.[17] For us, these positions are somewhat paradoxical, because they seem to presuppose that Equity has a monopoly on certain kinds of legal reasoning. We argue that whatever virtue is seen to exist in equity cannot, as a matter of logic, be seen to exist only in Equity. There is no particular reason that the procedural fusion of common law and Equity should limit, diminish or eliminate equity, when the latter is seen as a manner of legal reasoning or a goal of legal reasoning. On the contrary, we will argue that a general understanding of equity, not tied to Equity, will allow equity to flourish.

There is no shortage of equity in the common law, even when 'common law' is defined in the narrow sense that excludes Equity. This is not only a matter of showing that the royal courts of common law did equity before the Chancellor's intervention was established;[18] nor of observing that Lord Mansfield characterised the common law's action for money had and received as 'equitable';[19] nor of showing that in many settler jurisdictions, equity was delivered by courts of common law in the absence of any court or person possessed of Equitable jurisdiction.[20] We can look also at the living common law. Lord Nicholls of Birkenhead, while he was a Law Lord, published an article addressing aspects of socially conscious fiduciary investment.[21] Under the subheading 'Morality and the law', he observed that judge-made law must and does evolve as morality and social conditions evolve.[22] To illustrate this he cited five

[15] Recent examples of how they have indeed done so in US law relate to the availability of the defence of 'unclean hands' to legal claims: Restatement (Third) of Restitution and Unjust Enrichment, s 63; TL Anenson, *Judging Equity: The Fusion of Unclean Hands in US Law* (Cambridge, CUP, 2019). For brief discussion of this issue in English law: J Goudkamp, 'The Law of Illegality: Identifying the Issues' in S Green and A Bogg (eds), *Illegality After Patel v Mirza* (Oxford, Hart, 2018) 39, 56–57.

[16] Henry Smith articulates a view of Equity as law about law, or meta-law, or as a second-order safety valve, eg in HE Smith, 'Fusion of Law and Confusion of Equity' in D Klimchuk, I Samet, and H Smith (eds), *Philosophical Foundations of the Law of Equity* (Oxford, OUP, 2020) 210. See too H Smith's chapter in this volume.

[17] Irit Samet argues that Equity aims to promote a better correspondence between legal liability and moral responsibility: I Samet, *Equity: Conscience Goes to Market* (Oxford, OUP, 2018) 28–35.

[18] P Brand, 'The Equity of the Common Law Courts' in E Koops and W Zwalve (eds), *Law & Equity: Approaches in Roman Law and Common Law* (Leiden, Martinus Nijhoff, 2014) 39.

[19] A popular subject over the years: ET Bishop, 'Money Had and Received, an Equitable Action at Law' (1933) 7 *Southern California Law Review* 41; M McInnes, 'The Equitable Action in Unjust Enrichment: Ambiguity and Error' (2007) 45 *Canadian Business Law Journal* 253; B Kremer, 'Equity and the Common Counts: The Development of the Action for Money Had and Received' in JC Goldberg, HE Smith, and P Turner (eds), *Equity and Law: Fusion and Fission* (Cambridge, CUP, 2019) 203. Each author is primarily concerned to show that the 'action for money had and received' was (or is) not Equitable, even though it might have been (or might be) equitable.

[20] SR Liverant and WH Hitchler, 'A History of Equity in Pennsylvania' (1933) 37 *Dickinson Law Review* 156, 165–79; P Girard, 'At the Crossroads of Fusion: British North America/Canada, 1750–2000' in JC Goldberg, HE Smith, and P Turner (eds), *Equity and Law: Fusion and Fission* (Cambridge, CUP, 2019) 97.

[21] Lord Nicholls, 'Trustees and Their Broader Community: Where Duty, Morality and Ethics Converge' (1995) 9 *Trust Law International* 71.

[22] ibid 72.

decisions of the House of Lords from 1868 to 1993.[23] Only one of these landmark cases had anything to do with Equity.[24] But in our view, all of them can be seen as examples of equity.

From a civilian perspective, the idea that equity cannot survive without a distinct court of Equity or a distinct body of Equity is even harder to understand, since the civil law has no tradition of the separate administration of Equity or of equity.[25] It has, however, a long tradition of making room for equity, a tradition which began long before the Norman invasion that led to the invention of the common law. We tend to agree with Bentham: 'Explain the business of a court of [E]quity by a definition of equity? As well might you explain the business of the star-chamber by the definition of a star …'.[26]

The habit of thought is deeply engrained in common lawyers that equity comes from Equity and only from Equity. From this perspective, the suggestion that equity might be at play in the evolution of the common law over the centuries is puzzling and counter-intuitive. But when equity is better understood, this perspective can be seen to be misconceived. The reason that Equity is called Equity is that historically, it was a place to seek equity. That is a historically contingent reality, but not a logically necessary one. There is a coherent and widely shared understanding of equity that does not depend on Equity. Reflecting upon the fusion of the administration of common law and Equity is the perfect moment to assess how we can understand equity in a way that is independent of Equity.

III. WHAT KIND OF A THING IS EQUITY?

A. A Thing for Correcting or Supplementing the Law

Like many authors, we start with Aristotle, whose account of *epiekcia* is widely known.[27] Many translators into English render this word as 'equity' but at least one renders it as 'decency'.[28] Aristotle's discussion, which is part of an analysis of the virtue of justice, is about the relationship between justice and decency/equity.[29] He begins with a puzzle: if they are both virtuous and are both about doing justice, how are they different? How can justice be made more just? Part of Aristotle's answer is

[23] *Rylands v Fletcher* (1868) LR 3 HL 330; *Donoghue v Stevenson* [1932] AC 562 (HL); *Fibrosa Spolka Akcyjna v Fairbairn Lawson Combe & Barbour Ltd* [1943] AC 32 (HL); *Hedley Byrne & Co Ltd v Heller & Partners Ltd* [1964] AC 465 (HL); *Re M* [1994] 1 AC 377 (HL).

[24] *Re M* (n 23) was about whether an injunction could be granted against a department of state or a Minister of the Crown, and also whether they could be liable for contempt for violating such an injunction. The case turned on the constitutional issues and not on the Equitable pedigree of injunctions.

[25] To develop, in this direction, the point in the previous note, the idea that injunctions are equitable makes little sense to a civilian. Courts have the discretionary power to grant injunctions as a matter of law, not equity.

[26] Bentham (n 3) 328. We capitalise the first occurrence of 'Equity' to be consistent with our convention.

[27] Aristotle, *Nicomachean Ethics*, Book V, ch 10.

[28] Aristotle, *Nicomachean Ethics*, T Irwin tr, 2nd edn (Indianapolis, Hackett Publishing Co, 1999).

[29] Aristotle (n 27) Book V deals with justice.

that it is not unjust to follow the law, because the law aims at justice;[30] but where the law is deficient due to its generality, it may be rectified by decency/equity. This implies that it is better to be just *and* decent/equitable than to be just without so being; but again, in what sense is one being just, if one could be more just? In this sense, it has been argued that it is a mistake to characterise decency/equity as 'justice in the particular case', because there is no justice except in particular cases.[31]

The solution to this puzzle seems to be that there may be kinds of justice that apply in different domains.[32] Legal justice, or law-making justice, is the justice of making general rules. A general rule may be just according to legal justice, and it would not be unjust to follow the rule;[33] but the result may not be just according to a more general notion of justice, and in this respect, may need to be corrected by decency or equity.[34] The role of equity in 'correcting or supplementing' the law is easier to understand if what is being corrected is not justice itself, but is always a general rule which may, in its own sphere – that is, as a matter of law-making justice – be a just rule.[35]

We will suggest below that there are different ways to correct or supplement the law in this Aristotelian sense. But we observe here that it seems implicit in Aristotle's account that the one who may do equity is not a legislator. A legislator necessarily has a general power and authority to make and to change law. Aristotle's discussion of equity is hardly a manual for legislators. Indeed, it is not primarily a manual for judges; it speaks to citizens about how to be virtuous. A citizen may, in the name of being decent or equitable, demand less than what the law entitles her to take.[36] A citizen clearly has the *authority* to take less than that to which she is entitled by law; and decency/equity may give her a virtuous reason for so acting. Less frequently discussed in applying Aristotle's account to modern law is whether a judge has the authority to require (for example) a citizen to take less than that to which the citizen

[30] See Book V ch 1 paras [12]–[13].

[31] MJ Falcón y Tella, *Equity and Law*, tr P Muckley (Leiden, Martinus Nijhoff, 2008) 12–13. *cf* A Burrows, 'We Do This at Common Law But That in Equity' (2002) 22 *OJLS* 1, 2, on his question to students who say that Equitable remedies are concerned to achieve fairness and justice between the parties: 'Does that mean that all those rules and principles [of the common law] are designed to achieve *un*fairness and *in*justice between the parties?' See also S Milsom, *Historical Foundations of the Common Law*, 2nd edn (London, Butterworths, 1981) 83–84, which contains several arresting statements for students of legal history: 'In the fourteenth century there was no law of England, no body of rules complete in itself with known limits and visible defects; or if there was it was not the property of the common law courts or any others. … Not only was there no equity as a nascent body of rules different from those of the common law. There was no common law, no body of substantive rules from which equity could be different. And the idea that law could be unjust, if comprehensible at all, would have been abhorrent. Failures [in the processes that unfolded in courts] were mechanical.'

[32] A Beever, 'Aristotle on Equity, Law, and Justice' (2004) 10 *Legal Theory* 33.

[33] Aristotle (n 27) Book V, ch 1, para [12] which (on Irwin's translation (n 28)) refers to 'legislative science'; see Irwin's note on this text and his translation of it at 228.

[34] Since one wider sense of equity comes close to justice itself (text accompanying nn 6–7), the potential for confusion caused by the different senses is evident: equity corrects the law to bring it closer to … equity.

[35] See also D Klimchuk, 'Aristotle at the Foundations of the Law of Equity' in D Klimchuk, I Samet, and H Smith (eds), *Philosophical Foundations of the Law of Equity* (Oxford, OUP, 2020) 32, 34–36, 38–40.

[36] Aristotle (n 27) Book V, ch 10, para [8]: the decent person is one who is '… not an exact stickler for justice in the bad way, but taking less than he might even though he has the law on his side'.

is entitled by law. That does not seem to be part of Aristotle's argument, because he is not primarily addressing the authority of judges.[37] His argument provides perhaps a *justification* for such an authority, one which would also delimit the authority if it were accepted as justificatory of it (although there might be other justifications for other aspects of that authority). But while a judge clearly has the authority to apply the law, does she have the authority to require litigants to take less than their legal entitlement?[38] That authority could only come from a judge's power *over* the law, or to correct or modify the law, to which we will return.

Frequently invoked in Roman law was an idea of *aequitas* whose etymological connection to equity and to *équité, equità* and so on is evident. Many roles were assigned to *aequitas*; one textbook says that in the ancient texts it has 'so many senses that it is of no great use'.[39] Even in the present chapter, we have noted wider senses of 'equity' that are quite different from Aristotle's idea.[40] A striking analysis through etymology claims, however, that the many meanings of *aequitas* 'oscillate between' the essence, and the antithesis, of the positive law. One might say that it is, at one and the same time, what the law is striving to be but what it is not.[41] And this idea is not so far from Aristotle's, including in its puzzling paradoxality.

It has been argued that a similar idea of equity operated in the Middle Ages, when the law of God might prevail over secular law, even written law.[42] Every common lawyer knows that when the Chancellor first began to intervene in private disputes, he was not enforcing a system of rules or a system of law, but was aiming to protect the immortal soul of the defendant.[43] He was bringing non-law into a dispute to

[37] Aristotle's discussion of decency/equity in his *Rhetoric* is, however, at least partly addressed to judges or arbitrators: Beever (n 32) 41–43; Klimchuk (n 35) 38.

[38] See Beever (n 32) 42–43, 45.

[39] WW Buckland and P Stein, *A Text-Book of Roman Law*, 3rd edn (Cambridge, CUP, 1963) 55. See also A Biscardi, 'On Aequitas and Epiekia' in AM Rabello (ed), *Aequitas and Equity: Equity in Civil Law and Mixed Jurisdictions* (Jerusalem, Harry and Michael Sacher Institute for Legislative Research and Comparative Law, 1997) 1, 7: '… we find … such a multiplicity of meanings of the noun aequitas and of the corresponding adjective (*aequus*), with such a vast range of nuances, that we are not surprised that equity has been considered one of the most "elusive" notions of the legal experience of ancient Rome.' See also, in the same volume, A Watson, 'Equity in the Time of Cicero' 23, and HE Yntema, 'Equity in the Civil Law and the Common Law' (1966) 15 *American Journal of Comparative Law* 60, 66–73.

[40] See the text accompanying nn 6–7.

[41] Biscardi (n 39) 7. There is a link here to the idea of the 'equity of the statute' which has been present in the common law since its early days: D Ibbetson, 'A House Built on Sand: Equity in Early Modern English Law' in E Koops and W Zwalve (eds), *Law & Equity: Approaches in Roman Law and Common Law* (Leiden, Martinus Nijhoff, 2014) 55, 56–57; J Edelman, 'The Equity of the Statute' in D Klimchuk, I Samet, and H Smith (eds), *Philosophical Foundations of the Law of Equity* (Oxford, OUP, 2020) 352 (what Edelman calls the 'older sense' of the expression is the relevant one here).

[42] M Lupoi, 'English "Equity" and the Civil Law – A Tale of two Worlds' in E Calzolaio, R Torino and L Vagni (eds), *Liber Amicorum Luigi Moccia* (Rome, RomaTre Press, 2021) 81.

[43] Maitland (n 3) 5: 'I do not think that in the fourteenth century the Chancellors considered that they had to administer any body of substantive rules that differed from the ordinary law of the land.' See also Milsom (n 31) 82–86. Bills in the early period recited that the defendant's soul would be imperilled without the Chancellor's intervention; see for example the bill in *Bale v Marchall* (1457) 10 SS 143 set out in WP Baildon (ed), *Select Cases in Chancery, 1364–1471*, vol 10, publications of the Selden Society (London, Bernard Quartich, 1896) 145, alleging that the facts recited were 'ageynst all right feithe & good consciens, & to right hevy ensample & grete perill to the soule of the seide Thomas [defendant], w^t^out your gracious remedy'.

resolve it better; better in the service of the one justice, that might otherwise not be achieved.

> The key to understanding the role played by the Chancellors is that they kept morals and laws together whilst everywhere else in Europe the two were parting and did eventually part.[44]

In the common law, it is well known that the idea that the practice of the Chancellor or the Court of Chancery was founded on equity became established in the Tudor period.[45] This replaced, although it never completely eclipsed, the understanding that it was founded on conscience.

Is anything common to all these notions of equity? Aristotle's equity seems to have as its role the correction of only one aspect of the law: those defects that arise from the law's generality. What if the law instead needs correction to comply with the law of God or the demands of conscience as seen by an Archbishop Chancellor? Is this a defect arising from generality? And how do we understand Aristotle's equity 150 years after the Judicature Acts? One thing seems clear: we cannot try to make sense of the law by imagining that all equity is sourced in Equity; or, that all that equity today means is that a judge can somehow use Equity to correct the law that she herself would otherwise apply. We can do better than that.

This leads us to think about the law-making function of a judge. Judges make law, in both the common law and the civil law.[46] It is possible to imagine the judicial function without any law-making authority; but this is not the reality in western legal systems.[47] Even so, judges do not always make law; judges may well simply apply the law to decide a case, and they are still doing their job. When judges do make law, they do not do so in the legislative voice, some of whose defects Aristotle's equity aims to address. They make law as an incident or by-product of their primary function of resolving disputes.[48] Looking at the existing law, which may be composed

[44] Lupoi (n 42) 90; see also M Lupoi, 'Chancellors as Civil Lawyers – And the Equitable Notion of "Fraud"' (2022) 28 *Trusts and Trustees* 343.

[45] JH Baker, *An Introduction to English Legal History*, 5th edn (Oxford, OUP, 2019) 114–16; and see M McNair, 'Equity and Conscience' (2007) 27 *OJLS* 659; DR Klinck, *Conscience, Equity and the Court of Chancery in Early Modern England* (Farnham, Ashgate, 2010); Ibbetson (n 41); Klimchuk (n 35).

[46] Case law may not formally be a 'source of law' in civilian systems, but no one pretends that the courts do not make, change and develop the law in some sense, see M Devinat, *La règle prétorienne en droit civil français et dans la common law canadienne: etude de méthodologie juridique comparée* (Aix-en-Provence, Presses universitaires d'Aix-Marseille, 2005).

[47] One grievance of the French revolutionaries was that in the *ancien régime* there was an inadequate separation of powers, and they aimed to implement Montesquieu's idea that a judge should only pronounce the law, not have any authority over it (still routinely summarised in his maxim that the judge is *la bouche de la loi*, only the mouth who speaks the words of the law). This survives in the Civil Code's Art 5, unchanged since it came into force in 1804: 'Il est défendu aux juges de prononcer par voie de disposition générale et réglementaire sur les causes qui leur sont soumises'; our translation: 'Judges are forbidden from formulating general or regulatory norms in relation to the cases that are submitted to them.' The reality is that even in France, judges can modify the law; see Devinat (n 46) and the example of the *Boudier* decision which we provide below.

[48] J Gardner, 'Legal Positivism: 5½ Myths' (2001) 46 *American Journal of Jurisprudence* 199, 215–17; L Smith, 'The Rationality of Tradition' in T Endicott, J Getzler, and E Peel (eds), *Properties of Law: Essays in Honour of James Harris* (Oxford, OUP, 2005) 297; S Beswick, 'Prospective Overruling Unravelled' (2021) 41 *Civil Justice Quarterly* 29.

of enacted law or case law or both, the judge, in deciding a new case, enunciates some new principle or rule or qualification or exception. Necessarily, the judge thinks that the law as it existed was inadequate for the case at hand. But can judicial law-making generally be seen as an example of equity? Does judicial law-making respond to a defect in the law that can be characterised as arising from generality?

Aristotle's notion certainly seems well-suited to judicial law-making in the context of legislation, a context he himself addressed.[49] Almost from the moment it was enacted, English judges read various exceptions and limitations into the Statute of Frauds of 1677. This was not a process of interpretation as that word is normally used.[50] When we turn to the civil law, we may think of the Civil Code, which is a statute in constitutional terms, but one which purports to enact all of private law. In the famous *Boudier* decision of 1892, the French *Cour de cassation* recognised the *actio de in rem verso* as a source of obligations or a cause of action, despite its absence from the French Civil Code.[51] The plaintiff had improved the land of the defendant, but had no claim under the explicit terms of the Code. Academic writing had argued that such a claim, which had been known to the *ius commune*, should be permitted. The lower court had allowed a claim and the landowner appealed.[52] In dismissing the appeal, the *Cour de cassation* accepted the argument that some articles of the Civil Code, which did not directly assist the plaintiff, were illustrations of a general principle against unjust enrichment.[53] On the view illustrated by this case, and by the English cases on the Statute of Frauds, words can effectively be read into a statute to give effect to its genuine intention, not as a matter of interpretation of the text, but as a conclusion as to how the statute would have been written had the legislature foreseen the case at hand. This corrects a defect in the law; but how does the judge identify the statute as potentially defective in the absence of equitable intervention? Against what standard is the written law seen to be wanting? The answer must be, against the standard of what the legislator was trying to accomplish.[54]

Can judicial law-making in the evolution of the common law, apart from statute, be understood as equitable in this sense? Judges may develop the law incrementally, where previous cases do not seem to give a clear answer, by enunciating a new rule. Is this correcting a defect in the law *arising from its generality*? We would argue that

[49] Both Beever (n 32) 41–42 and Klimchuk (n 35) 35, 38 address Aristotle's discussion in his *Rhetoric* of when a judge should use equity to qualify the application of a law.

[50] See Edelman (n 41).

[51] *Cour de cassation, Chambre des requêtes*, 15 June 1892.

[52] Whether the facts of the case rightly gave rise to this action, which remains a matter of debate, is of no concern here.

[53] A similar holding was reached many years later in Quebec law in *Cie immobilière Viger v Lauréat Giguère Inc* [1977] 2 SCR 67; the action was codified in Quebec when the Civil Code of Québec came into force in 1994 (Arts 1493–94); and it was eventually codified also in France in amendments of 2016 (Arts 1303 to 1303–4). See A Popovici, 'Justifier l'enrichissement injustifié: un regard québécois' (2019) 4 *Tribonien* 154. In *Boudier* the principle against unjust enrichment was described as 'equitable' but this seems to be in the sense of 'fairness' (see text accompanying nn 6–7).

[54] Again, however, this is not the same exercise as what is often called 'purposive interpretation'. On the contrary, doing equity in this sense '… respects neither the intended meaning of the words nor the application to the facts that is required by that meaning. Rather, it involves *not* applying the meaning of the law that is actually enacted': Edelman (n 41) 353 (emphasis in original).

it can be seen as such.[55] Again, if we judge the law – here, the common law – against the standard of what the law is trying to accomplish, and find that it does not give the right answer in the particular case, then judicial development of the common law can be seen as equitable. Case law, when it needs adjusting, can often be said to have been too general. This is not because it is expressed in a general legislative form; on the contrary, it is because the maker of each decision, who needs to resolve the particular dispute, does not even try to address all future possibilities. That is not the judge's job. It is for subsequent judges to decide whether a prior decision is wide or narrow in its scope. What if a case law rule is clear, but is now thought to be out of date because society has changed? This too can be seen as a problem of over-generality: the case law rule is too general, if it is taken to be a forever unchanging rule.

Let us summarise. equity is not law, but it makes law work better. Whatever the law is intended to implement and accomplish, it may fail to do so perfectly. If private law aims to implement some system of interpersonal morality, it cannot always do so perfectly, especially when we remember that morality evolves.[56] There must be some authority for a judge to have access to the underlying justificatory principles, or (to use a more civilian expression) the general principles of the law, in order to permit the evolution of the law.[57] Every human creation is imperfect; equity is a justification for a judge's authority to modify the law to make it better. Again: not 'better' as a legislator might try to reform the law in one direction or another; rather, equity allows the law to be made better at what it is already trying to accomplish. Aristotle's argument is a justification for why that authority rightly exists and how it may rightly be used.

We do not say that all judicial development of the law partakes of equity. A decision interpreting a statute may be important, especially if it has precedential force, but does not purport to modify the law. A court's decision that the law as stated by another court is simply wrong may well modify the law, but its justification must lie outside of equity.

[55] In this we agree with Klimchuk (n 35) 34 fn 12.

[56] Samet (n 17). Many economic analysts of law may say that some legal principles respond to 'opportunism', even while being unable to provide a clear definition of this concept (eg, DG Smith, 'The Critical Resource Theory of Fiduciary Duty' (2002) 55 *Vanderbilt Law Review* 1399, 1402 fn 10). HE Smith, 'Why Fiduciary Law is Equitable' in AS Gold and PB Miller (eds), *Philosophical Foundations of Fiduciary Law* (Oxford, OUP, 2014) 267 defines 'opportunism' as '… behavior that is undesirable but that cannot be cost-effectively captured – defined, detected, and deterred – by explicit ex ante rulemaking …'. Interestingly, neither author defines opportunism as unlawful even though both argue that it attracts legal sanction. Although economic analysis of law generally operates on the assumption that the law is not informed by morality, opportunism (not being illegal) seems to be a deeply moralistic concept, one which may be understood to be introduced into law via a kind of equity (Smith, 'Fusion of Law and Confusion of Equity' (n 16) 212). See too, H Smith's chapter in this volume, especially section IIIA.

[57] In the codified civil law, uncodified 'general principles' can be inferred to lie behind the codal text, as in *Boudier*; again, compare the common law's 'equity of the statute' discussed in n 41. The Preliminary Disposition of the Civil Code of Québec refers expressly to general principles as part of the law with which the Code operates 'in harmony'. For civilian discussion of equity in terms of allowing the court to give effect to general principles, see JE Brierley and RA Macdonald (eds), *Quebec Civil Law: An Introduction to Quebec Private Law* (Toronto, Emond Montgomery, 1993) 128–30, 191–93; P Fréchette, *La restitution des prestations* (Montreal, Éditions Yvon Blais, 2018) 120–22.

B. Different Ways in Which equity May Operate

In some situations, the application of equity may be understood as 'decisional': as correcting the law but without creating new general rules.[58] Where judicial decisions make law (as is typical in the common law and often occurs in civilian systems as well), however, then the operation of equity may involve changing the law and making new legal rules.

This helps us to understand a development seen in both common law and civil law: what starts as equity may become law, by being integrated into the law in the form of general rules. In Republican Roman law, the praetor's edict, which could modify the strict law, was published and treated as governing by subsequent praetors.[59] In the recent history of Quebec civil law, a doctrine of abuse of rights was introduced by the courts on the basis of equity;[60] when the Civil Code was reformed, the rule was codified.[61] Turning to the common law, this is the sense in which, while all of Equity started out in some sense as equity, this is far from true today; nor has it been for a long time.[62] This creates the potential confusion that can arise when a legal rule is said to be a creature of equity: this may be true in a historical sense that speaks to the origin of the rule, while being misleading as to the current nature of the rule. To say it is a creature of equity is to say something about the (or a) *justification for the introduction of the rule in the past*, not about the rule as a rule, once it is in place.[63] To illustrate with a parallel: two different legal systems might have exactly the same rule for how to accept a contractual offer, but in System A it may be a legislative rule while in System B, a rule of case law. We could rightly point to this difference in the 'rule of recognition' that makes the rule into a legal rule; but this difference can coexist with the reality that the rule's content is identical in one system and the other.

[58] Fréchette (n 57) 125–26.

[59] Buckland and Stein (n 39) 5, 8–10; *cf* WW Buckland, *Equity in Roman Law* (London, University of London Press, 1911). See also Lord Kames, *Principles of Equity*, 5th edn (Edinburgh, Bell & Bradfute etc, 1825) 17–18.

[60] *Houle v National Bank of Canada* [1990] 3 SCR 122, 145h (referring to *équité* in the French text, to 'a just and fair approach' in English).

[61] Civil Code of Québec, Art 7; see also Arts 6, 1375 (good faith). We have already noticed (see n 53) that in both France and Quebec, the *actio de in rem verso* was first recognised as a matter of equity, and later codified into law.

[62] Ibbetson (n 41); Baker (n 45) 119, speaking of the eighteenth century: '*Rigor aequitatis* set in …'. In fact this arguably happened much earlier in the common law tradition with respect to land. Many of the 'proprietary' aspects of the use of land were settled within a few decades during the second half of the fifteenth century once the Chancellor began to intervene: see J Barton, 'The Medieval Use' (1965) 81 *LQR* 562, 569–70. Milsom (n 31) 88–90, 213–16 suggests that the early hardening of equity into law was essential because so much land was held to uses.

[63] In this regard, the judicial power known in Scots law as *nobile officium* has the feature that it is more obviously associated with the authority to modify the law than with the modification itself; but it does not seem possible to say that *nobile officium* simply *is* equity in Scots law. See DM Walker, *The Oxford Companion to Law* (Oxford, Clarendon Press, 1980) sv '*nobile officium*'; E Örücu, 'Equity in the Scottish Legal System' in AM Rabello (ed), *Aequitas and Equity: Equity in Civil Law and Mixed Jurisdictions* (Jerusalem, Harry and Michael Sacher Institute for Legislative Research and Comparative Law, 1997) 390–92; D Carr, 'Are Equity and Law in Scotland Fused, Separate or Intertwined?' in JC Goldberg, HE Smith, and P Turner (eds), *Equity and Law: Fusion and Fission* (Cambridge, CUP, 2019) 179, 190, 199.

One advantage of looking at equity in a comparative perspective is that it can help one to distinguish the operation of equity generically from those legal innovations that were, as a matter of contingent history, generated by Equity in English law, arguably relying on equity in the particular context of English law, but in a way that might have been quite unnecessary in another legal system. Each tradition has followed a different path, and may not have needed equity in the same situations. Thus, just as it may have equity without trusts, the civil law may have trusts without equity (or Equity).[64]

More generally this helps the civilian, and the common lawyer, to understand why some legal principles are treated as Equitable in the common law tradition, even though they do not have anything obvious to do with equity. Injunctions and specific performance are good examples. These orders are commonplace in civil law and no one connects them with equity; they have always been available to courts of law. In the very old days, the royal courts of common law ordered specific performance of promises, but they stopped sometime in the fourteenth century.[65] Then they regained this power by statute in 1854.[66] In between, the provision of such orders naturally fell to the Chancery and so is considered part of Equity. This historically contingent sequence of events does not imply that such orders are equitable, except perhaps inasmuch as their appearance, way back when, was a necessary supplement to the common law's decision to withhold such relief. That was a very contingent decision which the common law might not have made. In that system-specific and path-dependent sense, such orders were equitable, as well as Equitable; but following their introduction and establishment, their ongoing deployment is not obviously a matter of equity, even though it is a matter of Equity.[67]

The jurisdiction to award injunctions and specific performance is discretionary, in the civil law and in Equity; before procedural fusion, the royal courts of common law took the same view in relation to their statutory powers. This raises the much-discussed issue of the link between equity and discretion. Etymologically, 'discretion' means 'judgment'; it is related in this sense to 'discreet' and even 'discrete', since the exercise of judgment involves drawing justifiable distinctions. One sense of 'discretionary' is therefore 'involving the exercise of judgment', although this sense certainly does not imply that a discretionary power is unconstrained. We have suggested that equity is a justification for an authority to modify the law. That authority must be discretionary in this sense, that it involves the exercise of judgment; but the authority can manifest in different ways. The modification may be via the creation of a new non-discretionary rule; or it may be by a decision in the particular case that

[64] G Gretton, 'Trusts Without Equity' (2000) 49 *ICLQ* 599; T Honoré, 'Trusts: The Inessentials' in J Getzler (ed), *Rationalizing Property, Equity and Trusts: Essays in Honour of Edward Burn* (London, Butterworths, 2003) 7, 15–20; Civil Code of Québec, Arts 1260–98.

[65] Except, of course, in relation to promises to pay money. See Baker (n 45) 339–42.

[66] Common Law Procedure Act 1854, s 79.

[67] Stephen A Smith, writing on the common law of remedies, provides accounts of why injunctions and specific performance are rightly discretionary without any reference to equity: SA Smith, *Rights, Wrongs, and Injustices* (Oxford, OUP, 2019) 146–71; he argues that the connection to Equity is a matter of historical path-dependency: 296–69.

preserves the discretion to be exercised in future cases.[68] That part of Equity which is discretionary – including what is sometimes still called the concurrent jurisdiction, to grant specific performance or injunctions – preserves the discretion rather than casting it into rules. The judge in Equity can, in this sense, be understood to be doing decisional equity in each case where such an order is granted. But again, this is true in a path-dependent way; not every discretionary judicial authority is justified by equity. Under the Variation of Trusts Act 1958, the judge has the discretionary authority to approve, or not, of a proposed variation. The authority comes from the very text of the written law; and its justification comes from the sovereignty of Parliament.[69] For the same reason, the discretionary authority to order injunctions or specific performance is not understood as equitable in the civil law tradition, because it has always been part of the law. It was not introduced to correct or supplement the law.

C. Legislation and equity

We have noticed a wide sense of 'equity' that means fairness, or perhaps more specifically, treating like cases alike.[70] This is usually the sense that is intended when 'equity' is given as a reason for legislative intervention.[71] The legislature's authority to amend the law obviously has its own foundation.

But even when the word is confined more narrowly, perhaps in line with the working definition we offered above,[72] a lot of discourse is characterised by multiple meanings. As we noted at the start of this chapter, references to 'equity' often fail to distinguish between the *doing* of equity; the *authority* to do equity; and the *justification* for such an authority. The amendment to the law that may be brought about through the exercise of this authority, even if it is in the form of a rule, may also be described as equitable, since it was a creature of equity. In the common law, of course, still more equivocation is introduced by the presence of Equity.

For reasons that were explored in the preceding section, there may be a tendency to label other judicial powers 'equitable' if they are discretionary, even if such powers are creatures of legislation. This is because they allow a judge to do *what a judge might do* if the judge were exercising a non-legislative authority to refine the law in the name of equity, even though the judge's authority actually derives from legislation.[73] Perhaps the most conceptually challenging situation is one in which the legislator specifically authorises the judge to 'do equity'.[74] Again, in this situation the justification for the

[68] See n 58 and the accompanying text.

[69] Variation of Trusts Act 1958, s 1(1): '... the court may if it thinks fit by order approve ...'.

[70] See the text accompanying nn 6–7.

[71] Yntema (n 39) 73.

[72] See n 5 and the accompanying text.

[73] For a discussion of this kind of 'legislative equity' as well as 'judicial equity' in Quebec law, see P-G Jobin, 'L'equité en droit des contrats' in P-C Lafond (ed), *Mélanges claude masse: en quête de justice et d'equité* (Cowansville, Éditions Yvons Blais, 2003) 473.

[74] In the Civil Code of Québec, see Arts 975: 'In circumstances not provided for, the right of accession with respect to movable property is entirely subordinate to the principles of equity.'; and 1434: 'A contract validly formed binds the parties who have entered into it not only as to what they have expressed in it

judge's authority does not come from equity; it comes from legislation. In such a case, the authority's existence and its justification cannot be controverted; its scope, however, may be difficult to discern.

A well-known legislative example, which is a little more precise, is found in Article 1 of the Swiss Civil Code:[75]

> [1] The law applies according to its wording or interpretation to all legal questions for which it contains a provision.
>
> [2] In the absence of a provision, the court shall decide in accordance with customary law and, in the absence of customary law, in accordance with the rule that it would make as legislator.
>
> [3] In doing so, the court shall follow established doctrine and case law.

The closing words of Article 1[2] could be understood, in the narrow range of cases where they apply, to give the judge a very wide legislative authority to make new rules of law. But if these words were interpreted in line with our argument, they would be better expressed in this way: '… in accordance with the rule the legislator would have made if it had addressed the case at hand, the judge's decision being based on what the legislator has in fact otherwise provided.'

In relation to a discretionary authority in judges to refine the law, or to grant or withhold particular orders, some have objected that such discretion is inconsistent with the rule of law. In her study of Equity, Irit Samet includes a thorough discussion of the rule of law, one that responds to arguments suggesting that the presence of discretion, or of standards-based reasoning, does not comply with the rule of law.[76] In relation to equity as we have defined it, we would add this. Anyone who thinks that before the Judicature Acts the judges of the royal courts of common law could not do equity in the sense that we have defined must presumably take the position that the common law never changed, except by Act of Parliament. That is not a tenable position. The study of legal history is in large part the study of how the law evolves. To a great extent, it does so, and has always done so, by the authority of the judges, although in earlier times they might have felt forced to use legal fictions to pretend otherwise.[77]

but also as to what is incident to it according to its nature and in conformity with usage, equity or law.' The latter provision relates primarily to interpretation. See also Arts 389, 1345, 1408 (equitable/equitably). The Swiss Civil Code, Art 4, provides (unofficial translation of the Swiss Confederation, available at www.fedlex.admin.ch/eli/cc/24/233_245_233/en): 'Where the law confers discretion on the court or makes reference to an assessment of the circumstances or to good cause, the court must reach its decision in accordance with the principles of justice and equity.'

[75] In Swiss legislation, sub-sections of articles of a law are designated by superscripted numbers.

[76] Samet (n 17) ch 1.

[77] For how pleading fictions were used to change the law, see Baker (n 45), whose index section on fictions has over 50 entries. A few of the most outstanding examples: in order to allow suit for trespass in the King's courts, which formally required a breach of the King's peace, blacksmiths who had negligently injured horses were fictitiously alleged to have attacked them with weapons (68); in order to allow freeholders to use the action of ejectment that was formally only available to leaseholders, fictitious leases and ejectments were recited (320–22); and in order to allow creditors to sue in *assumpsit* rather than debt, so gaining trial by jury instead of by compurgation, the debtor was fictitiously said to have made a subsequent promise to pay the debt (363–70).

IV. THE FUTURE OF FUSION

What can this tell us about the future of the procedurally fused system of common law and Equity found in almost every common law jurisdiction today? Bernard Rudden showed that before procedural fusion, the judges of the royal courts of common law had an alibi.[78] They could choose not to do equity, because they knew that suitors could have access to equity (or at least to Equity) in another place.[79] The judges in a procedurally fused system are all capable of doing equity; and there are no other courts to which suitors can be sent.

The alibi is now gone. And just as the common law has lost its alibi, Equity has lost its mystery. equity is part of how the law, as a whole and as a system, evolves. We have argued that Aristotle's discussion of equity applies not only to how a judge deals with statutes, but also to how a judge deals with case law; and that it provides a justification for a large part of the authority of judges to develop the law through their decisions. Moreover, any judge can do equity in Aristotle's sense: can exercise a justified authority to correct, supplement and otherwise improve the law, so that the case at hand will be decided more truly to the legal system as a whole than it would be without that improvement. There is no longer any reason to pretend that equity belongs, somehow, to Equity.

How should we assess procedural fusion 150 years after the Judicature Acts? Fusion calls on us to 'forget your perfect offering'. Two thousand years of civil law, and almost a thousand years of common law, tell us that the law can never be made, once and for all, just right. It always needs a crack to let the light in.

[78] B Rudden, 'Equity as Alibi' in S Goldstein (ed), *Equity and Contemporary Legal Developments* (Jerusalem, Sacher Institute, 1992) 30. See also Milsom (n 31) 93: '… common law judges often welcomed applications to the chancery by litigants whom they were themselves unable to save from their own rules.'

[79] Paul Brand has shown that before the Chancellor's intervention was established, the royal courts of common law did do equity: Brand (n 18). And to repeat, on our definition of equity, even though the judges of the royal courts of common law might have had an alibi for not doing equity, they frequently did; otherwise, the law could never have evolved.

17

Equitable Meta-Law: The Spectrum of Property

HENRY E SMITH*

I. INTRODUCTION

PROPERTY LAW CONTRIBUTES more than its share of dichotomous thinking into the legal world. And, ironically or even paradoxically, with the decline of the famous dichotomy between law and equity this problem has only grown worse.

There is a tendency in property law to look for discrete answers to whether an interest is *in rem* or *in personam* or whether it is property or contract – and, relatedly, whether it is to be treated in a formalist or contextualised fashion. Basic interests like the fee simple are clearly *in rem* property interests, and they are for many purposes treated rather formally, at least in comparison to contract rights. *In rem* property rights tend to be more standardised than *in personam* contract rights, a phenomenon associated with the *numerus clausus*, which treats property and contract as being very different in this regard.[1]

And yet there are legal devices that fall between the purely *in rem* and *in personam*. These include the lease, the bailment, security interests, and trusts.[2] Even here, there is a tendency to push these intermediate legal institutions toward one end of the spectrum or the other: there is said to be a transformation from property to contract in leases,[3] and debate has raged over whether beneficial interests are

* Fessenden Professor of Law and Director of the Project on the Foundations of Private Law, Harvard Law School. Email: hesmith@law.harvard.edu.

[1] B Rudden, 'Economic Theory v Property Law: The *Numerus Clausus* Problem' in J Eekelaar and J Bell (eds), *Oxford Essays in Jurisprudence (Third Series)* (Oxford, OUP, 1987); TW Merrill and HE Smith, 'Optimal Standardization in the Law of Property: The *Numerus Clausus* Principle' (2000) 110 *Yale Law Journal* 55; B Akkermans, *The Principle of* Numerus Clausus *in European Law* (Antwerp, Intersentia, 2008) 169–252; HE Smith, 'Standardization in Property Law' in K Ayotte and HE Smith (eds), *Research Handbook on the Economics of Property Law* (Cheltenham, Elgar, 2011) 165–67.

[2] TW Merrill and HE Smith, 'The Property/Contract Interface' (2001) *Columbia Law Review* 773.

[3] RA Cunningham, 'The New Implied and Statutory Warranties of Habitability in Residential Leases: From Contract to Status' (1979) 16 *Urban Law Annual* 3; MA Glendon, 'The Transformation of American Landlord-Tenant Law' (1982) 23 *Boston College Law Review* 503; EH Rabin, 'Revolution in Residential

property or not.[4] And much confusion about bailment law stems from an attempt to see issues in bailment law through the lens of contract, rather than in light of basic notions of possession.[5]

These discontents are a symptom of a larger problem in US law: the law is losing the ability to achieve an articulated spectrum of property. One important way that Anglo-American law traditionally modulated the *in rem–in personam* spectrum was through equity. Among the 'intermediate' legal devices just mentioned is the trust, which is equity's greatest invention. Many doubt that it is particularly equitable in a substantive sense,[6] and some fusionists argue more generally that the distinction between property and contract is disappearing: because law and equity are not distinct, equitable property rights are in fact allowing obligations to become property.[7] This depends on what we mean by 'equity', 'property', 'obligations' and even 'disappear'. While a kind of bottom-line instrumentalism might point in the direction of this kind of thoroughgoing fusion, we have to ask whether the structure of equitable rights and equitable interventions persists – and should persist for functional reasons.[8]

And such a functionally motivated structure indeed exists. As I have argued elsewhere, a major theme of traditional equity has been what I call 'meta-law', and it is this second-order supplement to the law that is often the method by which the law creates a spectrum of property running from the *in rem* toward the *in personam*.[9] Meta-law is law about law; it presupposes law and supplements it,[10] sometimes overriding it, and occasionally modifying it, especially over time. Or, in Aristotle's formulation, equity corrects the law when the law fails on account of its generality.[11]

Landlord-Tenant Law: Causes and Consequences' (1984) 69 *Cornell Law Review* 517. See too S Bright, *Landlord and Tenant Law in Context* (Oxford, Hart, 2007) 30–33 and N Mrockova, 'The Meaning of Exclusive Possession after *Bruton*' [2021] *Conv* 183.

[4] Compare FW Maitland, *Equity: A Course of Lectures*, edn by AH Chaytor and WJ Whittaker (Cambridge, CUP, 1936) 29: '[T]he Chancellor begins to enforce a personal right … which in truth is a contractual right, a right created by a promise.'; JH Langbein, 'The Contractarian Basis of the Law of Trusts' (1995) 105 *Yale Law Journal* 625, 627, 669 (acknowledging that '[t]rust is a hybrid of contract and property', but maintaining that at bottom '[t]rusts are contracts') with AW Scott, 'The Nature of the Rights of the Cestui Que Trust' (1917) 17 *Columbia Law Review* 269, 289: '[T]he rights of the cestui que trust … are treated like property rights rather than like obligations.'; H Hansmann and U Mattei, 'The Functions of Trust Law: A Comparative Legal and Economic Analysis' (1998) 73 *New York University Law Review* 434, 454–59 (arguing for a property-based account of trusts); see also Merrill and Smith, 'The Property/Contract Interface' (n 2) 843–49 (analysing trust as an institution between *in rem* and *in personam*); Y-C Chang and HE Smith, 'An Economic Analysis of Civil Versus Common Law Property' (2012) 88 *Notre Dame Law Review* 1, 13 (discussing trusts in context of styles of legal systems).

[5] CM Newman, 'Bailment and the Property/Contract Interface' (2015) *George Mason Legal Studies Research Paper No LS 15–12*, available at ssrn.com/abstract=2654988.

[6] See, eg, M Oza, 'Book Review – Irit Samet, *Equity: Conscience Goes to Market*' (2020) 70 *University of Toronto Law Journal* 216, 219.

[7] S Worthington, 'The Disappearing Divide Between Property and Obligation: The Impact of Aligning Analysis and Commercial Expectation' in S Degeling and J Edelman (eds), *Equity in Commercial Law* (Sydney, Lawbook Co, 2005).

[8] See too, McFarlane's chapter in this volume.

[9] HE Smith, 'Equity as Meta-Law' (2021) 130 *Yale Law Journal* 1050.

[10] For an analysis of particular equitable rules as exemplifying this supplementary function, see Hudson's chapter in this volume.

[11] Aristotle, *The Nicomachean Ethics* (H Rackham tr, Cambridge, Harvard University Press, 1934) 1137b, at 314–15.

Meta-law is a function of equity triggered in certain circumstances, and once triggered ranges over the results of regular law, taking a broad swath of context into account. It applies a discretionary and fairness-based reasoning to override the result the law would otherwise produce. It is thus neither co-extensive with jurisdictional equity (some 'equity' is a matter of first-order rules), nor is it 'equity' writ large as a matter of morality untethered to doctrine.

In the Anglo-American legal tradition, this meta-law function was often (but not always) performed by doctrines emanating from the courts of equity, and it was the separation of courts of law and equity that promoted the development of equity as meta-law. This also fostered the property spectrum by making meta-law more readily available. Meta-law could operate on the law to create a host of rights that mimic the function of in rem property, more or less, without invoking the full machinery of property law with all its normative and informational implications.[12] Equity could modulate the exercise of existing rights thereby producing the effect of rights in others, without those rights putting third parties to the nonconsensual choice of either investigating and avoiding them or incurring liability for violating them.

Ready availability of meta-law is important. Although the common law narrowly construed might create a property spectrum, equity can play a role in creating and maintaining the property spectrum. Along this spectrum are 'quasi-property' in corpses and hot news,[13] borderline kinds of property associated with equitable remedies, and varieties of the constructive trust. Over time some of these interests were 'promoted' to something close to *in rem* status, as in the case of equitable servitudes. The spectrum serves a purpose, because there are situations in which robust protection of an entitlement is needed but not costly protection against the world at large. Highly targeted protection in terms of subject matter and duty bearers will do. In some of these situations, protection against others generally would burden them with the duty to avoid violations, in a non-consensual fashion. The conditioning of such rights can be highly tailored without large information costs. Functionally, the intermediate points on the spectrum may well be preferable to substitutes that are more purely *in rem* or *in personam*, which do not achieve property-style protection in such a limited or targeted way.

With the fusion of law and equity, the property spectrum is in danger. Existing intermediate devices become harder to understand and to deploy to their best effect. Even beneficial interests under trusts, familiar though they are, are apt to be misunderstood in their intersection with other bodies of law, like the law of torts.[14] Further, when new situations arise, intermediate solutions fall outside the modern legal imagination, and over time a fruitful source of law is choked off. Instead, the law veers between extremes and grasps for ad hoc and poorly conceived solutions to individual problems.

[12] Note the claim of Milsom that 'equity has proved that from the materials of obligation you can counterfeit the phenomena of property': SF Milsom, *Historical Foundations of the Common Law*, 2nd edn (London, Butterworths, 1961) 6.

[13] See the discussion in section III.

[14] B McFarlane, 'Equity and the Justification of Private Rights' in S Degeling, M Crawford, and N Tiverios (eds), *Justifying Private Rights* (Oxford, Hart, 2020) 221–46, and in particular the discussion there of *Shell UK Ltd v Total UK Ltd* [2010] EWCA Civ 180, [2011] QB 86.

This chapter will first set out what meta-law is and why it is used at all. More particularly, I will show how it serves to manage the boundaries of property and contract, notably by selectively overcoming the strictures of privity (section II).[15] Section III then shows how these meta-law interventions can provide 'near property' where property-style protection that is less than *in rem* is called for, especially if that kind of protection needs to respond to complex features of a context sounding in fairness and deceit. This near property has distinctive features designed to tap into the functional benefits of property in the given context whilst also avoiding some of the burdens it poses for third parties. Section IV turns to the dynamic process whereby meta-law provides new solutions which sometimes are transformed into law themselves and concludes with some thoughts on the implications of the property spectrum for the fusion of law and equity.

II. META-LAW AND THE PROPERTY SPECTRUM

It is no accident that equity is associated with intermediate spots in the property-obligation spectrum. For any legal institution like property, tort and contract, there are benefits and costs to providing different modes of protection. Within property law, exclusion strategies are a first cut at defining rights.[16] They have the advantage of providing robust protection: possessors need not prove much to vindicate their rights, because liability turns on simple on/off signals like boundary crossings and gross interferences with personal property. Conversely, the message sent to potential duty bearers is a simple one: keep off, unless you have permission. This simple regime's strength is its weakness: it does little on its own to foster multiple access, which would require monitoring uses in more detail.[17] We thus find the law turning to governance strategies, which focus on narrower classes of uses. Everything from the law of nuisance to servitudes to zoning and land use regulation all implement governance strategies. Nevertheless, these governance strategies, while more focused, are often still *in rem*.[18] For example, easements are protected against third-party interferences, and nuisance binds anyone who might commit one (even if the neighbours are the ones most likely to do so). Because these rights are all *in rem*, they bind others non-consensually.[19] And those third parties would have to expend effort at learning about and avoiding those rights or incur liability. In a sense, the information costs problem is the other side of the coin of the nonconsensual nature of *in rem* rights.[20]

[15] Smith, 'Equity as Meta-Law' (n 9) 1090–92.

[16] HE Smith, 'Exclusion Versus Governance: Two Strategies for Delineating Property Rights' (2002) 31 *Journal of Legal Studies* S453, S467–71.

[17] RC Ellickson, 'Property in Land' (1993) 102 *Yale Law Journal* 1315, 1327–28.

[18] Smith, 'Exclusion Versus Governance' (n 16) S471–74. See also CM Rose, 'Rethinking Environmental Controls: Management Strategies for Common Resources' [1991] *Duke Law Journal* 1, 9–36.

[19] Covenants are least likely to bind third parties, and they are more towards the contract end of the spectrum.

[20] This relates to the theory of the *numerus clausus*: see, eg, B McFarlane, 'The *Numerus Clausus* and Covenants Relating to Land' in S Bright (ed), *Modern Studies in Property Law* (Oxford, Hart, 2013) vol 6. Civilian legal theory emphasises its nonconsensual imposition on third parties: see, eg, K Larenz and M Wolf, *Allgemeiner Teil Des Bürgerlichen Rechts*, 9th edn (Munich, CH Beck, 2004) 250–51;

And yet there are many situations in which such *in rem* protection adds little if anything. The main actors who can contribute positively or negatively to the asset in question are a defined group of people.[21] In some such situations, contract may work, but the group may face high transaction costs (including not knowing they are the relevant group until a problem has arisen).[22] And contract may provide too little protection against third parties, especially successors.

Particularly where the nature of the group and its members' inter-relations are complex or uncertain, there is a rationale for meta-law.[23] Law like other systems employs higher-order components when it faces problems of high complexity and associated uncertainty.[24] In law, these typically stem from polycentric problems, conflicting rights and opportunism.[25] That is, where many elements interact, multiple presumptive rights come into play, or parties may be exploiting the structures of the law to achieve a surprise unfair advantage over another, the problem can often be more effectively addressed by ranging over the results at the primary level and adjusting ex post where needed. For example, if one wants to modulate the application of privity rules (to which I return below), one can use meta-law or one can spell out highly complicated or indeterminate (or both) exceptions at the primary level. In section III below, I discuss this in connection with liability of professionals to third parties who rely on their product. For another example that is functionally rather than jurisdictionally equitable: in the United States, the standard for nuisance liability has been couched either as a second-order reconciliation of conflicting presumptive rights or as a multi-factor balancing test.[26] In the kinds of intermediate property situations we are concerned with in this chapter, all of these problems are in play, and a second-order solution may be called for.

Some prototypical examples of equitable meta-law creating near-property will give some idea of how functionally motivated such interventions are. Consider the evolving scope of privity rules and the development of the trust.

M Wellenhofer, *Sachenrecht*, 34th edn (Munich, CH Beck, 2019) 2. This is intertwined with the information-cost problem emphasised in Merrill and Smith, 'Optimal Standardization in the Law of Property' (n 1). By creating new types of in rem rights, parties put third parties to the nonconsensual choice of expending effort at finding out about rights to avoid violating them or risking violating them and being liable.

[21] HE Smith, 'The Language of Property: Form, Context, and Audience' (2003) 55 *Stanford Law Review* 1105, 1151–53.

[22] GD Libecap, *Contracting for Property Rights* (Cambridge, CUP, 1989) 93–114.

[23] Smith, 'Equity as Meta-Law' (n 9) 1071–90.

[24] ibid 1055–56. For systems in general, see L von Bertalanffy, *General System Theory: Foundations, Development, Applications* (New York, George Braziller, 1968) 27–29, 74, 213–14 (discussing hierarchy in systems); JH Holland, *Hidden Order* (New York, Basic Books, 1995) 11–12 (discussing aggregation and meta-agents); AY Aulin-Ahmavaara, 'The Law of Requisite Hierarchy' (1979) 8 *Kybernetes* 259, 261–62 (discussing required property of higher-order control mechanisms); F Heylighen and C Joslyn, 'Cybernetics and Second-Order Cybernetics' in RA Meyers (ed), *Encyclopedia of Physical Science and Technology*, 3rd edn (San Diego, Academic Press, 2001) 2–4, 10 (discussing motivations for moving to higher orders in cybernetics and the notion of systems of systems).

[25] Smith, 'Equity as Meta-Law' (n 9) 1071–90.

[26] JCP Goldberg and HE Smith, 'Wrongful Fusion: Equity and Torts' in JCP Goldberg, HE Smith and PG Turner (eds), *Equity and Law: Fusion and Fission* (Cambridge, CUP 2019) 315–21. The current Restatement (Fourth) of Property project has proposed returning to a more structured approach to nuisance liability, in contrast with the Restatement (Second) of Torts which provided for a vague standard backed by the unguided balancing of numerous factors. Compare Restatement (Second) of Torts, ss 821D, 821F, 822, 824–31 with Restatement (Fourth) of Property, ss 2.1.2.1 and 2.1.2.2.

First, privity. Various rules of privity serve in a sense as the firewalls of private law. Their advantage is making information internal to a transaction of relevance to the transactors and not to others outside. Normally contractual liability does not extend to third parties, and the mechanism for ensuring this is to require privity of contract.

Privity is part of a system of boundaries between contract and other rights that prevents the detail of obligations from being relevant to third parties and to put them to the choice of becoming informed or risking violation. Privity requirements protect someone within the contractual relationship from liability to third parties. Protection runs in the other direction too, such that third parties are only liable in a highly limited way to the parties to a contract. Third parties are not liable for interfering with contracts unless they have notice (at least), and the duty to inform oneself is minimal: even under tortious interference with contract, one is not liable for contract breach (which might depend on all the details of the agreement) but only for willful inducement of breach, the kind that places a much lesser nonconsensual burden on an outsider.[27] In a similar vein, the 'boundaries' work together to prevent tortfeasors from being liable for pure economic loss such as arises from harm to someone with only a contract and not a property right in the damaged thing.[28]

Returning to privity, equity played a large role in modulating and selectively loosening its requirements in favour of third parties.[29] For example, should contracting parties be liable for the harm they might cause to third parties? Is faulty accounting or legal advice something over which a relying third party might be able to sue the professional? Traditionally the answer was no, although, in the United States, equity might loosen such constraints where the advice was targeted at the third party and could have a nearly fraudulent effect.[30] More recently with the decline of equity, such

[27] RA Epstein, 'Inducement of Breach of Contract as a Problem of Ostensible Ownership' (1987) 16 *Journal of Legal Studies* 1, 4, 24–26; FS McChesney, 'Tortious Interference with Contract Versus "Efficient" Breach: Theory and Empirical Evidence' (1999) 28 *Journal of Legal Studies* 131, 163–64; B McFarlane and A Televantos, 'Third Party Effects in Private Law: Form and Function' in P Miller and J Oberdiek (eds), *Oxford Studies in Private Law Theory* (Oxford, OUP, 2020) vol 1. See also *OBG Ltd v Allan* [2007] UKHL 21, [2008] 1 AC 1.

[28] HE Smith, 'Modularity and Morality in the Law of Torts' (2011) 4 *Journal of Tort Law* 1, 25–28.

[29] *Seaver v Ransom* (1918) 120 NE 639 (New York Court of Appeals) 640 (Pound J): 'It has been said that "the establishment of this doctrine has been gradual, and is a victory of practical utility over theory, of equity over technical subtlety." Brantly on Contracts (2d ed) p. 253. The reasons for this view are that it is just and practical to permit the person for whose benefit the contract is made to enforce it against one whose duty it is to pay.'; see also *New York State Energy Research & Development Authority v Nuclear Fuel Services Inc* (1983) 561 F Supp 954 (US District Court, Western District of New York) 979–80. Samuel Williston originally saw exceptions to the privity rule in favour of third parties as a matter of equity, and then later recast it as a rule; see MA Eisenberg, 'Third-Party Beneficiaries' (1992) 92 *Columbia Law Review* 1358, 1366 fn 37: '1 Samuel Williston on Contracts (1920) § 354, at 682–89 [equitable approach]. Later, as the Reporter for Restatement (First) of Contracts (1932), Williston included in the Restatement a rule that allowed third-party beneficiaries to bring suit even in courts of law, … but he regarded the rule as "an anomaly." See 5 A.L.I. Proc. 385 (1927) (remarks of Reporter Williston).' American commentators noted that English law stretched the equitable device of the trust to provide for rights in third party beneficiaries. See AL Corbin, 'Contracts for the Benefit of Third Persons' (1930) 46 *LQR* 12, 12, 14, 18; G Shalev, 'Third Party Beneficiary: A Comparative Analysis' (1976) 11 *Israel Law Review* 315, 324. This became a rule by legislation, see the Contracts (Rights of Third Parties) Act 1999.

[30] MJ Rizzo, 'A Theory of Economic Loss in the Law of Torts' (1982) 11 *Journal of Legal Studies* 281; HE Smith, 'Fusing the Equitable Function in Private Law' in K Barker, K Fairweather and R Grantham (eds), *Private Law in the 21st Century* (Oxford, Hart, 2017) 173, 188–91.

modulation has given way to some quite complicated (and unsatisfying) multi-factor balancing tests.[31]

Thus, equity would override the limits of privity in various situations. For example, in real servitudes, equity allowed covenants to create what amounted to easements.[32] It did so by disregarding privity and causing the easement-like substance to bind those with notice. This overcame the limits of real covenants and prevented opportunistic behaviour by those with notice.[33] It should also be noted that meta-law outside of equity can be brought to bear in such situations. John Goldberg and I have argued that Judge Cardozo's opinion in *MacPherson v Buick Motor Co*[34] employed an equity-style meta-law to overcome the privity-based limit on tort liability to the manufacturer's immediate purchasers (car dealers), thus allowing the ultimate purchasers to sue for defects.[35]

Another route to intermediate property is the trust. The literature on the nature of the trust is vast, and much of it focusses on the question of whether the trust is more like property or contract.[36] One could say it is intermediate, but from the perspective of meta-law what is interesting is how it is both. The trust allows much contract-style detail to reside internally to the trust, while the interface to the outside world is mostly but not quite the simple one of the trustee's legal ownership. Moreover, the law provides for asset partitioning in the trust: in defensive asset partitioning, creditors dealing with the trust cannot reach the trustee's other assets,[37] and in affirmative asset partitioning, the trustee's creditors cannot reach trust assets.[38] Affirmative asset partitioning is property like in that it defines a pool of assets in a way that would be impossible to replicate by contract alone.[39]

The result is a modular structure in which much information is hidden. As for third parties, the protection is not just intermediate but intermediate in a characteristically meta-law fashion. If the trustee wrongfully transfers to a third party the beneficiary can sue to get the rights restored to the proper trustee unless the third party is a good faith purchaser for value. Thus, equitable interests can be overridden by good faith purchase in a way that legal property cannot (especially in the United States with its narrow exceptions for good faith purchase). Beneficiaries are traditionally not allowed to sue on behalf of the trust; only the trustee may.[40]

[31] Smith, 'Fusing the Equitable Function in Private Law' (n 30).

[32] See, eg, AF Conard, 'Words Which Will Create an Easement' (1941) 6 *Missouri Law Review* 245.

[33] This is most associated with *Tulk v Moxhay* (1848) 2 Ph 774, 41 ER 1143. Ben McFarlane shows how this intervention grew out of a line of cases: B McFarlane, '*Tulk v Moxhay* (1848)' in C Mitchell and P Mitchell (eds), *Landmark Cases in Equity* (Oxford, Hart, 2012).

[34] (1916) 111 NE 1050 (New York Court of Appeals).

[35] Goldberg and Smith (n 26) 319–21.

[36] See n 4.

[37] Restatement (Third) of Trusts, ss 105–106; Uniform Trust Code, s 1010. In earlier law, as remains the case in English law, the trustee would be liable but could be indemnified from the trust's assets: see, eg, *Investec Trust (Guernsey) Ltd v Glenalla Properties Ltd* [2018] UKPC 7, [2019] AC 271 [59].

[38] RH Sitkoff, 'Trust Law as Fiduciary Governance Plus Asset Partitioning' in L Smith (ed), *The Worlds of the Trust* (Cambridge, CUP, 2013).

[39] ibid. The asset partitioning framework was developed in H Hansmann and R Kraakman, 'The Essential Role of Organizational Law' (2000) 110 *Yale Law Journal* 387.

[40] If a beneficiary happens to be in possession of the trust property, this may independently furnish standing to sue: see, eg, *Healy v Healy* [1915] 1 KB 938 (KBD).

As Ben McFarlane and Robert Stevens argue, this constellation of rights and standing follows from the structure of the trust if it is analysed as a right against a right.[41] Against non-good faith purchaser transferees, the beneficiary is suing to get the right back, whereas in property torts, the beneficiary has no direct interest in the trust res.[42]

Whether we take the beneficiary's interest to be a right against a right or see the trustee's ownership as subject to a second layer of duties to use its powers of ownership in favour of the beneficiary,[43] this second layer can be seen as meta-law.[44] Crucially the structure of the trust cannot be reduced to this or that rule or component. It is the synergy of the trust as a mini complex system that allows its results, especially property-like promotion of autonomy and stability of expectations at lower information cost and lesser imposition on third parties, to emerge as overall properties of the system.[45] The meta-law structure allows one to get most of the benefits of property without all of the costs.

The intermediate and more contextual approach offers parties more options to structure their relationships.[46] There are reasons of both cost and benefit to occupying the middle of the *in rem–in personam* spectrum. Moreover, not every way to be intermediate is equally good. Robust protection of an entitlement is at its maximum when it binds the world as duty bearers. Typically, when it does so, it cannot demand a great deal of information gathering and processing on the part of far-flung parties. Consistent with a very general informational tradeoff, one can send an informationally intense message to a less extensive audience or a less informationally intense message to a more extensive audience at equal cost.[47] Thus, in natural language we get more formal registers, with less context employed and less background information needed, when the message is to socially more distant audiences. Among familiars, much can be left unsaid, because more is brought to the communication.[48] So it is in

[41] B McFarlane and R Stevens, 'What's Special About Equity? Rights about Rights' in D Klimchuck, I Samet and HE Smith (eds), *Philosophical Foundations of The Law of Equity* (Oxford, OUP, 2019); B McFarlane and R Stevens, 'The Nature of Equitable Property' (2010) 4 *Journal of Equity* 1.

[42] B McFarlane and A Televantos, 'As Complex as ABC? Bona Fide Purchasers of Equitable Interests' in T Cheng-Han and PS Davies (eds), *Intermediaries in Commercial Law* (Oxford, Hart, 2022). McFarlane criticises the opinion in *Shell* (n 14), which allowed beneficiary standing to sue for negligence (for damage to the trust property), for both physical loss and foreseeable consequences, irrespective of whether the beneficiary had possession of that property: B McFarlane, 'Form and Substance in Equity' in A Robertson and J Goudkamp (eds), *Form and Substance in the Law of Obligations* (Oxford, Hart, 2019) 203–06.

[43] JE Penner, 'An Untheory of the Law of Trusts, or Some Notes Towards Understanding the Structure of Trusts Law Doctrine' (2010) 63 *Current Legal Problems* 653.

[44] Smith, 'Equity as Meta-Law' (n 9); McFarlane, 'Form and Substance in Equity' (n 42); R Stevens, 'Set-Off and the Nature of Equity' in PS Davies, S Douglas and J Goudkamp (eds), *Defences in Equity* (Oxford, Hart, 2018).

[45] J Hudson and C Mitchell, 'Justificanda' in S Degeling, J Hudson and I Samet (eds), *The Philosophical Foundations of the Law of Express Trusts* (Oxford, OUP, 2023). On emergent properties in private law, see also AS Gold and HE Smith, 'Sizing Up Private Law' (2020) 70 *University of Toronto Law Journal* 489; HE Smith, 'Systems Theory: Emergent Private Law' in A Gold et al (eds), *The Oxford Handbook of New Private Law* (Oxford, OUP, 2020).

[46] B McFarlane, 'Equity and the Justification of Private Rights' in S Degeling, M Crawford, and N Tiverios (eds), *Justifying Private Rights* (Oxford, Hart, 2021).

[47] Smith, 'The Language of Property' (n 21).

[48] See FI Dretske, *Knowledge and the Flow of Information* (Cambridge, Mass, MIT Press, 1981) 42–43.

law. A good example is custom, which tends to be both detailed and implicit when it is a matter of insiders but tends to be formalised when it is applied to third parties, especially when it is incorporated into the general law.

III. THE TWILIGHT ZONE OF PROPERTY

In this section, I will briefly canvas the spectrum of rights between property and obligation and show how they often arise though the intervention of meta-law. This appears at first glance to be a grab bag of miscellaneous rights. There is truth in that, which is part of their attraction. I will, however, argue that meta-law allows courts to craft useful rights with combinations of features, some more property-like and some more obligation-like. Not all rights in this intermediate or twilight zone between property and obligation are equal: some attain robustness of protection, tailoring to context and protection of third parties better than others nearby in the same space.

This twilight zone is not without traditional categorisation. Some such rights are equitable rights, although that is a category that itself embraces a miscellany of situations. Another possible category is 'quasi-property', which has sometimes been invoked in US law to denote rights that bear some resemblance to property but that are not full-blown property. How does quasi-property relate to meta-law?

In his insightful treatment of quasi-property, Shyamkrishna Balganesh argues that it embraces a certain kind of near property and for good reasons.[49] According to Balganesh, '[w]hat triggers courts' identification of these relationships (for their invocation of quasi-property) is (i) the status of the parties vis-à-vis each other, (ii) the unique environment or context within which they interact, (iii) the nature – wrongful or otherwise – of one party's actions, or (iv) a combination of these factors'.[50] This is the kind of multi-element and interactive context that is apt for treatment at a higher level. And, as we will see, in areas like hot news misappropriation, the nature of one party's actions sounds in opportunism or constructive fraud, a classic trigger for equity.

Quasi-property can be seen as a potential field for equitable meta-law. Balganesh contrasts quasi-property with other not-quite-property relations like equitable interests and prepossessory interests, restitutionary claims and entitlements, and the like, and identifies these as more metaphorical and not as quasi-property proper. Without taking a position on how to classify all these interests, what the meta-law perspective adds is that these interests fall between obligations and property and their heterogeneity is no accident. Meta-law can tweak interests on a large number of margins, making this initially look totally messy. However, because we can identify the benefits and costs of the use of meta-law, the actual instantiations of interests in this broad space is anything but accidental.

[49] S Balganesh, 'Quasi-Property: Like, But Not Quite Property' (2012) 160 *University of Pennsylvania Law Review* 1889.

[50] ibid 1902. For an application of quasi-property to reconceptualise the law of privacy, see LH Scholz, 'Privacy as Quasi-Property' (2016) 101 *Iowa Law Review* 1113.

Thus, new full-blown equitable rights may or may not be classified as quasi-property. At the other end, the 'mere equity' may not be quasi-property, but it is a right resulting from equity as meta-law within the twilight zone. In general, meta-law allows us to see some additional reasons for the workings of quasi-property and shows why different degrees of exclusion can be combined, in different ways, with different levels of protection against competing rights and immunities of third parties. Meta-law sets the stage for an account, based on the benefits and costs of managing complexity, of why we see the combinations we see, as well as of which ones we might want to see soon.

In property theory there are certain stock examples of borderline property – resources for which property treatment is a close or fraught question. These include hot news, body parts and certain kinds of information. For each of these, I will argue, there is less than meets the eye in terms of property and much more in a different dimension: the dimension of equity.

A. Misappropriation and Hot News

The notion of quasi-property is bound up with meta-law. Quasi-property's most famous instantiation, in hot news misappropriation, is, I have argued, a prime example of meta-law, and was at the time of its development conceived as an equitable intervention.[51] The hot news doctrine is a reference point for property theory because it seems at first blush to involve the courts in creating property rights in information, perhaps for Lockean reap-where-you-sow reasons. In the seminal case of *International News Service v Associated Press* ('*INS v AP*'),[52] the US Supreme Court held that one news organisation violated the rights of another news organisation by repackaging its stories and publishing the fresh news in its own member newspapers. The collecting organisation had a right to exclusive publishing of the news while it was still hot. Justice Brandeis's dissent sounds in the default freedom of information ('free as the air to common use') and the need for legislatures to be the prime creators of property rights.[53]

Regarded closely, the *INS* case is not one of property in the regular sense.[54] As the Court repeatedly noted, the case was in equity, and the rights that one competitor holds against another are quasi-property sounding in misappropriation, not full-blown property. The set of duty bearers is not the rest of the world or people generally as in classic *in rem* property, but an identified set of people engaging in identified similar activities under circumscribed conditions. The decision quite possibly draws on customs of the news business, although the Court gives little indication of this.[55]

[51] HE Smith, 'Equitable Intellectual Property: What's Wrong with Misappropriation?' in S Balganesh (ed), *Intellectual Property and the Common Law* (Cambridge, CUP, 2013) 42.

[52] (1918) 248 US 215 (US Supreme Court).

[53] ibid 262–67.

[54] Smith, 'Equitable Intellectual Property' (n 51).

[55] RA Epstein, '*International News Service v Associated Press*: Custom and Law as Sources of Property Rights in News' (1992) 78 *Virginia Law Review* 85; but see JE Rothman, 'The Questionable Use of Custom in Intellectual Property' (2007) 93 *Virginia Law Review* 1899.

To the extent there was such a custom of mutual respect for hot news, one can see the decision as not only not about property but also not about law: the court is intervening into the law by means of equity to protect the custom, including one of joint contribution to news gathering.[56]

Equity here as often elsewhere is functioning as meta-law or law about law. Law operates as a system with a certain degree of generality, but this very generality causes it to fail for complex reasons, typically of multipolar problems, conflicting rights, and opportunism.[57] Arguably all three were present in *INS*, and whatever the wisdom of protecting hot news, this kind of intervention is far more targetted and far less threatening to the freedom of information than would be a property rights version of *INS* that could become a fount of judge-created first-order intellectual property protection (as Justice Brandeis and later Judge Learned Hand feared).[58] Interestingly and consistently with patterns of fusion in the United States, *INS v AP* has been taken to be about 'property' rather than 'ethics' and it has famously been reformulated into a multi-factor test.[59]

Returning to the problem of complexity, the equitable intervention is limited in the ways one would expect from a concern about complexity. Equity is synergistic with law but in certain defined channels (equity's limited domain and its triggers based on custom and the like). Both as new intellectual property and especially as a free-floating *deus ex machina* of equity, misappropriation law could be much more open-ended and unmanageably complex than it is. The equitable meta-law version of misappropriation gets most of the benefit of property (competitors are those who can affect the value of the resource) and at minimal cost to third parties in terms of restricting them and obligating them to engage in avoidance. The rights are not *in rem* (with all their costs, especially in the realm of information), and the trigger is detailed and classically equitable. As such, it comes as less of a surprise to those who might be bound.[60]

B. Body Parts

Property rights can also be controversial or borderline for moral reasons. Should property extend to body parts?[61] This is sometimes thought to be a question of

[56] S Balganesh, '"Hot News": The Enduring Myth of Property in News' (2011) 111 *Columbia Law Review* 419.

[57] Smith, 'Equity as Meta-Law' (n 9).

[58] See *Cheney Bros v Doris Silk Co* (1929) 35 F.2d 279 (2nd Cir).

[59] See, eg, *National Basketball Association v Motorola* (1997) 105 F.3d 841 (2nd Cir) 852 (Winter J). See also ibid 853 (Winter J): 'INS is not about ethics; it is about the protection of property rights in time-sensitive information so that the information will be made available to the public by profit seeking entrepreneurs.' See also DG Baird, 'Common Law Intellectual Property and the Legacy of *International News Service v Associated Press*' (1983) 50 *University of Chicago law Review* 411, 428–29 (discussing *INS* as common-law intellectual property and as a source of property rights).

[60] On the kinds of 'acoustic separation' and audience design in equity, see Y Feldman and HE Smith, 'Behavioral Equity' (2014) 170 *Journal of Institutional and Theoretical Economics* 137.

[61] Recently, this issue has arisen in the context of patent law, in which the question is under what circumstances one can acquire a patent in genetic sequences. See, eg, *Association for Molecular Pathology v*

property, both conceptually and morally. And one can frame the question this way. However, some of the case law that supposedly illustrates the struggle with this question presents less than meets the eye in terms of property. Instead it is equity acting as meta-law.

Consider *Moore v Regents of the University of California*,[62] perhaps the most famous case on body parts in the United States and a staple of property courses. On one level, it presents a borderline property scenario, but there is more and less to it than that. In *Moore*, the doctors treating Moore's cancer deceived Moore into undergoing additional tests and used his spleen cells after treatment without telling him that they developed a patented cell line out of them. The majority disallowed conversion because they found the cells not to be Moore's property (or perhaps the other way around – no conversion, no property). In dissent, Justice Mosk famously applied a bundle-of-rights analysis to argue for property treatment. Among the majority's concerns with treating the spleen as property and applying conversion would be the potential conversion liability for downstream researchers using the cells in good faith without knowing their problematic origin. Functionally what the Court was doing was more equitable than it was like property or tort.[63] The majority did not leave Moore remediless in that it did allow him to sue for breach of fiduciary duty and lack of informed consent. The Court was enforcing custom and commercial morality filtered through a relationship of trust and vulnerability and thereby reconciling conflicting interests at one remove, without declaring *in rem* rights.

One of the advantages of the equitable approach is that it can provide some protection for those in Moore's position and downstream third parties, rather than requiring an all or nothing solution. The equity protecting Moore would bind only those third parties with notice, and we could calibrate the degree of inquiry required through the concept of inquiry notice. Such a solution is not costless: Moore would be protected even better by an *in rem* right and subjecting good faith downstream researchers to conversion liability. Under *Moore*, plaintiffs have no ability to hold downstream researchers to account. The equitable solution provides more protection than that and holds downstream researchers liable only if they have notice so their conscience is affected (as with third-party liability for misuse of confidential information). And in a sense the court in *Moore* was groping toward this solution, but missed it because of its focus purely on *in rem* and *in personam* to the exclusion of equity.

As with misappropriation of hot news, limiting the property-style treatment of a thing can be a way of containing complexity, especially where the implications of property treatment are troubling on substantive grounds.

Myriad Genetics Inc (2013) 569 US 576 (US Supreme Court); JL Contreras, '*Association for Molecular Pathology v Myriad Genetics*: A Critical Reassessment' (2020) 27 *Michigan Technology Law Review* 1.

[62] (1990) 793 P.2d 479 (Supreme Court of California).

[63] Goldberg and Smith (n 26).

C. Sensitive Information

As with misappropriation, we must be on guard not to let intellectual property rights in by the back door. An expansive approach chills expression, dampens certain kinds of creativity, and places an informational burden on third parties. Where certain targeted kinds of information might be protected, even against third parties, US law has had difficulty in framing the issue. This too may be a symptom of a dearth of equitable meta-law.

In English and Australian law, courts have gone some distance in allowing for liability for downstream third parties: in addition to the liability of one who has breached a duty of confidence, someone who receives the information can be liable for misusing it if they know that the information was confidential.[64] The calibration of liability sounds in equitable principles: one who has notice is one whose conscience is affected. This can extend to what someone ought to have known.[65] Nonetheless, the duty involved is not one of inquiry, but rather not ignoring the obvious.[66] This allows for protection against some third parties but without placing a heavy burden on those third parties.

In the United States, downstream third-party liability for misuse of confidential information is far less accepted, and the law and commentary has struggled with the issue. It has led to proposals for workarounds for parties who would like more protection beyond contracting parties than the law affords.[67] Because principles of equity and notice are less familiar as a living system, using these tools in the law of confidential information has not been as available as in other common law systems. An echo of these problems can be found in insider trading law with its constant struggles over its relationship to fraud and the vexing question of tippee liability.[68] The full use of equitable meta-law machinery could frame the problem better and possibly form part of the solution. This is especially true of downstream liability for those with notice.

D. Overview

There is a sense in which *Moore* and even *INS* are about property after all. In each of them, who gets to do what to whom is at stake. The interests involved – in body

[64] *Attorney General v Observer Ltd* [1990] 1 AC 109 (HL) 268. See P Stanley, *The Law of Confidentiality: A Restatement* (Oxford, Hart 2008) para [5] (Notice), 25–31.

[65] *Smith Kline & French Laboratories (Aust) Ltd v Secretary, Department of Community Services and Health* (1990) 22 FCR 73 (FCA) 96 (Gummow J): '[E]quity may impose an obligation of confidence upon a defendant having regard not only to what the defendant knew, but to what he ought to have known in all the relevant circumstances.' See too *Campbell v MGN Ltd* [2004] UKHL 22, [2004] 2 AC 457 [14] (Lord Nicholls) and [44]–[45] (Lord Hoffmann) and *Primary Group (UK) Ltd v Royal Bank of Scotland plc* [2014] EWHC 1082 (Ch), [2014] 2 All ER (Comm) 1121 [237] (Arnold J).

[66] Stanley (n 64) 30.

[67] W Hartzog, 'Chain-Link Confidentiality' (2012) 46 *Georgia Law Review* 657.

[68] Z Gubler, 'Insider Trading as Fraud' (2020) 98 *North Carolina Law Review* 533. See *Dirks v SEC* (1983) 463 US 646 (US Supreme Court) 659–64. See also the controversy over the misappropriation theory.

parts, in information one is using in one's news business, and so on – are the kind of interests that property institutions address. And in the sense of offering some protection to these interests, equity, restitution and even contract achieve a partial property-like effect. One can use non-property-like mechanisms to achieve the aims of property. In trust law, the beneficiary has rights against the trustee that the trustee use the powers of legal title for the beneficiary's benefit, and such rights carry over to some transferees but not all. Through the trust, one can achieve the effect of property by non-classic property means – second-order means that have become quite regularised.[69] In some technological situations, we worry that someone can use *in personam* contract on a mass scale to achieve property protection not afforded by copyright: if anyone encountering one's software can be forced by technological and legal means to contract, the effect is like a synthetic *in rem* right.[70] Trusts are the classic way of achieving idiosyncrasies in property rights without burdening many third parties with having to know much about them: legal title is the interface to most of the rest of the world under most circumstances. In *Moore*, full-blown property protection could easily lead to liability for good faith downstream researchers – a result that courts should not produce lightly and which can be avoided through the application of equity. The various routes to propertyhood in this functional or substantive sense are not equal, because they achieve protections with very different effects on third parties.

IV. THE DYNAMICS OF EQUITY AND FUSION

Robust meta-law does more than define intermediate points on the property spectrum. Even if at any given time, intermediate interests might look static and have no ongoing meta interventions, they may retain a two-tier structure. Equitable property rights (like those of a beneficiary of a trust) are an example. But meta-law can be seen as doing more if we examine its operation through time. Meta-law can provide a path to rights on a micro level, and it also can lead to the development of new property rights at a systemic level.

A. The Dynamic Equitable Process

The micro path to property should be familiar: we have seen it in the discussion of various situation-specific innovations to provide some kind of equitable right. A very

[69] McFarlane and Stevens, 'The Nature of Equitable Property' (n 41); McFarlane, 'Equity and the Justification of Private Rights' (n 14) 232–35; Smith, 'Equity as Meta-Law' (n 9).

[70] For an example that comes close to this, see *ProCD Inc v Zeidenberg* (1996) 86 F.3d 1447 (7th Cir); S Macaulay, 'Freedom from Contract: Solutions in Search of a Problem?' 2004 *Wisconsin Law Review* 777, 804: 'Was ProCD using the alchemy of a pretend contract to claim property in material that was and ought to remain in the public domain?'.

well-worn path is to use estoppel.[71] And equity generally regulates the path towards the acquisitions of rights.[72]

The importance of the dynamics of meta-law comes (again) from the trust. The obligational view of the beneficial interest, namely that it is a right against a right, has the advantage of compatibility with civil law.[73] Civil law has a notion of obligation and as long as a right can be its subject matter, one might think that the trust could be built directly out of these materials. And yet that is not what happened, and the trust has often been imported into civilian jurisdictions rather than being constructed out of home-grown materials.[74] The 'meta' step of allowing a right to be the subject matter of a right is easier to accomplish when one can use a second-order law as in English equity.[75] The separate courts made the functioning of the trust work smoothly, and it arose in an organic way (some problems were directed at one court or the other).[76] Creating a trust in a civil law system would require a much more conscious act of legal design. This is not impossible but more difficult. Greater attention to meta-law can unlock the potential of the law to accomplish these kinds of innovations without having to incur the burden of a dual-court system. And because post-merger, the common-law world also has no separate equity as a matter of jurisdiction, there too further innovative uses of equity will have to be more deliberate.

All of which is not to say that equity should be creating new property rights willy-nilly. Meta-law allows us to frame the issue, though: for example, it can forbid equity from doing so in contexts in which the nonconsensual informational burden on parties is likely to be high compared with the benefit of solving the problem at hand.

B. Problems of Fusion

Flattening meta-law means losing the ability to do a specific kind of intermediate property, less than full property but more than obligation, or doing it in an especially effective way. If equity is suited for intermediate property, then excessive

[71] B McFarlane, *The Law of Proprietary Estoppel*, 2nd edn (Oxford, OUP, 2022).

[72] L Katz, 'Pathways to Legal Rights: The Function of Equity' in I Samet, D Klimchuck and HE Smith (eds), *Philosophical Foundations of The Law of Equity* (Oxford, OUP, 2019).

[73] See McFarlane and Stevens, 'The Nature of Equitable Property' (n 41); P Matthews, 'The Compatibility of the Trust with the Civil Law Notion of Property' in L Smith (ed), *The Worlds of the Trust* (Cambridge, CUP, 2013).

[74] See, eg, L Smith (ed), *Re-Imagining the Trust: Trusts in Civil Law* (Cambridge, CUP, 2012); L Smith (ed), *The Worlds of the Trust* (Cambridge, CUP, 2013); L Ho and R Lee (eds), *Trust Law in Asian Civil Law Jurisdictions: A Comparative Analysis* (Cambridge, CUP, 2013); L Thévenoz, 'The Future of Trusts: A Swiss Perspective' (2013) 19 *Trusts and Trustees* 296. See also R Helmholz and R Zimmermann, *Itinera Fiduciae: Trust and Treuhand in Historical Perspective* (Berlin, Duncker & Humblot, 1998).

[75] See McFarlane's chapter in this volume.

[76] J Getzler, '"As If." Accountability and Counterfactual Trust' (2011) 91 *Boston University Law Review* 973, 979–80; Penner (n 43) 665–66; DJ Seipp, 'Trust and Fiduciary Duty in the Early Common law' (2011) 91 *Boston University Law Review* 969, 1014–22.

fusion raises the stakes for the *numerus clausus* and standardisation: losing the intermediate way means that the *numerus clausus* will be either more draconian or more ineffective.

In the United States, the process of fusion has proceeded in characteristically extreme ways. The process began as the natural rights paradigm was breaking down and reached its culmination in the era of legal realism.[77] I have argued that fusion in the United States has partaken of the general flattening of private law.[78] One sign of this fusion-abetted flattening is the replacement of equitable presumptions and principles with multi-factor balancing tests. A prominent example is the standard of liability for professionals to third parties relying on their work product. Multi-factor tests for property have also been devised for hot news misappropriation.[79]

The multi-factor balancing test is often the best one can do if one flattens out meta-law. Problems of complexity and uncertainty, involving multiple parties, conflicting rights or opportunism, are hard to solve at one level.[80] The solutions need to be themselves complex, often taking the form of many specified factors or unspecified and unguided balancing.

The flattening from fusion also shows up in the property spectrum in specific ways. If meta-law is not available to create detail in a walled-off way, then the stakes become higher. If protection is to be afforded a party, we have to choose complete property with all of its sweeping implications and information costs, or we have to go with obligation and risk lesser protection.

Returning to 'property' in body parts, courts are nervous about commodification and they worry about innocent downstream researchers facing conversion liability. And yet no protection is troubling. It is no accident that the Court in *Moore* made gestures to fiduciary law, which is equitable. If it followed out this idea it could even protect someone like Moore against downstream researchers with notice, through the imposition of some kind of equitable right, perhaps employing the constructive trust.

Or take the increasing attention to the mere equity in English and Australian law. The mere equity is not a full-blown property right, not even an equitable interest (on some accounts); it is a placeholder for an equitable remedy.[81] Some argue that it can be

[77] For England, see the Judicature Acts 1873–75. For the United States, see the Federal Rules of Civil Procedure 1938 (US); New York Code of Procedure of 1848, NY Laws Ch 379 (Field Code); K Funk, 'The Union of Law and Equity: The United States, 1800–1938' in JCP Goldberg, HE Smith and PG Turner (eds), *Equity and Law: Fusion and Fission* (Cambridge, CUP, 2019) 46; PI McMahon, 'Field, Fusion and the 1850s: How an American Law Reformer Influenced the Judicature Act of 1875' in PG Turner (ed), *Equity and Administration* (Cambridge, CUP, 2016).

[78] HE Smith, 'Fusion of Law and Confusion of Equity' in D Klimchuk, I Samet and HE Smith (eds), *Philosophical Foundations of the Law of Equity* (Oxford, OUP, 2020).

[79] See n 59.

[80] Smith, 'Equity as Meta-Law' (n 9).

[81] See, eg, GC Cheshire, 'A New Equitable Interest in Land' (1953) 16 *MLR* 1; AR Everton, '"Equitable Interests" and "Equities" – In Search of a Pattern' (1976) 40 *Conveyancer and Property Lawyer* 209; M Neave and M Weinberg, 'The Nature and Function of Equities' (1978) 6 *University of Tasmania Law Review* 24 and (1979) 6 *University of Tasmania Law Review* 115. See also S Cooper and E Lees, 'Interests, Powers and Mere Equities in Modern Land Law' (2017) 37 *OJLS* 435; RE Poole, 'Equities in the Making' (1968) 32 *Conveyancer and Property Lawyer* 98. See generally DC Jackson, *Principles of Property Law* (Sydney, Law Book Co, 1967) 47–118; J Wells, *What Is a Mere Equity?: An Investigation into the Nature*

employed in the law of restitution for unjust enrichment.[82] Crucially it can bind third parties, even if it is more vulnerable to good faith purchasers (eg, of equitable interests) than are true equitable interests. The equity, once featured in US law, dropped out of the legal toolkit sometime in the twentieth century. What has taken its place is un-thought-through invocations of estoppel, with scant regard to the question of third parties. Or courts simply grasp at cruder solutions, again without following out the implications.

In contrast to England and other common law jurisdictions,[83] the law of estoppel in the United States is underdeveloped. It is often treated as a dangerous *deus ex machina*. Recent scholarship has begun to make sense of estoppel,[84] but the courts need to consider what the triggering events are and what are the implications for third parties. This is exactly how questions are framed by meta-law, which could be resuscitated for this purpose.[85]

Another problem in American law has been the scope and nature of the constructive trust. Although it is famous through then-Judge Cardozo's pronouncement that the constructive trust is 'the formula through which the conscience of equity finds expression',[86] this gives little guidance.[87] And US law has gone all in for the remedial constructive trust, without a great deal of theorising behind it. That may be starting to change with the attention to equitable remedies in the Restatement (Third) of Restitution and Unjust Enrichment.[88] I have argued that the constructive trust can be understood as a mechanism of meta-law.[89] This is especially true of those aspects of the constructive trust that could be said to alter the underlying right, something that can be useful but needs to be cabined.[90] In the area of equitable conversion in the land sale transaction, US law could give more attention to the various equities that fall under the constructive trust and how these grow during the executory period.[91]

and Function of So-Called 'Mere Equities' (PhD thesis submitted at the University of York, 2019). For scepticism about the distinction between equities and equitable interests, see, eg, R Chambers, *Resulting Trusts* (Oxford, OUP, 1997) 171–84; PD White, 'The Illusion of the Mere Equity' (1967) 5 *Sydney Law Review* 499.

[82] R Chambers, 'Two Kinds of Enrichment' in R Chambers, C Mitchell and J Penner (eds), *Philosophical Foundations of the Law of Unjust Enrichment* (Oxford, OUP, 2009). See also Restatement (Third) of Restitution and Unjust Enrichment, s 55. For an argument against a proprietary account sounding in equity and inadequacy of the legal remedy, see W Swadling, 'Unjust Enrichment: Value, Rights, and Trusts' (2012) 137 *LQR* 56. For argument in favour of a powers model rather than one based on intermediate interests, see B Häcker, 'Proprietary Restitution after Impaired Consent Transfers: A Generalised Power Model' (2009) 68 *CLJ* 324.

[83] See, eg, M Barnes, *The Law of Estoppel* (Oxford, Hart, 2020); B McFarlane, *The Law of Proprietary Estoppel*, 2nd edn (Oxford, OUP, 2022); B McFarlane and P Sales, 'Promises, Detriment and Liability: Lessons from Proprietary Estoppel' (2015) 131 *LQR* 610.

[84] MP Gergen, 'Towards Understanding Equitable Estoppel' in C Rickett and R Grantham (eds), *Structure and Justification in Private Law: Essays for Peter Birks* (Oxford, Hart, 2008) 319–37.

[85] Even the tendency in the United States to treat covenants as servitudes, rather than as sometimes creating easements, may reflect the dearth of equitable meta-law.

[86] *Beatty v Guggenheim Exploration Co* (1896) 225 NY 380 (New York Court of Appeals) 386.

[87] *See* HJ Powell, '"Cardozo's Foot": The Chancellor's Conscience and Constructive Trusts' (1993) 56 *Law and Contemporary Problems* 7.

[88] Restatement (Third) of Restitution and Unjust Enrichment, s 55.

[89] Smith, 'Equity as Meta-Law' (n 9) 1134–35.

[90] See YK Liew, *Rationalising Constructive Trusts* (Oxford, Hart, 2017).

[91] See PG Turner, 'Understanding the Constructive Trust Between Vendor and Purchaser' (2012) *LQR* 582. See too Swadling's chapter in this volume.

As with the rest of the downplaying of equity, the law is led to overly dichotomous, polarised positions.

This kind of collapsing of the property spectrum has consequences. To take but one, consider the use of the (mere) equity to enforce a promise that someone can live somewhere for life, upon which promise the promisee reasonably relies.[92] In *Garner v Gerrish*,[93] the Court was faced with what purported to be a lease for life. Robert Donovan executed a lease on a printed form, with Lou Gerrish as the tenant. Rent was $100 a month and the lease provided that 'Lou Gerrish has the privilege of termination [sic] this agreement at a date of his own choice' (handwritten). Gerrish moved in and lived there until Donovan died several years later. David Garner, executor of Donovan's estate, served Gerrish with notice to quit. Under the *numerus clausus* implicit in US law, a lease for life is not possible (although one could create a 99-year lease terminable by the tenant). Traditionally, courts would treat a purported lease for life, a lease for the duration of the war, and the like, as a tenancy at will or periodic tenancy.[94] However, in a realist vein, the opinion in *Garner* is festooned with sneering references to feudalism and seisin.[95] Apparently seeing in Gerrish a tenant in need of protection, the Court rejected tenancy at will as not in accord with the parties' intent. The court was not clear on whether it considered the interest a life estate (some language supports this) or a lease (also supported). Ironically, recent work by Bernie Jones has shown that far from being a case of an overbearing landlord, Donovan was very ill and the lease was likely the product of unconscionability and undue influence by Gerrish on Donovan.[96]

Garner illustrates in multiple ways the pathology of eliminating meta-law. The opinion shows no awareness of the impact on third parties, whether successors, the heirs, or other potential transactors. The Court was not attuned to the equities of the situation because it was busy trying to effect the parties' 'intent'. The Court did not even consider the application of estoppel, perhaps because there was a written lease. The main lesson is that the court failed to consider a variety of possibilities and aspects of the situation, all of which would have been front and centre in a court more attuned to equitable meta-law. An opinion that purports to be nuanced manages to flop in exactly this regard. And the decision has had little impact.

V. CONCLUSION

Meta-law is associated with equity, and along with equity has been partially flattened out of the law. This is one of the major effects of the hyper-fusion of law and

[92] For consideration of a similar situation in English law, see, eg, *Errington v Errington* [1952] 1 KB 290 (CA). See Cheshire (n 81); Poole (n 81).

[93] (1984) 473 NE2d 223 (New York Court of Appeals).

[94] Merrill and Smith, 'Optimal Standardization in the Law of Property (n 1) 11–12. For the position in English law, see *Berrisford v Mexfield Housing Co-operative Ltd* [2011] UKSC 52, [2012] 1 AC 955.

[95] *Garner* (n 93) 224–25.

[96] BD Jones, '*Garner v Gerrish* and the Renter's Life Estate: Teaching a New Concept of "Home"' (2010) 2 *Faulkner Law Review* 1, 4.

equity in the United States. Equity is a specialised component or sub-system of the law that can be deep and contextualised without being general. Sometimes in the space between property and contract, that combination is called for on functional grounds. Although when and where it makes sense to employ meta-law, especially in the gap between property and obligation, turns on empirical questions, equity helps frame the question and offers concrete solutions with which we already have some experience.

18

Certainty of Loss of Chance in Equity

SIMONE DEGELING*

I. INTRODUCTION

THE CLAIMANT MAY have suffered a lost opportunity in the course of dealing that engages their equity for relief. For example, the claimant may have given up an existing career in reliance on a father's promise to leave them property on his death,[1] relinquished the opportunity to obtain a binding court order effecting a property settlement after a divorce[2] or they may have lost the opportunity to raise investor equity through a delinquent director's breach of fiduciary duty in appropriating that opportunity.[3] Such scenarios raise the conceptual problem of uncertainty of loss, since if this lost chance is relevant to establishing their equity for relief or the exercise of equitable discretion as to the appropriate relief, the claimant must necessarily have reference to past or future hypothetical events or value. The claimant asks what would have happened, in the past or the future, had the defendant not breached their equitable obligations or otherwise acted contrary to equitable standards of conduct.[4] Answering such questions requires the court to apply principles of certainty of loss. This chapter explores these issues largely by reference to Australian law, drawing on cases from other jurisdictions where relevant.

Certainty of loss is familiar in claims for compensatory damages at law. *McGregor on Damages* states that '[t]o justify an award of substantial damages where loss is asserted the claimant must satisfy the court both as to (i) the fact of damage, that is an adverse consequence; and (ii) as to its amount'.[5] Consistently with this requirement of

* Professor, University of New South Wales Faculty of Law and Justice. I thank Prof Ben McFarlane and Dr Steven Elliott KC, the organisers of the *Equity: 150 Years After the Judicature Reforms* conference, for their invitation to speak. I am indebted to the other conference participants, as well as Scott Donald, Chris Pearce and Allison Silink for comments and questions on a draft version of this chapter. I also thank Jack Zhou for his research assistance. All errors are mine.

[1] *Q v E* [2018] NSWSC 442.

[2] *Delaforce v Simpson-Cook* [2010] NSWCA 84, (2010) 78 NSWLR 483.

[3] *Ramsay v BigTinCan Pty Ltd* [2014] NSWCA 324.

[4] *cf* A Burrows, 'Uncertainty about Uncertainty: Damages for Loss of a Chance' [2008] *Journal of Personal Injury Law* 31, 34; A Burrows, *Remedies for Torts, Breach of Contract, and Equitable Wrongs*, 4th edn (Oxford, OUP, 2019) ch 2.

[5] J Edelman, *McGregor on Damages*, 21st edn (London, Sweet & Maxwell, 2021) para [10-001].

certainty, substantial damages may be recoverable at law for a loss of a chance despite the 'nature of the damage [preventing] absolute certainty of proof'.[6] As stated by Bowen LJ in *Ratcliffe v Evans*, 'as much certainty and particularity must be insisted on … [in] proof of damage, as is reasonable, having regard to the circumstances and to the nature of the acts themselves by which the damage is done'.[7] What is required is reasonable or relative certainty. Thus, in appropriate categories,[8] the value of any compensatory damages at law is capable of being calculated proportionate to the chances rather than according to the 'all or nothing' balance of probabilities test.[9] Given that equity also recognises and gives normative significance to lost chances, what is equity's approach to certainty?

This chapter identifies the principles by which equity makes reasonably certain the value of the claimant's lost opportunity. This may have significance for equitable analysis in at least two ways. First, the lost opportunity may as a factual matter satisfy an element of the claimant's equity for relief. Secondly, it may be relevant for the remedial inquiry. Thus, the principles by which the claimant's loss is made certain varies depending on the role played by the lost opportunity.[10] Each of these is outlined briefly below.

First, as in equitable estoppels, elements of the claimant's equity may as a factual matter be satisfied by the claimant's lost opportunity. As is outlined in section III, in equitable estoppels the defendant will be estopped where they have made 'a representation or assurance … to the claimant; reliance on [the representation or assurance] by the claimant; and detriment to the claimant in consequence of [their] (reasonable) reliance'.[11] The relevant detriment is that which would flow from a departure from the assurance. Thus, it is not the detriment accruing to the claimant simply from relying on the representation or assurance, but that which would flow from the claimant's 'change of position if the [representation or assurance] were deserted that led to it'.[12] As a factual matter, the claimant's lost opportunity may be used as evidence going to satisfy either or both the reliance on the assurance given by the defendant and also detriment. Equity tolerates a relatively high degree of uncertainty when establishing the existence and evaluating the significance of the lost chance for either of these inquiries. The court establishes the existence of any opportunity lost on a balance

[6] ibid para [10-009].

[7] *Ratcliffe v Evans* [1892] 2 QB 524 (CA) 532–33. Strictly speaking, this dictum is limited to actions derived from Case, and was given in the context of a consideration of the need to establish damage as an element of the cause of action. However, the dictum is 'generally taken as the *locus classicus* of the concept of certainty': M Tilbury, *Civil Remedies* (Sydney, Butterworths, 1990) vol I, para [3195]. See also *Parabola Investments Ltd v Browallia Cal Ltd* [2011] EWCA Civ 486, [2011] QB 477 [22]–[23] (Toulson LJ) with whom Rimer LJ (at [61]) and Mummery LJ (at [62]) agreed.

[8] eg, damages for loss of profit in contract, pure economic loss in negligence.

[9] *Palliser Ltd v Fate Ltd* [2019] EWHC 43 (QB), [2019] Lloyd's Rep IR 341 [27]; *Sellars v Adelaide Petroleum NL* (1994) 179 CLR 332 (HCA).

[10] Hypothetical value is not limited to the loss side of the ledger, it also flows into gain via an account of profits for future profits. See *Ancient Order of Foresters in Victoria Friendly Society Ltd v Lifeplan Australia Friendly Society Ltd* [2018] HCA 43, (2018) 265 CLR 1 and S Degeling 'Certainty in Calculating Monetary Remedies for Breach of Fiduciary Duty' in K Barker and R Grantham (eds), *Apportionment in Private Law* (Oxford, Hart, 2019) 221. This chapter focusses on loss.

[11] *Thorner v Major* [2009] UKHL 18, [2009] 1 WLR 776 [29] (Lord Walker).

[12] *Grundt v Great Boulder Pty Gold Mines Ltd* (1937) 59 CLR 641 (HCA) 674 (Dixon J).

of probabilities. However, what is the nature and extent of this loss? Or put another way, to what extent, does the court inquire as to the value of the lost opportunity? For reliance, there is limited qualitative evaluation such that the chance cannot be established, for example, via 'pure speculation'.[13] Similarly, in relation to detriment, the court applies a broad-brush evaluation of the significance of this opportunity, requiring only that the chances of success not be 'fanciful or unrealistic'.[14]

Secondly, the claimant's lost chance may have significance in a remedial inquiry. Specifically, this loss may be met via an award of equitable compensation or, as argued below, potentially via other monetary remedies consequent on rescission. Within the remedial inquiry, the court is concerned to establish the existence and value of the lost chance. The existence of the lost opportunity is required to be established on a balance of probabilities. However, the value of that opportunity depends upon various contingencies including the conduct of the claimant and also third parties. As discussed below, equity arguably has two techniques for making certain the claimant's lost chance as part of this remedial inquiry. The first explicitly applies probabilistic reasoning and discounts the value of the lost chance by reference to the impact of the conduct of the claimant and third parties. The second locates the inquiry within equitable discretion, applying presumptions and fact-finding principles which are weighted according to the conduct of the parties.

Understanding equity's approach to certainty of loss is important for a number of linked reasons. Most obviously, principled development of the law requires us to make explicit equity's approach. As this chapter demonstrates, equity has various approaches to lost opportunity, and these need to be identified and understood. Additionally, as a head of loss, lost opportunity has the potential to be a vehicle to recharacterise other losses. For example, at law, in a negligence claim against a testator's solicitor, an intended beneficiary sought to recharacterise the loss to the estate in a testator's family maintenance action as the testator's loss of opportunity to arrange his affairs differently. The claim failed as no duty of care was owed to the intended beneficiary and, even if it was, factual causation of loss was not established. However, the High Court of Australia did not hold that the possible recharacterisation of loss was unavailable.[15] By contrast, a claimant was not permitted to sue for the loss of a chance of a better medical outcome instead of physical injury in a case where medical negligence had been found.[16] Whilst claims for physical injury are not likely in equity,[17] the same propensity of some losses to shape shift into lost opportunities is potentially present. Therefore, it is essential to know equity's approach to making certain the value of lost opportunity, as part of a broader debate about the extent to which equity will award monetary remedies for those lost opportunities.

[13] *Steria Ltd v Hutchison* [2006] EWCA Civ 1551, [2007] ICR 445 [127] (Neuberger LJ).

[14] *Delaforce* (n 2) [5] (Allsop P).

[15] *Badenach v Calvert* [2016] HCA 18, (2016) 257 CLR 440 [37] (French CJ, Kiefel and Keane JJ) [92]–[93] (Gordon J).

[16] *Tabet v Gett* [2010] HCA 12, (2010) 240 CLR 537 [46] (Gummow A-CJ), [124] (Kiefel J), [100] (Crennan J), [68] (Hayne and Bell JJ).

[17] Contrast, eg, L Ho, 'Undue Influence and Equitable Compensation' in P Birks and F Rose (eds), *Restitution and Equity* (Oxford, Mansfield Press, 2000) 209.

The discussion proceeds as follows: Section II briefly sets out what is meant by a lost chance; section III considers principles of certainty as they are applied to a lost chance as an element of the claimant's equity for relief, considering equitable estoppels. The discussion then moves to consider equity's approach at the remedial inquiry, dealing separately with (section IV) equitable compensation; and (section V) monetary remedies consequent on rescission in equity. Section VI concludes the discussion.

II. WHAT IS A LOST CHANCE?

In *Talacko v Talacko*[18] the High Court observed that the language of loss of chance does not always distinguish between the following two categories, of which only the first is relevant for this chapter:[19]

> (i) instances where a defendant's [wrongful] act deprives a plaintiff of an opportunity or chance to which the plaintiff was not entitled but where such deprivation constitutes an immediate loss; and (ii) instances where a defendant's [wrongful] act reduces or extinguishes the value of a plaintiff's existing right, where the value might be quantified by reference to the likelihood of future events.

In both categories, 'once the lost opportunity or diminution in value of a right is proved', difficult issues of quantification may arise since value may be a function of 'estimating the significance of events which are, or may be, yet to come'.[20] However, only the first category embodies a lost opportunity. This is because in this category the wrongful act does not interfere with or impair an *existing right* of the claimant. In asserting a lost opportunity, it is therefore 'necessary to "identify the interest said to have been harmed by the defendant". That interest, whether described as a chance or opportunity, must be lost'.[21] Illustrations include the well-known case of *Sellars v Adelaide Petroleum NL*,[22] discussed in section IV, where the claimant lost an opportunity to contract with a third party on more favourable terms which would have been achieved but for the defendant's statutory wrongdoing.

By contrast, the Court in *Talacko* explained that the second category, in which 'the existence of a loss is sufficiently shown by proving that the [wrongdoing] caused a permanent impairment of the value of the plaintiff's existing right'[23] is better understood as a form of loss of value of property, relevantly a chose in action. Whilst the value of that loss may well be assessed by reference to 'events which did not happen', the Court emphasised that this 'has been said to have "nothing to do with loss of chance as such. It is simply the judge making a realistic and reasoned assessment

[18] [2021] HCA 15, (2021) 389 ALR 178.
[19] ibid [40] (the Court).
[20] ibid [41] (the Court) quoting *HTW Valuers (Central Qld) Pty Ltd v Astonland Pty Ltd* [2004] HCA 54, (2004) 217 CLR 640 [32] (the Court).
[21] ibid [42] (the Court), quoting *Tabet* (n 16) [53] (Gummow A-CJ).
[22] *Sellars* (n 9).
[23] *Talacko* (n 18) [43] (the Court).

of a variety of circumstances in order to determine what the level of loss has been"'.[24]

This chapter focuses on the first category, where the defendant's conduct in breach of an equitable obligation or contrary to an equitable standard, deprives the claimant of 'an opportunity or chance to which [they were] not entitled but where such deprivation constitutes an immediate loss'.[25] Such losses are inherently uncertain. In order for equitable principle to engage with that lost opportunity, the nature and extent of the loss must therefore be rendered reasonably or relatively certain. As discussed in the next two sections, equity's approach differs according to whether the lost chance satisfies part of the claimant's equity for relief or is an element in the remedial inquiry.

III. LOST CHANCE AS AN ELEMENT OF THE EQUITY FOR RELIEF – EQUITABLE ESTOPPELS

The use of loss of a chance to satisfy the claimant's equity for relief is prominent in equitable estoppels. As stated above, the defendant will be estopped where they have made 'a representation or assurance … to the claimant; reliance on [the representation or assurance] by the claimant; and detriment to the claimant in consequence of [their] (reasonable) reliance'.[26] The party relying on the estoppel must therefore demonstrate reliance, that '[they] would have acted differently in the absence of the relevant encouragement'[27] and that should the defendant be permitted to resile from that encouragement, they would suffer detriment 'by reason of [their] change of position in reliance on the encouraged expectation, if it were [now] to be departed from'.[28] The claimant's lost opportunity may as a factual matter be employed as evidence satisfying both the elements of reliance and detriment. Equity tolerates relative uncertainty when considering the existence and valuation of any such hypothetical event for the purpose of meeting the elements of equitable estoppels.

Equity recognises various forms of estoppel, including proprietary and promissory estoppel. Proprietary estoppel arises where 'the owner of property has encouraged another to alter their position in the expectation of obtaining a proprietary interest in that land and the other has changed their position to their detriment'.[29] Promissory estoppel arises when another party makes a promise or assurance to the claimant that the other will not enforce their strict legal rights against the claimant and that promise

[24] ibid, citing *Vasiliou v Hajigeorgiou* [2010] EWCA Civ 1475 [25] (Patten LJ).
[25] ibid [40] (the Court).
[26] *Thorner* (n 11) [29] (Lord Walker).
[27] *Q v E Co* [2020] NSWCA 220, (2020) 383 ALR 469 [88] (Meagher JA, with whom Leeming JA and Payne JA agreed).
[28] *Grundt* (n 12) 674–75 (Dixon J). This concept of detriment is applicable to proprietary estoppel, see *Donis v Donis* [2007] VSCA 89, (2007) 19 VR 577 [54] (Nettle JA) and *Delaforce* (n 2) [44] (Handley JA with whom Allsop P and Giles JA agreed), as well as promissory estoppel, see *Legione v Hateley* (1983) 152 CLR 406 (HCA) 437 (Mason and Deane JJ).
[29] *Allianz Australia Insurance Ltd v Delor Vue Apartments* [2021] FCAFC 121, (2021) 287 FCR 388 [453] (Derrington J).

or assurance is intended to affect the legal relations between them or is reasonably understood by the claimant to have that effect. The claimant must rely upon this promise or assurance, altering their position such that the claimant would suffer detriment if the other was permitted to resile from the promise or assurance.[30] In English law, the effect of a promissory estoppel is to prevent the defendant's assertion of their right against the claimant. Promissory estoppel therefore does not operate as a source of positive rights for the claimant against the defendant in that jurisdiction.[31] However, Australian law is unresolved as to whether promissory estoppel has a wider ambit and may operate as a cause of action.[32] To the extent that the doctrine encompasses a positive equity for relief, promissory estoppel therefore arises where the claimant 'assumed that a particular legal relationship then existed between .... [the parties] ... or expected that a particular legal relationship *would* exist between them and, in the latter case, that [the defendant] would not be free to withdraw from the expected legal relationship'.[33]

It lies beyond the scope of this discussion to resolve the true nature of promissory estoppel or indeed if there exists a broader unified doctrine of equitable estoppel.[34] Relevant is that the claimant's lost opportunity is capable of satisfying the key elements of reliance and detriment common across all equitable estoppels. Our focus is therefore on these two key elements, either of which may entail the need to make certain, or at least relatively certain, hypothetical value. In satisfaction of either, equity requires that the claimant establish the existence of the lost opportunity on a balance of probabilities. The nature and extent of the loss is also determined, although the valuation is not probabilistic and does not discount for the conduct of the claimant or third parties. I briefly discuss reliance and detriment below.

Turning first to reliance, an example is *Sidhu v Van Dyke*[35] where the claimant, who ultimately succeeded in raising a proprietary estoppel, pointed to the fact that, influenced by the defendant's assurances as to her ownership of 'Oaks Cottage', which was owned by the defendant, she had lost an opportunity to pursue a property settlement at the time of her divorce from her ex-husband.[36] In accepting this as evidence of her reliance, the Court was satisfied as to the existence of the claimant's

[30] *Grundt* (n 12).

[31] Promissory estoppel may also be invoked by B to prevent A raising a defence to B's claim or as an answer to a defence. See, eg, *Robertson v Minister of Pensions* [1949] 1 KB 227 (KBD).

[32] In *Saleh v Romanous* [2010] NSWCA 274, (2010) 79 NSWLR 453 [74] (Handley JA, with whom Giles JA and Sackville JA agreed), said that '[promissory estoppel] is a restraint on the enforcement of rights and ... must be negative in substance'. However, in *Ashton v Pratt* [2015] NSWCA 12, (2015) 88 NSWLR 281 [138] (Bathurst CJ, McColl JA agreeing), acknowledged 'significant dicta contrary to this limitation on promissory estoppel' and in *Mineralogy Pty Ltd v Sino Iron Pty Ltd (No 6)* [2015] FCA 825, (2015) 329 ALR 1 [769] Edelman J treated the matter as an open question. See also *Allianz* (n 29) [439] (Derrington J) and A Robertson, 'Three Models of Promissory Estoppel' (2013) 7 *Journal of Equity* 226.

[33] *Waltons Stores (Interstate) Ltd v Maher* (1988) 164 CLR 387 (HCA) 428–29 (Brennan J) (emphasis added).

[34] *The Commonwealth of Australia v Verwayen* (1990) 170 CLR 394 (HCA).

[35] [2014] HCA 19, (2014) 251 CLR 505.

[36] *Sidhu v Van Dyke* [2013] NSWCA 198, (2013) 301 ALR 769 [103] (Barrett JA, with whom Basten JA (at [1]) and Tobias JA (at [148]) agreed).

lost opportunity,[37] noting the claimant's evidence of its value.[38] Beyond this baseline inquiry as to the existence of the opportunity, there was no significant scrutiny of its value.[39] Whilst courts may vary on the strength of the evidence required to establish the existence of the lost chance,[40] this must have an evidential basis and the opportunity said to have been foregone by the claimant cannot be established by conjecture or speculation.[41]

A consideration of reliance in estoppel necessarily brings into view causation which is complex and contested, both as to the matters incorporating a causal element[42] and the appropriate test(s) of causation to be applied.[43] Resolution of these issues lies beyond the remit of this chapter. What is secure is that reliance requires satisfaction of two causal links: the claimant must have made an assumption as to a state of affairs induced by the defendant's assurance and that assumption must have caused them to change their behaviour.[44] Where the claimant's change of position is a forgone opportunity, it may be difficult to separate causation as a discrete element. A consideration of the likelihood and value of the hypothetical may be enmeshed in the inquiry. Asking whether the claimant has walked away from the path forgone in reliance on the assurance may also involve asking about the likelihood of the claimant pursuing the original path in any event. Broadly speaking, it is only a belief or expectation induced by the defendant, and only the claimant's change(s) of position in reliance on that belief or expectation, which will be relevant. Authority supports both the view that estoppel will be established if the assurance is merely a contributing cause or influenced[45] the claimant's change of position and also that the claimant

[37] *Sidhu v Van Dyke* [2012] NSWSC 118 [217] (Ward J).

[38] ibid [5] (Ward J): 'an opportunity the loss of which is asserted by her to be somewhere in the order of $35,000–$60,000'.

[39] By contrast, Ward J observed (at ibid [14] (emphasis added)) that '*had the issue of relief arisen* … [her Honour would have obtained independent expert evidence from a family law practitioner] as to what provision was likely to have been made had there been an application made for a property settlement at the relevant time'. This lost opportunity was not ultimately claimed as the detriment for which the claimant sought relief. Rather, for the purposes of relief, the relevant detriment was that flowing from the defendant's representation that he was willing to gift the cottage to her. This is discussed below.

[40] B McFarlane, *The Law of Proprietary Estoppel*, 2nd edn (Oxford, OUP, 2022) paras [3.267]–[3.269], citing as examples at the lower end of the evidentiary threshold *Greasely v Cook* [1980] 1 WLR 1306 (CA) 1311 (Lord Denning MR) and *Re JR (A Ward of Court)* [1993] IRLM 657 (High Court of Ireland) [12] (Costello J).

[41] *Steria Ltd* (n 13) [126]–[127] (Neuberger LJ). Note that Neuberger LJ (at [127]) appears to have countenanced that a lost chance may be established on the lower evidential threshold of 'possibility' rather than 'probability'.

[42] See generally E Cooke, *The Modern Law of Estoppel* (Oxford, OUP, 2000). See also Justice J Ward and S Puttick, 'Willpower Has No Voltage: Problems with Causation in Equitable Estoppel' (2022) 49 *University of Western Australia Law Review* 23.

[43] See generally McFarlane (n 40) paras [3.104]ff; J McGhee (ed), *Snell's Equity*, 34th edn (London, Sweet & Maxwell, 2020) paras [12-027], [12-043]; A Silink, 'Causation in Equitable Estoppel' (2016) 43 *Australian Bar Review* 320; Ward and Puttick (n 42).

[44] E Bant, *The Change of Position Defence* (Oxford, Hart, 2009) 28–31; E Bant, 'Causation and Scope of Liability in Unjust Enrichment' (2009) 17 *Restitution Law Review* 60, 62–63.

[45] *Q v E* (n 1) [901] (Ward CJ in Eq); *Moore v Aubusson* [2020] NSWSC 1466 [405] (Ward CJ in Eq) preferring the formulation of this test given in *Sidhu* (n 35) [91]–[93] (Gageler J); *Mineralogy* (n 32) [770]–[778] (Edelman J); *Priestly v Priestly* [2017] NSWCA 155 [136]–[137] (Emmett JA, McColl JA agreeing (at [1])).

would have acted differently 'but for'[46] the assurance. However, given that reliance is relevant in identifying whether the defendant's assurance induced the claimant's assumption, and whether that assumption influenced the claimant to change their behaviour, it is not surprising that courts do not further inquire into the value or likelihood of success of the lost chance. Such matters are not relevant to the causal inquiry. Beyond establishing the existence of the lost opportunity according to the civil standard of proof, further inquiries as to value do not assist in determining reliance.[47]

The next element is detriment, which can be 'any material disadvantage'[48] which would arise from permitting a departure from the assurance on the 'faith of which the [claimant] acted or refrained from acting'. The detriment must be 'substantial, although it need not be quantifiable in the same way as an order of damages'.[49] Detriment 'need not consist of expenditure or money or other quantifiable disadvantage'.[50] The object of estoppel has been said 'to prevent an unjust departure by one person from an assumption adopted by another as the basis of some act or omission which, unless the assumption be adhered to, would operate to that other's detriment'.[51] Detriment is examined when the defendant seeks to resile from their promise or assurance.[52] The court compares the position the claimant currently occupies and the position they would have occupied had they not changed their position in reliance on the assurance. An estoppel will be raised if the claimant would suffer prejudice or disadvantage by reason of their changes of position if the defendant were now to depart from that expectation.[53]

Opportunities forgone by the claimant in reliance on the defendant's promise or assurance may be given as evidence of detriment.[54] As above, courts must determine whether these past events are sufficiently certain and be satisfied as to two interrelated inquiries: first, as to the existence of the lost chance and secondly, as to the value or substance of the lost chance. As observed in *Allianz Australia Insurance Ltd v Delor Vue Apartments CTS 39788*:[55]

> Raising the existence of possible alternative courses of action does not establish detriment. Even though it is not necessary to establish the actual value of the opportunities

[46] *Sidhu* (n 35) [91]–[93] (Gageler J); *Stone v Stone* [2014] NSWSC 1655 [45]–[46] (Darke J); *Miller Heiman Pty Ltd v Sales Principles Pty Ltd* [2017] NSWCA 106, (2017) 94 NSWLR 500 [49], [62] (Macfarlan JA, McColl JA and Sackville AJA agreeing); *Priestly v Priestly* [2016] NSWSC 1096 [119]–[136] (White J) and on appeal *Priestly* (n 45) [16] (Macfarlan JA).

[47] McFarlane (n 40) para [3.269] argues for '… particularly intensive [scrutiny] where [the claimant's] claim rests on how [they] *might* have behaved' (emphasis in original).

[48] *Australian Financial Services and Leasing Pty Ltd v Hills Industries Ltd* [2014] HCA 14, (2014) 253 CLR 560 [150] (Gageler J) citing *Donis* (n 28) [20] (Nettle JA, with whom Maxwell ACJ (at [1]) and Ashley JA (at [66]) agreed) and *Verwayen* (n 34) 448 (Deane J), 461–62 (Dawson J).

[49] *AFSL* (n 48). See also *Ashton* (n 32) [147] (Bathurst CJ).

[50] *Donis* (n 28) [20] (Nettle JA).

[51] *Thompson v Palmer* (1933) 49 CLR 507 (HCA) 547 (Dixon J).

[52] *Gillett v Holt* [2001] Ch 210 (CA) 232 (Robert Walker LJ); *Allianz* (n 29).

[53] *Q v E Co* (n 27) [154] (Meagher JA).

[54] *Gillett* (n 52); *Delaforce* (n 2); *Waddell v Waddell* [2012] NSWCA 214, (2012) 292 ALR 788; *Walsh v Walsh* [2012] NSWCA 57; *AFSL* (n 48) [150] (Gageler J); *E v Q* (n 1) upheld on appeal in *E Co v Q (No 4)* [2019] NSWSC 429; *Moore* (n 45); *Allianz* (n 29); *Hansen v Marco Engineering (Aust) Pty Ltd* [1948] VLR 198 (VSC), 211 (Fullager J); *Harrison v Harrison* [2013] VSCA 170.

[55] *Allianz* (n 29) [500] (Derrington J).

> foregone, it is necessary to prove to the requisite degree that they were actually available, that they were able to be pursued, and that they would have been. To merely point to them as being potentially available does not establish detriment.

Q v E Co[56] illustrates equity's approach. In 2002 Q and his three sons (A, B and C) established a family farming business to be conducted on Q's land. The business was to be operated by E Co, in which Q's sons were quarter shareholders and directors. Q had encouraged an expectation that he would continue to own the land for use in the family business during his lifetime and on his death his sons would inherit the land. The sons each made a 'life changing decision' not to pursue other career options in reliance on this expectation. Q's relationship with his sons broke down when Q was convicted of sexually abusing two of B's children and later made a new will under which his sons were not intended to benefit. The sons successfully jointly made claims to an equitable proprietary estoppel against Q. Of relevance is the approach taken by the Court in establishing and evaluating this lost chance. How did the Court make the lost chance certain, or at least relatively certain?

Turning first to the existence of the lost chance, it was found that the civil standard had been met, despite the defendant Q arguing that A '[gave] no evidence of substance of other farming opportunities'.[57] Similarly, it was 'not necessary for [claimant, C] to articulate precisely what he would (counterfactually) have done'.[58] Ultimately, it was found that there were 'other [employment] avenues … available' to each son.[59] So long as some baseline inchoate level of lost opportunity was established, it was 'not fatal to [the claimant's] case that [they were] unable to state categorically, with the benefit of hindsight, how [they] would have acted differently'.[60]

The Court also considered the value or substance of the lost chance. The leading case is *Delaforce v Simpson-Cook*.[61] The claimant was the former wife of the deceased who refrained from obtaining orders from the Family Court formalising their property settlement in reliance on her then husband's promise that he would bequeath the property to her on his death. He did not. The claimant established a proprietary estoppel, relying on the legal effect of the deceased's promise.[62] She gave evidence that 'if the deceased had not been prepared to put the agreement [about the property] in writing "I would have sought orders from the Family Court"'.[63] On valuation, Allsop P stated that the lost chance must not be 'fanciful or otherwise doomed to fail'[64] such that the claimant would have been 'better off in the posited alternative reality'.[65] Thus, the hypothetical conduct of the claimant or third parties is not

[56] *Q v E Co* (n 27).
[57] *Q v E* (n 1) [1090] (Ward CJ in Eq).
[58] *Q v E Co* (n 27) [106].
[59] ibid [1168].
[60] *Priestly* (n 45) [147] (Emmett AJA). See also *Waddell* (n 54) [65], [67] (Campbell JA) with whom Allsop P (at [1]) and Sackville AJA (at [72]) agreed; *Walsh* (n 54) [25]–[26] (Meagher JA with whom Macfarlan JA (at [1]) and Barrett JA (at [35]) agreed); *Allianz* (n 29) [221] (McKerracher and Colvin JJ).
[61] (n 2).
[62] ibid [5] (Allsop P with whose additional comments Giles JA agreed), [29], [93] (Handley JA).
[63] ibid [26] (Handley JA).
[64] ibid [5] (Allsop P).
[65] ibid.

formally taken into account in assessing the degree of probability of success or value of the lost opportunity, beyond a threshold requirement that the prospect of success of the chance not be fanciful or unrealistic. In *Q v E Co* the opportunities forgone were held to be 'substantial'[66] and thus sufficiently certain.

Finally, we come to remedy. Courts do not speak with one voice as to whether the object of equitable relief is to prevent or remove the claimant's detriment or to enforce the claimant's reasonable expectation. However, in all cases, the court considers the extent of the equity for relief raised by the claimant's estoppel, observing 'the fundamental principle that equity is concerned to prevent unconscionable conduct [which] permeates all the elements of the doctrine … the court must look at the matter in the round'.[67] This directs attention to the fundamental role of proportionality between the claimant's expectation and the claimant's detriment. The claimant's equity may be established, but the disproportion between the claimant's detriment and their expectation is so great that conscience does not require relief or requires limited relief.[68] The court brings into the ledger any benefits which have accrued to the claimant in reliance on the assurance and the claimant's detriment, already established as part of the equity for relief, is again relevant.[69] In *Australian Financial Services and Leasing Pty Ltd v Hills Industries Ltd*[70] Justice Gageler stated that the material disadvantage or detriment 'need not be quantifiable in the same way as an award of damages'. This issue of the quantifiability of the claimant's detriment, as part of the proportionality inquiry, again raises the issue of certainty of loss where the detriment is a foregone opportunity.[71]

Independently of the inquiry as to the extent of the claimant's equity for relief is an inquiry as to what remedy will best satisfy that equity. This is an exercise of the court's remedial discretion and, as explained by Hudson,[72] will take into consideration a broader range of considerations beyond the prevention of unconscionable conduct which underpins the equity for relief. Thus, for example, the impact of the proposed remedy on third parties and clean break considerations may play a role. It lies beyond the scope of this chapter to consider all the possible remedies to equitable estoppels. Of relevance are two types of equitable compensation. The first is

[66] *Q v E Co* (n 27) [163] (Meagher JA) (see also [158] (Meagher JA)). See also *Allianz* (n 29) [217]–[225] (McKerracher and Colvin JJ).

[67] *Gillett* (n 52) 225 (Robert Walker LJ).

[68] *Sidhu* (n 35) [85]; *Giumelli v Giumelli* (1999) 196 CLR 101 (HCA) [40]–[48] (Gleeson CJ, McHugh, Gummow and Callinan JJ); *Delaforce* (n 2) [62], [76], [77] (Handley JA); *Moore* (n 45) [386] (Ward CJ in Eq).

[69] On the facts, the claimant may have benefitted in reliance on the assurance such that they would suffer no prejudice if the defendant were now permitted to resile: *Q v E Co* (n 27) [155] (Meagher JA).

[70] *AFSL* (n 48) [150]. See also French CJ (at [30]), noting that the valuation approach required for the change of position defence to a claim in unjust enrichment is conducted on an 'entirely different basis' from the 'detriment constituted by loss of economic opportunity, the kind of valuation approach undertaken in an assessment of damages for loss of opportunities [by reason of breach of contract]'.

[71] See, eg, *Harrison* (n 54) where the claimant's detriment lay in the lost entitlement to bring a family provision claim. The court rejected the argument that this lost opportunity should be made certain according to the common law probabilistic approach (at [159] citing *Sellars* (n 9)).

[72] J Hudson, 'Equitable Compensation for Equitable Estoppels' in S Degeling and J Varuhas (eds), *Equitable Compensation and Disgorgement of Profit* (Oxford, Hart, 2017) 226–30.

that the extent of the claimant's equity requires equitable compensation calculated according to the claimant's detriment. The second is that the defendant pay equitable compensation as a substitute for specific equitable relief.[73] As shown by *Giumelli v Giumelli*[74] and *Sidhu v Van Dyke*,[75] as a substitute for the prima facie measure of relief, the remedy necessary to satisfy the claimant's equity for relief may instead formally require 'the fixing of a money sum to represent the value of the equitable claim'.[76] In both *Giumelli* and *Sidhu*, the prima facie relief was that the defendant should hold the relevant land on constructive trust, with an order to transfer title to the claimant. However, in substitution for this specific relief, the court in both cases awarded a monetary sum,[77] taking into account various factors rendering specific relief unavailable. For example, in *Giumelli*, these factors included other litigation still pending between related parties, the need for a clean break and the desire to avoid injustice to third parties. The remedial inquiry is considered in further depth in the next two sections: equitable compensation (IV); and monetary orders consequent on equitable rescission (V).

IV. EQUITABLE COMPENSATION

Equitable compensation is an equitable monetary remedy given to restore the position of the claimant, including for lost opportunity. Traditionally equitable compensation was thought to be limited to claimants standing in an accounting relationship with the defendant. Modern equity is not so confined.[78] Thus, for example, equitable compensation is given to meet the equity raised by equitable estoppels,[79] equitable fraud constituted by fraud on the minority of members of an owner's corporation of a statutory strata title scheme,[80] unconscionable conduct,[81]

[73] See generally ibid.

[74] *Giumelli* (n 68).

[75] *Sidhu* (n 35).

[76] *Giumelli* (n 68) 125 (Gleeson CJ, McHugh, Gummow and Callinan JJ).

[77] ibid 126–27 (Gleeson CJ, McHugh, Gummow and Callinan JJ); *Sidhu* (n 35) [87] (French CJ, Kiefel, Bell and Keane JJ) affirming *Sidhu* (n 36) [142], [147] (Barrett JA with whom Basten JA (at [1]) and Tobias JA (at [148]) agreed).

[78] See J Ward, 'Equitable Compensation – An Overview' in S Degeling and J Varuhas (eds), *Equitable Compensation and Disgorgement of Profit* (Oxford, Hart, 2017) 69–71; Hudson (n 72) 230–36. See also *United States Surgical Corporation v Hospital Products International Pty Ltd* [1982] 2 NSWLR 766 (NSWSC) 816 (McLelland J) confirming the Court's 'inherent power to grant relief by way of monetary compensation for breach of fiduciary or other equitable obligation'.

[79] See, eg, *EK Nominees Pty Ltd v Woolworths Ltd* [2006] NSWSC 1172 [278], [281], [283], [291] (White J).

[80] *Houghton v Immer (No 155) Pty Ltd* (1997) 44 NSWLR 46 (NSWCA) 54, 56, 48, 57, 59, 60 (Handley JA, with whom Mason P (at 48) and Beazley JA (at 60) agreed).

[81] *Karam v ANZ Banking Group Ltd* [2001] NSWSC 709 [425]–[428] (Santow J) (reversed on other grounds in *Australia and New Zealand Banking Group v Karam* [2005] NSWCA 344, (2005) 64 NSWLR 149. The possibility of equitable compensation for equitable unconscionability was also recognised in *Paroz v Paroz* [2010] QSC 41, [133]–[135] (Lyons J) with limited support also given in *Hrycenko v Hrycenko* [2019] VSC 700 [13], [17] (Lyons J) where the availability of this remedy was conceded (appeal at [2020] VSCA 324 failed). See also *Tillett v Varnell Holdings Pty Ltd* [2009] NSWSC 1040 [101] (Brereton J), where his Honour would have ordered equitable compensation had unconscionability been established and other remedies not been appropriate. However, McLure J in *Australia and New Zealand Banking Group Ltd v*

undue influence[82] and for breach of a fiduciary duty inherent in the giving of advice,[83] where there is no agency or holding of a fund. However, in order to understand the extent to which equity makes certain any loss (or, conversely, tolerates relative *uncertainty* of loss), where equitable compensation is given for the claimant's lost opportunity, we need briefly to return to the traditional position where the availability of equitable compensation was apparently limited to those standing in accounting relationships.

As stated in *Associated Alloys*, '[b]efore a party can be ordered to account, liability to account must be established'.[84] Accounting relationships are typified by the fact that the accounting party 'controls property that [they] must hold and apply for another person's (eg, the beneficiary or principal's) benefit'.[85] It is not necessary to prove a breach of duty to obtain an order for account. The beneficiary or principal in an accounting relationship may call for an account as of right. It is through the account that the claimant therefore identifies and quantifies any deficit in the fund and seeks a remedy by which the deficit may be made good, 'either *in specie* or in money'.[86] Equitable compensation may be the subsequent equitable remedy sought by the claimant following this accounting process.

Two forms of equitable accounting are relevant.[87] The first is an order for common account[88] in which the defendant is required to account for what they have actually received. The claimant may falsify and/or surcharge this record. Thus, if the account discloses an unauthorised disbursement, the claimant may falsify that item or 'ask for [it] … to be disallowed'.[89] Similarly, a 'surcharge is the showing of an omission for which credit ought to have been given'.[90] Thus, value on the incoming side of the account may be missing, and therefore surcharged. The inquiry in common account is limited to amounts *actually* received by the accounting party and not credited to the fund or expended without authority. Where the defendant is ordered to make good the deficit by the payment of money, that remedy has been described as equitable compensation. Importantly, as emphasised by Lord Millett in *Libertarian Investments*, the award is 'not compensation for loss but … restorative. The amount

Dziencial [2001] WASC 305 [413] observed that the usual remedies in unconscionability are to rescind or resist enforcement of the suspect transaction together with consequential orders as are necessary to achieve practical justice, leaving open the further issue of whether equitable compensation was an available response. Stronger doubt was expressed in *Perpetual Trustees Victoria Ltd v Burns* [2015] WASC 234 [249] (Heenan J).

[82] This may conceal two deeper taxonomic categories: (a) a wrong of abuse of influence and (b) the unjust factor related to undue influence. See, eg, *Smith v Glegg* [2004] QSC 443, [2005] 1 Qd R 561; *Mahoney v Purnell* [1996] 3 All ER 61 (QB); *Lawrie v Hwang* [2012] QSC 422; *McFarlane v McFarlane* [2021] VSC 197.

[83] *ABN AMRO Bank NV v Bathurst Regional Council* [2014] FCAFC 65, (2014) 224 FCR 1 [1084], [1090]–[1098] (the Court).

[84] *Associated Alloys Pty Ltd v ACN 001 452 106 Pty Ltd (in liq)* [2000] HCA 25, (2000) 202 CLR 588 [56] (Gaudron, McHugh, Gummow and Hayne JJ).

[85] C Mitchell, 'Stewardship of Property and Liability to Account' (2014) 78 *The Conveyancer* 215, 219.

[86] *Libertarian Investments Ltd v Hall* [2013] HKCFA 93, [2014] 1 HKC 368 [168] (Millett NPJ).

[87] There is a third possibility, the account of profits, which is directed to an unauthorised surplus in the account and is not the focus of this discussion.

[88] *Glazier Holdings v Australian Men's Health (No 2)* [2001] NSWSC 6 [38] (Austin J).

[89] *Libertarian Investments* (n 86) [168] (Millett NPJ).

[90] *Glazier Holdings* (n 88) [38] (Austin J).

of the award is measured by the objective value of the property lost determined at the date when the account is taken and with the full benefit of hindsight'.[91] In this sense, the monetary remedy is in substitution for the performance of the accounting party's duty rather than reparation of a loss.[92] Hence 'substitutive compensation', based on common account, 'describes a claim for the substituted value of the assets dissipated without authority: it demands that the trustee perform [their] ... duty to maintain the assets or fund'.[93] Correlatively with the position that the award is in substitution of the defendant's duty, 'considerations of causation, foreseeability and remoteness do not readily enter the matter'.[94] Rather, the necessary causal connection may be established, for example, 'merely [by showing] ... that the [defendant accounting party] made the transfer without authority'.[95]

The second form of equitable accounting is that taken on the basis of wilful default which is 'entirely grounded on misconduct'.[96] The account is taken not of what the defendant has actually received, but of 'what [they] might have received had it not been for the default'.[97] The processes of surcharge and falsification are similarly available. The object of the award is to put the fund or claimant in the position 'as if the defendant had performed his duty and obtained [the property or income or investment] for the benefit of [the claimant or fund]'.[98] Thus, '[t]he exercise of quantifying loss on a wilful default basis is necessarily hypothetical'.[99] In this measure, '[s]ince *ex hypothesi* the property has not been acquired, the defendant will be ordered to make good the deficiency by the payment of money, and [the award is] ... akin to the payment of damages as compensation for loss'.[100] Therefore, 'reparative compensation', based on the account taken in wilful default, 'describes a claim for reparation for the loss suffered by breach of duty'.[101] In the reparative measure the claimant must establish causation. Whilst the appropriate causal approach may vary according to the policy settings underlying the particular equity for relief, it is clear causation is an element required to be met.

A subset of modern cases discloses a third possibility, which is that courts dispense with the need for an intermediate accounting process. Rather, cases are directly argued and decided on 'the liability of a trustee who commits a breach of trust to compensate the beneficiaries for such a breach.'[102] Any equitable compensation ordered in such a case is therefore not directed to any particular accounting procedure.

[91] *Libertarian Investments* (n 86) [168] (Millett NPJ).

[92] McGhee (n 43) paras [20-028]–[20-035]; S Elliott, 'Remoteness Criteria in Equity' (2002) 65 *MLR* 588, 589–91 and S Elliott, 'Compensation Claims Against Trustees' (DPhil Thesis, University of Oxford, 2002); *Agricultural Land Management Ltd v Jackson [No 2]* [2014] WASC 102, (2014) 48 WAR 1 [336]–[346] (Edelman J).

[93] *Agricultural Land Management* (n 92) [349] (Edelman J), citing the work of Dr Elliott.

[94] *Re Dawson (deceased); Union Fidelity Trustee Co Ltd v Perpetual Trustee Co Ltd* [1966] 2 NSWLR 211 (NSWSC) 215 (Street J).

[95] *Agricultural Land Management* (n 92) [368] (Edelman J).

[96] *Glazier Holdings* (n 88) [39] (Austin J).

[97] ibid.

[98] *Libertarian Investments* (n 86) [170] (Millett NPJ).

[99] ibid [123] (Ribeiro PJ).

[100] ibid [170] (Millett NPJ).

[101] *Agricultural Land Management* (n 92) [349] (Edelman J), citing the work of Dr Elliott.

[102] *Target Holdings Ltd v Redferns* [1996] AC 421 (HL) 428 (Lord Browne-Wilkinson). See also *AIB Group (UK) plc v Mark Redler & Co Solicitors* [2014] UKSC 58, [2015] AC 1503.

Finally, beyond formal processes of equitable accounting, equitable compensation may also be ordered in cases which lie outside accounting relationships. This category includes equitable compensation given to meet equitable estoppels (including as a substitute for specific relief), unconscionability, undue influence and non-custodial fiduciary relationships such as advising solicitors. Outside rescission (considered separately below), courts may also order equitable compensation as one of the terms on which equitable relief is given, fashioned to meet the particular facts and circumstances of the case.[103]

The claimant's lost opportunity is capable of recognition in all measures of equitable compensation. All measures may therefore entail the need to make certain hypothetical value. Equity arguably employs two alternate methods of making certain the claimant's lost opportunity. The first relies on probabilistic reasoning. The second resolves certainty by reference to the exercise of equitable discretion. Neither correlates with any particular measure of loss. However, all are limited by the normative commitments and settings of the particular equity for relief being met by equitable compensation.

A. Probabilistic Reasoning

A probabilistic approach makes certain the value of lost chances by reference to the probability of the lost opportunity occurring and the value of that opportunity, discounted according to contingencies. Analysis proceeds in two steps. The first requires the claimant on a balance of probabilities to demonstrate the existence of the lost opportunity. The second is a valuation exercise, by which the value of the opportunity is assessed by reference to the likelihood of that opportunity having come to fruition is established. The normative settings and commitments of the particular equity for relief constrain this discounting process.

A leading example is *Ramsay v BigTinCan Pty Ltd*,[104] which involved the reparative measure. BigTinCan ('BTC') was a start-up company requiring an injection of capital. In breach of his equitable fiduciary obligations, a director of BTC established a rival corporate entity ('Newco') with the objective of acquiring BTC's assets and operating its business, including by diverting funding opportunities from BTC to Newco. There had been parties willing to invest in BTC, but the director pursued the interests of Newco not BTC in diverting the opportunity to raise funds. BTC sought equitable compensation from the director arguing that, as a result of the director's conduct, it lost the opportunity to raise capital and should be compensated for that lost opportunity.[105] At trial it was established that BTC had a 25 per cent chance of raising $1,200,000.[106] However, the New South Wales Court of Appeal confirmed

[103] See, eg, *E Co v Q (No 4)* (n 54) [16], [653] (Ward CJ in Eq) and *Gillett* (n 52) 237 (Robert Walker LJ, with whom Waller and Beldam LJJ (at 238) agreed).

[104] *Ramsay* (n 3). See also *Hart Security Pty Ltd v Boucousis* [2016] NSWCA 307, (2016) 339 ALR 659; *Anderson v Canaccord Genuity Financial Ltd* [2022] NSWSC 58.

[105] *Ramsay v BigTinCan* [2013] NSWSC 1248 [88] (Ball J).

[106] ibid [101] (Ball J).

that BTC's failure to obtain funding was not itself the loss. The Court held that in valuing the lost commercial opportunity, it was necessary to demonstrate that the opportunity would have been put to a profitable use.[107] As stated by Macfarlan JA,[108]

> the raising of funds would only have been of benefit to BTC if it could have done something useful with them. Otherwise, whilst [BTC] would have received money, it would have incurred a liability to the investor to repay an equivalent amount, either as a debt due to a creditor or as share capital ultimately to be returned to a shareholder. If the evidence established that funding would, or might, have enabled BTC to earn profits, the absence of that funding might fairly be regarded as causally related to a financial loss. Otherwise, it could not be so regarded.

Relying on *Sellars v Adelaide Petroleum NL*,[109] BTC was therefore required to demonstrate on a balance of probabilities the existence of an opportunity to raise capital. Having done so, the question was what was the value of that lost opportunity? Valuation was to be 'ascertained by reference to the degree of probabilities or possibilities'[110] or 'informed estimation'[111] on which BTC's counterfactual of what it could have done with the funds rested. Taking into consideration the 'very significant business contingencies to which the prospect of deriving the anticipated profit was subject',[112] a majority of the court assessed the value of the lost opportunity at $300,000.[113]

Sellars concerned a claim for damages under section 82 of the Trade Practices Act 1974 (Cth). When applied to the calculation of compensatory damages for breach of contract, or damages under the statute, application of the *Sellars* 'degree of probabilities or possibilities' approach requires the court to assess the 'prospects of success of the [lost opportunity] had it been pursued'.[114] *Sellars* was a claim by Adelaide Petroleum, which was in simultaneous negotiations with rival companies Pagini and Poseidon, with a view to selling to the successful party the director's shareholding in Adelaide Petroleum. As a result of Poseidon's misleading conduct in breach of the Trade Practices Act, Adelaide's negotiations with Pagini were interrupted. Adelaide subsequently resumed talks with Pagini, which resulted in an agreement. However,

[107] *Ramsay* (n 3) [69] and [72] (Macfarlan JA, with whom McColl JA (at [2]) agreed). Gleeson JA (at [123]–[141]) came to a lower valuation overall, but his Honour's reasoning similarly rests on the need to incorporate the various contingencies affecting whether the funding would have enabled BTC to obtain a financial benefit (see [119]).

[108] ibid [69] (Macfarlan JA).

[109] *Sellars* (n 9) 355 (Mason CJ, Dawson, Toohey and Gaudron JJ), 362–64 (Brennan J).

[110] ibid 355 (Mason CJ, Dawson, Toohey and Gaudron JJ).

[111] ibid 368 (Brennan J): 'hypotheses and possibilities the fulfilment of which cannot be proved must be evaluated to determine the amount or value of the loss suffered. Proof on the balance of probabilities has no part to play in the evaluation of such hypotheses or possibilities: evaluation is a matter of informed estimation.'

[112] *Ramsay* (n 3) [84] (Macfarlan JA, with whom McColl JA (at [2]) agreed). Gleeson JA assessed the value of the lost opportunity at $65,000 (see [141]), as his Honour placed a higher value on the discount to be applied to the contingencies involved, ruling that BTC held only a 10% prospect of success had it obtained the funding (see [139]).

[113] Thereby confirming the quantum of equitable compensation awarded at trial but not the method of valuation: see ibid [83] (Macfarlan JA).

[114] *Sellars* (n 9) 355 (Mason CJ, Dawson, Toohey and Gaudron JJ), approved in *Berry v CCL Secure Pty Ltd* [2020] HCA 27, (2020) 271 CLR 151 [32] and [35] (Bell, Keane and Nettle JJ).

Adelaide established there was 'more than a mere speculative possibility'[115] that Pagini would have contracted on more favourable terms had the negotiations not been interrupted by Poseidon's conduct. This lost opportunity also entailed the risk that the conditions precedent to the agreement may not have been fulfilled. Adelaide succeeded in obtaining damages for the lost commercial opportunity. Bearing in mind the various contingencies, and in recognition of the fact that there was a 40 per cent chance that the original Pagini agreement would not have proceeded, the Court therefore discounted the award by 40 per cent. Thus, on this approach, a certain value of loss was achieved by incorporating into analysis any impact of the hypothetical conduct of third parties and the hypothetical conduct of the claimant.[116]

Care is required when applying this reasoning to making certain the value of a lost opportunity in equity. This is because the process of discounting should not run contrary to the underlying normative commitments of the particular equity for relief. This has particular traction when seeking equitable compensation for a lost opportunity for a breach of fiduciary duty. Whilst at law it may be permissible to discount the award for the risk that the *claimant* would not have pursued the opportunity,[117] where the claimant is the principal in a fiduciary relationship this runs counter to the fiduciary's strict obligation of loyalty. Within the scope of the fiduciary relationship, the fiduciary must not put themselves in a position of conflict or possibility of conflict between duty and self-interest or conflicting fiduciary duties owed to more than one principal, and must not make a profit by reason or use of position. Unless the principal has given informed consent, the principal will have an equity for relief which may include an account of profits or equitable compensation. Crucially, in relation to liability to account for profit, 'it is no defence that the plaintiff was unwilling, unlikely or unable to make the profits for which an account is taken …'.[118] Thus, the court is not permitted to discount the value of an account of profits by the risk that the claimant/principal would not have pursued the opportunity, and I argue that the same calculus should similarly be impermissible in relation to equitable compensation for the lost opportunity. Further, as emphasised in *E-T China.com International Holdings Ltd v Cheung* the evidence must support a 'reliable starting point'.[119] If the contingencies are too 'many and varied', and are themselves affected by the underlying allegations of wrongdoing, a probabilistic approach may not reliably value a lost opportunity.[120]

Research has only identified the use of the probabilistic approach in relation to calculating equitable compensation for lost chance on breach of fiduciary duty. However, to the extent that equitable compensation is available for other equitable

[115] *Sellars* (n 9) 347 (Mason CJ, Dawson, Toohey and Gaudron JJ).

[116] *Heenan v Di Sisto* [2008] NSWCA 25, [32]–[33] (Giles JA with whom Mason P and Matthews AJA agreed).

[117] ibid.

[118] *Warman v Dwyer* (1995) 182 CLR 544 (HCA) 558 (Mason CJ, Brennan, Deane, Dawson and Gaudron JJ) relying on *Regal (Hastings) Ltd v Gulliver* [1967] 2 AC 134 (HL) and *Boardman v Phipps* [1967] 2 AC 46 (HL).

[119] *E-T China.com International Holdings Ltd v Cheung* [2021] NSWCA 24, (2021) 388 ALR 128 [276] (Bell P with whom Bathurst CJ (at [1]) and Leeming JA (at [287]) agreed).

[120] ibid [276]–[278] (Bell P).

wrongs, such as undue influence[121] and unconscionability, there is no reason of principle why this method of making certain the claimant's lost opportunity should not be employed. Relief in such cases typically takes the form of setting aside or rescinding the impugned transaction or resisting its enforcement, together with such consequential orders as are necessary to achieve practical justice.[122] However, it is not difficult to construct facts involving a lost opportunity. Take *McFarlane v McFarlane*.[123] A mother gifted title to her house to her abusive son. Richards J found that 'she was frightened of him, and of what he might do to her if she refused to sign the transfer'.[124] The mother moved into residential aged care and, as a result of Centrelink looking through the transfer and deeming the house to be an income-producing asset, she lost an entitlement to her pension, reducing her annual payments. She was also subject to an increased contribution fee to her aged care provider.[125] Thus, she was left without title to her home and in parlous financial circumstances. Richards J determined that the gift was tainted by both undue influence and unconscionability and ordered that the transfer be set aside.[126] The Court also awarded equitable compensation, stating that '[e]quitable compensation may be ordered to remedy a wide variety of equitable misbehaviour, beyond cases involving a breach of trust or other fiduciary duty'.[127] On the facts, the claimant suffered no lost chance as, going back to *Talacko*, her pension losses related to an existing entitlement.[128] However, if we vary the facts such that the mother lost an opportunity to invest in a commercial opportunity only offered to home-owners on her street, a lost chance comes into view. Arguably the probabilistic method of making certain this loss should be available.

B. Embedded within Equitable Discretion

At least in making relatively certain losses flowing from a breach of fiduciary duty, there is evidence of an alternative method which embeds the certainty inquiry within equitable discretion. According to this approach, the court may[129]

> [f]irst, ... be able to take the fiduciary at his own word and use his falsehoods to establish the facts as if they were true even though they are known to be untrue. Secondly the court

[121] To the extent that equitable compensation is available, and the remedy sought is 'other than the mere reversal of the transaction' the relevant event is arguably 'wrongful influence' in which there may be a requirement that the defendant's conduct involves an 'abuse of trust': *Anderson v McPherson [No 2]* [2012] WASC 19, [245] (Edelman J); J Edelman and E Bant, *Unjust Enrichment*, 2nd edn (Oxford, Hart, 2016) 242–50. See also *Mahoney* (n 82) 90–91 (May J); *Smith* (n 82) 575–76; D Heydon, 'Equitable Compensation for Undue Influence' (1997) 113 *LQR* 8; Ho (n 17) 193–210.

[122] *Commercial Bank of Australia Ltd v Amadio* (1983) 151 CLR 447 (HCA); *Bridgewater v Leahy* (1998) 194 CLR 457 (HCA); *Australia and New Zealand Banking Group Ltd v Dzienciol* (n 81) [413] (McLure J).

[123] (n 82).

[124] ibid [45].

[125] ibid [65].

[126] ibid [63].

[127] ibid [64].

[128] ibid [67].

[129] *Libertarian Investments* (n 86) [174] (Millett NPJ).

> is entitled to make every assumption against the party whose conduct has deprived it of necessary evidence. And thirdly the court is entitled to be robust and do rough and ready justice without having to justify the amount of its award with any degree of precision.

Libertarian Investments Ltd v Hall[130] also concerned the reparative measure. Libertarian Investments Ltd was wholly owned by Mr Woods. The defendant Mr Hall controlled a fund containing moneys belonging to Libertarian and owed fiduciary duties to Libertarian and Woods in respect of the fund.[131] Hall had undertaken to use the money to acquire on behalf of Libertarian/Woods a 10 per cent share in This Sporting Exchange Ltd ('TSE') which was not publicly listed at the time of the relevant transaction but was later listed on the London Stock Exchange. It was contemplated that Woods/Libertarian would later on-sell their stake in TSE for a profit. However, in breach of fiduciary duty, Hall misappropriated the money for his own purposes and no TSE shares were purchased. Woods sought an account on the basis of wilful default[132] and reparative equitable compensation for Libertarian's lost opportunity to on-sell TSE shares in the market.

In making certain the value of this lost opportunity it was necessary to determine the price a potential buyer would have been prepared to pay Libertarian for a hypothetical shareholding in TSE at a time 10 years earlier. In resolving these 'evidential difficulties' the Court relied on the position of Handley JA in *Houghton v Immer (No 155) Pty Ltd*: 'In my judgment the Court should assess the compensation in a robust manner, relying on the presumption against wrongdoers, the onus of proof, and resolving doubtful questions against the party "whose actions have made an accurate determination so problematic."'[133]

Applying this approach to the facts of *Libertarian Investments*, the hypothetical share balance was valued using the traded share price and robustly assuming that this price was the same as the TSE shares that Hall should have purchased on behalf of Woods.[134] This was the value of the opportunity lost.

Beyond breach of fiduciary duty, there is also evidence of an approach which similarly values lost opportunity according to a discretionary approach, again moulded according to the settings and values of the particular equity for relief. An example is the remedial phase of proprietary estoppel according to which relief is fashioned to ensure that the remedy satisfies the claimant's equity for relief. In *E Co v Q*,[135] the claimant sons established an equity for relief in proprietary estoppel[136] and the properties subject to the expectation were declared to be held by the defendant on

[130] ibid.
[131] ibid [35], [106]–[107] (Ribeiro PJ).
[132] ibid [113] (Ribeiro PJ).
[133] *Libertarian Investments* (n 86) [138] (Ribeiro PJ) (see also [123] (Ribeiro PJ) and [174] (Millett NPJ)), citing *Houghton* (n 80) 59 (Handley JA, with whom Mason P (at 48) and Beazley JA (at 60) agreed). This approach has been reaffirmed in calculating equitable compensation for breach of fiduciary duty, albeit not for a lost chance, in *Australian Executor Trustees (SA) Ltd v Kerr* [2021] NSWCA 5, (2021) 151 ACSR 204 [128], [133] (Gleeson JA, with whom Leeming JA (at [336]) and Emmett AJA (at [337]) agreed) and *Blong Ume Nominees v Semweb Nominees* [2019] SASCFC 151, (2019) 135 SASR 385 [99]–[101] (the Court).
[134] *Libertarian Investments* (n 86) [139] (Ribeiro PJ).
[135] *E Co v Q (No 4)* (n 54).
[136] *Q v E* (n 1) [47] (Ward CJ in Eq).

institutional constructive trust for them. However, in the remedial phase, given that E Co[137] was entitled as lessee to use the properties to conduct farming activities, and the need for a clean break between Q and his sons, Ward CJ in Eq accelerated the sons' interests.[138] The sons were ordered to pay equitable compensation to Q in an amount representing the net present value of rent in respect of the transferred properties, calculated by reference to the nine years of Q's life expectancy.[139] Q's entitlement to lost rent was not presented in the case as a lost opportunity. However, conceptually, it comes very close. Given that the constructive trust was said to be institutional and, moreover, that there was an order for the transfer to the sons of the legal title to the relevant properties,[140] it is difficult to conceive of Q's loss of rent as an accrued loss. Arguably, it was an opportunity lost in virtue of the fact that title to the property was being transferred. The Court did not value this loss by reference to probabilities, but took a robust approach, approximating the lost future income stream for the property.[141] In terms of meeting the values of the equity for relief, the overarching inquiry was to fashion a remedy which made good the sons' expectation as to ownership and E Co's expectation as to the use of the properties.[142] The imperative for a clean break was strong, justifying acceleration of the sons' expectations. The remedy was proportionate to the equity raised, in part precisely because of the equitable compensation on account of lease payments. Further, Ward CJ in Eq noted that, had Q not resiled from the expectations, he still would not have had access to the properties as they would have been subject to ongoing leases and for part of the period he was serving a custodial prison sentence.[143]

V. MONEY ADJUSTMENTS FOLLOWING RESCISSION IN EQUITY

A claimant may have an equity to rescind a contract made pursuant to undue influence, unconscionable conduct, in breach of equitable fiduciary duty and non-fraudulent misrepresentations. Gifts may also be rescinded in equity if the donor was suffering a causative unilateral mistake of sufficient gravity, such that it would be unconscionable not to grant relief.[144] Further, rescission is available in equity on the grounds for rescission recognised at law: duress and fraudulent misrepresentation. On particular facts, rescission in equity may be motivated by the fact that, as discussed below, the requirement of *restitutio in integrum* is applied more strictly at law than in equity. Claimants who are barred from rescission at law may thus nonetheless be entitled to equitable relief.

[137] E Co was owned partly by the sons with Q's shares also declared to be held on constructive trust for his sons: *Q v E Co* (n 27) [10] (Meagher JA), [1] and [10] (Meagher JA).
[138] ibid [10] (Meagher JA).
[139] *E Co v Q (No 4)* (n 54) [16], [658]–[661] (Ward CJ in Eq).
[140] ibid [16], [653] (Ward CJ in Eq).
[141] ibid [658]–[663] (Ward CJ in Eq).
[142] ibid [638]–[639] (Ward CJ in Eq).
[143] *Q v E* (n 1) [1216] (Ward CJ in Eq).
[144] *Pitt v Holt* [2013] UKSC 26, [2013] AC 108 [122], [124]–[126], [128] (Lord Walker with whom the other members of the Court agreed).

The effect of rescission in equity is *ab initio* to extinguish the agreement between the parties or, where relevant, set aside a gift. The object of equity's intervention is to restore the parties as near as possible to their original positions[145] such that they are 'not to be replaced in exactly the same position in all respects, otherwise [the claimant would be entitled to recover damages at law] but … to be replaced … so far as regards the rights and obligations which have been created by the contract'.[146] As part of this 'unravelling'[147] both parties must be able to restore the other to their original positions, or near enough, to do what is 'practically justice'.[148] Thus, equity requires *substantial restitutio in integrum*. This is facilitated by equitable accounting and the ability to award the money substitute of benefits received, including for chattels, land and services. Moreover, as an equitable remedy, rescission is discretionary, and may be subject to terms including the making of further financial adjustments between the parties.[149] These include accounting for profits for the use of assets, an indemnity for burdens assumed under the contract and compensation or a money sum reflecting improvements, repairs, deterioration and depreciation of any assets.

Of relevance is the possibility that these financial adjustments may include compensation for losses, including lost opportunities. Thus, in *Newbigging v Adam* the claimant was a military officer serving in India. Induced by the defendant's innocent misrepresentations about the financial state of what proved to be an unsuccessful textile business, he 'gave up his commission, returned to England [and] entered into the business'.[150] As required by their contract, he paid £9,700 into the business and just over £324 to discharge the existing liabilities of the partnership.[151] The claimant successfully obtained rescission of the contract. In upholding the claimant's right to rescind, the Court of Appeal confirmed the claimant's right to an 'indemnity' for the burdens assumed by the claimant under the contract.[152] Bant[153] argues that, to the extent that the claimant had relieved the defendant of the burden of an inevitable expense in meeting the creditors, the indemnity orders in *Newbigging* are restitutionary. On other facts, however, these adjustments are directed to the claimant's loss. Could this include the claimant's lost opportunity?

In *Newbigging*, at least in relation to the indemnity orders, Cotton LJ gave an answer in the negative, observing that the claimant 'may have been induced by these

[145] *Erlanger v The New Sombrero Phosphate Co* (1878) 3 App Cas 1218 (HL) 1278–79 (Lord Blackburn); *Newbigging v Adam* (1886) 34 Ch D 582 (CA) 588–89 (Cotton LJ); *Brown v Smitt* (1924) 34 CLR 160 (HCA) 165–66 (Knox CJ, Gavan Duffy and Starke JJ).

[146] *Newbigging* (n 145) 592–93 (Bowen LJ), his Honour intending that phrase to have limited meaning such that '[i]t is only the immediate consequences of the contract itself which must be reversed': D O'Sullivan, S Elliott and R Zakrzewksi, *The Law of Rescission*, 2nd edn (Oxford, OUP, 2014) para [13.04]. See also *Brown* (n 145) 166 (Knox CJ, Gavan Duffy and Starke JJ).

[147] O'Sullivan, Elliott and Zakrzewksi (n 146) para [13.06].

[148] *Erlanger* (n 145) 1279 (Lord Blackburn).

[149] *Nadinic v Drinkwater* [2017] NSWCA 114, (2017) 94 NSWLR 518 [29], [30], [32] (Leeming JA).

[150] (n 145).

[151] ibid 583.

[152] ibid 589 (Cotton LJ), 596 (Fry LJ), 592–94 (Bowen LJ).

[153] E Bant, 'Rescission, Restitution and Compensation' in S Degeling and J Varuhas (eds), *Equitable Compensation and Disgorgement of Profit* (Oxford, Hart, 2017) 277, 290–95, esp 293–94 pointing to the fact that the defendant was required to re-assume the burden.

misstatements to give up a commission in the army … but he could not in such an action as the present obtain any relief in respect of it'.[154] However, it must be asked whether Cotton LJ's negative indication should be seen as a closed door on all arguments by the claimant for financial adjustments consequent on rescission on account of lost opportunities. As this chapter has attempted to demonstrate, equity has a growing competence in making certain the nature and extent of a claimant's lost opportunity. Could either the probabilistic or the discretionary approach to certainty offer the means by which equity may within its discretion make consequential adjustments following rescission to reflect the claimant's lost opportunity?[155] The tentative answer is yes, but only to the extent that the lost opportunity is eligible for recognition via a financial adjustment. Put another way, equity will not adjust for opportunities lost as a result of the contract simply because it has available techniques more coherently to appreciate the nature and extent of those losses. The fundamental question remains whether the *contract* obliges the claimant to give up the opportunity.[156] Lost opportunities incurred in connection with the contract, but not pursuant to it, will not qualify for monetary adjustments following rescission. Thus, in *Brown v Smitt*, a plaintiff purchased farmland relying on the defendant's fraudulent misrepresentations, including that the soil was of good quality and that the 'farm was a first-class dairying property'.[157] The contract was rescinded and the plaintiff received a monetary adjustment following rescission reflecting his 'expenditure occasioned by the contract'.[158] Title was reconveyed to the defendant who likewise sought an adjustment for his lost opportunity to grow a hay crop[159] since he would receive the farm back without growing hay on it and too late in the season to sow another crop.[160] The defendant's claim was rejected by the High Court.[161] That equity is able to make reasonably or relatively certain the value of a lost opportunity would not affect the outcome in this type of case.

VI. CONCLUSION

The claimant's loss of opportunity may arise in the course of dealing establishing the claimant's equity for relief or be relevant for the remedial inquiry and the exercise of the court's discretion as to the nature and extent of equitable relief. However, lost opportunities are by their nature inherently uncertain. Whilst the claimant may be able to establish the existence of the opportunity lost on a balance of probabilities, the nature and extent of that loss or the *value of the opportunity lost* will be contingent.

[154] *Newbigging* (n 145) 589 (Cotton LJ).

[155] Albeit taking a slightly different approach, Bant, 'Rescission, Restitution and Compensation' (n 153) 301–05 has similarly argued that where the giving up of a valuable opportunity is substantial and not speculative (at 301), the lost opportunity might be recognised as the claimant's change of position as part of the overall calculus in respect of the claimant's liability to make counter-restitution.

[156] *Newbigging* (n 145) 592–94 (Bowen LJ).

[157] *Brown v Smitt* [1924] VLR 333 (VSC) 336, 337 (Mann J).

[158] ibid (Mann J).

[159] ibid.

[160] *Brown* (n 145) 164 (Knox CJ, Gavan Duffy and Starke JJ).

[161] ibid 166 (Knox CJ, Gavan Duffy and Starke JJ).

It may depend, for example, on the hypothetical conduct of the defendant, of third parties, or indeed of the plaintiff themselves. As this chapter has attempted to demonstrate, depending on the function of the lost opportunity in equitable analysis, equity requires differing standards of certainty, and has various techniques capable of making the value of the opportunity lost relatively certain.

The core example in which the claimant's lost opportunity satisfies elements of the claimant's equity for relief is equitable estoppels. Once the existence of the lost opportunity is established on a balance of probability, there is only a minimal qualitative inquiry into the value of that opportunity. However, in the remedial inquiry, greater certainty is required. This is most prominent in equitable compensation, where the claimant's lost opportunity is a recognised head of loss. Once again, the existence of the lost opportunity is required to be established on a balance of probabilities. In rendering the nature and extent of this loss reasonably certain, equity employs two techniques. The first explicitly applies probabilistic reasoning and discounts the value of the lost chance by reference to the impact of the conduct of the claimant and third parties. The second locates the inquiry within equitable discretion, applying presumptions and fact-finding principles which are weighted according to the conduct of the parties. These techniques in principle should also be available to determine the nature and extent of any lost opportunity as part of any financial adjustments made following equitable rescission, assuming that loss is eligible to be brought into the ledger (which may rarely, if ever, occur). Finally, equity's methods of making lost opportunities sufficiently certain must not run counter to the underlying normative commitments of the particular equity for relief. Thus, for example, when considering equitable compensation for breach of fiduciary duty, where the plaintiff principal has lost an opportunity, the court should not discount for the risk that the plaintiff would not have pursued the opportunity. This is consistent with the position in calculating an account of profits for the same fiduciary breach.[162]

[162] See n 118.

19

Dishonesty and Unconscionability in Contractual Performance – A Role for Equity?

THE HONOURABLE MADAM JUSTICE MARY V NEWBURY*

I. INTRODUCTION

WRITING IN A well-known article in 1998, Lord Millett expressed the view that '[e]quity's place in the law of commerce, long resisted by commercial lawyers, can no longer be denied'.[1] This was a good thing, he suggested, because there had never been a 'greater need to impose on those who engage in commerce the high standards of conduct which Equity demands'.[2] His Lordship went on to describe recent developments in the equitable concepts of fiduciary duty and constructive trust, which in his opinion demonstrated a worrying lack of agreement among commercial lawyers about the fundamental principles of equity and their application to commerce.

Now, 25 years later, there is no reason to believe the need for high standards in commerce is any less pressing. However, the focus of commentators and lawyers in the commercial world has shifted somewhat to the concept of good faith in contract – a concept that has been described as including reasonableness, honesty, 'fair dealing' and even 'legitimate expectations' between contracting parties.[3] Good faith in

* The author wishes to acknowledge with thanks the contribution of her law clerks at the Court of Appeal for British Columbia in preparing this paper, namely Will Eberle and Jennifer Rogers.

[1] P Millett, 'Equity's Place in the Law of Commerce' (1998) 114 *LQR* 214.

[2] ibid 216.

[3] See, eg, SM Waddams, 'Good Faith, Unconscionability and Reasonable Expectations' (1995) 9 *Journal of Contract Law* 55; J Cartwright, 'Protecting Legitimate Expectations and Estoppel in English Law' (2006) 10 *Electronic Journal of Comparative Law*; and E McKendrick, 'Good Faith in the Performance of a Contract in English Law' in L DiMatteo and M Hogg (eds), *Comparative Contract Law* (Oxford, OUP, 2016). For some time, it was thought a duty of good faith might amount to a fiduciary duty, but that idea has now largely dissipated. See generally JD McCamus, 'Abuse of Discretion, Failure to Cooperate and Evasion of Duty: Unpacking the Common Law Duty of Good Faith Contractual Performance' (2004) 29 *Advocates' Quarterly* 72; DW Little, 'Fiduciary Duties in Construction Projects: Much Higher than Good Faith' (2017) *Journal of the Canadian College of Construction Lawyers* 171.

contract has been the subject of countless academic articles in the common law world, but courts outside the United States[4] have not seen fit to adopt it as a 'free-standing' doctrine of general application, confining it to only certain types of contracts.

I do not intend to add to the literature on good faith. Rather, I will discuss how judges have developed the common law or equitable rules[5] applying to dishonest or simply misleading statements made by one contracting party to the other, relating to the parties' rights under a concluded contract or to its performance. Where such a statement is relied on by the representee to his or her detriment, the law (including equity) may provide a defence against the enforcement of the contract, or even provide a cause of action by which the detriment suffered by the representee may be 'avoided'.[6] However, the jurisprudential route by which courts have arrived at this outcome over the last few decades has varied significantly among jurisdictions.

In this chapter, I review, 'from 30,000 feet', the broad contours of these varying responses, in each of Canada, Australia and England,[7] to 'dishonest performance' or unconscionable conduct in the form of statements of the kind I have described. For the most part, this will be a story of the relationship between rules of contract law – most obviously, the doctrine of consideration, which with one exception[8] has been retained unaltered in England – and the development of a broader and more principled doctrine of (equitable) estoppel. Put in even broader terms, it is a reflection of the tension between certainty in contract law and the discretionary nature of equity. Of course, this tension has been ongoing since at least the enactment of the Judicature Act 150 years ago.

In Canada, the Supreme Court declined in 2014 to adopt the idea of a duty of good faith in contract, recognising it as (and *only* as) a 'general organising principle'. At the same time, the Court imposed a narrower and more concrete 'duty of honest performance' intended to accord with the reasonable expectations of contracting parties and enhance commercial certainty. Equity did not figure in the Court's reasoning – this was a new 'common law' duty. Arguably, it represented a reach at the 'low-hanging fruit' of the good faith principle, making it unnecessary to define good

[4] See, eg, Uniform Commercial Code ('UCC'), s 1–304. See generally EA Farnsworth, 'Good Faith Performance and Commercial Reasonableness Under the Uniform Commercial Code' (1963) 30 *University of Chicago Law Review* 666; H Dubroff, 'The Implied Covenant of Good Faith in Contract Interpretation and Gap-Filling: Reviling a Revered Relic' (2006) 80 *St John's Law Review* 559; P MacMahon, 'Good Faith and Fair Dealing as an Underenforced Legal Norm' (2015) 99 *Minnesota Law Review* 2051.

[5] This chapter does not consider legislative responses, such as the prohibition on misleading or deceptive conduct in trade or commerce imposed by s 18 of the Australian Consumer Law: see Competition and Consumer Act 2010, Sch 2.

[6] Of course, the tort of deceit is available where the elements set out in *Derry v Peek* (1889) 14 App Cas 337 (HL), including fraud on the part of the representor, are present. The tort is beyond the scope of this paper.

[7] For discussion of the use of the concept of 'unconscionability' in linked areas (including proprietary estoppel) in Hong Kong and Singapore, see Yip's chapter in this volume.

[8] See *Williams v Roffey Bros* [1991] 1 QB 1 (CA); *cf Re Selectmove Ltd* [1995] 2 All ER 531 (CA); and *Rock Advertising Ltd v Business Exchange Centres Ltd* [2018] UKSC 24, [2018] 2 WLR 1603 [18]. In Canada, *Williams* was discussed favourably in *Greater Fredericton Airport Authority Inc v NAV Canada* 2008 NBCA 28, 290 DLR (4th) 405 [26]–[32]; *Rosas v Toca* 2018 BCCA 191, 9 BCLR (6th) 293; and in B MacDougall, *Estoppel*, 2nd edn (Toronto, LexisNexis Canada, 2019) paras [5.64]–[5.77].

faith exhaustively, but still addressing one type of unacceptable conduct and leaving the door open for further specific 'manifestations' of the organising principle.

A very different approach has been taken in Australia. The High Court looked to equity, and what it called 'equitable estoppel' in particular, to ensure that where 'unconscionable conduct' (meaning conduct that is 'unfair', 'unjust' or 'against conscience') is shown – here in the form of a statement by one contracting party that is relied on by the other to his or her detriment – a suitable remedy may be fashioned, either to compel the representor to make good the expectation he or she created or, more commonly, to compensate for its falsity. The High Court re-examined many of the longstanding obstacles to the application of estoppel in this context, expessing the hope that a unifying principle of unconscionability may subsume at least the traditional categories of estoppel in equity.

Except in certain types of contracts (particularly 'relational' ones[9]), English courts have preferred to address would-be good faith obligations indirectly through long-standing rules of contractual interpretation and the implying of terms, attempting to ensure certainty and predictability above all. Conversely, they have been reluctant to rationalise equitable principles to address conduct between contracting parties that is 'against conscience', retaining the highly compartmentalised nature of estoppel and the peculiarities of each of its categories. Even so, commentators have expressed the fear that equity is getting 'out of control in the marketplace'.[10] An argument *could* be made that English courts have carried on the fine tradition, observed by Professor Waddams in 1976, of taking general concerns that engage equity, slicing them into carefully defined categories, laying out narrow exceptions, and ultimately 'suppressing the true principle'.[11]

II. CANADA

I begin with Canada, however, where the Supreme Court's 2014 decision in *Bhasin v Hrynew*[12] effected an important change in contract law. The plaintiff, Bhasin, was an 'enrolment director' who sold education savings plans for the defendant, Can-Am, under an evergreen contract that could be terminated by either party's giving six months' notice at the end of each three-year term. The relationship was somewhat similar to a franchise arrangement. Can-Am began to encourage a merger between Bhasin and the second defendant, Hrynew, a competitor of Bhasin's. Bhasin was opposed to the idea. Hrynew was brought in by Can-Am to assist with the provincial securities commission, and for this purpose carried out audits of Can-Am's enrolment directors, acquiring confidential information about them. Bhasin objected

[9] See D Campbell (ed), *The Relational Theory of Contract: Selected Works of Ian Macneil* (London, Sweet & Maxwell, 2001); and D Campbell, 'Good Faith and the Ubiquity of the "Relational" Contract' (2014) 77 *MLR* 475. For a recent example of a case applying the English rules of interpretation to a relational contract, see *Bates v Post Office* [2019] EWHC 606 (QB) [702ff].

[10] See, eg, Lord Briggs of Westbourne, 'Equity in Business' (2019) 135 *LQR* 567, 567, 583.

[11] SM Waddams, 'Unconscionability in Contracts' (1976) 39 *MLR* 369, 391.

[12] *Bhasin v Hrynew* 2014 SCC 71, [2014] 3 SCR 494.

but was repeatedly assured, falsely, that his information would be kept confidential. He was also given equivocal answers concerning the possible merger, which in fact was a 'done deal' as far as Can-Am was concerned. Can-Am finally gave notice of termination of the contract. Bhasin sued Can-Am for breach of contract (specifically, breach of a duty of good faith), and Hrynew for intentional inducement of breach of contract and civil conspiracy. The trial judge found that Bhasin had lost the value of his business and lost most of his workforce to Hrynew's agency.

Prior to the Supreme Court's decision in *Bhasin*, the position in Canada was similar to that in England: although good faith was implied by law as an incident of certain categories of contract, no *general* doctrine was recognised. Thus the Alberta Court of Appeal wrote in *Bhasin* itself that '[t]here is no duty to perform most contracts in good faith'.[13]

On appeal, however, the Supreme Court observed that good faith in contractual dealings underlies 'many elements of modern contract law', in particular the law relating to implied terms and contractual interpretation. The phrase 'good faith' appeared in various statutes, including those dealing with franchises and labour law. Good faith considerations were also evident in the employment, insurance and tendering contexts. It was time, the Court decided, to enunciate a 'general organizing principle of good faith'.

Speaking for the Court, Cromwell J described the organising principle as '… simply that parties generally must perform their contractual duties honestly and reasonably and not capriciously or arbitrarily'.[14] It was not a free-standing rule, but a 'standard that underpins and is manifested in more specific legal doctrines and may be given different weight in different situations'. It was to be applied in a manner consistent with the importance given by contract law to the freedom of parties to pursue their individual self-interest, and so as to avoid 'veer[ing] into a form of *ad hoc* judicial moralism or "palm tree" justice'.[15]

The contract at issue in *Bhasin*, however, was said not to fit into any of the categories (franchise agreements or relational contracts, for example) in which a duty of good faith had been found to exist; and the 'entire agreement' clause was found to preclude the implying of such a duty. The Court therefore decided to 'create' a new duty of 'honesty in contractual performance' under the umbrella of good faith. Cromwell J defined 'dishonest performance' as referring to an incorrect or misleading statement by one contracting party to the other, who acts on it to his or her detriment. He framed the duty as a straightforward concept – a 'simple requirement not to lie or mislead the other party about one's contractual performance'. It was not to be treated as an implied term of contract, but as a 'general doctrine of contract law that imposes … a minimum standard of honest contractual performance'.[16]

One might object that the word 'performance' was being used very broadly here – surely a contractual 'duty' or 'obligation' is either performed or it is not.

[13] *Bhasin v Hrynew* 2013 ABCA 98, 362 DLR (4th) 18 [27].
[14] *Bhasin* (n 12) [63].
[15] ibid [70].
[16] ibid [74].

Unless the term is very unusual, 'honesty' is beside the point. However, from the examples provided by the Court and subsequent cases, it appears the duty relates to the exercise of a power (using the term loosely) or discretion one party has under the contract. It might refer, for example, to a right or power to order an increased number of widgets, to fix a market rent in a lease, or to pay a bonus in certain conditions; or more widely, to a party's statement that he or she intends to act in a particular way in the future under, or despite, the terms of the contract. The court in *Bhasin* seems to have assumed that without the new duty, such a statement would not constitute the breach of a *contractual* obligation per se, although it did not explain why a term could not be implied to the effect that Can-Am's discretion to terminate had to be exercised honestly or in a manner consistent with the objectives of the contract. Indeed, the Court noted elsewhere in its reasons that the implying of terms 'plays a functionally similar role in common law contract law to the doctrine of good faith in civil law jurisdictions by filling in gaps in the written agreement of the parties'.[17]

The duty of honest performance would operate irrespective of the parties' intentions (and perhaps even contrary to them), and could not be contracted out of – even though the 'entire agreement' clause was effective to preclude the duty of good faith. In this sense, the new duty was said to be analogous to equitable doctrines, such as unconscionability, that impose limits on freedom of contract.[18] Cromwell J expressed the hope that taken together with the organising principle, the duty would bring 'certainty and coherence' to this area of the law in a manner 'consistent with reasonable commercial expectations'.[19]

Finally, the duty of honest performance was not 'subsumed' by the existing law relating to 'civil fraud' or estoppel: it did not require proof that the representor intended his or her statement to be relied on (although on the facts of *Bhasin* there could be little doubt it was so intended); and it was not 'subject to the uncertainty around whether estoppel can be used to found an independent cause of action'. Further, statements of future intention as well as those of existing fact, would seem to be subject to the duty. Although it was 'extra-contractual', a breach of the new duty would support a claim for damages in contract[20] – a result that would normally be precluded by the *Photo Production* line of cases[21] followed in Canada in *Hunter Engineering Ltd v Syncrude Canada Ltd*.[22]

Having recognised a new doctrine of contract law that applied regardless of the parties' intentions – no mean feat – the Court agreed with the trial judge that the defendant Can-Am had 'acted dishonestly' toward the plaintiff in invoking the termination clause. It had 'equivocated' in what it told him about its intention to merge Bhasin's agency with Hrynew's, and repeatedly misrepresented the nature

[17] ibid [44] (Cromwell J) citing SM Waddams, *The Law of Contracts*, 6th edn (Aurora Ont, Canada Law Book, 2010) paras [499]–[506].
[18] ibid [74].
[19] ibid [62].
[20] ibid [88].
[21] *Photo Production Ltd v Securicor Transport Ltd* [1980] AC 827 (HL).
[22] [1989] 1 SCR 426.

of its obligations to the securities authorities. At one point the court said that Can-Am was liable 'on the basis of what Mr Bhasin's economic position would have been had Can-Am fulfilled that duty'.[23] However, the damages award was not calculated to put him in the position he would have been in if the contract had been honestly performed: recall that Can-Am was entitled to terminate (ie, not renew) the contract on giving six months' notice *in any event*. Instead, the plaintiff was compensated for the detriment he had suffered, to the extent that, and for as long as, it had been reasonable for him to rely on the mis-statements – the reliance measure of damages.

In a subsequent case, *CM Callow Inc v Zollinger*,[24] the Court muddied the waters somewhat. The facts were simple: the defendant condominium corporations 'actively deceived' the plaintiff into believing his contract (which was terminable on 10 days' notice) for providing winter maintenance services would be renewed, leading him to provide extra work in the spring and summer free of charge to the defendants. In fact they had already decided not to renew. The plaintiff sued for 'bad faith' in contract, and unjust enrichment. The Supreme Court was split, with the majority sometimes conflating the duty of honest performance with the organising principle of good faith. The majority found a breach of the duty of honest performance, but also ruled that a contractual right to terminate for convenience 'cannot be exercised in a manner that transgresses the core expectations of honesty required by good faith in the performance of contracts'.[25] The minority clearly limited the case to the duty of honest performance[26] and acknowledged that the damages awarded in *Bhasin* had been aimed at making good the detriment resulting from the plaintiff's reliance on Can-Am's dishonest statements. The minority also questioned the appropriateness of referring to the doctrine of 'abuse of right' in the civil law of Quebec (a doctrine firmly founded in the representor's subjective state of mind) to support the majority's interpretation of good faith and honest performance.

As observed by Professor MacDougall,[27] the new Canadian duty of honest performance does not sit comfortably with the law of contract. As a stand-alone wrong, it looks more like a tort, albeit arising in a contractual context. The purpose of damages for breach of the duty is usually to negate the effect of the detriment rather than to enforce the plaintiff's expectations. In addition, the duty of honest performance has many of the characteristics of estoppel by representation, although the intention required for estoppel is largely objective: if the representee would reasonably interpret the statement as one intended to be relied on, a presumption of intention on the part of the representor normally arises.[28] The Supreme Court has not clarified why, given the objective nature of contract law, a (subjective) intention to induce reliance must be shown for a breach of the new duty; nor has it indicated whether the awarding of

[23] *Bhasin* (n 12) [108] (Cromwell J).
[24] 2020 SCC 45, 452 DLR (4th) 44.
[25] ibid [84] (Kasirer J).
[26] ibid [124], [138].
[27] B MacDougall, *Misrepresentation and (Dis)Honest Performance in Contracts,* 2nd edn (Toronto, LexisNexis Canada, 2021) para [7.109].
[28] MacDougall, *Estoppel* (n 8) para [4.64].

damages is discretionary or whether the foreseeability of damage is relevant. Finally, it has not commented on whether the tort of deceit could have performed the function of the new duty of honesty in contract law.

III. AUSTRALIA

The Australian High Court, which it must be said has historically been much more 'equity-friendly' than Canadian courts,[29] has taken a very different approach to the problem of mis-statements (a wider concept than dishonest statements) made by one contracting party to the other. The obvious focal point is *Waltons Stores*,[30] which built upon earlier judgments, including *Thompson v Palmer*,[31] *Grundt v Great Boulder Pty Gold Mines Ltd*,[32] and *Legione v Hateley*.[33] Whilst *Waltons Stores* itself concerned pre-contractual conduct, the principles discussed are also relevant to statements made by one contracting part to another and relied on by that other to his or her detriment.

The facts of *Waltons Stores* were complicated and four sets of reasons were delivered. The case involved an '*almost-formed*' agreement rather than the 'performance' of a concluded and enforceable contract. Under the Conveyancing Act 1919, an exchange of signed documents had to take place for the planned lease to become enforceable. Chief Justice Mason and Wilson J, in a joint judgment, found that the respondents, the owners of the property, had been led to believe *not* that the lease had been signed by Waltons, but that an 'agreement' existed and that the signing and exchange of documents were mere formalities that would follow. On this assumption, the owners had begun demolition of an old building on the property and construction of a store to Waltons' urgent specifications. Unbeknownst to the owners, however, Waltons changed its mind at the last minute and decided not to sign the lease or to erect a store there. It failed to inform the owners until seven weeks later, by which time the construction was 40 per cent complete.

Given this view of the facts, then, the owners were not relying on a representation of *fact* but one as to Waltons' future intention – a circumstance that would normally preclude the application of both common law estoppel by representation (relied on by the trial judge) and estoppel based on an omission to correct a unilateral mistake (favoured by the New South Wales Court of Appeal).[34] *Promissory* estoppel (traditionally concerned with making good the expectations of the representee) was available for statements or 'promises' as to *future* intentions or conduct[35] but

[29] See generally K Maharaj, 'An Action on the Equities: Re-Characterizing *Bhasin* as Equitable Estoppel' (2017) 55 *Alberta Law Review* 199, 202–23, citing *Canson Enterprises Ltd v Boughton & Co* [1991] 3 SCR 534, 577–78.

[30] *Waltons Stores (Interstate) Ltd v Maher* (1988) 164 CLR 387 (HCA).

[31] (1933) 49 CLR 507 (HCA).

[32] (1937) 59 CLR 641 (HCA).

[33] (1983) 152 CLR 406 (HCA).

[34] *Waltons Stores* (n 30) 398 (Mason CJ).

[35] In promissory estoppel, usually a statement that the speaker would not strictly enforce his or her rights under the contract. See the discussion in *Legione v Hateley* (n 33) 432–34 (Mason and Deane JJ).

thus far, only as a 'defensive equity' – a 'shield not a sword'.[36] The owners asked the Court to go one step further by using promissory estoppel to *enforce*, in the absence of a 'pre-existing relationship', a non-contractual 'promise' or statement (in this case, one made by silence) on which they had relied to their detriment. Arguably, of course, such a result would 'outflank' the principles of contract law, specifically the requirement for consideration to make a promise enforceable.[37]

Drawing support from *Crabb v Arun District Council*[38] and *Attorney General for Hong Kong v Humphreys Estate Ltd*,[39] however, the joint judgment fastened on the doctrine of unconscionability. In cases of *promissory* estoppel, he said, the elements of reliance and detriment usually attracted equitable intervention 'on the basis that it is unconscionable for the promisor to depart from his promise if to do so will result in detriment to the promisee'.[40] Suggestions to this effect could be found in English cases such as *Amalgamated Property Co v Texas Bank*[41] (at the trial level by Goff J)[42] and in the law of *proprietary* estoppel explored in *Taylors Fashions Ltd v Liverpool Victoria Trustees' Co Ltd*.[43] The common thread of these cases was that equity will come to the relief of a party who has acted to his or her detriment on the basis of an assumption where the other party has 'played such a part in the adoption of the assumption that it would be unfair or unjust if he were left free to ignore it'.[44] The equity thus arising could lead to the granting of various forms of relief, including the recognition of rights in property 'without [the representee's] having to pay for them', since equitable estoppel 'has its basis in unconscionable conduct, rather than the making good of representations'.[45] In *Crabb* and the seminal *Ramsden v Dyson*,[46] proprietary remedies had been recognised that 'came into existence as the only appropriate means by which the defendants could be effectively estopped from exercising their existing legal rights'.[47]

On the facts of *Waltons Stores*, Mason CJ and Wilson J concluded that it was unconscionable for Waltons, 'knowing that the [property owners] were exposing themselves to detriment by acting on the basis of a false assumption, to adopt a course of inaction which encouraged them in the course they had adopted'. In the 'language of promissory estoppel', Waltons was estopped from retreating from its implied promise to complete the contract.[48]

[36] *Waltons Stores* (n 30) 400, citing *Hughes v Metropolitan Railway Co* (1877) 2 App Cas 439 (HL) and *Combe v Combe* [1951] 2 KB 215 (CA). See generally DE Jackson, 'Estoppel as a Sword' (1965) 81 *LQR* 223.
[37] *Waltons Stores* (n 30) 400.
[38] [1975] All ER 865 (CA).
[39] [1987] AC 114 (PC).
[40] *Waltons Stores* (n 30) 401 (Mason CJ and Wilson J).
[41] [1982] QB 84 (CA) 107.
[42] [1981] 2 WLR 554 (QBD).
[43] [1982] QB 133 (Ch).
[44] *Waltons Stores* (n 30) 404 (Mason CJ and Wilson J).
[45] ibid 405 (Mason CJ and Wilson J).
[46] (1866) LR 1 HL 129.
[47] *Waltons Stores* (n 30) 404 (Mason CJ and Wilson J).
[48] ibid 407–08.

Brennan J adopted the same view concerning the factual assumption made by the property owners. He contrasted estoppel by representation, commonly said to be only a rule of evidence[49] that requires the representor to 'adhere to the assumption that the contract exists', with equitable estoppel or an 'equity created by estoppel'. Citing *Chalmers v Pardoe*,[50] a case of proprietary estoppel, he described *equitable* estoppel as *the source of a legal obligation* arising on an *actual* (rather than assumed) state of affairs. It binds the conscience of the representor to do or abstain from doing something in order to prevent detriment to the other as a result of having acted in reliance on the induced assumption.[51] The assumption or expectation might be one of fact or law, or even an error of law, but must be intended or understood by both parties as affecting their legal relationship.[52]

Brennan J preferred the term 'equitable estoppel' to the traditional categories of estoppel, which he found not to be helpful. In his words:

> If cases of equitable estoppel are in truth but particular instances of the operation of the general principles of equity, there is little purpose in dividing those cases into the categories of promissory and proprietary estoppel … I do not find it generally helpful to divide into classes the cases in which an equity created by estoppel has been held to exist. However, the familiar categories serve to identify the characteristics of the circumstances which have been held to give rise to an equity in the party raising the estoppel.[53]

He cited English cases including *Combe v Combe* in support of this equitable estoppel. In that case, Lord Denning had said the promisor or representor must accept his legal relations with the promisee 'subject to the qualification which he himself has so introduced, even though it is not supported in point of law by any consideration but only by his word'.[54]

Depending on the facts, various remedies could be granted to give effect to the equity thus created; but as a court of conscience, the Court would go 'no further than is necessary to prevent unconscionable conduct'.[55] Since the object of the equity is the avoidance of the detriment suffered by the representee, its measure 'varies according to what is necessary to prevent detriment resulting from unconscionable conduct'.[56] So regarded, equitable estoppel did not elevate non-contractual promises to the level of contractual ones and the doctrine of consideration was not 'blown away by a side-wind'.[57] In *Waltons Stores* itself, the equity was satisfied by treating Waltons as though it had executed and delivered the lease, thus 'avoiding' the detriment suffered by the owners. Their action to enforce the equity was not brought 'upon any contract' (which would be prohibited by the *Conveyancing Act*), but arose 'out of the circumstances'.

[49] *Low v Bouverie* (1891) 3 Ch 82 (CA); and see Jackson (n 36) 96–99.
[50] [1963] 1 WLR 677 (PC).
[51] *Waltons Stores* (n 30) 416.
[52] ibid 421.
[53] ibid 420.
[54] *Combe* (n 36) 220. No estoppel was recognised in *Combe*.
[55] *Waltons Stores* (n 30) 419 (Brennan J).
[56] ibid 425 (Brennan J). See also J Campbell, '*Waltons v Maher*: History, Unconscientiousness and Remedy – The "Minimum Equity"' (2013) 7 *Journal of Equity* 171.
[57] *Waltons Stores* (n 30) 427.

Indeed, Brennan J observed, the Statute of Frauds 1677 had 'never stood in the way of a decree to enforce a proprietary estoppel' and there was no reason it should do so when any other form of estoppel is applied.[58]

Unlike their colleagues, each of Deane and Gaudron JJ proceeded on the basis that the owners had believed a binding (ie, enforceable) agreement *had* come into existence when they began work on the subject property. For Deane J, Waltons' 'deliberate silence' was sufficient to found an estoppel by conduct that precluded it from denying the 'assumed fact' that a binding agreement existed 'where there was in fact none'. That being so, estoppel 'outflanked' the Conveyancing Act and there was no room for its intrusion into the assumed facts.[59] His Honour also addressed the notion that estoppel may be used only as a defence. He found that previous judgments of the High Court dealing with estoppel by conduct had been framed in general terms and did not support such a 'constriction'. Insofar as other decisions supported such a view, he said, they should not be accepted as law in Australia.[60]

For our purposes, the most interesting part of Deane J's analysis was that dealing with estoppel by conduct pre- and post-fusion. In his words, the operation of estoppel is

> an area in which it is necessary for care to be taken to avoid the risk that a consciousness of past separateness of common law and equitable doctrines may lead to a tendency to discount the full substantive effects of their fusion … To ignore the substantive effects of the interaction of doctrines of law and equity within that fused system in which unity, rather than conflict, of principle is now to be assumed is, however, unduly to preserve the importance of past separation and continuing distinctness as a barrier against the orderly development of a simplified and unified legal system which fusion was intended to advance.[61]

Even before fusion, he said, there had been a general consistency, or 'unity', in context and rationale between common law and equitable principles regarding estoppel by conduct. This had been emphasised by the majority in *Jorden v Money* itself.[62] In ordinary cases of estoppel by conduct precluding the denial of an existing fact, 'particularly in the context of mistaken notions that estoppel by conduct was but a rule of evidence', there was no point in maintaining independent equitable and common law doctrines under a fused system. In connection with estoppel relating to a representation or assumption of *future* action or inaction, on the other hand, the doctrine of consideration had 'routed' estoppel, although estoppel by conduct had continued to appear in some pockets of the law as 'an equity'.[63] The 'sourcing' of these to the modern doctrine of promissory estoppel had led to the mistaken perception that it was exclusively equitable. In fact, he said, the rule that the representation or assumption in question must not relate to future action or intentions

[58] ibid 433.
[59] ibid 444–46 (Deane J).
[60] ibid 444–45.
[61] ibid 446–47.
[62] (1854) 5 HL Cas 185, 212–13. See, also, Jackson (n 36) 88–95.
[63] *Waltons Stores* (n 30) 448 (Deane J), citing, eg, *Hughes v Metropolitan Railway Co* (n 36).

had arisen both in courts of equity and those of common law and could be justified in *either* context 'by deference to the primacy of the doctrine of consideration'.[64] The rule had always sat uncomfortably with the 'notions of good conscience and fair dealing which underlay common law, as well as equitable doctrines of estoppel by conduct'.[65]

Proceeding on the basis that estoppel by conduct was a doctrine of substantive law rather than merely a rule of evidence, Deane J saw no reason why it could not be applied to statements as to a future state of affairs just as effectively as to an existing fact. On this basis, he agreed that *Jorden v Money* and cases following it should no longer be seen as good law. The extension of this estoppel to cases involving facts like those in *Waltons Stores* would not, he suggested, undermine the doctrine of consideration; rather, that principle would be strengthened 'by overcoming its unjust operation in special circumstances with which it is inadequate to deal'.[66]

Gaudron J gave the fourth set of reasons. Like Deane J, she found on the facts that the property-owners had assumed that the exchange of contracts *had* occurred. This made it unnecessary for her to decide the 'future conduct' issue. In her analysis, 'common law' or 'evidentiary' estoppel compels adherence to an assumption of fact, while equitable estoppel operates with reference to an assumption as to rights.[67] Where the latter occurs and adherence can be compelled only by the recognition of an 'equitable entitlement to a positive right' in the person claiming estoppel, she said, the resulting estoppel is generally referred to as 'proprietary estoppel'. Where, on the other hand, adherence to an assumption of rights may be compelled by precluding the representor from asserting existing rights, the term 'promissory estoppel' is generally used.[68]

In *Waltons Stores* itself, Gaudron J noted, an assumption that the contracts *would be* exchanged could be seen as an assumption of future fact or conduct – which, if *Jorden v Money* applied, would not found a common law estoppel. But it could also be seen as an assumption as to future rights, and thus might found an equitable estoppel. The answer to this problem might depend on whether proprietary and promissory estoppel were discrete categories of equitable estoppel or merely illustrative of different assumptions as to rights.[69]

Gaudron J did not find it necessary to decide this question, instead proceeding with reference to the assumption that exchange *had* taken place. Following *Grundt*[70] and *Thompson v Palmer*,[71] she asked whether Waltons had 'so contributed to the assumption that exchange [of documents] had taken place that it would be unjust

[64] *Waltons Stores* (n 30) 448–49 (Deane J), citing *Jorden v Money* (n 62).
[65] ibid 449 (Deane J).
[66] ibid 451–53 (Deane J).
[67] ibid 458.
[68] ibid 458–59.
[69] ibid 459–60. See more recently *Crown Melbourne Ltd v Cosmopolitan Hotel (Vic) Pty Ltd* [2016] HCA 26, (2016) 260 CLR 1 [146].
[70] (n 32).
[71] (n 31) 547.

or unfair if it were left free to ignore it'.[72] She concluded that once it had come to Waltons' knowledge that construction had begun, Waltons had been under a duty to inform the owners that the situation had changed – Waltons no longer wanted to build at that site. Its 'imprudence' in doing nothing was a 'proximate cause' of the owners' making and acting on the assumption, with the result that it would be unfair to 'allow departure from that assumption'.[73]

In the end, all five justices agreed that the lower court's order requiring Waltons to pay damages in lieu of specific performance of the lease should be affirmed.

Two years later, in *Commonwealth v Verwayen*,[74] the Court revisited *Waltons Stores* in the context of a personal injury lawsuit brought by a member of the Navy against the Commonwealth for negligence. The Commonwealth told the plaintiff's solicitor that it proposed to admit liability and to waive the limitations statute. Later the Government changed its mind on both points and sought to amend its pleading. The Supreme Court of Victoria ruled that the Government had not waived the defences, but that it was estopped from resiling from its promise not to plead limitation. The plaintiff received damages for his out-of-pocket expenses incurred by reason of the Commonwealth's change of mind.

The High Court allowed the Government's appeal on the basis that this remedy was disproportionate to the detriment the plaintiff had suffered. Indeed, no detriment had been found by the trial court flowing from his reliance on the assumption that limitation would not be pleaded. This time, seven sets of reasons were delivered, making it difficult to extract a ratio. Their Honours did seem to accept that a legal relationship (even if not a contractual one) was sufficient for the operation of promissory estoppel.

In his reasons, Chief Justice Mason stated that there should now be

> but one doctrine of estoppel, which provides that a court of common law or equity may do what is required, but not more, to prevent a person who has relied upon an assumption as to a present, past or future state of affairs ... which assumption the party estopped has induced him to hold, from suffering detriment in reliance upon the assumption as a result of the denial of its correctness.

A central element of that doctrine was proportionality between the remedy and the detriment it was intended to avoid.[75] Writing extra-judicially some time later, the Chief Justice described *Verwayen* as a 'staging post along the way towards recognition of an over-arching unity embracing the various classes of estoppel'.[76]

A more useful case on virtually identical facts (but much stronger evidence of detrimental reliance) is *Commonwealth v Clark*,[77] where the Supreme Court of

[72] *Waltons Stores* (n 30) 461.

[73] Campbell (n 56) 14 concludes that the ratio of the judgments of both Deane and Goudron JJ was that *common law* estoppel applied.

[74] *Commonwealth v Verwayen* (1990) 170 CLR 394 (HCA).

[75] ibid 413.

[76] AF Mason, 'Contract, Good Faith and Equitable Standards in Fair Dealing' (2000) 116 *LQR* 66, 91. A few years after *Verwayen*, in *Giumelli v Giumelli* (1999) 196 CLR 101 (HCA), the court declined the opportunity to decide whether a 'single overarching doctrine' of estoppel by conduct should be recognised.

[77] *Commonwealth v Clark* [1994] 2 VR 333 (Supreme Court of Victoria).

Victoria held that equitable estoppel was made out and that the minimum required to do justice was to prohibit the Commonwealth from amending its pleading to assert the limitations statute. Three sets of reasons were given, the longest by Ormiston J, who subjected the *Verwayen* reasons to a very detailed analysis, ultimately concluding it would be 'grossly unfair'[78] to allow the Commonwealth to depart from the assumptions it had induced in the mind of the plaintiff, who continued to suffer severe psychiatric *sequelae* of the accident.

Not all Australian courts and academics, however, happily threw off the categories of equitable estoppel for a unified one, or adopted the notion that estoppel can generally operate to found a cause of action.[79] As Professor Robertson observes, although the 'independent source of rights model' of promissory estoppel is 'taken by some judges to be unquestionably well established in Australian law, others treat it as unquestionably wrong'.[80] Many state courts have found it possible to avoid applying *Waltons Stores* in one way or another; others have been overtly critical. At the end of the day, it appears that as the authors of *Spencer Bower on Estoppel by Misrepresentation* suggested in their 2004 edition, the various conclusions expressed in *Waltons Stores* and *Verwayen* are 'probably best regarded as works in progress'.[81]

IV. ENGLAND

I now turn now to England, where most courts have resisted the notion of a stand-alone duty of good faith implied by law in the performance of commercial contracts generally. Professor McKendrick suggests that English courts regard the development of such a duty as contrary to the incremental approach preferred in English law, which is to fashion 'particular solutions in response to particular problems rather than by enforcing broad overreaching principles'.[82] He writes that a good faith duty in contract is seen as inconsistent with the 'ethos of individualism' that underlies contract law and as undermining the goal of contractual certainty by introducing 'vague and subjective' obligations.[83] Again, I do not propose to discuss good faith per se,

[78] ibid 384.

[79] See *Saleh v Romanous* [2010] NSWCA 274, (2010) 79 NSWLR 453; *DHJPM Pty Ltd v Blackthorn Resources Ltd* [2011] NSWCA 348, (2011) 83 NSWLR 728 [47], [92]–[93]; *Hammond v JP Morgan Trust Australia Ltd* [2012] NSWCA 295, [2013] ALMD 926; *Character Design Pty Ltd v Kohlen* [2013] WASC 112; *Ashton v Pratt* [2015] NSWCA 12, (2015) 88 NSWLR 281 [138]; *Mineralogy Pty Ltd v Sino Iron Pty Ltd* [2015] FCA 825, (2015) 329 ALR 1 [769]; and see generally A Robertson, 'Three Models of Promissory Estoppel' (2013) 7 *Journal of Equity* 226.

[80] Robertson (n 79) 245.

[81] P Feltham, D Hochberg and T Leech (eds), *Spencer Bower: Estoppel by Representation*, 4th edn (West Sussex, Tottel Publishing, 2004) para [XIV.5.10].

[82] McKendrick (n 3) 203–05. See, also, the suggestion of PD Finn, 'The Fiduciary Principle' in TG Youdan (ed), *Equity, Fiduciaries and Trusts* (Toronto, Carswell, 1989) 2–3 that a legal system 'with a commitment to uphold individual responsibility and self-reliance may be less prepared to oblige parties to be their "brother's keeper" than one committed to social cooperation and neighbourhood responsibilities'; and *Pakistan International Airlines Corp v Times Travel (UK) Ltd* [2021] UKSC 40, [2021] 3 WLR 727 [27].

[83] E McKendrick, *Contract Law*, 9th edn (Oxford, OUP, 2020) 221–22, quoted by Leggatt J in *Yam Seng Pte v International Trade Corp Ltd* [2013] EWHC 111 (QB), [2013] 1 All ER (Comm) 1321 [123].

except to say that it is percolating away at lower levels of the courts in England and has gained some support at the appellate level.[84]

I am not aware of any appellate cases from England that consider the idea of a substantive duty of honest performance in contract similar to that created by *Bhasin* in Canada. That idea might be slightly more acceptable in England than a general duty of good faith in contract. However, the creation of such a duty might be unnecessary. The observations of Mr Justice Leggatt (now of course Lord Leggatt) in *Yam Seng Pte v International Trade Corp Ltd*[85] are perhaps best-known in this regard: after emphasising that all contracts are made against the background of unstated shared understandings that inform their meaning, he observed that a 'paradigm example' of a general norm underlying almost all contractual relationships is the expectation of honesty, which is essential to commerce, and which depends critically on trust.[86] As far as contractual construction is concerned, he said, it is hard to imagine any contract that would not be reasonably understood as requiring honesty in its performance.[87] Similarly, with respect to the implying of terms, 'the requirement that parties will behave honestly is so obvious that it goes without saying. Such a requirement is also necessary to give business efficacy to commercial transactions'.[88]

A necessarily brief review of some key English cases will illustrate the recent thinking concerning equitable estoppel since *Waltons Stores* was decided, and of the continuing issues that arise in the interaction of contract law with equitable doctrines. But realising that one cannot embark on such a review without an old chestnut from Lord Denning, I begin with *Texas Bank*,[89] decided shortly before *Waltons Stores*. It involved a guarantee given to a bank, which was intended by both parties to cover liability under a particular loan. In the event, the loan was made by a subsidiary of the bank, rather than the bank itself. When the guarantor went into liquidation, its liquidator took the position that it was not bound to pay the shortfall, as the written agreement did not in fact apply to the loan it had been intended to guarantee.

At trial, Robert Goff J ruled that it would be unconscionable for the guarantor to seek to take advantage of the mistake, which both parties had shared. More important to his analysis, the guarantor had encouraged the bank's mistaken belief by various acts and correspondence, both before and after the guarantee was executed. Goff J observed that '… it can only be unconscionable for the encourager or representor to enforce his strict legal rights if the other party's conduct has been influenced by the encouragement or representation'.[90] He described equitable estoppel as one of the 'most flexible' doctrines, adding that although courts had enunciated various

[84] *Interfoto Picture Library Ltd v Stiletto Visual Programmes Ltd* [1987] 1 QB 433 (CA) 439; *Socimer International Bank Ltd v Standard Bank London Ltd* [2008] EWCA Civ 116, [2008] 1 Lloyd's Rep 558; *Braganza v BP Shipping Ltd* [2015] UKSC 27, [2015] 4 All ER 639.

[85] (n 83).

[86] ibid [135].

[87] ibid [136] citing *HIH Casualty v Chase Manhattan Bank* [2003] UKHL 6, [2003] 2 Lloyds Rep 61.

[88] ibid [137]. See also Leggatt J, speaking extra-judicially, in 'Contractual Duties of Good Faith' (Lecture to the Commercial Bar Association, 18 October 2016), available at www.judiciary.uk/wp-content/uploads/2016/10/mr-justice-leggatt-lecture-contractual-duties-of-faith.pdf.

[89] (n 41).

[90] *Texas Bank* (n 42) 571.

principles concerning various types of estoppel, '… all these have been statements of aspects of a wider doctrine; none has sought to be exclusive. … it cannot be right to restrict equitable estoppel to certain defined categories, and indeed some of the proposed categories are not easy to defend'.[91] It is not surprising, he continued, to 'discover a tendency in the more recent authorities to reject any rigid classification of equitable estoppel into exclusive and defined categories'.[92]

In the Court of Appeal, Lord Denning MR took a similar view, and spoke in similar terms, famously stating that '[t]he doctrine of estoppel is one of the most flexible and useful in the armoury of the law' and that its different manifestations, such as proprietary and promissory estoppel, could 'now be seen to merge into one general principle shorn of limitations'.[93] He found that this 'general principle' applied in the case before him.

But this endorsement of a unified doctrine of estoppel was not the view of the majority in *Texas Bank*, who found in any case that the terms of the contract did in fact cover the intended liability. Brandon LJ, with whom Eveleigh LJ agreed on this point, nonetheless considered the position if that interpretation of the contract were incorrect. If so, he would have characterised the case as one of estoppel *by convention:* both parties had assumed certain facts and acted upon them; each would be estopped as against the other from questioning the truth of the facts so assumed. In response to the argument that the bank was seeking to use estoppel as a sword, Brandon LJ described the matter as one of 'semantics'.[94] If the bank had sued the guarantor before it had gone into liquidation, the bank would have pleaded the guarantee; the guarantor would have argued that on its true construction, it was bound to pay only what was owed to the *bank*, and not to its *subsidiary*; and then the bank would have replied that the guarantor was 'precluded' from questioning the interpretation that both parties had assumed to be true in their dealings. In this way, Brandon LJ observed that 'the bank, while still in form using the estoppel as a shield, would in substance be founding a cause of action on it'.[95] The 'true proposition of law', he said, was that while a party 'cannot in terms found a cause of action on an estoppel, he may, as a result of being able to rely on an estoppel, succeed on a cause of action on which, without being able to rely on that estoppel, he would necessarily have failed'.[96]

The doctrine of estoppel by convention was recently examined by the Supreme Court in *Tinkler v Revenue and Customs Commissioners*,[97] where it was applied to prevent a taxpayer from denying an assumption, shared by him and the Revenue, that a valid enquiry into his tax return had been opened. One of the requirements of such an estoppel was that, by action in reliance on the common assumption, the party asserting the estoppel had suffered some detriment, or the other party had received

[91] ibid 569.
[92] ibid 570.
[93] *Texas Bank* (n 41) 122.
[94] ibid 131.
[95] ibid.
[96] ibid 131–32.
[97] [2021] UKSC 39, [2021] 3 WLR 697.

some benefit, 'sufficient to make it unjust or unconscionable for the latter to assert the true legal (or factual) position'. Unconscionability was thus recognised as an underlying basis of the doctrine,[98] and Lord Burrows also noted that most estoppel doctrines

> are nowadays usually regarded as equitable doctrines not least because there is a heavy emphasis in the case law on 'unconscionability' (although, wherever possible, one should seek to clarify what that vague phrase means in relation to the particular facts in play).

Nonetheless, Lord Burrows did not draw on the role of unconscionability as a means to argue for the unification of these forms of estoppel, noting instead that 'such unification has proved elusive and the different types of estoppel continue to be seen as having their own particular requirements and effects'.[99] He cited in support *Baird Textile Holdings Ltd v Marks and Spencer plc*.[100] In that case, no relevant contract was found to exist between the parties; the estoppel sought by Baird relied only on 'assurances' and a 'conventional understanding'. The court below declined to strike out Baird's case, saying that '[i]f ever a case were fit to test the limits of the doctrine of estoppel by convention then this is it'.[101]

The Court of Appeal, however, disagreed. Judge LJ mentioned two 'specific aspects of the current principles of the law of estoppel which may be open for reconsideration' – first, whether the various principles associated with estoppel should 'cease to be treated as if they were individually compartmentalised' (a suggestion that, as Millett LJ had observed in *First National Bank v Thomson*,[102] had never won general acceptance'); and second, whether the 'misleading aphorism that estoppel is a shield, not a sword' should be consigned to history.[103] Judge LJ acknowledged that the possible development of the law of estoppel on these points might have justified allowing the case to proceed to trial, but he was ultimately persuaded there was no 'real prospect of the claim succeeding unless and until the law is developed, or corrected, by the House of Lords'.[104] Being bound to apply the law as it is and 'not as it may possibly one day become',[105] he joined in allowing the appeal.[106]

Mance LJ in *Baird Textile* also reviewed different forms of estoppel and its relationship to contract at some length, but emphasised that the requirements of contract formation could not be 'bypassed' to found an estoppel. He found no authority to support the proposition that estoppel could achieve 'so expanded an application, simply by limiting recovery to reliance loss'.[107] Any such development in English law 'could and should … now take place in the highest court'.[108] His Lordship also

[98] ibid. See too Lord Briggs at [89].
[99] ibid [28].
[100] [2001] EWCA Civ 274, [2002] 1 All ER (Comm) 737.
[101] *Baird Textile Holdings Ltd v Marks and Spencer plc* (QBD, 29 June 2000) [20] (Morison J).
[102] [1996] Ch 231 (CA) 236.
[103] *Baird Textile* (n 100) [52].
[104] ibid [55].
[105] ibid.
[106] ibid.
[107] ibid [91].
[108] ibid.

acknowledged that the court might have reached a similar result to that reached in *Waltons Stores*, albeit by different reasoning. In *Waltons Stores*, there had been complete agreement on the terms of the lease; thus in Mance LJ's analysis, the recognition of an estoppel might not result in using the doctrine 'as giving a cause of action in itself'[109] and almost certainly would not undermine the necessity of consideration in contract. It would only have precluded Waltons from raising a 'collateral objection' to the binding nature of the lease.[110]

Moving ahead to 2008, we find the seminal *Cobbe v Yeoman's Row Management Ltd*,[111] which weakened hopes that the House of Lords would grasp the nettle of a unified doctrine of equitable estoppel. In *Cobbe*, the parties had reached an oral 'agreement in principle' for the development and purchase of land owned by the corporate defendant. The agreement was incomplete, but even if complete, would not give rise to a contract as it did not comply with the requirement of signed writing in section 2 of the Law of Property (Miscellaneous Provisions) Act 1989. The claimant, an experienced property developer, had been aware of this requirement, but in reliance on the agreement in principle had expended time and money to obtain planning permission for the development of the property. The oral agreement contemplated that once permission was obtained, the parties would enter into a written contract under which the plaintiff would purchase the property for an initial payment of £12 million. Then, after selling the six houses to be built on the property, he would pay the corporate defendant an additional 50 per cent of any amount by which the gross proceeds exceeded £24 million.

Perhaps not surprisingly, the corporate defendant (represented by its director, the defendant LM) withdrew from the arrangement as soon as planning permission was obtained. The claimant sued on various grounds, including that the defendants had acted unconscionably in knowingly inducing and encouraging him to believe the property would be sold to him, and then refusing to honour the oral agreement. The lower court allowed his claims in proprietary estoppel and constructive trust on this basis.

Again, not surprisingly, the House of Lords reversed. First, estoppel did not fit the facts of the case: in the analysis of Lord Scott (concurred in by Lord Hoffmann, Lord Brown and Lord Mance) there was nothing the defendants would be estopped from denying if proprietary estoppel were applied; nor would the claimant be assisted by estoppel – he would still have only an oral, and therefore unenforceable (as well as incomplete) agreement.[112] He had not spent his money and time *in reliance on* a

[109] ibid [98].

[110] ibid citing also H Beale (ed), *Chitty on Contracts*, 28th edn (London, Sweet & Maxwell, 1999) para [3-095].

[111] [2008] UKHL 55, [2008] 1 WLR 1752.

[112] Section 2(5) of the Law of Property (Miscellaneous Provisions) Act 1989 excepted constructive, resulting or implied trusts from the requirement that an agreement be in writing but made no exception for proprietary estoppel. Lord Scott (*Cobbe* (n 111) [29]) expressed the tentative view that proprietary estoppel could not 'contradict the statute'. Lord Walker did not express a view on that point (see *Cobbe* (n 111) [93]) and later cases have demurred from Lord Scott's opinion: see, eg, *Farrar v Miller* [2018] EWCA Civ 172, [2018] 2 P & CR DG3 [57]–[63] and note too Lord Neuberger, 'The Stuffing of Minerva's Owl? Taxonomy and Taxidermy in Equity' (2009]) 68 *CLJ* 537, 546–47.

mistaken belief that the agreement was legally enforceable; rather, he had consciously taken a chance on LM's acting honourably – an 'acknowledgement that she was not legally bound'.[113] The fact that LM had taken unconscionable advantage of Mr Cobbe could not itself create a 'proprietary estoppel equity'.[114] Without clarity as to what the defendants were to be estopped from denying, and the nature of the property interest that would be defeated, Lord Scott observed, proprietary estoppel would 'lose contact with its roots and risk becoming unprincipled and therefore unpredictable, if it has not already become so'.[115]

Lord Walker also gave reasons, with which Lord Brown also concurred. Lord Walker warned that equitable estoppel is 'not a sort of joker or wild card' to be used whenever the court disapproves of the conduct of a litigant who 'seems to have the law on his side', and that it must be 'formulated and applied in a disciplined and principled way'.[116] After reviewing some of the incomplete gift and unilateral mistake cases, he characterised *Cobbe* as a case of 'common expectation' if anything. But Mr Cobbe had really been only a *hope*, given his awareness of the requirement that a sale agreement be evidenced in writing. 'Hope' had not been enough to constitute an *expectation* in *Ramsden v Dyson*;[117] nor was it enough in *Cobbe*. In the imperfect gift cases, in contrast, the parties successfully raising an estoppel had more than hope: they relied to their detriment on assurances they believed were binding and irrevocable.[118]

In response to LM's argument that it would not have been unconscionable in any event for her to insist on her legal rights, Lord Walker observed that unconscionability 'plays a very important part in the doctrine of equitable estoppel, in unifying and confirming … the other elements' of the doctrine. But Mr Cobbe had known LM was 'bound in honour only, and so in the eyes of equity her conduct, although unattractive, was not unconscionable'.

Ultimately, Lord Walker concluded that the Court of Appeal had 'stretched the boundaries of the doctrine of equitable estoppel too far' in granting relief that went well beyond the restitutionary relief to which the claimant was held to be entitled. If the Court of Appeal's decision were to stand, it would tend to introduce uncertainty into commercial negotiations. In short, although equity has some important functions in regulating commercial life, 'those functions must be kept within proper bounds'.[119]

Whilst it is possible that the decision of the Supreme Court in *Guest v Guest*[120] may bring greater clarity, decisions since *Cobbe* have not yet added noticeably to an understanding of the 'proper bounds' of equitable estoppel in England, nor to a 'firmer

[113] *Cobbe* (n 111) [27] echoing Lord Cranworth in *Ramsden v Dyson* (n 46)145–46.
[114] *Cobbe* (n 111) [28].
[115] ibid.
[116] ibid [46].
[117] (n 46). See too *Attorney General for Hong Kong v Humphrey's Estate* (n 39).
[118] *Cobbe* (n 111) [66]. See also Lord Neuberger (n 112) 541–44 (speaking extra-judicially).
[119] *Cobbe* (n 111) [85].
[120] On appeal from *Guest v Guest* [2020] EWCA Civ 387, [2020] 1 WLR 3480. The Supreme Court heard the appeal in December 2021, but judgment had not been handed down by the time this chapter was finalised at the end of September 2022.

concept' of unconscionability.[121] Professor Handley has suggested not only that the idea of a unified doctrine has become 'unfashionable' in England (was it ever fashionable?) but that the role, if any, of unconscionability itself is now being downplayed in comparison to the early years of this century.[122] His view is that '[u]nconscionability has no real work to do and is nothing more than a confusing label although it still appears in some judgments'.[123]

With respect, I believe it is clear even in England that unconscionability (or 'unfairness' or 'injustice') plays and has for many decades played an important role in those types of estoppel that require detrimental reliance.[124] To be sure, there is a debate as to whether it is a 'separate' or 'additional' element, as opposed to being inherent in the other three. Most commentators now seem to take the latter view; the authors of the fifth edition of *Spencer Bower*, for example, write that if the three elements are satisfied, 'then it is unfair or unconscionable; if they are not, then it is not; and if that is not the result produced, then the answer must be further to refine or adjust the requirements themselves so that it is'.[125]

I am inclined to the opposite view – that rather than 'adjusting' the other elements to reach the right result, 'something more' is required for an equity to arise, and that that 'something' is a finding (perhaps only implicit) of unconscionability or unfairness. As we have seen, the representor may have been labouring under a mistake of fact or even law in making the statement – even acting in good faith! – but it is the representor's *conduct* that is scrutinised, not his or her state of mind.[126] In my respectful view, the court must exercise its discretion in deciding whether it would be 'contrary to conscience' to permit the representor, *in the particular circumstances before the court*,[127] simply to walk away from the detriment he or she has caused. This analysis is not reminiscent of the 'moral standards of the vicarage';[128] it seeks fairness as between contracting or otherwise related parties, one of whom has acted to his or her detriment in reliance on a statement made by the other. Thus I agree with the opinion expressed by Deane J in *Verwayen*:

> In this, as in other areas of equity-related doctrine, conduct which is 'unconscionable' will commonly involve the use of or insistence upon legal entitlement to take advantage of another's special vulnerability or misadventure ... in a way that is unreasonable and

[121] M Dixon, 'Proprietary Estoppel and Formalities in Land Law and the Land Registration Act 2002: A Theory of Unconscionability' in E Cooke (ed), *Modern Studies in Property Law*, vol 2 (Oxford, Hart, 2002) 176.

[122] K Handley, *Estoppel by Conduct and Election*, 2nd edn (London, Thomson Reuters, 2016) para [1-030].

[123] ibid para [1-032]. See, also, P Feltham and others (eds), *Spencer Bower: Reliance-Based Estoppel*, 5th edn (London, Bloomsbury Professional, 2017) para [1.70].

[124] See too the discussion above of *Tinkler* (n 97).

[125] Feltham and others (n 123) para [1.71]. See also Macdougall, *Estoppel* (n 8) para [1.6.5].

[126] See Lord Walker in *Cobbe* (n 111) [91]. In each of *Taylors Fashions* (n 43) and *Tinkler* (n 97), for example, an estoppel operated against a party who had innocently shared the assumption of the relying party.

[127] See, eg, *Walton v Walton* (CA, 14 April 1994) 4, where Hoffmann LJ stated that equitable estoppel 'looks backwards from the moment when the promise falls due to be performed and asks whether, in the circumstances which have actually happened, it would be unconscionable for the promise not to be kept'.

[128] See *UBSAG (London Branch) v Kommunale Wasserwerke Leipzig GMBH* [2017] EWCA Civ 1567, [2017] 2 Lloyd's Rep 621 [347].

> oppressive to an extent that affronts ordinary minimum standards of fair dealing. That being so, the question whether conduct is or is not unconscionable in the circumstances of a particular case involves a 'real process of consideration and judgment'... in which the ordinary processes of legal reasoning by induction and deduction from settled rules and decided cases are applicable but are likely to be inadequate to exclude an element of value judgment ...[129]

Lord Walker observed in *Cobbe* that if the three objective elements 'appear to be present but the result does not shock the conscience of the court, the analysis needs to be looked at again'.[130] In my view, what needs to be looked *for* is the 'shocking' (or perhaps 'offending') nature of the representor's conduct to one's conscience. Conversely, even where the three elements are shown, there may be circumstances that lead to the conclusion that the conduct, though relied upon, is *not* unconscionable.[131] For example, circumstances arising after the representations and reliance may mean it is no longer unconscionable for a party to refuse to honour a promise to transfer land.[132]

Setting this debate aside, it seems unlikely that courts in England will follow the lead of *Waltons Stores* and adopt a unified or overarching doctrine of 'equitable estoppel' in the near to medium term.[133] Where certainty or predictability in contract law is seen to be jeopardised, the courts find a way to leave the topic for another day. Admittedly, they have become less formulaic than in previous generations (recall the 'five probanda' of *Willmott v Barber*[134] and the 'Procrustean bed constructed from some unalterable criteria' referred to in *Taylors Fashions*[135]). They seem now to be more concerned with the principles at stake in a given case than with the type(s) of estoppel involved. Because of this, the differences between categories of estoppel – especially proprietary and promissory estoppel – have begun to blur somewhat. Only in cases of *proprietary* estoppel have the rules against the enforcement of what contract law regards as gratuitous promises been largely overcome – 'assimilating' (in the words of Brennan J in *Waltons Stores*) the 'relationship arising from equitable estoppel to the relationship arising in contract'.[136] But again, an overarching doctrine is some distance away.

[129] *Verwayen* (n 74) 440–41; and see M Dixon, 'Confining and Defining Proprietary Estoppel: The Role of Unconscionability' (2010) 30 *Legal Studies* 408. Dixon, 'Proprietary Estoppel and Formalities in Land Law' (n 121) 177 writes that if unconscionability exists *by definition* wherever the elements of assurance, reliance and detriment exist, the concept of unconscionability, which he describes as lying at the heart of proprietary estoppel, is robbed of 'any discernible meaning. It is a non-definition'.

[130] *Cobbe* (n 111) [92].

[131] P Feltham, D Hochberg and T Leech (n 81) para [XIV 3.13].

[132] See the example discussed by Lord Scott in *Thorner v Major* [2009] UKHL 18, [2009] 1 WLR 776 [88], where the promisor needs to sell the land in order to pay for medical care. For the effect of a change of circumstances, see too *Habberfield v Habberfield* [2019] EWCA Civ 890, [2019] 2 P & CR DG13 and note B McFarlane, *The Law of Proprietary Estoppel*, 2nd edn (Oxford, OUP, 2020) paras [5.89–5.114] and [7.64–7.65].

[133] Although note that a recent work, M Barnes, *The Law of Estoppel* (London, Hart, 2020) 22–27 attempts to set out general issues which are common to the four 'reliance-based' estoppels of estoppel by representation, estoppel by convention, proprietary estoppel, and promissory estoppel.

[134] (1880) 15 Ch D 96 (Ch).

[135] (n 43) 154 (Oliver J).

[136] *Waltons Stores* (n 30) 424.

An obstacle to the recognition of a unifying doctrine embracing the types of equitable estoppel is often expressed – the concern that unconscionability is simply too 'abstract' or operates at too high a level of generality to provide any guidance to courts or businesspeople in the complicated world of 'real events and real transactions'.[137] Without the strict enforcement of the categories of estoppel, it has been said, an 'uncontrolled invasion of equity into commerce' may be expected.[138] I cannot agree that the notion of unconscionability is all that abstract or uncertain, at least in the context of equitable estoppel. Unconscionability – which at bottom asks what the *conscientious* person would think of the representor's conduct – is no more difficult than the concept of negligence, which asks what a *reasonable* person would have done in the defendant's shoes. Both concepts are bread and butter to most judges, who apply them to a multitude of fact situations the categories of which are never closed. I have seen no indication that courts are 'out of control' in determining whether given conduct in the commercial context is against conscience. As we have seen, if anything judges in England have been astute to avoid the issue in many instances, basing their decisions on the absence of one of the three *objective* elements.

As for concerns about 'palm-tree justice', the specific requirements of each category of estoppel can of course provide assistance in 'unifying and confirming' claims of unconscionability – as opposed to constituting pigeonholes into which each case *must* be fitted if estoppel is to be applied. As the authors of *Spencer Bower* wrote in their 2004 edition, the doctrine of estoppel exists to remedy *not all forms* of unfairness, but only the 'particular unfairness of a party suffering because he was induced to act on a proposition made by another and the other resiled from it'.

So it seems to me, with respect, that unconscionability is an understandable concept that has real meaning and can be applied with some predictability in the 'real world' of commerce. Lord Neuberger's suggested formulation of the unified doctrine of equitable estoppel seems about right:

> At least in broad terms, may not estoppel now be seen to be a generic term for a claim by a claimant who has changed his position in the reasonable and foreseeable belief that a defendant's act, statement, silence or inaction has a particular consequence, so that it would now be unconscionable for the defendant to repudiate that consequence (wholly or to an extent), at least without giving the claimant some compensation?[139]

V. CONCLUSION

We have seen three very different ways of addressing false or incorrect statements made in the context of contractual relationships. In England, terms of honesty and even good faith may be implied in some types of contracts, but certainty and predictability have thus far trumped unifying and modernising tendencies in the law of estoppel. In Australia, the High Court in *Waltons Stores* confronted almost every

[137] Lord Briggs of Westbourne (n 10) 567, 583.
[138] ibid 583. See too Yip's chapter in this volume.
[139] Lord Neuberger (n 112) 547–48. See also Waddams 'Unconscionability in Contracts' (n 11) 390–91.

substantive issue that stands in the way of a unified doctrine of equitable estoppel, and did so in a principled and scholarly way. However, it is difficult to extract a ratio from *Waltons Stores*, and the Court may have gone 'too far' for other courts in Australia. The result seems to be that the varieties of estoppel, with their rules and exceptions, effectively remain in force. Partly because of this perceived difficulty, the Supreme Court of Canada sidestepped equity in *Bhasin*, borrowing instead from the civil law of Quebec to impose a narrow and ill-fitting duty of 'honest performance' as a common law 'manifestation' of good faith in contract. Looking at it 'from 30,000 feet', it appears that equity's role in addressing statements made in commerce that are dishonest or otherwise misleading is still relevant in this sesquicentennial year – but also problematic.

20

Equity in Commerce: Too Much and Too Little?

MAN YIP

I. INTRODUCTION

THE INTERACTION AND clash between equity and commerce have attracted much attention from judges[1] and academics[2] in recent years. Commercial lawyers may complain about equity introducing uncertainty into commercial endeavours and at times, (mis-)applying the 'moral standards of the vicarage' to actors in commercial dealings.[3] However, the objections are not directed at all aspects of equity, but are usually addressed to some 'disfavoured parts of it', such as the creation of a new obligation or discretionary remedies.[4] On the other hand, from the perspective of equity lawyers, equity's interplay with commerce may lead to the contractualisation or commercialisation of equitable doctrines,[5] thereby lowering the standards that equity traditionally expects of actors such as trustees and fiduciaries.[6]

Lord Briggs, writing extra-judicially, stated that the important task is to investigate how 'to set bounds upon the role of equity in business and commerce, so as

[1] See, for example, The Honourable Justice MJ Beazley, 'Conflicts in Commercial Trusts' (Annual Commercial and Corporate Law Conference, Supreme Court of New South Wales, 2016); Lord Briggs of Westbourne, 'Equity in Business' (2019) 135 *LQR* 567; M Leeming, 'The Role of Equity in 21st Century Commercial Disputes – Meeting the Needs of Any Sophisticated and Successful Legal System' (2019) 47 *Australian Bar Review* 137; The Hon Geoffrey Nettle AC, 'Trust and Commerce in Historical Perspective' (2021) 15 *Journal of Equity* 2. See too, Newbury's chapter in this volume.

[2] See, for example, J Penner and P Davies (eds), *Equity, Trusts and Commerce* (Oxford, Hart, 2017); P Devonshire and R Havelock (eds), *The Impact of Equity and Restitution on Commerce* (Oxford, Hart, 2019); I Samet, *Equity: Conscience Goes to Market* (Oxford, OUP, 2018).

[3] *UBS AG (London Branch) v Kommunale Wasserwerke Leipzig GmbH* [2017] EWCA Civ 1567, [2017] 2 Lloyd's Rep 621 [347] (Gloster LJ dissenting). See also *Cobbe v Yeoman's Row Management Ltd* [2008] UKHL 55, [2008] 1 WLR 1752 [81] (Lord Walker). *cf* M Harding, 'Equity and the Value of Certainty in Commercial Life' in P Devonshire and R Havelock (eds), *Impact of Equity and Restitution on Commerce* (Oxford, Hart, 2019) 147.

[4] Leeming (n 1) 151.

[5] M Yip and J Lee, 'The Commercialisation of Equity' (2017) 37 *Legal Studies* 647.

[6] See, eg, L Ho and R Nolan, 'The Performance Interest in the Law of Trusts' (2020) 136 *LQR* 402.

to keep its important role from getting out of hand'.[7] Focussing on modern English developments, Lord Briggs concluded that judges, academics and advocates have succeeded only in parts in keeping equity to its proper role.[8] But what is equity's proper role in commerce? It must be tied to the basic principles and the boundaries that are set in respect of these principles' operation in each context. But whatever equity's role may be in contemporary commerce, it undoubtedly takes some of its colour from its historical and non-commercial origins.

This chapter contributes to discussion of the operation of modern equity in commerce by introducing a comparative perspective: it considers how equity has developed in recent years in other common law jurisdictions, such as Hong Kong and Singapore. This international perspective is crucial for three reasons. First, equity has taken root in other jurisdictions beyond England and Wales and has resulted in developments of potential value to English law for law reform purposes. Second, commerce is transnational and the quality of common law (including equitable principles) in other jurisdictions is one of the factors which may influence where parties wish to have their international commercial disputes resolved. Third, a comparative review of Hong Kong and Singapore developments is meaningful because they are both financial centres whose laws have historically hewed closely to English law. Moreover, foreign judges (sitting or former judges) can exert some degree of direct influence on the laws in both jurisdictions.[9]

This chapter examines two areas: first, the modern courts' recourse to 'unconscionability'; and secondly, the irreducible core of trusteeship and duty limitation and liability exemption clauses. The first area is at the heart of the 'disfavoured' parts of equity which are said to generate uncertainty in commerce. The second area relates to the converse complaints from equity scholars that commercial considerations lower the standards set in equity. The analysis will show that the interaction between commerce (and to a large extent, contract law) and equity in these two areas demonstrates the interplay between certainty and flexibility in law. In the area of 'unconscionability', equity exhibits the trait of flexibility in a commercial context traditionally dominated by the principle of certainty. In the area of duty limitation and liability exemption clauses, on the other hand, equity exhibits the trait of certainty by providing a baseline standard which commerce attempts to make malleable based on the principle of party autonomy. It is perhaps not so much a clash between equity and commerce as a tension between certainty and flexibility in the enterprise of developing law and administering justice. The bounds that need to be set are determined by the role that equity plays in each context, informed by the values championed by each jurisdiction based on its unique culture, experience and the attitudes of the individual judges.

[7] Lord Briggs (n 1) 569.
[8] ibid 568.
[9] In Hong Kong, overseas judges are appointed to join the local judges in hearing appeals in the Hong Kong Court of Final Appeal: www.hkcfa.hk/en/about/who/judges/npjs/index.html. In Singapore, foreign judges are appointed as International Judges to hear cases in the SICC and the appeals from the SICC to the Singapore Court of Appeal: www.sicc.gov.sg/about-the-sicc/judges.

II. THE COMMERCIAL CONTEXT

It is apposite to make a preliminary remark about what is meant by 'commerce' and 'business' in this chapter. The commercial and domestic distinction is not a bright-line division.[10] However, 'context' is not used in this chapter as a determinant of the applicable tool of analysis. Instead, context is used more generally as the background against which to appreciate the application and adaptation of equitable principles. I therefore use the terms 'commerce' and 'business' widely, and so include business dealings that are not at arms' length.

Crucially, it is accepted that commercial and domestic contexts fall on a continuum and do shade into each other at some point. Further, the analysis is anchored on the observation that what might be traditionally perceived as the domestic context can be underlined by compelling commercial considerations such that it becomes a form of business. This is evident in the field of private client/wealth management practice, the context in which we will examine the law on duty limitation and liability exemption clauses in section IV. Relevantly, as the analysis will show, the 'commercial context' is a generalised label that in fact comprises different contexts. There is a need to differentiate between them.

III. UNCONSCIONABILITY

A. The Meaning of 'Unconscionability'

In *Gillett v Holt*, Walker LJ explicitly acknowledged that 'the fundamental principle of equity' is to 'prevent unconscionable conduct'.[11] The problem with the language of 'conscience' (and cognate labels)[12] is that it is vague and connotes intuitions that are inimical to the objectivity required by law.[13] Examples of judicial criticism and caution on the direct use of 'unconscionability' as a free-standing doctrine abound.[14] As do judicial efforts in setting limits to restrain the excesses of 'unconscionability' in modern law. In *Gavin Edmondson Solicitors Ltd v Haven Insurance Co Ltd*,[15] for example, Lord Briggs rejected as unprincipled an argument that the law on a solicitor's equitable lien should protect solicitors from 'any unconscionable interference

[10] See, eg, *Chan Yuen Lan v See Fong Mun* [2014] SGCA 36, [2014] 3 SLR 1048 [155]: the Singapore Court of Appeal categorically rejected the unclear domestic and commercial distinction that has emerged from *Stack v Dowden* [2007] UKHL 17, [2007] 2 AC 432.

[11] *Gillett v Holt* [2001] Ch 210 (CA) 225.

[12] For an examination of the historical meaning and usage of terms like 'conscience' and 'unconscionability', see R Havelock, 'The Evolution of Equitable "Conscience"' (2014) 8 *Journal of Equity* 128.

[13] See P Birks, 'Equity, Conscience, and Unjust Enrichment' (1999) 23 *Melbourne University Law Review* 1; R Havelock, 'Conscience and Unconscionability in Modern Equity' (2015) 9 *Journal of Equity* 1, 3–4; G Virgo, 'Whose Conscience? Unconscionability in the Common Law of Obligations' in A Robertson and M Tilbury (eds), *Divergences in Private Law* (Oxford, Hart, 2016).

[14] See, eg, *Royal Brunei Airlines Sdn Bhd v Tan* [1995] 2 AC 378 (PC) 392 (Lord Nicholls); *Wee Chiaw Sek Anna v Ng Li-Ann Genevieve (sole executrix of the estate of Ng Hock Seng, deceased)* [2013] SGCA 36, [2013] 3 SLR 801 [100]–[103].

[15] [2018] UKSC 21, [2018] 1 WLR 2052.

with their expectations in relation to recovery of their charges'.[16] In respect of the element of 'unconscionability' in the equitable doctrine of knowing receipt, both the Hong Kong and Singapore courts have clarified its application in the commercial context. Under Hong Kong law, the defendant must have 'actual knowledge of the facts which render it unconscionable for the defendant to retain the benefit of the receipt'.[17] Under Singapore law, whilst actual knowledge of breach of trust is not 'invariably required', the Singapore Court of Appeal said that unconscionability could be shown in the commercial context 'where there are circumstances in a particular transaction that are so unusual, or so contrary to accepted commercial practice'.[18]

B. The Modern Embrace of 'Unconscionability'

Yet, the general wariness of 'unconscionability' in modern law has not halted courts from embracing it in some contexts. As Lord Briggs astutely points out, 'unconscionability' may 'sometimes help … in preventing equity being reduced to a set of arcane rules, and becoming detached from its fundamental purpose'.[19] The modern function of 'unconscionability' is as a tool wielded by courts to decide cases in a fact-sensitive way, whether in responding to new facts or in taking the full facts of the case into consideration. Its curse is its very charm: the lack of complete definitional precision. In English law, we have seen the endorsement of 'unconscionability' as part of the test for setting aside a voluntary disposition on the basis of mistake in *Pitt v Holt*.[20] In Australia, 'unconscionability' is very much alive,[21] both in statutes (commonly referred to as 'statutory unconscionability'),[22] as well as in judge-made law.[23]

More recently, in Singapore and Hong Kong, we see judicial recourse to 'unconscionability' by the apex courts in extending existing principles and developing new doctrines in 'hard cases'. In both jurisdictions, 'unconscionability' provides the justification for the law to decide the outcome in a fact-sensitive way. The inherent difficulty with a fact-sensitive approach is in ensuring that it does not undermine certainty, a value that is considered paramount in the commercial context. The introduction of new principles or the extension of existing ones based on a fact-sensitive approach

[16] ibid [58].

[17] *Hing Yip Holdings (Hong Kong) Ltd v Cellmark China Ltd* [2021] HKCFI 1396 [209], citing *Thanakharn Kasikorn Thai Chamkat (Mahachon) v Akai Holdings Ltd* [2010] HKCFA 63, (2010) 13 HKCFAR 479.

[18] *George Raymond Zage III v Ho Chi Kwong* [2010] SGCA 4, [2010] 2 SLR 589 [32] (VK Rajah JA).

[19] Lord Briggs (n 1) 583.

[20] [2013] UKSC 26, [2013] 2 AC 108 [124]–[125]. For an application in the commercial context, see *Co-operative Bank Plc v Hayes Freehold Ltd* [2017] EWHC 1820 (Ch).

[21] However, Justice Leeming notes extra-judicially that based on a sample of commercial list judgments from 2014 to 2018, a large percentage of the claims based on allegations of unconscionable conduct failed. See Leeming (n 1) 1513–14.

[22] See, eg, Australian Securities and Investments Commission Act 2001, s 12CB and Australian Consumer Law, s 21.

[23] See discussion in Havelock, 'Conscience and Unconscionability in Modern Equity' (n 13) 15–19.

is even more concerning. I examine these decisions below and investigate how courts balance certainty, flexibility and innovation in modern equity, and thus how proper bounds on equity operating in commerce are set.

i. The Narrow Doctrine of Unconscionability: BOM v BOK

BOM v BOK[24] is a landmark ruling of the Singapore Court of Appeal. The Court's decision was delivered by Andrew Phang JA (since redesignated as JCA) who was a contract law scholar prior to joining the bench. The case, in which Singapore law recognised the narrow doctrine of unconscionable transactions,[25] arose in the family context between a married couple whereby the wife misled her husband into giving up his inheritance by asking him to sign a trust deed at a time when he was undergoing acute grief over the passing of his mother. The husband alleged that the wife had misrepresented to him that the trust of all of his assets in favour of his infant son was to take effect on his death when in fact it took effect immediately, a matter he belatedly learnt after signing the deed. The Singapore Court of Appeal agreed that the trust deed could be set aside on the grounds of misrepresentation, mistake, undue influence and unconscionability.

In respect of the doctrine of unconscionability under Singapore law, the Singapore Court of Appeal formulated a two-stage test.[26] Under stage one, the plaintiff bears the burden to show that he or she suffered from an infirmity of sufficient gravity and evident to the counterparty which the counterparty exploited in procuring the transaction. On satisfying this requirement, the burden then shifts to the defendant at stage two to show that the transaction was fair, just and reasonable. The Court of Appeal emphasised that the Singaporean version of unconscionable bargains is one that sits between the narrow version endorsed in cases such as *Fry v Lane*[27] and *Cresswell v Potter*[28] and the broad version exemplified by *Commercial Bank of Australia Ltd v Amadio*.[29] Notably, the Singapore Court of Appeal was of the view that the *Amadio* doctrine – which is based on the test of 'special disadvantage' – is too uncertain and can lead to subjective judicial analysis.[30] The Singaporean doctrine also expanded the list of recognised infirmities laid down in the aforementioned English cases to include physical, mental or emotional infirmities, beyond poverty and ignorance.[31] The point appears to be this: the doctrine needs to be fact-sensitive, but it must clearly define what facts may be admitted for evaluation. The decision has attracted

[24] [2018] SGCA 83, [2019] 1 SLR 349.

[25] *cf Esben Finance Ltd v Wong Hou-Lianq Neil* [2022] SGCA 1, [2022] 1 SLR 136 [246]. In this subsequent decision, the Singapore Court of Appeal seemed to have taken a more tentative stance in respect of the place of the free-standing doctrine of unconscionability in Singapore law. Phang JCA, delivering the unanimous judgment of the court, described the doctrine as 'putative' and commented that it had not been rejected entirely in *BOM v BOK*.

[26] *BOM v BOK* (n 25) [141]–[142].

[27] (1888) 40 Ch D 312 (Ch).

[28] [1978] 1 WLR 255 (Ch).

[29] (1983) 151 CLR 447 (HCA).

[30] *BOM v BOK* (n 25) [133].

[31] ibid [141].

trenchant criticisms from Bigwood, especially in respect of the court's characterisation of *Amadio* as representing a broad doctrine of unconscionability.[32] This is not the occasion to examine Bigwood's criticisms in detail. Instead, I wish to raise three other points regarding *BOM v BOK* that are tied to the theme of my chapter.

First, the *BOM v BOK* doctrine of unconscionability also applies to contractual transactions,[33] although the Singapore Court of Appeal does not appear to draw any distinction between the principles to be applied in the commercial and non-commercial contexts. This is consistent with the same court's approach in *Chan Yuen Lan v See Fong Mun*,[34] a case concerning beneficial ownership of property, in which it laid down a six-step framework that is to apply in both commercial and non-commercial contexts. That the same principles apply does not mean that there is no distinction at all in the application in each context – the Court acknowledged that 'in principle', it would be easier to rebut the presumption of resulting trust in the domestic context.[35] Reading the two cases together, and to borrow Hopkins' terminology,[36] the Singapore courts favour a 'context-neutral, outcome-specific' approach. That is, the same principles are applied regardless of the context, but the context affects the application and therefore the outcome of the case.[37]

Second, the Singapore Court of Appeal was wary of introducing uncertainty and unpredictability by the recognition of 'unconscionability' as a free-standing doctrine, even in the domestic context. It tried to dissociate 'unconscionability' from historical usage and perception and imbue it with modern sensibility. This grave concern must be read against the wider backdrop of the country's ambition to become a leading hub for international dispute resolution. It explains the Court's lengthy discussion of the various meanings of 'unconscionability' and the distinction between unconscionability operating as an overarching rationale and unconscionability operating as a substantive doctrine.[38] The discussion has a signalling effect: to avoid any perception that Singapore equity – particularly in the context of equitable intervention in contracts – descends into wide discretion and uncertainty. More importantly, the Court is clearly vigilant against introducing uncertainty and unpredictability through the embrace of unconscionability even in the domestic context. The application of these principles in the commercial context, on a 'context-neutral, outcome-specific' approach, ensures that the principles are not subject to further adaptation which could potentially lead to greater uncertainty.

Third, it may be questioned as to whether the Court of Appeal's concern over uncertainty was somewhat overstated to the point that it colours its view of *Amadio*.

[32] R Bigwood, 'Knocking Down the Straw Man: Reflections on *BOM v BOK* and the Court of Appeal's "Middle-Ground" Narrow Doctrine of Unconscionability for Singapore' [2019] *Singapore Journal of Legal Studies* 29.

[33] *BOM v BOK* (n 25) [176].

[34] (n 11) [147].

[35] ibid [157], citing PS Davies and G Virgo, *Equity and Trusts: Cases and Materials* (Oxford, OUP, 2013).

[36] N Hopkins, 'Regulating Trusts of the Home: Private Law and Social Policy' (2009) 125 *LQR* 310, 316.

[37] See *BOM v BOK* (n 25) [112]. This is evident in the Singapore Court of Appeal's treatment of the issue as to whether there was an implied retainer between the wife (a lawyer) and the husband in relation to the former's advice as to the effect of the trust deed to the latter. The court took note of the marital context and said that it is 'far removed from the commercial contexts in which implied retainers are typically found'.

[38] *BOM v BOK* (n 25) [117]–[126].

The answer would depend on one's perspective. Here, I agree with Bigwood's point that 'the interpretation of another legal system's doctrinal formulation is to a significant and unavoidable extent perspectival',[39] but I do so in affirmation of the value of a comparative perspective. The treatment of equity in a particular legal system is always tied to its unique legal culture and history, and to some degree, influenced by the personality and training of the judges involved.[40] A person internal to the legal system may consider an external viewpoint on the laws of her own country as a misinterpretation, having acquired familiarity with how the laws are applied locally and perceived by the local legal community. In relation to the doctrine of unconscionability, Bigwood points out that the Australian doctrine should not be perceived as a wide doctrine because *Amadio* has been reined in by a series of subsequent decisions.[41] On the other hand, the external viewpoint is often expressed in the process of assessing the suitability of transplanting that law to a different legal system. The two perspectives are equally valuable and pertinent to the understanding of the development of equity in each jurisdiction. In particular, on this occasion in *BOM v BOK*, Phang JA was concerned with adopting the language of 'special disadvantage', which potentially admits a wide margin of discretion, in Singapore law. No matter how Australian courts might have circumscribed *Amadio* in subsequent cases, it cannot be denied that the nuances in post-*Amadio* Australian case law could become lost in transplantation.[42] In discussing perspective, I should also add that Phang JA was likely influenced by the paramount status of certainty in Singapore contract law in his treatment of equity in the domestic context, especially as the doctrine is equally applicable in the contractual context.[43] Indeed, the tolerance for flexibility and discretion would certainly vary from jurisdiction to jurisdiction,[44] and even from one judge to the next.[45] This helps to explain the difference in approach to the doctrine of unconscionability between the different jurisdictions. I will return to this point shortly in my discussion of *Quoine Pte Ltd v B2C2 Ltd*.[46]

[39] Bigwood (n 33) 138.

[40] Yip and Lee (n 5) 649–50.

[41] Bigwood (n 33) 51–54, referring to, eg, *ACCC v C G Berbatis Holdings Pty Ltd* [2003] HCA 18, (2003) 214 CLR 51 and *Kakavas v Crown Melbourne Ltd* [2013] HCA 25, (2013) 250 CLR 392.

[42] In *Stubbings v Jams 2 Pty Ltd* [2022] HCA, [2022] 399 AL 409 [39] Kiefel CJ, Keane and Gleeson JJ explained that considerations of knowledge, special disadvantage and unconscientious exploitation under the *Amadio* doctrine are not 'to be addressed separately as if they were separate elements of a cause of action in tort' and the court, in determining equitable relief, is entitled to take 'a more comprehensive view' based on an examination of the facts of the case.

[43] Phang JA (as he then was) has referred to the Singapore court's rejection of an implied duty of good faith in contract law: see *BOM v BOK* (n 25) [125]. Put another way, the learned judge approached the matter from the standpoint of transactional certainty, rather than through the lenses of equity.

[44] See E McKendrick, 'Commercial Contract Law: How Important Is the Quest for Certainty?' [2021] *Lloyd's Maritime and Commercial Law Quarterly* 72, 96.

[45] The Honourable Justice Peter Young OA, then Chief Judge in Equity in New South Wales, had made this point extra-judicially in the context of comparing the judicial attitude towards time clauses, citing the Privy Council decision in *Union Eagle Ltd v Golden Achievement Ltd* [1997] AC 514 (PC) (an appeal from Hong Kong) as illustration. See PW Young, 'Equity, Contract and Conscience' in S Degeling and J Edelman (eds), *Equity in Commercial Law* (Sydney, Lawbook Co, 2005) 503.

[46] [2020] SGCA(I) 02, [2020] 2 SLR 20.

ii. Unilateral Mistake in Equity and Unconscionable Conduct

The *BOM v BOK* doctrine not only applies in the commercial context, but it potentially functions as a control as to how much equity should be introduced in the commercial setting in Singapore law, especially in novel situations. In *Quoine*, the Singapore Court of Appeal was confronted with an appeal from the Singapore International Commercial Court ('SICC') concerning cryptocurrency trades carried out on the defendant's currency exchange platform as a result of a prior computer system glitch. The contracts were concluded pursuant to the parties' respective deterministic algorithms without human participation or foreknowledge. This resulted in the plaintiff selling Ethereum for Bitcoin at a rate that was approximately 250 times the then prevailing market rate, and the sale proceeds were automatically credited to the plaintiff's account. On the defendant's discovery of the system error and the trades made, it unilaterally cancelled the trades and reversed the debit and credit transactions. The plaintiff sued the defendant, amongst other claims, for breach of contract.

One of the defences raised was unilateral mistake in equity.[47] The defendant argued that the counterparties to the contracts had mistakenly believed that they would be trading at prices which approximated the prevailing true market value. It further contended that the plaintiff's programmer had actual or constructive knowledge of this mistake because his main objective in programming the trading software which allowed trades at disproportionate prices to take place under certain conditions was to 'unconscionably profit' from potential errors of the other market participants.[48] Both the majority and the dissenting judgment from Mance IJ relied on *BOM v BOK*, but to different effects.

The majority (comprising Menon CJ, Phang JA, Prakash JA and French IJ) rejected the defence on the basis that there was neither constructive knowledge of the mistaken party's mistake nor unconscionable conduct, which are requirements under current Singapore law,[49] on the part of the programmer to justify setting aside the contract on the basis of unilateral mistake in equity.[50] By way of obiter, the majority referred to the discussion of 'unconscionable conduct' in *BOM v BOK* in its consideration as to whether 'the same narrow conception of unconscionability should apply in the context of unilateral mistake in equity', although it was not necessary for the Court to decide the point in the dispute.[51] This obiter comment, whilst contemplative in nature, indicates inclination on the majority's part to unify the definition of 'unconscionable conduct' under Singapore law, for the purpose of legal certainty.

[47] The Singapore Court of Appeal assumed without deciding that the defence of unilateral mistake could be availed by the defendant as a defence to the breach of contract claim mounted by the plaintiff, even though the alleged mistake related to contracts entered into between the plaintiff and the counterparties. See *Quoine* (n 47) [78].

[48] ibid [112].

[49] The majority took the view that the court's task was to 'apply existing law on the doctrine subject to incremental adjustments being made in order to suit the particular context'. A more fundamental reform would require legislative intervention: ibid [79].

[50] ibid [126]–[127].

[51] ibid [109]–[110].

Mance IJ, in dissent, took the position that the defendant should have succeeded in its defence of unilateral mistake in equity, not based on current principles but through an adaptation of the current principles to uphold justice 'in the new world of algorithmic programmes and artificial intelligence'.[52] As the parties had entrusted the transactions to computers, there was no human involvement or consciousness at the time the transactions took place.[53] Hence, it would not be meaningful to apply the existing law on unilateral mistake which necessarily asks if the counterparty had actual knowledge or constructive notice of the mistake.[54]

To fashion a new set of principles for the algorithmic world, Mance IJ first emphasised the attributes of equity as being *flexible* and *supplemental* to the common law to provide relief relating to unilateral mistake.[55] Mance IJ said that '[e]quity's conscience must be capable of being affected by behaviour in seeking to retain the benefit of the mistake, once it is discovered'.[56] This provides justification to fashion a test that focuses on a reasonable trader's reaction upon learning of the transactions. If a reasonable trader would have recognised that a fundamental computer error had occurred on discovering the transactions, and the mistake could be readily corrected without detriment to the non-mistaken party or prejudice to third-party interests, it would be unconscionable to allow the trader to retain the benefit.[57] As Mance IJ explained, it is the failure to 'do the honourable thing and return the benefit' in such circumstances that amounts to unconscionability.[58]

Importantly, Mance IJ referred to *BOM v BOK* in his analysis as a point of distinction. He said a distinction needs to be made between, on the one hand, unconscionability being used as the sole criterion for relief (as in *BOM v BOK*) which justifies a narrow scope of operation and, on the other hand, unconscionability being used as an additional criterion to a primary basis of relief,[59] which permits a greater scope of flexibility 'to meet the equity of the case'.[60] In other words, unlike the majority, he confined the narrow view of unconscionability in *BOM v BOK* to a defined context of application which does not implicate areas that lie beyond. Following from this analysis, Mance IJ's proposed principles for unilateral mistake in equity applied to algorithmic contracting would not be subject to the narrow view of unconscionability in *BOM v BOK*. Unconscionability or unconscionable conduct is not used as the sole criterion for relief. On one view, Mance IJ's proposed adaptation of the principles of unilateral mistake is reminiscent of the *Pitt v Holt* test for setting aside a voluntary disposition on the basis of mistake. The *Pitt v Holt* test requires a causative mistake of sufficient gravity which would render it unjust or unconscionable to leave the mistake uncorrected.[61] The court would consider all the circumstances of the case

[52] ibid [193].
[53] ibid [182].
[54] ibid [178] and [204].
[55] ibid [163] and [166].
[56] ibid [171]–[172].
[57] ibid [195].
[58] ibid [206].
[59] As suggested in relation to unilateral mistake in equity in *Chwee Kin Keong v Digilandmall.com Pte Ltd* [2005] SGCA 2, [2005] 1 SLR(R) 502.
[60] ibid [169]–[170].
[61] *Pitt v Holt* (n 21) [126].

to determine if the transaction should be reversed. Similarly, Mance IJ's proposed test of unilateral mistake may be recast as requiring a very serious computer error to have occurred and in determining whether to reverse the transaction, the court is to consider the circumstances of the case. The factors to take into account include: whether the party seeking to retain the benefit of the transaction would have realised that a very serious mistake had occurred on learning of the transaction; whether the party seeking to retain the benefit would have suffered any detriment if the transaction were reversed; whether any third party interests have intervened;[62] and whether the party seeking to set aside the contract were so egregiously at fault that he should be denied relief.[63] On this interpretation, there is a primary basis (a very serious or fundamental mistake) to which the additional consideration of 'unconscionability' attaches. Pertinently, as with the *Pitt v Holt* test but unlike the traditional test for unilateral mistake in equity, Mance IJ's test does not depend on particular kinds of egregious conduct. It is concerned with whether the circumstances of the case, holistically assessed, require a transaction to be set aside. The test therefore does not seek to define 'unconscionable conduct'.

Crucially, Mance IJ's proposed adaptation results in a test that is no longer concerned with unilateral mistake, terminology which suggests that only one party is mistaken. Rather, a new doctrine concerned with computer error was proposed by Mance IJ. On one level, *Quoine* is a testament to the contrasting views on the modern recourse to unconscionability and equity's relationship with contractual certainty. Interestingly, this contrast in views – which may be fairly described as a clash between the internal and external perspectives on 'unconscionability' and certainty – played out in an 'international and commercial'[64] dispute governed by Singapore law in a national court designed to be 'international' in character.[65] Indeed, it may be said that the majority looked at the doctrine of mistake in equity through the prism of contract, a standpoint which would lead to an impulse to restrain equitable intervention in the name of safeguarding contractual certainty. Mance IJ, on the other hand, considered the matter through the lens of equity which quite naturally brought to the fore the role and qualities of equity in delivering fair and just outcomes. In his own words, '[t]here are cases where justice outweighs in the balance the interests of legal certainty'.[66] This contrast in views also bears on a point of reflection: is the admired quality of a jurisdiction's commercial law attributed primarily to its certainty? Mance IJ's dissenting judgment will draw sympathy from those who attach greater weight to delivering fair and just outcomes. The answer would differ between jurisdictions, and even between judges. In *Vauxhall Motors Ltd v Manchester Ship Canal Co Ltd*,[67] in accounting for the high regard which English law enjoys in the world, Lord Briggs placed greater emphasis on the value of certainty,[68] whilst Lady Arden

[62] ibid [167].
[63] ibid [195].
[64] The SICC only hears 'international and commercial' disputes.
[65] It may be that, for this reason, former English judges feel less inhibition in expressing their views in the SICC than in the English courts. cf *Lehtimäki v Cooper* [2020] UKSC 33, [2022] AC 155 [236] (Lord Reed).
[66] *Quoine* (n 47) [184].
[67] [2019] UKSC 46, [2020] AC 1161.
[68] ibid [2] and [41].

accorded greater weight to the delivery of fair and just outcomes and credited that attribute of English law to its equitable principles.[69]

iii. Discretionary Remedialism – 'Unconscionability' and Controls

The contrast in views between the majority and Mance IJ in *Quoine* also bears on the judicial techniques used to set proper bounds to the operation of equity in commerce. Beyond defining 'unconscionability', there are other techniques (some deliberate and others incidental) which work towards the same end. In this subsection, we examine controls of excessive discretion in the commercial context in relation to two controversial equitable doctrines: the remedial constructive trust and proprietary estoppel.

Whilst English law has explicitly rejected the remedial constructive trust,[70] it has been recognised in Australia, Canada and Singapore. The remedial constructive trust affords courts the flexibility to award proprietary relief based on the circumstances of the case. Unlike the Australian model, the Singaporean model has generally escaped intense scrutiny, in part, because its framework remained underdeveloped for a long time.[71] And in most cases in which the remedy was sought, the claim had been unsuccessful.

Importantly, 'unconscionability' lies at the core of the Singaporean model of remedial constructive trust. It is 'predicated on a state of knowledge which renders it unconscionable for the recipient to keep the [asset which will be subject to the trust]'.[72] It is thus well accepted that under Singapore law, fault is required for a remedial constructive trust to be awarded. To date, the one case in which the claim for remedial constructive trust succeeded concerned commercial fraud.[73] A seemingly narrow definition of 'unconscionability' notwithstanding, the remedial constructive trust could potentially lead to widely available proprietary relief in both domestic and commercial settings. Many causes of action recognised under Singapore law entail an element of fault. And it is by no means clear where the line between new categories of institutional constructive trust and new instances in which a remedial constructive trust could arise is to be drawn.[74]

Beyond the requirement of fault, the only doctrinal controls appear to be that: (a) the remedial constructive trust does not establish a cause of action and operates only as a remedy awarded at the court's discretion;[75] (b) there must be a proprietary

[69] ibid [63].

[70] *Bailey v Angove's Pty Ltd* [2016] UKSC 47, [2016] 1 WLR 3179 [27].

[71] See generally M Yip, 'Singapore's Remedial Constructive Trust: Lessons from Australia?' (2014) 8 *Journal of Equity* 77. cf *Ok Tedi Fly River Development Foundation Ltd v OK Tedi Mining Ltd* [2021] SGHC 205 [106].

[72] *Wee Chiaw Sek Anna* (n 15).

[73] *National Bank of Oman SAOG Dubai Branch v Dhamala* [2020] SGHC 199, [2020] 3 SLR 943. The cause of action in response to which the remedy was granted was the tort of unlawful means conspiracy.

[74] eg, under Singapore law, a constructive trust imposed over unauthorised gains received in breach of fiduciary duty is institutional in nature: see *Guy Neale v Nine Squares Pty Ltd* [2014] SGCA 64, [2015] 1 SLR 1097.

[75] *Ok Tedi* (n 72) [109].

connection between the assets claimed and the plaintiff's own assets;[76] and (c) the court can tailor the remedy to the circumstances of the case to prevent prejudice to third parties' interests.[77] In practice, the remedial constructive trust under Singapore law has been kept in check as a result of judicial restraint prevailing at the High Court level. The restraint is expressed in a variety of ways, including scepticism that the remedy has been firmly recognised under Singapore law;[78] advice that the remedy is to be 'sparingly' imposed;[79] and a general unwillingness to discuss the remedy where the case could be resolved through other means.[80] That being the case, a general judicial disclination against awarding or even engaging with the remedy does not amount to setting *proper bounds* on this equitable remedy. To ensure that the remedial constructive trust does not become an instrument of subjective justice, the immediate task is to develop proper principles to guide the exercise of discretion.

It has been said that the modern function of proprietary estoppel 'is to deal, in a fact-sensitive way, with some of the risks arising from the existence of legal powers, such as the power to transfer property to another'.[81] The Hong Kong Court of Final Appeal's decision in *Cheung Lai Mui v Cheung Wai Shing (No 2)*[82] appears to have taken an overly expansive view of a fact-sensitive approach on the basis of unconscionability.

The case arose in the domestic context, arising from a dispute between a successor to title to the land and an occupier who claimed that a promise was made to him by the predecessor co-owners of the land. The Court was confronted with the question whether there was 'reasonable detrimental reliance' of the promisee before the death of the promisor (in this case, the last surviving co-owner) and whether detrimental reliance after the promisor's death could be taken into account. Sidestepping the issue of whether the detriment suffered by the occupier was *substantial* prior to the promisor's death, the Court simply took the view that the occupier's reliance was reasonable having regard to the family culture and his relative youth at the material time. On the issue of appropriate relief, in a disappointingly brief analysis, Ribeiro PJ and Gummow NPJ simply held that 'dispossessing' the occupier in circumstances where he had not invested in any other properties and had instead maintained strong sentimental and emotional attachment to the land which was his family home for many years would be *unconscionable* in the sense used by Walker LJ in *Gillett v Holt*.[83] The Court gave no explanation as to why Hong Kong law, at the remedial

[76] *Zhou Weidong v Liew Kai Lung* [2017] SGHC 326, [2018] 3 SLR 1236 [81]–[82]. The claim would fail if the claimant's assets have been dissipated.

[77] *Ong Chai Koon v Ong Chai Soon* [2021] SGHC 76 [185].

[78] *Ok Tedi* (n 72) [106].

[79] *CPIT Investments Ltd v Qilin World Capital Ltd* [2017] 5 SLR 1 (SICC) [199] (Vivian Ramsay IJ).

[80] See, eg, *Sabyasachi Mukherjee v Pradeepto Kumar Biswas* [2018] SGHC 271 [19]; *Philip Antony Jeyaretnam v Kulandaivelu Malayaperumal* [2019] SGHC 214, [2020] 3 SLR 738 [23]–[24].

[81] J Mee and B McFarlane, 'Estoppel Remedies: Switching to Expectation When It is Difficult to Quantify Detriment' (*University of Oxford Property Law Blog*, 15 March 2022), www.law.ox.ac.uk/research-and-subject-groups/property-law/blog/2022/03/estoppel-remedies-switching-expectation-when.

[82] [2021] HKCFA 19, [2021] 5 HKC 185.

[83] (n 12) 225 and 232.

stage, should start with expectation relief[84] and how detriment was assessed to determine if that starting point ought to be displaced. Whilst direct financial expenditure is not required to establish detriment, the Court appears to be overly sympathetic towards the occupier's sentimental and emotional attachment to the home. Further, the occupier and his family had enjoyed rent-free accommodation for many years, a countervailing benefit that should be taken into account in the Court's exercise of discretion.

How would the *Cheung Lai Mui* decision affect the application of proprietary estoppel in the commercial context? Whilst the decision appears to endorse the exercise of strong discretion, it may be that the commercial context is somewhat insulated from the impact of *Cheung Lai Mui*. It is generally difficult to succeed on the doctrine where the claim arose out of failed contractual negotiations where the parties knew that the terms agreed to were not binding.[85] In Singapore, the judicial sentiment is that a claim in proprietary estoppel should not be imposed too readily in the commercial setting, as parties 'dealing at arm's length' would expect to arrange their dealings through contract.[86] Hong Kong courts further acknowledge that communications in the family context are more informal and equivocal in terms than communications in the commercial context.[87] The judicial impulse to protect reliance is far less powerful in the commercial context.

IV. DUTY LIMITATION AND EXEMPTION CLAUSES IN MODERN TRUSTS

A. Autonomy, Beneficiary Protection and the Needs of a Valid Trust in the Modern Age

Duty limitation and exemption clauses raise 'the question of the appropriate balance between settlor autonomy and the protection of the interests of beneficiaries and the needs of a valid trust in the modern age'.[88] Academic commentary is generally focused on the concept of the irreducible core of trustee obligations, an idea first developed by Hayton[89] and then formulated into law by Millett LJ in *Armitage v Nurse*: 'The duty of the trustees to perform the trusts honestly and in good faith for the benefit of the beneficiaries is the minimum necessary to give substance to the trusts …'.[90]

[84] This matter has yet to be settled under Hong Kong law: see Y Liew, 'Proprietary Estoppel Remedies in Hong Kong: Lessons from Singapore, England, and Australia' (2020) 50 *Hong Kong Law Journal* 109. See also *Shun Pong Ltd v Chan Koo Kai Felix* [2018] HKEC 3507 (HC) [93].

[85] *Cobbe* (n 3); *Motivate Publishing FZ LLC v Hello Ltd* [2015] EWHC 1554 (Ch); *Smoke Club Ltd (In Administration) v Network Rail Infrastructure Ltd* [2021] UKUT 78 (LC).

[86] *Day, Ashley Francis v Yeo* [2020] SGHC 93, [2020] 5 SLR 514 [192].

[87] *East Surplus Investment Ltd v Tincho Industrial Co Ltd* [2012] HKEC 1343 (DC) [19].

[88] T Graham and D Russell, 'Exemption Clauses in the Modern Age: Do They Result in an "Institution in Crisis"?' (2022) 28 *Trusts & Trustees* 54, 57.

[89] D Hayton, 'The Irreducible Core Content of Trusteeship' in AJ Oakley (ed), *Trends in Contemporary Trust Law* (Oxford, OUP, 1996).

[90] *Armitage v Nurse* [1998] Ch 241 (CA) 253–54.

Millett LJ's beneficiary-centred formulation echoes Hayton's comment that 'there is a strong contract-like basis for gratuitous family trusts to be regarded as "deals" made with trustees for the benefit of the beneficiaries'.[91] Even so, the formulation, which adopts the common law definition of dishonesty, has been criticised as being too 'permissive' and 'laissez faire' for the law of trusts.[92] Millett LJ's suggestion that professional trustees may exclude liability for gross negligence at common law[93] has also been criticised for setting the baseline standard a little too low.[94]

More generally, the irreducible core of trustee obligations calibrates a balance between settlor autonomy and beneficiary protection by prescribing the 'outer limits of trust drafting' beyond which the transaction may not take effect as a trust.[95] What is rarely investigated is the needs of a valid trust in the modern age and how this consideration interacts with the considerations of settlor autonomy and beneficiary protection. The discussion below shows that modern trusts are multifarious and in a number of instances, business considerations underline both the practice as well as the development of trust law. This is because modern trusts are not exclusively or even predominantly of the traditional gratuitous family trust variety. Two types of trusts are examined below.

B. Debt Securitisation

In the specialised context of debt securitisation, it is clear that the trust structure is deployed in the transaction not for the sole benefit of the beneficiaries who are the noteholders. Instead, the trust is utilised 'as a means of enforcing collective action for the issuer's protection'.[96] By consolidating the enforcement rights in the hands of the trustee, the trust structure prevents the noteholders from individually pursuing their rights as creditors of the issuer, a course of conduct that could trigger drastic financial consequences for the latter which would in turn harm the collective interests of the noteholders. Hence, the trustee's role is not a custodian to protect the noteholders but 'a gatekeeper' to restrict investors' ability to enforce their rights against the issuer.[97] The most that can be said is that the trustee's role is to balance the interests of both the note issuer and the noteholders.

It is only with an appreciation of the commercial reality that one can understand the English Court of Appeal's decision in *Citibank NA v MBIA Assurance SA*.[98] In that case, the senior notes were guaranteed by MBIA. To ensure its position was

[91] Hayton (n 90) 62.
[92] Graham and Russell (n 89).
[93] *Armitage* (n 91) 256.
[94] See, eg, Graham and Russell (n 89); A Usilova, 'Reliance on a Professional Trustee: A Case for a Change to the Rule in *Armitage v Nurse*' (2016) 8 *Trusts & Trustees* 923.
[95] D Fox, 'Non-Excludable Trustee Duties' (2011) 17 *Trusts & Trustees* 17, 26.
[96] M Yip, 'The Commercial Context in Trust Law' [2016] *Conv* 347.
[97] P Rawlings, 'Reinforcing Collectivity: The Liability of Trustees and the Power of Investors in Finance Transactions' (2009) 23 *Trust Law International* 14.
[98] [2007] EWCA Civ 11, [2007] 1 All ER (Comm) 475.

protected, MBIA was accorded the right to give Citibank, the security trustee, mandatory instructions concerning the latter's exercise of certain powers and discretions. The trust deed explicitly provided that in acting on MBIA's instructions, Citibank 'need not have regard to the interests of the noteholders'. This raised the question as to whether Citibank's acting in accordance with MBIA's mandatory instruction would be inconsistent with the irreducible core of trusteeship.

Arden LJ took the view that Citibank's powers were not so reduced that it ceased to be a trustee, as Citibank owed an obligation of good faith at all times and the trust deed conferred real discretions on Citibank in other respects which it had to exercise independently.[99] In other words, the trust was valid, and Citibank could act in accordance with the provisions in the trust deed. However, it has been challenged that there was a meaningful trust for the noteholders because MBIA effectively held control over the exercise of all important powers of the trust.[100] And an essential aspect of the trustee obligation – that is to act for the benefit of the beneficiaries – was certainly missing. Yet, to hold to the contrary would mean either that the trust was not valid or that the relevant clause was unenforceable. Either outcome would have an impact on the industry. Would a guarantor have come on board without the duty modification clause in the trust deed and, if so, at what additional costs? If we bear in mind that a security trustee is a gatekeeper to balance the interests of the note issuer and the noteholder, and not a traditional trustee who acts for the sole interests of the beneficiaries, the result appears less exceptional. The prioritisation of contractual freedom (party autonomy) in this instance is arguably justified.[101]

C. Modern Family Trust Practice

More worrying is the trend of a laissez faire approach towards duty limitation and exemption clauses in modern family trust practice. The trust industry has seen a decline in small or medium-sized family trusts.[102] Instead, many clients are wealthy individuals who desire to retain significant control over assets (especially their business assets or empires) which are settled on trusts for family members. The modern family trust is thus not necessarily set up with intergenerational distribution of wealth as the immediate objective because the settlors are usually still in their prime. How does the trust industry respond? It has switched to the language of professional services and trust markets and relabelled family trust practice as 'private client work' which expression indicates that the focus is on taking care of the interests of the settlor. Business considerations undoubtedly infiltrate the trust deals made between settlors and trustees who are in a client–service provider relationship. The rise of settlor-directed trust products is a testament to this business reality.

[99] ibid [82].

[100] A Trukhtanov, 'The Irreducible Core of Trust Obligations' (2007) 123 *LQR* 342, 345.

[101] See too the commercially motivated approach to interpretation of a 'no action' clause in a bond issue taken by Lawrence Collins LJ in *Elektrim SA v Vivendi Holdings 1 Corp* [2008] EWCA Civ 1178, [2009] 2 All ER (Comm) 213.

[102] R Walker, 'The Changing Face of Trust Law' (2017) 31 *TLI* 19, 21.

Nor are governments, lawmakers and courts blind to the business reality. How should the law balance the economic objective of growing a local trust industry and the legal imperative of ensuring sufficient beneficiary protection? On the one hand, we see steps to raise the baseline standard of protection. For example, where professional trustees are concerned, an objective test of dishonesty is applicable,[103] instead of a subjective test as endorsed in *Armitage v Nurse*. Further, it has been questioned as to whether it is right to exempt professional trustees from liability for gross negligence.[104] Various jurisdictions (including established wealth management centres) have taken the position, by way of judge-made law or legislative intervention, that trustee exemption clauses cannot exclude liability for gross negligence.[105] On the other hand, there is increasing acceptance that fiduciary duties may be modified by contract, including a trustee's fiduciary duties so long as they are not reduced below the 'irreducible core' formulated in *Armitage v Nurse*.[106]

The tension between the two objectives can be seen in the recent *Zhang Hong Li v DBS Bank (Hong Kong) Ltd*[107] litigation which involved a robustly drafted anti-*Bartlett* provision. Where the shares of a private company are settled on trust and the trust holds a controlling interest in the corporate entity, an anti-*Bartlett* provision is frequently, though not invariably, included in the trust deed to override the trustee's *Bartlett* duty.[108] A *Bartlett* duty requires the trustee to supervise the progress of corporate affairs by making inquiries and consulting with the company's directors from time to time to ensure that she has an adequate flow of information on corporate management. The practical effect of an anti-*Bartlett* provision is to keep the trustee out of the way of corporate management.

In *Zhang v DBS*, a married couple (the settlors) set up a family trust, governed by Jersey law, of the sole share in a private investment company ('Wise Lords') owned by the wife, Ji. The beneficiaries of the trust were the settlors and their children. The trustee was a subsidiary company of DBS Bank (which was the settlors' banker) and it nominated DBS Bank's corporate services subsidiary as the sole director of Wise Lords to manage its daily operations. To retain control over Wise Lords' investment activities, Ji was appointed as its investment advisor and authorised to give investment instructions to DBS Bank directly. The trust deed contained robustly drafted anti-*Bartlett* provisions which effect was that the trustee had no duty to interfere with or supervise the corporate management of Wise Lords save where it acquired actual knowledge of dishonesty at the corporate level. Specifically, the trustee was entitled to assume that corporate management was competent, without taking any

[103] See *Walker v Stones* [2001] QB 902 (CA) 939; *Fattal v Walbrook Trustees (Jersey) Ltd* [2010] EWHC 2767 (Ch), [2012] Bus LR D7 [81]. cf *Spread Trustee Co Ltd v Hutcheson* [2011] UKPC 13, [2012] 2 AC 194 [107] (Lord Mance).

[104] See the dissenting judgments of Lady Hale and Lord Kerr in *Spread Trustee* (n 104).

[105] See, eg, Canada, Hong Kong, Jersey, New Zealand and Scotland.

[106] *Lehtimäki* (n 66) [82] (Lady Arden), citing her own decision in *MBIA* (n 100). It should be borne in mind that not all situations of conflicts are harmful to the interests of the beneficiaries: see JH Langbein, 'Questioning the Trust Law Duty of Loyalty: Sole Interest or Best Interest' [2005] *YLJ* 931.

[107] (2019) 22 HKCFAR 392.

[108] Derived from the case of *Bartlett v Barclays Bank Trust Co Ltd (No 2)* [1980] Ch 515 (Ch). See further Man Yip, 'Trust-owned companies: understanding the trustees' duties' (2018) 31 *TLI* 185.

steps of verification or obtaining any information regarding Wise Lords' affairs. Further, it would be exempted for liability for any losses arising from: (a) acts or omissions of directors or other persons regardless of the degree of culpability; and (b) not obtaining information about Wise Lords or verifying the veracity of information received.

Ji's investment strategy led to huge losses suffered by Wise Lords during the 2008 financial crisis which she, together with the husband, sought to recover by suing (in their capacity as objects of the trust) for breach of trust. All levels of the Hong Kong courts affirmed the validity of the anti-*Bartlett* provisions under Jersey law, but they differed on whether the trustee nevertheless still owed a duty of supervision which was breached in the circumstances. Notably, the Court of Final Appeal rendered a detailed judgment even though the parties had already reached a settlement just prior to the release of the judgment. It did so because the case 'involves issues of law of general importance, and … has attracted considerable public interest in Hong Kong and internationally'.[109] Although the Hong Kong court was technically ruling on a matter governed by Jersey law, its views on the anti-*Bartlett* provisions and the irreducible core of trusteeship more generally reflect the position under Hong Kong law, which either fosters or shakes the confidence of settlors in Hong Kong as a wealth management centre. It was therefore an opportune occasion for the apex court of Hong Kong to share its views on trust law, especially at a time when Hong Kong was undergoing instability.

For the purposes of present analysis,[110] it suffices to contrast the views of the Hong Kong Court of Final Appeal against the views of the Hong Kong Court of Appeal. Both courts relied on the expert report given by Professor Paul Matthews as an expert on Jersey law, but they disagreed as to what Professor Matthews meant by 'a residual obligation' on the trustees which the anti-Bartlett provisions, whilst valid, did not exclude. The expert report states:[111]

> Although the trustee has no obligation to interfere in the business of the company, and no obligation to obtain information regarding the company, it still has a power to do so, because it is a member of the company. If circumstances were to arise where no reasonable trustee could lawfully refrain from exercising those powers, a failure to do so in such a case would amount to a breach of trust …

The decision of the courts was arrived at based on the written report. The Court of Appeal held that notwithstanding the validity of the anti-*Bartlett* provisions, there remained a residual supervisory duty on the trustee to intervene in corporate operations and make inquiries 'where no reasonable trustee could lawfully refrain from exercising those powers'.[112] Following the Court of Appeal's holding, the trustee could not simply rely on the anti-*Bartlett* provisions and routinely approve the investments

[109] *Zhang v DBS* (n 109) [6].

[110] For a detailed analysis of the judgments reached at all three levels of Hong Kong court, see R Lee and M Yip, 'Exclusion of Duty and the Irreducible Core Content of Trusteeship: A Re-Assessment' (2020) 14 *Journal of Equity* 131.

[111] For the relevant excerpt of the report, see *Zhang v DBS* (n 109) [55].

[112] *Zhang Hong Li v DBS Bank (Hong Kong) Ltd* [2018] HKCA 435 [6.8]–[6.10].

directed by Ji. It should have intervened in the high-risk transactions directed by Ji that led to the huge losses sustained by the trust.

The Hong Kong Court of Final Appeal, in a unanimous judgment delivered by Ribeiro PJ, Fok PJ and Lord Neuberger NPJ, held that the Court of Appeal's decision was self-contradictory because the 'residual obligation' conceptualised by the Court of Appeal would be clearly inconsistent with the express terms of the trust.[113] A non-contradictory reading of the relevant paragraphs of the expert report was to be preferred: that is, the anti-*Bartlett* clauses did not exclude an obligation on the trustee to act in cases where it had actual knowledge of dishonesty.[114] On the facts, since the trustee did not possess actual knowledge of dishonesty, it was not under a duty to intervene and there was therefore no breach of trust. Whilst the outcome was defensible on the facts,[115] Lee and I have argued that the residual, high-level supervisory obligation endorsed by the Hong Kong Court of Appeal could be justified on the basis of a reanalysed account of the irreducible core of trustee obligations.[116] Essentially, we argued for a higher baseline standard based on an expanded scope of the irreducible core to include liability for gross negligence where professional trustees are concerned. I will not rehash those arguments here.

The point to make is that the contrast in views between the two Hong Kong courts belies a difference in opinion as to the balance between settlor autonomy and the minimum level of beneficiary protection in the modern trust industry involving professional trustees. Unlike the debt securitisation context, the trustee in a modern family trust remains a steward of trust assets for the benefit of the beneficiaries. In this context, certain standards set by equity are mandatory and cannot be modified by contract. A court that privileges settlor autonomy would set a very low minimum standard, to enable the settlor to enjoy a wider span of choice in structuring the trust deal. A court that privileges beneficiary protection would set a higher standard, as the Hong Kong Court of Appeal did, which therefore restricts the settlor's freedom of choice.

The root of the problem is *Armitage v Nurse*. In choosing the common law definition of dishonesty as opposed to the more malleable concept of 'equitable fraud', and in excluding liability for gross negligence (a concept that is difficult to define) from the irreducible core, Millett LJ was privileging certainty. A baseline which is certain would facilitate the creation of family trusts by enabling settlors and trustees to know beforehand what terms they could put into the trust deed. However, Millett LJ dealt with a simple, traditional family trust, without anticipating how his formulation of the irreducible core could impact family trusts of a very different variety to enable reservation of (excessive) settlor control. There is no reason why certainty and flexibility cannot go hand in hand in equity by allowing a calibrated approach towards the irreducible core of trusteeship. Such a calibration, distinguishing between

[113] *Zhang v DBS* (n 109) [64].

[114] ibid [63].

[115] Zhang and Ji had bargained for the right to direct an investment of their choice. It was only when Ji's investment decisions had gone wrong that they decided to sue the trustee for breach of trust to recoup their losses.

[116] Lee and Yip (n 112) 138–47.

a professional trustee and a lay trustee, has already been made in respect of the statutory duty of care.[117] The differentiation in standards, when applied in the context of duty limitation and liability exemption clauses, reins in the excessive desire of the settlor to retain control over assets settled on trust, which fee-earning trustees are in practice unable to push back against. Such an approach facilitates the establishment of a healthy modern trust industry.

V. REFLECTIONS

A single chapter cannot make a comprehensive review of all recent developments in the law of equity, much less across all common law jurisdictions. My objective is not to propose a generalised role of equity in modern commerce. My analysis of the selected handful of cases, however, indicates that the role of equity would differ in each context. 'Unconscionability' has been wielded by courts as a tool to apply a fact-sensitive approach, especially in responding to new situations arising from complex human dealings. It confirms the value of equity in commerce to provide intervention and innovation. The cases demonstrate that the courts of different jurisdictions and even judges of the same court may have different views as to the proper balance between certainty and flexibility, as well as the means to achieve that balance. Even more fundamentally, these terms must be understood in a native legal environment and against the experience of the particular judges pronouncing them.

My analysis of the concept of the irreducible core content of trustee obligations and duty limitation and liability exemption clauses reveals a similar line of tension between certainty and flexibility. Equitable standards appear to be displaced in favour of commercial considerations. I have explained that the role of standard setting must be understood with reference to the objective of the trust. Where the trust is not utilised in the traditional paradigm of protecting the beneficiaries against trustee abuse, its traditional standards arguably do not apply with full rigour. Where it does, however, courts should not readily allow the equitable standards to be displaced by settlor autonomy. In clearly endorsing equity's place and standards in the modern practice of family trust, for instance, equity facilitates the establishment of a healthy trust industry.

Finally, and more generally, each jurisdiction has its own philosophy, motivations and techniques in invoking equity in commerce. To fully appreciate the underlying philosophy, motivations and techniques, it is sometimes helpful to examine their origin and development in the domestic context, as the discussion above has shown. Further, as a result of these differences, courts must take great care in assessing the persuasive value of foreign case law concerning the same or similar doctrine in the development of its own law.[118]

[117] Trustees Act 2000, s 1.

[118] See, eg, M Leeming, 'Equity in Australia and the United Kingdom: Dissonance and Concordance' Institute of European and Comparative Law, Oxford Law Faculty (25 October 2019), www.supremecourt.justice.nsw.gov.au/Documents/Publications/Speeches/2019%20Speeches/Leeming_20191025.pdf.

Index

www.ingramcontent.com/pod-product-compliance
Ingram Content Group UK Ltd.
Pitfield, Milton Keynes, MK11 3LW, UK
UKHW020228290926
15470UKWH00001B/411

9 781509 960071